Learning to Use
WordPerfect 5.0/5.1
Lotus 1-2-3 Release 2.2
and dBASE III PLUS
Alternate Edition

GARY B. SHELLY   **THOMAS J. CASHMAN**

RUTH GURGEL   **JAMES S. QUASNEY**   **PHILIP J. PRATT**

boyd & fraser

The Shelly/Cashman Series
boyd & fraser publishing company

THE SHELLY/CASHMAN SERIES

Essential Computer Concepts
Computer Concepts
Computer Concepts with BASIC §
Computer Concepts with Microcomputer Applications (Lotus® version) §
Computer Concepts with Microcomputer Applications (VP-Planner Plus® version) §
Learning to Use WordPerfect® (version 4.2), Lotus 1-2-3®, and dBASE III PLUS® §
Learning to Use WordPerfect® 5.0/5.1, Lotus 1-2-3®, and dBASE III PLUS® §
Learning to Use WordPerfect® 5.0/5.1, Lotus 1-2-3®, and dBASE III PLUS® Alternate Edition
Learning to Use WordPerfect® 5.0/5.1, Lotus 1-2-3® Release 2.2, and dBASE III PLUS® §
Learning to Use WordPerfect® 5.0/5.1, Lotus 1-2-3® Release 2.2, and dBASE III PLUS® Alternate Edition
Learning to Use WordPerfect® (version 4.2), VP-Planner Plus®, and dBASE III PLUS® §
Learning to Use WordPerfect® (version 4.2) §
Learning to Use WordPerfect® 5.0/5.1 §
Learning to Use VP-Planner Plus® §
Learning to Use Lotus 1-2-3® §
Learning to Use Lotus 1-2-3® Release 2.2 §
Learning to Use dBASE III PLUS® §
Learning to Use dBASE IV®
Computer Fundamentals with Application Software
    Workbook and Study Guide to Accompany Computer Fundamentals with Application Software
Learning to Use SuperCalc®3, dBASE III®, and WordStar® 3.3: An Introduction
Learning to Use SuperCalc®3: An Introduction
Learning to Use dBASE III®: An Introduction
Learning to Use WordStar® 3.3: An Introduction
BASIC Programming for the IBM Personal Computer
RPG II, RPG III, and RPG/400

§ ClassNotes and Study Guide available

© 1990 by boyd & fraser publishing company
A Division of South-Western Publishing Company
Boston, MA 02116

Developed by Susan Solomon Communications
Manufactured in the United States of America

Library of Congress Cataloging-in-Publication Data

ISBN 0-87835-707-6

2 3 4 5 6 W 3 2 1 0

CONTENTS

Introduction to Computers

Introduction to DOS

Word Processing Using WordPerfect 5.0/5.1

Spreadsheets Using Lotus 1-2-3 Release 2.2

PROJECT 1   BUILDING A WORKSHEET   L 2

PROJECT 2   FORMATTING AND PRINTING A WORKSHEET   L 48

PROJECT 3 ENHANCING YOUR WORKSHEET   L 97

PROJECT 6   SORTING AND QUERYING A WORKSHEET DATABASE   L 231

APPENDIX—COMMAND STRUCTURE CHARTS FOR RELEASE 2.2   L 263

Database Management Using dBASE III PLUS

PREFACE

Today over 30 million microcomputers are used in businesses, schools, and homes throughout the world. A new generation of software, commonly called application software, has been developed to use the power of these computers. The most widely used software applications are word processing, spreadsheet, and database; thus, respectively, this textbook includes detailed instructions on WordPerfect 5.0/5.1, Lotus 1-2-3 Release 2.2, and dBASE III PLUS. This texbtook assumes no previous experience with computers and is written with continuity, simplicity, and practicality in mind. After completing this textbook, students will be able to implement a wide variety of tasks using these three software packages.

This textbook is a derivative of earlier works by Shelly and Cashman. Great care has been taken to maintain the content and philosophy of the original works, as well as the Shelly and Cashman pedagogy and teaching style — a style which has proven effective in educating millions of students.

ABOUT THE ALTERNATE EDITION

*T*he difference between this book and our other book covering the same versions of the same packages lies in our coverage of WordPerfect 5.0/5.1. This *Alternate Edition* teaches WordPerfect using inches on the status line and in the display of margins and tab settings, and showing position numbers and line numbers in decimal notation.

ORGANIZATION OF THE TEXTBOOK

*T*his textbook consists of two introductory chapters and six projects for *each* software package.

An Introduction to Computers

Introduction to Computers covers computer hardware and software concepts important to first-time microcomputers users. These concepts include the functions of the computer and the components of a typical microcomputer system.

An Introduction to DOS

To use a computer effectively, students need practical knowledge of operating systems. The second chapter in this text, therefore, is *Introduction to DOS*—an introduction to the most commonly used DOS commands—such as loading DOS, formatting a diskette, and copying files.

Six Problem-Oriented Projects for Each Application

Detailed instruction on each of the three software packages follows the basic microcomputer and DOS concepts. This instruction is divided into six projects for each package. In each project students learn by the unique Shelly/Cashman problem-oriented approach; various problems are presented and then *thoroughly* explained step-by-step. Numerous, carefully labeled screens and keystroke sequences illustrate exactly what is necessary to solve the problems presented. This approach visually guides students as they enter the various commands and quickly learn how to use the software.

End-of-Project Summaries

Two helpful learning and review tools are included at the end of each project—the Project Summary and the Keystroke Summary. The Project Summary lists the key concepts covered in the project. The Keystroke Summary is an exact listing of each keystroke used to solve the project's problem.

Student Assignments

An important feature of this textbook is the numerous and wide variety of Student Assignments provided at the end of each project. These assignments include the following: true/false questions; multiple choice questions; assignments that require students to write and/or explain various commands; a series of realistic problems for students to analyze and solve by applying what they have learned in the project, and minicases for the dBASE projects.

THE SUPPLEMENTS TO ACCOMPANY THIS TEXT

even teaching and learning materials supplement this textbook. They are the Instructor's Guide and Answer Manual, Test Bank, MicroSWAT, Transparency Masters, Instructor's Diskette, HyperGraphics, Instructor's Manual to Accompany HyperGraphics, and *ClassNotes and Study Guide*.

Instructor's Guide and Answer Manual

This manual includes Lesson Plans and Answers and Solutions. The Lesson Plans begin with chapter or project behavioral objectives. Next an overview of each chapter or project is included to help the instructor quickly review the purpose and key concepts. Detailed outlines of each chapter and/or project follow. These outlines are annotated with the page number of the textbook on which the outlined material is covered; notes, teaching tips, and additional activities that the instructor might use to embellish the lesson; and a key for using the Transparency Masters. Complete answers and solutions for the Student Assignments are included to ease course administration.

Test Bank

This is a hard copy version of the test questions. It is comprised of three types of questions—true/false, multiple choice, and fill-in. Each project has approximately 50 true/false, 25 multiple choice, and 35 fill-ins. Answers to all of these test questions are included.

MicroSWAT

MicroSWAT, a computerized test generating system, is available free to adopters of this textbook. It includes all of the questions from the Test Bank included in the Instructor's Materials for this book. MicroSWAT is an easy to use menu-driven package that provides instructor's testing flexibility and allows customizing of testing documents. For example, a user of MicroSWAT can enter his or her own questions and can generate review sheets and answers keys. MicroSWAT will run on any IBM PC, IBM PS/2, or IBM compatible systems with two diskette drives or a hard disk.

Transparency Masters

A Transparency Master is included for *every* figure in the textbook.

Instructor's Diskette

This free supplement contains the letters and memos used to teach the WordPerfect projects, the project worksheets and Student Assignment worksheet solutions for Lotus 1-2-3, the databases that students will create and use in the dBASE minicases, and the data for the dBASE employee database example.

HyperGraphics®

How instructors teach has changed very little in the last few decades. After all the flag waving about computer tutorials, CAI, and the like, we have learned that the human instructor is neither replaceable by a machine nor by someone who is untrained. HyperGraphics is a tool that acknowledges these facts.

What Is HyperGraphics? HyperGraphics is an instructional delivery system; it is a piece of software that presents all of the Shelly and Cashman textbook content with the use of graphics, color, animation, and interactivity. It is a powerful software tool that enhances classroom instruction. It is a state-of-the-art, computer-based teaching and learning environment that promotes interactive learning and self-study.

What Hardware Do You Need for HyperGraphics? You need three pieces of hardware to run HyperGraphics; two additional pieces are optional.

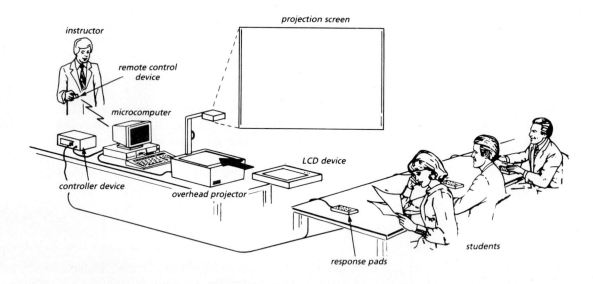

1. An IBM Personal Computer or PS/2 Series computer (or compatible) with a standard CGA graphics card.
2. A standard overhead projector and projection screen.
3. A standard projection device, such as a color projector or a liquid crystal display (LCD), that fits on the projection area of the overhead projector. The projection device is connected to the personal computer, resulting in the projection of the computer's screen.
4. A hand-held remote control device (*optional*), that allows the instructor to navigate throughout the presentation materials and still move freely around the classroom.
5. A set of at least eight response pads (*optional*), small pads consisting of 10 digit keys, that can be pressed to indicate a student's response. (These pads are linked to the microcomputer by a controller device.)

How Does the Instructor Use HyperGraphics? HyperGraphics is very easy to use. The instructor presses the appropriate keys on the hand-held remote control device or the keyboard and thereby controls the screen display. This display is projected through the LCD to the overhead projector. The instructor has complete control over the order and pacing of how the lessons are taught. By pushing one or more keys he or she can do such things as:

- View and select from the lesson menu
- Deliver the lesson's instructional materials in sequence
- Repeat any portion of a lesson to reinforce or review material

- Move ahead to specific portions of the lesson
- View the chapter objectives at any time
- View one or more questions about the lesson at any time
- Have students respond to one or more questions via the response pads
- Log students' responses to questions
- Randomly select students to respond to a question
- End a lesson
- Return directly to that point in the lesson where he or she stopped in the previous class meeting

What Are the Benefits of Using the Student Response Pads? Instructors have never before had the opportunity to assess student comprehension and retention of class instruction immediately and accurately. They can now do so if they use HyperGraphics with the student response pads.

For example, suppose the instructor presents a multiple choice question on the screen at the end of a segment of a lesson. Students will see an indication light illuminate on their response pads, and they'll have a period of time (controlled by the instructor) to press the button corresponding to the answer of their choice. The answers are tabulated by the microcomputer, and an optional aggregate bar chart of the answers selected is immediately available for viewing by the entire class. Each student's answer is also available on disk for later analysis or review. Thus, the progress of the entire class as well as each student can be tracked throughout the course.

Using these response pads results in substantial and *measurable* benefits to instructors as well as to students. The pads provide a rich teaching and learning experience and actively promote student participation.

What Does HyperGraphics Cost? HyperGraphics is *free* to adopters of this textbook. The only cost is for the computer and the projection device and screen, equipment that most educational institutions already possess. (Student response pads and the controller device are available at an extra charge.) HyperGraphics revolutionizes classroom instruction. It brings classroom instruction alive through graphic imagery and interactivity, and it can provide immediate and direct feedback to students and instructors.

Instructor's Manual to Accompany HyperGraphics

This manual contains teaching tips and guidelines for enhancing your classroom instruction using HyperGraphics. Easy-to-follow installation instructions are also included.

ClassNotes and Study Guide

The active learning experience of HyperGraphics can also be promoted if students purchase this supplement. As its title suggests, the *ClassNotes and Study Guide* serves three purposes. First, it relieves students from laborious and tedious notetaking responsibilities, freeing them to concentrate on the instruction. Second, if used with HyperGraphics, it provides an active learning experience for students to fill in key terms and key concepts during classroom instruction. Third, used without HyperGraphics this supplement provides a chance for students to review and study independently, as they can with traditional study guides.

ACKNOWLEDGMENTS

Learning to Use WordPerfect 5.0/5.1, Lotus 1-2-3 Release 2.2, and dBASE III PLUS would not be the quality textbook it is without the help of many people. We would like to express our appreciation to the following people, who worked diligently to assure a quality publication: Mel Martin, special consultant on WordPerfect; Jeanne Huntington, typesetter; Michael Broussard, Anne Craig, and Ken Russo, artists; Ginny Harvey, manuscript editor; Becky Herrington, director of production and art coordinator; Susan Solomon, director of development; and Tom Walker, publisher and vice president of Boyd & Fraser.

ORDER INFORMATION AND FACULTY SUPPORT INFORMATION

For the quickest service, refer to the map below for the South-Western Regional Office serving your area.

1 ORDER INFORMATION
5101 Madison Road
Cincinnati, OH 45227-1490
General Telephone–513-527-6945
Telephone: 1-800-543-8440
FAX: 513-527-6979
Telex: 214371

FACULTY SUPPORT INFORMATION
5101 Madison Road
Cincinnati, OH 45227-1490
General Telephone–513-527-6950
Telephone: 1-800-543-8444

Alabama	Massachusetts	Ohio
Connecticut	Michigan	Pennsylvania
Delaware	Minnesota	Rhode Island
Florida	Mississippi	South Carolina
Georgia	Missouri	South Dakota
Illinois	Nebraska	Tennessee
Indiana	New Hampshire	Vermont
Iowa	New Jersey	Virginia
Kentucky	New York	West Virginia
Maine	North Dakota	Wisconsin
Maryland	North Carolina	District of Columbia

2 ORDER INFORMATION
13800 Senlac Drive
Suite 100
Dallas, TX 75234
General Telephone–214-241-8541
Telephone: 1-800-543-7972

FACULTY SUPPORT INFORMATION
5101 Madison Road
Cincinnati, OH 45227-1490
General Telephone–513-527-6950
Telephone: 1-800-543-8444

Arkansas	Louisiana	Texas
Colorado	New Mexico	Wyoming
Kansas	Oklahoma	

3 ORDER INFORMATION and FACULTY SUPPORT INFORMATION
6185 Industrial Way
Livermore, CA 94550
General Telephone–415-449-2280
Telephone: 1-800-543-7972

Alaska	Idaho	Oregon
Arizona	Montana	Utah
California	Nevada	Washington
Hawaii		

Introduction to Computers

Introduction to Computers

OBJECTIVES

- Define computer and discuss the four basic computer operations: input, processing, output and storage.
- Define data and information.
- Explain the principal components of the computer and their use.
- Describe the use and handling of diskettes and hard disks.
- Discuss computer software and explain the difference between application software and system software.

*T*he computer is an integral part of the daily lives of most individuals. Small computers, called microcomputers or personal computers (Figure 1), have made computing available to almost everyone. Thus, your ability to understand and use a computer is rapidly becoming an important skill. This book teaches you how to use a computer by teaching you how to use software applications. Before you learn about the application software, however, you must understand what a computer is, the components of a computer, and the types of software used on computers. These topics are explained in this Introduction.

FIGURE 1
Microcomputers: The IBM PS/2 Model 30 (left) and Compaq Deskpro 386S (right) are two examples of popular microcomputer systems.

WHAT IS A COMPUTER?

A **computer** is an electronic device, operating under the control of instructions stored in its own memory unit, that accepts input or data, processes data arithmetically and logically, produces output from the processing, and stores the results for future use. All computers perform basically the same four operations:

1. **Input operations**, by which data is entered into the computer for processing.
2. **Arithmetic operations**, are addition, subtraction, multiplication, and division. **Logical operations** are those that compare data to determine if one value is less than, equal to, or greater than another value.
3. **Output operations**, which make the information generated from processing available for use.
4. **Storage operations**, which store data electronically for future reference.

These operations occur through the use of electronic circuits contained on small silicon chips inside the computer (Figure 2). Because these electronic circuits rarely fail and the data flows along these circuits at close to the speed of light, processing can be accomplished in millionths of a second. Thus, the computer is a powerful tool because it can perform these four operations reliably and quickly.

FIGURE 2
This microprocessor is shown "packaged" and ready for installation in a microcomputer.

Data - Raw facts

WHAT IS DATA AND INFORMATION?

T he four operations that can be performed using a computer all require data. **Data** is raw facts, the numbers and words that are suitable for processing in a predetermined manner on a computer to produce information. Examples of data include the hours posted to a payroll time card or the words comprising a memo to the sales staff. A computer accepts data, processes data and, as a result of the processing, produces output in the form of useful information. **Information** can therefore be defined as data that has been processed into a form that has meaning and is useful.

WHAT ARE THE COMPONENTS OF A COMPUTER?

T o understand how computers process data into information, it is necessary to examine the primary components of the computer. The four primary components of a computer are:

    1. input devices   3. output devices
    2. processor unit   4. auxiliary storage units

Figure 3 illustrates the relationship of the various components to one another.

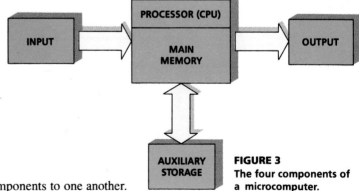

FIGURE 3
The four components of a microcomputer.

Input Devices

Input devices enter data into main memory. Several input devices exist. The two most commonly used are the keyboard and the mouse.

The Keyboard.   The input device you will most commonly use on computers is the **keyboard** on which you manually "key in" or type the data (Figures 4a and b). The keyboard on most computers is laid out in much the same manner as a typewriter. Figures 4a and b show two styles of IBM keyboards: the original standard keyboard and a newer enhanced keyboard. Although the layouts are somewhat different, the use of the keys is the same.

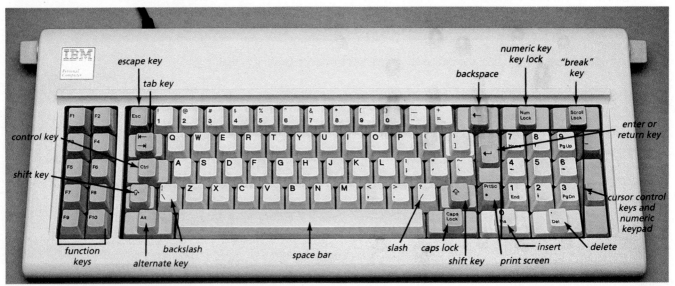

FIGURE 4a The IBM standard keyboard

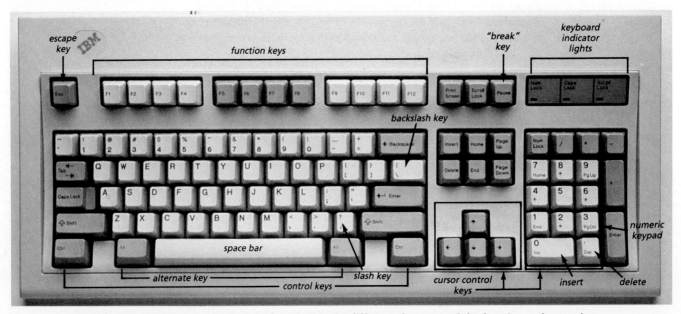

FIGURE 4b The enhanced IBM PS/2 keyboard. Note the different placement of the function and cursor keys.

A numeric keypad in the 10-key adding machine or calculator key format is located on the right side of both keyboards. This arrangement of keys allows you to enter numeric data rapidly. To activate the numeric pad on the keyboards you press the Num Lock key, located above the numeric keys. On the enhanced keyboard, a light turns on at the top right of the keyboard to indicate that the numeric keys are in use. You may also invoke the number keys by using the shift key together with the number keys located across the top of the typewriter keys.

Cursor control keys determine where data is displayed on the screen. The **cursor** is a symbol, such as an underline character, which indicates where on the screen the next character will be entered. On the keyboards in Figures 4a and b the cursor control keys or arrow keys are included as part of the numeric keypad. The enhanced keyboard has a second set of cursor control keys located between the typewriter keys and the numeric keypad. If you press the **Num Lock** key at the top of the numeric keypad, numeric characters appear on the screen when you press the numeric key pad keys. You can still use the cursor control keys by pressing the Shift key together with the desired cursor control key. If the Num Lock key is engaged (indicated by the fact that as you press any numeric key pad key, a number appears on the screen) you can return to the standard mode for cursor control keys by pressing the Num Lock key.

The cursor control keys allow you to move the cursor around the screen. Pressing the **Up Arrow** key ↑ causes the cursor to move upward on the screen. The **Down Arrow** key ↓ causes the cursor to move down; the **Left** ← and **Right** → **Arrow** keys cause the cursor to move left and right on the screen.

The other keys on the keypad—(PgUp), (PgDn), Home, and End—have various uses depending on the microcomputer software you use. Some programs make no use of these keys; others use the **(PgUp)** and **(PgDn)** keys, for example, to display previous or following pages of data on the screen. Some software uses the **Home** key to move the cursor to the upper left corner of the screen. Likewise, the **End** key may be used to move the cursor to the end of a line of text or to the bottom of the screen, depending on the software.

Function keys on many keyboards can be programmed to accomplish specific tasks. For example, a function key might be used as a help key. Whenever that key is pressed, messages appear that give instructions to help the user. Another function key might be programmed to cause all data displayed on the CRT screen to be printed on a printer whenever the key is pressed. In Figure 4a, ten function keys are on the left portion of the standard keyboard. In Figure 4b, twelve function keys are located across the top of the enhanced keyboard.

Other keys have special uses in some applications. The **Shift** keys have several functions. They work as they do on a typewriter, allowing you to type capital letters. The Shift key is always used to type the symbol on the upper portion of any key on the keyboard. Also, to use the cursor control keys temporarily as numeric entry keys, you can press the Shift key to switch into numeric mode. If, instead, you have pressed the Num Lock key to use the numeric keys, you can press the Shift key to shift temporarily back to the cursor mode.

The keyboard has a Backspace key, a Tab key, an Insert key and a Delete key that perform the functions their names indicate.

The **Escape (Esc)** key also has many different uses. In some microcomputer software it is used to cancel an instruction but this use is by no means universally true.

As with the Escape key, many keys are assigned special meaning by the microcomputer software. Certain keys may be used more frequently than others by one piece of software but rarely used by another. It is this flexibility that allows the computer to be used in so many different applications.

The Mouse   An alternative input device you might encounter is a mouse. A **mouse** (Figure 5) is a pointing device that can be used instead of the cursor control keys. You lay the palm of your hand over the mouse and move it across the surface of a table or desk. The

mouse detects the direction of your movement and sends this information to the screen to move the cursor. You push buttons on top of the mouse to indicate your choices of actions from lists displayed on the computer screen.

FIGURE 5
A mouse can be used as a cursor control device.

The Processor

The **processor unit** is composed of the central processing unit (CPU) and main memory (see Figure 3). The **central processing unit** contains the electronic circuits that actually cause processing to occur. The CPU interprets instructions to the computer, performs the logical and arithmetic processing operations, and causes the input and output operations to occur.

    Main memory consists of electronic components that store numbers, letters of the alphabet, and characters such as decimal points or dollar signs. Any data to be processed must be stored in main memory.

    The amount of main memory in microcomputers is typically measured in **kilobytes** (K or KB), which equal 1,024 memory locations. A memory location, or byte, usually stores one character. Therefore, a computer with 640K can store approximately 640,000 characters. The amount of main memory for microcomputers may range from 64K to several million characters, also called a **megabyte (MB)**, or more.

FIGURE 6
This dot matrix printer, the IBM Proprinter II, is often used to print documents from an IBM PC and other popular microcomputers.

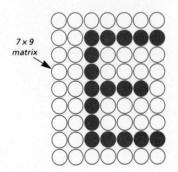

7×9 matrix

Output Devices

Output devices make the information resulting from processing available for use. The output from computers can be presented in many forms, such as a printed report or color graphics. When a computer is used for processing tasks, such as word processing, spreadsheets, or database management, the two output devices most commonly used are the **printer** and the televisionlike display device called a **screen**, **monitor**, or **CRT** (cathode ray tube).

    Printers   Printers used with computers can be either impact printers or nonimpact printers.

    An **impact printer** prints by striking an inked ribbon against the paper. One type of impact printer often used with microcomputers is the dot matrix printer (Figure 6). To print a character, a **dot matrix printer** generates a dot pattern representing a particular character. The printer then activates vertical wires in a print head contained on the printer, so that selected wires press against the ribbon and paper, creating a character. As you see in Figure 7, the character consists of a series of dots produced by the print head wires. In the actual size created by the printer, the characters are clear and easy to read.

Dot matrix printers vary in the speed with which they can print characters. These speeds range from 50 characters per second to over 300 characters per second. Generally, the higher the speed, the higher the cost of the printer.

Many dot matrix printers also allow you to choose two or more sizes and densities of character. Typical sizes include condensed print, standard print, and enlarged print. In addition, each of the three print sizes can be printed with increased density, or darkness (Figure 8).

FIGURE 8
These samples show condensed, standard, and enlarged print. These can all be produced by a dot-matrix printer.

```
This line of type is in CONDENSED Print
AaBbCcDdEeFfGgHhIiJjKkLlMmNnOoPpQqRrSsTtUuVvWwXxYyZz 0123456789

This line of type is in STANDARD Print
AaBbCcDdEeFfGgHhIiJjKkLlMmNnOoPpQqRrSsTtUuVvWwXxYyZz 0123456789

This line of type is in ENLARGED Pr
AaBbCcDdEeFfGgHhIiJjKkLlMmNnOoPpQqR
UuVvWwXxYyZz 0123456789
```

Another useful feature of dot matrix printers is their ability to print graphics. The dots are printed not to form characters, but rather to form graphic images. This feature can be especially useful when working with a spreadsheet program in producing graphs of the numeric values contained on the worksheet.

When users require printed output of high quality, such as for business or legal correspondence, a letter-quality printer is often used. The term **letter quality** refers to the quality of the printed character that is suitable for formal or professional business letters. A letter-quality printed character is a fully formed, solid character like those made by typewriters. It is not made up of a combination of dots, as by a dot matrix printer.

The letter-quality compact printer most often used with microcomputers is the **daisy wheel printer**. It consists of a type element containing raised characters that strike the paper through an inked ribbon.

Nonimpact printers, such as ink jet printers and laser printers, form characters by means other than striking a ribbon against paper (Figure 9). An **ink jet printer** forms a character by using a nozzle that sprays drops of ink onto the page. Ink jet printers produce relatively high-quality images and print between 150 and 270 characters per second.

FIGURE 9
Two nonimpact printers: a laser printer (left) and inkjet printer (right)

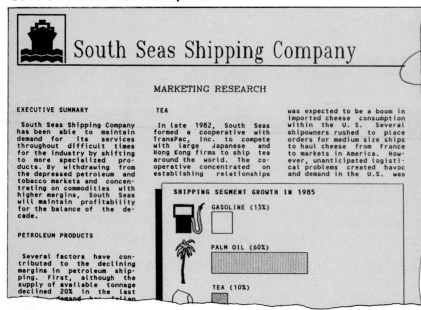

FIGURE 10
Sample output from a laser printer

Laser printers convert data from the personal computer into a beam of laser light that is focused on a photoconductor, forming the images to be printed. The photoconductor attracts particles of toner that are fused onto paper to produce an image. An advantage of the laser printer is that numbers and alphabetic data can be printed in varying sizes and type styles. The output produced is very high quality (Figure 10), with the images resembling professional printing rather than typewritten characters. Laser printers for microcomputers can cost from $1,500 to over $8,000. They can print six to eight pages of text and graphics per minute.

Computer Screens

The computer you use probably has a screen sometimes called a **monitor** or **CRT** (cathode ray tube). The **screen** displays the data entered on the keyboard and messages from the computer.

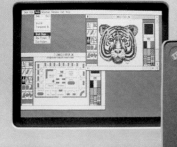

FIGURE 11
A computer display screen may be a monochrome or color unit.

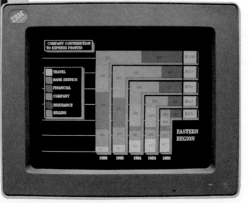

Two general types of screens are used on computers. A **monochrome** screen (Figure 11) uses a single color (green, amber, or white) to display text against a dark background. Some monochrome screens are designed to display only characters; others can display both characters and graphics. Although they cannot display multiple colors, some monochrome screens simulate full color output by using up to 64 shades of the screen's single color.

The second type of screen is a color display. These devices are generally able to display 256 colors at once from a range of more than 256,000 choices.

Computer graphics, charts, graphs, or pictures, can also be displayed on a screen so that the information can be easily and quickly understood. Graphics are often used to present information to others, for example, to help people make business decisions.

Auxiliary Storage

Main memory is not large enough to store the instructions and data for all your applications at one time, so data not in use must be stored elsewhere. **Auxiliary storage** devices are used to store instructions and data when they are not being used in main memory.

Diskettes   One type of auxiliary storage you will use often with microcomputers is the **diskette**. A diskette is a circular piece of oxide-coated plastic that stores data as magnetic spots. Diskettes are available in various sizes. Microcomputers most commonly use diskettes that are 5¼ inches or 3½ inches in diameter (Figure 12).

To read data stored on a diskette or to store data on a diskette, you insert the diskette in a diskette drive (Figure 13). You can tell that the computer is reading data on the diskette or writing data on it because a light on the disk drive will come on while read/write operations are taking place. Do not try to insert or remove a diskette when the light is on. You could easily cause permanent damage to the data stored on it.

The storage capacities of diskette drives and the related diskettes can vary widely (Figure 14). The number of characters that can be stored on a diskette by a diskette drive depends on three factors: (1) the number of sides of the diskette used; (2) the recording density of the bits on a track; and (3) the number of tracks on the diskette.

Early diskettes and diskette drives were designed so that data could be recorded only on one side of the diskette. These drives are called **single-sided drives**. **Double-sided diskettes**, the typical type of diskette used now, provide increased storage capacity because data can be recorded on both sides of the diskette. Diskette drives found on many microcomputers are 5¼-inch, double-sided disk drives that can store approximately 360,000 bytes on the diskette. Another popular type is the 3½-inch diskette, which, although physically smaller, stores from 720,000 to 1.44 million bytes—over twice the capacity of the 5¼-inch diskette. An added benefit of the 3½-inch diskette is its rigid plastic housing, which protects the magnetic surface of the diskette.

The second factor affecting diskette storage capacity is the **recording density** provided by the diskette drive. (The recording density is stated in technical literature as the bpi—the number of bits that can be recorded on a diskette in a one-inch circumference of the innermost track on the diskette.) For the user, the diskettes and diskette drives are identified as being **single density, double density**, or **high density**. You need to be aware of the density of diskettes used by your system because data stored on high-density diskettes, for example, cannot be processed by a computer that has only double-density diskette drives.

The third factor that influences the number of characters that can be stored on a diskette is the number of tracks on the diskette. A **track** is a very narrow recording band forming a full circle around the diskette (Figure 15 on the following page). The width of this recording band depends on the number of tracks on the diskette. The recording bands are separated from each other by a very narrow blank gap. The tracks are established by the diskette drive using the diskette, and they are not visible.

FIGURE 12
Diskettes come in both 5 1/4-inch and 3 1/2-inch sizes. One advantage of the 3 1/2-inch type is its rigid plastic housing, which helps prevent damage to the diskette.

FIGURE 13
To read from a diskette or to store data on it, you must insert the diskette into the computer's diskette drive.

DIAMETER SIZE (INCHES)	DESCRIPTION	CAPACITY (BYTES)
5.25	Single-sided, double-density	160KB/180KB
5.25	Double-sided, double-density	320KB/360KB
5.25	High-capacity, double-density	1.25MB
3.5	Double-sided	720KB
3.5	Double-sided, double-density	1.44MB

FIGURE 14
Types of diskettes and their capacities

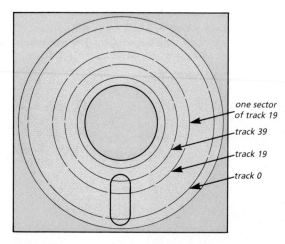

FIGURE 15
How a diskette is formatted

one sector
of track 19

track 39

track 19

track 0

Each track on a diskette is divided into sectors. Sectors are the basic units for diskette storage. When data is read from a diskette, a minimum of one full sector is read. When data is stored on a diskette, one full sector is written at one time. The number of sectors per track and the number of characters that can be stored in each sector are defined by a special formatting program that is used with the computer.

Data stored in sectors on a diskette must be retrieved and placed into main memory to be processed. The time required to access and retrieve data, called the access time, can be important in some applications. The access time for diskettes varies from about 175 milliseconds (one millisecond equals 1/1000 of a second) to approximately 300 milliseconds. On average, data stored in a single sector on a diskette can be retrieved in approximately 1/5 to 1/3 of a second.

Diskette care is important to preserve stored data. Properly handled, diskettes can store data indefinitely. However, the surface of the diskette can be damaged and the data stored can be lost if the diskette is handled improperly. A diskette will give you very good service if you follow a few simple procedures (Figure 16):

Don't touch the disk surface. It is easily contaminated, which causes errors.

Don't use near magnetic field including a telephone. Data can be lost if exposed.

Keep disk in protective envelope when not in use.

Don't bend or fold the disk.

Don't place heavy objects on the disk.

Don't use rubber bands or paper clips on the disk.

Insert disk carefully. Grasp upper edge and place it into the disk drive.

Don't expose the disk to excessive heat for sunlight.

Don't write on the index label with pencil or ballpoint. Use felt-tip pen only.

Don't use erasers on the disk label.

FIGURE 16
How to care for and handle diskettes

1. Store the diskette in its protective envelope when not in use. This procedure is especially necessary for the 5¼-inch diskette that has an oval opening, the **access window**, which permits the read/write heads to access the diskette but also allows the diskette to be easily damaged or soiled.

2. Keep diskettes in their original box or in a special diskette storage box to protect the diskette from dirt and dust and prevent it from being accidentally bent. Store the container away from heat and direct sunlight. Magnetic and electrical equipment, including telephones, radios, and televisions, can erase the data on a diskette so do not place diskettes near such devices. Do not place heavy objects on the diskette, because the weight can pinch the covering, causing damage when the disk drive attempts to rotate the diskette.

3. To affix one of the self-adhesive labels supplied with most diskettes, write or type the information on the label *before* placing the label on the diskette. If the label is already on the diskette, *do not* use an eraser to change the label. If you must write on the label after it is on the diskette, use only a felt-tip pen, *not* a pen or pencil, and press lightly.

4. To use the diskette, carefully remove it from the envelope by grasping the diskette on the side away from the side to be inserted into the disk drive. Slide the diskette carefully into the slot on the disk drive. If the disk drive has a latch or door, close it. If it is difficult to close the disk drive door, do not force it—the diskette may not be inserted fully, and forcing the door closed may damage the diskette. Reinsert the diskette if necessary, and try again to close the door.

The diskette **write-protect** feature (see Figure 17) prevents the accidental erasure of the data stored on a diskette by preventing the diskette drive from writing new data or erasing

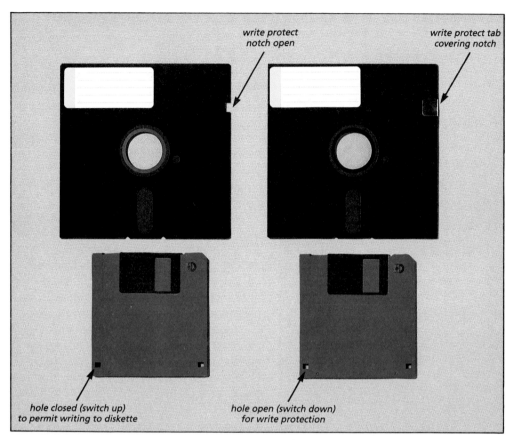

write protect
notch open

write protect tab
covering notch

hole closed (switch up)
to permit writing to diskette

hole open (switch down)
for write protection

FIGURE 17
The write-protect notch of the 5 1/4-inch disk on the left is open and therefore data could be written to the disk. The notch of the 5 1/4-inch disk on the right, however, is covered. Data could not be written to this disk. The reverse situation is true for the 3 1/2-inch disk. Data cannot be written on the 3 1/2-inch disk on the right because the small black piece of plastic is not covering the window in the lower left corner. Plastic covers the window of the 3 1/2-inch disk on the left, so data can be written on this disk.

existing data. On a 5¼-inch diskette, a **write-protect notch** is located on the side of the diskette. A special **write-protect label** is placed over this notch whenever you want to protect the data. On the 3½-inch diskette, a small switch can slide to cover and uncover the write protection notch. On a 3½-inch diskette, when the notch is uncovered the data is protected.

Hard Disk   Another form of auxiliary storage is a hard disk. A **hard disk** consists of one or more rigid metal platters coated with a metal oxide material that allows data to be magnetically recorded on the surface of the platters (Figure 18). Although hard disks are available in cartridge form, most hard disks cannot be removed from the computer and thus are called "fixed disks." As with diskettes, the data is recorded on hard disks on a series of tracks. The tracks are divided into sectors when the disk is formatted.

The hard disk platters spin at high rate of speed, typically 3,600 revolutions per minute. When reading data from the disk, the read head senses the magnetic spots that are recorded on the disk along the various tracks and transfers that data to main memory. When writing, the data is transferred from main memory and is stored as magnetic spots on the tracks on the recording surface of one or more of the disks. Unlike diskette drives, the read/write heads on a fixed disk drive do not actually touch the surface of the disk.

The number of platters permanently mounted on the spindle of a hard disk varies from one to four. On most drives each surface of the platter can be used to store data. Thus, if a hard disk drive uses one platter, two surfaces are available for data. If the drive uses two platters, four sets of read/write heads read and record data from the four surfaces. Storage capacities of fixed disks for microcomputers range from five million characters to over 100 million characters.

FIGURE 18
Cutaway of typical hard disk construction.

SUMMARY OF THE COMPONENTS OF A COMPUTER

*T*he components of a complete computer are illustrated in Figure 19. (Compare this illustration to the computer you will be using.) Input to the computer occurs through the keyboard. As data is keyed on the keyboard, the data is transferred to main memory. In addition, the keyed data is displayed on the computer display screen. The output may be printed on a printer or may be displayed on the computer screen.

The processor unit, which contains main memory and the central processing unit (CPU), consists of circuit boards inside a housing called the **system unit**. In addition to the CPU and main memory, circuit boards inside the system unit contain electronic components that allow communication with the input, output, and auxiliary storage devices.

Data can be transferred from main memory and stored on a diskette or a hard disk. Computers may have a single diskette drive, two diskette drives, one diskette drive and one hard disk drive, or several other combinations. The keyboard, system unit, printer, screen, and auxiliary storage devices are called **computer hardware**.

FIGURE 19
A computer system

WHAT IS COMPUTER SOFTWARE?

A computer's input, processing, output, and storage operations are controlled by instructions collectively called a **computer program** or **software**. A computer program specifies the sequence in which operations are to occur in the computer. For example, a person may give instructions that allow data to be entered from a keyboard and stored in main memory. Another time the program might issue an instruction to perform a calculation using data in main memory. When a task has been completed, a program could give instructions to direct the computer to print a report, display information on the screen, draw a color graph on a color display unit, or store data on a diskette. When directing the operations to be performed, a program must be stored in main memory. Computer programs are written by computer programmers.

Most computer users purchase the software they need for their computer systems. The two major categories of computer software are (1) application software and (2) system software.

Application Software

Application software allows you to perform an application-related function on a computer. A wide variety of programs is available, but for microcomputers the three most widely used types of application software are word processing, spreadsheet, and database management.

Word Processing Software   **Word processing software** such as WordPerfect enables you to use a computer to create documents.

As you use a word processing program, words are keyed in, displayed on the screen, and stored in main memory. If necessary, you can easily correct errors by adding or deleting words, sentences, paragraphs, or pages. You can also establish margins, define page lengths, and perform many other functions involving the manipulation of the written word.

After you have created and corrected your text, you can print it and store it on auxiliary storage for reuse or future reference.

Spreadsheet Software   **Spreadsheet software** is used for reporting and decision making within organizations. At home, you can use a spreadsheet program for budgeting, income tax planning, or tracking your favorite team's scores. You might choose VP Planner or Lotus 1-2-3 to enter the values and formulas needed to perform the desired calculations.

One of the more powerful features of spreadsheet application software is its ability to handle "what-if" questions such as, "What would be the effect on profit if sales increased 12% this year?" The values on the worksheet could easily be recalculated to provide the answer.

Database Software   **Database software** is used to store, organize, update, and retrieve data. Packages such as **dBASE III Plus** store data in a series of files. A **file** is a collection of related data. The data can be organized in the manner you select for your particular application. Once stored in the database, data can be retrieved for use in a variety of ways. For example, data can be retrieved based on the name of an employee in an employee file and full reports can be generated.

System Software

System software consists of programs that start up the computer—load, execute, store, and retrieve files—and perform a series of utility functions. A part of the system software available with most computers is the operating system. An **operating system** is a collection of programs that provides an interface between you or your application programs and the computer hardware itself to control and manage the operation of the computer.

System software, including operating systems, available on computers performs the following basic functions: (1) booting, or starting, the computer operation, (2) interfacing with users, and (3) coordinating the system's access to its various devices.

"Booting" the Computer   When a computer is turned on, the operating system is loaded into main memory by a set of instructions contained internally within the hardware of the computer. This process is called **booting** the computer. When the operating system is loaded into main memory, it is stored in a portion of main memory.

Interface with Users   To communicate with the operating system, the user must enter commands that the operating system can interpret and act upon. The commands can vary from copying a file from one diskette to another, to loading and executing application software.

Coordinating System Devices   Computer hardware is constructed with electrical connections from one device to another. The operating system translates a program's requirements to access a specific hardware device, such as a printer. The operating system can also sense whether the devices are ready for use, or if there is some problem in using a device, such as a printer not being turned on and, therefore, not ready to receive output.

SUMMARY OF INTRODUCTION TO COMPUTERS

 s you learn to use the software taught in this book, you will also become familiar with the components and operation of your computer system. You can refer to this introduction when you need help understanding how the components of your system function.

SUMMARY

1. A **computer** is an electronic device operating under the control of instructions stored in its memory unit.
2. All computers perform basically the same four operations: input, processing, output, and storage.
3. **Data** may be defined as the numbers, words, and phrases that are suitable for processing on a computer to produce information. The production of information from data is called **information processing**.
4. The four basic components of a computer are input unit, processor unit, output unit, and auxiliary storage units.
5. The **keyboard** is the most common input unit. It consists of typewriterlike keys, a numeric keypad, cursor control keys, and programmable function keys.
6. The computer's **processing unit** consists of the central processing unit (CPU) and main memory.
7. Output units consist primarily of displays and printers. **Displays** may be single color (monochrome) or full color. **Printers** may be impact or nonimpact printers.
8. A **dot matrix printer**, the type most commonly used for personal computing, forms characters by printing series of dots to form the character.
9. **Auxiliary storage** on a personal computer is generally disk storage. Disk storage may be on a 5¼-inch or 3½-inch **diskette**, or it may be on an internal **hard disk**.
10. New diskettes must be formatted before they can be used to store data.
11. Computer software can be classified as either **system software**, such as the **operating system**, or as **application software**, such as a word processing, spreadsheet, or database program.

STUDENT ASSIGNMENTS

True-False Questions

Instructions: Circle T if the statement is true or F if the statement is false.

T F   1. The basic operations performed by a computersystem are input operations, processing operations, output operations, and storage operations.
T F   2. Data may be defined as numbers, words, or phrases suitable for processing to produce information.
T F   3. A commonly used input unit on most personal computers is the keyboard.
T F   4. A mouse is a hand-held scanner device for input.
T F   5. The central processing unit contains the processor unit and main memory.
T F   6. Typical personal computer memory is limited to a range of approximately 256,000 to 512,000 bytes of main memory.
T F   7. Auxiliary storage is used to store instructions and data when they are not being used in main memory.
T F   8. The diskette or floppy disk is considered to be a form of main memory.

(T) F   9. A commonly used 5¼-inch double-sided double-density diskette can store approximately 360,000 characters.

T (F) 10. Diskettes can normally store more data than hard disks.

(T) F 11. A computer program is often referred to as computer software.

T (F) 12. A computer program must be permanently stored in main memory.

T (F) 13. Programs such as database management, spreadsheet, and word processing software are called system software.

T (F) 14. The cursor is a mechanical device attached to the keyboard.

(T) F 15. PgUp, PgDn, Home, and End are Function keys.

T (F) 16. A laser printer is one form of impact printer.

(T) F 17. A dot matrix printer forms characters or graphics by forming images as a closely spaced series of dots.

(T) F 18. Application software is the type of program you will use to perform activities such as word processing on a computer.

(T) F 19. The operating system is a collection of programs that provides an interface between you and the computer.

Multiple Choice Questions

1. Which of the following activities will a personal computer *not* be able to perform?
   a. word processing
   b. taking orders in a restaurant
   c. making airline reservations
   (d.) replacing human decision making

2. The four operations performed by a computer include
   (a.) input, control, output, storage
   b. interface, processing, output, memory
   c. input, output, arithmetic/logical, storage
   d. input, logical/rational, arithmetic, output

3. Data may be defined as
   a. a typed report   c. a graph
   (b.) raw facts   d. both a and c

4. PgUp, PgDn, Home, and End keys are
   a. word processing control keys
   (b.) function keys
   c. optional data entry keys
   d. cursor control keys

5. A hand-held input device that controls the cursor location is
   a. the cursor control keyboard
   (b.) a mouse
   c. a scanner
   d. the CRT

6. A printer that forms images without striking the paper is
   a. an impact printer   (c.) an ink jet printer
   (b.) a nonimpact printer   d. both b and d

7. A screen that displays only a single color is
   a. a multichrome monitor
   b. an upper-lower character display
   c. a 7-by-9 matrix screen
   (d.) a monochrome screen

8. Auxiliary storage is the name given to
   a. the computer's main memory
   b. diskette drives
   c. instruction storage buffers
   (d.) none of the above

9. A diskette
   a. is a nonremovable form of storage
   b. is available in 5¼- and 3½-inch sizes
   c. is a form of magnetic data storage
   (d.) both b and c

10. The amount of storage provided by a diskette is a function of
    a. whether the diskette records on one or both sides
    b. the recording pattern or density of bits on the diskette
    c. the number of recording tracks used on the track
    (d.) all of the above

11. Some diskettes have an access window that is used to
    a. pick up and insert the diskette into a diskette drive
    b. provide access for cleaning
    (c.) provide access for the read/write head of the diskette drive
    d. verify data stored on the diskette

12. When not in use, diskettes
    a. should be placed in their protective envelopes
    b. should be stored away from heat, magnetic fields, and direct sunlight
    c. should be stored in a diskette box or cabinet
    (d.) all of the above

13. A hard disk is
    a. an alternate form of removable storage
    b. a rigid platter with magnetic coating
    (c.) a storage system that remains installed in the computer
    d. both a and b

14. Storage capacities of hard disks
    a. are about the same as for diskettes
    b. range from 80,000 to 256,000 bytes
    c. range from five million to over 100 million
    d. vary with the type of program used

15. Software is classified as
    a. utility and applied systems
    b. operating systems and application programs
    c. language translators and task managers
    d. word processing and spreadsheet programs

Projects

1. Popular computer magazines contain many articles and advertisements that inform computer users of the latest in computing trends. Review a few recent articles and report on the apparent trends you have noted. Discuss which hardware features seem to be the most in demand. What are the differences between the alternative hardware choices? Discuss the implications these choices may have on the type of software chosen by a computer owner.
2. Software changes as computer users become more knowledgeable. According to your reading of computer magazines, what software innovations seem to have the greatest promise? Which specific features or styles of user interfaces seem to offer new computing capabilities? Discuss any particular program that seems to be a style setter in its field.
3. Visit local computer retail stores to compare the various types of computers and supporting equipment available. Ask about warranties, repair services, hardware setup, training, and related issues. Report on the knowledge of the sales staff assisting you and their willingness to answer your questions. Does the store have standard hardware "packages," or are they willing to configure a system to your specific needs? Would you feel confident about buying a computer from this store?

INDEX

Photo Credits: **Opening Page**, International Business Machines Corp.; **Figure 1**, International Business Machines Corp.; Compaq Computer Corp.; **Figure 2**, Intel Corp.; **Figure 4**, (a) Curtis Fukuda, (b) International Business Machines Corp.; **Figure 5**, Logitech, Inc.; **Figure 6**, International Business Machines Corp.; **Figure 9 and 10**, Hewlett-Packard Company; **Figure 11**, (left) Wyse Technology; (right) International Business Machines Corp.; **Figures 12, 13, and 17**, Curtis Fukuda; **Figure 18**, Seagate Technology; **Figure 19**, International Business Machines Corp.

Word Processing Using WordPerfect 5.0/5.1

PROJECT 1

Typing, Saving, and Printing a Simple Letter

Objectives

You will have mastered the material in this project when you can:

- Load WordPerfect into main memory
- Explain the function of the WordPerfect template
- Move the cursor in all directions
- View the reveal codes
- Type, save, and print a short letter
- Exit WordPerfect and return to the DOS prompt

WordPerfect, developed by **WordPerfect Corporation**, Orem, Utah is a best-selling word processing program. WordPerfect 5.0 and 5.1 are available for use on most microcomputers on the market. You will learn how to use WordPerfect 5.0 and 5.1 on an IBM personal computer (PC, XT, AT, PS/2, and compatibles) operating under MS-DOS, or PC-DOS. The differences between 5.0 and 5.1 are identified by the phrase "For 5.1 Users." Like all word processing programs, WordPerfect is used to produce printed documents and is especially useful when documents require precise formatting and presentation. These documents can be prepared for many different applications, from business memos to student term papers.

In the following projects all the features of WordPerfect will not be explained. For an explanation of those features not covered, refer to the WordPerfect Reference Manual supplied with the software package by WordPerfect Corporation.

For the following Projects using WordPerfect we assume you are using a keyboard with the function keys at the *left* of the keyboard.

THE KEYBOARD

In Project 1 you will become familiar with the keyboard and the template used with WordPerfect. To learn the position and feel of the keys, you will practice pressing certain keys before turning the computer on. Then, after turning the computer on and loading WordPerfect, you will type, save, and print the short letter in Figure 1-1. You will then practice moving the cursor on a blank screen, after which you will exit the WordPerfect program.

```
December 1, 1990


Mr. Joseph Wright
236 Santo Domingo Cir.
Fountain Valley, CA 92708

Dear Mr. Wright:

I received your letter today and wish to thank you for it.

Sincerely,


Mary Martinez
Director
```

FIGURE 1-1
Letter for Project 1.

The **keyboard** is used as an **input** device to input data into the computer. Look over the entire keyboard in Figure 1-2. In addition to the familiar typewriter keyboard keys, you will see some other keys. To the left of the typewriter section (or on top of the keyboard, depending on which keyboard you are using), you will notice keys F1 through F10. These are called **function keys** (some computers also have function keys 11 and 12). To the right of the keyboard is a **numeric keypad**, which looks similar to a 10-key adding machine. In addition to numbers, most keys on this numeric keypad have arrows pointing in different directions, or words such as Home and End.

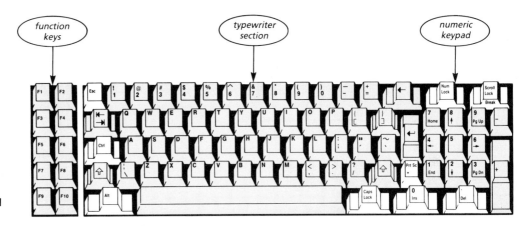

FIGURE 1-2
The computer keyboard (console).

The Typewriter Section

Most keys in the typewriter section have the automatic repeat feature. For example, if you hold down the "a" key, the letter "a" will repeatedly appear on the screen. When you are asked in this book to press a specific key, try to tap the key quickly rather than pressing down and holding the key down. This will eliminate unwanted repeat characters.

Keys that do not have the automatic repeat feature are the Shift, Ctrl (Control) and Alt (Alternate) keys, which all act like the Shift key on a traditional typewriter. To type a CAPITAL LETTER or the symbols above the numbers (#, $, %, &, *, etc.), hold down the Shift key and press the desired key. The Shift, Ctrl, and Alt keys (Figure 1-3) are used with the function keys to achieve specific word processing goals.

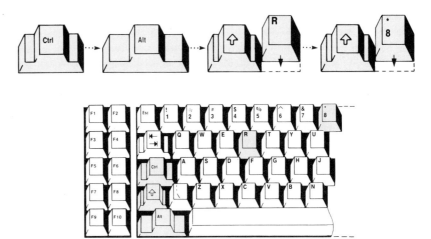

FIGURE 1-3
The Ctrl, Alt, and Shift keys.

To become familiar with these keys *before* you turn on the computer, press the Ctrl key down, then let it up. Now press the Alt key, then let it up. Press the Right Shift key down and while holding it press the R key, then let them both up. Now hold the Left Shift key down and press the 8 key. Had the machine been on and WordPerfect loaded, the R key would have typed a capital R and the 8 key would have typed the asterisk, *.

The **Tab** key (Figure 1-4) is used for indenting to the next tab setting to the right, just as on a typewriter. Press the Tab key, and notice that there is one arrow that faces forward → and one arrow that faces backward ←. That is because this key, when pressed with the Shift key, also allows you to release the left margin. Hold the Shift key down firmly and press the Tab key. Had the machine been on and WordPerfect loaded, the margin would have been released to the next tab setting to the *left* of the cursor.

The **Return** key (Figure 1-5), is used to do the same thing that the Return key is used for on a typewriter—to begin a new line. On most keyboards, however, the word **Enter** is on the key along with an arrow that looks like this ←. That is because this key is also used to enter information into the computer.

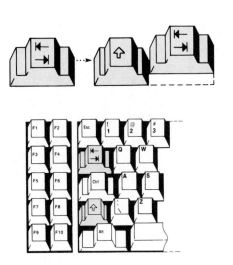

FIGURE 1-4 The Tab key.

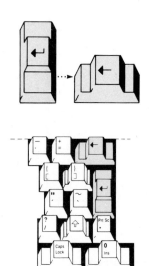

FIGURE 1-5 The Return or Enter and Backspace keys.

Often while using a word processing package, such as WordPerfect, you will type a command and the letters or numbers you typed will stay on the screen; you may wonder what to do next. A good rule of thumb is that *if you have given a command and nothing happens, press Enter* ←. In other words, the command you typed is only on the screen. It will not be entered into the memory of the computer until you press the Enter key. The few exceptions to this will be discussed individually. Now, for practice, press the Enter key.

Although Enter and Return are the same key, remember that sometimes the key will be referred to as Enter and sometimes as Return. When you were loading DOS into the computer, you may have had to type the date. After the date, you pressed the Enter key, because you wanted the date entered into the computer memory. When you press this key at the end of a paragraph or a short line, or when you want to add a blank line in your text, you refer to the key as the Return key, as you normally would if you were typing on a typewriter. Since the Enter (Return) key has an arrow like this ←, many times throughout these projects you will see this arrow instead of the word Enter or Return. When you see the arrow, press the Enter key.

The **Backspace** key (Figure 1-5) is used to move the cursor backward on the screen, much like the Backspace key on a typewriter. However, in WordPerfect, as you backspace, the character or space directly to the left of the cursor (_) is deleted. Try pressing the Backspace key.

The Numeric Keypad

Figure 1-6 shows the numeric keypad. The keys on the numeric keypad can be used to type numbers, but for most purposes it's better to use the number keys in the typewriter section of the keyboard to type numbers. It's more important to use the keys on the numeric keypad to move the cursor through the text on the screen. An enhanced keyboard has an extra set of cursor keys, which frees the numeric keypad for typing only numbers. The arrow pointing to the left will move the cursor one character to the left. Press the **Left Arrow** key ← several times. The arrow pointing right will move the cursor one character to the right. Press the **Right Arrow** key → several times. The arrow pointing up will move the cursor up one line. Press the **Up Arrow** key ↑ several times. The arrow pointing down will move the cursor down one line. Press the **Down Arrow** key ↓ several times.

If you wish to use the numeric keypad to type numbers instead of using it to move the cursor, you will have to "lock" the numbers to the "on" position by pressing the Num Lock key. For practice, press the Num Lock key several times.

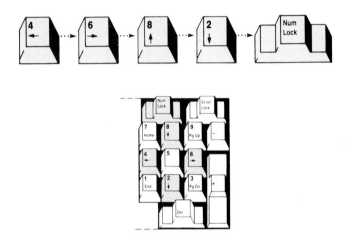

FIGURE 1-6 The Numeric Keypad.

The Function Keys

Find the function keys on the far left side of the keyboard (or at the top). They are numbered 1 to 10 (or 11 and 12 on the enhanced keyboard), with an F in front of each number. These function keys are special keys programmed to execute commonly used commands. Functions can be margin changes, tab setting changes, boldfacing, correcting the spelling of a document, and so on.

To understand how the function keys work, first look at the keyboard. If you have any typing experience, you know that if you were to type the G key, you would see a lowercase g on the screen. If you hold down the Shift key and type the *same* G key, the Shift key changes the function of that key and makes it a capital G. You type the same key, but you get a different value, depending on whether you press the key alone or hold down the Shift key and press the G key.

The Function keys are very similar. If you press a function key alone, you will be able to perform a certain function, such as saving a document. But if you hold the Shift key down and press the same function key, you will be able to perform an entirely different function, such as centering.

Further, you can hold down the Alt key or the Ctrl key and press the same Function key to perform additional functions such as moving parts of your text. *Each* function key can have *four* different values, depending on whether you press it alone or with the Ctrl, Alt, or Shift keys.

THE WORDPERFECT TEMPLATE

Figure 1-7 shows two versions of the WordPerfect **Template**. One template fits around the function keys. The other lays above the function keys. Most word processors show command messages on the screen that take up valuable space. The template takes command messages off the screen and puts them next to the function keys to which they correspond. This not only makes it easier to learn the keystrokes, it also unclutters the screen, making it easier to read.

The template is color coded, starting at the bottom with black, then blue, green, and red on the top. The colors signify the following:

Black means you press the key alone.

Blue means you hold down the **Alt** key firmly while pressing the desired F key.

Green means you hold down the **Shift** key firmly while pressing the desired F key.

Red means you hold down the **Ctrl** key firmly while pressing the desired F key.

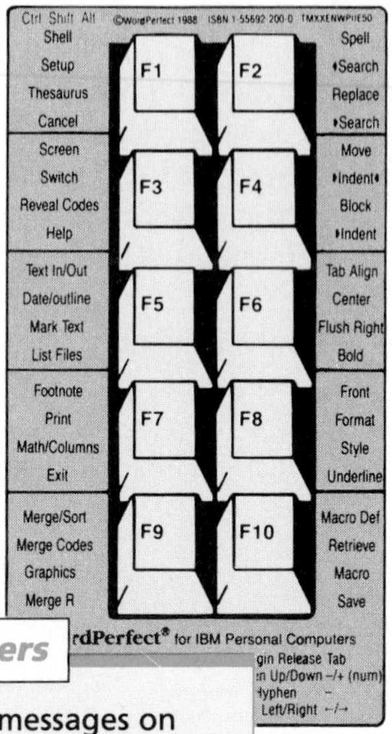

For 5.1 Users

The command messages on your template will be slightly different, but your keystrokes will remain the same.

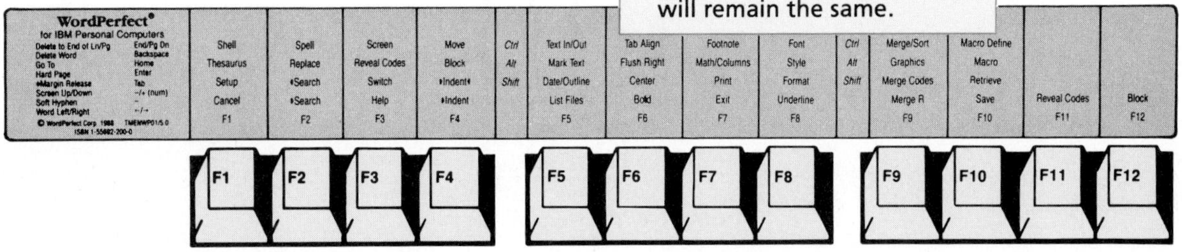

FIGURE 1-7 Templates for the Function keys.

To understand how to use this template and its color coding, look next to the F6 key on the template. Notice that the bottom item, in black, says Bold. Therefore, if you desire to have your typing boldfaced you would press the F6 key alone. For practice, press the F6 key. If the computer had been turned on and WordPerfect was loaded, after you pressed the F6 key, any typing you did would have been boldfaced, until you "turned off" the boldface by pressing the F6 key again.

Let's try another example. Look at the template next to the F2 key. You will see the word Spell in red. Because red signifies the Ctrl key on the template, hold down the Ctrl key firmly and while holding it, lightly press the F2 key to perform the Spell function. For practice, hold down the Ctrl key and press the F2 key. If the machine had been turned on and WordPerfect was loaded, it would have been ready to check the spelling of your text.

In summary, whenever you see Ctrl, Alt, or Shift followed by a hyphen and a function key—such as Ctrl-F8 or Alt-F3—remember to hold down the first key and, while holding it down, lightly press the function key.

Common mistakes made by users of WordPerfect are that they try to press the Ctrl, Alt, or Shift key *simultaneously* with the function key, or they press the Ctrl, Alt, or Shift key, release that key, and then press the function key. If you make either of those mistakes, the computer will react as if you had pressed the function key *only*.

If you press the function keys in error and get a message on the lower left corner of the screen that you wish to remove, press the F1 (Cancel) key. That will usually undo that error and remove the message.

Practice on the keyboard for a few minutes to feel more comfortable with it. After you have practiced with the Ctrl, Alt, and Shift keys, you will have just the right touch.

DEFAULTS

One word that you will see throughout this text is **default**. This word simply means that *unless instructed otherwise* this is the action to be taken. For example, you will often be asked to give a yes or no answer, as in the message in Figure 1-8. You may type Y or N, whichever is your choice. (You do not need to type the whole word Yes or No.) Notice that after the (Y/N), WordPerfect displays an option outside the parentheses, and the cursor will be under that option. The choice above the cursor is WordPerfect's default choice. If you want the default choice, you can type Y or N, or you can press the Enter key, which automatically accepts the default choice.

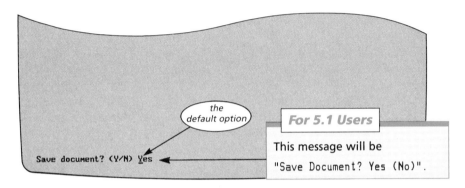

the default option

For 5.1 Users

This message will be "Save Document? Yes (No)".

Save document? (Y/N) Yes

FIGURE 1-8

LOADING WORDPERFECT

WordPerfect 5.0 and 5.1 are normally installed on a hard disk system, because of the memory required to store this word processing software. If you are using a hard disk system, or running on a networked version of WordPerfect, your instructor will show you how to access the WordPerfect program. Also be sure to put a formatted floppy disk into drive A so you can save your documents to a floppy disk.

If you are running WordPerfect on a floppy disk system, use the following instructions. First load DOS into memory so that the A> prompt is displayed. Remove the DOS disk and place the WordPerfect disk into drive A. Also place a formatted data disk into drive B to save your documents. At the A> prompt, type wp and press the Enter key, as shown in Figure 1-9. This instructs the computer to load the WordPerfect program into the computer's memory.

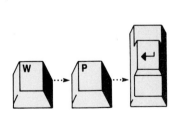

```
Current date is Tue 1-01-1980
Enter new date: 12-1-90
Current time is   0:00:15.32
Enter new time:

The IBM Personal Computer DOS
Version 2.10 (C)Copyright IBM Corp 1981, 1982, 1983

A> wp
```

FIGURE 1-9

You hear the drives working, loading the WordPerfect program into the memory of the computer. (If the last person to use WordPerfect exited WordPerfect improperly, you may be stopped before this screen and asked, "Are other copies of WordPerfect currently running (Y/N)? Yes" If you get this message, type N and WordPerfect will continue.)

After WordPerfect is loaded, an almost blank screen appears, as shown in Figure 1-10. The only things on this screen are the status line and a blinking cursor. This blank screen is your work space, just as if you had put a blank piece of paper in your typewriter. The **cursor** is a visual reminder of where you are in the document. The **status line** informs you at all times about the exact document, page, line, and position of your cursor. For example, in Figure 1-10 the status line tells you that the cursor is in Document 1, on page 1, line 1", position 1". Line 1" means that the cursor is one inch from the top of the page. Pos 1" means that the cursor is one inch from the left edge of the page (Figure 1-11).

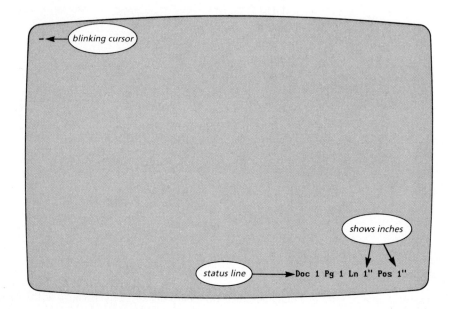

FIGURE 1-10

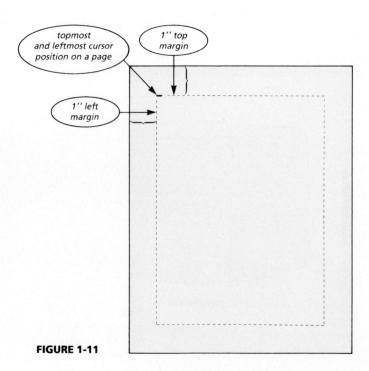

FIGURE 1-11

One of the differences between WordPerfect 4.2 and WordPerfect 5.0/5.1 is that 5.0/5.1 introduces the use of inches on the status line and in the display of margins and tab settings. In WordPerfect 5.0/5.1 the position and line numbers appear as decimal numbers, such as Ln 2.67" Pos 3.7". In WordPerfect 4.2, the same information appears in whole numbers, such as Ln 2 Pos 37. The use of inches is becoming the accepted standard for word processing, and so inches will be used in this book. Please note that depending upon the make and model of your computer, the numbers that appear on your screen may not exactly match those shown in the book. For example, 3.33" may appear on your screen as 3.34". WordPerfect version 5.0 and 5.1 can be changed to the 4.2 format. If you are using the 5.0 or the 5.1 version of the program, and if your version is set to the 4.2 format, you should change to the 5.0/5.1 format as follows:

First enter the Setup menu by holding down the Shift key and pressing F1 (step 1 in Figure 1-12). If you are using Word-Perfect 5.1, also press the number 3 (For 5.1 Users box in step 1 in Figure 1-12). Press the number 8 for Units of Measure (step 2 in Figure 1-12). Press 1 for Display and Entry of Numbers, and then hold down the Shift key and press the single/double quotes key, which is also used for the inches symbol (") (step 1 in Figure 1-13). Next, press 2 to select Status Line Display, and again hold down the Shift key and press the inches key (") (step 2 in Figure 1-13). To exit to the document screen press F7 (step 3 in Figure 1-13). Your screen will then look like Figure 1-14.

Step 1: View Setup Menu

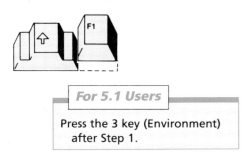

For 5.1 Users

Press the 3 key (Environment) after Step 1.

Step 2: Select Units of Measure

```
Setup

    1 - Backup

    2 - Cursor Speed                    Normal

    3 - Display

    4 - Fast Save (unformatted)         Yes

    5 - Initial Settings

    6 - Keyboard Layout

    7 - Location of Auxiliary Files

    8 - Units of Measure




Selection: 0
```

FIGURE 1-12

Step 1: Select Display and Entry of Numbers, and choose inches

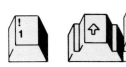

Step 2: Select Status Line Display and choose inches

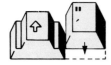

Step 3: Exit to the document

```
Setup: Units of Measure

    1 - Display and Entry of Numbers        "
            for Margins, Tabs, etc.

    2 - Status Line Display                 u


Legend:

    " = inches
    i = inches
    c = centimeters
    p = points
    u = 1200ths of an inch
    u = WordPerfect 4.2 Units (Lines/Columns)





Selection: 0
```

FIGURE 1-13

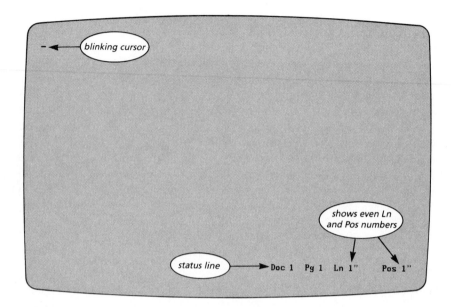

FIGURE 1-14

Before you proceed, you must do two things: check the default drive to verify that documents you type will be saved to your diskette, and select what is called the Standard Printer Definition. To check the default drive, press the F5 key. If the prompt in the lower left corner reads Dir A:*.* for hard drive users or Dir B:*.* for two disk drive users, then you do not have to change the default drive. Notice on the bottom right corner of the screen that you can type the equals sign (=) to change the default directory. If you do need to change the default drive, press the equals sign and, following the prompt "New directory = ", type a: (if you are using a hard disk system) or type b: (if you are using a two disk drive system). Then press Enter, and notice that the default directory has changed. Press F1 to return to the document screen.

Next we will select the Standard Printer Definition, in other words, we will define the specifications WordPerfect will send to the printer when we print a document. A document can look very different depending upon which printer definition we select. All of the projects in this book use what is called the **Standard Printer Definition**. If you have another printer definition selected, your documents may look different than the screen illustrations throughout this book. Thus, you must be sure that you *use the Standard Printer Definition in this and all future projects in this book*. To be sure that you use the Standard Printer Definition, first press Shift-F7. To the right of Select Printer, you see the words Standard Printer. If not, press S for Select Printer. A list of printer files appears. Move the cursor down to highlight the Standard Printer, then press 1 to select that printer definition. *If the Standard Printer is not listed*, press 2 for Additional Printers. Then press 4 to List Printer Files. Look for the STANDARD.PRS file on this list, and move the cursor to highlight it. (If you cannot find the STANDARD.PRS file see your instructor.) Press 1 to select it. A message tells you that no help is provided. Then press F7 to exit this screen, and press F7 again to exit the list of printers. The Standard Printer is now highlighted on the screen. Press 1 to select the Standard Printer, and Press F7 to exit to a blank screen.

THE SCREEN (OR WINDOW)

A **screen** or "window" is what appears on the computer monitor. Although you may have a four-page document, you can only view 24 lines down or 80 characters across at any one time on a screen. Imagine yourself looking out a window. You can only see a portion of the landscape outside. This does not mean that the rest of the world is not there, just that *your* view of the world is limited. If you went to another window, you would have a different view. This is the same as your "window" on your document. As Figure 1-15 shows, you can only see one screenful at a time. This does not mean that the rest of the document does not exist. Your view of your document depends on where your screen or "window" is situated.

If you were typing on a typewriter, you would put one sheet of paper in at a time. Figure 1-15 illustrates how in Word-Perfect all the pages seem to be attached together, with a so-called perforation between the pages. WordPerfect is programmed to advise you where the bottom of the page is and when you have started typing on the next page. When you have moved onto the next page, a line that looks much like a perforation will appear across the screen. After this line appears, the status line indicates that you are on the next page.

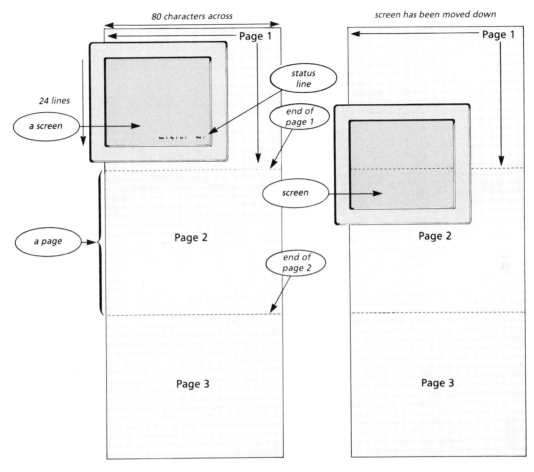

FIGURE 1-15

THE HELP FUNCTION

*I*f you need help, you could use the **Help Function**. This is a collection of screens that you can access any time you are working on a document. These screens contain quick reminders on how to use WordPerfect. For example press F3. You can press any letter to view an alphabetical list of features, or you can press any function key to view information about the use of the key. Telephone numbers for customer support are also given. To exit the Help screen, press Enter or the spacebar.

CREATING A DOCUMENT

*N*ow we are ready to create the letter to Mr. Wright (recall Figure 1-1). As you type, remember that if you type a mistake, all you need to do is press the Backspace key. As you do, your typing to the left of the Backspace key will be deleted. You can then retype correctly. If something unexpected happens, pressing the Backspace key may help. If you press a function key in error and you see a message at the bottom left corner of the screen, try pressing the **F1 (Cancel)** key.

Begin typing the first line of Figure 1-16, which is the date. As you type, notice that the position indicator (Pos) on the status line changes with each letter or space you add.

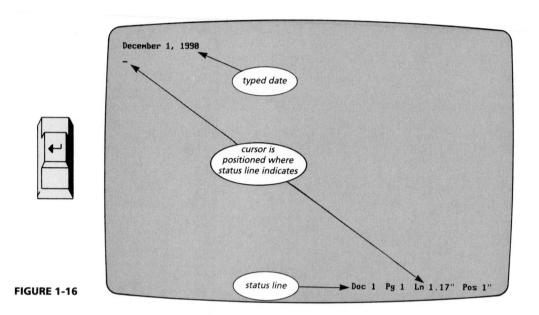

FIGURE 1-16

After typing the date, press the Return key. Pressing the Return key to start a new line is called a **hard return**. The cursor is now at line 1.17". Look at the status line for verification of the line where the cursor is. In order to insert four blank lines between the date and the addressee's name, press the Return key four more times. The status line now shows that the cursor is on line 1.83". Type the words Mr. Joseph Wright and then press the Return key, which takes the cursor to line 2". Type 236 Santo Domingo Cir. and press the Return key. The status line now indicates that the cursor is on line 2.17". Type the words Fountain Valley, CA 92708 and press the Return key. Figure 1-17 shows what your screen looks like with the date, name, and address.

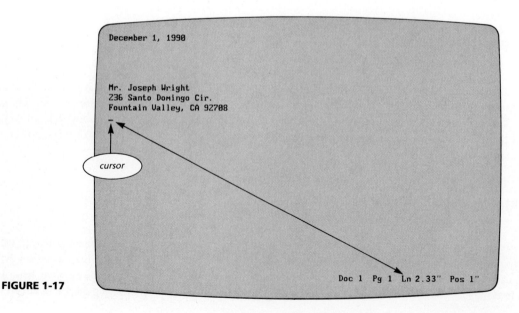

FIGURE 1-17

Now that you have typed the name and address, you want a blank line between the last address line and the greeting to Mr. Wright. Simply press the Return key. That will insert a blank line. Your status line now indicates that the cursor is on line 2.5", position 1". Type the words Dear Mr. Wright: and press the Return key. Press the Return key again to insert another blank line. On line 2.83", type: I received your letter today and wish to thank you for it. Press the Return key. Press it again to insert a blank line. On line 3.17", type the word Sincerely, and press the Return key, which will move the cursor to line 3.33", position 1" (Figure 1-18).

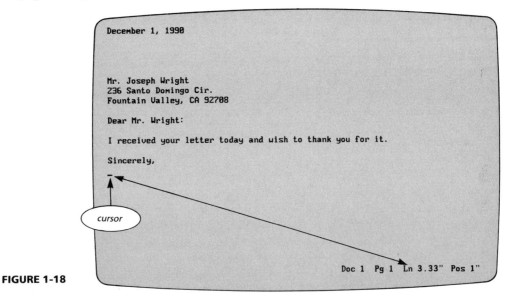

FIGURE 1-18

To add three more blank lines, press the Return key three more times. On line 3.83" type the words Mary Martinez followed by a Return. Type the word Director. The status line shows line 4", position 1.8". Press the Return key one more time, taking the cursor to line 4.17", position 1".

Figure 1-19 shows how the finished document should look on your screen.

If you neglected to insert a blank line somewhere, move the cursor to the beginning of that line and press Enter. If you omitted a word, move the cursor to the point where you wish to insert the word and type. All other text will move to accommodate the new text.

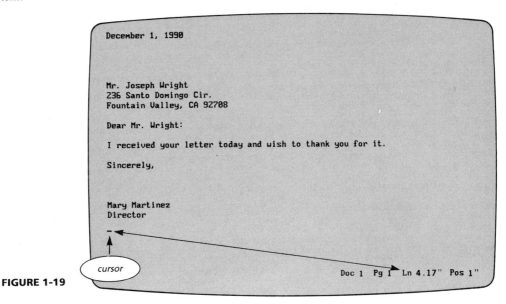

FIGURE 1-19

REVEAL CODES

*T*he WordPerfect software "remembers" each keystroke you make, whether a letter, number, or space. In addition, when you change margins or when you press the Return key, the Tab key, or other keys, the WordPerfect software embeds **codes** into the text, thereby recording each key you have pressed. To keep the screen clean and free of codes, WordPerfect stores these embedded codes in a hidden screen. You can view the codes at any time, however, by using the Alt and F3 keys. To learn about these codes first press the Up Arrow key until the cursor is at the top of the document.

Learning How to Read the Reveal Codes

For each function you perform in WordPerfect, a unique code is embedded into the text. When you type a line and then perform a hard return, for example, that hard return is registered by the WordPerfect software and the code **[HRt]** is entered into the text at that point.

As you look at the screen you cannot see any of the codes, because they are on a hidden screen. Hold down the Alt key firmly and press the F3 key. Your screen will look similar to Figure 1-20. [For 5.1 Users – The Reveal Codes screen will display fewer lines.]

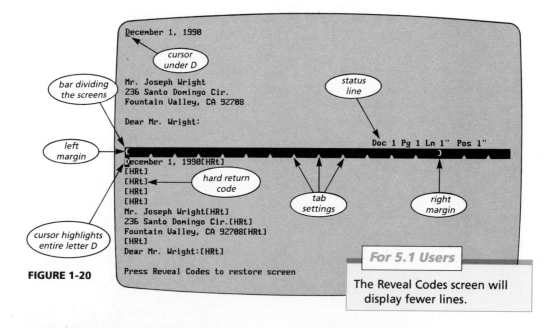

FIGURE 1-20

For 5.1 Users

The Reveal Codes screen will display fewer lines.

Step 1: Move cursor one space to the right

Step 2: Move cursor down one line at a time

Step 3: Exit reveal codes

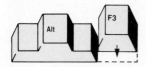

If you are using an enhanced keyboard you will find two function keys labeled F11 and F12. WordPerfect allows you to access the reveal codes by pressing F11 instead of Alt-F3. You can also press F11 to exit the reveal codes. You will not be told this each time we look at the reveal codes, but if you are using an enhanced keyboard you can press F11 whenever you are instructed to press Alt-F3.

Look at your screen carefully. It appears that you have two different screens separated by a bar. First, look at the upper portion of the screen, at the numbers and letters above the bar. This is the screen you are used to viewing. You cannot see any codes, and your status line can still be viewed.

In the middle of the screen there appears to be a bar. On the left side you will notice a brace {. This indicates where your left margin is located. On the right side you will notice a brace also. This indicates where your right margin is located. The triangles (▲) you see between these symbols indicate where the tabs are currently set. Default is every five spaces.

On the bottom portion of the screen, notice that the text of the letter is the same as that on the top of the screen, with some differences. This lower screen is where your **reveal codes** are displayed. All the codes are in boldface. This is so that the codes will be easily recognized. The cursor in the reveal codes screen highlights or makes a reverse video of the letter or code where the cursor is currently placed. If the cursor is *under* the D in the upper screen the *entire* D is highlighted in the lower screen.

Figure 1-20 also shows, on the lower screen, that at the end of the first line you typed, you inserted a hard return. At the end of that line the code **[HRt]** is inserted, indicating that you pressed the Return key to start a new line.

Move your cursor one character to the right by pressing the Right Arrow → (step 1 in Figure 1-20). Notice that the cursor on the upper screen moves *underneath* each character, while the cursor on the lower screen moves *over* each character. Now move your cursor down one line by pressing the Down Arrow key ↓ (step 2 in Figure 1-20). Notice how both cursors move at the same time. They are, in fact, the same cursor, and move in relationship to each other.

Continue pressing the Down Arrow key ↓ until the status line indicates the cursor is on line 2.33". As you do this, notice how each time you pressed the Return key in the letter, the reveal codes indicate that a hard return code was embedded into the document. The reveal codes function is a valuable feature of WordPerfect. As you become more familiar with this feature, you will notice how much control you have over your word processing.

To exit from the reveal codes press Alt-F3 (step 3 in Figure 1-20).

Because you will be instructed many times in this text to display the reveal codes, practice this a few times. Hold down the Alt key, then press the F3 key. See how quickly the reveal codes are displayed. Press Alt-F3 to exit the reveal codes.

SAVING A DOCUMENT

*T*he letter to Mr. Wright is now completed. Whenever a document is completed, it should be **saved** on a disk so that it can be retrieved for printing or modification at a later time. Look at the template next to the F10 key (Figure 1-21).

For 5.1 Users

The command messages on your template will be slightly different, but your keystrokes will remain the same.

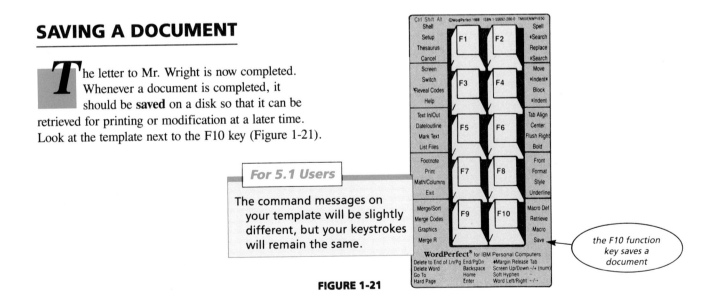

the F10 function key saves a document

FIGURE 1-21

Notice that the word Save is in black, indicating that the key is to be pressed alone. Now press the F10 key. At the lower left corner of your screen you will see the message "Document to be Saved:" (Figure 1-22).

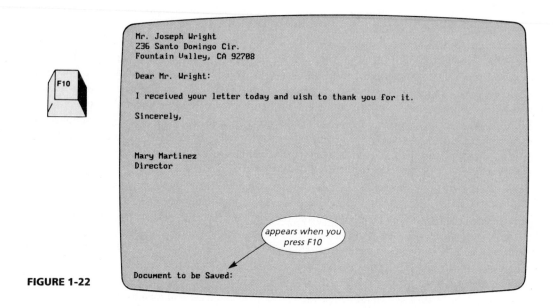

FIGURE 1-22

Type the name Wright (in uppercase, lowercase, or a combination). After you have typed Wright you will notice that nothing else happens. Remember: When nothing happens, press Enter (Figure 1-23).

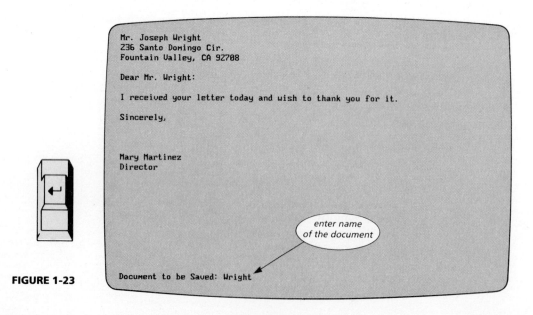

FIGURE 1-23

After you have pressed the Enter key you will notice that the light on drive A or drive B goes on, indicating that the document is being saved to that drive. Remember that at the beginning of this project you changed the default drive to A if you are using a hard disk system or drive B if you are using a floppy disk system.

Your document is now named and saved. The name of your document appears in the lower left corner of your screen. As shown in Figure 1-24, the disk drive and directory that the document was saved to (B:\) are also displayed along with the document name.

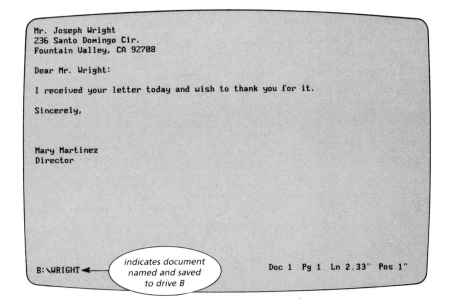

```
Mr. Joseph Wright
236 Santo Domingo Cir.
Fountain Valley, CA 92708

Dear Mr. Wright:

I received your letter today and wish to thank you for it.

Sincerely,



Mary Martinez
Director




B:\WRIGHT ◄─        indicates document        Doc 1  Pg 1  Ln 2.33"  Pos 1"
                    named and saved
                    to drive B
```

FIGURE 1-24

PRINTING A DOCUMENT

fter the document is typed and stored on the disk, you usually want to **print** it on paper. Before continuing, be sure that your printer has continuous feed paper inserted and that the printer is turned on and ready to print. To print your document look at the template next to the **F7** key. Notice the word Print in green (Figure 1-25).

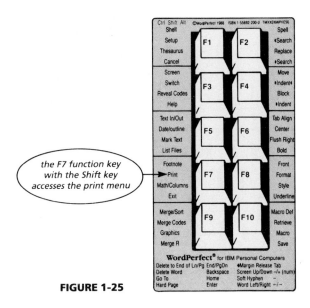

the F7 function key with the Shift key accesses the print menu

FIGURE 1-25

Hold down the Shift key and press the F7 key (step 1 in Figure 1-26). You will see on your screen the Print menu shown in Figure 1-26.

Since we want to print the full text of this document, press the number 1 for full text (step 2 in Figure 1-26). At this point the printer will begin printing your document. The printed letter should look like Figure 1-1 on page WP 2.

Step 1: Retrieve the Print menu

Step 2: Print the full text

FIGURE 1-26

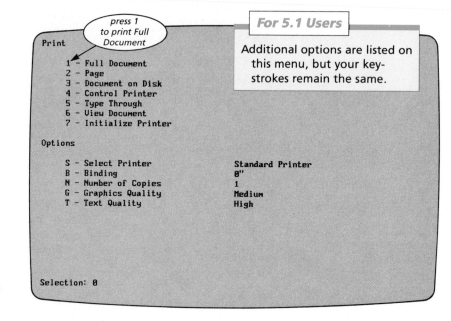

```
                                    press 1
                                   to print Full
                                    Document            For 5.1 Users
 Print
                                                    Additional options are listed on
       1 - Full Document                              this menu, but your key-
       2 - Page                                        strokes remain the same.
       3 - Document on Disk
       4 - Control Printer
       5 - Type Through
       6 - View Document
       7 - Initialize Printer

 Options

       S - Select Printer           Standard Printer
       B - Binding                  0"
       N - Number of Copies         1
       G - Graphics Quality         Medium
       T - Text Quality             High




 Selection: 0
```

MOVING THE CURSOR ON A BLANK SCREEN

N ow that the letter to Mr. Wright has been typed, saved, and printed, we will use a blank screen to practice the Return, Tab, and spacebar functions shown in Figure 1-27. These are helpful keys for moving the cursor. To be sure you are at the end of this document, press the **Home** key *two times*, then press the Down Arrow key ↓ one time (step 1 in Figure 1-28). This places the cursor at the end of your document. Press the Return key to insert a hard return (step 2 in Figure 1-28). This moves the cursor to a new line.

FIGURE 1-27

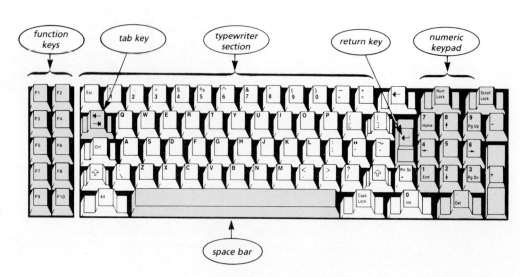

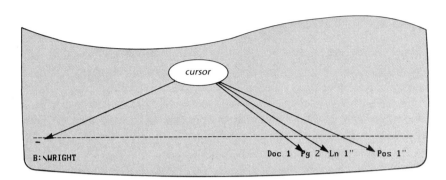

FIGURE 1-28

Step 1: Move cursor to the end of the document   **Step 2: Move cursor to a new line**   **Step 3: Move to page 2, line 1**

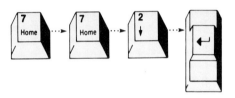   

Recall that when you press the Return key, the cursor moves down one line at a time. The status line also indicates when the cursor has moved down a line. Press the Return key until the status line indicates that the cursor is on page 1, line 9.83''. If you then press the Return key one more time (step 3 in Figure 1-28), a dotted line appears on the screen. This dotted line marks the end of page 1. The status line indicates that the cursor is now on page 2, line 1'' as shown in Figure 1-28.

Press the Tab key once and you will see the cursor move to the right 1/2'' at a time. The status line also indicates with the position number that the cursor has moved 1/2'' at a time.

Press the spacebar and you will see the cursor move to the right 1'' at a time. The status line will also indicate with the position number that the cursor has moved 1'' at a time.

Remember also that you cannot move the cursor into an area of the screen where text has not already been entered. For example, on line 2.5'' you cannot move beyond position 2.6'', the position of the hard return.

Now that you understand the meanings of Pg (page), Ln (line), and Pos (position) on the status line, you may wonder about Doc (document) 1. WordPerfect allows you to work on two different documents at the same time. For example, suppose you were working on a 30-page document and you needed to stop and quickly type a letter and print it out. You could switch to Doc (document) 2. In fact, you could switch back and forth between the two documents, making changes, printing, saving, and so on. The changes or printing of document 1 would not affect document 2 at all. This is like having two computers.

Look at the template next to the F3 key and notice the word Switch in green (Figure 1-29). To see document 2, hold down the Shift key firmly and press the F3 key (step 1 in Figure 1-30 on the next page). You could type, save, and print a letter in document 2 without disturbing your letter to Mr. Wright in document 1. When finished with the letter in document 2, you could switch back to document 1. Your cursor will revert to where it was in document 1, allowing you to continue.

the F3 function key with Shift key switches to a different document

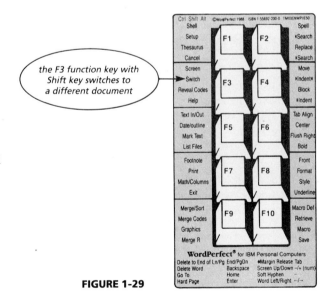

FIGURE 1-29

To return to document 1, hold the Shift key down and press the F3 key (step 2 in Figure 1-30). You are now back in document 1.

Since you have pressed the Return key, the spacebar, and the Tab key, you have changed your document. This altered document, with more spaces, tabs, and hard returns, has not been saved permanently to the disk, and we do not wish to do so. Remember that the *typed* portion of the document was saved. That saved portion was not changed on the disk. Since we want to exit from this document without saving again we will not use F10. To prepare to exit WordPerfect, move the cursor to the top of the document by pressing the Home key twice, then press the Up Arrow key ↑ (Figure 1-31). It is not necessary to move to the top of a document when exiting. We do so here to show that the letter to Mr. Wright is still in memory.

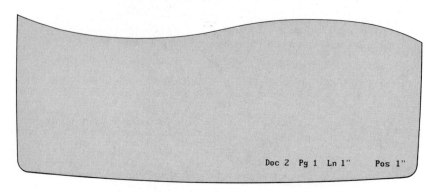

Doc 2   Pg 1   Ln 1"   Pos 1"

Step 1: Switch to Doc 2   Step 2: Return to Doc 1

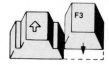   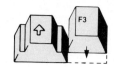   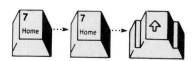

FIGURE 1-30   **FIGURE 1-31**

EXITING WORDPERFECT

To exit this document, as well as WordPerfect, first look at the template next to the F7 key. The word Exit is in black, indicating that you press only the F7 key (Figure 1-32).

Press the F7 key (step 1 in Figure 1-33). The message "Save Document? (Y/N) Yes" is shown in the lower left corner of the screen. [For 5.1 Users – The message will be "Save Document? Yes (No)".]

the F7 function key exits WordPerfect

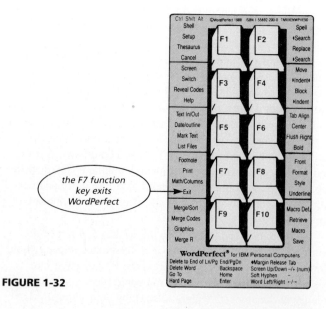

FIGURE 1-32

Step 1: Initiate exit

Step 2: Choose not to save document

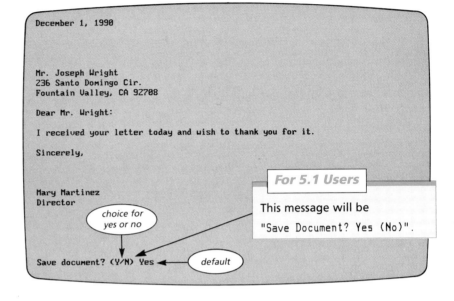

December 1, 1990

Mr. Joseph Wright
236 Santo Domingo Cir.
Fountain Valley, CA 92708

Dear Mr. Wright:

I received your letter today and wish to thank you for it.

Sincerely,

Mary Martinez
Director

choice for yes or no

For 5.1 Users

This message will be "Save Document? Yes (No)".

Save document? (Y/N) Yes   *default*

FIGURE 1-33

The (Y/N) means that if you press the Y (for yes) you want to save the document. If you press the N (for no) you do not want to save the document. The Yes outside the parentheses means that the WordPerfect software has defaulted the answer to yes, so if you press either the Enter key or the spacebar the computer will accept yes as the default. However, type N for no (step 2 in Figure 1-33). You will then see "Exit WP? (Y/N) No" on your screen (Figure 1-34). Since we do want to exit the program, type Y. (If you failed to complete the printing of the document you may see the message "Cancel all print jobs (Y/N)?No". If this appears, type Y for yes.) [For 5.1 Users – The message will be "Exit WP? **No** (**Yes**)" and "Cancel all print jobs? **No** (**Yes**)".]

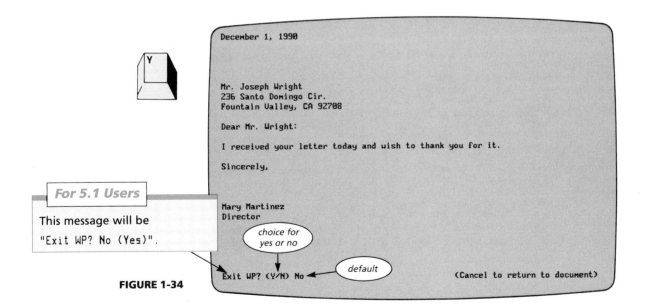

December 1, 1990

Mr. Joseph Wright
236 Santo Domingo Cir.
Fountain Valley, CA 92708

Dear Mr. Wright:

I received your letter today and wish to thank you for it.

Sincerely,

Mary Martinez
Director

choice for yes or no

For 5.1 Users

This message will be "Exit WP? No (Yes)".

Exit WP? (Y/N) No   *default*   (Cancel to return to document)

FIGURE 1-34

The DOS prompt or the DOS screen should then appear indicating that WordPerfect is no longer in the computer's main memory.

PROJECT SUMMARY

*T*his project demonstrated how to use the function keys with the WordPerfect template. You learned how to enter the WordPerfect program and type a document using the hard return at the end of short sentences. You also learned the importance of reveal codes to a document, and that the hidden codes can be found by holding down the Alt key and pressing the F3 key. You learned how to save and print the document and how to move the cursor on a blank screen. Finally, you exited WordPerfect.

The following is a summary of the keystroke sequence we used in Project 1:

SUMMARY OF KEYSTROKES—Project 1

STEPS	KEY(S) PRESSED	STEPS	KEY(S) PRESSED
1	wp [at the A> prompt or as instructed for hard disk or networked version]	23	↵
		24	I received your letter today and wish to thank you for it.
2	↵		
3	(F5)	25	↵
4	=	26	↵
5	b: [for a two disk drive system or a: for a hard disk system]	27	Sincerely,
		28	↵
6	↵	29	↵
7	(F1)	30	↵
8	December 1, 1990	31	↵
9	↵	32	Mary Martinez
10	↵	33	↵
11	↵	34	Director
12	↵	35	↵
13	↵	36	(Alt-F3) [notice codes]
14	Mr. Joseph Wright	37	(Alt-F3)
15	↵	38	(F10)
16	236 Santo Domingo Cir.	39	Wright
17	↵	40	↵
18	Fountain Valley, CA 92708	41	(Shift-F7)
19	↵	42	1
20	↵	43	(F7)
21	Dear Mr. Wright:	44	N
22	↵	45	Y

The following list summarizes the material covered in Project 1.

1. The **keyboard** is used as an input device to input data into the computer.
2. **Function keys** numbered F1 through F10 are located to the left or at the top of the keyboard. Each function key has been assigned four specific functions to execute commonly used commands.
3. The keys on the **numeric keypad**, to the right of the keyboard, are used to move the cursor. When the Num Lock key is pressed, these keys can also be used to type numbers.
4. The **Shift key** is used to make lowercase letters into capital letters and to type the symbols above the numbers. It is also used with the function keys to accomplish specific word processing goals.
5. The **Ctrl** key, used in tandem with function keys, performs special functions.
6. The **Alt** key, used in tandem with function keys, also performs special functions.
7. The **Tab** key moves the cursor to the next tab setting, and when used with the Shift key releases the left margin.
8. The **Enter** or **Return** key is used to enter data in the computer, or as a **hard return** at the end of a line or paragraph.
9. The **Backspace** key moves the cursor backward on the screen, deleting the character to the left of the cursor.
10. The **Left Arrow** key moves the cursor one character to the left.
11. The **Right Arrow** key moves the cursor one character to the right.
12. The **Up Arrow** key moves the cursor up one line.
13. The **Down Arrow** key moves the cursor down one line.
14. A color-coded **template** is placed over the function keys to identify the keys to be used for specific functions.
15. The **Help function** is a collection of screens that gives reminders on how to use WordPerfect.
16. A **default** option is a preassigned choice. Unless instructed otherwise, the default option will be chosen.
17. The **cursor** is the blinking underscore on the screen that designates the current position in a document.
18. The **status line**, at the bottom right of the screen, identifies the exact location of the cursor.
19. The **screen** (window) is the monitor of the computer. It shows what has been entered into the computer.
20. Press the **Cancel (F1)** key when an undesired message appears at the bottom left of the screen.
21. **Reveal codes** are the commands embedded in the document by the WordPerfect software. They control how the input document appears on the screen, as well as how it is printed on a printer.
22. The **hard return [HRt]** code indicates the end of a short line or paragraph, or where a blank line is to be inserted into the document.
23. Press the Alt and F3 keys to view the screen that reveals the embedded codes that control the format of the document.
24. After a document has been entered into the computer, it must be **saved** to a disk for later retrieval or reference.
25. **Printing** a document that has been typed and stored produces a copy of the document on paper.

STUDENT ASSIGNMENTS

STUDENT ASSIGNMENT 1: True/False

Instructions: Circle T if the statement is true and F if the statement is false.

T F 1. The Ctrl, Alt, or Shift keys are used to execute WordPerfect commands without having to press a second key.
T F 2. A good rule of thumb is, if nothing happens on the screen, press Enter.
T F 3. The WordPerfect template fits above or around the function keys.
T F 4. When saving a document the file name must be typed in all capital letters.
T F 5. To exit WordPerfect, use the F7 key.
T F 6. To save a file, use the F10 key.
T F 7. The numeric keypad is usually on the left side of the keyboard.
T F 8. To print a document, use the Ctrl-F8 keys.
T F 9. On most monitors, you can only view 24 lines of typing at a time.
T F 10. To add a blank line, press the spacebar.

STUDENT ASSIGNMENT 2: Multiple Choice

Instructions: Circle the correct response.

1. The WordPerfect template is used in conjunction with the
   a. numeric keypad
   b. alphabet keys
   c. function keys
   d. 1 through 10 keys
2. On the template, functions typed in red are used with the
   a. Ctrl key
   b. Shift key
   c. Alt and Ctrl key
   d. none of the above
3. The numeric keypad can be used to
   a. type numbers
   b. move the cursor
   c. neither a nor b
   d. both a and b
4. When some function keys are pressed a message may appear at the
   a. upper left corner of the screen
   b. lower left corner of the screen
   c. upper right corner of the screen
   d. lower right corner of the screen
5. After you press some function keys and a message appears on the screen, you can cancel the message by pressing the
   a. F2 key
   b. F7 key
   c. Shift-F10 keys
   d. F1 key
6. The Right Arrow key moves the cursor
   a. one character or space to the right
   b. one word to the right
   c. to the right end of the line
   d. one line down
7. To exit from reveal codes you can
   a. press the Right Arrow key
   b. press Alt-F3
   c. press the Down Arrow key
   d. press the Home key twice, then the Up Arrow key
8. The Return key is used to
   a. end a paragraph
   b. put a [HRt] code in the document
   c. insert a blank line
   d. all of the above

STUDENT ASSIGNMENT 3: Matching

Instructions: Put the appropriate number next to the words in the second column.

1. Red	_____	Alt plus a function key
2. Blue	_____	Alt-F3
3. Black	_____	Shift-F7
4. Cancel	_____	Ctrl plus a function key
5. Save	_____	Shift plus a function key
6. Print	_____	F7
7. Bottom of document	_____	F1
8. Green	_____	Function key alone
9. Exit	_____	Home, Home, Up Arrow
10. Reveal codes	_____	Home, Home, Down Arrow
11. Top of document	_____	F10

STUDENT ASSIGNMENT 4: Fill in the Blanks

1. To enter the WordPerfect program while using a floppy disk system at the A> prompt, type _____ and then press _____ .
2. When WordPerfect has been brought into the memory of the computer, a screen appears that is blank except for a _____ line at the lower right corner of the screen.
3. When you view a new screen for the first time, the status line displays Doc _____ Pg _____ Ln _____ Pos _____ .
4. The screen or window can show _____ lines of the document at any one time.
5. If something unexpected happens on the screen—for example, an extra space or a hard return—pressing the _____ key may help.
6. When you press the Return key at the end of a line, the code that is embedded into the document is _____ .
7. When the screen is split to reveal codes, the codes can be viewed in the _____ screen.
8. The Down Arrow moves the cursor down _____ line(s).
9. "Document to be Saved:" appears on the screen when you press the _____ key.
10. If an unwanted message appears on the screen, you can usually press the _____ key to cancel the message.

STUDENT ASSIGNMENT 5: Fill in the Blanks

1. When pressing Ctrl, Alt, or Shift with a function key, it is incorrect to press the keys simultaneously. The correct way is _____ .
2. The ↵ key can be called either the _____ or the _____ key.
3. After pressing Shift-F7 to print, if you wish to print the full text, you must press the number _____ .
4. If you accept the tab default settings, the cursor will move _____ inch/inches when you press the Tab key.
5. After you press the Shift-F3 keys, the cursor will move to document _____ .
6. When you wish to exit, press the _____ key.
7. After you have pressed the Exit key, instead of exiting immediately, WordPerfect prompts: _____ Document? (Y/N) Yes.
8. If you press N in answer to the message in question 7, the next prompt is: _____ WP? (Y/N) No.
9. If you press Y in answer to the message in question 8 you will then _____ from the WordPerfect program.

STUDENT ASSIGNMENT 6: Naming the Keys

Instructions: On the keyboard shown here, label the keys with the names given below.

Ctrl
Shift (both keys)
Alt
Backspace
Tab
Enter (Return)
Spacebar
Caps Lock

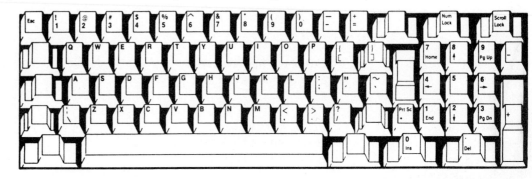

On the numeric keypad,
fill in the correct direction
of the cursor arrows.

Label function keys 1 through 10
(write F1, F2, etc.).

STUDENT ASSIGNMENT 7: Correcting Errors

Instructions: The document illustrates the first part of a memo that is being prepared using WordPerfect. An error was made when typing the memo. The last word was typed todya. The word should be today. Explain in detail the steps necessary to correct the error.

Method of correction: _____

_____

_____

_____

_____

_____

_____

```
December 1, 1990



Mr. Joseph Wright
236 Santo Domingo Cir.
Fountain Valley, CA 92708

Dear Mr. Wright:

I received your letter todya_
```

STUDENT ASSIGNMENT 8: Correcting Errors

Instructions: The screen illustrates a letter that has been prepared using WordPerfect. There are no hard returns between the body of the letter and the word Sincerely, and there is no space between the words thankyou. Explain in detail the steps required to add a blank line above the word Sincerely, and to put a space between the words thankyou.

```
December 1, 1990



Mr. Joseph Wright
236 Santo Domingo Cir.
Fountain Valley, CA 92708

Dear Mr. Wright:

I received your letter today and wish to thankyou for it.
Sincerely,



Mary Martinez
Director
```

Method of correction: _____

_____

_____

_____

STUDENT ASSIGNMENT 9: Viewing Reveal Codes

Problem 1: Prepare the memo illustrated. Follow the step-by-step instructions you learned in this project.

```
TO:  All Employees
FROM:     Personnel Department
SUBJECT:  Vacation Schedules

The following are the rules for vacations:

1.   Each employee will have two weeks vacation.
2.   Vacations must be taken in June, July or August.
3.   You must notify personnel 4 weeks in advance.
4.   You must obtain approval from your supervisor.

Janet Fisher
Personnel Administrator
```

Problem 2: After you have typed the letter, press the Alt-F3 keys to reveal the codes. To send what is on your screen to the printer press the PrtSc (Print Screen) key (on some computers there is a Print Screen key, and on others you must press Shift-PrtSc). After you have a hard copy of what is on the screen, circle all [HRt] codes on the page.

Problem 3: Save on disk as schedule.1.

STUDENT ASSIGNMENT 10: Creating and Printing a Document

Instructions: Perform the following tasks.

1. For hard disk systems load WordPerfect as you are directed by your instructor.
   For two disk drive systems, load DOS into main memory. Remove the DOS disk, and replace it with the WordPerfect disk. Type wp and press Enter.
2. Verify that the status line is in inches format and that the default drive is drive A for hard disk systems or drive B for two disk drive systems. Check to be sure that you have defined the Standard Printer as we did in Project 1. Begin this project on a clean screen.

Problem 1: Prepare the letter illustrated at the right.

```
March 15, 1990

Ms. Roberta Weitzman
President, SpaceTek Inc.
44538 Scroll Avenue
Monnett, NJ 08773

Dear Ms. Weitzman:

This letter confirms our purchase of 13 Pin Brackets.

James R. McMillan, AirFrame Inc.
```

Problem 2: Save the document on disk. Use the file name Weitzman.1.
Problem 3: After the document has been saved on disk, produce a printed copy of the letter.

STUDENT ASSIGNMENT 11: Creating and Printing a Document

Instructions: Perform the following tasks.

1. For hard disk systems load WordPerfect as you are directed by your instructor.
   For two disk drive systems, load DOS into main memory. Remove the DOS disk, and replace it with the WordPerfect disk. Type wp and press Enter.
2. Verify that the status line is in inches format and that the default drive is drive A for hard disk systems or drive B for two disk drive systems. Check to be sure that you have defined the Standard Printer as we did in Project 1. Begin this project on a clean screen.

Problem 1: Prepare the letter illustrated at the right.

```
March 15, 1990


Dear Employees:

You must notify the Personnel department of your vacation plans.

Janet Fisher
Personnel Administrator
```

Problem 2: Save the document on disk. Use the file name Vacation.
Problem 3: After the document has been saved on disk, produce a printed copy of the letter.

PROJECT 2

Creating a Document with Word Wrap

Objectives

You will have mastered the material in this project when you can:

- Type documents using word wrap
- Move the cursor using more efficient keystrokes
- Delete and restore text

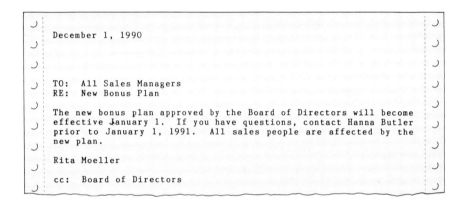

```
December 1, 1990


TO:  All Sales Managers
RE:  New Bonus Plan

The new bonus plan approved by the Board of Directors will become
effective January 1.  If you have questions, contact Hanna Butler
prior to January 1, 1991.  All sales people are affected by the
new plan.

Rita Moeller

cc:  Board of Directors
```

FIGURE 2-1

Loading the WordPerfect Program

If you are working on a hard disk system, load WordPerfect as your instructor directs you. If you are working on a two disk drive system, at the A> prompt (with the WordPerfect disk in drive A and the data disk in drive B), type wp and press Enter. Word-Perfect loads into main memory. As in Project 1, verify that the status line is in inches format. Also as in Project 1, use the F5 key to change the default drive to drive A for hard disk systems, or drive B for two disk drive systems. You should then see a clean screen with only the status line in the lower right corner, indicating Doc 1 Pg 1 Ln 1" Pos 1". Finally, check to be sure that you have defined the Standard Printer as we did in Project 1. In this project we will type and save the letter in Figure 2.1.

LEARNING ABOUT WORD WRAP

When you type on a typewriter, the first thing you do after putting the paper in is set the margins. In WordPerfect, the default margins are one inch on the left and one inch on the right. *Default* means that the margins have been preset at these positions. Unless you instruct the software otherwise, these are the margins it will follow.

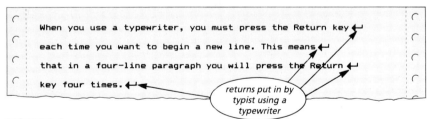

```
When you use a typewriter, you must press the Return key↵

each time you want to begin a new line. This means↵

that in a four-line paragraph you will press the Return↵

key four times.↵
```

returns put in by typist using a typewriter

FIGURE 2-2

When you type on a typewriter with the margins set, every time you approach the end of a line, you hear a "ding" from the typewriter. This indicates that the margin is approaching and you should finish typing the current word and press the Return ↵ key to return the carriage to the next line, as illustrated in Figure 2-2.

Most word processing software, unlike a typewriter, allows you to type continuously. The software automatically "wraps" the typing to the next line when it reaches the right margin, as illustrated in Figure 2-3. The term for this is **word wrap**. The only time you need to press the Return ↵ key is when you reach the end of a paragraph, when you want to insert a blank line, or when you want to terminate the line before word wrap can take effect. Such is the case in the first three lines of the memo you will be typing (Figure 2-1). Word wrap allows you to enter data much faster than if you had to press Return after each line. The word wrap feature is a major advantage of most word processing programs, including WordPerfect.

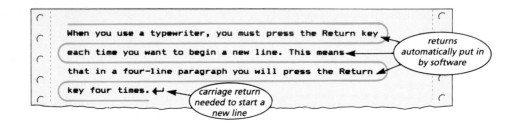

FIGURE 2-3

Typing a Letter

Check to be sure that you have defined the Standard Printer as we did in Project 1. Begin typing the memo in Figure 2-1. As you learned in Project 1, each time you press a key on the keyboard to enter a character, the cursor moves one position to the right, and the position number on the status line changes to indicate the cursor's position. The date line is not long enough to wrap. Therefore, after typing the date, press the Return ↵ key. The status line shows the cursor on line 1.17", position 1". Press the Return ↵ key four more times to move the cursor to line 1.83", position 1". Type TO: and press the Tab key, moving the cursor to position 1.5"; then type the words All Sales Managers and press the Return ↵ key, putting the cursor on line 2", position 1". Type RE: and press the Tab key; then type the words New Bonus Plan. Press the Return key two times (↵ ↵), taking the cursor to line 2.33, position 1" (Figure 2-4).

Now type the paragraph of the memo. As you type remember to press the spacebar twice after each period at the end of each sentence. Also, remember *not* to press the Return key at the end of each line. As you approach the end of the first line, watch the screen. When you begin to type the word effective, notice that the word is too long to fit on the line. But before the word is completely typed it wraps down to the next line.

Type the entire paragraph. After you have typed the last word, plan, followed by a period, the cursor is on line 2.83", position 1.9". Press the Return ↵ key because this last line of the paragraph is too short to wrap. Press the Return key again, moving the cursor to line 3.17", position 1". Type the name Rita Moeller and press the Return ↵ key two times. The cursor is now on line 3.5", position 1". Type the abbreviation cc:, then press the Tab key. Type the words Board of Directors.

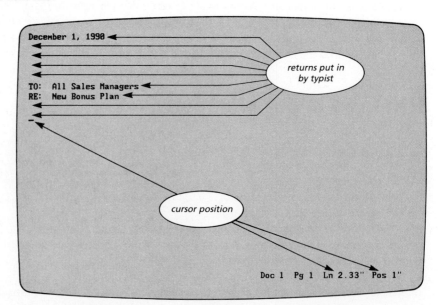

FIGURE 2-4

The cursor should be on line 3.5", position 3.3". Press Return ↵, thereby putting the cursor on line 3.67", position 1" (Figure 2-5).

In Figure 2-5, all the text in the body of the memo has been typed. It consists of three full lines of text and a partial fourth line. Word wrap occurred for the three full lines of text. When you typed the fourth line of the paragraph, you reached the end of the text before word wrap took effect, so you pressed the Return to cause a hard return. When word wrap causes text to be moved to the next line, a **soft return** is said to have occurred.

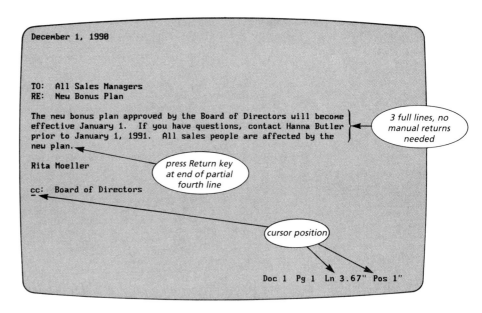

FIGURE 2-5

Checking the Reveal Codes

It is always necessary to be conscious of the codes being embedded into your document. The entire format of your document is determined by the codes, and the printer is governed by codes. If something does not print the way you anticipated, it is wise to check the codes. As you learned in Project 1, the codes are embedded into the document automatically by the software and saved when the document is saved. Before you look at the codes, return to the top of the document. Press the Home, Home, Up Arrow ↑ keys (Figure 2-6). This takes the cursor immediately to the top of the document, line 1", position 1".

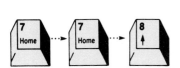

FIGURE 2-6

Look at the template next to the F3 key. Notice the words Reveal Codes in blue. Hold down the Alt key firmly and press the F3 key. When you do, the screen shown in Figure 2-7 appears.

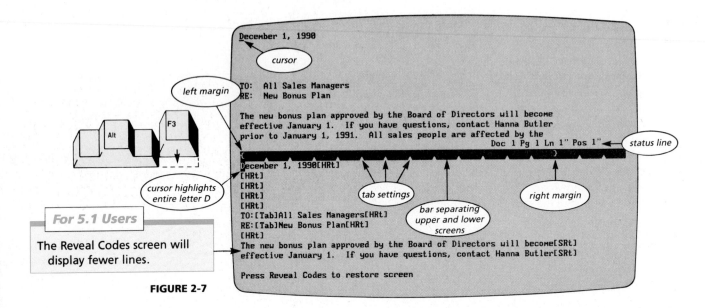

For 5.1 Users

The Reveal Codes screen will display fewer lines.

FIGURE 2-7

Look at your screen carefully. The bar indicating the left and right margins and tab settings separates the upper and lower screens. Above the bar is the screen you are familiar with. You cannot see any codes, and your status line can still be viewed.

Below the bar is the reveal codes screen. Notice that the typing is the same as on the upper screen, except the codes also appear. All the codes are in boldface so that they are easily recognizable (if you have a color monitor, boldface may appear as a particular color; in that case the codes will be that boldface color). The cursor in the lower screen highlights or makes a reverse video of the character or code where it is placed.

In Figure 2-8, notice the [HRt] code at the end of line 1" where you typed the date. Move the cursor down to line 1.83" with the Down Arrow ↓ key. Notice that both cursors move at the same time. They are, in fact, the same cursor and move in relationship to each other.

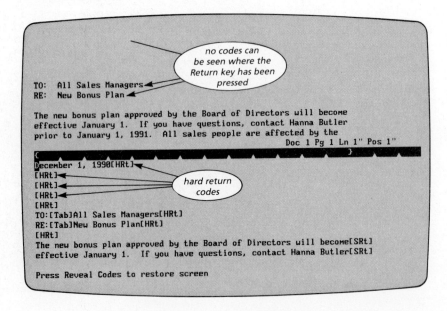

FIGURE 2-8

As you move the cursor, notice that wherever you inserted a hard return there is the [HRt] code. In Figure 2-9, on line 1.83" after TO: and on line 2" after RE: where you pressed the Tab key, notice the code **[Tab]**. Each of those lines is followed by a hard return.

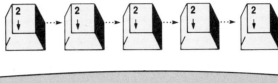

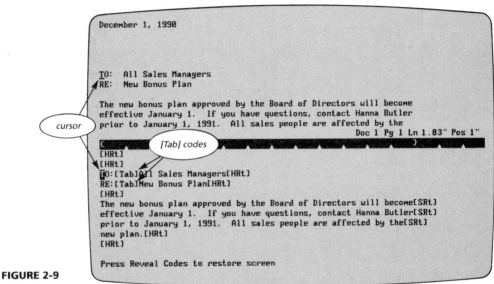

FIGURE 2-9

Looking only at the lower screen, continue moving the cursor down with the Down Arrow ↓ key. When you get to the paragraph you typed, notice that instead of [HRt] codes at each line end, there are **[SRt]** codes (Figure 2-10). These are the lines where you allowed word wrap to occur, so there is a soft return [SRt] code at the end of each line.

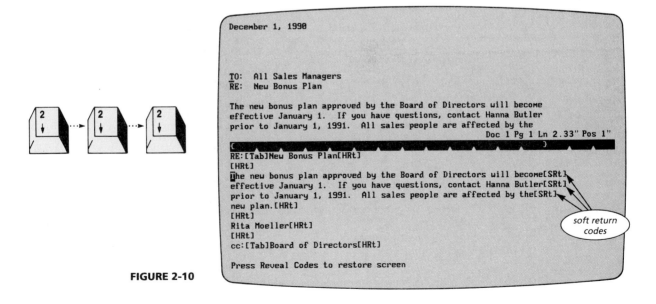

FIGURE 2-10

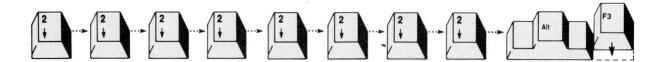

With the Down Arrow ↓ key continue moving the cursor down to the end of the document, shown in Figure 2-11. The last code in the document is [HRt]. To exit from the reveal codes screen, press Alt-F3.

Saving a Document

The memo to the sales managers shown in Figure 2-1 is completed. Whenever a document is completed, it should be saved onto the disk so that it can be retrieved for printing or modification at a later time. Look at the template next to the F10 key. Notice the word Save in black. Press the F10 key (step 1 in Figure 2-12). At the lower left corner of your screen you see the message "Document to Be Saved:". To name the document type the word MEMO as shown in step 2 in Figure 2-12 (you can type it in uppercase, lowercase, or a combination). After you have typed MEMO, notice that nothing else happens. Press the Enter key ↵.

After you press the Enter key, notice that the light on the default drive goes on, indicating that the document is being saved to the diskette in the default drive (drive A for hard disk systems, drive B for floppy disk systems).

Your document is now named and saved. The name of the document appears in the lower left corner of your screen.

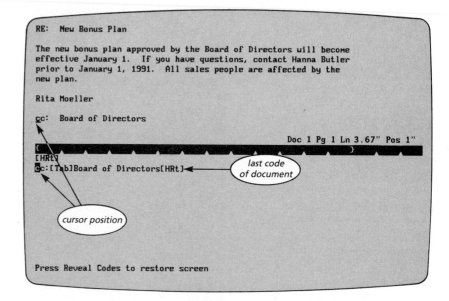

FIGURE 2-11

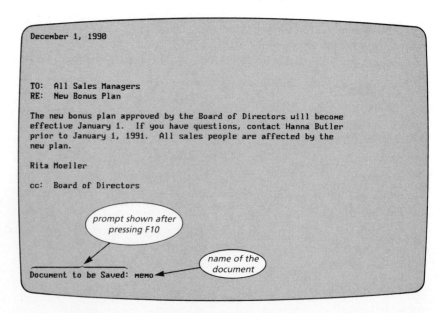

Step 1: Save the document   Step 2: Name the document

FIGURE 2-12

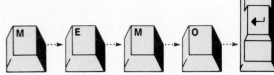

Although you did not enter B:\ before you typed the name, because at the beginning of this project we defaulted to drive B, B:\ appears to remind you that the document is saved to the diskette in drive B.

Figure 2-13 shows that that designation is now part of the name of this document.

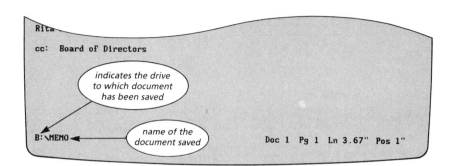

FIGURE 2-13

Printing a Document

After the file is entered and stored on the disk, the next task is normally to print the document. Wordperfect 5.0 and 5.1 allow you to view your document before you print, to see how it will appear when it is printed. The View Document function is found on the print menu. While holding down the Shift key, press the F7 key. Figure 2-14 shows that when you press those keys the print menu appears on the screen. To view the document, press 6 and notice how the screen shows the letter on what looks like a miniature piece of paper (Figure 2-15). You cannot read the words in the letter, because they have been made small enough to show the entire page. To view a smaller portion of the page, thus making the words more legible, press 1 to view the document at 100%. If you wish to make the words even larger, you could press the number 2 for 200%. To exit this screen, press F1 to cancel, which returns you to the print menu. If you press F7 to exit, you will return to your document. If this happens, press Shift-F7 to restore the print menu.

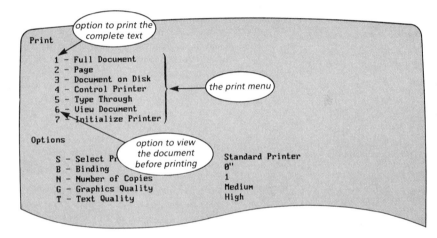

FIGURE 2-14

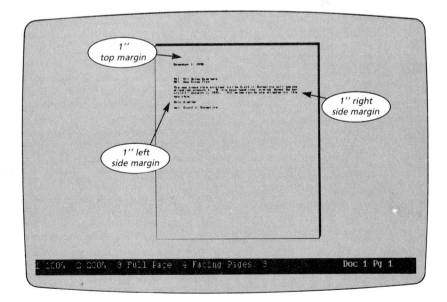

FIGURE 2-15

Be sure your printer has paper inserted correctly and that the printer is turned on and is ready to print. Since you wish to print the full text of this document, press the number 1 for full text, and the printer begins printing your document. The printed document should appear like the letter in Figure 2-1, page 29.

MOVING THE CURSOR

Arrow Keys

As you have learned, the arrow keys are used to move the cursor on the screen. However, to save time by moving more efficiently through your document, WordPerfect allows many combinations of cursor movements. Table 2-1 presents a comprehensive list of cursor movements. Refer to the table during the following discussion about cursor movements.

TABLE 2-1   Summary of Cursor Keystrokes

KEYSTROKES	RESULTS
←	Moves cursor one character or space to the left.
→	Moves cursor one character or space to the right.
↑	Moves cursor up one line.
↓	Moves cursor down one line.
Ctrl →	Moves cursor to the first letter of the next word.
Ctrl ←	Moves cursor to the first letter of the previous word.
Home →	Moves cursor to the right edge of the current screen. If there are more screens to the right and you continue to press Home, Right Arrow, the cursor moves to the right edge of the next screen to the right.
Home ←	Moves cursor to the left edge of the current screen. If there are more screens to the left and you continue to press Home, Left Arrow, the cursor moves to the left edge of the next screen to the left.
Home ↑	Moves cursor to the top of the current screen, then to the top of the previous screen.
Home ↓	Moves cursor to the bottom of the current screen, then to the bottom of the next screen.
⊖ (on numeric keypad)	Moves cursor to the top of the current screen, then to the top of the previous screen (same as Home, Up Arrow).
⊕ (on numeric keypad)	Moves cursor to the bottom of the current screen, then to the bottom of the next screen (same as Home, Down Arrow).
Home Home ↑	Moves cursor to the top of the document, but not in front of all codes.
Home Home ↓	Moves cursor to the bottom of the entire document.
Home Home →	Moves cursor to the right end of the current line.
Home Home ←	Moves cursor to the beginning of the current line.
Home Home Home ←	Moves cursor in front of all codes and characters at the beginning of the current line.
Home Home Home ↑	Moves cursor in front of all codes and characters at the beginning of the document.
End	Moves cursor to the right end of the current line.
PgDn	Moves cursor to line 1 of the next page.
PgUp	Moves cursor to line 1 of the previous page.
Ctrl-Home, page number, ←	"Go to" command. When "Go to" appears on the screen, type the page number desired and press Enter. Moves cursor to line 1 of page indicated.
Ctrl-Home ↑	Moves cursor to line 1 of current page.
Ctrl-Home ↓	Moves cursor to last line of current page.
Ctrl-Home Alt-F4	Moves cursor to the beginning of a block.
Ctrl-Home Ctrl-Home	Returns cursor to previous position of cursor.
Esc	Repeats the keystroke command the number of times indicated. The default number is 8. To change the number, type in the desired number when n = 8 appears on the screen. Refer to WordPerfect manual to change the default number permanently.
Esc ↓	Moves cursor down the number of lines indicated, i.e., if n = 8, the cursor would move down 8 lines.
Esc ↑	Moves cursor up the number of lines indicated.
Esc →	Moves cursor right the number of characters indicated.
Esc ←	Moves cursor left the number of characters indicated.
Esc PgDn	Moves cursor down the number of pages indicated. Cursor will be placed on line 1 of the new page.
Esc PgUp	Moves cursor up the number of pages indicated. Cursor will be placed on line 1 of the new page.
Tab	Moves the cursor right to the next tab setting, on the current line only when the Insert key has been pressed and the word Typeover appears on the screen. (Caution: if Typeover is not on, a [Tab] code will be inserted.)

Home Key Used with Arrow Keys

Move to the top of the document by pressing Home, Home, and then the Up Arrow key (Figure 2-16). To move to the end of the document, press Home, Home, and the Down Arrow key (step 1 in Figure 2-17). The cursor will go to the bottom of the document. Note that Home, Home, Up Arrow moves the cursor to the top of the document text. Home, Home, Home, Up Arrow moves the cursor to the top of the *entire* document, even if codes are embedded at the beginning of the document.

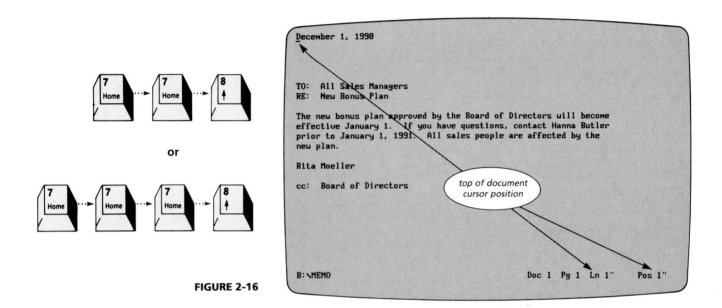

FIGURE 2-16

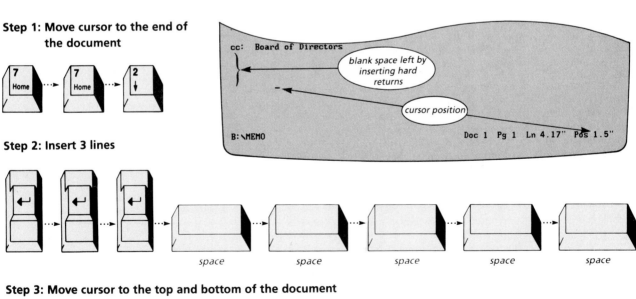

FIGURE 2-17

The cursor cannot move past the bottom of the document, that is, it cannot move where there is no typing or codes. Press the Return key three times to put the cursor on line 4.17". Note the status line. Press the spacebar five times (step 2 in Figure 2-17), placing the cursor on line 4.17", position 1.5". Press Home, Home, and the Up Arrow key. The cursor returns to line 1", position 1". Then press Home, Home, and the Down Arrow key (step 3 in Figure 2-17). The cursor returns to line 4.17", position 1.5".

Many cursor movements can only be demonstrated over several pages of text. Since you have not yet typed several pages, do the following exercise first so you can practice additional cursor movements.

First, press a hard return ↵, which moves the cursor to line 4.33", position 1". Type the letter o followed by a hard return ↵. Continue to type the letter o followed by a hard return ↵ until the cursor is on line 9.83" of page 1 (this may seem awkward right now, but you will see its usefulness when we begin to move the cursor). Next type one more o followed by a hard return ↵ and as you do, watch for a dotted line to appear across the screen. This dotted line indicates that there has been a *page break*, which means that the document has moved from page 1 to page 2. Figure 2-18 shows that the status line also indicates that the cursor is now on page 2, line 1".

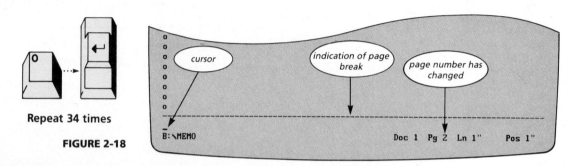

Repeat 34 times

FIGURE 2-18

On page 2, line 1" type the letter a, then press the Enter key ↵. Continue to do this until another page break appears and the status line indicates that the cursor is on page 3, line 1", as shown in step 1 in Figure 2-19. To complete this exercise, type the letter u and press the Enter key ↵. Continue to do so until the cursor is on line 2.5", position 1" of page 3 (step 2 in Figure 2-19). If you could now see your entire document, it would look like Figure 2-20.

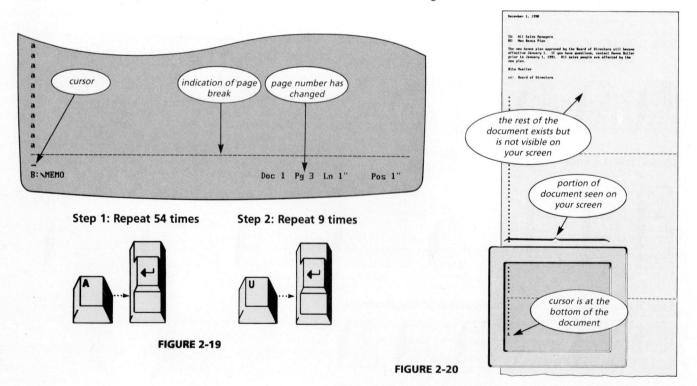

Step 1: Repeat 54 times   **Step 2: Repeat 9 times**

FIGURE 2-19

FIGURE 2-20

The cursor is at the bottom of your document. That is, the *last* position of the cursor is the end of the document. Now press Home, Home, Up Arrow to move to the beginning of your document, page 1, line 1", position 1" (step 1 in Figure 2-21). Press the Down Arrow until you are on line 2.33" of page 1, the paragraph portion of your letter (step 2 in Figure 2-21).

To move the cursor to the right, press the Right Arrow → (step 3 in Figure 2-21). This moves the cursor to the right one character at a time. To move the cursor to the left, press the Left Arrow ← (step 4 in Figure 2-21). This moves the cursor to the left one character at a time.

Step 1: Move the cursor to top of the document

Step 2: Move the cursor to line 2.33"

Step 3: Practice using the Right Arrow key

Step 4: Practice using the Left Arrow key

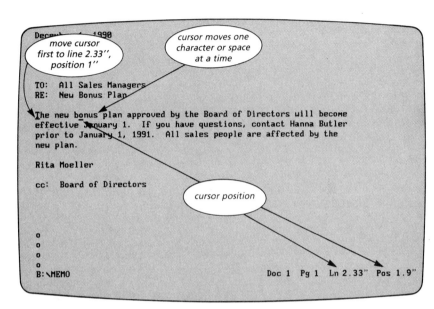

FIGURE 2-21

Control Key Used with Arrow Keys

Move the cursor to position 4.1" of line 2.33" so that it is under the letter t in the word the (step 1 in Figure 2-22). To move one word at a time, hold the Ctrl key down firmly and while holding, press the Right Arrow key → (step 2 in Figure 2-22). If you continue to press the Right Arrow key, the cursor moves one word at a time. Hold down the Right Arrow key firmly while holding the Ctrl key; notice how fast the cursor moves through the document.

Hold down the Ctrl key and press the Left Arrow key ←. The cursor moves to the left one word at a time (step 3 in Figure 2-22).

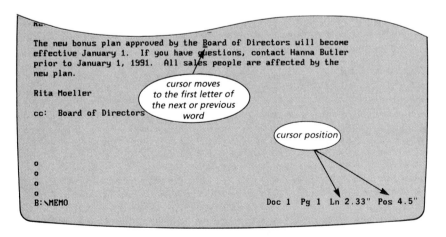

Step 1: Move the cursor to line 2.33", position 4.1"

Step 2: Move the cursor to the beginning of the next word

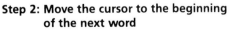

Step 3: Move the cursor to the beginning of previous words

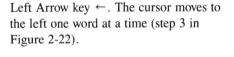

FIGURE 2-22

End Key

Move the cursor again to line 2.33", position 1". Note that you are at the left edge of the line. Press the End key. Figure 2-23 shows how the End key moves the cursor to the end of the line.

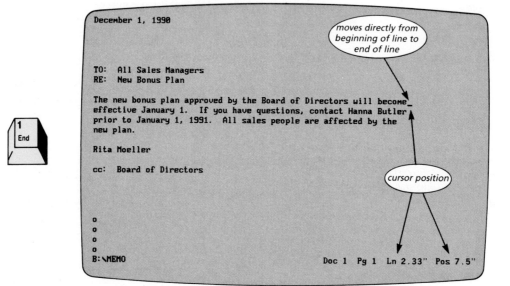

FIGURE 2-23

More Home Key, Arrow Key Sequences

Move to the top of the document again by pressing Home, Home, Up Arrow. The cursor is now on page 1, line 1", position 1".

As you learned in Project 1, you may have a large document, but the monitor can only show you one screenful at a time. If you wish to move the cursor to the top, the bottom, the left, or the right edges of your present screen, press the Home key *once*, then the Up, Down, Left, or Right Arrow keys. Try pressing the Home key, then the Down Arrow key ↓. That moves the cursor to line 4.83" (step 1 in Figure 2-24). Press the Home key, then the Up Arrow key ↑. That moves the cursor to line 1" (step 2 in Figure 2-24). Press Down Arrow ↓ to move the cursor down to line 2.33". Now press Home, then Right Arrow →. The cursor moves to the right end of the line (step 3 in Figure 2-24). Press Home, then Left Arrow ←. The cursor moves to the left edge of the screen, in this case the left end of the line (step 4 in Figure 2-24). Thus, pressing the Home key once in combination with an arrow key moves the cursor to the edges of the screen.

Step 1: Move the cursor to the bottom of the screen

Step 2: Move the cursor to the top of the screen

Step 3: Move the cursor to the right of the screen

Step 4: Move the cursor to the left of the screen

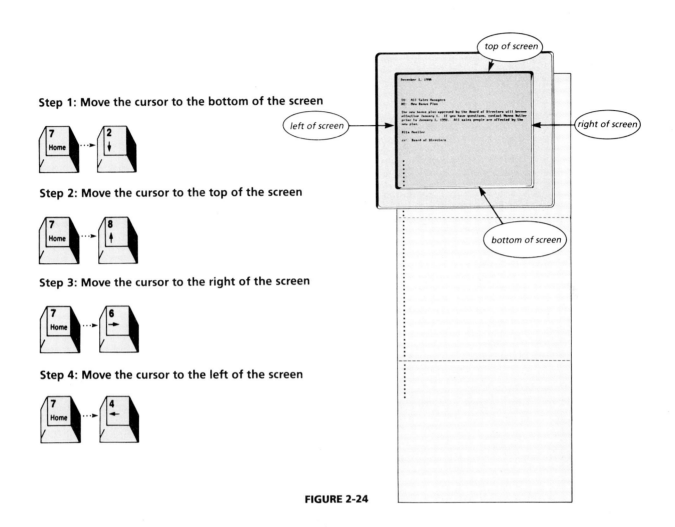

FIGURE 2-24

The margins of your document can be very wide, extending beyond the left or right edges of your screen, and you may wish to be able to move quickly to the left or right ends of a line in your document. With the cursor still on page 1, line 2.33", press Home, Home, Right Arrow (step 1 in Figure 2-25 on the next page). Notice that the cursor moves to the right end of the line, to position 7.5". Press Home, Home, Left Arrow, and the cursor moves back to position 1" at the left end of the line (step 2 in Figure 2-25). The cursor movements caused by Home, Right or Left Arrow, and Home, Home, Right or Left Arrow appear to be the same. But if you had lines longer than could be shown on one screen, you would notice that Home, Left or Right Arrow moves the cursor only to the edges of the screen you are viewing. Figure 2-25 illustrates that Home, Home, Right or Left Arrow causes the cursor to move immediately to the right or left ends of the line, even if the ends of the line cannot be seen on the current screen.

In addition to the Home, Home, Left Arrow function, you can use Home, Home, Home, Left Arrow. This keystroke sequence moves the cursor to the beginning of the line, even if codes are embedded at the beginning of the line. When text is moved, the codes have to be moved too.

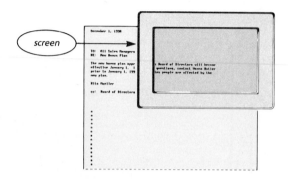

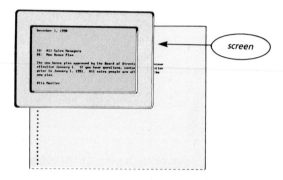

Step 1: Move the cursor to the right end of the line

Step 2: Move the cursor to the left end of the line

FIGURE 2-25

Move your cursor to the bottom of the screen by pressing Home, Down Arrow ↓ (step 1 in Figure 2-26). The cursor is now on page 1, line 4.83", position 1". To go to the bottom of the *next* screen, press Home, Down Arrow ↓ (step 2 in Figure 2-26). The cursor is now on page 1, line 8.83", position 1".

When you press Home, Down Arrow or Home, Up Arrow, you will not miss viewing any lines of typing. The cursor moves down one screen at a time or up one screen at a time, without skipping any portions of the document. Figure 2-26 shows how the screen moves. Because WordPerfect automatically breaks a page after line 9.83", the next screen down shows the remainder of the lines on page 1, then the dotted line showing the break between the pages. The cursor is on line 3.67" of page 2. Press Home, Down Arrow again and again until the cursor is at the bottom of the document (page 3, line 2.5"). Since that is as far as the cursor has been before, it cannot be moved any farther. To move the cursor up one screen at a time, press Home, Up Arrow ↑. The cursor moves to the top of the screen. Continue pressing Home, Up Arrow and watch how the cursor moves a screen at a time (watch the status line as well as the screen). Continue pressing Home, Up Arrow until the cursor is on page 1, line 1".

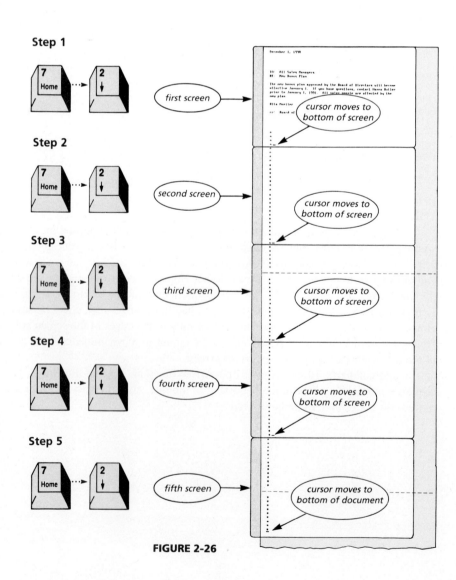

FIGURE 2-26

Plus and Minus Keys on the Numeric Keypad

The **Plus** and **Minus** keys on the numeric keypad, when the Num Lock key is "off", perform the same functions as the Home, Up Arrow and Home, Down Arrow keys (Figure 2-27).

Look on the numeric keypad at the Plus (+) and the Minus (–) keys. Press the Plus key. Notice that the cursor moves to line 4.83", as shown in Figure 2-28.

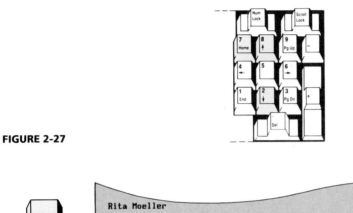

FIGURE 2-27

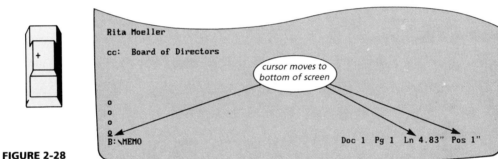

FIGURE 2-28

Press the Plus key again and the cursor moves to line 8.83" (Figure 2-29). This is the same result you would get from pressing the Home, Down Arrow keys. Press the Minus key and the cursor moves to the top of the screen, line 5" (Figure 2-30 on the next page), just as if you had pressed the Home, Up Arrow keys. Press the Minus key again and the cursor moves to line 1" of page 1.

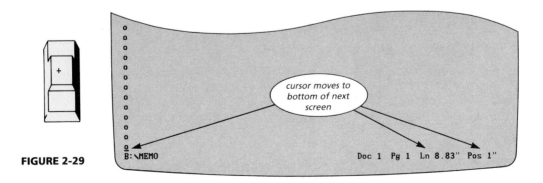

FIGURE 2-29

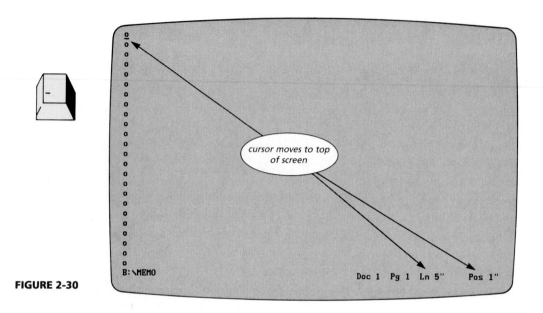

FIGURE 2-30

Page Down and Page Up Keys

The **PgDn** (Page Down) key moves the cursor to line 1" of the *next* page. The **PgUp** (Page Up) key moves the cursor to line 1" of the *previous* page.

With the cursor on page 1, line 1", press the PgDn key (step 1 in Figure 2-31). Notice that the cursor moves to line 1" of page 2. Press the PgDn key again and the cursor moves to line 1" of page 3 (step 2 in Figure 2-31).

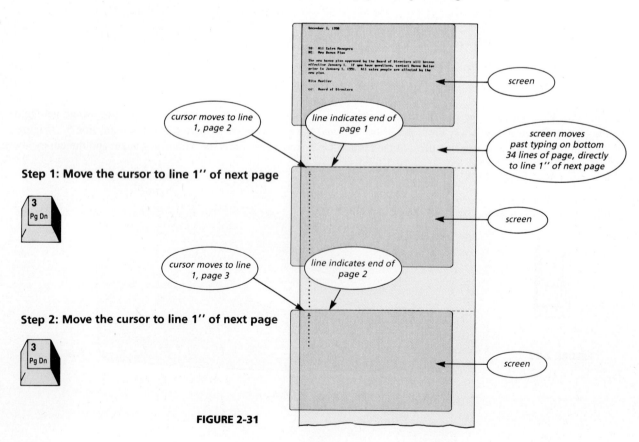

Step 1: Move the cursor to line 1" of next page

Step 2: Move the cursor to line 1" of next page

FIGURE 2-31

Now move the cursor up only one line by pressing the Up Arrow ↑ key (step 1 in Figure 2-32). The cursor moves to line 9.83" of page 2. Press the PgDn key (step 2 in Figure 2-32). Note that the cursor moves only one line, but the status line indicates the cursor is on page 3 because PgDn moved the cursor to line 1" of page 3.

Press the Up Arrow ↑ one time, moving the cursor to line 9.83" of page 2. Because the status line states page 2, you know that the previous page is page 1. Therefore the PgUp key will take the cursor almost two full pages to line 1", page 1. Press the PgUp key.

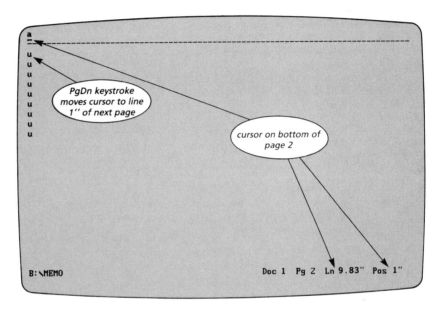

FIGURE 2-32

Step 1: Move cursor up one line
to line 9.83" of page 2

Step 2: Move cursor to line 1" of
page 3

"Go to" Cursor Function

There may be times when you want to go directly to a specific page, but repeatedly pressing the PgDn key would take too long. For example, if you had a 30-page document and you wished to go to page 15, pressing PgDn 15 times would be too time consuming.

To move directly to a particular page, hold down the Ctrl key and while holding it, press the Home key (step 1 in Figure 2-33). You see the message "Go to" in the lower left corner of the screen. Type the number 3 and then press Enter ↵ (step 2 in Figure 2-33).

Step 1: Invoke the "Go to" message

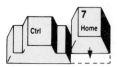

Step 2: Go to page 3

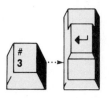

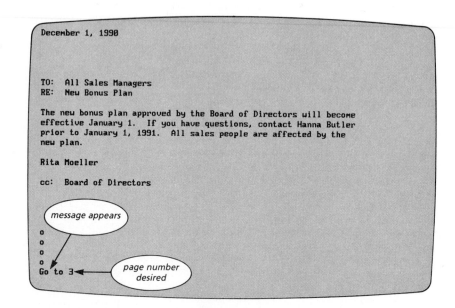

FIGURE 2-33

Notice that the cursor moves to page 3, line 1". To "Go to" a particular page, you can also go backward. While on page 3, line 1", hold the Ctrl key down and press the Home key (step 1 in Figure 2-34). The "Go to" message appears again. Type the number 2 and then press the Enter ↵ key (step 2 in Figure 2-34). The cursor is now on page 2, line 1". The cursor will always go to line 1" of the page number that you type.

Step 1: Invoke the "Go to" message

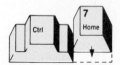

Step 2: Go to page 2

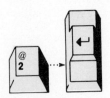

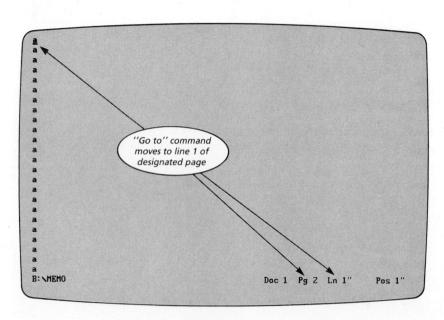

FIGURE 2-34

Another "Go to" command will take you either to the last line or the first line of the page you are currently on. The cursor should be on page 2, line 1". Hold down the Ctrl key and press the Home key. The "Go to" message appears. Press the Down Arrow key ↓ (Figure 2-35). Look at the status line and notice that the cursor stayed on page 2, but went to the last line of that page, line 9.83".

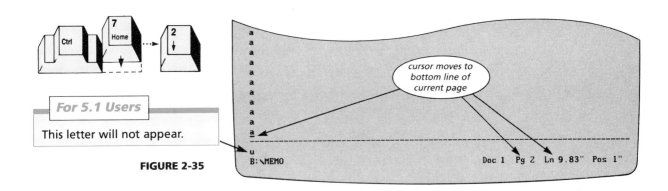

FIGURE 2-35

To move the cursor to the first line of page 2, hold the Ctrl key down and press the Home key. The "Go to" message appears. Press the Up Arrow ↑ key (Figure 2-36). The cursor moves to page 2, line 1".

One more "Go to" function allows you to return to the position in which the cursor was last placed. Press Ctrl-Home, then Ctrl-Home again. The cursor returns to its last position as shown in Figure 2-35.

To move the cursor to the top of your document, press Home, Home, Up Arrow. The cursor is on page 1, line 1".

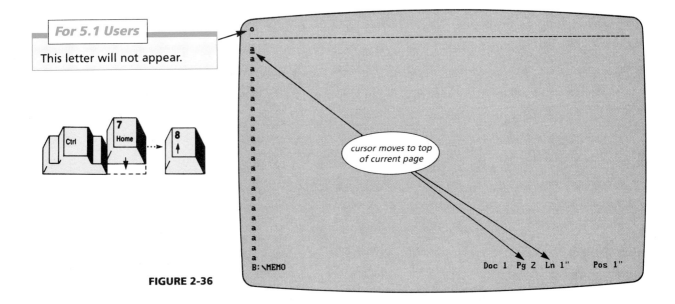

FIGURE 2-36

Esc Key

Another key used to move the cursor is the **Esc** key. This is called a repeating key because it will repeat almost any stroke, whether a character or a cursor movement. For our purposes now, we will use it only to move the cursor.

Press the Esc key. Figure 2-37 shows the message "Repeat Value = 8" at the bottom left corner of the screen. The message means that the default number is 8. Whatever keystroke you choose will be repeated eight times. After pressing Esc, press the Down Arrow ↓ key (step 1 in Figure 2-38). Instead of moving down one line, the cursor moves down eight lines, from line 1" to line 2.33". Press the Esc key again. The message "Repeat Value = 8" appears again. Now press the Right Arrow key → (step 2 in Figure 2-38). The cursor moves to position 1.8" on line 2.33", moving eight characters to the right instead of just one.

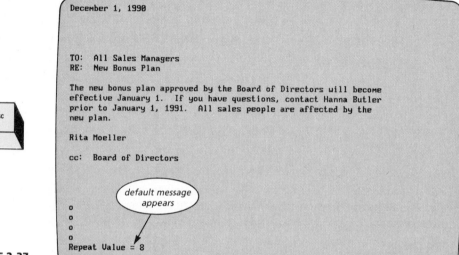

FIGURE 2-37

Step 1: Move cursor down 8 lines

Step 2: Move cursor 8 characters to the right

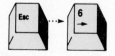

FIGURE 2-38

You can also change the number of lines or characters that the cursor will move. Press the Esc key. The message "Repeat Value = 8" appears on the screen. Instead of accepting the default, type the number 15. The 8 is replaced by the number 15 in the message. Next, press the Down Arrow key. The cursor moves down 15 lines to line 4.83", as shown in Figure 2-39.

You can see how important it is to memorize the keystroke sequences that move the cursor. You will save a lot of time by learning to use WordPerfect efficiently.

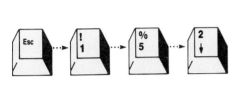 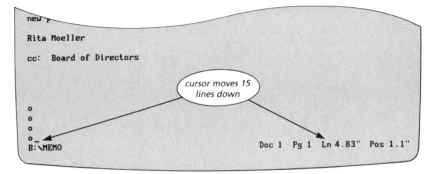

FIGURE 2-39

DELETING TEXT

*L*earning how to use the deletion keys is as important as learning the cursor movements. Table 2-2 presents a comprehensive list of deletion keystrokes. Refer to the table during the following discussion about using the deletion keys.

Before we start, move the cursor to the bottom of the document by pressing Home, Home, Down Arrow. The cursor should be on page 3, line 2.5".

TABLE 2-2 Summary of Deletion Keystrokes

KEYSTROKES	RESULTS
[F1] 1	Restores deleted text. F1 highlights deleted text, then 1 restores that text.
[Backspace]	Deletes the character or code to the left of the cursor.
[Delete]	Deletes the character or code above the cursor moving to the right (as text is deleted, the typing to the right of the cursor moves left to the cursor).
[Home] [Backspace]	Deletes the word to the left of the cursor. (Let up on Home before pressing Backspace.)
[Ctrl-Backspace]	Deletes the word above the cursor (as words are deleted, the typing to the right of the cursor moves left to the cursor). (Hold down Ctrl while pressing Backspace.)
[Ctrl-End]	Deletes from the cursor to the end of the current line.
[Ctrl-PgDn]	The prompt "Delete Remainder of page? (Y/N) No" appears. Type the letter Y to delete from the cursor to the end of the current page.
[Alt-F4] [Delete]	To delete a block place the cursor at the beginning of a block. Hold down the Alt key and press F4. Move the cursor to identify and highlight a block of text. Press the Delete key. At the prompt "Delete Block? (Y/N) No" type the letter Y.

Using the Backspace Key and Restoring Deleted Text

Type these words: This is how to use the Backspace key (see Figure 2-40). The cursor is now at position 4.6" in a blank space just to the right of the y in the word key. Think of the **Backspace** key as deleting *backward*. Press the Backspace key and notice that the character to the *left* of the cursor is deleted. Continue to press the Backspace key until you've deleted the words Backspace and key (Figure 2-40).

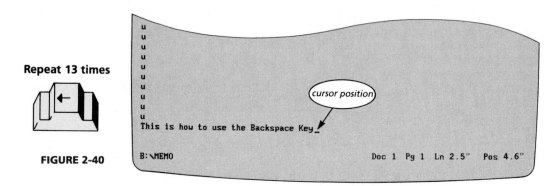

Repeat 13 times

FIGURE 2-40

If you deleted text in error, and you have not moved the cursor to another position in the document, you can restore your text. Look at the template next to the F1 key. Notice the word Cancel in black. Press the F1 key. The text that was deleted reappears and is highlighted on the screen. The menu on the bottom of the screen shows that pressing the numeric key 1 will "undelete" or restore the highlighted text. Press 1 to see the text restored, putting the cursor back to position 4.6" to the right of the y (Figure 2-41).

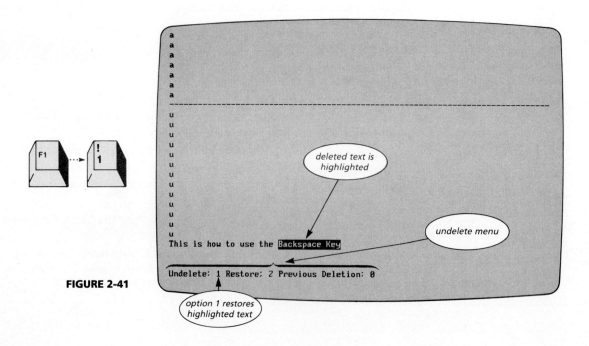

FIGURE 2-41

Using the Delete Key and Restoring Deleted Text

The other key used to delete text is the Delete key. The **Delete** key deletes the space or character directly *above* the cursor. Think of the Delete key as deleting text going *forward*.

Press the Return key to move the cursor to page 3, line 2.67". Type these words: This is how to use the Delete Key (Figure 2-42). Press Home, Left Arrow to move the cursor to the beginning of the line, putting the cursor under the T in This. Press the Delete key and notice that the T that was directly above the cursor is deleted. Delete these words: This is how.

As before, to restore this deleted text press the F1 key. The "undelete" menu appears at the bottom of the screen. Press 1 to restore the highlighted text. The text is restored with the cursor on position 2.1".

Repeat 11 times

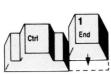

FIGURE 2-42

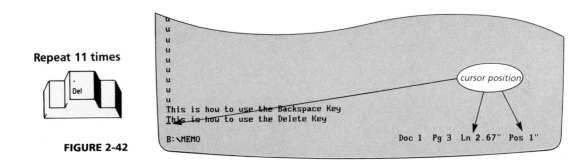

Deleting One Line at a Time

To delete a line from where the cursor is to the end of the line, hold the Ctrl key down and press the End key. Figure 2-43 shows that the text from position 2.1" to the end of the line is deleted. To restore the deleted text, press the F1 key, then number 1.

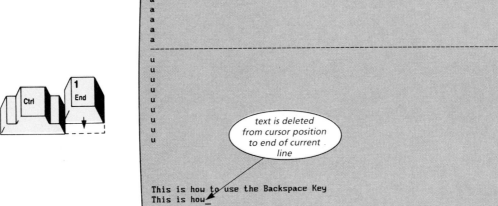

Deleting One Page at a Time

The Ctrl-PgDn keys are used if you wish to delete from where the cursor is to the bottom of the page. Press Home, Home, Up Arrow to move the cursor to page 1, line 1". Since the cursor is on line 1", Ctrl-PgDn will delete from there to line 9.83", which is the bottom of this page. If your cursor were on line 2.33", Ctrl-PgDn would delete from there down to line 9.83". Hold down the Ctrl key and press the PgDn key (Figure 2-44). Since an entire page can contain a lot of work, WordPerfect has a built-in precaution. The message "Delete Remainder of page? (Y/N) No" appears at the bottom left corner of the screen. The No at the end of the message means that the default is no. Therefore, if you press any key (besides Y), the answer no is accepted and nothing is deleted. Type the letter Y. Figure 2-45 shows that typing the letter Y deletes the entire text of page 1, bringing the text that was below page 1 up to line 1" of page 1. [For 5.1 Users – The message will be "Delete Remainder of page? No (Yes)" with the cursor under the **N**.]

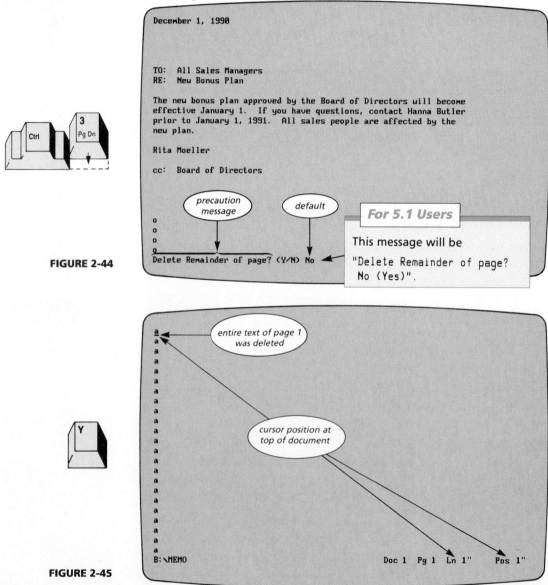

FIGURE 2-44

FIGURE 2-45

To restore the entire deleted text, press F1 to undelete and highlight the deleted text, then press the number 1 to restore the entire deleted text, bringing the cursor to line 9.83" on page 1. Press Home, Home, Up Arrow, moving the cursor to page 1, line 1". The entire text is restored.

Deleting One Word at a Time

There will be times when you want to delete three or four words on a line. Move the cursor under the T in The, hold down the Ctrl key, and press the Backspace key. Figure 2-46 shows that instead of just one character, the entire word The plus the space after it is deleted, bringing the first character of the next word to the cursor. Ctrl-Backspace deletes one word at a time going *forward* through the text. Continuing to hold down the Ctrl key and pressing the Backspace key, delete these words: new bonus plan. Then, to restore the deleted text, press the F1 key. Notice the highlight on the words The new bonus plan. Press the number 1 to restore those words to the text.

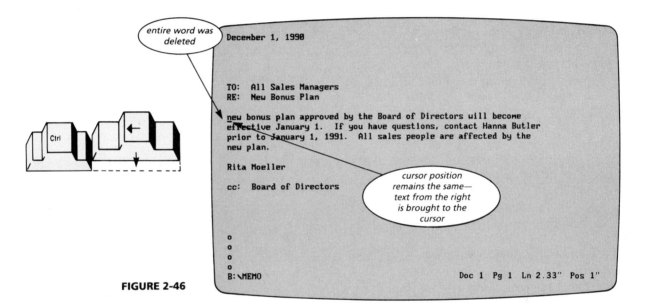

entire word was deleted

December 1, 1990

TO: All Sales Managers
RE: New Bonus Plan

new bonus plan approved by the Board of Directors will become effective January 1. If you have questions, contact Hanna Butler prior to January 1, 1991. All sales people are affected by the new plan.

Rita Moeller

cc: Board of Directors

cursor position remains the same— text from the right is brought to the cursor

o
o
o
o
B:\MEMO   Doc 1 Pg 1 Ln 2.33" Pos 1"

FIGURE 2-46

The cursor is at position 2.9" under the letter a in the word approved. To delete one word at a time going *backward* in your text, press the Home key once, then press the Backspace key (be sure to let up on the Home key before pressing the Backspace key). Notice that the word plan to the left of the cursor is deleted. Again press Home, then Backspace. The word bonus is deleted. Press Home, Backspace two more times, deleting first the word new and then the word The (Figure 2-47).

To restore these four words, press the F1 key and then the number 1. The four words are restored to their original position. To restore the paragraph to its original format, it may be necessary to press the Down Arrow key three or four times.

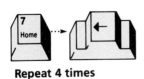

Repeat 4 times

December 1, 1990

cursor position moves to the left

TO: All Sales Managers
RE: New Bonus Plan

approved by the Board of Directors will become effective January 1. If you have questions, contact Hanna Butler prior to January 1, 1991. All sales people are affected by the new plan.

Rita Moeller

cc: Board of Directors

o
o
o
o
B:\MEMO   Doc 1 Pg 1 Ln 2.33" Pos 1"

FIGURE 2-47

Deleting One Block at a Time

Sometimes you may wish to delete an entire block of text. The **Block** feature highlights an area or "block" of text, thereby isolating that text from the rest of the document. Once the desired text is highlighted you can invoke the desired function.

Press Home, Home, Up Arrow to move the cursor to the top of your document (page 1, line 1"). Press the Esc key, then the Down Arrow ↓ key, moving the cursor to page 1, line 2.33".

Look at the template next to the F4 key. You see the word Block in blue. Hold down the Alt key and press the F4 key (step 1 in Figure 2-48). The "Block on" message blinks in the lower left corner of your screen. To highlight text you must move the cursor in any of the ways you have learned in this project (step 2 in Figure 2-48). For example, press the Right Arrow → key and as you continue to press it, you see the word The highlighted. To highlight one *word* at a time, hold down the Ctrl key and while holding it, press the Right Arrow → key two or three times. Notice that words are highlighted one at a time. Press Down Arrow ↓ and notice that you can highlight one line at a time. Move the cursor to line 2.83", position 1.9", thereby highlighting the entire paragraph. Figure 2-49 shows how the entire paragraph should be highlighted.

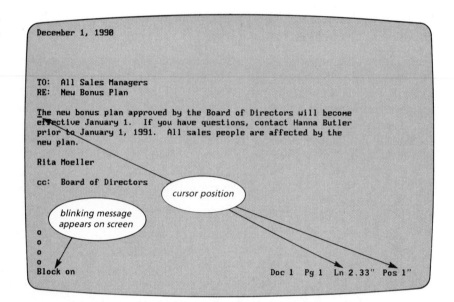

Step 1: Invoke Block on   **Step 2: Use cursor movements to highlight paragraph**

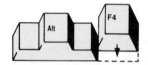   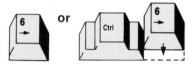

FIGURE 2-48

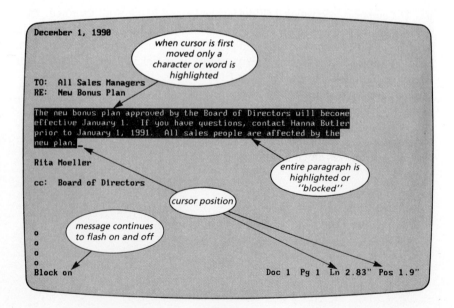

FIGURE 2-49

Now that the desired text is highlighted, press the Del key. Figure 2-50 shows that when you do, the message "Delete Block (Y/N)? No" appears at the bottom left corner of the screen. Delete the block of text you have highlighted by typing the letter Y. Restore the deleted text by pressing the F1 key. The deleted text is highlighted again. Press the number 1 and the text is restored. [For 5.1 Users – The message will be "Delete Block? No (Yes)".]

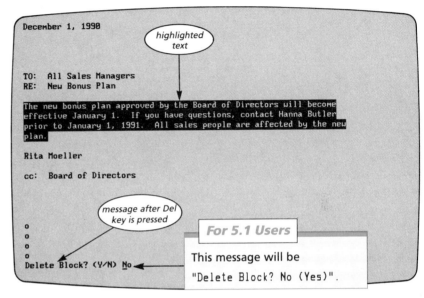

FIGURE 2-50

EXITING PROJECT 2

Move the cursor to the top of the document by pressing Home, Home, Up Arrow. Look at the template next to the F7 key. Notice the word Exit in black. Press the F7 key (step 1 in Figure 2-51). The message "Save Document? (Y/N) Yes" is shown in the lower left corner of the screen. [For 5.1 Users – The message will be "Save Document? Yes (No)" with the cursor under the Y.]

The (Y/N) indicates that if you press Y for yes, you would like to save the document. If you press N for no, you do not wish to save the document. The Yes outside the brackets indicates that the default response to this question is yes, which means that if you press either the Enter key or the spacebar the software will process yes as your answer. In this project you altered the document since you last saved it to the disk. To save this latest version with the ability to practice cursor movements, press Y for yes (step 2 in Figure 2-51).

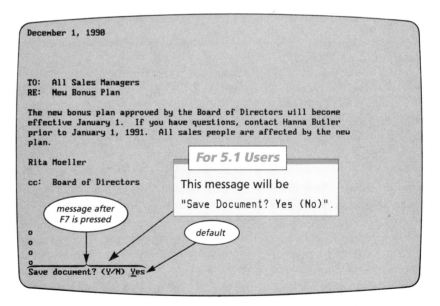

Step 1: Invoke Exit   **Step 2: Save the document**

FIGURE 2-51

Figure 2-52 shows that the message "Document to be Saved: B:\MEMO" appears at the bottom of the screen. Because the memo as it was originally saved will be retrieved in Project 4, it is necessary to give this new version a new name. Type memo.cur and press Enter.

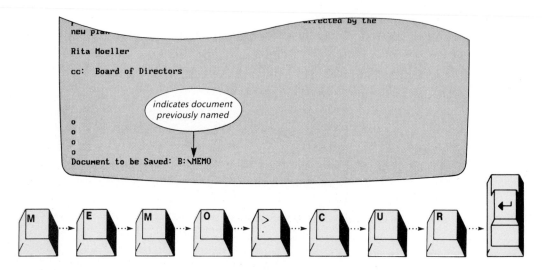

FIGURE 2-52

The light on the default drive turns on, indicating that the document is being saved in its new form to the disk, under the new name.

Next, a message "Exit WP? (Y/N) No" appears (Figure 2-53). Type the letter Y. (If you failed to complete the printing of the document you may see the message "Cancel all print jobs (Y/N)? No" If this appears, type the letter Y for yes.)

As you learned in Project 1, you are returned to the DOS prompt or the DOS screen.

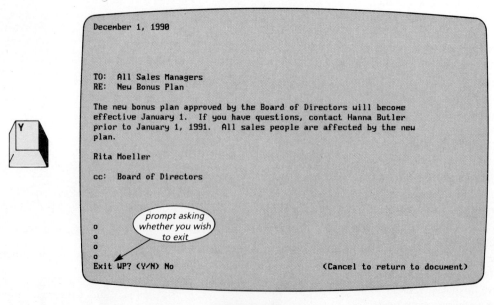

FIGURE 2-53

PROJECT SUMMARY

*I*n Project 2 you learned how to type a document using the word wrap feature. After the document was typed, you learned more about the reveal codes, including how to read the [Tab] code, the hard return [HRt] code, and the soft return [SRt] code.

After saving the document, you printed it. To understand how the cursor moves through several pages of text, you added typing to page 3. Then you practiced several keystrokes that help to move the cursor quickly through a document. You learned that the screen can only show certain portions of the document at a time. You also learned how to edit the text by using several deletion keystrokes or functions.

The following is a list of the keystroke sequence we used in Project 2. Check to be sure that you have defined the Standard Printer as we did in Project 1.

SUMMARY OF KEYSTROKES—Project 2

STEPS	KEY(S) PRESSED	STEPS	KEY(S) PRESSED
1	wp [for two disk drive systems with wp disk in drive A and data disk in drive B]	26	↵
2	↵	27	The new bonus plan approved by the Board of Directors will become effective January 1. If you have questions, contact Hanna Butler prior to January 1, 1991. All sales people are affected by the new plan.
3	F5		
4	=		
5	b: [for two disk drive systems with data disk in drive B] or a: [for hard disk systems with data disk in drive A]	28	↵
		29	↵
6	↵	30	Rita Moeller
7	F1 [to return to blank screen]	31	↵
8	December 1, 1990	32	↵
9	↵	33	cc:
10	↵	34	Tab
11	↵	35	Board of Directors
12	↵	36	↵
13	↵	37	F10
14	Caps Lock	38	Memo
15	TO:	39	↵
16	Caps Lock	40	Shift-F7
17	Tab	41	1
18	All Sales Managers	42	[practice in text cursor movements and deleting text]
19	↵		
20	Caps Lock	43	F7
21	RE:	44	Y
22	Caps Lock	45	memo.cur
23	Tab	46	↵
24	New Bonus Plan	47	Y
25	↵	48	[remove disk(s) from diskette drive(s)]

The following list summarizes the material covered in Project 2:

1. The **word wrap** function eliminates the need to press the Return (Enter) key until you come to the end of a paragraph, short line, or command, or if you want to insert a blank line.
2. A **soft return** has occurred when word wrap automatically moves text to the next line.
3. The **[SRt]** code is embedded in the document when a soft return occurs.
4. Pressing the Tab key embeds the **[Tab]** code into the document.
5. Cursor movement keys are the single keys or combinations of keys that move the cursor efficiently throughout the document (see Table 2-1).
6. The **Plus** and **Minus** keys on the numeric keypad perform the same functions as the Home, Up Arrow and Home, Down Arrow keys.
7. To move the cursor to line 1 of the next page, press the **PgDn** key. To move the cursor to line 1 of the previous page, press the **PgUp** key.
8. To move directly to a particular page, press Ctrl-Home, then enter the desired page number in response to the "**Go to**" message on the screen, and press Enter.
9. The **Esc** key lets you repeat a character or a cursor movement.
10. Deletion keys are the single keys or combinations of keys that delete a character, a word, a page, or blocks of text (see Table 2-2).
11. The **Backspace** key deletes the character or code to the left of the cursor.
12. The **Delete** key deletes the space or character directly above the cursor, moving to the right.
13. The **Block** function highlights a block of text in the document so that a specific function can be performed, such as deleting the text.

STUDENT ASSIGNMENTS

STUDENT ASSIGNMENT 1: True/False

Instructions: Circle T if the statement is true and F if the statement is false.

T F   1. When typing a paragraph at the computer, if you continue typing, the words will automatically wrap to the next line.
T F   2. When word wrap occurs, the code inserted in the document is [HRt].
T F   3. To view the reveal codes screen, press the Alt key, release it, and press F3.
T F   4. When a word is in black on the template, it signifies that the function key is to be pressed alone.
T F   5. To move the cursor to the bottom of the screen, press Home, Down Arrow.
T F   6. To move the cursor to the top of the current screen you press Home, Up Arrow.
T F   7. To move the cursor to the bottom of the document press the PgDn key.
T F   8. The Backspace key deletes the character or space above the cursor.
T F   9. To restore deleted text, press the F1 key, then 1.

STUDENT ASSIGNMENT 2: Multiple Choice

Instructions: Circle the correct response.

1. To load WordPerfect into main memory on a two disk drive system, with the WordPerfect disk in drive A, type
   a. the characters WPC at the DOS A > prompt
   b. the word WORDPERFECT at the DOS A > prompt
   c. the characters wp at the DOS A > prompt
   d. the word WORDPERFECT at the DOS B > prompt
2. Which of the following is a valid file name?
   a. MEMO
   b. memo
   c. Memo
   d. all of the above
3. When typing a paragraph
   a. press the Enter key at the end of each sentence
   b. press the Enter key at the end of each line
   c. press the Enter key at the end of each paragraph
   d. press the Enter key at the end of the document
4. The command to move the cursor to line 1" of the next page is
   a. Home, Home, Down Arrow
   b. Home, Down Arrow
   c. End
   d. PgDn
5. The command to delete from the cursor to the end of the line is
   a. End
   b. Ctrl-End
   c. Delete
   d. Ctrl-Backspace
6. If the cursor is on line 9.83" of page 1, how many lines will the cursor move if you press the PgDn key?
   a. 1
   b. 54
   c. 53
   d. 2
7. To repeat a certain keystroke, you can press the Esc key before the keystroke. The default number of keystrokes is (Repeat value = ?)
   a. 10
   b. 9
   c. 8
   d. 6
8. The Cancel key can be used to restore a deletion. The Cancel key is
   a. Esc
   b. F1
   c. Shift-F1
   d. Alt-F1
9. The command Ctrl-PgDn can be used to delete
   a. the current page from the cursor down
   b. the entire current page, no matter where the cursor is
   c. to the end of the document
   d. half a page

10. To invoke the Block function, press
    a. Ctrl-F4
    b. F4
    c. Shift-F4
    d. Alt-F4

STUDENT ASSIGNMENT 3: Matching

Instructions: Put the appropriate number next to the words in the second column.

1. PgDn   _____   one word to the left
2. Home, Home, Down Arrow   _____   line 1" of previous page
3. Right Arrow   _____   line 1", page 3
4. Ctrl-Left Arrow   _____   top of document
5. Esc, Down Arrow   _____   bottom of document
6. PgUp   _____   right end of line
7. End   _____   bottom line of current page
8. Ctrl-Home, Down Arrow   _____   line 1" of next page
9. Ctrl-Home, 3, Enter   _____   next right character
10. Home, Home, Up Arrow   _____   8 lines down

STUDENT ASSIGNMENT 4: Fill in the Blanks

Instructions: Next to each keystroke or keystroke sequence, describe its effect.

Keystroke(s)   **Effect**

1. PgDn   _____
2. PgUp   _____
3. Right Arrow   _____
4. Left Arrow   _____
5. Down Arrow   _____
6. Up Arrow   _____
7. Home, Home, Up Arrow   _____
8. Home, Home, Down Arrow   _____
9. Ctrl-Left Arrow   _____
10. Ctrl-Right Arrow   _____
11. Home, Down Arrow   _____
12. Home, Up Arrow   _____
13. Home, Left Arrow   _____
14. Home, Right Arrow   _____

STUDENT ASSIGNMENT 5: Fill in the Blanks

Instructions: Next to each delete function below, describe the effect of that deletion.

Delete Function   **Effect**

1. Backspace   _____
2. Delete   _____
3. Ctrl-Backspace   _____
4. Ctrl-End   _____
5. Ctrl-PgDn, Y   _____
6. Alt-F4, Home, Home,
      Down arrow, Delete, Y   _____
7. F1, 1   _____
8. Home, Backspace   _____

STUDENT ASSIGNMENT 6: Deleting Text

Instructions: The screen illustrates a memo that was prepared using WordPerfect. The words approved by the Board of Directors are to be deleted from the memo. Assume that the cursor is under the B in the word Board. Explain in detail the steps necessary to delete the words.

```
TO:   All Sales Managers
RE:   New Bonus Plan

The new bonus plan approved by the Board of Directors will become
effective January 1.  If you have questions, contact Hanna Butler
prior to January 1, 1991.  All sales people are affected by the
new plan.

Rita Moeller

cc:   Board of Directors




B:\DIRECTOR                              Doc 1  Pg 1  Ln 2.67" Pos 1.5"
```

Method of correction: _____

_____

_____

_____

STUDENT ASSIGNMENT 7: Reformatting the Text

Instructions: The screen illustrates a memo that was prepared using the word wrap feature in WordPerfect. Words were then deleted in the first line of the paragraph. Explain in detail the steps necessary to reformat the text so that all lines wrap at the margins.

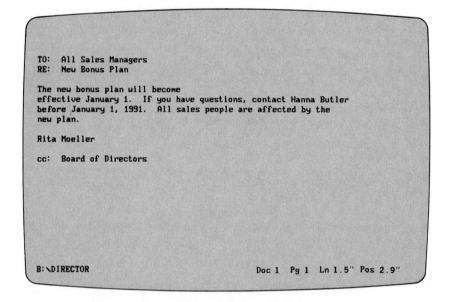

```
TO:   All Sales Managers
RE:   New Bonus Plan

The new bonus plan will become
effective January 1.  If you have questions, contact Hanna Butler
before January 1, 1991.  All sales people are affected by the
new plan.

Rita Moeller

cc:  Board of Directors




B:\DIRECTOR                                    Doc 1  Pg 1  Ln 1.5"  Pos 2.9"
```

Method of correction: _____

_____

_____

STUDENT ASSIGNMENT 8: Modifying a WordPerfect Document

Instructions: Perform the following tasks.

1. For hard disk systems, load WordPerfect as you are directed by your instructor.
   For two disk drive systems, load DOS into main memory. Remove the DOS disk, and replace it with the WordPerfect disk. Type wp and press Enter.
2. Verify that the status line is in inches format and change the default drive to drive A for hard disk systems or drive B for two disk drive systems. Check to be sure that you have defined the Standard Printer as we did in Project 1. Begin this project on a clean screen.

Problem 1: Type the letter illustrated at right without corrections.

Problem 2: Make the corrections indicated and save the document. Name the document Director.

Problem 3: Print the document.

```
TO:  All Sales Managers
RE:  New Bonus Plan
           new
The bonus  plan  approved  by  the  Board of Directors  will become
effective January 1. If you have questions, contact  Hanna Butler
  prior to  January 1,  1991. All  sales people are affected by the
new plan.  before
Rita Moeller

cc: Board of Directors
```

STUDENT ASSIGNMENT 9: Modifying a WordPerfect Document

Instructions: Perform the following tasks.

1. For hard disk systems, load WordPerfect as you are directed by your instructor.
   For two disk drive systems, load DOS into main memory. Remove the DOS disk, and replace it with the WordPerfect disk. Type wp and press Enter.
2. Verify that the status line is in inches format and change the default drive to drive A for hard disk systems or drive B for two disk drive systems. Check to be sure that you have defined the Standard Printer as we did in Project 1. Begin this project on a clean screen.

Problem 1: Type the document illustrated below. Then make the following changes to the document. *NOTE:* In pencil, note the changes to the memo on this page before modifying the document using WordPerfect. The document should appear like the second document shown here.

```
TO:  All Employees
FROM:  Personnel Department
SUBJECT:  Vacation Schedule

All employees that have been employed for more than one  year are
eligible for  two weeks vacation each year. The vacations must be
taken during the  months  of  June,  July,  or  August.  You must
notify the  Personnel Department at least 4 weeks in advance. You
must also obtain approval from your immediate supervisor.

Janet Fisher
Personnel Administrator
```

1. Begin the memo on line 2.83" of the page.
2. Add the current date on the line above the word TO.
3. Delete the words each year from the second line of the body of the memo.
4. Insert the word May, a comma, and a space before the word June in the third line of the body of the memo.
5. Delete the sentence You must notify the Personnel Department at least 4 weeks in advance.
6. Delete the word also from the last sentence.
7. Delete the period after the word supervisor in the last sentence and add these words to the last sentence: at least 4 weeks in advance.

Problem 2: Save the modified document. Name the document Schedule.2.

Problem 3: Print the modified document.

```
DATE:       January 1, 1991
TO:  All Employees
FROM:  Personnel Department
SUBJECT:  Vacation Schedule

All employees that have been employed for more than one  year are
eligible  for  two  weeks  vacation.  The vacations must be taken
during the months of May,  June,  July,  or August.  You  must obtain
approval  from  your  immediate  supervisor  at  least 4 weeks in
advance.

Janet Fisher
Personnel Administrator
```

[handwritten: Morrison]

[handwritten: F7 name exit word Perfect]

STUDENT ASSIGNMENT 10: Modifying a WordPerfect Document

Instructions: Perform the following tasks.

1. For hard disk systems, load WordPerfect as you are directed by your instructor.
   For two disk drive systems, load DOS into main memory. Remove the DOS disk, and replace it with the WordPerfect disk. Type wp and press Enter.
2. Verify that the status line is in inches format and change the default drive to drive A for hard disk systems or drive B for two disk drive systems. Check to be sure that you have defined the Standard Printer as we did in Project 1. Begin this project on a clean screen.

Problem 1: Type the document illustrated below. Then make the following changes to the document. *NOTE:* In pencil, note the changes on the letter on this page before modifying the document using WordPerfect.

1. Begin the letter on line 8 of the page.
2. Change the name to Ms. Roberta A. Morrison.
3. Change the address to 222 Edwards Drive.
4. Delete the words effective immediately beginning on the first line of the text.
5. Add this sentence at the end of the first paragraph: I am currently employed as a programmer/analyst with Rockview International, Redlands, California.
6. Change the last sentence to: Thank you for providing this valuable service to those employed in the computer industry.

Problem 2: Save the modified document. Name it Morrison. The document should appear like the second document shown here.

Problem 3: Print the modified document.

```
January 10, 1990


Ms. Roberta A. Morrison
Editor, Computer Magazine
222 Edwin Drive
Arlington, VA 22289

Dear Ms. Morris:

Please enter   my  subscription  to your  magazine effective
immediately.   It  is  my  understanding  that  you  provide  free
subscriptions to those employed in the computer industry.

Thank  you  for  providing  this valuable service to the computer
industry.

Sincerely,


Rodney C. Caine
Programmer/Analyst
Rockview International
111 Riverview Drive
Redlands, CA 92393
```

```
January 10, 1990



Ms. Roberta A. Morrison
Editor, Computer Magazine
222 Edwards Drive
Arlington, VA 22289

Dear Ms. Morrison:

Please enter   my  subscription to your  magazine.  It  is  my
understanding  that  you  provide  free  subscriptions  to  those
employed  in  the  computer   industry.  I am currently employed as a
programmer/analyst  with  Rockview  International,  Redlands,
California.

Thank  you  for providing  this valuable service to those employed
in the computer industry.

Sincerely,


Rodney C. Caine
Programmer/Analyst
Rockview International
111 Riverview Drive
Redlands, CA 92393
```

PROJECT 3

Learning Special Features

Objectives

You will have mastered the material in this project when you can:

- Arrange text flush right and centered
- Underline and boldface text
- Insert text and type over existing text
- Indent text using the indent key and the left/right indent function
- Save and replace a document

In Project 3 you will create the document shown in Figure 3-1. If you are working on a hard disk system, load Word-Perfect as your instructor directs you. If you are working on a two disk drive system, at the A> prompt (with the WordPerfect disk in drive A and the data disk in drive B), type wp and press Enter. WordPerfect loads into main memory. As in Project 1, verify that the status line is in inches format. Also as in Project 1, use the F5 key to change the default drive to drive A for hard disk systems, or drive B for two disk drive systems. You should then see a clean screen with only the status line in the lower right corner, indicating Doc 1 Pg 1 Ln 1" Pos 1".

Check to be sure that you have defined the Standard Printer as we did in Project 1. Note that correct typing practice requires you to press the spacebar *two times* after typing the period at the end of a sentence. Also note that Project 3 gives some instructions that do not coincide with the document shown in Figure 3-1. This is done purposely. Later in the project you will learn how to move the cursor back to these positions to change and correct the typing, so that eventually your document will be exactly like the one in Figure 3-1. Finally, we will hereafter abbreviate instructions whenever you are asked to hold down one key and, while holding it down, press another key. For example, Alt-F3, means hold down the Alt key and while holding it down press the F3 key.

```
                                        December 15,1990

            LICENSING AGREEMENT

You should carefully read the following terms and conditions.
Your use of this program package indicates your acceptance of
them. If you do not agree with them, you should not use this
software package. Instead, you should return the package and your
money will be returned to you.

PerSoft Inc. provides this program and licenses you to use it.
You assume responsibility for the selection of this program to
achieve your intended results. PerSoft Inc. assumes no
responsibility for the results you obtain from the use of this
software package.

LICENSE

You may perform the following functions:

  a.  Use the program on a single machine only. Use on more
      than one machine is considered "pirating" this
      software.

  b.  Copy the program into any machine readable or printed
      form for backup or modification purposes in support of
      your use of the program on a single machine. Certain
      programs from PerSoft Inc., however, may contain
      mechanisms to limit or inhibit copying. These program
      are marked "copy protected."

  c.  Modify or merge the program into another PerSoft Inc.
      program for use on the single machine. Any portion of
      the program merged into another program will continue
      to be subject to the terms and conditions of this
      License.

You MAY NOT use, copy, modify, or transfer the program, in whole
or in part, except as expressly permitted in this Licensing
Agreement. PerSoft Inc. also reserves the right to do the
following:

    Withdraw your license if this software package is used for
any illegal or immoral purpose which, in the sole judgment of
PerSoft Inc., may damage the reputation of PerSoft Inc.

If you transfer possession of any copy, modification, or merged
portion of the program to another person, YOUR LICENSE IS
AUTOMATICALLY TERMINATED.
```

FIGURE 3-1

MOVING TEXT FLUSH RIGHT

*I*n Figure 3-1, notice that the date is against the right margin. The term to describe this placement of text is **flush right**. Look at the template next to the F6 key, as shown in Figure 3-2. You see the words Flush Right in blue.

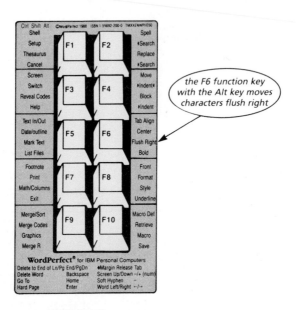

FIGURE 3-2

Press Alt-F6, (step 1 in Figure 3-3). The right margin defaults at position 7.4" (or a one inch right margin). Notice on the status line that the cursor is on position 7.5", just to the right of position 7.4". As you type, the text will move to the left of position 7.5". Type the date December 15, 1990. Figure 3-3 shows how the cursor is anchored at position 7.5" and how the letters move to the left as you type them. To end the Flush Right command press the Return key ← (step 2 in Figure 3-3).

Step 1: Align text flush right

Step 2: Stop aligning text flush right

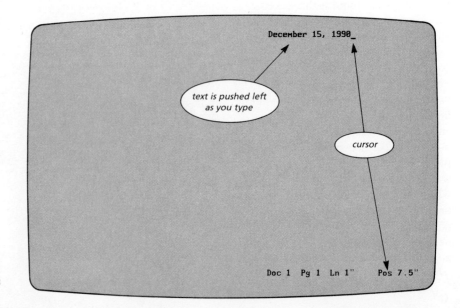

FIGURE 3-3

Now, view the code that is inserted when you align text flush right. Press Alt-F3 (step 1 in Figure 3-4). Figure 3-4 shows how the screen is divided. The lower screen reveals the codes that were embedded in your document. The first code you see is **[Flsh Rt]**, followed by the date. The [Flsh Rt] signifies the *beginning* of a Flush Right command. After the date, notice the code **[C/A/Flrt]**, which signifies the end of a Flush Right command. After the [C/A/Flrt] code is the [HRt] code, which indicates the hard return you pressed after typing the date. [For 5.1 Users – The code **[C/A/Flrt]** will not appear and the reveal codes screen will display fewer lines.] To exit the reveal codes screen and return to your typing screen, press Alt-F3. Next, insert two blank lines by pressing Return twice ↵ ↵, placing the cursor on line 1.5", position 1".

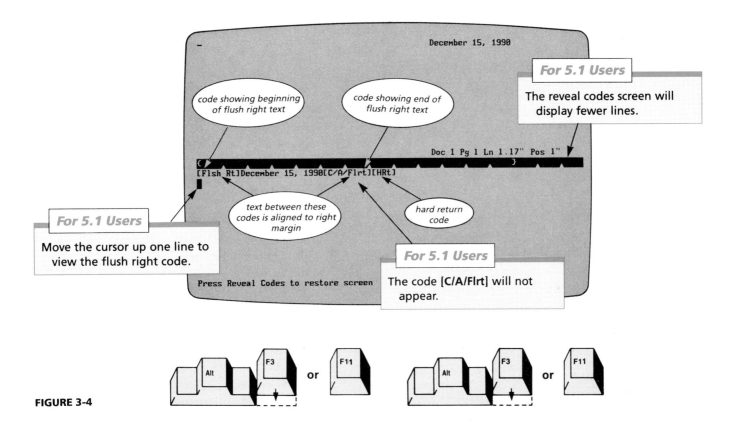

FIGURE 3-4

CENTERING TEXT

Center Text is a useful command and one that is commonly used, such as when you wish to center a heading. In Projects 1 and 2, you learned that the margins in WordPerfect are preset at (or default to) a one inch margin on the left and one inch on the right. Instead of figuring the middle of the text by hand, as you would with typewriting, when you invoke the center function in WordPerfect, the program does all the figuring automatically.

Look at the template next to the F6 key. You see the word Center in green. While holding down the Shift key, press the F6 key (step 1 in Figure 3-5). The status line indicates you are at position 4.25", which is the middle position between the left and right margins. Before you begin typing, note that the title in Figure 3-1 is in capital (uppercase) letters. To capitalize your title, press the Caps Lock key (step 2 in Figure 3-5). Look at the status line. Figure 3-5 shows that the letters Pos are now POS. This is your indication that anything you type now will be in uppercase letters. The Caps Lock key is a *toggle* key, which means you turn it off the same way you turn it on. In other words, you press it once to activate the capitalization function and press it again to turn it off. For practice you may want to press the Caps Lock key a few times.

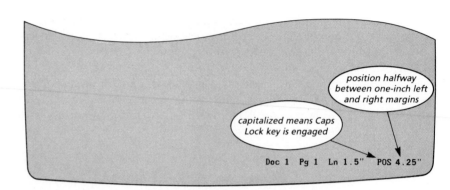

position halfway between one-inch left and right margins

capitalized means Caps Lock key is engaged

Doc 1 Pg 1 Ln 1.5"   POS 4.25"

Step 1: Center text   **Step 2: Capitalize text**   **Step 3: Stop centering text**

FIGURE 3-5

When you are ready to continue with the project, be sure you see POS on the status line, indicating that type will be in uppercase letters. Type the words LICENSING AGREEMENT and as you do, notice that the text is automatically centered. To end the centering of text, press the Return key ← (step 3 in Figure 3-5). To insert a blank line, press the Return key one more time ←, placing the cursor on line 1.83", position 1".

Now, to see the codes that are embedded when you use the centering function, hold down the Alt key and press the F3 key (step 1 in Figure 3-6).

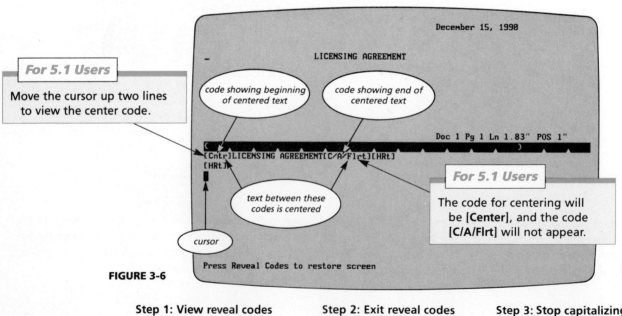

December 15, 1990

LICENSING AGREEMENT

For 5.1 Users

Move the cursor up two lines to view the center code.

code showing beginning of centered text

code showing end of centered text

Doc 1 Pg 1 Ln 1.83" POS 1"

[Cntr]LICENSING AGREEMENT[C/A/Flrt][HRt]
[HRt]

text between these codes is centered

For 5.1 Users

The code for centering will be [**Center**], and the code [**C/A/Flrt**] will not appear.

cursor

Press Reveal Codes to restore screen

FIGURE 3-6

Step 1: View reveal codes   **Step 2: Exit reveal codes**   **Step 3: Stop capitalizing text**

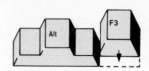

On the line where you centered text, you see the code **[Cntr]**, indicating the beginning of centering. At the end of the text is the code **[C/A/Flrt]** followed by another [HRt] code, indicating the end of centering. (Because centering is ended by pressing a hard return, which embeds the [C/A/Flrt] code, if you were to look at the codes before you inserted the hard return, you would not see the [C/A/Flrt] code.) In addition to the [HRt] after the [C/A/Flrt] code you also see another [HRt] code, which inserted the blank line. [For 5.1 Users – The code for centering will be **[Center]**, and the code **[C/A/Flrt]** will not appear.] To exit from the reveal codes, press Alt-F3 (step 2 in Figure 3-6). You are returned to your document. To turn off the capitalizing function, press the Caps Lock key (step 3 in Figure 3-6) and notice on the status line that POS is again Pos.

BOLDFACING TEXT

*C*ontinue by typing the words You should, and then press the spacebar. The cursor is on line 1.83", position 2.1". Note that in Figure 3-1 the word carefully is in darker, bolder type. When letters are presented this way in a document, they are said to be **boldfaced** or in boldface type. Look at the template next to the F6 key. You see the word Bold in black. Press the F6 key (step 1 in Figure 3-7) and as you press it look at the position number. If you have a monochrome monitor, the number itself becomes bolder. If you have a color monitor, the number changes to a different color. For practice, press the F6 key several times while watching the position number on the status line.

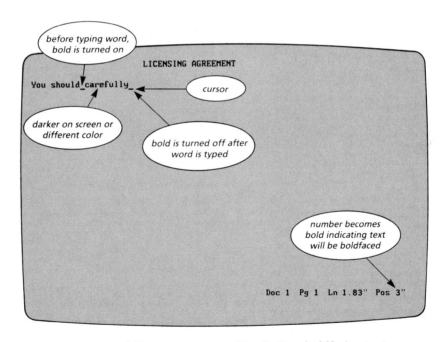

FIGURE 3-7

Step 1: Boldface text   Step 2: Stop boldfacing text

Be sure that the Bold command is on, and type the next word in Figure 3-1, which is the word carefully. As shown in Figure 3-7 the cursor is on line 1.83", position 3". Because you only want one word boldfaced, press F6 again to turn off the Bold command (step 2 in Figure 3-7). To view the codes that are inserted when typing in boldface mode, press Alt-F3 (step 1 in Figure 3-8). Figure 3-8 illustrates that preceding the word carefully is the code **[BOLD]**, indicating the beginning of bold-facing. At the end of the word carefully is the code **[bold]**, indicating the end of boldfacing. When the document is printed, the printer reads the codes, and only the typing between the boldface codes will be in boldface. To exit from the reveal codes press Alt-F3 (step 2 in Figure 3-8), and you are returned to your document.

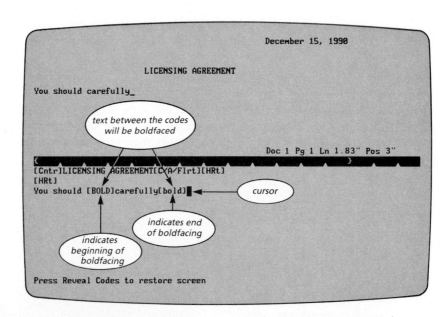

FIGURE 3-8

Step 1: View reveal codes   **Step 2: Exit reveal codes**

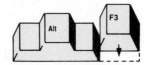

To continue, press the spacebar one time and type these words:

> read the following terms and conditions. Your use of this program package indicates your acceptance of them. If you do

Then press the spacebar. The cursor is now on line 2.17", position 2.7".

UNDERLINING TEXT

At times, you may want your type to be underscored with a line. You would then want to use the **underline** function. Look at the template next to the F8 key. Note the word Underline in black. Press the F8 key (step 1 in Figure 3-9). The position number on the status line is underlined, indicating that any text you type now will be underlined. (If you have a color monitor, the color of the number will change.) For practice, press the F8 key several times, so that you can see how your monitor indicates that the words or letters you type will be underlined. Before you begin typing, be sure that the underline command is on. Type the word not. Then, before typing or even spacing, press the F8 key again and notice on the status line that the underline command is off (step 2 in Figure 3-9). The cursor is at position 3.0".

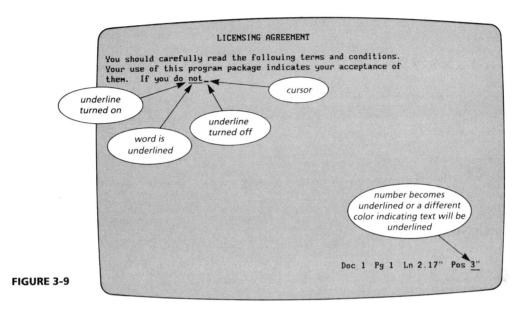

FIGURE 3-9

Step 1: Underline text   Step 2: Stop underlining text

To view the codes used for underlining, press Alt-F3 (step 1 in Figure 3-10). Figure 3-10 shows in the lower screen that before the word not is the code **[UND]**, indicating the beginning of underlining. After the word not is the code **[und]**, indicating the end of underlining. To exit from the reveal codes, press Alt-F3 and you are back to your document.

To finish typing the paragraph, press the spacebar and, with the cursor at position 3.1", type these words:

> agree with them, you should not use this software package. Instead, you should return the package and your money will be returned to you.

Next, press the return ↵ key twice, placing the cursor on line 2.83", position 1". Now type the second paragraph in Figure 3-1. Beginning on line 2.83", position 1", type these words:

> PerSoft Inc. provides this program and licenses you to use it.

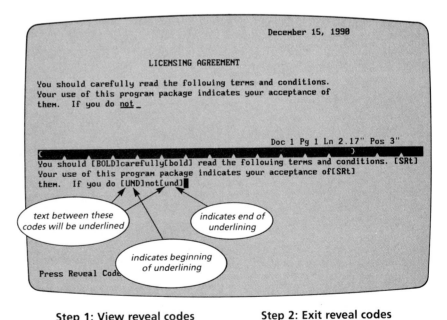

Step 1: View reveal codes   Step 2: Exit reveal codes

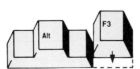

FIGURE 3-10

After typing the period, press the spacebar twice, placing the cursor on line 2.83", position 7.4". Since the next word is to be underlined, press the F8 key (step 1 in Figure 3-11). Before you type, let's see how the codes appear. Press Alt-F3 (step 2 in Figure 3-11). The lower screen shows both the underline codes together, with the cursor highlighting the right code. To demonstrate that you can type while still in reveal codes, type the word You. Notice how the right code is pushed to the right as you type.

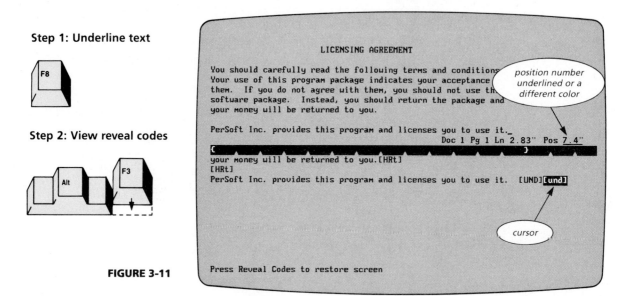

Step 1: Underline text

Step 2: View reveal codes

FIGURE 3-11

Before you turn off the underline command, look at the lower screen of reveal codes. Your screen will look like the one in Figure 3-12. [For 5.1 Users – The underline codes and the word you will move to the next line.] Notice how the lowercase **[und]** code moved to the right and the word you typed appears between the codes. In addition, notice that because the Underline command is still turned on, the cursor still highlights the [und] code.

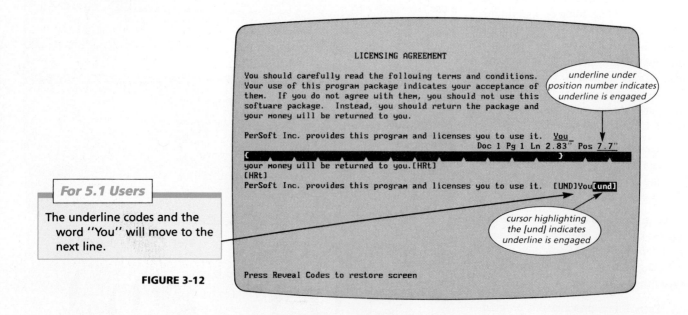

For 5.1 Users

The underline codes and the word "You" will move to the next line.

FIGURE 3-12

Now, press the F8 key to turn off the Underline command (step 1 in Figure 3-13). By turning off the Underline command, you have moved the cursor to the right of the [und] code. Press Alt-F3 to exit the reveal codes (step 2 in Figure 3-13).

Step 1: Stop underlining text

Step 2: Exit reveal codes

For 5.1 Users

The underline codes and the
word "You" will move to the
next line.

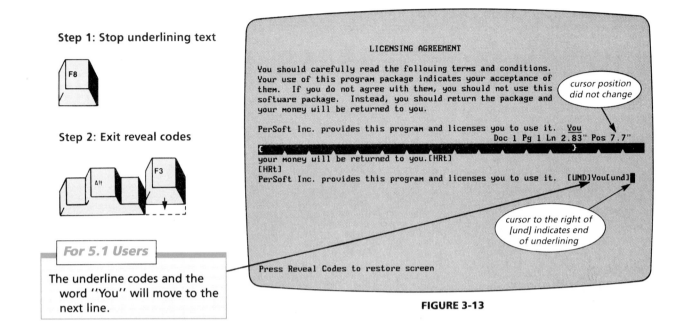

LICENSING AGREEMENT

You should carefully read the following terms and conditions.
Your use of this program package indicates your acceptance of
them. If you do not agree with them, you should not use this
software package. Instead, you should return the package and
your money will be returned to you.

PerSoft Inc. provides this program and licenses you to use it. You
                                              Doc 1 Pg 1 Ln 2.83" Pos 7.7"

your money will be returned to you.[HRt]
[HRt]
PerSoft Inc. provides this program and licenses you to use it. [UND]You[und]

Press Reveal Codes to restore screen

*cursor position
did not change*

*cursor to the right of
[und] indicates end
of underlining*

FIGURE 3-13

INSERTING TEXT

Sometimes you may wish to insert text between existing text. WordPerfect defaults to the **Insert Text** mode, which
means that as you type, text will be inserted wherever the cursor is located.

Press the spacebar to make the line wrap and move the cursor to line 3", position 1.4". Type these words:

assume responsibility for the selection of this program to achieve your intended results. PerSoft Inc. assumes no responsibility for the results you obtain from the use of this package.

When you finish, the cursor is on line 3.5", position 1.8". Compare what you typed to Figure 3-1. You see that you omitted
the word software before the last word, package. Press the Left Arrow ← key to move the cursor to the left to position it under
the p in the word package. Type
the word software and as you do,
notice that the word is inserted into
the text and the word package is
moved to the right (Figure 3-14).
Finally, press the spacebar once to
insert a space between the last two
words of the paragraph.

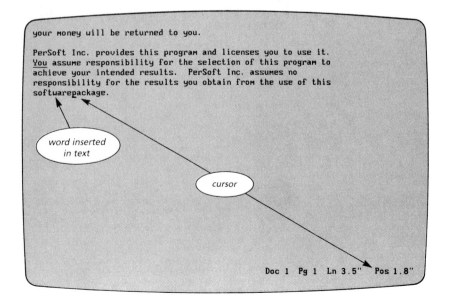

your money will be returned to you.

PerSoft Inc. provides this program and licenses you to use it.
You assume responsibility for the selection of this program to
achieve your intended results. PerSoft Inc. assumes no
responsibility for the results you obtain from the use of this
softwarepackage.

*word inserted
in text*

cursor

Doc 1 Pg 1 Ln 3.5"   Pos 1.8"

FIGURE 3-14

USING THE BACKSPACE KEY TO CORRECT ERRORS

As you know, if you make a mistake in typing a word, you can press the Backspace key to delete the error. At other times you can use the Backspace key to correct other errors such as hard returns and spacing. For example, you may accidentally press the Return/Enter key ↵, thereby splitting lines of text on the screen. With the cursor still under the p in package, press the Return key ↵. Figure 3-15 shows how this splits the line. Press the Backspace key. Figure 3-16 shows how the word package returns to line 3.5".

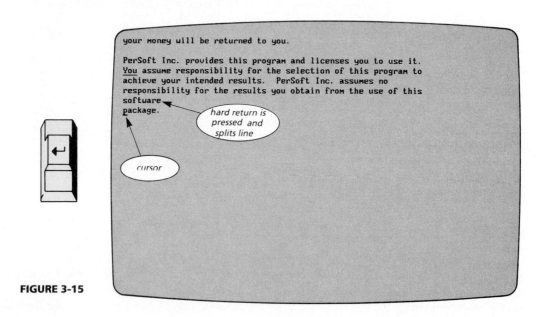

FIGURE 3-15

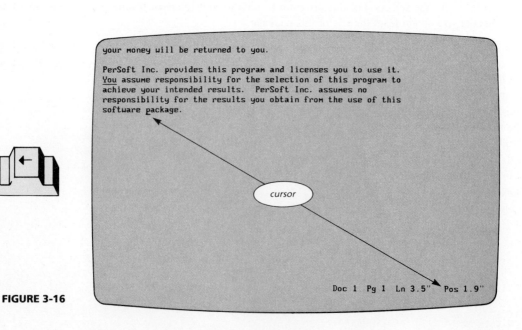

FIGURE 3-16

You can also use the Backspace key if you press the spacebar in error. Press the Spacebar two times (step 1 in Figure 3-17). To delete these extra spaces, press the Backspace key two times (step 2 in Figure 3-17) to return the word package to its original position.

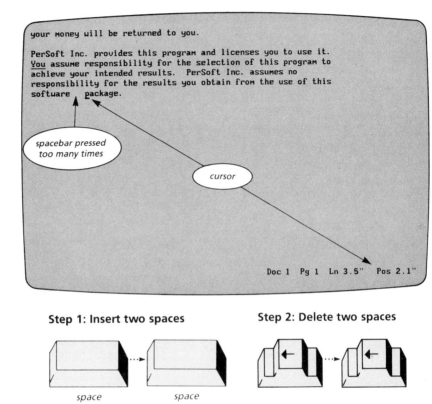

FIGURE 3-17

Step 1: Insert two spaces

Step 2: Delete two spaces

space   space

Because you wish to end the paragraph, press Home, then Right Arrow →, placing the cursor to the right of the period, on line 3.5", position 2.7". To end the paragraph, press Return ↵. To insert a blank line press Return ↵ again, placing the cursor on line 3.83", position 1".

USING THE TYPEOVER COMMAND

s explained earlier, WordPerfect defaults to the Insert mode. However, if you wish to type over existing text instead of using the insert function, you must turn on the Typeover command. The Insert key is a toggle key, which means you turn it off the same way you turn it on.

Beginning at position 1" on line 3.83" type the word License. Comparing the word with the one in Figure 3-1 you note that it should have been typed in capital letters rather than uppercase and lowercase letters. One way to do this is to delete the word and then retype it completely. However, you can also use the **Typeover** mode to accomplish this.

Move the cursor to the left under the i in License as shown in Figure 3-18. Before you begin typing press the Caps Lock key, then press the Insert key (step 1 in Figure 3-18). At the bottom left corner of your screen you see the word "Typeover." It means that anything you type will type over existing text. Type the letters ICENSE and as you do notice how the lowercase letters become uppercase letters. When finished, press the Insert key to turn the Typeover command off. The word "Typeover" in the left corner of the screen disappears. Press the Caps Lock key to change from uppercase to lowercase typing (step 2 in Figure 3-18). Press the Return key ↵ to move the cursor to line 4", then press the Return key ↵ again to insert a blank line and move the cursor to line 4.17", position 1".

Type the words You may perform the following functions: followed by a hard return ↵. To insert a blank line press the hard return ↵ again, placing the cursor on line 4.5", position 1".

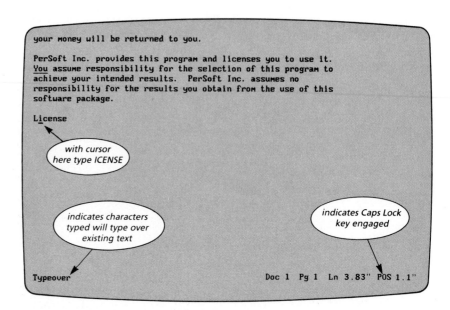

FIGURE 3-18   **Step 1: Type over text with capitalized letters**

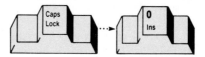

Step 2: Return to Insert mode and stop capitalizing text

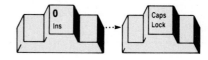

USING THE INDENT KEY

Without actually changing the margin settings you may wish to change the left margin temporarily so that lines wrap to a specific position setting, making a wider margin, as shown in Figure 3-19. To accomplish this you must use the →**Indent** key, which is the F4 key. Look at the template next to the F4 key. You see the word →Indent in black. When you use the Indent key you will notice that the cursor always moves to where the Tabs are set. In WordPerfect the tabs setting defaults to every 1/2 inch, or 0, .5, 1.0, 1.5, 2.0, and so on.

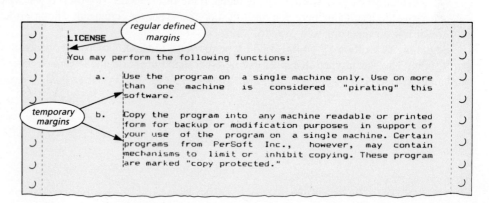

FIGURE 3-19

With the cursor at position 1", press the F4 key. The cursor moves to position 1.5", which is where the first tab is found to the right of the margin. At position 1.5" type a. then press the F4 key again. As shown in Figure 3-20, the cursor moves to position 2", which is now the new temporary left margin. All text typed will wrap around to position 2".

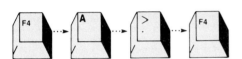

FIGURE 3-20

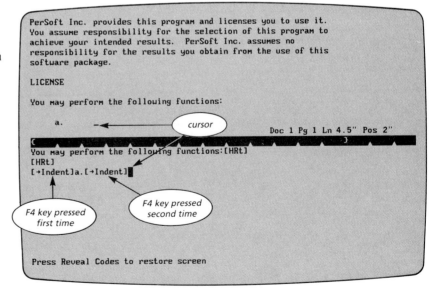

To view the code that is embedded into the text when you press the Indent key, press Alt-F3. Figure 3-21 shows the reveal codes screen. You see the first [→Indent] code, then the letter a. Next you see the second [→Indent] code, which will change the left margin temporarily. Press Alt-F3 to exit from the reveal codes (step 2 in Figure 3-21).

FIGURE 3-21

Step 1: View reveal codes   Step 2: Exit reveal codes

Beginning on line 4.5", position 2" type these lines:

Use the program on a single machine only. Use on more than one machine is considered "pirating" this software.

At the end of the first line when you begin typing the word than, notice that the word wraps to the next line, to position 2", which is the new temporary margin. After typing the word software followed by a period, end indenting by pressing the Return key ↵. The cursor moves to line 5", position 1", which is the default left margin.

To insert a blank line, press Return ↵ to move the cursor to line 5.17", position 1" (step 1 in Figure 3-22). Since you need to indent the next paragraph, press the F4 key and type b. then press the F4 key again (step 2 in Figure 3-22). With the cursor on position 2", type this paragraph:

Copy the program into any machine readable or printed form for backup or modification purposes in support of your use of the program on a single machine. Certain programs from PerSoft Inc., however, may contain mechanisms to limit or inhibit copying. These programs are marked "copy protected."

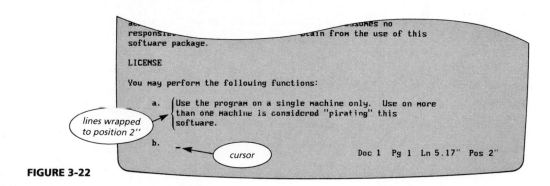

FIGURE 3-22

Step 1: Return to default margin
and insert blank line

Step 2: Create temporary margin

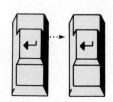
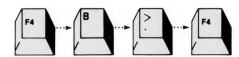

When you have finished typing the paragraph the cursor will be on line 6", position 4.8". Press the Return key ↵ to end the indenting for this paragraph. Press the Return key ↵ again to insert a blank line, placing the cursor on line 6.33", position 1" (step 1 in Figure 3-23).

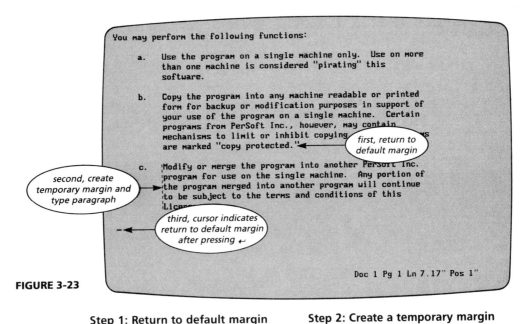

FIGURE 3-23

Step 1: Return to default margin and insert blank line

Step 2: Create a temporary margin

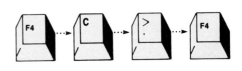

Step 3: Return to default margin

Before typing the last indented paragraph, press the F4 key and type c. then press the F4 key again (step 2 in Figure 3-23). Beginning on position 2", type this paragraph:

> Modify or merge the program into another PerSoft Inc. program for use on the single machine. Any portion of the program merged into another program will continue to be subject to the terms and conditions of this License.

To end indenting the paragraph press the Return key ← (step 3 in Figure 3-23). This moves the cursor to line 7.17" position 1". Then press the Return key ← again to insert a blank line. With the cursor on Ln 7.33" Pos 1" type these words:

You MAY NOT use, copy, modify, or transfer the program, in whole or in part, except as

Then press the spacebar, placing the cursor on line 7.5", position 3.2".

BOLDFACING AND UNDERLINING AT THE SAME TIME

To emphasize important words in a document, you may wish to use boldface as well as underlining. Remember how to underline text: Press the F8 key. To boldface text, press the F6 key (step 1 in Figure 3-24). Type the words: expressly permitted. Figure 3-24 shows how your screen will look with the words both boldfaced and underlined (if you have a color screen, the words to be boldfaced and/or underlined appear in different colors). Before you resume typing you must turn off the Boldface and Underline commands. Press F8 to turn off the Underline, then press F6 to turn off the Boldface (step 2 in Figure 3-24).

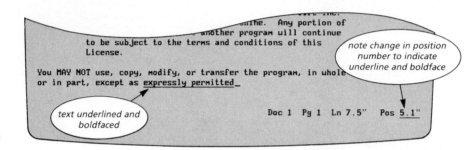

FIGURE 3-24

Step 1: Underline and Boldface text   **Step 2: Stop underlining and boldfacing**

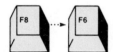   

To view the codes in this document, press Alt-F3 (step 1 in Figure 3-25). Figure 3-25 shows both the underline [UND][und] and boldface [BOLD][bold] codes at the beginning and end of the two words. Press Alt-F3 to exit from the reveal codes (step 2 in Figure 3-25).

Press the spacebar to insert a space after the word permitted and continue typing:

in this Licensing Agreement. PerSoft Inc. also reserves the right to do the following:

To end the paragraph press the Return key ↵ followed by another Return ↵ to insert a blank line. The cursor should now be on line 8.17", position 1".

Step 1: View reveal codes

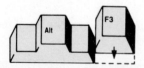

Step 2: Exit reveal codes

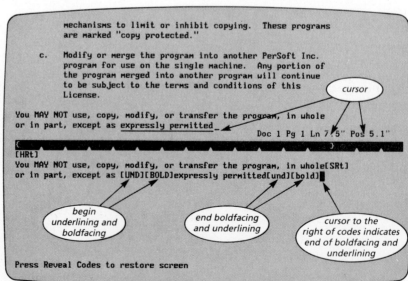

FIGURE 3-25

USING THE LEFT/RIGHT INDENT KEY

*I*f you wish to define wider left and right margins temporarily, you can use the **Left/Right Indent** key. The Left/Right Indent key can be used for long quotes that will be indented from both the left and right margins. The left/right indent moves to where the tabs are currently set. When you use the left/right indent, the right margin will move in the same number of spaces as the left margin.

Look at the template next to the F4 key. You see the word →**Indent**← in green. Press Shift-F4 (step 1 in Figure 3-26). To see the embedded code, press Alt-F3 (step 2 in Figure 3-26). In the lower screen shown in Figure 3-26 notice the code [→**Indent**←], indicating that any text that follows will be indented from both the left and right margins. To exit from the reveal codes, press Alt-F3 (step 3 in Figure 3-26).

Now type the left/right indented paragraph:

> Withdraw your license if this software package is used for any illegal or immoral purpose which, in the sole judgment of PerSoft Inc., may damage the reputation of PerSoft Inc.

When you finish typing this paragraph, the cursor is on line 8.67", position 2.7". To end the Left/Right Indent command, press the Return key ↵, then press the Return key ↵ again to insert a blank line, placing the cursor on line 9", position 1". Beginning on line 9", position 1", type the last paragraph of the licensing agreement:

> If you transfer possession of any copy, modification, or merged portion of the program to another person, YOUR LICENSE IS AUTOMATICALLY TERMINATED.

The entire document is now typed.

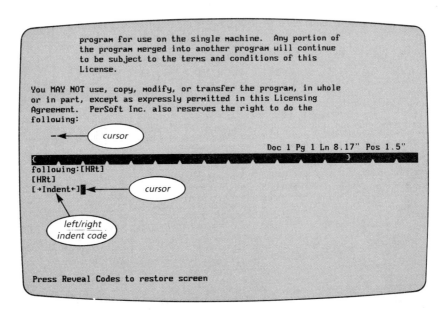

Step 1: Indent text   **Step 2: View reveal codes**   **Step 3: Exit reveal codes**

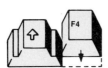      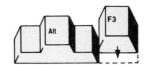

FIGURE 3-26

SAVING A FILE TO THE DISK

It is necessary to save the document to disk so that it can be retrieved for printing or modification later. To save, follow the procedure you learned in Projects 1 and 2. Save this document under the name LICENSE.

UNDERLINING AND BOLDFACING EXISTING TEXT

At the beginning of Project 3 you were told that you would be creating the document in Figure 3-1. If you compare the document in Figure 3-1 with your completed document as shown in Figure 3-27, you will notice the following differences:

1. In the title, the words LICENSING AGREEMENT are not underlined in Figure 3-27.
2. Farther down, the word LICENSE is not in boldface type.
3. The words MAY NOT are not underlined.
4. The last five words of the agreement are not in bold-face type.

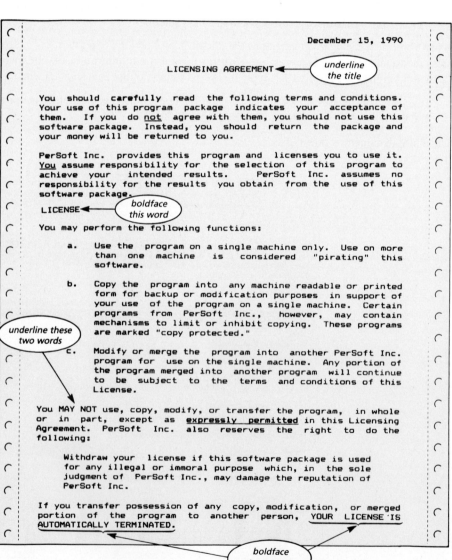

FIGURE 3-27

The comparison of the two figures shows that sometimes you need to boldface or underline *existing* text. It is not necessary to delete the text and retype it in boldface or underline mode. Move the cursor to the top of the document by pressing Home, Home, Up Arrow ↑. As the cursor moves to the top of the document, the word "Repositioning" appears in the lower left corner of the screen, advising you that the cursor is in the process of moving.

Move the cursor down so that it is under the L in LICENSING AGREEMENT. The cursor will be on line 1.5", position 3.3".

As we learned in Project 2, the block function highlights specified text, thereby isolating that text from the rest of the document. Once the desired text is highlighted you can perform the requested function. Here we use the **block** function to underline and then boldface a block of text.

Look at the template next to the F4 key. You see the word Block in blue. Press Alt-F4 (step 1 in Figure 3-28). The "Block on" message begins blinking in the lower left corner of the screen. To highlight or block the words LICENSING AGREEMENT, move the cursor to the right one character at a time with the Right Arrow → key, or move the cursor more quickly by pressing the Home key followed by the Right Arrow key → (step 2 in Figure 3-28). When the cursor is on position 5.2" just to the right of the letter T in AGREEMENT, the two words are blocked. You have now isolated these words from the rest of the document and can underline them. As noted on the template, the F8 key is used for underlining. Press the F8 key (step 3 in Figure 3-28). When you do, notice that the "Block on" message turns off on the screen and at the same time the block of text is underlined.

If you have an enhanced keyboard you can also use the F12 key to turn on block mode and to turn off block mode. You will not be told this each time we turn on or turn off block mode, but if you have the F12 key available and you are instructed to press Alt-F4, you can choose to press F12.

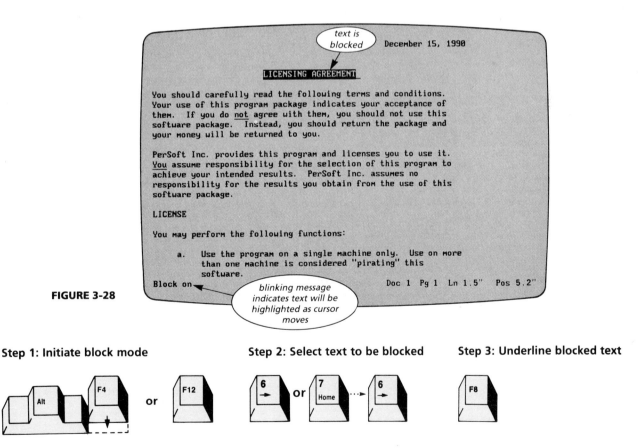

FIGURE 3-28

Step 1: Initiate block mode   Step 2: Select text to be blocked   Step 3: Underline blocked text

Move the cursor down to line 3.83", position 1" so that it is under the L in the word LICENSE. This is existing text you wish to boldface. The same method that was used to underline existing text is used to boldface existing text. Press Alt-F4 (step 1 in Figure 3-29). With the "Block on" message flashing in the lower left corner of your screen, move the cursor to the right to highlight the word LICENSE (step 2 in Figure 3-29). When the word is highlighted, note that the word Bold is in black next to the F6 key, and press the F6 key (step 3 in Figure 3-29). The blocked text is turned off and the word LICENSE is boldfaced.

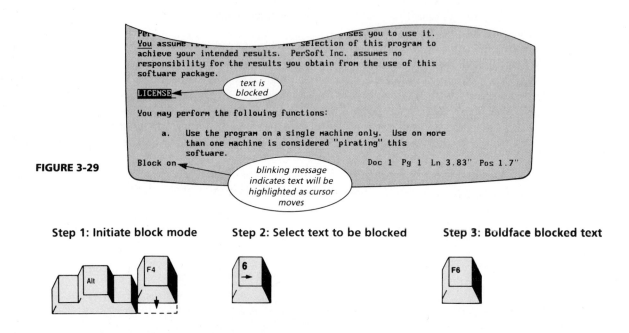

FIGURE 3-29

Step 1: Initiate block mode   **Step 2: Select text to be blocked**   **Step 3: Boldface blocked text**

Move the cursor down to line 7.33" of your document, then to position 1.4". The cursor should be under the M in the word MAY. To block the words MAY NOT, press Alt-F4 (step 1 in Figure 3-30). With the message "Block on" flashing, move the cursor to the right to highlight the words MAY NOT (step 2 in Figure 3-30). When the words are highlighted, press the F8 key (step 3 in Figure 3-30). The block is turned off and the words are underlined.

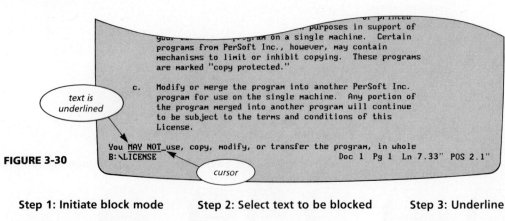

FIGURE 3-30

Step 1: Initiate block mode   **Step 2: Select text to be blocked**   **Step 3: Underline blocked text**

Move the cursor down to line 9.17". To move to the right, while holding down the Ctrl key, press the Right Arrow →
until the cursor is under the letter Y in the word YOUR. The cursor should be at position 5.2". To highlight the last five
words of the document, press Alt-F4 (step 1 in Figure 3-31). With the message "Block on" flashing, move the cursor to highlight the last five words of the document, YOUR LICENSE IS AUTOMATICALLY TERMINATED (step 2 in Figure 3-31).
With the desired text highlighted, press the F6 key (step 3 in Figure 3-31). "Block on" is turned off and the text is placed in
boldface mode.

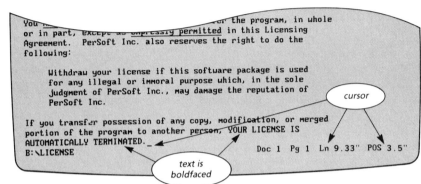

FIGURE 3-31

Step 1: Initiate block mode   **Step 2: Select text to be blocked**   **Step 3: Boldface blocked text**

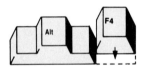   or

To view your last command in the
reveal codes, press Alt-F3 (step 1 in Figure 3-32). In the lower screen the **[BOLD]**
code (beginning boldface) was placed
before the Y and the **[bold]** code (ending
boldface) was placed after the period.
When the document is printed, all type
between those codes will be printed in
boldface. To exit the reveal codes, press
Alt-F3 (step 2 in Figure 3-32).

For 5.1 Users

Move the cursor up one line to
see both codes.

Step 1: View reveal codes   **Step 2: Exit reveal codes**

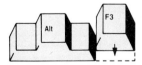   

FIGURE 3-32

SAVING AND REPLACING A DOCUMENT

When you finished typing this document, you saved it to your disk. But after saving it, you made several changes to the document on your screen. Those changes have not been saved to the disk. If there were a power failure or if you turned off the computer, the revised document in the main memory would be lost. Therefore, you must save the changes to the disk, replacing the old text with the new text. When you instruct the computer to replace the old document with the new one, the entire document will be saved, including any changes or additions.

To **save and replace** your document, press the F10 key (step 1 in Figure 3-33). Notice the message "Document to be Saved:" in the lower left corner of the screen, along with the name you previously gave your document. Once you have named a document, it is not necessary to type the name each time you wish to save and replace. Since that is the name you wish to keep, you only need to press the Enter ↵ key (step 2 in Figure 3-33). When you do, the message "Replace B:\LICENSE? (Y/N) No" appears on the screen (Figure 3-34). [For 5.1 Users – The message will be "Replace B:\LICENSE? No (Yes)".] Since you want to replace the old document with the new one, type the letter Y for yes. You will hear the default drive whirring and see the light go on, indicating that the document is being saved to the diskette and that the new version is replacing the old version.

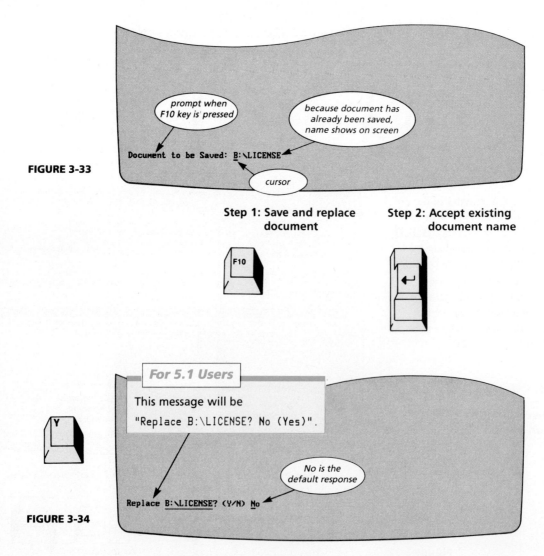

FIGURE 3-33

prompt when F10 key is pressed

because document has already been saved, name shows on screen

Document to be Saved: B:\LICENSE

cursor

Step 1: Save and replace document

Step 2: Accept existing document name

F10

For 5.1 Users

This message will be "Replace B:\LICENSE? No (Yes)".

No is the default response

Replace B:\LICENSE? (Y/N) No

Y

FIGURE 3-34

PRINTING A DOCUMENT

N ow you can print the document in its final form. As shown in Project 2, WordPerfect 5.0 and 5.1 allow you to view your document before you print, to see how it will appear when it is printed. The View Document function is found on the print menu. While holding down the Shift key, press the F7 key. Figure 3-35 shows that when you press those keys the print menu appears on the screen. To view the document, press 6 and notice how the screen shows the letter on what looks like a miniature piece of paper (Figure 3-36). To exit this screen, press F1 to cancel, which returns you to the print menu. If you press F7 to exit, you will return to your document. If this happens, press Shift-F7 to restore the print menu.

Be sure your printer has paper inserted correctly and that the printer is turned on and is ready to print. Since you wish to print the full text of this document, press the number 1 for full text, and the printer begins printing your document. The printed document should appear like the letter in Figure 3-1, page 66.

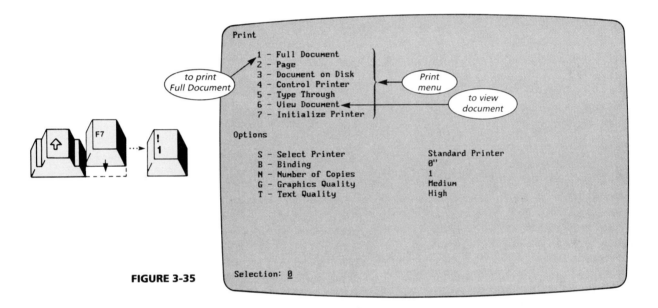

FIGURE 3-35

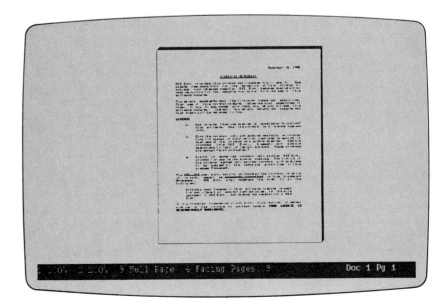

FIGURE 3-36

EXITING PROJECT 3

*I*n order to exit this document press the F7 key (step 1 in Figure 3-37). The message "Save Document? (Y/N) Yes" appears in the lower left corner of the screen.

Remember that you have already saved this document in its new form to the disk, so it is not necessary to save it again. Look at the right corner of the screen in Figure 3-37. Notice the message "(Text was not modified)." That message is your assurance that everything in your document has been saved. If that message were completed it would say "Text was not modified since you last saved to disk." If you are ever exiting a document you wish to save and you do not see the "(Text was not modified)" message, be sure to save and replace as you exit.

Since you do see the message and are assured that your document has been saved in its entirety, you can answer the prompt by pressing the letter N for no (step 2 in Figure 3-37).

The screen then displays the prompt "Exit WP? (Y/N) No" as shown in Figure 3-38. Since you do wish to exit the program, type the letter Y as you have done in Projects 1 and 2 to return to the DOS prompt or DOS screen.

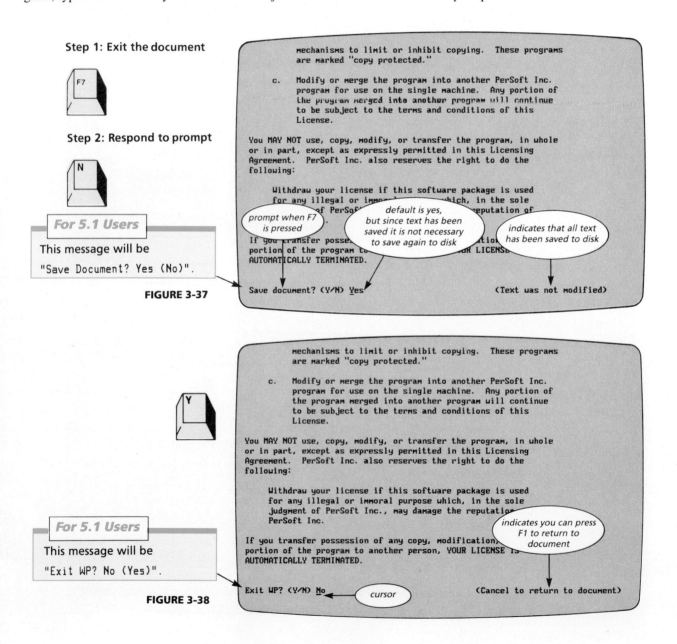

Step 1: Exit the document

F7

Step 2: Respond to prompt

N

For 5.1 Users

This message will be
"Save Document? Yes (No)".

FIGURE 3-37

prompt when F7 is pressed

default is yes, but since text has been saved it is not necessary to save again to disk

indicates that all text has been saved to disk

Save document? (Y/N) Yes   (Text was not modified)

Y

For 5.1 Users

This message will be
"Exit WP? No (Yes)".

FIGURE 3-38

indicates you can press F1 to return to document

Exit WP? (Y/N) No   cursor   (Cancel to return to document)

PROJECT SUMMARY

*I*n Project 3 you learned how to arrange text flush right and centered, how to boldface and underline text, and how to indent text. You saved the document to disk, then returned to existing text and boldfaced and underlined some key words. Then you saved the revised document to the disk, replacing the first version. You printed the document, making a hard copy of the text. Throughout the project, you practiced viewing the reveal codes screen to become familiar with the various codes that are embedded as you create a document.

The following is a list of the keystroke sequence we used in Project 3. Check to be sure that you have defined the Standard Printer as we did in Project 1.

SUMMARY OF KEYSTROKES—Project 3

STEPS	KEY(S) PRESSED	STEPS	KEY(S) PRESSED
1	wp [for two disk drive systems with wp disk in drive A and data disk in drive B]	35	space
		36	space
2	↵	37	F8
3	F5	38	You
4	=	39	F8
5	b: [for two disk drive systems with data disk in drive B] or a: [for hard disk systems with data disk in drive A]	40	space
		41	assume responsibility for the selection of this program to achieve your intended results. PerSoft Inc. assumes no responsibility for the results you obtain from the use of this software package.
6	↵		
7	F1 [to return to blank screen]		
8	Alt-F6	42	↵
9	December 15, 1990	43	↵
10	↵	44	Caps Lock
11	↵	45	LICENSE
12	↵	46	Caps Lock
13	Shift-F6	47	↵
14	Caps Lock	48	↵
15	LICENSING AGREEMENT	49	You may perform the following functions:
16	Caps Lock	50	↵
17	↵	51	↵
18	↵	52	F4
19	You should	53	a.
20	space	54	F4
21	F6	55	Use the program on a single machine only. Use on more than one machine is considered "pirating" this software.
22	carefully		
23	F6		
24	space	56	↵
25	read the following terms and conditions. Your use of this program package indicates your acceptance of them. If you do	57	↵
		58	F4
		59	b.
26	space	60	F4
27	F8	61	Copy the program into any machine readable or printed form for backup or modification purposes in support of your use of the program on a single machine. Certain programs from PerSoft Inc., however, may contain mechanisms to limit or inhibit copying. These programs are marked "copy protected."
28	not		
29	F8		
30	space		
31	agree with them, you should not use this software package. Instead, you should return the package and your money will be returned to you.		
		62	↵
32	↵	63	↵
33	↵	64	F4
34	PerSoft Inc. provides this program and licenses you to use it.	65	c.

SUMMARY OF KEYSTROKES—Project 3 (continued)

STEPS	KEY(S) PRESSED	STEPS	KEY(S) PRESSED
71	c.	98	[space]
72	[F4]	99	[Caps Lock]
73	Modify or merge the program into another PerSoft Inc. program for use on the single machine. Any portion of the program merged into another program will continue to be subject to the terms and conditions of this License.	100	YOUR LICENSE IS AUTOMATICALLY TERMINATED.
		101	[Caps Lock]
		102	[F10]
		103	license
		104	← [wait for document to be saved]
74	←	105	[Home][Home]↑
75	←	106	[move cursor to line 4, position 33 under the L in LICENSING AGREEMENT]
76	You	107	[Alt-F4]
77	[space]	108	[→ to highlight or block LICENSING AGREEMENT]
78	[Caps Lock]	109	[F8]
79	MAY NOT	110	[move cursor down to line 18, position 10 under the L in LICENSE]
80	[Caps Lock]		
81	[space]	111	[Alt-F4]
82	use, copy, modify, or transfer the program, in whole or in part, except as	112	[→ to highlight or block LICENSE]
		113	[F6]
83	[space]	114	[move cursor to line 39, position 14 under the M in MAY NOT]
84	[F8]		
85	[F6]	115	[Alt-F4]
86	expressly permitted	116	[→ to highlight or block MAY NOT]
87	[F8]	117	[F8]
88	[F6]	118	[press cursor keys to move cursor to line 50, position 52 under the Y in YOUR]
89	[space]		
90	in this Licensing Agreement. PerSoft Inc. also reserves the right to do the following:	119	[Alt-F4]
		120	[press cursor keys to highlight the words YOUR LICENSE IS AUTOMATICALLY TERMINATED.]
91	←		
92	←	121	[F6]
93	[Shift-F4]	122	[F10]
94	Withdraw your license if this software package is used for any illegal or immoral purpose which, in the sole judgment of PerSoft Inc., may damage the reputation of PerSoft Inc.	123	←
		124	Y [wait for document to be saved]
		125	[Shift-F7]
		126	1 [wait for document to be printed]
95	←	127	[F7]
96	←	128	N
97	If you transfer possession of any copy, modification, or merged portion of the program to another person,	129	Y [wait for DOS prompt or DOS screen]
		130	[remove disks from both drives]

The following list summarizes the material covered in Project 3:

1. The term **flush right** describes text that is aligned to the right margin. The embedded codes are **[Flsh Rt]** and **[C/A/Flrt]**.
2. The **Center Text** command centers text between the margins. The embedded codes are **[Cntr]** and **[C/A/Flrt]**.
3. **Boldfaced text** appears darker or bolder. The embedded codes are **[BOLD]** and **[bold]**.
4. The **underline** function is used to underline text. The embedded codes are **[UND]** and **[und]**.
5. When you **insert** text, existing text is moved to the right.
6. Use the **Typeover** command to type over existing text by pressing the Insert key.

7. The **Indent** key sets a temporary left margin. The embedded code is [→**Indent**]. The temporary margin is removed with a hard return.
8. Use the **Left/Right Indent** key to set temporary left and right margins. The embedded code is [→**Indent**←]. Temporary margins are removed with a hard return.
9. Use the **block** function to highlight text, to isolate it from the rest of the document so that you can underline or boldface it.
10. If you have **saved** a document to disk and then made changes in it on the screen, you must **replace** the old document with the new version by saving it again to disk.

STUDENT ASSIGNMENTS

STUDENT ASSIGNMENT 1: True/False

Instructions: Circle T if the statement is true and F if the statement if false.

T F   1. To use the flush right function you would use the Shift-F6 keys.
T F   2. The paired codes to indicate boldfacing are [BOLD] and [bold].
T F   3. The Indent key moves the cursor to the next tab setting.
T F   4. To turn off the block function you could press the Exit (F7) key.
T F   5. With the Insert key turned on, the message "Typeover" appears on the screen.
T F   6. The command Alt-F6 can be used to cause boldface characters.
T F   7. Pressing the Indent key temporarily changes the left margin until a hard return is pressed.
T F   8. The Ctrl-F4 keys are used to turn on the block function.
T F   9. The left/right indent function is invoked with the Shift-F4 keys.
T F 10. To exit a document you can use the F1 (Cancel) key.

STUDENT ASSIGNMENT 2: Multiple Choice

Instructions: Circle the correct response.

1. When the F6 key is pressed
   a. the position number changes appearance
   b. the codes [BOLD] and [bold] are embedded into the document
   c. boldface typing will occur until the F6 key is pressed again, turning boldfacing off
   d. all of the above
2. To underline a word in the body of the text
   a. the user must backspace and underline the characters just typed
   b. press the F8 key, type the text to be underlined, then press F8 again
   c. press the F6 key, type the text to be underlined, then press F6 again
   d. press the F8 key, type the text to be underlined, then press the F7 (Exit) key
3. The boldface function can be specified by pressing
   a. the F8 key
   b. the Shift-F8 keys
   c. the F6 key
   d. none of the above

Student Assignment 2 (continued)

4. To center a heading on a page,
    a. the spacebar must be used to cause spaces to appear to the left
    b. the Shift-F6 keys must be pressed
    c. a hard return must be pressed after the text has been typed
    d. both b and c are correct
5. The F4 or Indent key will do the following:
    a. temporarily change the left margin
    b. temporarily change the left and right margins
    c. move the cursor to the next tab stop setting
    d. both a and c are correct
6. The code(s) that are inserted when the Alt-F6 keys are pressed (followed by a hard return) are

    For 5.0 Users   *For 5.1 Users*
    a. [Flsh Rt]   a. [HRt]
    b. [Flsh Rt] [C/A/Flrt]   b. [Flsh Ryt]
    c. [HRt]   c. [Flsh Ryt] [Flsh Ryt]
    d. [SRt]   d. [SRt]
7. To invoke Boldfacing mode,
    a. press F6 at the beginning and end of the type to be boldfaced
    b. press F6 at the beginning and a hard return at the end of the type to be boldfaced
    c. press F8 at the beginning and end of the type to be boldfaced
    d. press Shift-F6 at the beginning of typing, and F7 at the end of the type to be boldfaced
8. To underline existing text,
    a. delete existing text, press F8, type text again, press F8
    b. put the cursor at the beginning of the text, press F8, then press the spacebar under the text
    c. block the existing text using the Alt-F4 keys, then press F8
    d. none of the above

STUDENT ASSIGNMENT 3: Matching

Instructions: Put the appropriate number next to the words in the second column.

			For 5.0 Users		*For 5.1 Users*
1.	Underline codes	_____	[Cntr] [C/A/Flrt]	_____	[Center]
2.	Typeover	_____	Alt-F4	_____	Alt-F4
3.	Boldface codes	_____	F6	_____	F6
4.	Left/Right Indent	_____	Insert key	_____	Insert key
5.	Center codes	_____	Shift-F6	_____	Shift-F6
6.	Indent key(s)	_____	[BOLD] [bold]	_____	[BOLD] [bold]
7.	Boldface key(s)	_____	[UND] [und]	_____	[UND] [und]
8.	Flush Right code	_____	F4	_____	F4
9.	Flush Right key(s)	_____	Shift-F4	_____	Shift-F4
10.	Center key(s)	_____	[Flsh Rt] [C/A/Flrt]	_____	[Flsh Ryt]
11.	Block function	_____	Alt-F6	_____	Alt-F6

STUDENT ASSIGNMENT 4: Writing WordPerfect Commands

Instructions: Next to each command, write its effect.

Command	Effect

1. Alt-F6 _____
2. F6 _____
3. Shift-F6 _____
4. F8 _____
5. Insert key _____
6. Caps Lock key _____
7. F4 _____
8. Shift-F4 _____
9. Alt-F4 (plus cursor keys) _____
10. F10 _____
11. Shift _____
12. F7 _____

STUDENT ASSIGNMENT 5: WordPerfect Commands

Instructions: The heading shown below was typed in capital letters, centered and underlined. Describe in detail each of the keystrokes that were used to produce this heading.

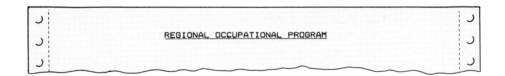

REGIONAL OCCUPATIONAL PROGRAM

STUDENT ASSIGNMENT 6: WordPerfect Commands

Instructions: The illustration below is the beginning of a document. After typing it, the user realized that the heading should have been underlined. Explain in detail how this existing text can be underlined without deleting the text.

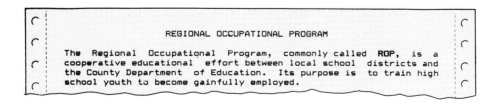

REGIONAL OCCUPATIONAL PROGRAM

The Regional Occupational Program, commonly called **ROP**, is a cooperative educational effort between local school districts and the County Department of Education. Its purpose is to train high school youth to become gainfully employed.

STUDENT ASSIGNMENT 7: WordPerfect Commands

Instructions: The text in sample A below is typed incorrectly because the margins after each letter should be indented temporarily. The text in sample B is typed correctly. Identify the one function key that made the difference in appearance, and describe in detail where that key should have been used.

```
a.   Copy the program into any machine readable or printed form
for backup or modification purposes in support of your use of the
program on a single machine.  Certain programs from PerSoft Inc.,
however, may contain mechanisms to limit or inhibit copying.
These programs are marked "copy protected."

b.   Modify or merge the program into another PerSoft Inc.
program for use on the single machine.   Any portion of the
program merged into another program will continue to be subject
to the terms and conditions of this License.
```

Sample A

```
a.   Copy the program into any machine readable or printed form
     for backup or modification purposes in support of your use
     of the program on a single machine.  Certain programs from
     PerSoft Inc., however, may contain mechanisms to limit or
     inhibit copying.   These programs are marked "copy
     protected."

b.   Modify or merge the program into another PerSoft Inc.
     program for use on the single machine.  Any portion of the
     program merged into another program will continue to be
     subject to the terms and conditions of this License.
```

Sample B

STUDENT ASSIGNMENT 8: WordPerfect Commands

Instructions: The text in sample A below is typed normally. The text in the first paragraph of sample B is indented five spaces from both the left and right margins. The text in the second paragraph of sample B is indented ten spaces from both the left and right margins. Describe in detail the keystrokes that were used to make the margins in both the first and second paragraphs of sample B.

```
Copy the program into any machine readable or printed form for
backup or modification purposes in support of your use of the
program on a single machine.  Certain programs from PerSoft Inc.,
however, may contain mechanisms to limit or inhibit copying.
These programs are marked "copy protected."

Modify or merge the program into another PerSoft Inc. program for
use on the single machine.  Any portion of the program merged
into another program will continue to be subject to the terms and
conditions of this License.
```

Sample A

```
Copy the program into any machine readable or printed
form for backup or modification purposes in support of
your use of the program on a single machine.  Certain
programs from PerSoft Inc., however, may contain
mechanisms to limit or inhibit copying.  These programs
are marked "copy protected."

     Modify or merge the program into another
     PerSoft Inc. program for use on the single
     machine.  Any portion of the program merged
     into another program will continue to be
     subject to the terms and conditions of this License.
```

Sample B

STUDENT ASSIGNMENT 9: Creating a Document

Instructions: Create the document below and save it under the name Regional. Then print the document.

1. For hard disk systems, load WordPerfect as you are directed by your instructor.

   For two disk drive systems, load DOS into main memory. Remove the DOS disk, and replace it with the WordPerfect disk.

   Type wp and press Enter.
2. Verify that the status line is in inches format, and that the default drive is set to drive A for hard disk systems or drive B for two disk drive systems. Check to be sure that you have defined the Standard Printer as we did in Project 1. Begin this project on a clean screen.

Reg. 1

```
              REGIONAL OCCUPATIONAL PROGRAM

The Regional Occupational Program, commonly called ROP, is a
cooperative educational effort between local school districts and
the County Department of Education.  Its purpose is to train high
school youth to become gainfully employed.

ROP has served and trained over 95,000 students in some 42 trades
since 1988.

ROP plays an important role in the application of basic skills in
the world of work, endeavoring to assist the unskilled and
undertrained to become gainfully employed.  ROP works in
cooperation with 1,054 local businesses in the community to provide
students on-the-job training.  About 500 members of business and
industry are involved in an advisory committee role to assure
meaningful job skill training, a verified labor market demand, and
a high potential for student placement in every course offered
through ROP.

Important features of the Regional Occupational Program are:

     1.   Students from many schools meet at a centralized
          classroom.  The teacher has a credential in the field
          being taught plus at least 5 years of directly related
          work experience.

     2.   Students are assigned to business training sites to
          receive realistic on-the-job skill development.  An
          individualized training plan is developed for each
          student at each job training site.

     3.   Periodically students return to the classroom for
          additional training and to review progress from an
          employment point of view.


Courses are offered for three semesters during the year.
Enrollment time varies depending on the course topic or trade area.
Some programs permit entry on any day, others at the start of each
semester.
```

STUDENT ASSIGNMENT 10: Correcting a Document

Instructions: The document that you created in Student Assignment 9 needs to be changed to look like the document below. Make the following corrections:

1. The characters ROP should appear in boldface type.
2. The heading should be underlined.
3. Add paragraph 4 after paragraph 3 as follows:

    4. There is no tuition charge for any ROP class.

4. Save the new document under the name Regional.2, then print the document.

REGIONAL OCCUPATIONAL PROGRAM

The Regional Occupational Program, commonly called **ROP**, is a cooperative educational effort between local school districts and the County Department of Education. Its purpose is to train high school youth to become gainfully employed.

ROP has served and trained over 95,000 students in some 42 trades since 1988.

ROP plays an important role in the application of basic skills in the world of work, endeavoring to assist the unskilled and undertrained to become gainfully employed. **ROP** works in cooperation with 1,054 local businesses in the community to provide students on-the-job training. About 500 members of business and industry are involved in an advisory committee role to assure meaningful job skill training, a verified labor market demand, and a high potential for student placement in every course offered through **ROP**.

Important features of the Regional Occupational Program are:

1. Students from many schools meet at a centralized classroom. The teacher has a credential in the field being taught plus at least 5 years of directly related work experience.

2. Students are assigned to business training sites to receive realistic on-the-job skill development. An individualized training plan is developed for each student at each job training site.

3. Periodically students return to the classroom for additional training and to review progress from an employment point of view.

4. There is no tuition charge for any **ROP** class.

Courses are offered for three semesters during the year. Enrollment time varies depending on the course topic or trade area. Some programs permit entry on any day, others at the start of each semester.

PROJECT 4

Modifying a WordPerfect Document

Objectives

You will have mastered the material in this project when you can:

- Retrieve a document
- Format a document
- Adjust left and right margins and top and bottom margins
- Justify and unjustify text
- Center text on a page
- Set tabs

RETRIEVING A DOCUMENT

*I*f you are working on a hard disk system, load WordPerfect as your instructor directs you. If you are working on a two disk drive system, at the A> prompt (with the WordPerfect disk in drive A and the data disk in drive B), type wp and press Enter. WordPerfect loads into main memory. As instructed in Project 1, verify that the status line is in inches format and that the default drive is set to drive A for hard disk systems or drive B for two disk drive systems. You should then have a clean screen with only the status line in the lower right corner, indicating Doc 1 Pg 1 Ln 1" Pos 1". Also check to be sure that you have defined the Standard Printer as we did in Project 1.

In many word processing applications, a document must be modified after it has been created. In this project you will make some changes to the memo you created in Project 2. The old memo (Figure 4-1a) contains instructions for corrections to be made. The corrected memo is shown in Figure 4-1b.

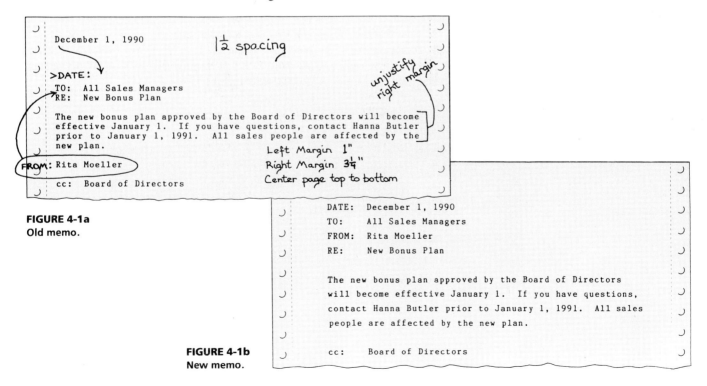

FIGURE 4-1a
Old memo.

FIGURE 4-1b
New memo.

In Project 2 you created a document, named it Memo, and saved it. Now you'll retrieve that document and modify it. Look at the template next to the F10 key. The word Retrieve is in green. Press Shift-F10 (step 1 in Figure 4-2). The message "Document to be Retrieved:" appears. Type the name memo, then press Enter ↵ (step 2 in Figure 4-2). The light on the default drive goes on, and the memo is retrieved from memory and displayed on the screen.

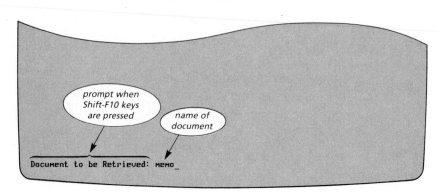

FIGURE 4-2

Step 1: Retrieve a document   Step 2: Specify name of document to be retrieved

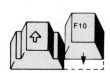   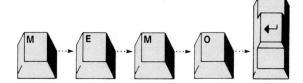

INSERTING CHANGES INTO TEXT

*I*n a memo's heading, the word DATE: is typed in front of the actual date and the name of the person sending the memo is placed at the top of the document after FROM:. Thus, the first task to modify the old memo is to add the word DATE: in front of the date. With the cursor on line 1", position 1", under the D in December, press the Caps Lock key and type the word DATE:. The date is pushed to the right and the word DATE is inserted (Figure 4-3). With the cursor still under the D in December, press the Tab key. The cursor moves to position 2" (step 1 in Figure 4-4).

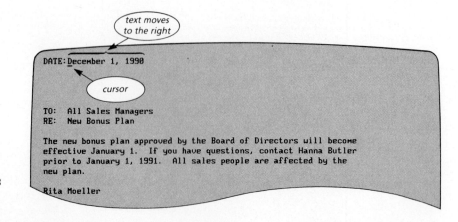

FIGURE 4-3

Now, remove the hard returns between the date and the line: TO: All Sales Managers. Press the Down Arrow ↓ to move the cursor to line 1.17", position 1", then press the Del key four times until the cursor is under the T in TO: on line 1.17", position 1" (step 2 in Figure 4-4). Press the Down Arrow ↓ to move the cursor under the R in RE: on line 1.33", position 1", then press Return ↵.

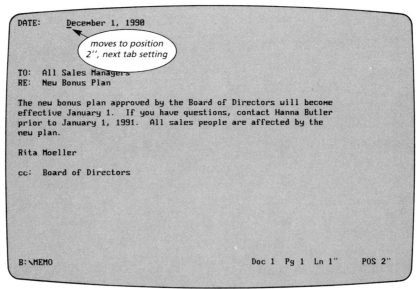

FIGURE 4-4

Step 1: Move cursor to the first tab setting

Step 2: Delete 4 lines

You see a blank line inserted, as shown in Figure 4-5. Press the Up Arrow ↑ key to put the cursor on position 1" of line 1.33", the blank line. With Caps Lock still on, type the word FROM:. To turn off capitalizations, press the Caps Lock key.

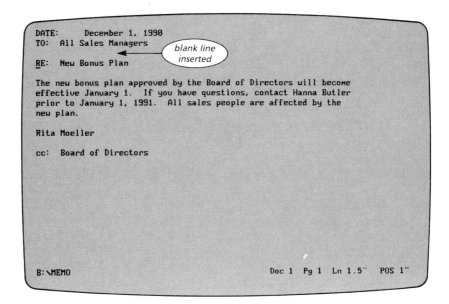

FIGURE 4-5

Press the Tab key and type the name Rita Moeller (Figure 4-6). Notice that although you pressed the Tab key only once after each heading, the tabbed lines begin at different positions. Later in this project we will change the tab settings so that they line up.

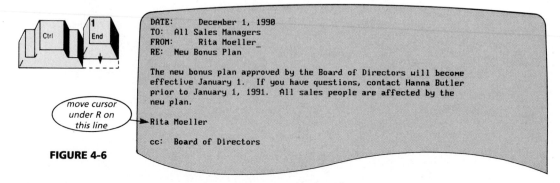

move cursor
under R on
this line

FIGURE 4-6

It is now necessary to remove the name that was typed at the bottom of the memo. Move the cursor to line 2.67", position 1". Press Ctrl-End. The line is deleted. Press the Del key two times. You see the last line of typing move up to line 2.67".

DEFAULT SETTINGS

 he appearance of the documents in Projects 1, 2, and 3 is governed by a number of default settings established by WordPerfect. In other words, if you do not change or add codes, your document will print with the parameters that have been set. You can, however, change the format of a document either before or after typing it.

LEFT AND RIGHT MARGINS

A normal page of typing paper is 8 1/2 inches wide by 11 inches long. The WordPerfect default settings have the length of a line of type 6 1/2 inches wide, leaving a 1-inch margin on both the left and right.

Traditionally, typewriters used **pica** or **elite** type. Pica type fits 10 characters into 1 inch of space on a line, and elite type fits 12 characters into that same space. Therefore pica is the larger type and elite is the smaller. Some typewriters can type very small, placing 15 characters within 1 inch of space. When you use a word processor, some of the terminology is different. If you have used different type elements, you may have used the term "typing ball." The term used in word processing is **type font**. Instead of pica or elite, the term used is **10 pitch** (10 characters per inch) or **12 pitch** (12 characters per inch) (Figure 4-7). You could also use a *15-pitch font*. WordPerfect's default is a *10-pitch font*.

FIGURE 4-7

Whatever the size of the type font you choose, WordPerfect 5.0 allows you to set the left and right margins. WordPerfect adjusts to accommodate different-sized type fonts, even if the different sizes are on the same line, because the margins are absolute and set in inches, not by so many characters per line.

TOP AND BOTTOM MARGINS

*F*igure 4-8 shows that a normal piece of paper is 11 inches long. Normal typewriting spacing allows for 6 lines per inch, making 66 lines from the top edge to the bottom edge of the paper. WordPerfect allows for 6 lines or a 1-inch top margin, and 6 lines or a 1-inch bottom margin. If you subtract the 6 lines on top and the 6 lines on the bottom (12 lines) from the total of 66, you know that there are 54 lines available for text. If you double-space your typing, you will have 27 lines of type and 27 blank lines.

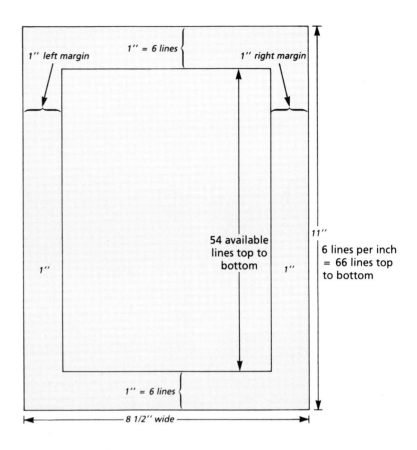

FIGURE 4-8
WordPerfect default margins.

FORMATTING

*A*ll the default settings we have discussed—pitch, font, lines per inch, line spacing, margin settings, tab settings, or anything that has to do with how the typing will appear on paper—are aspects of **formatting**. Any default setting can be changed by inserting a code, which will be embedded into the particular document on which you are working. You will learn many of the formatting functions in this project. To become familiar with the codes you will refer to the reveal codes screen many times. If you make an error in formatting, refer to the codes and analyze them to decide how they have affected the look of your document.

All the format settings are on the Format key, which is Shift-F8. Next we will make several changes from the default settings.

LINE FORMATTING

*T*o change anything having to do with the left or right margins, the line spacing, right justification, or the tab settings on the line, we must use the **Line Format** screen.

Changing Margin Settings

Look at the memo to be corrected in Figure 4-1a. Notice that the margins are to be changed to one inch on the left and 3.25 inches on the right. With the total width of the paper being 8 1/2 inches wide, and a total of 4 1/4 inches for the margins, you can calculate that the length of the line will be 4 1/4 inches long.

To change the margins, you must insert the margin code at the very beginning of the document, because a code takes effect starting from where it is inserted. Be sure the cursor is at the top of the document by pressing Home, Home, Up Arrow.

Look at the template next to the F8 key. Notice that the word Format is in green. Press Shift-F8, and the menu shown in Figure 4-9 appears. Press 1 for Line Format.

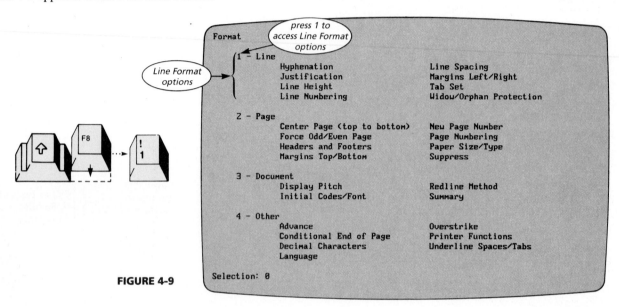

FIGURE 4-9

Next press 7 for Margins, Left and Right. Press Enter ← to accept the 1-inch left margin, and then type 3.25 for the new right margin. Press Enter ← to actually change the right margin (Figure 4-10). Press F7 (Exit) to return to the document on the screen. (If you press Enter to exit the screen, you return to the format screen, and you must press Enter again to return to the document.)

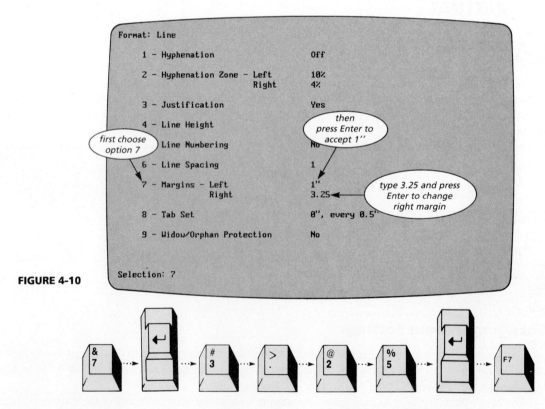

FIGURE 4-10

Since the screen does not reflect the new margin setting, you must rewrite the screen. Look at the template next to the F3 key. In red you see the word Screen. Press Ctrl-F3. Figure 4-11 shows that 0 will rewrite. Note that the cursor is under the number 0, the default, so it is only necessary to press Enter. Press Enter ↵ to rewrite the screen. [For 5.1 Users – Number 3 will rewrite, and the default is number 3.]

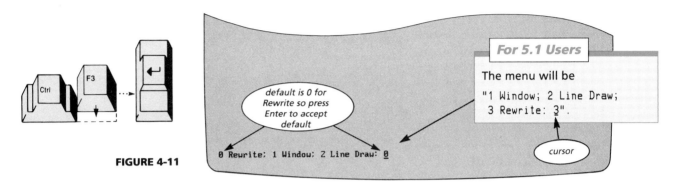

For 5.1 Users

The menu will be

"1 Window; 2 Line Draw; 3 Rewrite: 3".

cursor

default is 0 for Rewrite so press Enter to accept default

0 Rewrite; 1 Window; 2 Line Draw: 0

FIGURE 4-11

To see that a code for the new margin setting has been embedded into the document, look at the codes using Alt-F3 (Figure 4-12). Notice that the cursor is to the right of the code highlighting the letter D in DATE. Press the Left Arrow ← one time. Notice that an entire code is enclosed within brackets [ ] and that the cursor highlights the entire code. Also notice, on the bar that separates the two screens, that the right bracket has moved to show the new margin setting. When you read a novel, you read from left to right, one line after another. You only understand what you have already read, not what might be coming. It is the same with how the codes work in WordPerfect. Think of the cursor reading left to right, line after line. When the cursor is to the left of the code or highlighting a code, the cursor follows the default setting of 1 inch for left and right margins. When you move the cursor to the right of the code, the cursor in a sense "reads" or "interprets" that code, and the bracket on the bar moves according to what is read.

This code we have just embedded controls the margin until it is replaced by a different code. To see this, press Home, Home, Home, Up Arrow to move the cursor to not only the top of the document, but also in front of all codes. (Note that the code is highlighted.) Press Alt-F3 to exit the reveal codes. Let's suppose that you decide that the right margin is too wide and that you wish to change it to 1.75 inches. Press Shift-F8. Press the number 1 for Line Format, then press the number 7 for margins. Press Enter ↵ to accept the 1-inch left margin. Type 1.75 and press Enter ↵ for the right margin. Press F7 to exit this screen and return directly to the document.

When you look at this document you will notice that even though we have embedded a new code to change the margin, you cannot see any changes to the length of the line. In Project 2 you learned that most problems with WordPerfect can be solved by analyzing the codes. Press Alt-F3.

```
DATE:      December 1, 1990
TO:  All Sales Managers
FROM:      Rita Moeller
RE:  New Bonus Plan

The new bonus plan approved by the Board
of Directors will become effective January
1.  If you have questions, contact Hanna
Butler prior to January 1, 1991.  All
sales people are affected by the new plan.

A:\MEMO.EDT                          Doc 1 Pg 1 Ln 1" Pos 1"
[                                    ]
[L/R Mar:1",3.25"]DATE:[Tab]December 1, 1990[HRt]
TO:[Tab]All Sales Managers[HRt]
FROM:[Tab]Rita Moeller[HRt]
RE:[Tab]New Bonus Plan[HRt]
[HRt]
The new bonus plan                   d[SRt]
of Directors wil                     ry[SRt]
1.  If you have q                    a[SRt]
Butler prior to Janu                 ll[SRt]
sales people are affected by the new plan.[HRt]

restore screen
```

first, the cursor is to the right of margin set code highlighting the D

bracket shows new right margin

Left Arrow moves cursor to highlight entire margin set code

For 5.1 Users

The Reveal Codes screen will display fewer lines.

FIGURE 4-12

As you see in Figure 4-13 you have two margin setting codes, with the cursor over the right code. The first code is the new margin setting of 1", 1.75". That code is in effect until it is overridden by a new code. As you see, it is immediately overridden by the old code of 1", 3.25". Therefore, the typing will follow the command of the right code instead of the left code. Since you want the document to follow the left code, you need to delete the right code. Because you wish to delete the right code, you wish to delete the code that is highlighted. Press the Delete key once. Be careful when you delete the code. It is only necessary to press the Delete key one time. Then press Alt-F3 to exit the reveal codes. Figure 4-14 shows how the new margin setting affects the document.

To emphasize one more time the importance of where you insert a code, move the cursor down to line 2.17", position 1", under the c in contact. Press Shift-F8, and then the number 1 for Line Format. Press the number 7 for margins. For the left margin type 2 and press Enter. Type 3.5 and press Enter for the right margin. Press F7 to return to the document. To rewrite the text press Ctrl-F3, and then press Enter. You see now that the code at the top of the memo remains in effect until it is overridden by a new code. Because the new code was inserted later in the document, the new code overrides the old code and will affect typing from where it is inserted *downward*. To view the new code, press Alt-F3 (Figure 4-15). You see the new code on the screen. The cursor is to the right of the code. Press the Backspace key *only one time* to delete the 2", 3.5" code, allowing the 1", 1.75" code to take effect again. Press Alt-F3 to exit the reveal codes, and Press Home, Home, Up Arrow to go to the top of the document.

After completing this exercise you can understand how important it is to have the cursor in the proper position before you invoke a code. You cannot be at the end of a document, then decide that you want to change the margins of the entire document, without pressing Home, Home, Up Arrow to place the code at the beginning of the text of the document.

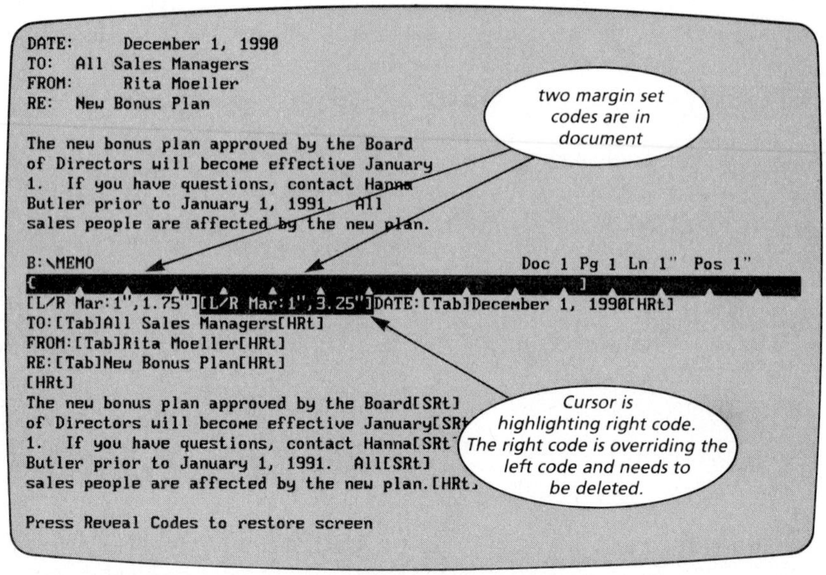

FIGURE 4-13

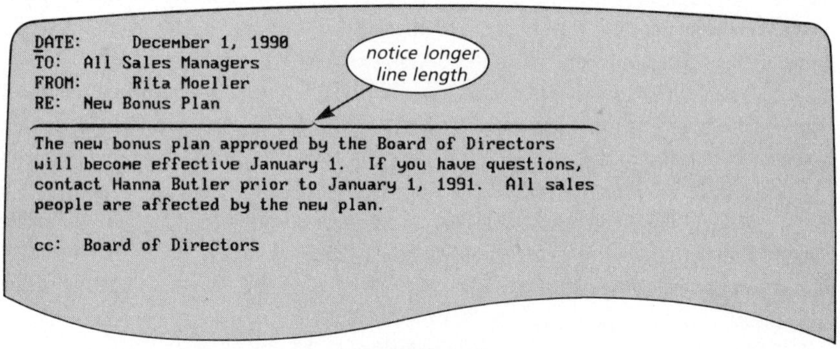

FIGURE 4-14

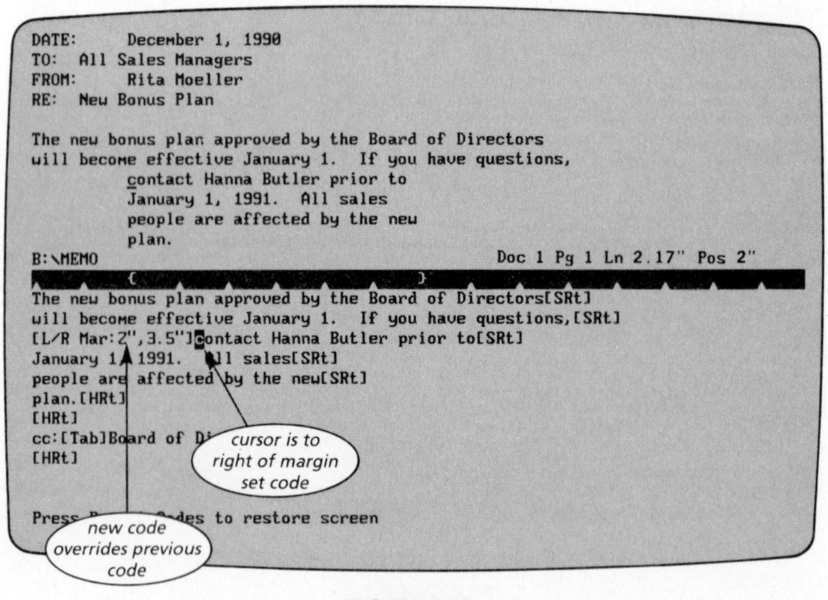

FIGURE 4-15

Changing Tab Settings

Notice in Figure 4-16 that the words December, All, Rita, and New do not align on the left as shown in Figure 4-1b. So that these words will align, you need to add a tab setting at position 1.7" and delete the tab setting at position 1.5". Press Shift-F8, number 1 for Line Format, then number 8 for Tabs. [For 5.1 Users – Notice that a plus sign (+) appears in front of each inch number. This plus sign indicates that tabs are set relative to the left margin. To proceed, press T for Type, then 1 for Absolute. Selecting Absolute measures the tab from the left edge of the paper.] Figure 4-16 shows the tab settings on the lower portion of the screen.

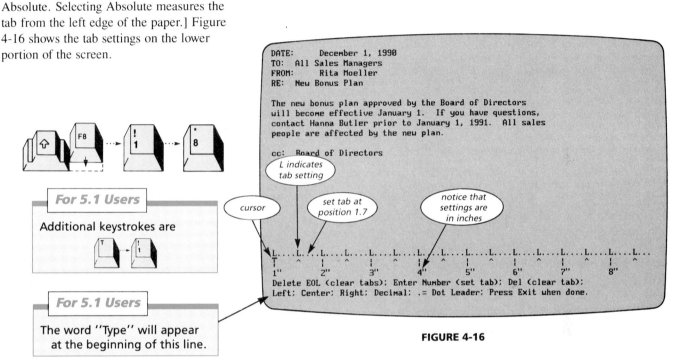

FIGURE 4-16

Type the number 1.7 and press Enter ↵ (step 1 in Figure 4-17). Notice that there is an L on position 1.7. To delete the tab setting on position 1.5, press the Left Arrow two times ← ← to move the cursor under the L on position 1.5. Press the Delete key one time (step 2 in Figure 4-17). The message on the screen instructs you to press Exit when done. This is how you exit the tab setting screen properly. If you press the Cancel key, you will exit but the changes will not be made. Press F7, therefore, to exit the tab setting screen, then press F7 again to exit to the document (step 3 in Figure 4-17).

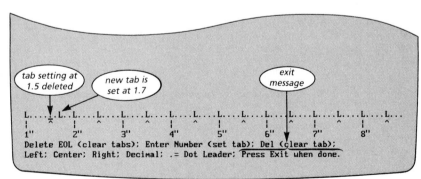

FIGURE 4-17

Step 1: Set tab at 1.7"

Step 2: Delete tab at 1.5"

Step 3: Save tab changes and exit tab settings then exit formatting screen

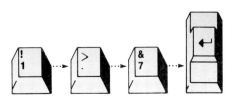

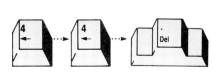

Now notice how the tabs have lined up properly, as in Figure 4-18.

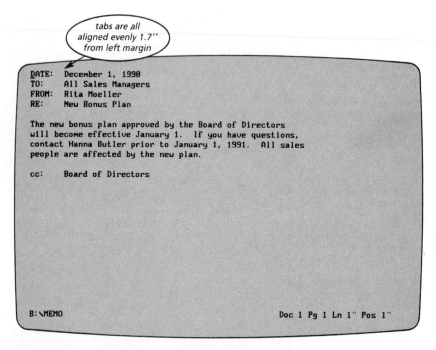

FIGURE 4-18

To view the embedded codes, press Alt-F3 (Figure 4-19). All the tab settings that were present when you inserted the one at position 1.7" are listed. Remember that codes are within brackets [ ]. Therefore, this is only *one* code. Press the Left Arrow ← and notice that the entire code is highlighted. Press the Right Arrow → and the cursor moves to the right of the code. To exit the reveal codes press Alt-F3.

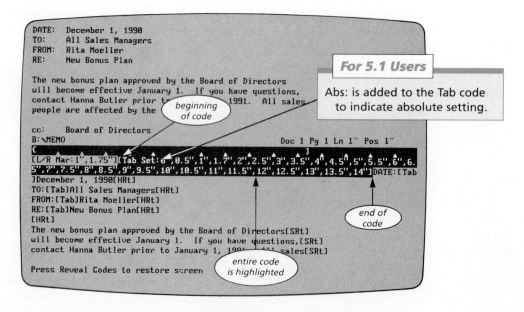

FIGURE 4-19

Changing the Line Spacing

The next change to make in the memo is to change the line spacing from single-space to 1 1/2 spacing. To change the line spacing, you must call up the line format menu. Press Shift-F8. At the Format menu, press the number 1 for Line Format, (step 1 in Figure 4-20). Next, press the number 6 for Line Spacing. Type the number 1.5 and press Enter ↵ (step 2 in Figure 4-20). To exit to the document press F7 (step 3 in Figure 4-20).

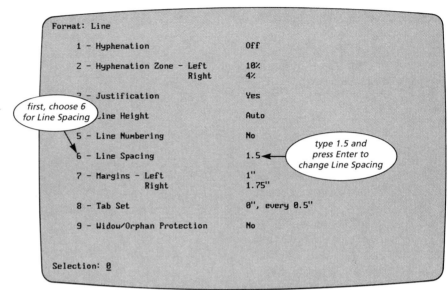

Step 1: View Line Format menu

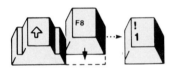

Step 2: Choose Line Spacing and change line spacing

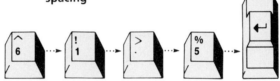

Step 3: Exit to document

FIGURE 4-20

To view the code that was inserted, press Alt-F3 (Figure 4-21). If you ever want to change back to single-spacing, you can simply delete the code. WordPerfect would then return to the default, which is single-spacing. If you wish to change to double-spacing, you must be sure that the cursor *follows* any code you wish to override.

To exit the reveal codes, press Alt-F3. The lines on the screen will appear to be double-spaced. That is because the screen cannot show 1 1/2 spacing. However, the printer will read the code and print in 1 1/2 spacing. Watching the status line, press the Down Arrow ↓.

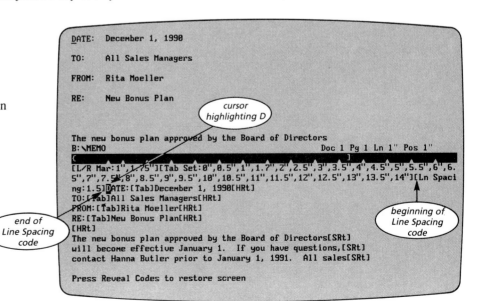

FIGURE 4-21

Figure 4-22 shows how the code is interpreted: the next line is line 1.25". Continue pressing the Down Arrow ↓ and notice that the spacing changes in increments of .25". Press Home, Home, Up Arrow to move the cursor to the top of the document.

Right Justified Text

Turning the justification on and off is also part of the line formatting process for a document. To view the Line Format screen, press Shift-F8, number 1 (step 1 in Figure 4-23). Press number 3 for Justification, then press N for No. [For 5.1 Users – Do not press N, press 1 for Left.] Notice that the justification is now turned off, in other words, is left justified (step 2 in Figure 4-23). Press F7 to exit the line format screen and return to the document (step 3 in Figure 4-23). To view the code that was inserted, press Alt-F3. Figure 4-24 shows the embedded code that turned the justification off. To exit the reveal codes, press Alt-F3.

```
DATE:    December 1, 1990
TO:      All Sales Managers
FROM:    Rita Moeller
RE:      New Bonus Plan


The new bonus plan approved by the Board of Directors
will become effective J          e questions,      press Down Arrow
                                                    once to move cursor
contact Hanna Butler pr              1.   All sales  to line 1.25''
people are affected by the new plan.


cc:      Board of Directors


B:\MEMO                                      Doc 1 Pg 1 Ln 1.25" Pos 1"
```

FIGURE 4-22

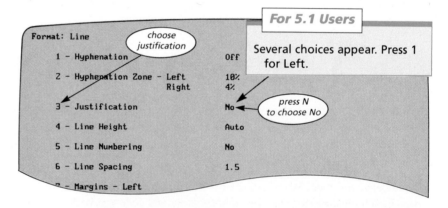

```
Format: Line                    choose
                                justification

    1 - Hyphenation                          Off

    2 - Hyphenation Zone - Left              10%
                          Right              4%

    3 - Justification                        No        press N
                                                       to choose No
    4 - Line Height                          Auto

    5 - Line Numbering                       No

    6 - Line Spacing                         1.5

    7 - Margins - Left
```

For 5.1 Users

Several choices appear. Press 1 for Left.

FIGURE 4-23

Step 1: View the Line Format screen   **Step 2: Turn off right justification**   **Step 3: Exit to document**

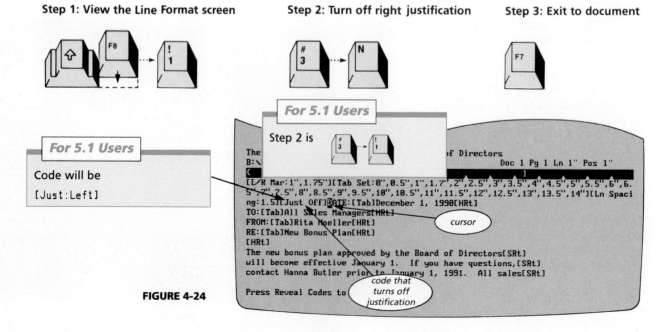

For 5.1 Users

Code will be

[Just:Left]

For 5.1 Users

Step 2 is

```
The                                  f Directors
B:\                                       Doc 1 Pg 1 Ln 1" Pos 1"
[
[L/R Mar:1",1.75"][Tab Set:0",0.5",1",1.7",2",2.5",3",3.5",4",4.5",5",5.5",6",6.
5",7",7.5",8",8.5",9",9.5",10",10.5",11",11.5",12",12.5",13",13.5",14"][Ln Spaci
ng:1.5][Just Off]DATE:[Tab]December 1, 1990[HRt]
TO:[Tab]All Sales Managers[HRt]
FROM:[Tab]Rita Moeller[HRt]
RE:[Tab]New Bonus Plan[HRt]
[HRt]
The new bonus plan approved by the Board of Directors[SRt]
will become effective January 1.  If you have questions,[SRt]
contact Hanna Butler prior to January 1, 1991.  All sales[SRt]
Press Reveal Codes to
```
cursor

code that turns off justification

FIGURE 4-24

PAGE FORMATTING

Centering Page Top to Bottom

Because your memo is short, when it is printed it will only cover the top portion of the page as shown in Figure 4-1a. To print your document in the center of the paper, as shown in Figure 4-1b, with even margins on the top and the bottom of the page, you must choose the **Center Page Top to Bottom** option from the page format screen. Press Shift-F8 and then number 2 (step 1 in Figure 4-25). The page format screen appears. Press the number 1 for Center Page (top to bottom), and notice how the No automatically changes to Yes as soon as the number 1 is pressed (step 2 in Figure 4-25). [For 5.1 Users – Your options will be No (Yes). Press Y for Yes.] Press F7 to exit to the document (step 3 in Figure 4-25).

Step 1: View Page Format menu

Step 2: Select the Center Page (top to bottom) option

Step 3: Exit to the document

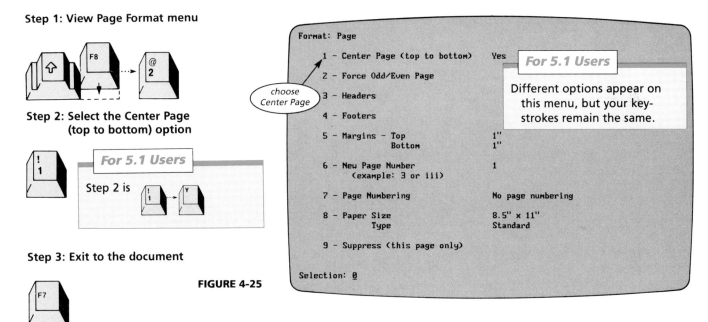

FIGURE 4-25

To view the inserted code, press Alt-F3. Figure 4-26 shows the code that directs the printer to center the page, giving it even top and bottom margins. To exit the reveal codes, press Alt-F3. You have now made all the desired changes requested in Figure 4-1a. Now you must save the document in its new form, view the document, and then print the document.

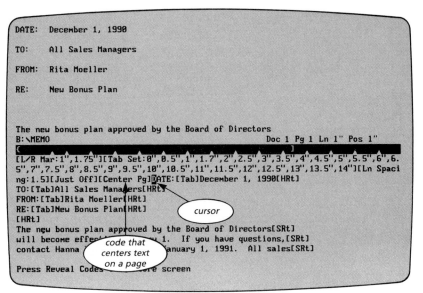

FIGURE 4-26

SAVING, REPLACING, VIEWING, AND PRINTING THE DOCUMENT

W hen you finished typing this document in Project 2, you saved the document to your disk. Since that time, you have made several changes to the document on your screen. However, those changes have not been saved to the disk. As you learned in Project 3, it is necessary to save these changes to the disk, replacing the old text with the new text. Keep in mind that you are not just adding but also replacing text. Save and replace your document now as you did in Project 3 (F10, Enter, Y).

Also, as shown in Projects 2 and 3, you can view your text exactly as it will be printed. Press Shift-F7 to reveal the Print menu, then press the number 6 to view the document (step 1 in Figure 4-27). Figure 4-27 shows you exactly how your document will be printed. Notice that the document is centered evenly between the top and bottom of the page. The text has an unjustified right margin. The left margin remains 1 inch and the right margin reflects the new 1.75-inch margin. If your revised memo appears correct, press F7 to exit to the document (step 2 in Figure 4-27).

Step 1: View document   **Step 2: Exit to document**

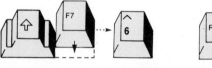

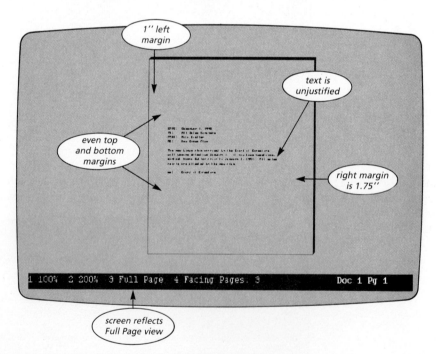

FIGURE 4-27

The document is now ready to be printed. Be sure that your printer has paper inserted and that the printer is turned on and ready to print. As you have done in previous projects, print the full text of this document. The printed document generated should look like Figure 4-1b.

OTHER PAGE FORMAT FEATURES

 ow that the document has been changed, saved, viewed, and printed, we can learn some other page format features. Let's return to the page format screen by pressing Shift-F8, and then the number 2.

Top and Bottom Margins

Another useful page formatting feature is the top and bottom margin. Although we will not change the margins here, press Shift-F8 and then the number 2 for the Page Format menu. Notice that the number 5 for margins gives you the option to make the top and bottom margins larger or smaller. The top and bottom margins are defaulted at 1 inch each or, in other words, 6 lines on the top and 6 lines on the bottom. The default is 6 lines of type per inch. This spacing would change if you were to have larger type faces. Press F7 to exit to the document.

Paper Size and Type

When we last viewed the document in this Project the page appeared vertical. This vertical view is called the *portrait* view of the page, where the page is 8 1/2 inches wide by 11 inches long. If you were to turn the page sideways, the 11-inch side would be the width and the 8 1/2-inch side would be the length. This view is called the *landscape* view of the page (Figure 4-28). Without changing any of the formatting features, such as margins, justification, and so on, you will now change the paper size to landscape.

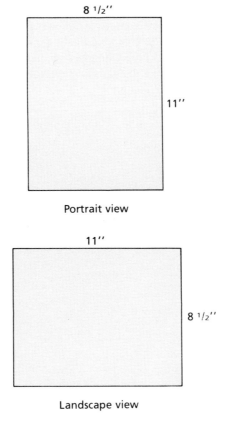

Portrait view

Landscape view

FIGURE 4-28

For formatting, press Shift-F8. Press 2 for Page Formatting. Under the number 8 notice that the paper size is 8.5" ×
11". Press the number 8 for Paper Size and Type. [For 5.1 Users – This paper size will be under the number 7, so press 7.]
Your screen will look like Figure 4-29.

Step 1: View Page Format menu

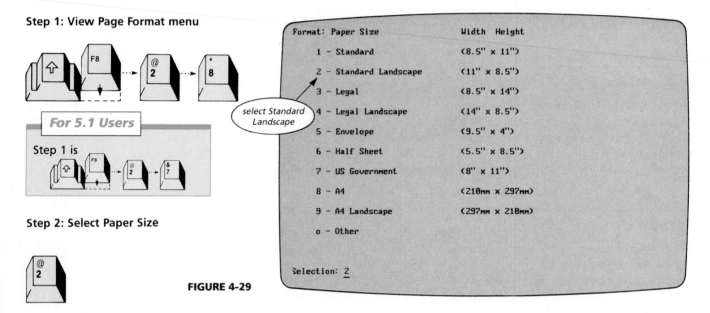

FIGURE 4-29

[For 5.1 Users – *Please note*. The differences between WordPerfect 5.0 and 5.1 for choosing paper size are significant.
Ignore Step 2 in Figure 4-29 and all of Figure 4-30, and proceed as follows: press 2 to Add, press 1 for Standard, press 1 for
Paper Size, press 2 for Standard Landscape, press F7 to Exit, and finally press 1 to Select. This series of keystrokes will take
you to a screen similar to Figure 4-31. Paper Size and Type will appear as number 7.]

To choose the Standard Landscape paper size, press the number 2 and the screen in Figure 4-30 appears.

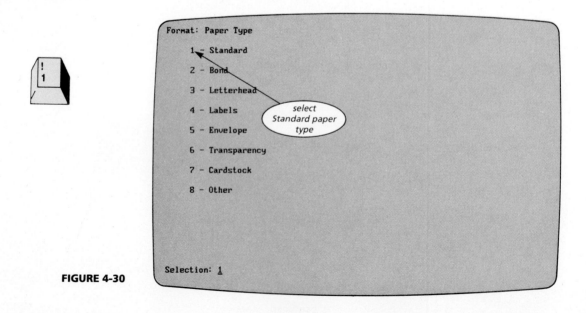

FIGURE 4-30

For Standard paper type press 1, and the screen should then look like Figure 4-31. Notice how the paper size has now changed from 8.5" × 11" to 11" × 8.5". Press F7 to exit to the document.

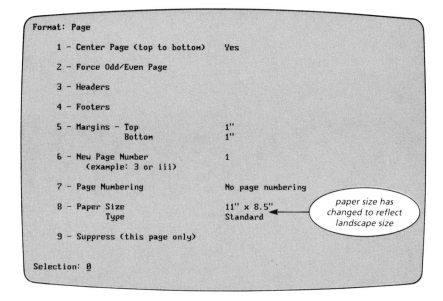

FIGURE 4-31

To view how this has changed the look of the typed document, press Shift-F7, then the number 6 to view the document. Figure 4-32 shows how your screen should look. Notice that all the formatting features have not changed: there is still a 1" left margin and a 1.75" right margin; the text is still centered top to bottom and right unjustified. Press F7 to exit to the document.

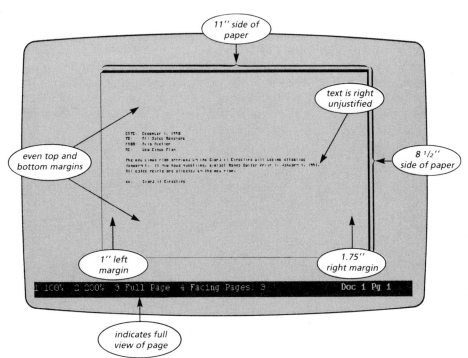

FIGURE 4-32

To view the code that was inserted to change the paper size and type, press Alt-F3 (Figure 4-33). Your cursor should be just to the right of the code. To restore the original portrait view, delete the code by pressing the Backspace key once. To exit reveal codes, press Alt-F3.

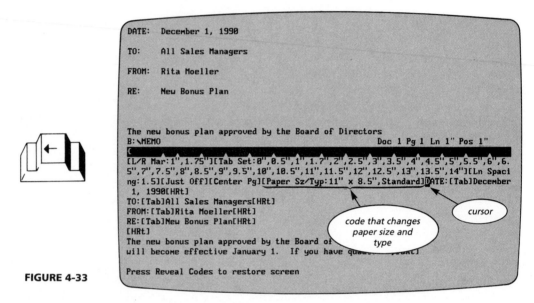

FIGURE 4-33

ADVANCED TAB SETTINGS

*H*ere we will learn some of the more advanced tab setting features. You do not want to confuse this lesson with the memo on your screen. WordPerfect has the capability to have two documents in memory and to let you switch quickly back and forth between the two documents. As we learned in Project 1, we can switch to document 2, while keeping document 1 as it is. Refer to the template next to the F3 key. You'll see that Shift-F3 will shift documents. Press Shift-F3. Your typing disappears, and you have a blank screen. Notice that the status line indicates document 2. This is a new blank screen; anything you do in this screen will be totally separate from document 1. For practice, press Shift-F3 and notice that you are back in document 1. Press Shift-F3 again and you are in document 2.

Recall that tabs are set by pressing Shift-F8, then the number 1 (Line Format), and finally the number 8 for tabs (Figure 4-34). [For 5.1 Users – Press T for type and 1 for absolute.] The default for tab settings are indicated by the letter L.

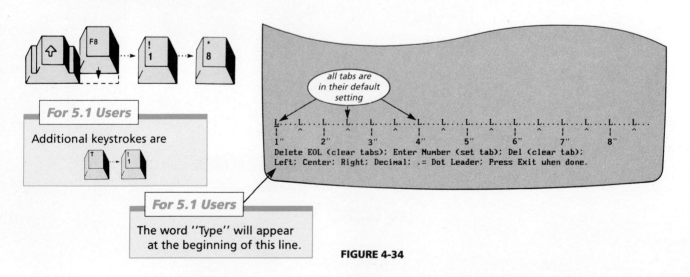

FIGURE 4-34

First we need to clear all tab settings. Press Home, Home, Left Arrow to move the cursor to position 0. As the bottom of the screen indicates, "Delete EOL" (Delete End of Line) will clear all tabs. Press Ctrl-End and all tab settings will clear (Figure 4-35).

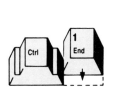

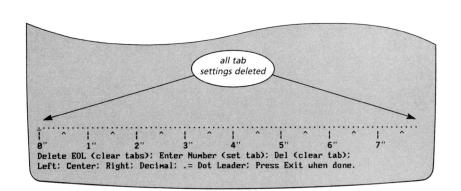

FIGURE 4-35

Now, let's set the desired tab settings; then their functions will be explained. Type the number 1.5 and press Enter ↵. You see an L above the 1.5″ position. Type the number 3 and press Enter ↵. You see an L above the 3″ position. Press the letter c and notice how the L changes to a capital C. Type the number 4.5″ and press Enter ↵. Press the letter r and notice how the L changes to a capital R. Type the number 6 and press Enter ↵. Press the letter d and notice once more how the L changes to a capital D. The screen should now look like the Figure 4-36.

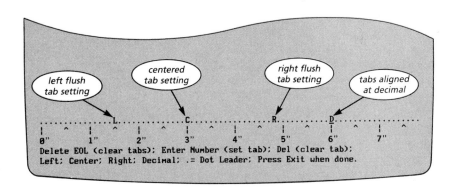

FIGURE 4-36

When you set each tab, the default of L appeared first at each setting. Imagine that the tab settings are like anchors. Wherever there is an L, the typing anchors to the *left* and the typing flows to the *right*. When you changed the L at position 3″ to C, you were instructing WordPerfect to anchor in the *center*, so the typing will be centered over the tab setting as it does when you use the center function. When you changed the L at position 4.8″ to R, you were instructing WordPerfect to anchor at the right, so the typing flows to the left as it does when you use the flush right function. When you changed the L at position 6″ to D, you were instructing WordPerfect to anchor at a decimal point (a period).

Figure 4-37 illustrates how each tab setting will be anchored and where the type will flow from the specific tab setting.

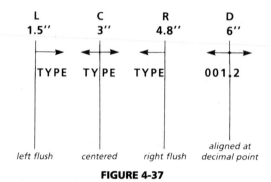

FIGURE 4-37

To exit from the tab setting screen, press F7. Press F7 again and you are returned to the blank screen of document 2. To view the inserted codes, press Alt-F3. Figure 4-38 shows that each tab setting is identified. To exit the codes press Alt-F3.

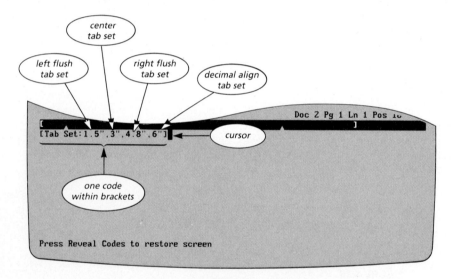

FIGURE 4-38

To use each tab setting, first press the Tab key. The cursor stops at the first tab setting, which is 1.5". The type will flow to the right of the tab setting. Type the two words Now is, and press the Tab key again. The cursor moves to position 3", the next tab setting. This is where the C for center was placed. Type the word Heading. As you do, try to watch the screen and notice how the word centers over position 3". Press the Tab key again and the cursor moves to position 4.8", the next tab setting. This is where an R was placed for right justified. Type the amount $1,000.00 and as you do notice how the typing anchors at the right on the tab setting and flows to the left of the tab, making the number flush right. For the last setting, press the Tab key, moving the cursor to position 6" where the D was placed, for aligning at the decimal point. In the lower left corner of the screen you see the message "Align Char = ." As you type now, try to watch the screen so you can see how the type anchors at the decimal point and the last two zeros are placed to the right of the decimal. Type the amount $2,000.00. The screen should look like Figure 4-39.

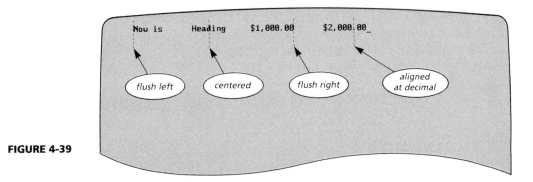

FIGURE 4-39

Press the hard return ↵ so you can use each tab setting one more time. The cursor should be on line 1.17", position 1". Press the Tab key and type these two words: the time. As you do so watch the typing anchor at the left. Press the Tab key again and type the word Head, and the typing centers at the tab setting. Press the Tab key again and type the number 60.00, and notice how the typing anchors at the right. Press the Tab key one more time. Type the number 120.345 and the typing will anchor at the decimal point, putting the 345 to the right of the decimal. Note the difference between the flush right and decimal settings. Sometimes you may have numbers with more than two digits to the right of the decimal. To align all numbers on the decimal, no matter how many digits are after the decimal, you can use the D or decimal tab setting. Press the hard return two times ↵ ↵, placing the cursor on line 1.5", position 1".

There is one more tab setting that is also very useful. To use it we must change the present tab settings. As before, press Shift-F8, number 1 for line format, and then number 8 for tabs. To delete the present settings press Ctrl-End. Type the number 7.4" and press Enter. An L is placed above position 7.4". Press the letter r, changing the L to an R. Now type . (a period) and notice how the R is shown in reverse video (Figure 4-40). You know that the R setting will anchor at the right and the text will flow to the left, as in flush right. By placing the decimal over the R, you are indicating that you want *leader dots* to be inserted automatically from where the cursor is to the tab setting. While you are only placing a period over the R in this particular exercise, you can also place a period over the L (left flush) or D (decimal align) settings. You cannot place a period over the C (center) tab setting. [For 5.1 Users – Leader dots can be used with the Center Tab.]

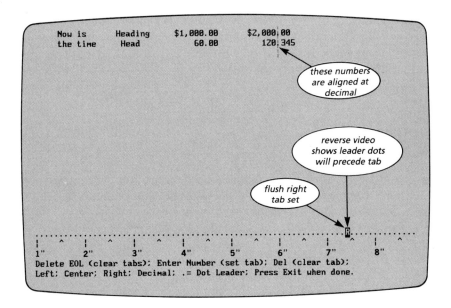

FIGURE 4-40

To exit from the tab setting screen, press F7. Press F7 again and you are returned to your document. To demonstrate how this tab setting works, we will type this as if it were part of a program you may be typing. With the cursor on line 1.5", position 1", type the words Piano Prelude, then press the Tab key. The cursor moves to position 7.4", which is the tab setting, and as it does, leader dots are inserted from the end of your typing to the tab setting. Now type the name Francis Holt and notice how the type moves to the left of the tab. As it does, it eliminates leader dots where the name is typed (Figure 4-41).

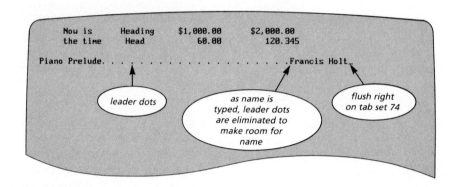

FIGURE 4-41

Leader dots can be used as above in programs, or, for example, in a table of contents. The dots lead the reader's eye to the right to follow the line of typing.

Save this document under the name Tabs. Press F10, type Tabs, then press Enter.

EXITING PROJECT 4

Y ou may remember that document 1 still remains in memory. You will not be able to exit WordPerfect without seeing a reminder that another document remains in memory. Press F7. Because you have already saved this document, press N to the prompt "Save document? (Y/N) Yes". The next prompt is "Exit Doc 2? (Y/N) No". It indicates that MEMO is still in memory in document 1. Type the letter Y to exit document 2 and return to document 1. If you had typed the letter N for no, you would have remained in document 2 and received a blank screen. Then you would have had to use the Shift-F3 function to return to document 1.

Save document 1 again as you exit. Press F7 and then Y (for yes to save). Press Enter ↵ to accept the current name, press Y to replace, and finally press Y to exit WordPerfect.

PROJECT SUMMARY

I n Project 4 you retrieved an existing document and made changes to it. You learned how to change the default settings for the margins, tab settings, and line spacing. You learned how to justify and unjustify text. You learned about the page format functions that center a short document on the page, control top and bottom margins, and change the paper size and type. Finally, you practiced advanced tab setting functions and moving back and forth between two documents in memory.

The following is a list of the keystroke sequence we used in Project 4. These keystrokes assume that the status line is in inches format and that the default drive has been correctly set to save the files to a diskette. Check to be sure that you have defined the Standard Printer as we did in Project 1.

SUMMARY OF KEYSTROKES—Project 4

STEPS	KEY(S) PRESSED	STEPS	KEY(S) PRESSED	STEPS	KEY(S) PRESSED
1	Shift-F10	53	Ctrl-F3	103	↵
2	memo	54	↵	104	c
3	↵	55	Alt-F3	105	4.8
4	Caps Lock	56	Backspace	106	↵
5	DATE:	57	Alt-F3	107	r
6	Tab	58	Home Home ↑	108	6
7	↓	59	Shift-F8	109	↵
8	Del	60	1	110	d
9	Del	61	8 [For 5.1 Users – Press 8 and then press T and then 1.]	111	F7
10	Del			112	F7
11	Del	62	1.7	113	Tab
12	↓	63	↵	114	Now is
13	↵	64	←	115	Tab
14	↑	65	←	116	Heading
15	FROM:	66	Del	117	Tab
16	Caps Lock	67	F7	118	$1,000.00
17	Tab	68	F7	119	Tab
18	Rita Moeller	69	Shift-F8	120	$2,000.00
19	[move cursor to line 2.67″, position 1″, under R in Rita]	70	1	121	↵
		71	6	122	Tab
20	Ctrl-End	72	1.5	123	the time
21	Del	73	↵	124	Tab
22	Del	74	F7	125	Head
23	Home Home ↑	75	Shift-F8	126	Tab
24	Shift-F8	76	1	127	60.00
25	1	77	3	128	Tab
26	7	78	n [For 5.1 Users – Press F instead of N.]	129	120.345
27	↵			130	↵
28	3.25	79	F7	131	↵
29	↵	80	Shift-F8	132	Shift-F8
30	F7	81	2	133	1
31	Ctrl-F3	82	1 [For 5.1 Users – Press 1 and then press Y.]	134	8
32	↵			135	Ctrl-End
33	Home Home Home ↑	83	F7	136	7.4″
34	Shift-F8	84	F10	137	↵
35	1	85	↵	138	r
36	7	86	y	139	.
37	↵	87	Shift-F7	140	F7
38	1.75	88	6	141	F7
39	↵	89	F7	142	Piano Prelude
40	F7	90	[be sure printer is on]	143	Tab
41	Alt-F3	91	Shift-F7	144	Francis Holt
42	Del	92	1	145	F7
43	Alt-F3	93	Shift-F3	146	y
44	[move cursor to line 2.17″, position 1″]	94	F7	147	tabs
		95	Shift-F8	148	↵
45	Shift-F8	96	1	149	y
46	1	97	8 [For 5.1 Users – Press 8 and then press T and then 1.]	150	F7
47	7			151	y
48	2	98	Home Home ←	152	↵
49	↵	99	Ctrl-End	153	y
50	3.5	100	1.5	154	y
51	↵	101	↵		
52	F7	102	3		

The following list summarizes the material covered in Project 4:

1. The term **type font** refers to the typeface or print style of a document.
2. Traditionally, typewriters used the terms **pica** or **elite** to describe type size. Pica type fits 10 characters into 1 inch of space on a line; elite type fits 12 characters into 1 inch of space.
3. Instead of pica or elite, the terms used in word processing are **10-pitch font** and **12-pitch font**.
4. **Formatting** is the process of defining how a document will look when printed.
5. The **Line Format** key is used to define tab settings, margins, and line spacing.
6. The **preview** function allows the user to see how a document will look when it is printed.
7. The **Center Page Top to Bottom** option from the page format screen centers the print on a page evenly between the top and bottom of the page.

STUDENT ASSIGNMENTS

STUDENT ASSIGNMENT 1: True/False

Instructions: Circle T if the statement is true and F if the statement is false.

T F   1. On the template, the word Retrieve is in red, meaning the user presses Ctrl-F10 to retrieve a document.
T F   2. WordPerfect default margin settings are at one inch on the left and one inch on the right.
T F   3. A piece of paper that is 11 inches long has 60 typing lines from the top edge of the paper to the bottom edge.
T F   4. To change any of the line format settings, press Shift-F8, and then the number 1.
T F   5. The default letter setting for tabs is the letter L.
T F   6. When changing the line spacing to 1 1/2 spacing, press Shift-F8, then 1, 6, then type 1.5 and press Enter.
T F   7. To change the type to be unjustified on the right margin, press the number 3 and then N on the line format screen. [For 5.1 Users – Press the number 3 and then the number 1.]
T F   8. When setting tab stops, if the user changes the L to R, the type will anchor at the right.
T F   9. When setting tab stops, changing the L to D will cause leader dots to be typed on the screen.
T F   10. When setting tab stops, changing the L to C will enable type to be centered over the tab stop.

STUDENT ASSIGNMENT 2: Multiple Choice

Instructions: Circle the correct response.

1. Circle all answers that refer to formatting functions.
   a. Shift-F8, 1
   b. Shift-F8, 5
   c. Shift-F8, 2
   d. Shift-F8
2. It is possible to invoke leader dots when setting a tab stop by pressing which key?
   a. D for decimal
   b. L for leaders
   c. . (period)
   d. none of the above
3. To change the line spacing to double-space, press the following keys:
   a. Shift-F8, 2, 6, 2, Enter
   b. Shift-F8, 2, Enter
   c. Shift-F8, 1, 6, 2, Enter
   d. Shift-F8, 3, 2, Enter

4. To turn off right justification, press the following keys:

For 5.0 Users	*For 5.1 Users*
a. Shift-F8, 1, 3, N	a. Shift-F8, 1, 3, 1
b. Shift-F8, 1, 3, Y	b. Shift-F8, 1, 3, 4
c. Shift-F8, 2, 3, N	c. Shift-F8, 1, 3, 2
d. Shift-F8, 3, 1, N	d. Shift-F8, 1, 3, 3

5. The code embedded into the document to signify that right justification has been turned off is:

For 5.0 Users	*For 5.1 Users*
a. [Just Off]	a. [Just: Left]
b. [Right Just Off]	b. [Just: Full]
c. [R Just Off]	c. [R Just: Off]
d. [Rt Just Off]	d. [Rt Just: Off]

6. When the tab setting has been changed to one tab stop at 3", the code embedded into the document shows the following:

For 5.0 Users	*For 5.1 Users*
a. [Tab Set]	a. [Tab:Abs: 3"]
b. [Tab Set: 3"]	b. [Tab Set:Abs: 3"]
c. [Tab Set: Pos 3"]	c. [Tab Set: 3"]
d. [Tab Set: L3"]	d. [Tab:Abs: L3"]

7. If the user were to change the margins to 1 1/2" on the left and 2" on the right, the code embedded into the document would read:

    a. [Margin Set]
    b. [L/R Mar: 1.5", 2"]
    c. [Margin Set: 1.5 left, 2 right]
    d. none of the above

STUDENT ASSIGNMENT 3: Matching

Instructions: Put the appropriate number next to the words in the second column.

1. Margin set	_____	Shift-F8
2. Top margin line default	_____	Home, Home, Up arrow
3. Default tab set letter	_____	Shift-F8, 1, 7
4. Justification off	_____	Shift-F8, 1, 8
5. Line format	_____	Shift-F8, 2, 1
6. Page format	_____	1 inch (or 6 lines)
7. Tab set	_____	L
8. Top of document	_____	Shift-F8, 1, 3, N [For 5.1 Users – Shift-F8, 1, 3, L]
9. Line spacing	_____	Shift-F8, 2
10. Center page, top to bottom	_____	Shift-F8, 1, 6

STUDENT ASSIGNMENT 4: Understanding WordPerfect Commands

Instructions: Next to each command, describe its effect.

Command	**Effect**
Shift-F8, 1, 8	_____
Shift-F8, 1, 7	_____
Shift-F8, 1, 6	_____
Shift-F8, 1, 3	_____
Shift-F8, 2, 1	_____
Shift-F7, 1	_____

STUDENT ASSIGNMENT 5: Identifying Default Settings

Instructions: Describe what default means. Then identify the default settings for the following commands.

Command	Default setting
Top margin	_____
Bottom margin	_____
Left margin	_____
Right margin	_____
Line spacing	_____
Lines per inch	_____
Pitch	_____
Right justification (on or off)	_____
Tab settings	_____
Letter tab setting	_____
Lines from top edge of paper to bottom edge	_____
Number of single-spaced text lines	_____

STUDENT ASSIGNMENT 6: Modifying a WordPerfect Document

Instructions: The screen below illustrates a memo that was prepared using WordPerfect. The margins are to be changed to 1 1/2" on the left and 1" on the right. The letter is to be centered top to bottom, and the right justification is to be turned off. Explain in detail the steps necessary to perform those changes.

```
DATE:        December 15, 1990
TO:   All Sales Managers
FROM:        Rita Moeller
RE:   New Bonus Plan

The new  bonus plan will become effective January 1.  If you have
questions, contact Hanna Butler.  All  sales people  are affected
by the new plan.
```

STUDENT ASSIGNMENT 7: Creating a WordPerfect Document

Instructions: Perform the following tasks.

1. For hard disk systems, load WordPerfect as you are directed by your instructor.
   For two disk drive systems, load DOS into main memory. Remove the DOS disk, and replace it with the WordPerfect disk. Type wp and press Enter.
2. Verify that the status line is in inches format and that the default drive is set to drive A for hard disk systems or drive B for two disk drive systems. Check to be sure that you have defined the Standard Printer as we did in Project 1. Begin this project on a clean screen.

Problem 1:
1. Set the left margin to 1.5" and the right margin to 3".
2. Turn the right justification off.
3. Center the page top to bottom.
4. Type the letter on the following page.

```
March 15, 1990

Ms. Roberta Weitzman
President, SpaceTek Inc.
44538 Scroll Avenue
Monnett, NJ 08773

Dear Ms. Weitzman:

This letter confirms our purchase of
thirteen DF-132 Modular Pin Brackets
from your company, delivery by April 1.

James R. McMillan, AirFrame Inc.
```

Problem 2: Save the document, using the name Weitzman.
Problem 3: Print the document.

STUDENT ASSIGNMENT 8: Modifying a WordPerfect Document

Instructions: Perform the following tasks.

1. For hard disk systems, load WordPerfect as you are directed by your instructor.
   For two disk drive systems, load DOS into main memory. Remove the DOS disk, and replace it with the WordPerfect disk. Type wp and press Enter.
2. Verify that the status line is in inches format and that the default drive is set to drive A for hard disk systems or drive B for two disk drive systems. Check to be sure that you have defined the Standard Printer as we did in Project 1. Begin this project on a clean screen.

Problem 1:
1. Retrieve the document named Weitzman, created in Student Assignment 7.
2. Change the margins to 1" on the left and 2 1/2" on the right (Hint: Either delete the old margin codes or be sure the new margin code is to the right of the old one. The last code governs).
3. The correct address is 44358 Scroll Street.
4. Change the purchase to 35 Pin Brackets.
5. Remove the words from your company on line 2 and end the sentence following the word Brackets.
6. Insert the words We expect in front of the word delivery on the second line.
7. The last name of the sender of the letter is MacMillan, not McMillan.

Problem 2: Save the document again, replacing the old version with the new version.
Problem 3: Print the modified document. It should look like the letter below.

```
March 15, 1990

Ms. Roberta Weitzman
President, SpaceTek Inc.
44358 Scroll Street
Monnett, NJ 08773

Dear Ms. Weitzman:

This letter confirms our purchase of 35 DF-132
Modular Pin Brackets.  We expect delivery by April
1.

James R. MacMillan, AirFrame Inc.
```

STUDENT ASSIGNMENT 9: Advanced Tab Settings

Instructions: Perform the following tasks.

1. For hard disk systems, load WordPerfect as you are directed by your instructor.
   For two disk drive systems, load DOS into main memory. Remove the DOS disk, and replace it with the WordPerfect disk. Type wp and press Enter.
2. Verify that the status line is in inches format and that the default drive is set to drive A for hard disk systems or drive B for two disk drive systems. Check to be sure that you have defined the Standard Printer as we did in Project 1. Begin this project on a clean screen.

Problem 1:
1. Set margins to 1.5" on the left and 2" on the right.
2. Center page top to bottom.
3. Center and capitalize heading, followed by three hard returns.
4. Change line spacing to 2 (double-space).
5. Clear all tab settings. Place one tab stop at position 6.4". Change the L to R. Type a . (period) over the R. Exit out of tab setting.
6. Type remaining portion of program.

Problem 2: Save the document to disk as Program.
Problem 3: Print the document.

```
                        GRADUATION PROGRAM


       Opening Procession. . . . . . . . Graduating Class

       Flag Ceremony . . . . . . . . . . . . . . . ROTC

       Greeting. . . . .Vice President of Student Affairs

       Special Number. . . . . . . . . . String Quartet

       Remarks . . . . . . . . . . . University President

       Song. . . . . . . . . . . . . . A Cappella Choir

       Presentation of Diplomas. . . . . .College Deans

       School Song . . . . . . . . . . Graduating Class
                          Recessional


                             *****


          Refreshments served in the foyer


                             *****
```

STUDENT ASSIGNMENT 10: Advanced Tab Settings

Instructions: Perform the following tasks.

1. For hard disk systems, load WordPerfect as you are directed by your instructor.

   For two disk drive systems, load DOS into main memory. Remove the DOS disk, and replace it with the WordPerfect disk. Type wp and press Enter.
2. Verify that the status line is in inches format and that the default drive is set to drive A for hard disk systems or drive B for two disk drive systems. Check to be sure that you have defined the Standard Printer as we did in Project 1. Begin this project on a clean screen.

Problem 1:
1. Center and capitalize the heading, followed by three hard returns.
2. Enter the tab setting screen, clear all current tab stops.
3. Enter a C (Center) tab stop at 2", 4.2", 6.2".
4. Type the first line of headings (Products, Wholesale Price, Retail Price).
5. After typing the column headings, press two hard returns. Enter the tab setting screen again and change the tab designations at 4.2" and 6.2" to a D.
6. Type the remainder of the price list.

Problem 2: Save the document to disk, using the name Price.
Problem 3: Print the document.

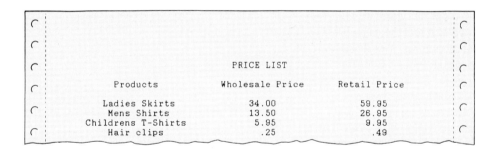

```
                        PRICE LIST

        Products        Wholesale Price       Retail Price

      Ladies Skirts          34.00                59.95
      Mens Shirts            13.50                26.95
   Childrens T-Shirts         5.95                 9.95
       Hair clips              .25                  .49
```

PROJECT 5

Formatting Functions, File Management, and Macros

Objectives

You will have mastered the material in this project when you can:

- Invoke the List Files option
- Change page length and insert hard page breaks
- Add headers and footers
- Specify date format and employ the date function
- Create and invoke macros

FILE MANAGEMENT

Load WordPerfect as you have in the previous projects. If you are working on a hard disk system, load WordPerfect as your instructor directs you. If you are working on a two disk drive system, at the A> prompt (with the WordPerfect disk in drive A and the data disk in drive B), type wp and press Enter. WordPerfect loads into main memory. As in Project 1, verify that the status line is in inches format. Also as in Project 1, verify that the default drive is set to drive A for hard disk systems, or drive B for two disk drive systems. You should then see a clean screen with only the status line in the lower right corner, indicating Doc 1 Pg 1 Ln 1" Pos 1". Finally, check to be sure that you have defined the Standard Printer as we did in Project 1. In this project you will revise a document to look like Figure 5-1. In Project 4 you retrieved a file using the Shift-F10 (retrieve) function. At the prompt you typed the name of the file to be retrieved. It is possible that you may not remember the name of the file, or perhaps you need to see how many bytes of memory a particular file uses. In these situations and to perform other file management functions, it is not necessary to exit WordPerfect, you can use the **List Files** function.

December 15, 1990

LICENSING AGREEMENT

You should **carefully** read the following terms and conditions. Your use of this program package indicates your acceptance of them. If you do <u>not</u> agree with them, you should not use this software package. Instead, you should return the package and your money will be returned to you.

PerSoft Inc. provides this program and licenses you to use it. <u>You</u> assume responsibility for the selection of this program to achieve your intended results. PerSoft Inc. assumes no responsibility for the results you obtain from the use of this software package.

LICENSE

a. Use the program on a single machine only. Use on more than one machine is considered "pirating" this software.

b. Copy the program into any machine readable or printed form for backup or modification purposes in support of your use of the program on a single machine. Certain programs from PerSoft Inc., however, may contain mechanisms to limit or inhibit copying. These programs are marked "copy protected."

c. Modify or merge the program into another PerSoft Inc. program for use on the single machine. Any portion of the program merged into another program will continue to be subject to the terms and conditions of this License.

- 1 -

Licensing Agreement   December 15, 1990

You <u>MAY NOT</u> use, copy, modify, or transfer the program, in whole or in part, except as <u>**expressly permitted**</u> in this Licensing Agreement. PerSoft Inc. also reserves the right to do the following:

Withdraw your license if this software package is used for any illegal or immoral purpose which, in the sole judgment of PerSoft Inc., may damage the reputation of PerSoft Inc.

If you transfer possession of any copy, modification, or merged portion of the program to another person, **YOUR LICENSE IS AUTOMATICALLY TERMINATED.**

- 2 -

FIGURE 5-1

Look at the template next to the F5 key. You see the words List Files in black. Press the F5 key. Figure 5-2 shows that the message "Dir B:*.*" appears in the lower left corner of your screen if you are using a two disk drive system or "Dir A:*.*" if you are using a hard disk system. As you learned in the Introduction to DOS, the asterisk (*) is a global character. B:*.*, therefore, stands for drive B and *all the files* (*) before the period and *all the files* (*) after the period. To accept the default drive and to see all the files on the default drive, press the Enter key.

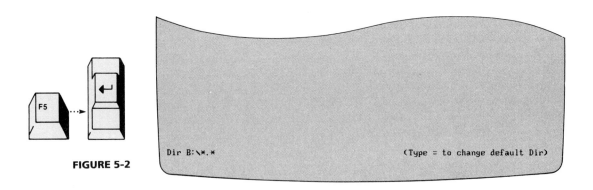

FIGURE 5-2

Dir B:*.*   (Type = to change default Dir)

Figure 5-3 shows a screen similar to what your screen will look like. (The names of the files you see may differ.)

The top left corner shows the date and updated time you entered when you loaded WordPerfect into main memory. At the top middle is the directory you are currently in. Also in the middle, you are shown the disk space that is still free. As each file is saved, bytes (each character or space is approximately equivalent to one byte) are subtracted from the free disk space. The Current Directory and Parent Directory are helpful for management of a hard disk. All files are listed in alphabetical order. After the name of the file, you see a dot or period and then the file extension name, if any. To the right of the file name are the number of bytes used by that particular file, then the date and time that particular file was saved. If you have since saved and then replaced a file, the last date and time of saving is shown. This is one reason why it is so important to enter the date when turning on the computer. Because all files are saved by date, you can often find a particular file you are looking for just by knowing when you last saved it. The Files menu at the bottom of the screen shows all the options that are available.

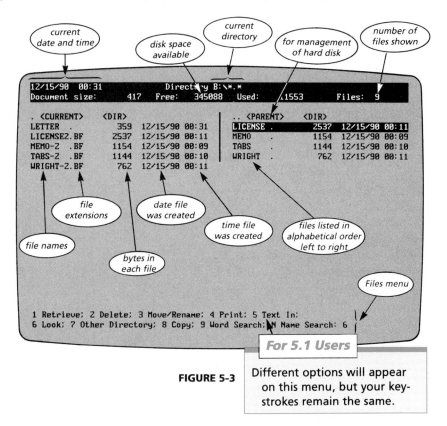

FIGURE 5-3

For 5.1 Users

Different options will appear on this menu, but your key-strokes remain the same.

To invoke any of the options, you must highlight a file. To do this, press the Down Arrow ↓ and then the Right Arrow →. Notice how the cursor highlights one file at a time. If you have many files you may have more than one screenful of file names. To view other files you can press PgDn or Home, Down Arrow to move down a screen at a time. To move up a screen at a time, press PgUp or Home, Up Arrow. To move to the last document listed (even if it were several screens down), press Home, Home, Down Arrow. To move to the top of the files listing, press Home, Home, Up Arrow.

Notice that there is a file named MEMO. Look at the last option on the menu at the bottom of the screen. **Name Search** allows you to search for a specific file name. Press the letter n for Name Search. Figure 5-4 shows that the menu at the bottom of the screen disappears, so that you can begin the Name Search. Press the letter M (capital or lowercase). When you press a letter in Name Search, the first file beginning with that letter is highlighted. If you do not wish to type any more letters to view other files, press Enter to bring the menu back. (If you happen to lose the List Files screen, press F5 and then Enter to retrieve it.)

At the files screen, press Home, Home, Up Arrow to move the cursor to the top of the list of files. You now wish to highlight the document you saved as LICENSE. If there is more than one file that begins with the letter L it may be necessary to type more than just L. Type n for Name Search (step 1 in Figure 5-5). Next, type L (lowercase or capital) (step 2 in Figure 5-5). Notice how the file LETTER is highlighted and the letter L is shown at the bottom of the screen. Type the letter I and notice in step 3 in Figure 5-5 how the highlighting moves to the first file that begins with LI. If you had many files, you could continue typing more letters of a file name, or you could move the cursor to the desired file name. Press Enter, and the menu is restored (step 3 in Figure 5-5). To exit the List Files menu, press the spacebar (step 4 in Figure 5-5). You can now see that you have a blank screen or a clean workspace.

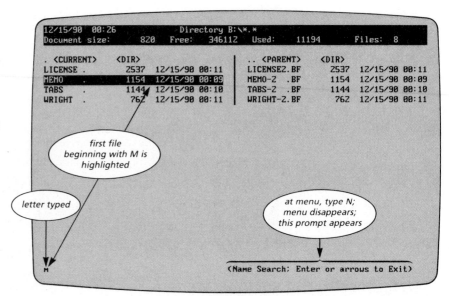

FIGURE 5-4

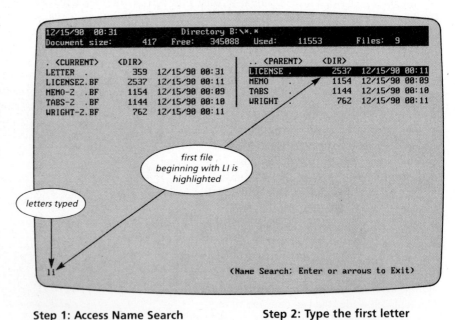

Step 1: Access Name Search

Step 2: Type the first letter of the file name

Step 3: Type the second letter of the file name. To retrieve the menu press Enter

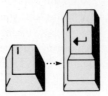

Step 4: Exit the List Files function

space

FIGURE 5-5

Look Function and Retrieving a Document

You will now retrieve a copy of a file from disk and place it into main memory. Note that you have a blank screen on which to retrieve that file. If you tried to retrieve a new document into the same screen where another document is present, you would see a message "Retrieve into current document? (Y/N) No". If you do retrieve a document on the screen, text that was on the screen would be pushed down below the incoming text. Since it might not be visible, you'd think it was gone, but you might find later that you saved two documents together. Remember to *clean the workspace* before you retrieve a new document into memory. The workspace can only be cleared using the Exit (F7) key.

To look at the entire listing of files on the default drive, press F5, then Enter ↵. To work on the file named LICENSE, you need to retrieve a copy of that file into the main memory of the computer. The term "copy" is used because the original file remains on the disk, and only a copy of that file is retrieved and placed in main memory. You will be changing that file, but all changes are made to the copy in main memory. To save all the changes, you will have to use the Save key and then replace the old file on disk with the new changes that are in main memory.

Press n for Name Search. Type LI and the document LICENSE that you created is highlighted. Press Enter to restore the menu. Since there are many files, you would waste time if you retrieved the wrong document into memory only to have to exit out again. WordPerfect includes an option to look at a document that is on the disk without actually retrieving a copy into main memory.

Look at the menu at the bottom of the screen as shown in Figure 5-6. Next to number 6 is the word Look. Press number 6 and the document LICENSE is displayed on your screen. Figure 5-7 shows, however, that you are just viewing the document. The bar at the top of the screen tells you which file you are looking at and how large the file is. At the bottom of the screen you are told to use the cursor keys to see more text. [For 5.1 Users – A different message will appear.] The document looks the same as you typed it. But in some documents (such as those that have columns or tabbed numbers) the typing may appear strange. Since the document has not been loaded into main memory you cannot do any editing. You can move the cursor up or down or even press the PgDn and PgUp keys to view more of the document.

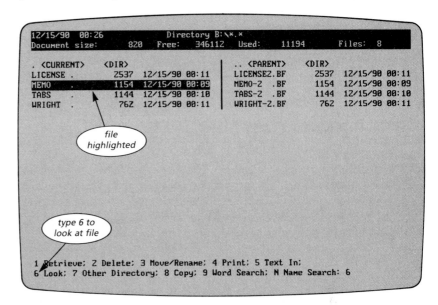

FIGURE 5-6

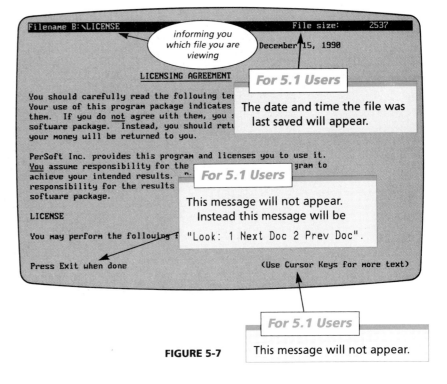

FIGURE 5-7

To return to the Files menu, press either Enter or the F7 key. The file you were just viewing remains highlighted in the Files menu.

Because the highlighted file you just viewed is the file you wish to retrieve, look at the menu at the bottom of the screen. Next to the number 1, notice the word Retrieve. With the file name LICENSE still highlighted, press the number 1. The document named LICENSE, which you typed in Project 3, is retrieved and placed in memory and displayed on your screen.

Press F5 and then Enter ↵. You now see the list files screen again. You would not want to now highlight another document and then retrieve it by pressing the number 1 because you would be retrieving another document on top of the one already in main memory. Press the spacebar, and you are returned to your document still on the screen.

Now that you have the document named LICENSE retrieved and loaded into main memory, you will use this document to learn more formatting features. First, it is necessary to delete a line of type in the document. It may seem that the line is needed in the text, but deleting it rearranges the page breaks so that you can learn more formatting features in this project.

To delete the line of type, press the Down Arrow 19 times to move the cursor to line 4.17", position 1". Then press Ctrl-End. Press the Delete key two times to delete the blank lines. Press Home, Home, Up Arrow to move the cursor to the top of the document.

MORE FORMATTING FEATURES

Now that you have deleted the one line, note that the body of the text should be in 1 1/2 spacing instead of single spacing. Since you do not want to change the spacing for the date and heading, press the Down Arrow ↓ five times to place the cursor on line 1.83", position 1" under the Y in You. To change the line spacing press Shift-F8. Press number 1 for Line Format, then number 6 for Line Spacing. Type 1.5 and press Enter ↵. Press F7 to exit to the document. Figure 5-8 shows that typing below the code is now in 1 1/2 line spacing.

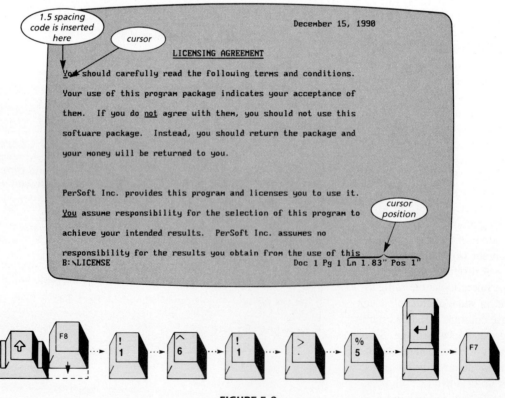

FIGURE 5-8

Before printing any document, it is important to view each screen to see if the format and the page breaks make reading easier. To do this, press the Plus (+) key on the numeric keypad to move to the bottom of the current screen. To move to the bottom of the next screen, press the + key again. The cursor moves to line 7.08". Press the + key a third time, and notice a dotted line across the screen, indicating a page break. The cursor should be on page 2, line 1.25". [For 5.1 Users – The cursor will be on page 2, line 1".] To view the reveal codes screen, press Alt-F3. The code **[SPg]** is inserted because the page break was invoked by the computer, causing a **soft page break**. [For 5.1 Users – Press the Up Arrow key one time to view the soft page break code, **[HRt-SPg]**]. To exit the reveal codes, press Alt-F3.

The page break comes at an awkward place; the four lines of the paragraph should be kept together. There are three ways in which the document can be formatted to keep these lines together. All three ways will now be demonstrated. When you type other documents in the future, you can decide which way will be most advantageous for each document.

Changing Top and Bottom Margins

As discussed in Project 4, WordPerfect defaults to a one-inch margin on the top and bottom of each page; that is why, when WordPerfect is formatted for single spacing, the page breaks at 9.83" (1 line less the 10"). Knowing that there are six single spaced lines to the inch, we can adjust the top and bottom margins to allow the four lines from page two to appear on page one. Remember to place codes that effect the entire document at the beginning of the document. Press Home, Home, Up Arrow to move to line 1" position 1". Look at the template next to the F8 key. Press Shift-F8 for the format screen. Press 2 for Page format. Press 5 for Margins, top and bottom. The menu shown in Figure 5-9 appears on the screen.

Type .7 and press Enter for the top margin. Notice how 0.7" appears on the screen. Next type .7 and press Enter for the bottom margin. Press F7 to exit to the document.

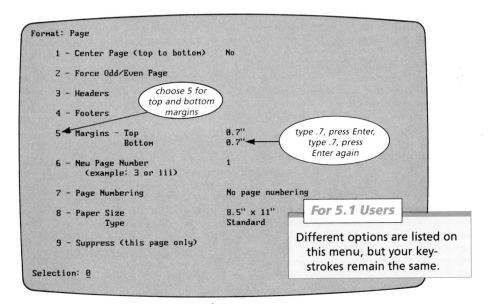

Step 1: Access top and bottom margin changes   Step 2: Exit to document

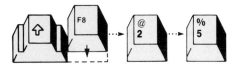

FIGURE 5-9

To view the code that was embedded into the document, press Alt-F3. The embedded code [T/B Mar:0.7",0.7"] shows the top and bottom margins set to 0.7" (Figure 5-10). Press the Pg Dn key one time and the Up Arrow key four times. Notice that the four lines are now together at the bottom of page one (Figure 5-11).

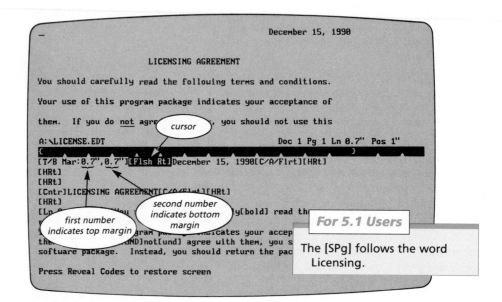

FIGURE 5-10

To try another way to keep the four lines together, it is necessary to delete the code that was just inserted into the document. Press Home, Home, Up Arrow to highlight the Flush Right code. To delete backward, press the Backspace key one time; the Top and Bottom margin code is deleted. Press Alt-F3 to exit the reveal codes. Press the Pg Dn key one time and the Up Arrow key one time [For 5.1 Users – Press the Up Arrow key one more time.], so that the cursor is under the Y in You on line 9.58", position 1". Press Ctrl-F3 and Enter to Rewrite the screen. Observe that the four lines are again split by a dotted line, indicating the page break.

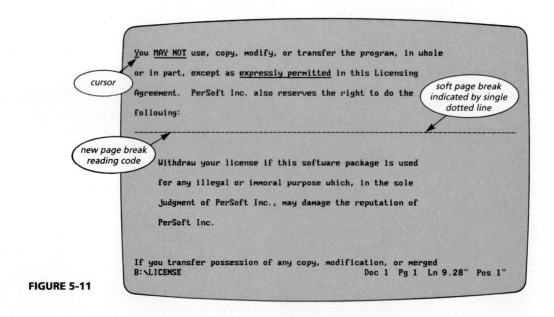

FIGURE 5-11

Hard Page Break

When you see a dotted line across the page, you know that it is a page break invoked by the WordPerfect software as it interprets the top and bottom margin codes, or the conditional end of page. You have viewed the [SPg] code that is embedded when the computer interprets top and bottom margin commands. There could be times when you wish to invoke a page break code to ensure that no typing can be inserted below a certain point on a page. This is called a **hard page break**. Even if margins (top/bottom or left/right) are redefined, the hard page break will continue to be invoked by the software as long as the code exists.

With the cursor on line 9.58" under the Y in You, press Ctrl-Enter. You can see how the page break has occurred (Figure 5-12), and you can also see that instead of a single dotted line, WordPerfect uses a double dotted line when you invoke a hard page break.

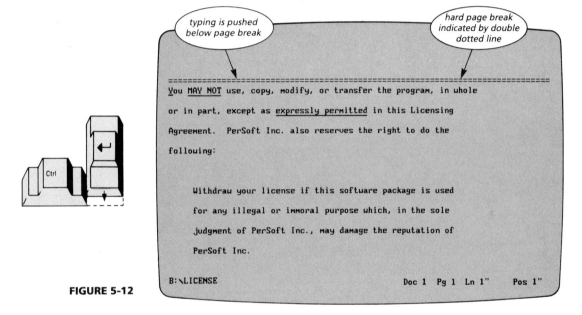

FIGURE 5-12

To view the code, press Alt-F3. Notice that above the first line of the paragraph a **[HPg]** code is embedded (Figure 5-13). [For 5.1 Users – Press Up Arrow to view the [HPg] code.] To delete the hard page break, press the Backspace key. [For 5.1 Users – Also press the Delete key.] Press Alt-F3 to exit the codes.

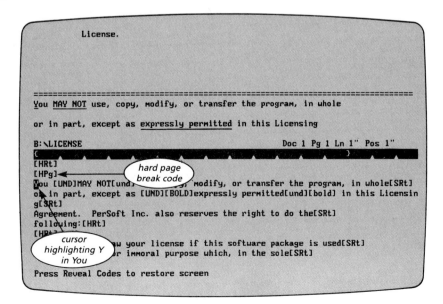

FIGURE 5-13

Conditional End of Page

Another formatting feature, **conditional end of page**, is found on the Other Format menu. This feature keeps a specified number of lines together on one page. If the current page is not long enough, it will move all lines specified to the next page. This is helpful if you have a table or graph that must be kept on one page.

The cursor must be *above* the lines to be kept together, so press the Up Arrow ↑ to move the cursor to line 9.33", which is the blank line before the paragraph. Press Shift-F8. Then press 4 for Other. The Other Format menu appears. Press number 2 for conditional end of page. The message "Number of Lines to Keep Together:" appears on the screen. Type the number 4 (because there are four lines you wish to keep together), as shown in Figure 5-14. Press Enter ↵, then press F7 to exit the Other Format menu and return to the document. The lines will reformat after you have looked at the codes.

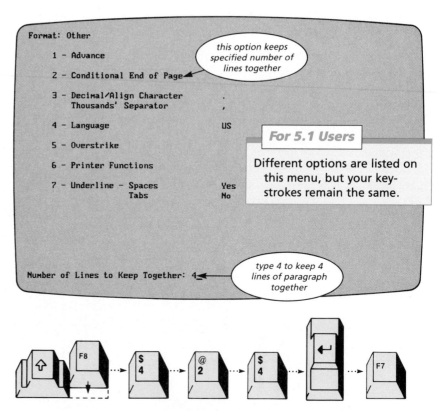

FIGURE 5-14

To view the code that was inserted, press Alt-F3. Figure 5-15 shows the conditional end of page code, **[Cndl EOP]**, embedded in your document. Before you exit the codes, notice that the [SPg] code again follows the word whole. [For 5.1 Users – The [SPg] code follows the word Licensing.]

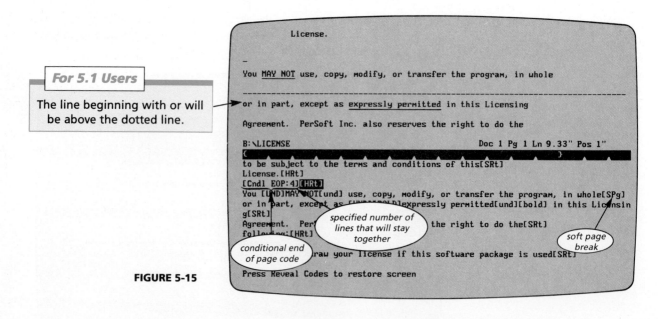

FIGURE 5-15

Press Alt-F3 to exit the codes. As you do, notice that all four lines have been kept together by being moved down to the next page below the dotted line (Figure 5-16).

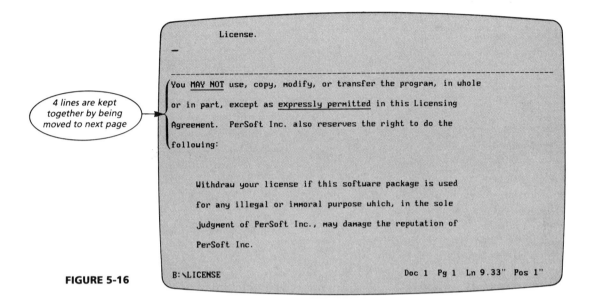

License.

—

_____

You MAY NOT use, copy, modify, or transfer the program, in whole

or in part, except as expressly permitted in this Licensing

Agreement. PerSoft Inc. also reserves the right to do the

following:

    Withdraw your license if this software package is used

    for any illegal or immoral purpose which, in the sole

    judgment of PerSoft Inc., may damage the reputation of

    PerSoft Inc.

B:\LICENSE   Doc 1 Pg 1 Ln 9.33" Pos 1"

4 lines are kept together by being moved to next page

FIGURE 5-16

HEADERS AND FOOTERS

Whenever your document contains more than one page, you will most likely wish to number the pages. You may also wish to have a heading at the top or bottom of each page, or perhaps both. A heading and page number placed at the top of a page is called a **header**; placed at the bottom of a page, it is called a **footer**. You may have noticed headers and footers in your textbooks. It is not necessary to type headers and footers on each and every page when you compose a document. It can be done once for the entire document.

WordPerfect allows you to have as many as two headers and/or two footers per page, which is helpful if you are typing a document that will have facing pages. Facing pages are normally used in books or magazines. You have probably noticed that in books odd pages are normally on the right side and even pages on the left side, either at the top or bottom of the page. This type of numbering is called facing pages numbering. For our exercise, we will use only one position for the numbering.

After you type headers and footers, a code is embedded and they are held in screens separate from the normal typing screen. When the pages are printed, headers will be printed at the top of each page and footers at the bottom of each page. WordPerfect allows one blank line to be inserted between either the header or footer and the body of the text. The lines required for the headers and/or footers are typed within the 54 lines of typing, leaving the top and bottom margins intact. Headers and footers should always be typed at the beginning of a document. If you have invoked a margin set change, the headers and footers code should follow the margin set code.

Headers

To move to the top of the document, press Home, Home, Up Arrow ↑. Headers and footers are found on the Page Format menu. Press Shift-F8 and then number 2. The Page Format menu appears on the screen.

For this document, you will define one header and then one footer. Press the number 3 for header A (step 1 in Figure 5-17). Then press 1 for header A (step 2 in Figure 5-17).

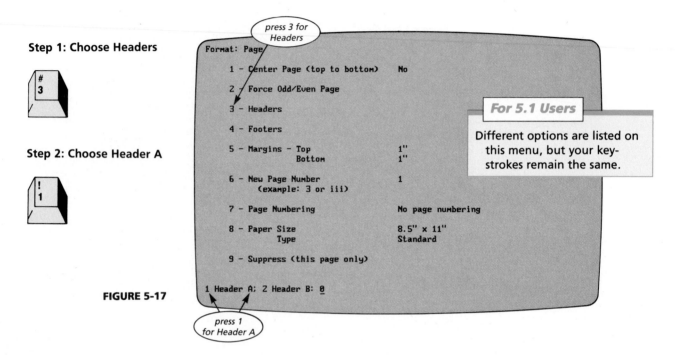

Step 1: Choose Headers

Step 2: Choose Header A

FIGURE 5-17

To place the header on every page type the number 2 (Figure 5-18). A totally blank screen with a mini status line appears. This screen is reserved for header A. What you type is held in reserve and will be printed when the document is sent to the printer. Type the words Licensing Agreement. Because you also want the date to appear in the upper right corner, you must add the date flush right. Press Alt-F6. The cursor moves to position 75. Type the date December 15, 1990 (or the current date, if you wish).

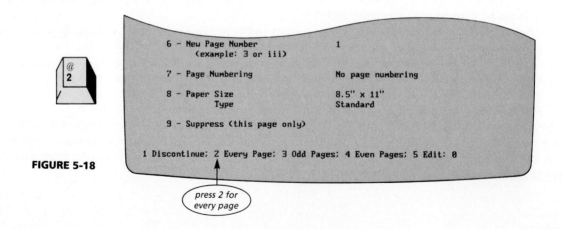

FIGURE 5-18

WordPerfect allows for one blank line between the header and the body of the text. Because you want an extra blank line between the header and the text, press the hard return ← key. Your screen should look like Figure 5-19. As indicated on the screen, press F7 to exit. You are returned to the Page Format menu.

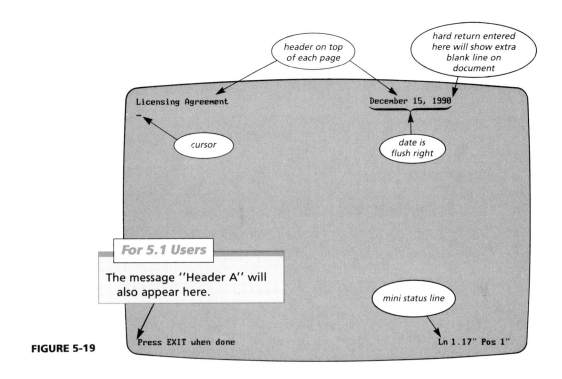

FIGURE 5-19

Footers

Because you also wish to add a footer, press the number 4 for footers. Press 1 for footer A. Next, press the number 2 for every page. Again you have a blank screen, which is reserved for footer A. The typing will be printed at the bottom of the page, and you want an extra blank line between the body of the text and the footer, so first press the hard return ↵ key. The cursor should be on line 1.17″, position 1″. Because you are going to put in page numbering, which you want centered at the bottom of each page, you must center the typing. Press Shift-F6. The cursor moves to position 4.2″. Type a hyphen (–) followed by the spacebar. At this point you would normally type the number. You need to put in a code that will merge with the status line, so that, for instance, when page 2 is typed, the printer will read the status line and invoke that particular page number. To put in a numbering merge code, hold down the Ctrl key and type the letter B. Press the spacebar and then type another hyphen. The screen should look like Figure 5-20. Press F7 to exit. You are returned to the page format screen.

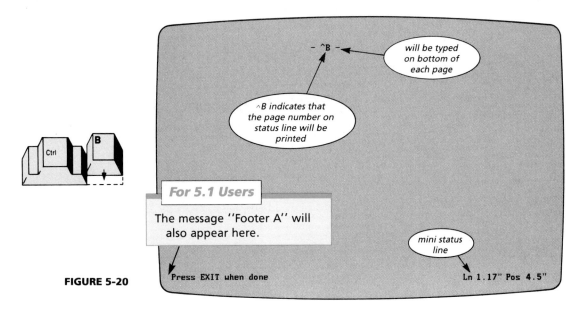

FIGURE 5-20

Suppress for Current Page Only

The codes for headers and footers are being invoked at the top of your document, but you do not wish to have the header typed on the first page, since that page has its own heading. To suppress the header for page 1, which is the current page, press the number 9 for Suppress (this page only) (step 1 in Figure 5-21). [For 5.1 Users – Press the number 8.] The menu in Figure 5-21 shows that you can suppress any number of options. You only wish to suppress the header, not the footer, so press the number 5 (step 2 in Figure 5-21), and then press y for Yes (step 3 in Figure 5-21) to turn off header A. Finally, press F7 to exit to the document (step 4 in Figure 5-21).

Step 1: Choose Suppress (this page only)

Step 2: Choose Suppress Header A

Step 3: Select Yes option

Step 4: Exit to document

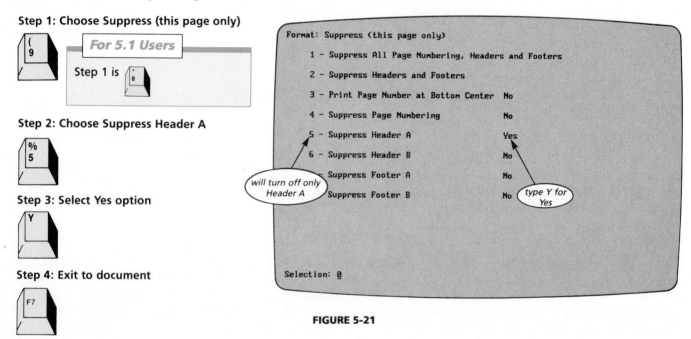

FIGURE 5-21

To view the three codes you just invoked, press Alt-F3. Figure 5-22 shows that first you have the header code, then the footer code, and then the suppress code. To exit the reveal codes, press the Alt-F3.

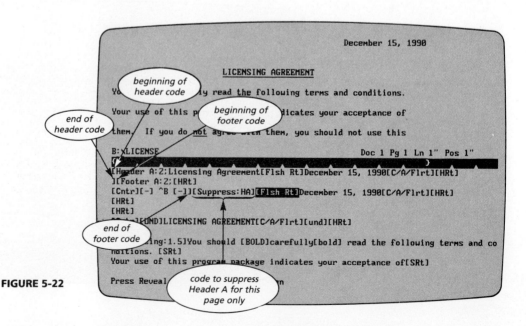

FIGURE 5-22

SAVING AND REPLACING A DOCUMENT

Whan you finished typing this document in Project 3, you saved the document to your disk. However, you have now made several changes to the document on your screen, but those changes have not been saved to the disk. As you learned in Projects 3 and 4, it is possible to save these changes to the disk by replacing the old text with the new text. In this case, you want to save both the version made in Project 3 as well as the changes made here in Project 5. Therefore, when you save you will give this document a different name.

To save your document, press the F10 key. At the prompt "Document to be Saved: B:\LICENSE", type the new name license.2 and press Enter. The document is saved to the disk in the default drive.

PRINTING A DOCUMENT

You have saved and replaced your document, and it is now ready to be printed. To view the document, press Shift-F7, then number 6 (step 1 in Figure 5-23). To move to page 2 in the view mode, press PgDn (step 2 in Figure 5-23). To exit to the document, press F7. At this point be sure that your printer has paper inserted, and that the printer is on and ready to print.

Press Shift-F7. You will see the Print menu screen. Because you wish to print the full text of this document, press the number 1 for full text. At this point, the printer begins printing your document. The printed document will look like Figure 5-1 at the beginning of this project.

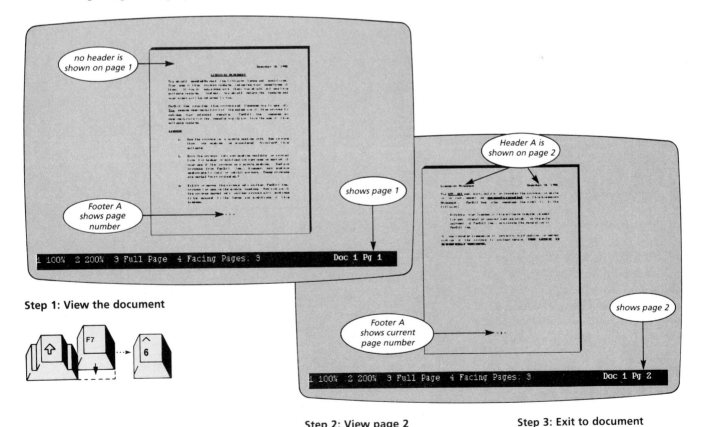

Step 1: View the document

Step 2: View page 2

Step 3: Exit to document

FIGURE 5-23

EXITING A DOCUMENT

Your document has been saved to disk and printed. It is now necessary to exit the document and clear the screen, but not exit the WordPerfect program.

Press the F7 key. At the prompt "Save Document? (Y/N) Yes", type the letter N because the document has already been saved. At the prompt "Exit WP? (Y/N) No", type the letter N. The document exits and a clear screen appears.

DATE FORMAT FUNCTION

When you first turned on your computer you were prompted to enter the date. It is always important to enter the date, because all files are saved by their date. Another good reason for inserting the date is that you can invoke the date with the F5 key. But when you use F5, the date you invoke will be the date you entered when first turning the machine on. Some computers today have automatic dates.

Look at the template next to the F5 key. Notice the words Date/Outline in green. Press Shift-F5. The menu shown in Figure 5-24 appears. Press the number 1 to enter today's date on your blank screen. Press a hard return ↵ to move the cursor to line 2.

choose 1 to insert Date Text

choose 2 for Date Code

1 Date Text; 2 Date Code; 3 Date Format; 4 Outline; 5 Para Num; 6 Define: 0

FIGURE 5-24

Whatever date you entered when you booted DOS will appear on the screen. For example, if you had entered 12–15–90 you would see December 15, 1990—the same date but in a different form. (If you did not enter a date you will see the system default date.) You can understand why the date appears in the form it does by viewing the **Date Format** menu.

To view the Date Format menu, press Shift-F5 and type the number 3. Figure 5-25 shows what your screen will look like. At the bottom in boldface typing you see "Date Format: 3 1, 4". The numbers are the default characters used. To understand the meaning of each number, look at the menu above. The 3 1, 4 stands for the following: 3 = month (word), 1 = day of the month (a comma is placed after the day because if you were typing it you would include a comma), 4 = year (all four digits). This explains how a date can be displayed or printed in one format when it was inserted in a different format. Press F7 to exit the Date Format menu.

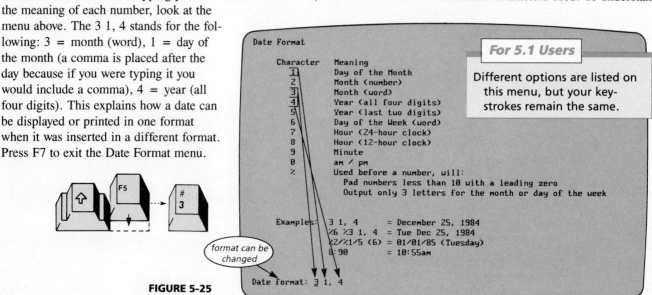

format can be changed

FIGURE 5-25

```
Date Format

     Character    Meaning
        1         Day of the Month
        2         Month (number)
        3         Month (word)
        4         Year (all four digits)
        5         Year (last two digits)
        6         Day of the Week (word)
        7         Hour (24-hour clock)
        8         Hour (12-hour clock)
        9         Minute
        0         am / pm
        %         Used before a number, will:
                     Pad numbers less than 10 with a leading zero
                     Output only 3 letters for the month or day of the week

     Examples:  3 1, 4        = December 25, 1984
                %6 %3 1, 4    = Tue Dec 25, 1984
                %2/%1/5 (6)   = 01/01/85 (Tuesday)
                8:90          = 10:55am

Date format: 3 1, 4
```

For 5.1 Users

Different options are listed on this menu, but your keystrokes remain the same.

With the Date menu at the bottom of the screen, now press the number 2 for Date Code. As you can see on the screen, the date is typed again.

To see the difference between 1 Date Text and 2 Date Code, you need to view the codes. Press Alt-F3. [For 5.1 Users – Also press the Up Arrow key one time.] The screen in Figure 5-26 shows that in the upper screen the date appears twice in exactly the same format. But the codes show that two different things happen. The first date is when you inserted text, exactly as if you had typed the date by hand. If you were to save this document and bring it up tomorrow, it would still have the same typing you see now. The second date is not a date at all in the codes. All you see is the code [Date: 3 1, 4]. The code inserts the current month, day, and year, which you entered when turning on the computer. If you were to bring this document up tomorrow, the date that would be invoked by the code would have tomorrow's date on the screen. This is especially useful if you type a letter today, but will be printing it out at some time in the future. Press Alt-F3 to exit the reveal codes.

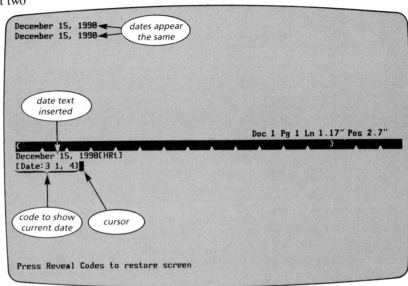

FIGURE 5-26

MACROS

Probably the single most time-saving feature of WordPerfect is its capability of using macros. Simply stated, a **macro** stores frequently used keystrokes that make up phrases, paragraphs, or commands, so that instead of having to press a sequence of keystrokes each time, you only have to press a few keys. If any typing or string of commands is used frequently, you can make a macro of those keystrokes. You will learn how to create two macros, and then whenever keystrokes become repetitive, you can create and then invoke your own macros.

You have just learned how to invoke a date function. You will now learn how to put those keystrokes into a macro.

Press a hard return ↵ to move to a clean line. To define a macro look at the template next to the F10 key. You see the words Macro Def in red. Press Ctrl-F10. The prompt "Define Macro:" appears on your screen (step 1 in Figure 5-27). First, you must name the macro. You can use letters of the alphabet or a word or abbreviation to name a macro. To save time, you should make the name short and representative of what the macro does. In this case hold down the Alt key and press the letter D for date (step 2 in Figure 5-27).

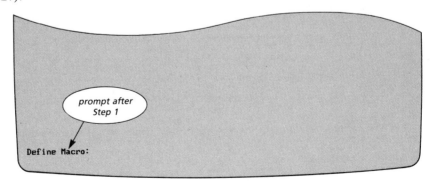

FIGURE 5-27

Step 1: Invoke macro function   Step 2: Ready the software to receive the macro

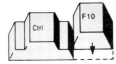

The prompt "Description:" is displayed as shown in Figure 5-28. (If you fail to get this prompt, and instead see a message "ALTD.WPM is Already Defined. 1 Replace; 2 Edit: 0", press 1 to replace the old macro with your new macro.) At the prompt "Description:", you can type a description of what this macro will do, or you can bypass this prompt by pressing Enter ↵. If you wish to type a description, type the words Current Date, and then press Enter ↵. If you do not wish to type a description, just press Enter ↵.

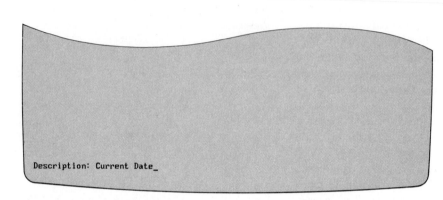

FIGURE 5-28

Description: Current Date_

Step 1: Type description of macro   Step 2: Enter description

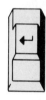

The prompt "Macro Def" begins flashing in the lower left corner of the screen (Figure 5-29). Any and all keys you press now will be stored in sequence until you turn the macro define off. Recalling what we did before to retrieve the current date, press Shift-F5. When you receive the Date menu, press the number 2 for Date Code (step 1 in Figure 5-29). The current date appears on the screen.

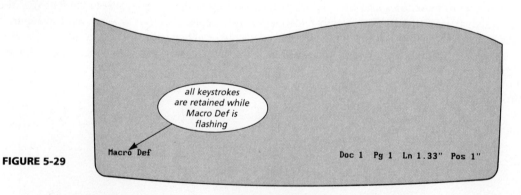

all keystrokes are retained while Macro Def is flashing

Macro Def   Doc 1 Pg 1 Ln 1.33" Pos 1"

FIGURE 5-29

Step 1: Type the macro   Step 2: Save the macro and escape from macro define mode

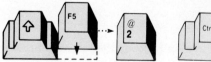   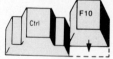

Turn off the macro define the same way you turned it on, by pressing Ctrl-F10 (step 2 in Figure 5-29). The macro is saved to the disk. The prompt then stops flashing. Press a hard return ↵ to put the cursor on a clean line. To invoke or retrieve the macro, press Alt-D. Immediately you see the date on the screen.

When you use this macro, the date will be inserted wherever the cursor is. To make the date flush right, press Alt-F6. When the cursor is flush right, press Alt-D. The date types out flush right. Press a hard return ↵ to move the cursor to a clean line. To center the date, press Shift-F6. With the cursor centered, press Alt-D. Press a hard return. The date types out centered.

Because the macro has the code of 3 1, 4, no matter on which date you invoke the macro, the current date will appear on the screen in the form of month (word), day, and year (all four digits).

To learn the second way to invoke a macro it is best to clear the screen. Press F7 then the letter N to not save the document, then the letter N again to not exit WordPerfect.

The second macro you will learn is the ending of a letter. This is a sequence of keystrokes that is often repeated. To define a macro, press Ctrl-F10. Name the macro by typing the letters SY (for sincerely yours), and press Enter ↵. Describe the macro as "letter ending", and press Enter. When "Macro Def" begins flashing, press the Tab key eight times, moving the cursor to position 5". (If you go too far or make a mistake, backspace and correct the error.) When the cursor is on position 5", type the phrase Sincerely yours, then press a hard return ↵. Press a hard return three more times ↵ ↵ ↵. Press the Tab key eight times to move to position 5". Type the name Francis Morris and press a hard return ↵. Press the Tab key eight times to move to position 5" again. Type the word Manager and press hard return. All your keystrokes are now defined. To turn off the macro define, press Ctrl-F10, and the macro is saved to the disk. To clear the screen, press F7, N, N.

To invoke the macro this time, look at the template next to the F10 key. Notice the word Macro in blue. Press Alt-F10. The prompt "Macro:" appears. Type the letters SY (uppercase or lowercase) and press Enter ↵. The macro is invoked and the typing appears on the screen.

A key point to remember is that you invoke a macro depending upon how the macro is named. If the name includes Alt, for example ALTD, you invoke the macro by pressing Alt-D. If the name of the macro does not include Alt, you invoke it by pressing Alt-F10 and then typing the name of the macro and pressing Enter ↵.

To view how WordPerfect lists the macros, look at the List Files menu. Press F5 and then Enter ↵ (step 1 in Figure 5-30). Notice that the macro files have the extension of WPM, which stands for WordPerfect Macro (Figure 5-30). Do not try to retrieve the macro files from this screen. If you do try to retrieve a macro file from the List Files menu, you will receive the message "ERROR: Incompatible file format". Press the spacebar to exit from this screen (step 2 in Figure 5-30).

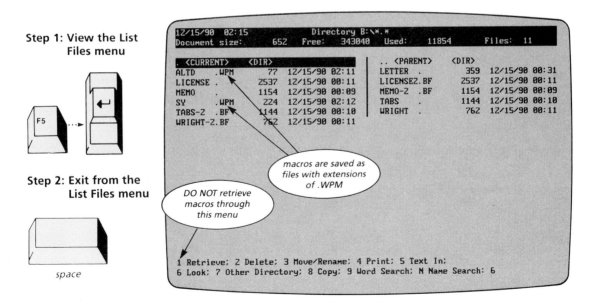

FIGURE 5-30

EXITING WORDPERFECT

s you have done before, exit this document and WordPerfect. It is not necessary to save this document because the macros have already been saved to disk.

PROJECT SUMMARY

*I*n Project 5 you learned about file management with the List File options. You retrieved the document you typed in Project 3 and practiced more formatting features on that document. You changed the top and bottom margins, put in a conditional end of page, and used a hard page break. You added a header and a footer to the document. After you saved, replaced, and exited the document, you learned about the date format and how to create macros.

The following list summarizes the material covered in Project 5:

1. **File Management** is done through the **List Files** menu. After a file is highlighted, it can be retrieved, renamed, printed, looked at, or copied under another name or to another directory. A word search can also be done through the List Files menu.
2. A **soft page break** is one invoked by the software. The embedded code is **[SPg]**.
3. **Changing the top and bottom margins** is a page format function that can be used to add more lines or lessen the number of lines on a page.
4. A **hard page break** is invoked by the user to prevent typing from being inserted past a certain point on the page. The embedded code is **[HPg]**.
5. The **conditional end of page** feature keeps a specified number of lines together on one page. The embedded code is **[Cndl EOP]**.
6. A **header** is typing found at the top of every page. Headers only have to be typed one time, then they are held in reserve to be printed on top of every page. Headers can consist of several lines of type, or perhaps just a code so the printer will print the current page number.
7. A **footer** is typing found at the bottom of every page. Footers only have to be typed one time, then they are held in reserve to be printed on the bottom of every page. Footers can consist of several lines of type, or perhaps just a code so the printer will print the current page number.
8. The **Suppress (this page only)** function can instruct the printer *not* to print a combination of page numbering or headers and footers on specified pages.
9. The **date code** function allows you to place a code in a document, so that the current date (or the date entered when loading DOS into the computer) will always be present in a document. Any combination of date formats can be used, such as day of month first, month as a word, and year in all four digits.
10. A **macro** is defined and invoked by the user to replace a sequence of keystrokes that is used frequently. When a macro is defined, all keystrokes are stored under one short name and can be invoked quickly by pressing just a few keys.

The following is a list of the keystroke sequence we used in Project 5. These keystrokes asssume that the status line is in inches format and that the default drive is set to save the files to a diskette. Check to be sure that you have defined the Standard Printer as we did in Project 1.

SUMMARY OF KEYSTROKES—Project 5

STEPS	KEY(S) PRESSED	STEPS	KEY(S) PRESSED	STEPS	KEY(S) PRESSED
1	F5	52	Alt-F3	104	Alt-F3 [view codes]
2	↵	53	↑ (to Ln 9.33″)	105	Alt-F3
3	n	54	Shift-F8	106	↵
4	li	55	4	107	Ctrl-F10
5	↵	56	2	108	Alt-D
6	1	57	4	109	current date
7	[↓ 19 times to line 5.33″, position 1″]	58	↵	110	↵
8	Ctrl-End	59	F7	111	Shift-F5
9	Del	60	Alt-F3 [view codes]	112	2
10	Del	61	Alt-F3	113	Ctrl-F10
11	Home Home ↑	62	Home Home ↑	114	↵
12	↓	63	Shift-F8	115	Alt-D
13	↓	64	2	116	Alt-F6
14	↓	65	3	117	Alt-D
15	↓	66	1	118	↵
16	↓	67	2	119	Shift-F6
17	Shift-F8	68	Licensing Agreement	120	Alt-D
18	1	69	Alt-F6	121	↵
19	6	70	December 15, 1990	122	F7
20	1.5	71	↵	123	n
21	↵	72	F7	124	n
22	F7	73	4	125	Ctrl-F10
23	+ (on numeric keypad)	74	1	126	sy
24	+	75	2	127	↵
25	+	76	↵	128	letter ending
26	↑	77	Shift-F6	129	↵
27	Home Home ↑	78	–	130	Tab [8 times to move cursor to position 5″]
28	Shift-F8	79	Space	131	Sincerely yours,
29	2	80	Ctrl-B	132	↵
30	5	81	Space	133	↵
31	.7	82	–	134	↵
32	↵	83	F7	135	↵
33	.7	84	9 [For 5.1 Users – Press 8 instead.]	136	Tab [8 times to move cursor to position 5″]
34	↵	85	5	137	Francis Morris
35	F7	86	y	138	↵
36	Alt-F3 [view codes]	87	↵	139	Tab [8 times to move cursor to position 5″]
37	Pg Dn	88	F7	140	Manager
38	↑	89	F10	141	↵
39	↑	90	license.2	142	Ctrl-F10
40	↑	91	↵	143	↵
41	↑	92	Shift-F7	144	↵
42	Home Home ↑	93	1	145	Alt-F10
43	Backspace [delete code]	94	F7	146	sy
44	Pg Dn	95	n	147	↵
45	↑ [For 5.1 Users – ↑ again.]	96	n	148	F5
46	Ctrl-F3	97	Shift-F5	149	↵ [view .WPM files]
47	Ctrl-Enter	98	1	150	Space
48	Ctrl-F3	99	↵	151	F7
49	↵	100	Shift-F5	152	n
50	Alt-F3	101	3	153	y
51	Backspace [delete code]	102	F7		
		103	2		

STUDENT ASSIGNMENTS

STUDENT ASSIGNMENT 1: True/False

Instructions: Circle T if the statement is true and F if the statement is false.

T F 1. Headers and footers are found on the Alt-F8 keys.

T F 2. To delete a file from the List Files menu, highlight the file, press the number 2, and respond Y for yes.

T F 3. WordPerfect lets you define two headers and two footers.

T F 4. WordPerfect defaults at 50 single lines of type per page.

T F 5. To list the files on the default drive, press F5 and Enter.

T F 6. To suppress a header/footer for the current page only, choose option 9 in the Page Format menu. [For 5.1 Users – Press 8 instead.]

T F 7. To access the Macro Define option, press Alt-F8.

T F 8. The date function is found by pressing Shift-F5.

T F 9. Each time a document is saved, the name must be retyped.

T F 10. To cause a hard page break, press the Scroll Lock/Break key.

STUDENT ASSIGNMENT 2: Multiple Choice

Instructions: Circle the correct response.

1. It is possible to delete a file by
   a. highlighting the file in List Files and pressing the Cancel key
   b. highlighting the file in List Files and pressing the 2 key, then Y
   c. highlighting the file in List Files and pressing the Exit key
   d. pressing Ctrl-F5
2. When defining headers and footers, WordPerfect allows for
   a. one header and one footer
   b. two headers and one footer
   c. either two headers or two footers but not both
   d. two headers and/or two footers
3. The Date Format, Date Text and Date Code can be found on the following key(s):
   a. F5
   b. Ctrl-F5
   c. Alt-F5
   d. Shift-F5
4. To invoke a macro,
   a. define the macro with Ctrl-F10
   b. while "Macro Def" is flashing, press all keys to be stored
   c. call up the macro through either Alt-F10 or Alt-(letter)
   d. all of the above
5. When defining a conditional end of page,
   a. press Shift-F8, 4, 2, and all lines will be kept together until you press a hard return
   b. press Shift-F8, 4, 2, and designate how many lines are to be kept together
   c. press Shift-F8, 2, 1, and designate how many lines to an inch
   d. none of the above

6. By pressing Ctrl-Enter, a hard page break occurs. The code embedded in the document for a hard page break is:
   a. [HPg]
   b. [HPgBrk]
   c. [Hard Page]
   d. [Page Brk]
7. In the List Files function, feature 6 will
   a. retrieve the document into memory
   b. allow the user to look at the entire document, without retrieving it into memory
   c. not allow the user to do any editing in the document
   d. both b and c
8. "Suppress (this page only)" will
   a. allow the user to cancel all headers and/or footers
   b. allow the user to cancel specific headers
   c. allow the user to cancel specific footers
   d. all of the above

STUDENT ASSIGNMENT 3: Matching

Instructions: Put the appropriate number next to the words in the second column.

1. Delete a file   _____ Shift-F8, 2, 5
2. Conditional end of page _____ Ctrl-Enter
3. Macro define   _____ 2 on List Files menu
4. Look option on List
   Files menu   _____ Shift-F5, 2
5. Date format   _____ 6 on List Files menu
6. Hard page break   _____ Shift-F8, 4, 2
7. Retrieve a file   _____ 1 on List Files menu
8. Change top and
   bottom margins   _____ Ctrl-F10
9. Define a header   _____ Shift-F5, 3
10. Insert date code   _____ Shift-F8, 2, 3

STUDENT ASSIGNMENT 4: Understanding WordPerfect Commands

Instructions: Next to each command, describe its effect.

Command	Effect
Shift-F8, 4, 2	_____
Ctrl-F10	_____
Ctrl-Enter	_____
Shift- F8, 2, 5	_____
F5, Enter	_____
1 on List Files menu	_____
2 on List Files menu	_____
6 on List Files menu	_____
Shift-F8, 2, 9	_____
Shift-F8, 2, 3 or 4	_____

STUDENT ASSIGNMENT 5: Describing a Footer

Instructions: At the bottom of the following document is a footer created on WordPerfect. Describe in detail how that footer was created.

The Regional Occupational Program, commonly called ROP, is a cooperative educational effort between local school districts and the County Department of Education. Its purpose is to train high school youth to become gainfully employed.

ROP has served and trained over 95,000 students in some 42 trades since 1988.

ROP plays an important role in the application of basic skills in the world of work, endeavoring to assist the unskilled and under-trained to become gainfully employed. ROP works in cooperation with 1,054 local businesses in the community to provide students on-the-job training. About 500 members of business and industry are involved in an advisory committee role to assure meaningful job skill training, a verified labor market demand, and a high potential for student placement in every course offered through ROP.

Important features of the Regional Occupational Program are:

1. Students from many schools meet at a centralized classroom. The teacher has a credential in the field being taught plus at least 5 years of directly related work experience.

2. Students are assigned to business training sites to receive realistic on-the-job skill development. An individualized training plan is developed for each student at each job training site.

3. Periodically students return to the classroom for additional training and to review progress from an employment point of view.

Courses are offered three semesters during the year. Enrollment time varies depending on the course topic or trade area. Some programs permit entry on any day, others at the start of each semester.

Regional Occupational Program   Page number 1

STUDENT ASSIGNMENT 6: Identifying the List Files Menu

Instructions: Look at this screen of a List Files menu. Circle the following areas and place the identifying number within the circle.

1. Amount of free disk space
2. Columns with names of files
3. Columns with names of extensions
4. Number of bytes used for files
5. Dates files were made
6. Directory of files

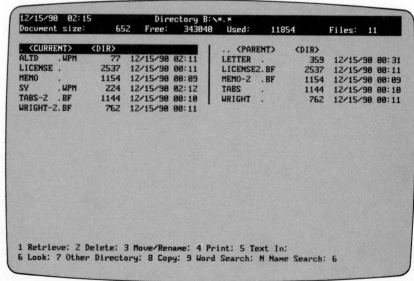

STUDENT ASSIGNMENT 7: Identifying Codes

Instructions: This screen shows several codes. Circle the entire code and identify it with the appropriate number from the list below.

1. Left/Right margin setting
2. Header
3. Tab setting
4. Date code
5. Suppress (this page only)
6. Hard page break
7. Top/Bottom margin setting
8. Conditional End of Page
9. Footer

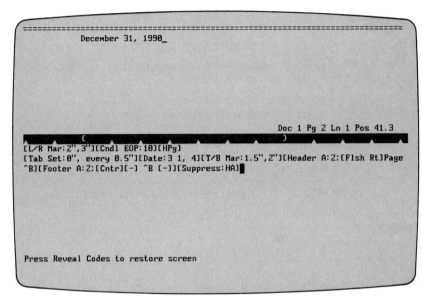

STUDENT ASSIGNMENT 8: Making a Macro

Instructions: This heading will be used frequently.

```
Robert B. Jones
Attorney
Jones, Richards, and Smith
534 Harrison Blvd.
Salt Lake City, UT 84106
```

Problem 1: Define the heading as a macro. Define the name as HEAD. Describe the macro as "name heading".
Problem 2: Practice retrieving the heading with Alt-F10.
Problem 3: Print the page of typing.

STUDENT ASSIGNMENT 9: Making a Macro

Instructions: Here is an ending that will be used frequently.

Problem 1: Define the ending as a macro. Define the name by using Alt-M. Describe the macro as "letter ending".
Problem 2: Practice retrieving the ending with Alt-M.
Problem 3: Print the page of typing.

```
Sincerely yours,


Robert B. Jones
Attorney
Jones, Richards, and Smith

RBJ/rg
```

STUDENT ASSIGNMENT 10: Modifying a Document

Instructions: Perform the following tasks.

1. For hard disk systems, load WordPerfect as you are directed by your instructor.
   For two disk drive systems, load DOS into main memory. Remove the DOS disk, and replace it with the WordPerfect disk. Type wp and press Enter.
2. Verify that the status line is in inches format and that the default drive is set to drive A for hard disk systems or drive B for two disk drive systems. Check to be sure that you have defined the Standard Printer as we did in Project 1. Begin this project on a clean screen.

Problem 1:
1. Retrieve the file named Regional.
2. Change the margins to 1 1/2" on the left and 1" on the right.
3. Delete all existing tabs. Set tab stops at 2" and 2.4".
4. Change the line spacing to 2.
5. Create a footer as follows:
   Regional Occupational Program (flush left)
   Page number (flush right)
6. Suppress the footer for the first page only.

Problem 2: Save the new document to disk under the new name of Regional.3.
Problem 3: Print the revised document; it should look like the document below.

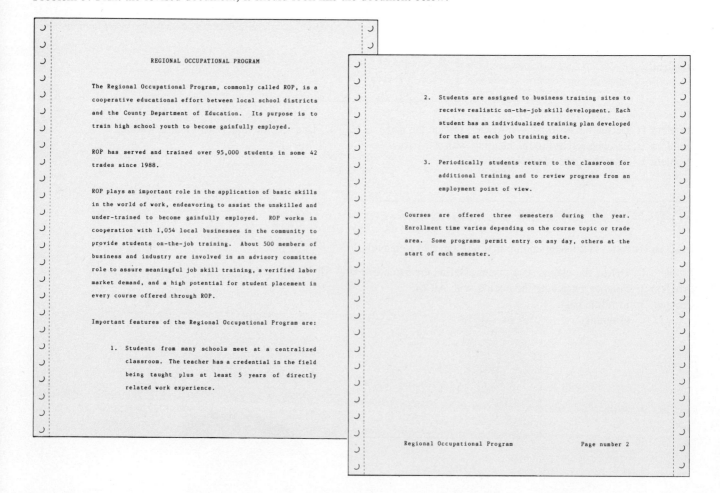

PROJECT 6

Advanced WordPerfect Features

Objectives

You will have mastered the material in this project when you can:

- Search and reverse search the text of a document
- Employ the search and replace function
- Practice using the thesaurus and speller demonstration example

*I*f you are working on a hard disk system, load WordPerfect as your instructor directs you. If you are working on a two disk drive system, at the A> prompt (with the WordPerfect disk in drive A and the data disk in drive B), type wp and press Enter. WordPerfect loads into main memory. As in Project 1, verify that the status line is in inches format. Also as in Project 1, verify that the default drive is set to drive A for hard disk systems, or drive B for a two disk drive system. You should then see a clean screen with only the status line in the lower right corner, indicating Doc 1 Pg 1 Ln 1" Pos 1".

Check to be sure that you have defined the Standard Printer as we did in Project 1. Retrieve License.2, the document you saved in Project 5, by pressing Shift-F10. Type the name License.2 and press Enter ↵. The document appears on the screen.

Let's assume that we must modify this document because PerSoft Inc. has been acquired by a company called UMC Corp. The modified document to be prepared is shown in Figure 6-1. Six changes must be made to the existing licensing agreement so that it can be used for the new company's products:

1. Remove the one-and-one-half spacing.
2. Emphasize the fact that the company assumes no responsibility.
3. Change the word License to License Agreement in section c.
4. Replace all occurrences of the name Per-Soft Inc. with the name UMC Corp.
5. Switch the order of the first and second paragraphs.
6. Switch the order of the two sentences in section a.

FIGURE 6-1

SEARCH FUNCTIONS

Searching for Codes

Before you begin manipulating text in the license, you decide that you do not want the document double-spaced. Knowing that a code was inserted, you can **search** or look for that code among the reveal codes. But instead of manually searching for it, you can issue a command in WordPerfect to have the program search for you. A search can be conducted within or outside the reveal codes screen. In this case, let's search in reveal codes, so press Alt-F3. Look at the template next to the F2 key. Notice the word Search in black. Press the F2 key. The message "→Srch:" appears on your screen. Notice that the arrow is pointing forward, indicating a forward search. To search for a code, you must invoke it the way you invoked the original code. Recall that spacing is invoked by pressing Shift-F8 and then number 1 for Line Format. The screen in Figure 6-2 appears.

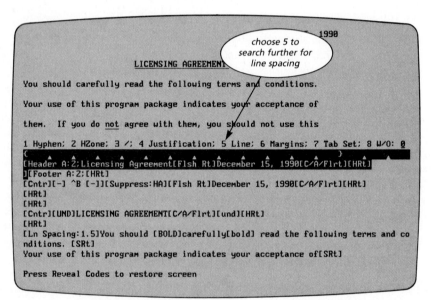

FIGURE 6-2

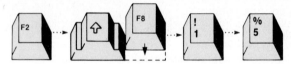

Since you do not see the line spacing option on this screen, you must seach further in Line Format. Press 5 and the screen in Figure 6-3 appears. For Line Spacing press the number 3.

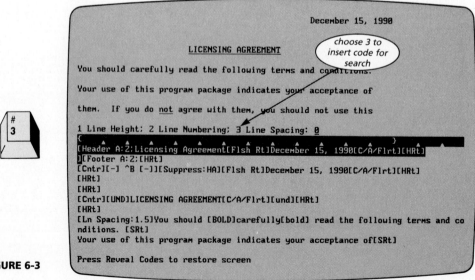

FIGURE 6-3

Figure 6-4 shows that your screen now displays the search command followed by the invoked code **[Ln Spacing]**. To invoke the search, press F2. Your tendency will be to press the Enter key. But if you do that a [HRt] code will be inserted, and you will need to backspace to delete the [HRt] code.

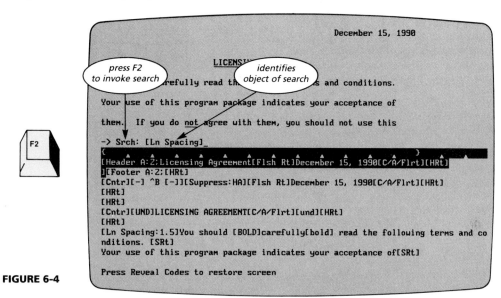

FIGURE 6-4

As you press the F2 key, notice that the cursor moves to the right of the first code it finds (Figure 6-5).

To delete the code, press the Backspace key (step 1 in Figure 6-5). Because there may be more than one spacing code, you want to continue the search. To be sure there are no more spacing set codes, press the F2 key again. The code "[Ln Spacing]" will appear again to remind you that you are searching for spacing set codes. Press the F2 key again to continue the search. If you find any more line spacing codes, delete them. When the prompt "* Not Found *" appears, you are assured that all spacing codes have been deleted. Press Alt-F3 to exit the reveal codes screen.

Step 1: Delete the code

Step 2: Continue to search if other codes exits

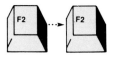

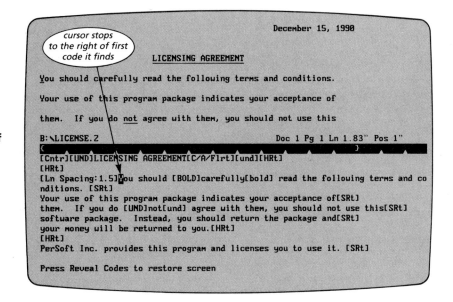

FIGURE 6-5

Forward Search

Move the cursor to the top of the document by pressing Home, Home, Up Arrow.

In the second paragraph of the document, you wish to emphasize the fact that the company assumes no responsibility. You can do this by searching for the word assumes and inserting the word absolutely, so the phrase will read: assumes absolutely no responsibility. To search forward for the word assumes, press the F2 key. The last command to search for, Ln Spacing code, is still within brackets next to the search forward prompt. But you do not wish to use that command. Type the word assumes, because that is the object of your search (step 1 in Figure 6-6). The code "Ln Spacing" is deleted and the word assumes appears next to the Srch: command. To begin the search, press the F2 key (step 2 in Figure 6-6). The cursor moves immediately to the right of the word. Press the spacebar and type the word absolutely.

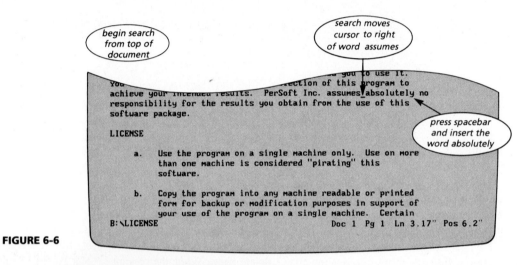

FIGURE 6-6

Step 1: Specify the object of the search

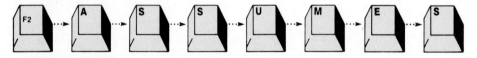

Step 2: Begin the search

Reverse Search

Move the cursor to the bottom of the document by pressing Home, Home, Down Arrow. At the end of section c is the word License, which you want to change to License Agreement. You may search backward with the Reverse Search key, which is Shift-F2. Press Shift-F2, and you will see the message "←Srch:" at the bottom left corner of the screen. Notice that the arrow points in the reverse direction, indicating that the search will be going backward from the cursor position. Type the word license in all lowercase letters. This causes WordPerfect to search for a word in lowercase, uppercase, or a combination of the two. If, however, you type in uppercase or both uppercase and lowercase letters, WordPerfect will look only for those exact characters. Press the F2 key to begin the search. The cursor stops at the first license it finds, even though it is in uppercase letters. This is not the one you wish to change. To continue the search backward through the document, press Shift-F2, then press F2 again. The cursor stops again at the word license but it is still not the one you desire. To continue, press Shift-F2, then the F2 key. The cursor stops at the desired spot. Press the spacebar and type the word Agreement. The period moves to the right as the word is inserted into the text (Figure 6-7).

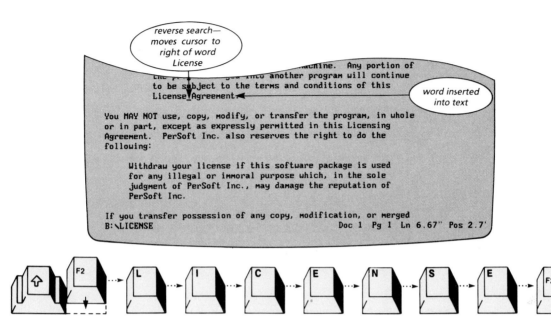

FIGURE 6-7

Search and Replace

Move the cursor to the top of the document by pressing Home, Home, Up Arrow.

WordPerfect provides commands that allow you to search the document for specific characters and, after finding these characters, automatically replace them with other characters. This series of commands is called **Search and Replace**.

Recall that we are changing the document named License because the company for which the document was prepared, PerSoft Inc., has been acquired by a company called UMC Corp. Look at the template next to the F2 key. Notice the word Replace in blue. Press Alt-F2. A prompt message appears asking if you want to confirm each occurrence of the change. Type the letter Y for yes. You are prompted with "→Srch:". Type the name PerSoft Inc. (Figure 6-8).

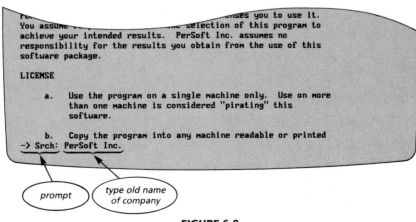

FIGURE 6-8

Press F2 to produce the prompt "Replace with:" (Figure 6-9).

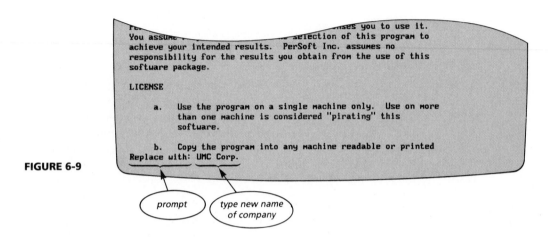

FIGURE 6-9

Type the name UMC Corp., then press the F2 key again. The cursor stops at the first occurrence of PerSoft Inc. and prompts "Confirm? (Y/N) No" (Figure 6-10). [For 5.1 Users – The prompt will be "Confirm? **No** (**Yes**)".] You may see the message "please wait" prior to seeing the prompt. Type the letter Y to change the name. The name will change and the cursor will move to the next occurrence of the name PerSoft Inc. and prompt again "Confirm? (Y/N) No". Type Y and the process will repeat itself. At each occurrence of the name, to confirm type Y until the prompt no longer appears at the lower left corner of the screen. That is your indication that there are no more occurrences of the name PerSoft Inc.

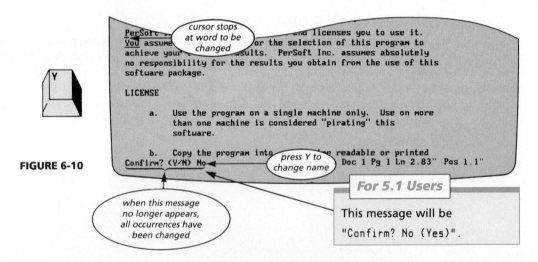

FIGURE 6-10

As you can see, you also could have typed N to not confirm each change. The WordPerfect software would have automatically made each change without stopping at each occurrence. You must be sure, however, that you do wish to change all occurrences of the searched-for word. For instance, you may have typed U.S. throughout a document and decided to change all occurrences of U.S. to United States. But you may have typed U.S. Grant for Ulysses S. Grant, in which case, had you not confirmed each change, his name would be changed to United States Grant. If you are *sure* all occurrences should be changed, there is no need to confirm.

MOVING TEXT WITHIN A DOCUMENT

Cut and Paste a Paragraph

*T*o move the cursor to the top of the document, press Home, Home, Up Arrow.

There are times when you wish to move text from one place in a document to another place. This is called **cut and paste**. Recall that you want to reverse paragraphs one and two. To **move** an entire paragraph, first you must move the cursor to the beginning of the paragraph. Press the Down Arrow to move to line 1.83", position 1" so that the cursor is under the Y in You in the first paragraph. Look at the template next to the F4 key. Notice the word Move in red. Press Ctrl-F4 (step 1 in Figure 6-11). The menu shown in Figure 6-11 gives you three options to move text, then an option to retrieve text. Notice the options to move a sentence, paragraph, or page. Type the number 2 for paragraph (step 2 in Figure 6-11).

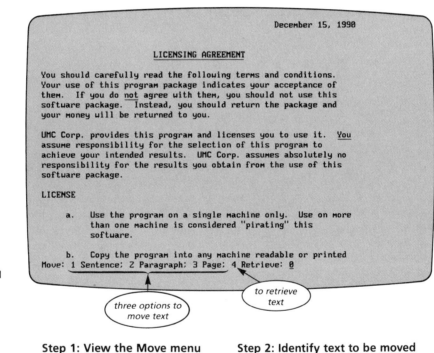

December 15, 1990

LICENSING AGREEMENT

You should carefully read the following terms and conditions. Your use of this program package indicates your acceptance of them. If you do <u>not</u> agree with them, you should not use this software package. Instead, you should return the package and your money will be returned to you.

UMC Corp. provides this program and licenses you to use it. <u>You</u> assume responsibility for the selection of this program to achieve your intended results. UMC Corp. assumes absolutely no responsibility for the results you obtain from the use of this software package.

LICENSE

    a.   Use the program on a single machine only. Use on more than one machine is considered "pirating" this software.

    b.   Copy the program into any machine readable or printed
Move: 1 Sentence; 2 Paragraph; 3 Page; 4 Retrieve: 0

three options to move text

to retrieve text

FIGURE 6-11

Step 1: View the Move menu

Step 2: Identify text to be moved

Figure 6-12 shows how the entire paragraph following the cursor is highlighted, indicating the text to be cut and pasted elsewhere. The figure also shows that at the bottom of the screen, you are given the options to move (cut), copy, or delete the highlighted text. Press the number 1 to cut the text for placement elsewhere (step 1 in Figure 6-12). The text of the highlighted first paragraph is cut and the second paragraph moves up to be in the first paragraph's position. Although the text of the first paragraph has been deleted from the screen, it has not been deleted from memory. Imagine that the text has been placed on a clipboard, and will be held there until the cursor has been moved to the desired new position, at which time you will retrieve the text from the clipboard.

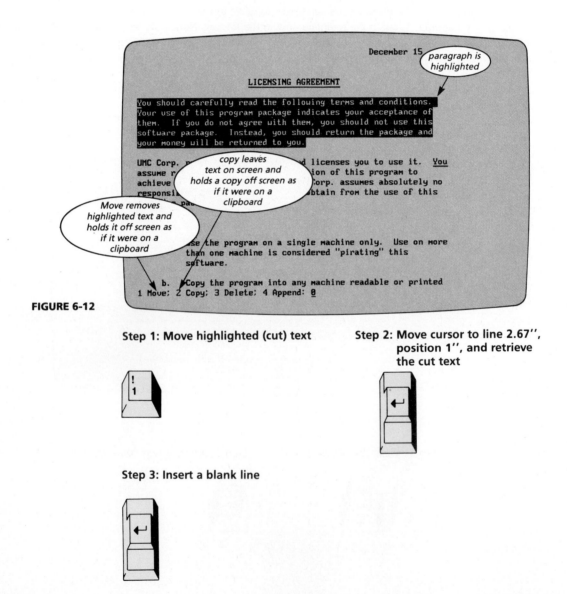

FIGURE 6-12

Step 1: Move highlighted (cut) text

Step 2: Move cursor to line 2.67'', position 1'', and retrieve the cut text

Step 3: Insert a blank line

Press the Down Arrow ↓ to move the cursor to line 2.67", position 1" so that it is on a blank line above the word License. When the text is retrieved, text will be moved down to make room for the incoming paragraph. Now, to retrieve the text that was cut, press Enter. You can see that another hard return is needed between the paragraphs. Press Return ↵ to make a blank line. The cut text is inserted and text at the cursor is moved down. Now move the cursor to Line 3.83" Pos 1" and press Delete to remove the extra line. As you can see, if a code or text is not moved in cut and paste, it can be added after the text is retrieved.

Cut and Paste a Block

Sometimes you may wish to move a specific block of text rather than a whole sentence, paragraph, or page. To illustrate this, you will reverse the two sentences of section a. Move the cursor down to line 4.17", position 6.3" so that it is under the U in the word Use (if you only inserted one space between the sentences, the cursor would be on position 6.2").

As you have learned, to turn the block on, press Alt-F4 and notice the message "Block on" flashing in the lower left corner of the screen. To highlight the sentence you can either move the cursor to the right one character at a time or press the Down Arrow key two times ↓ ↓ to highlight the entire sentence, as shown in Figure 6-13.

Using the block function, you can be exact about the text you wish to cut and paste. To learn another way to move the cursor when the block is on, first, press F1 to stop the flashing Block on. To return to the last cursor position, press the Go to command, Ctrl-Home, then press Ctrl-Home again. [For 5.1 Users – Move the cursor to Ln 4.17" Pos 6.3".] The cursor should be under the U in Use. Turn the block function on again by pressing Alt-F4. With Block on flashing, you can move the cursor directly to a character or code by pressing the desired character or code. Press a period (.) and notice that the cursor moves directly to the first period it finds and blocks the text to that point.

FIGURE 6-13

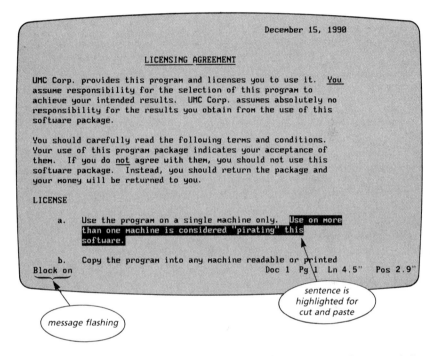

message flashing

sentence is highlighted for cut and paste

To move this highlighted or blocked text, press Ctrl-F4. The message "Move: 1 Block 2 Tabular Column 3 Rectangle" appears. Press 1 for Block (Figure 6-14).

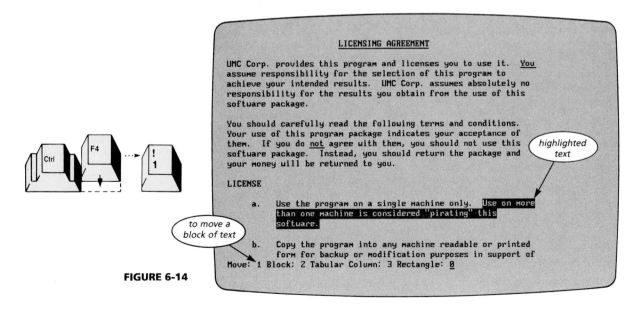

highlighted text

to move a block of text

FIGURE 6-14

Press 1 to move the block (step 1 in Figure 6-15). Move the cursor to line 4.17", position 2" under the U in Use. To retrieve the text from the "clipboard," press Enter ↵ (step 2 in Figure 6-15). The text needs to be rewritten [For 5.1 Users – The text is automatically rewritten.], so press Ctrl-F3 and then Enter, and the paragraph is properly rewritten (step 3 in Figure 6-15).

Step 1: Move the block

Step 2: Move cursor, and retrieve and insert cut text

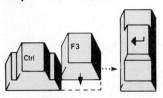

Step 3: Rewrite the text

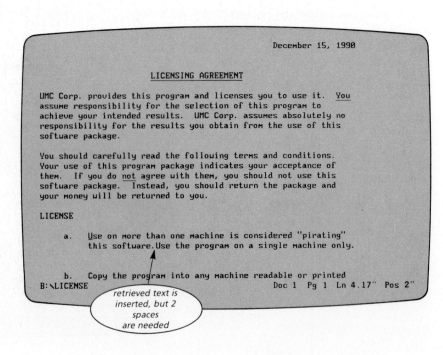

FIGURE 6-15

Figure 6-16 shows no spaces between the first and second sentence. If you have spaces between the first and second sentences, it is not necessary to add any more. However, if you have no spaces, move the cursor down one line and to the right, under the U in Use. Press the spacebar two times to insert the two needed spaces. Press the Down Arrow key two times ↓ ↓ to reformat the text.

FIGURE 6-16

SAVING THE DOCUMENT UNDER A NEW NAME

Now that the document has been changed, you decide that you wish to leave the document as it is on the disk, saved as it was in Project 5. You also wish to save this new version of the document. Therefore, as you save this document, you must give it another name. Look at the template by the F10 key. Notice the word Save in black. Press the F10 key. At the prompt "Document to be Saved:", type License.3 and press the Enter ↵ key. The document is saved under the new name.

PRINTING A DOCUMENT

Now that you have saved your document, it is ready to be printed. Before you print the document, however, let's view it to see how it will appear when printed. Press Shift-F7 for the print menu. Press number 6 for View Document. The screen shown in Figure 6-17 appears, and you can tell that the document will be printed as you wish. To return to the document, press F7. If you press F1 for cancel, you are returned to the Print menu. With the document on your screen, press Shift-F7. You again see the Print menu. Press number 1 for full text. At this point the printer will begin printing your document. The printed document generated is illustrated in Figure 6-1 at the beginning of this project.

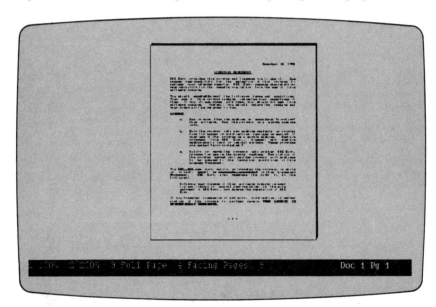

FIGURE 6-17

EXITING A DOCUMENT

Your document has been saved to disk and printed. It is now necessary to exit the document and clear the screen, but not exit the WordPerfect program.

Press the F7 key. At the prompt "Save Document? (Y/N) Yes", type N because the document has already been saved. At the prompt "Exit WP? (Y/N) No", type N. The document is exited and a clear screen appears.

THE THESAURUS

A thesaurus is a collection of words and their synonyms and antonyms. We will use the WordPerfect thesaurus to choose different words for a famous saying. If you are using a two disk drive system, remove the data disk from drive B and replace it with the WordPerfect Thesaurus disk. If you are using a hard disk system, you do not need to change disks. To learn how to use the thesaurus, first type: Fools rush in where angels fear to tread.

Move the cursor under the F in Fools. Look at the template next to the F1 key. Notice the word Thesaurus in blue. Press Alt-F1. Figure 6-18 shows the list of nouns (n), verbs (v), and antonyms (ant) that relate to the word Fools. A letter of the alphabet is next to each word in the first column, which will facilitate choosing a replacement for the word Fools. The words with dots are called **headwords**. If you wish to see other possible choices you can look up a word using one of the headwords. Press the number 3. The prompt "Word:" appears in the lower left corner of the screen. Type the word idiot and press Enter ↵.

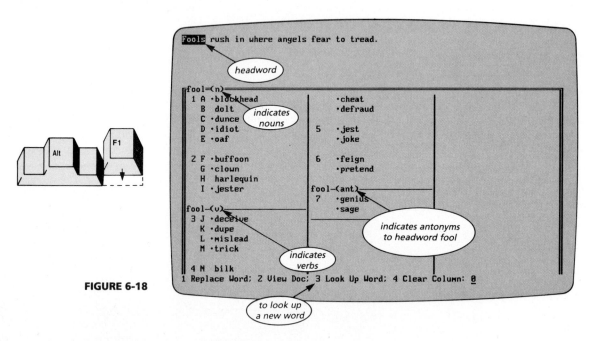

FIGURE 6-18

The screen will look like Figure 6-19. Notice that the second column shows the word idiot as the headword, giving synonyms and an antonym. The letter choices have moved from the first column to the second column. To look for more choices, press the number 3 again, then type the word simpleton and press Enter ↵.

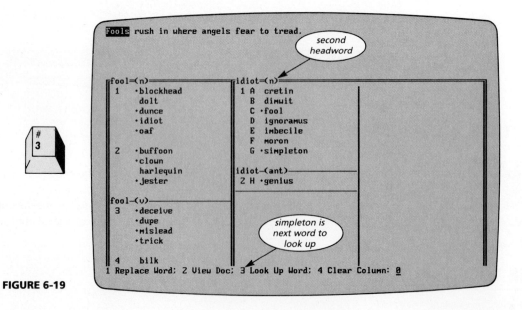

FIGURE 6-19

Figure 6-20 shows that the third column is now headed by the word simpleton and that the letters for choices have moved to the third column. Because you do not wish to use any of the words in columns two or three, press the Left Arrow ← to move the letter choices to the middle column. Instead of moving the cursor again to the left, notice that option number 4 is to clear a column. Type the number 4 and notice how the simpleton list is moved from column three to column two and that the letter choices are by the words in column two. Type the number 4 again and the letter choices are moved to column one (step 1 in Figure 6-20). Notice that the word clown is next to the letter G. To replace the word Fools with Clown, press the number 1. The prompt "Press letter for word" appears on the screen. Press the letter G and notice that the word Fools is replaced by the word Clown. Type an s to make clown plural (step 2 in Figure 6-20). Because the word you are replacing, Fools, begins with a capital letter, the lowercase c in clown in the thesaurus will become uppercase when inserted into the document.

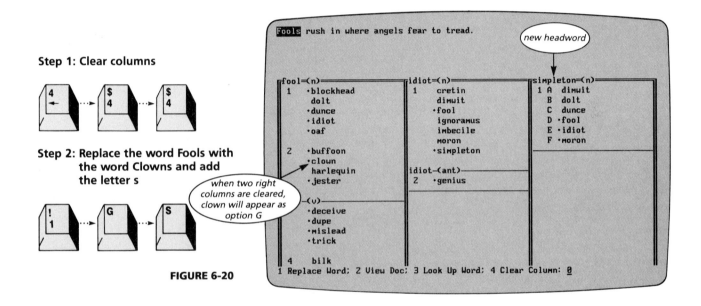

Step 1: Clear columns

Step 2: Replace the word Fools with the word Clowns and add the letter s

when two right columns are cleared, clown will appear as option G

FIGURE 6-20

Continue practicing with the thesaurus. Press the Right Arrow → to move to the word angels. Press Alt-F1. Synonyms and an antonym appear on the screen (Figure 6-21).

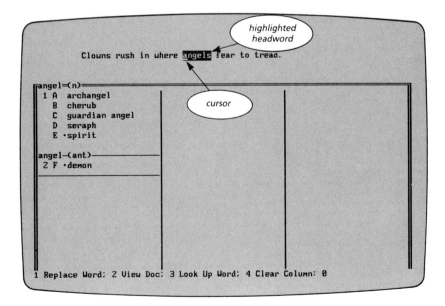

FIGURE 6-21

Press the number 1 to replace the word. Type the letter c and notice how angels changes to guardian angel. Type an s to make angel plural. Figure 6-22 shows how the corrected sentence appears. To exit this screen without saving the sentence on the screen, press F7 to exit, press N not to save the document, then press N not·to exit WordPerfect. A clean screen appears. If you are using a two disk drive system, replace the Thesaurus disk in drive B with your data disk.

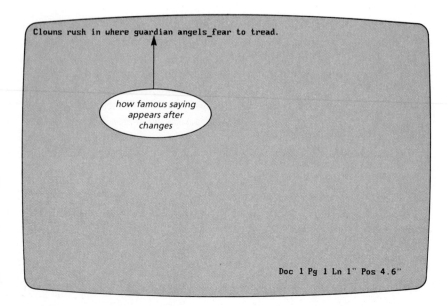

FIGURE 6-22

THE SPELLER

Many word processing programs include a **speller**, a feature that checks the spelling of words you have typed. To demonstrate the WordPerfect speller, first type the following sample paragraph *exactly* as you see it. Be sure to include all of the errors.

December 31st, 1990
We hold theese truths to be self-evedent, that all men are are created equal, that they are endoud by their Creator with certain unalienable rights, that maong these are life, liberty andthe prusuit of happiness. That to secure these rights, Gvermnts are instituted among men, deriving their just powers from the consent of the governed.

Save this paragraph to the disk under the name Speller. If you are using a two disk drive system, after you have saved the paragraph, remove the data disk from drive B and replace it with the WordPerfect Speller disk. If you are using a hard disk system, you do not need to change disks.

Look at the template next to the F2 key. Notice the word Spell in red. Press Ctrl-F2. Figure 6-23 shows the menu at the bottom of the screen. Since the sample paragraph has only one page of typing, press the number 2 for Page.

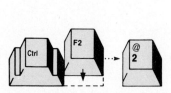

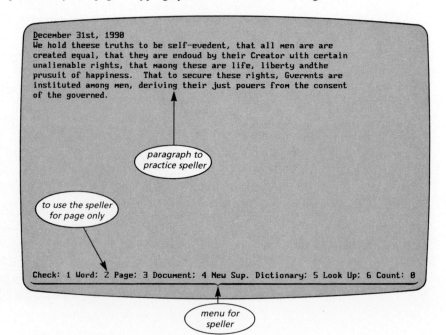

FIGURE 6-23

Each word on the page will be matched against the words in the speller. If the WordPerfect speller does not recognize a word, it scans its dictionary containing almost 120,000 words. If a word is not in its dictionary, the word will be highlighted. Then a list will appear from which you can make a choice of what you wish to do with that particular highlighted word. If you do not wish to use any of the choices listed, you must make a choice from the menu at the bottom of the screen. In the event that the highlighted word is a word you want to add to the dictionary, you can press the number 3. Once a word is added it will not be highlighted in future spell-checking.

The first word to be highlighted is 31st, because the WordPerfect Speller does not recognize words that mix letters and numbers. Look at the menu on the screen. If you were to choose the number 6, the speller would ignore all words in your document that contain both numbers and letters. You will not select number 6 here. Because the word 31st is correct in this paragraph, you should skip over it without changing it. WordPerfect provides you with two choices to skip over text. Number 1 skips over the word once, then picks it up if it appears again. Number 2 skips over all occurrences of this word for this spell check only. Because you know that 31st appears only once, press number 1 to skip over it without changing it. The speller then skips over 31st and highlights the next word it does not recognize.

The next word to be highlighted is the misspelled word theese (Figure 6-24). Press the letter A, then notice on the screen how the misspelling is corrected and evedent, the next misspelled word, is highlighted. Some choices appear. Press the letter A again to correct the word.

Next you see that the same two words were typed together. The speller recognizes

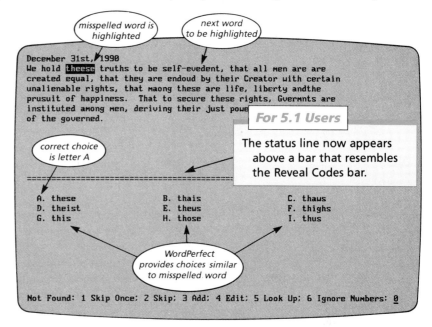

FIGURE 6-24

double words and gives you the menu shown in Figure 6-25. There are times when you purposely type two words together, such as in the sentence I had had enough. In that case you would skip over the double words. In the case shown on the screen, the second are is not needed, so press the number 3. The second are is deleted and the next word to be highlighted as misspelled is endoud. Press the letter D, for the word endowed to correct the misspelling.

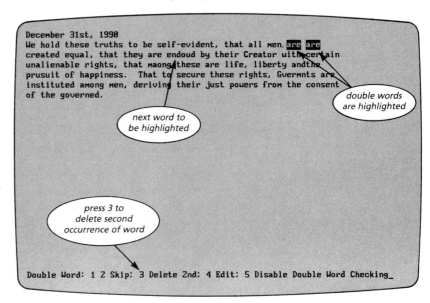

FIGURE 6-25

The next word to be highlighted is maong, which should be among (Figure 6-26). Press the letter A for among.

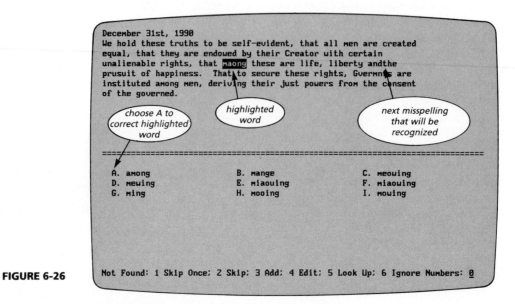

FIGURE 6-26

Next to be highlighted are the words andthe, which were typed with no space in between. The speller recognizes this as a misspelling but cannot find it in its word lists. Since you know what the problem is, you can correct the error. Press the number 4 for Edit and the cursor moves to the beginning of the misspelled word. Press the Right Arrow → three times to move the cursor under the t in the. Press the spacebar to insert a space between the words (Figure 6-27). As noted on the screen, press F7 when done. The speller recognizes the two words as correct and moves on to highlight the word prusuit. Press the letter A to correct the word.

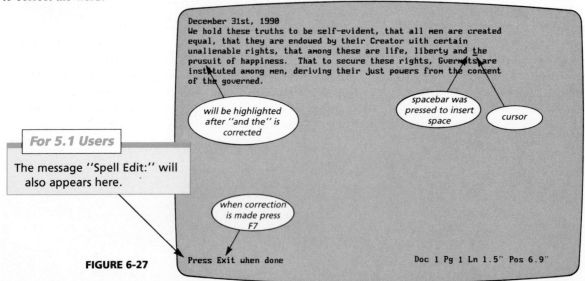

FIGURE 6-27

The next word that the speller does not recognize is Gvermnts (Figure 6-28). Although the word governments is in the speller, there are not enough vowels in the misspelling for the speller to recognize it and give you an option on the lower screen. If you were not sure how to spell this word and were typing on a typewriter, you would probably go to the dictionary and look up the word. In WordPerfect you can also *look up* a misspelled word. Look at the menu at the bottom of the screen. Press the number 5 for Look Up. The prompt ''Word or word pattern:'' appears on the screen. Type the word gov*ts. Because you know the word begins with gov and ends with ts, but you may not be sure what is in between, you place the asterisk (*)

between the beginning and the end. As you learned in *Introduction to DOS*, the asterisk is a global command. Using it in the look-up function causes WordPerfect to look in its dictionary for all words that begin with gov and end with ts, no matter how many letters are in between. If you were to type g*s it would look for all words that begin with g and end with s. You can see there probably would be many more words given as an option if you were to type g*s. If you are not sure how a word ends, you could also type gov* and the speller would look for all the words that begin with gov no matter what the ending. Using the question mark can also help, but the question mark can only stand in the place of one character. For instance, the word pattern could be gover?ments and the speller would find the n where the question mark is. Since the asterisk stands for one or more characters, it is better to use the asterisk.

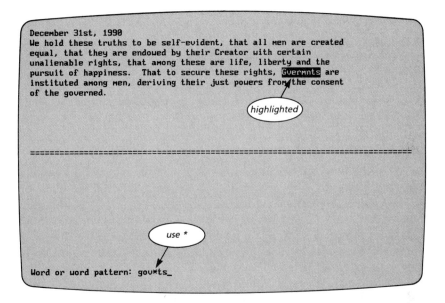

FIGURE 6-28

With gov*ts on the screen as the word pattern, press the Enter ↵ key. The word governments is shown under the letter A. Press the letter A and the word is spelled correctly in the document. Because the word you are replacing begins with a capital letter, the lowercase g in government in the speller will become uppercase when inserted into the document.

Since there are no more misspelled words, the speller reviews how many words it has spell-checked and displays that number on the screen as the word count (Figure 6-29).

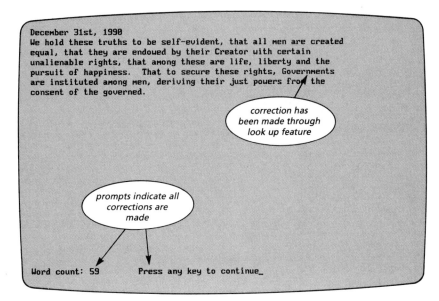

FIGURE 6-29

Press the spacebar to continue. The original menu appears again and shows that you have the option to look up a word directly from the speller without having it highlighted in a document. The option is number 5, the same option you use when looking up the spelling of a word. To exit from the speller, press the spacebar. You are returned to your document. If you are using a two disk drive system, replace the Speller disk in drive B with your data disk.

It is important to remember that all corrections that you made to your document with the speller have been made only in the memory of the computer and have not been saved to disk. Immediately after checking the spelling of a document, save and replace the corrected version to the disk. Then exit the WordPerfect program by pressing F7, N to save the document, and finally Y to exit WordPerfect.

PROJECT SUMMARY

 *I*n Project 6 you learned how to use the search function, the reverse search function, search and replace, and the move function. You used these functions to make changes to your document. In addition, you learned how to use the Word-Perfect thesaurus and speller to change words in your document and to correct misspelled words.

The following list summarizes the material covered in Project 6:

1. The **search** function allows you to find a character, a code, or a string of text within a document.
2. **Search and replace**, also known as a global search and replace, allows you to look for every occurrence of a specified character, code, or string of text and either delete them or replace them with another specified code or text.
3. The **move** function allows you to highlight a specific block of text, then cut or copy the text, move it to another part of the document or to another document, and retrieve the cut or copied text.
4. The **thesaurus** allows you to point to a specific word, then invoke a search for possible replacement words. The thesaurus displays not only synonyms but also antonyms for the marked word. Use **headword** to look up other words in the thesaurus.
5. The **speller** provided with WordPerfect has a dictionary of almost 120,000 words with which it checks the spelling of the words in a document. You can add up to 20,000 words to the speller.

The following is a list of the keystroke sequence we used in Project 6. These keystrokes assume that the status line is in inches format and the default drive is set to save the files to a diskette. Check to be sure that you have defined the Standard Printer as we did in Project 1.

SUMMARY OF KEYSTROKES—Project 6

STEPS	KEY(S) PRESSED	STEPS	KEY(S) PRESSED	STEPS	KEY(S) PRESSED
1	[Be in WP at a blank screen]	47	[↓ to line 2.67″, position 1″ under L in License]	92	[→ to the word angels]
2	Shift-F10	48	↵	93	Alt-F1
3	License.2	49	↵	94	1
4	↵	50	[↓ to line 3.83″, position 1″]	95	C
5	Alt-F3	51	Delete	96	s
6	F2	52	[↓ then → to line 4.17″, position 6.3″ under U in Use]	97	F7
7	Shift-F8			98	N
8	1	53	Alt-F4	99	N
9	5	54	↓	100	December 31st, 1990
10	3	55	↓		We hold theese truths to be self-evedent, that all men are are created equal, that they are endoud by their Creator with certain unalienable rights, that maong these are life, liberty andthe prusuit of happiness. That to secure these rights, Gvermnts are instituted among men, deriving their just powers from the consent of the governed.
11	F2	56	Ctrl-F4		
12	Backspace	57	1		
13	F2	58	1		
14	F2 [″Not Found″ should appear on screen]	59	[← to line 4.17″, position 2″ under U in Use]		
15	Alt-F3	60	↵		
16	Home Home ↑	61	[↓ then → to U in Use]		
17	F2	62	Space		
18	assumes	63	Space	101	F10
19	F2	64	↓	102	speller
20	Space	65	↓	103	↵
21	absolutely	66	F10	104	Ctrl-F2
22	Home Home ↓	67	License.3	105	2
23	Shift-F2	68	↵	106	1
24	license	69	Shift-F7	107	A
25	F2	70	6 [view document]	108	A
26	Shift-F2	71	F7	109	3
27	F2	72	Shift-F7	110	D
28	Shift-F2	73	1 [wait for document to be printed]	111	A
29	F2			112	4
30	Space	74	F7	113	→
31	Agreement	75	N	114	→
32	Home Home ↑	76	N	115	→
33	Alt-F2	77	Fools rush in where angels fear to tread	116	Space
34	Y			117	F7
35	PerSoft Inc.	78	[position cursor under F in Fools]	118	A
36	F2			119	5
37	UMC Corp.	79	Alt-F1	120	gov*ts
38	F2	80	3	121	↵
39	Y	81	idiot	122	A
40	Y	82	↵	123	Space
41	[continue to type Y to change each occurrence of PerSoft Inc. to UMC Corp.]	83	3	124	Space
		84	simpleton	125	F10
		85	↵	126	↵
		86	←	127	y
42	Home Home ↑	87	4	128	F7
43	[↓ to line 1.83″, position 1″, under Y in You]	88	4	129	N
		89	1	130	Y
44	Ctrl-F4	90	G		
45	2	91	s		
46	1				

STUDENT ASSIGNMENTS

STUDENT ASSIGNMENT 1: True/False

Instructions: Circle T if the statement is true and F if the statement if false.

T F 1. When you invoke the search function, the cursor stops to the left of what you are searching for.
T F 2. A reverse search is invoked by pressing Shift-F2, typing what is to be searched for, then pressing F2.
T F 3. The search feature cannot search for codes embedded in the document.
T F 4. When moving text, either move (cut) or copy a block of text.
T F 5. The move function is invoked through Ctrl-F4.
T F 6. Alt-F1 will access the thesaurus.
T F 7. The reveal codes function can be accessed through Alt-F4.
T F 8. The speller will only spell words that are typed on the screen; it cannot look up words.

STUDENT ASSIGNMENT 2: Multiple Choice

Instructions: Circle the correct response.

1. The move function can
   a. move paragraphs
   b. move sentences
   c. move specific blocks of text
   d. all of the above
2. When invoking the search function and the desired code or words are defined, the user must
   a. press Enter
   b. press F2
   c. press Alt-F2
   d. press Shift-F2
3. When using the speller the user can
   a. look up a word by giving the word pattern
   b. skip over words whose spelling is not to be changed
   c. add words to the dictionary
   d. all of the above

STUDENT ASSIGNMENT 3: Matching

Instructions: Put the appropriate number next to the words in the second column.

1. Ctrl-F2 _____ Reverse Search
2. Ctrl-F4 _____ Search
3. Alt-F1 _____ Speller, Look Up
4. Ctrl-F2, 5 _____ Move function

5. Alt-F3 _____ Speller
6. F2 _____ Reveal codes
7. Shift-F2 _____ Thesaurus
8. Alt-F2 _____ Search and Replace

STUDENT ASSIGNMENT 4: Moving Text

Instructions: In the paragraph below, it is necessary to move the second sentence in the paragraph to be the first sentence. Describe in detail the steps to accomplish this.

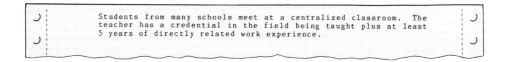

```
Students from many schools meet at a centralized classroom.  The
teacher has a credential in the field being taught plus at least
5 years of directly related work experience.
```

STUDENT ASSIGNMENT 5: Using Search and Replace

Instructions: Perform the following tasks.

1. For hard disk systems, load WordPerfect as you are directed by your instructor.

   For two disk drive systems, load DOS into main memory. Remove the DOS disk, and replace it with the WordPerfect disk. Type wp and press Enter.
2. Verify that the status line is in inches format, and that the default drive is set to drive A for hard disk systems or drive B for two disk drive systems. Check to be sure that you have defined the Standard Printer as we did in Project 1. Begin this project on a clean screen.

Problem 1:

1. Create the resume as shown at the right. The titles in the left column should be in boldface type. (Hint: Don't forget the Indent [F4] key, or the hanging indent function [F4, Shift-Tab].)
2. Save the document under the name Cook.
3. Print the document.

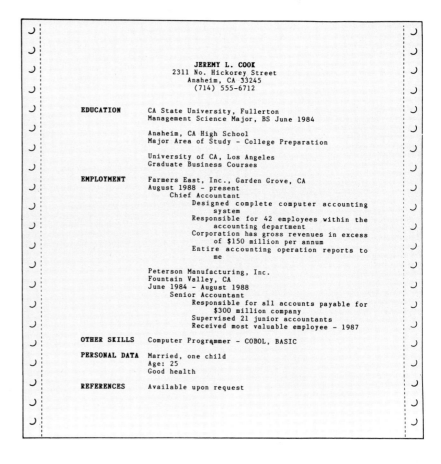

```
                         JEREMY L. COOK
                      2311 No. Hickorey Street
                         Anaheim, CA 33245
                         (714) 555-6712

     EDUCATION        CA State University, Fullerton
                      Management Science Major, BS June 1984

                      Anaheim, CA High School
                      Major Area of Study - College Preparation

                      University of CA, Los Angeles
                      Graduate Business Courses

     EMPLOYMENT       Farmers East, Inc., Garden Grove, CA
                      August 1988 - present
                         Chief Accountant
                            Designed complete computer accounting
                               system
                            Responsible for 42 employees within the
                               accounting department
                            Corporation has gross revenues in excess
                               of $150 million per annum
                            Entire accounting operation reports to
                               me

                      Peterson Manufacturing, Inc.
                      Fountain Valley, CA
                      June 1984 - August 1988
                         Senior Accountant
                            Responsible for all accounts payable for
                               $300 million company
                            Supervised 21 junior accountants
                            Received most valuable employee - 1987

     OTHER SKILLS     Computer Programmer - COBOL, BASIC

     PERSONAL DATA    Married, one child
                      Age: 25
                      Good health

     REFERENCES       Available upon request
```

Student Assignment 5 (continued)

Problem 2:

1. Beginning at the top of the document, search for all designations of CA and replace them with California. (Hint: Type Y to confirm.)
2. Save the document as Cook.2.
3. Print the document.

```
                         JEREMY L. COOK
                      2311 No. Hickorey Street
                      Anaheim, California 33245
                           (714) 555-6712

        EDUCATION      California State University, Fullerton
                       Management Science Major, BS June 1984

                       Anaheim, California High School
                       Major Area of Study - College Preparation

                       University of California, Los Angeles
                       Graduate Business Courses

        EMPLOYMENT     Farmers East, Inc., Garden Grove, California
                       August 1988 - present
                            Chief Accountant
                                 Designed complete computer accounting
                                     system
                                 Responsible for 42 employees within the
                                     accounting department
                                 Corporation has gross revenues in excess
                                     of $150 million per annum
                                 Entire accounting operation reports to
                                     me

                       Peterson Manufacturing, Inc.
                       Fountain Valley, California
                       June 1984 - August 1988
                            Senior Accountant
                                 Responsible for all accounts payable for
                                     $300 million company
                                 Supervised 21 junior accountants
                                 Received most valuable employee - 1987

        OTHER SKILLS   Computer Programmer - COBOL, BASIC

        PERSONAL DATA  Married, one child
                       Age: 25
                       Good health

        REFERENCES     Available upon request
```

STUDENT ASSIGNMENT 6: Modifying a Document with the Move Function

Instructions: Perform the following tasks.

1. For hard disk systems, load WordPerfect as you are directed by your instructor.

   For two disk drive systems, load DOS into main memory. Remove the DOS disk, and replace it with the WordPerfect disk. Type wp and press Enter.
2. Verify that the status line is in inches format, and that the default drive is set to drive A for hard disk systems or drive B for two disk drive systems. Check to be sure that you have defined the Standard Printer as we did in Project 1. Begin this project on a clean screen.

Problem 1:

1. Retrieve the document named Cook.2 created in Student Assignment 5.
2. Using the block function, move the whole section of type under EDUCATION to be second after the heading EMPLOY-MENT as shown below.

```
                              JEREMY L. COOK
                            2311 No. Hickorey Street
                            Anaheim, California 33245
                                (714) 555-6712

        EMPLOYMENT      Farmers East, Inc., Garden Grove, California
                        August 1988 - present
                            Chief Accountant
                                Designed complete computer accounting
                                    system
                                Responsible for 42 employees within the
                                    accounting department
                                Corporation has gross revenues in excess
                                    of $150 million per annum
                                Entire accounting operation reports to
                                    me

                        Peterson Manufacturing, Inc.
                        Fountain Valley, California
                        June 1984 - August 1988
                            Senior Accountant
                                Responsible for all accounts payable for
                                    $300 million company
                                Supervised 21 junior accountants
                                Received most valuable employee - 1987

        EDUCATION       California State University, Fullerton
                        Management Science Major, BS June 1984

                        Anaheim, California High School
                        Major Area of Study - College Preparation

                        University of California, Los Angeles
                        Graduate Business Courses

        OTHER SKILLS    Computer Programmer - COBOL, BASIC

        PERSONAL DATA   Married, one child
                        Age: 25
                        Good health

        REFERENCES      Available upon request
```

Problem 2: Save the document to disk as Cook.3.

Problem 3: Print the revised document.

STUDENT ASSIGNMENT 7: Using the Speller

Instructions: Perform the following tasks.

1. For hard disk systems, load WordPerfect as you are directed by your instructor.
   For two disk drive systems, load DOS into main memory. Remove the DOS disk, and replace it with the WordPerfect disk. Type wp and press Enter.
2. Verify that the status line is in inches format, and that the default drive is set to drive A for hard disk systems or drive B for two disk drive systems. Check to be sure that you have defined the Standard Printer as we did in Project 1. Begin this project on a clean screen.

Problem 1: Create the document exactly as written below, even the spelling errors.

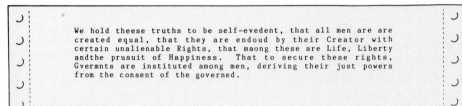

We hold theese truths to be self-evedent, that all men are are created equal, that they are endoud by their Creator with certain unalienable Rights, that maong these are Life, Liberty andthe prusuit of Happiness. That to secure these rights, Gvermnts are instituted among men, deriving their just powers from the consent of the governed.

Problem 2: Save the document to disk as Speller.

Problem 3: Print the document.

Problem 4: Invoke the speller and correct any misspellings.

Problem 5: Save the corrected document to disk as Speller.1.

Problem 6: Print the revised document.

STUDENT ASSIGNMENT 8: Using the Thesaurus

Instructions: Perform the following tasks.

1. For hard disk systems, load WordPerfect as you are directed by your instructor.
   For two disk drive systems, load DOS into main memory. Remove the DOS disk, and replace it with the WordPerfect disk. Type wp and press Enter.
2. Verify that the status line is in inches format, and that the default drive is set to drive A for hard disk systems or drive B for two disk drive systems. Check to be sure that you have defined the Standard Printer as we did in Project 1. Begin this project on a clean screen.

Problem 1: Type the sentence: Fools that rush to step on me.

Problem 2: Position the cursor under the word Fools. Invoke the Thesaurus. Press the Print Screen option to print a hard copy of the screen as shown below.

Problem 3: Repeat the process in problem 2 for the words rush and step, making a print screen hard copy as shown below.

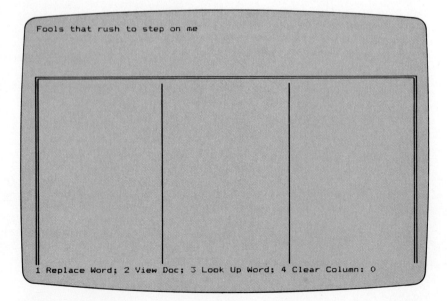

Fools that rush to step on me

1 Replace Word; 2 View Doc; 3 Look Up Word; 4 Clear Column: 0

WordPerfect Index

![black bar]

Spreadsheets Using Lotus 1-2-3 Release 2.2

PROJECT 1

Building a Worksheet

Objectives

You will have mastered the material in this Project when you can:

- Start 1-2-3
- Describe the worksheet
- Move the cell pointer around the worksheet
- Enter labels, numbers, and formulas into a worksheet
- Save a worksheet

- Print the screen image of the worksheet
- Correct errors in a worksheet
- Use the UNDO command
- Answer your questions regarding 1-2-3 using the online help facili
- Quit 1-2-3

 n Project 1 we will develop the worksheet illustrated in Figure 1-1. It contains a company's first quarter sales report. To build this worksheet, we will enter the revenues and costs for January, February, and March. 1-2-3 calculates the profit for each month by subtracting the cost from the revenue.

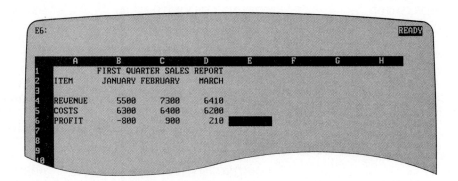

FIGURE 1-1
The worksheet we will build in
Project 1.

STARTING 1-2-3

B oot the computer following the procedures presented earlier in the Introduction to DOS. Next, follow the steps listed below if your computer has no fixed disk. If your computer has a fixed disk, follow the steps at the bottom of the next page. Several seconds will elapse while the 1-2-3 program is loaded from the disk into main computer memory. The red light on the disk drive turns on during this loading process. After 1-2-3 is loaded into main computer memory, it is automatically executed. The first screen displayed by 1-2-3 contains the copyright message shown in Figure 1-2. After a few seconds the copyright message disappears, leaving the worksheet illustrated in Figure 1-3.

Computer with No Fixed Disk Drive

To start 1-2-3 from a computer with no fixed disk drive, do the following:

1. Replace the DOS disk in drive A with the 1-2-3 system disk. If you have two disk drives, place your data disk in drive B.
2. At the A > prompt, type 123 and press the Enter key.
3. If you have only one disk drive, replace the system disk in drive A with your data disk after the program is loaded.

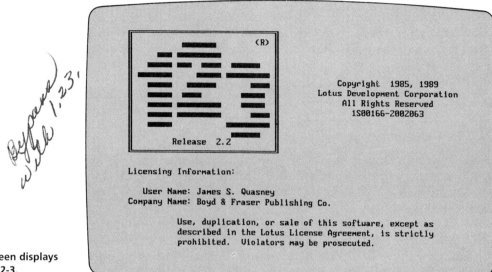

FIGURE 1-2
The copyright screen displays
when you load 1-2-3.

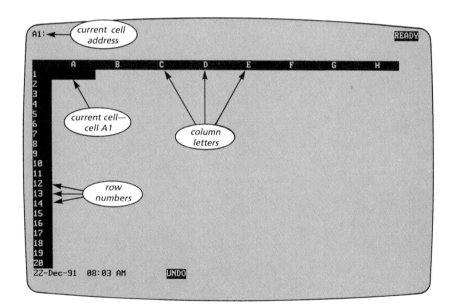

FIGURE 1-3
The worksheet.

Computer with a Fixed Disk Drive

To start 1-2-3 from a fixed disk drive, do the following:

1. Use the DOS command CD to change to the subdirectory containing the 1-2-3 program.
2. Place your data disk in drive A.
3. At the DOS prompt, type 123 and press the Enter key.

THE WORKSHEET

*T*he worksheet is organized into a rectangular grid containing columns (vertical) and rows (horizontal). In the border at the top, each **column** is identified by a column letter. In the border on the left side, each **row** is identified by a row number. As shown in Figure 1-3 on the previous page, eight columns (A to H) and twenty rows (1 to 20) of the worksheet appear on the screen.

Cell, Cell Pointer, and Window

Within the borders is the worksheet. It has three parts: cell, cell pointer, and window. A **cell** is the intersection of a column and a row. It is referred to by its **cell address**, the coordinates of the intersection of a column and a row. When you specify a cell address, you must name the column first, followed by the row. For example, cell address D3 refers to the cell located at the intersection of column D and row 3.

One cell on the worksheet is designated the current cell. The **current cell** is the one in which you can enter data. The current cell in Figure 1-3 is A1. It is identified in two ways. First, a reverse video rectangle called the **cell pointer** displays over the current cell. Second, the **current cell address** displays on the first of three lines at the top of the screen. It is important to understand the layout of the worksheet and how to identify all cells, including the current cell.

1-2-3 has 256 columns and 8,192 rows for a total of 2,097,152 cells. Only a small portion of the rectangular worksheet displays on the screen at any one time. For this reason, the area between the borders on the screen is called a **window**. Think of your screen as a window through which you can see parts of the worksheet as illustrated in Figure 1-4.

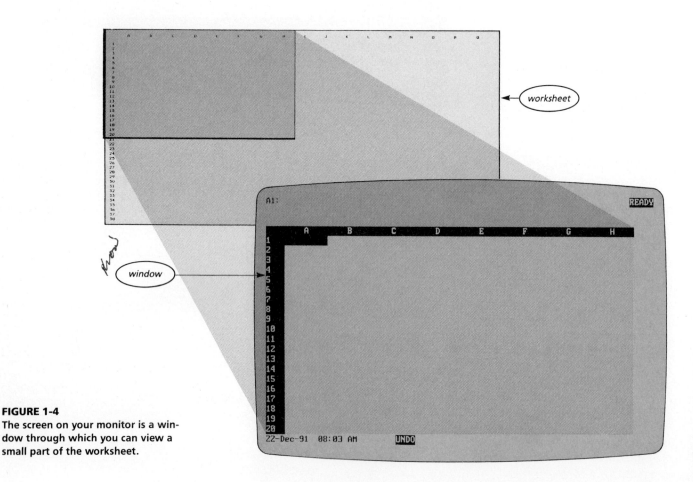

FIGURE 1-4
The screen on your monitor is a window through which you can view a small part of the worksheet.

The Control Panel and the Indicator Line

The three lines above the window at the top of the screen display important information about the worksheet. The three lines—status line, input line, and menu line—are collectively called the **control panel**. Below the window, at the bottom of the screen, is the indicator line. These four lines are illustrated in Figure 1-5.

Status Line   The first line in the control panel at the top of the screen is the **status line**. It identifies the current cell address and displays the mode of operation. If data is already in the current cell, the status line also shows the type of entry and its contents.

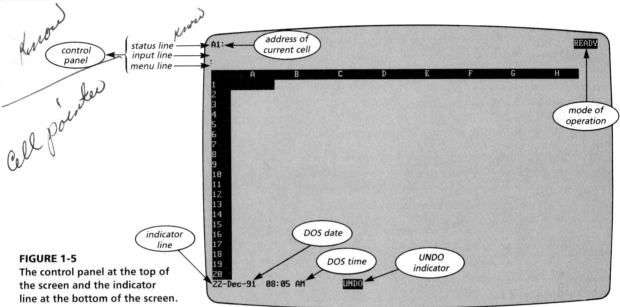

FIGURE 1-5
The control panel at the top of the screen and the indicator line at the bottom of the screen.

The mode of operation displays on the right side of the status line at the top of the screen. Mode indicators, like EDIT, ERROR, LABEL, MENU, POINT, READY, VALUE, and WAIT tell you the current mode of operation of 1-2-3. For now you should know that when the mode READY displays (Figure 1-5), 1-2-3 is ready to accept your next command or data entry. When the mode indicator WAIT displays in place of READY, 1-2-3 is busy performing some operation that is not instantaneous, like saving a worksheet to disk.

Input Line   Just below the status line is the input line. The **input line** displays one of three things: the characters you type as you enter data or edit cell contents; the command menu; or input prompts asking for additional command specifications.

Menu Line   The **menu line**, the third line in the control panel, displays information about the menu item highlighted on the input line when 1-2-3 is in the MENU mode.

Indicator Line   The line at the very bottom of the screen is the **indicator line**. It displays three items: the date, the time of day as maintained by DOS, and the status indicators of 1-2-3. Status indicators, like UNDO, CALC, CAPS, CIRC, END, NUM, OVR, and SCROLL, tell you which keys are engaged and alert you to special worksheet conditions. Note where the indicator UNDO appears at the bottom of Figure 1-5. When this indicator is on, you can use the UNDO command to restore the worksheet data and settings to what they were the last time 1-2-3 was in READY mode. We'll discuss this command in more detail later in this project.

MOVING THE CELL POINTER ONE CELL AT A TIME

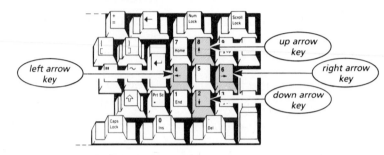

FIGURE 1-6 The arrow keys on the keyboard.

Before you can build a worksheet, you must learn how to move the cell pointer to the cells in which you want to make entries. Several methods let you easily move to any cell in the worksheet. The most popular method is to use the four arrow keys located on the numeric keypad. Figure 1-6 illustrates a numeric keypad on a computer keyboard.

On some computers, you have a choice of two sets of arrow keys. One set, as shown in Figure 1-6, is part of the numeric keypad. The other set is located just to the left of the numeric keypad. If you have two sets of arrow keys on the keyboard, the set to the left of the numeric keypad is always active. The set of arrow keys on the numeric keypad is active only when the **Num Lock key** is disengaged. You know that the Num Lock key is disengaged when the NUM indicator is not displayed on the indicator line at the bottom of the screen.

For these projects we will use the arrow keys located on the numeric keypad. The arrow keys work as follows:

1. **Down Arrow key** (↓) moves the cell pointer directly down one cell.
2. **Left Arrow key** (←) moves the cell pointer one cell to the left.
3. **Right Arrow key** (→) moves the cell pointer one cell to the right.
4. **Up Arrow key** (↑) moves the cell pointer directly up one cell.

In the sample worksheet in Figure 1-1, the title FIRST QUARTER SALES REPORT begins in cell B1. Therefore, we must move the cell pointer from cell A1, where it is when 1-2-3 starts, to cell B1 so we can enter the title. Do this by pressing the Right Arrow key one time, as shown in Figure 1-7. Notice that the current cell address on the status line in the upper left corner of the screen changes from A1 to B1. Remember, the current cell address on the status line always identifies the current cell—the one where the cell pointer is.

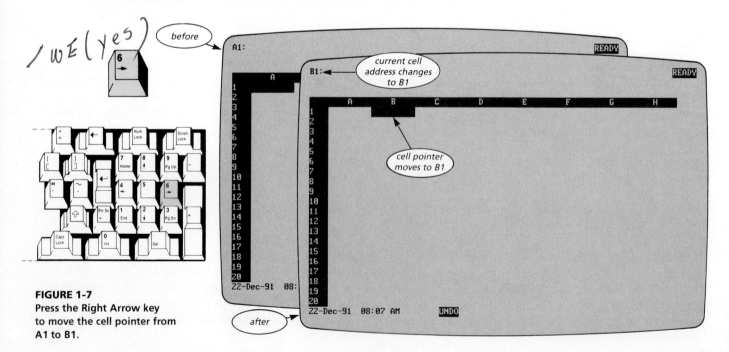

FIGURE 1-7
Press the Right Arrow key to move the cell pointer from A1 to B1.

ENTERING LABELS

With the cell pointer on the proper cell (B1), we can enter the title of the worksheet. In the title FIRST QUARTER SALES REPORT, all the letters are capitals. While it is possible to enter capital letters by holding down one of the Shift keys on the keyboard each time we type a letter, a more practical method is to press the **Caps Lock key** one time (Figure 1-8).

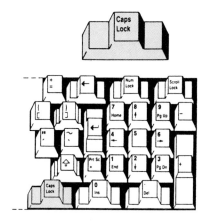
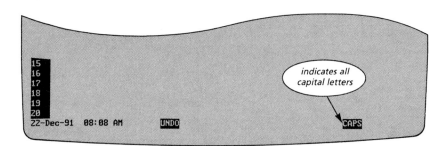

FIGURE 1-8 Press the Caps Lock key to type all capital letters.

The word CAPS on the indicator line at the bottom of the screen in Figure 1-8 tells you that the Caps Lock key is engaged. Therefore, all subsequent letters you type will be accepted by 1-2-3 as capital letters. Note, however, that both uppercase and lowercase letters are valid in a worksheet, and that the letters appear in the same case as they are entered. The Caps Lock key affects only the keys representing letters. Digit and special-character keys continue to transmit the lower character on the key when you press them, unless you hold down a Shift key while pressing the key. To enter a lowercase letter when the Caps Lock key is engaged, hold down the Shift key while typing the letter.

Labels That Begin with a Letter

Entering the title is simple. Just type the required letters on the computer keyboard. Type the words FIRST QUARTER SALES REPORT on the keyboard to get the display shown in Figure 1-9.

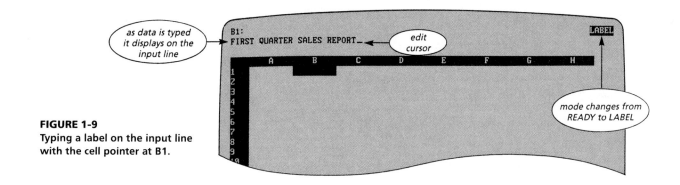

FIGURE 1-9
Typing a label on the input line with the cell pointer at B1.

Figure 1-9 shows two important features. First, as soon as we enter the first character of the report title, the mode on the status line changes from READY to LABEL. 1-2-3 determines that the entry is a **label** and not a number because the first character typed is a letter.

Second, as we type the report title, it displays on the input line followed immediately by the edit cursor. The **edit cursor** is a small, blinking underline symbol. It indicates where the next character typed will be placed on the input line.

Although the data appears at the top of the screen on the input line, it still is not in cell B1. To assign the title to cell B1, press the Enter key as shown in Figure 1-10. This causes the report title displayed on the input line to be placed in the worksheet beginning at cell B1, the cell identified by the cell pointer.

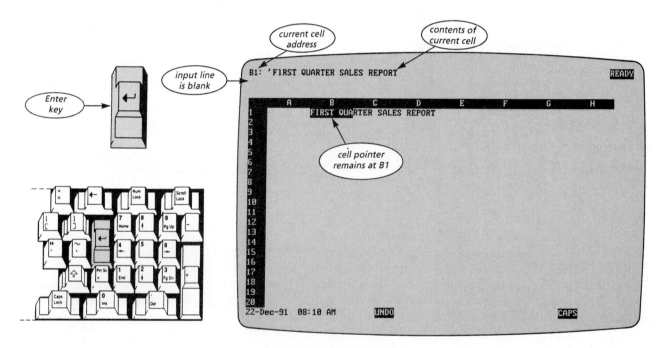

FIGURE 1-10 Pressing the Enter key assigns the label on the input line to cell B1. The cell pointer remains at B1.

If you type the wrong letter and notice the error while it is on the input line at the top of the screen, use the **Backspace key** (above the Enter key on the keyboard) to erase all the characters back to and including the ones that are wrong. If you see an error in a cell, move the cell pointer to the cell in question and retype the entry.

When you enter a label, a series of events occurs. First, the label is positioned left-justified in the cell where it begins. Therefore, the F in the word FIRST begins in the leftmost position of cell B1.

Second, when a label has more characters than the width of the column, the characters are placed in adjacent columns to the right so long as these columns are blank. In Figure 1-10, the width of cell B1 is nine characters. The words we entered have 26 characters. Therefore, the extra letters display in cell C1 (nine characters) and cell D1 (eight characters), since both cell C1 and cell D1 were blank when we made the 26-character entry in cell B1.

If cell C1 had data in it, only the first nine characters of the 26-character entry in cell B1 would show on the worksheet. The remaining 17 characters would be hidden, but the entire label that belongs to the cell displays in the upper left corner of the screen on the status line whenever the cell pointer is moved to cell B1.

Third, when you enter data into a cell by pressing the Enter key, the cell pointer remains on the cell (B1) in which you make the entry.

Fourth, a label, in this case FIRST QUARTER SALES REPORT, appears in two places on the screen: in the cell and on the status line, next to the cell address. Note that 1-2-3 adds an apostrophe (') before the label on the status line (Figure 1-10). This apostrophe identifies the data as a left-justified label.

With the title in cell B1, the next step is to enter the column titles in row 2 of the worksheet. Therefore, move the cell pointer from cell B1 to cell A2 by using the arrow keys (Figure 1-11). Press the Down Arrow key and then the Left Arrow key. Pressing the Down Arrow key once causes the cell pointer to move to cell B2. Then pressing the Left Arrow key once causes the cell pointer to move to cell A2. Remember that pressing an arrow key one time moves the cell pointer one cell in the direction of the arrow. The current cell address changes on the status line from B1 to A2.

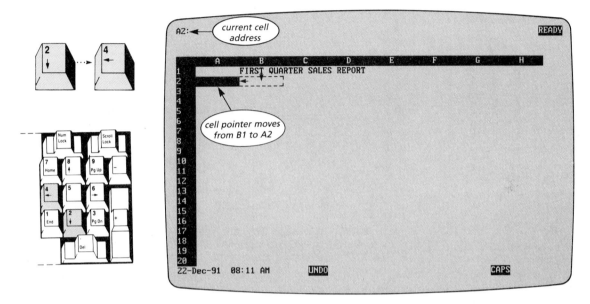

FIGURE 1-11 Moving the cell pointer from B1 to A2 using the arrow keys.

With the cell pointer on A2, enter the label ITEM as shown on the input line in Figure 1-12. Since the entry starts with a letter, 1-2-3 positions the label left-justified in the current cell. To enter the label in cell A2 we could press the Enter key as we did for the report title in cell B1. But another way is to press any one of the four arrow keys, as shown in Figure 1-13 on the next page. In this case, press the Right Arrow key. This is the better alternative because not only is the data entered into the current cell, but the cell pointer also moves one cell to the right. The cell pointer is at cell B2, the location of the next entry.

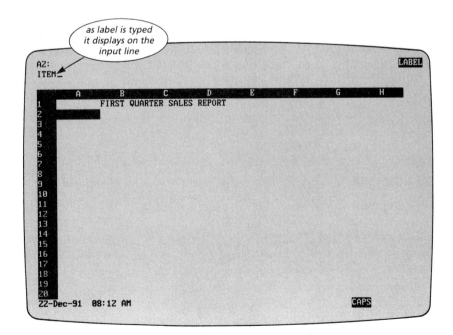

FIGURE 1-12
Typing a label on the input line.

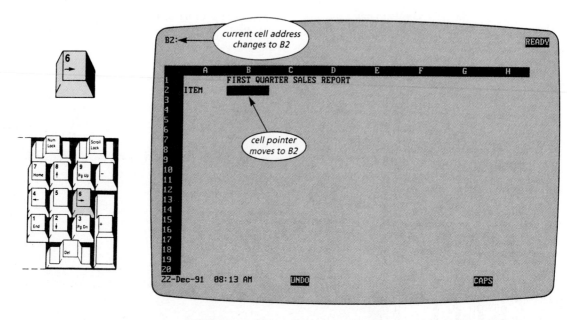

FIGURE 1-13 Pressing the Right Arrow key rather than the Enter key assigns the label on the input line to cell A2 and moves the cell pointer one cell to the right to B2.

Labels Preceded by a Special Character

The worksheet in Figure 1-1 that we are in the process of building requires that the column headings JANUARY, FEBRUARY, and MARCH be positioned right-justified in the cell, rather than left-justified. There are three different ways to position labels in a cell: left-justified, right-justified, or centered. Remember that the first character of the entry instructs 1-2-3 how to place the label in the cell.

If a label begins with a letter or apostrophe ('), 1-2-3 positions the label left-justified in the current cell. If a label begins with a quotation mark ("), it is positioned right-justified. Finally, if a label begins with a circumflex (^), it is centered within the cell. When the first character is an apostrophe, quotation mark, or circumflex, 1-2-3 does not consider the special character to be part of the label and it will not appear in the cell. However, the special character will precede the label on the status line when the cell pointer is on the cell in question. Table 1-1 summarizes the positioning of labels in a cell.

TABLE 1-1 Positioning Labels within a Cell

FIRST CHARACTER OF DATA	DATA ENTERED	POSITION IN CELL	REMARK
1. Letter	ITEM	ITEM	Left-justified in cell.
2. Apostrophe (')	'9946	9946	Left-justified in cell. The label 9946 is a name, like the address on a house, and not a number.
3. Quotation Mark (")	"MARCH	MARCH	Right-justified in cell. This always results in one blank character at the end of the label in the cell.
4. Circumflex (^)	^MARCH	MARCH	Centered in the cell.

With the cell pointer located at cell B2, enter the column heading JANUARY preceded by a quotation mark (") as shown in Figure 1-14, and then press the Right Arrow key. The word JANUARY appears, right-justified, in cell B2 and the cell pointer moves to cell C2 in preparation for the next entry (Figure 1-15).

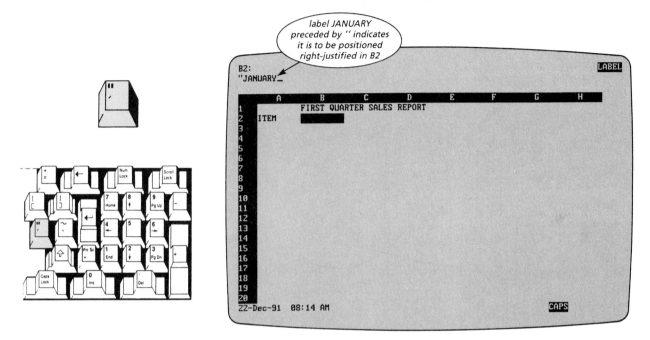

FIGURE 1-14 Begin a label with a quotation mark (") to make it right-justified.

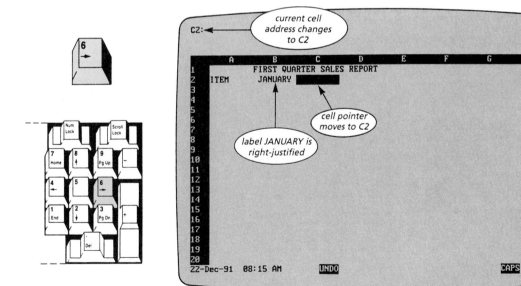

FIGURE 1-15 Pressing the Right Arrow key assigns the label on the input line to cell B2 and moves the cell pointer one cell to the right to C2.

Next, enter the month name FEBRUARY in cell C2 and the month name MARCH in cell D2. Enter both labels right-justified. That is, precede each month name with the quotation mark ("). Press the Right Arrow key after typing each label. With these latest entries, the worksheet appears as illustrated in Figure 1-16.

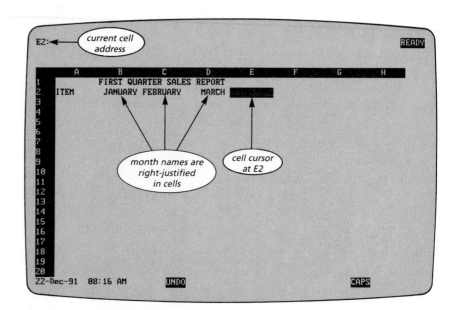

FIGURE 1-16
The three month names entered right-justified.

The cell pointer is now located at cell E2. According to Figure 1-1 no data is to be entered into cell E2. The next entry is the label REVENUE in cell A4. Therefore, move the cell pointer from cell E2 to cell A4. Press the Down Arrow key twice and the Left Arrow key four times, as shown in Figure 1-17.

With the cell pointer at A4, type the label REVENUE and press the Right Arrow key. The cell pointer moves to cell B4 as shown in Figure 1-18.

FIGURE 1-17
Using the arrow keys to move the cell pointer from E2 to A4.

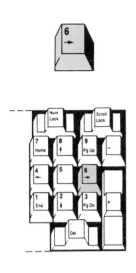

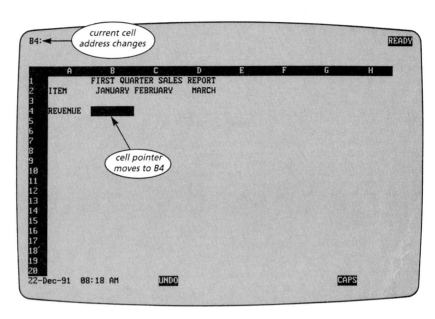

FIGURE 1-18 Pressing the Right Arrow key assigns the label on the input line to cell A4 and moves the cell pointer to B4.

ENTERING NUMBERS

umbers are entered into cells to represent amounts. Numbers are also called **values**. 1-2-3 assumes that an entry for a cell is a number or a formula if the first character you type is one of the following:

0 1 2 3 4 5 6 7 8 9 (@ + - . # $

Whole Numbers

With the cell pointer located at cell B4, enter the revenue amount for January. As shown in Figure 1-1, this amount is 5500. Type the amount 5500 on the keyboard without any special character preceding the number. The screen should now look like Figure 1-19 on the next page. Remember, the CAPS indicator affects only the keys that represent letters on the keyboard. Therefore, never hold down a Shift key to enter a number.

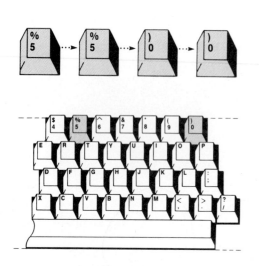

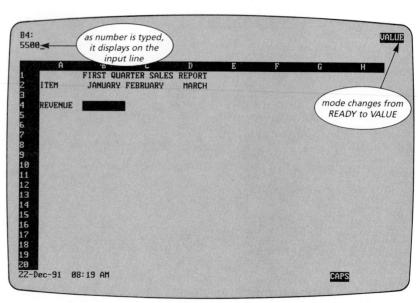

FIGURE 1-19 Entering a number on the input line.

As soon as we enter the first digit, 5, the mode of operation on the status line changes from READY to VALUE. As we type the value 5500, it displays in the upper left corner of the screen on the input line followed immediately by the edit cursor.

Press the Right Arrow key to enter the number 5500 in cell B4 and move the cell pointer one cell to the right. The number 5500 displays right-justified in cell B4 as shown in Figure 1-20. Numbers always display right-justified in a cell. As with right-justified labels, a blank is added to the right side of a number when it is assigned to a cell.

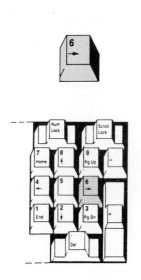

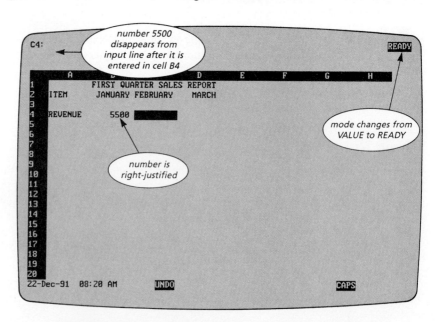

FIGURE 1-20 Pressing the Right Arrow key assigns the number on the input line to cell B4 and moves the cell pointer to C4.

After we enter the data in cell B4, the cell pointer moves to cell C4. At this point, enter the revenue values for February (7300) and March (6410) in cells C4 and D4 in the same manner as we entered the number 5500 into cell B4. After we make the last two revenue entries, the cell pointer is located in cell E4 as shown in Figure 1-21.

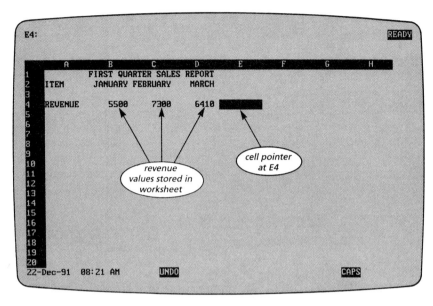

FIGURE 1-21 The revenues for the three months entered into cells B4, C4, and D4.

Decimal Numbers

Although the numeric entries in this project are all whole numbers, you can enter numbers with a decimal point, a dollar sign, and a percent sign. However, the dollar sign and percent sign will not appear in the cell. Other special characters, like the comma, are not allowed in a numeric entry. Table 1-2 gives several examples of numeric entries.

TABLE 1-2 Valid Numeric Entries

NUMERIC DATA ENTERED	CELL CONTENTS	REMARK
1.23	1.23	Decimal fraction numbers are allowed.
32.20	32.2	Insignificant zero dropped.
320.	320	Decimal point at the far right is dropped.
$67.54	67.54	Dollar sign dropped.
47%	.47	Percent converted to a decimal fraction.

MOVING THE CELL POINTER MORE THAN ONE CELL AT A TIME

After entering the revenue values for the three months, the cell pointer resides in cell E4. Since there are no more revenue values to enter, move the cell pointer to cell A5 so that we can enter the next line of data. While we can use the arrow keys on the right side of the keyboard to move the cell pointer from E4 to A5, there is another method that is faster and involves fewer keystrokes. This second method uses the GOTO command.

The GOTO Command

The **GOTO command** moves the cell pointer directly to the cell you want. GOTO is one of many commands that you enter through the use of the function keys. As shown in Figure 1-22, each function key, except for F6, is assigned two commands — one when you press only the function key, and the other when you hold down the Alt key (or the Shift key) and then press the function key.

The function keys may be located at the far left side or at the top of the keyboard. In either case, the function keys work the same. For these projects, we assume that the function keys are located at the far left side of the keyboard (Figure 1-23). Issue the GOTO command by pressing function key F5. 1-2-3 responds by displaying the message "Enter address to go to: E4" in the upper left corner of the screen and changing the mode from READY to POINT. This is illustrated in Step 1 of Figure 1-23. When the mode is POINT, 1-2-3 is requesting a cell address.

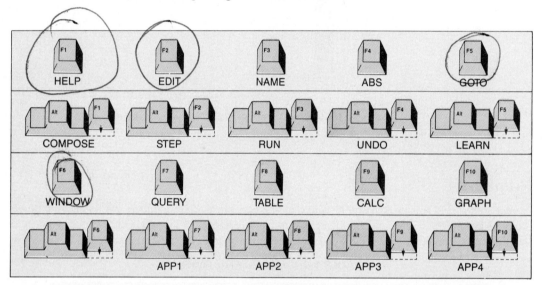

FIGURE 1-22 The commands associated with the function keys on the keyboard.

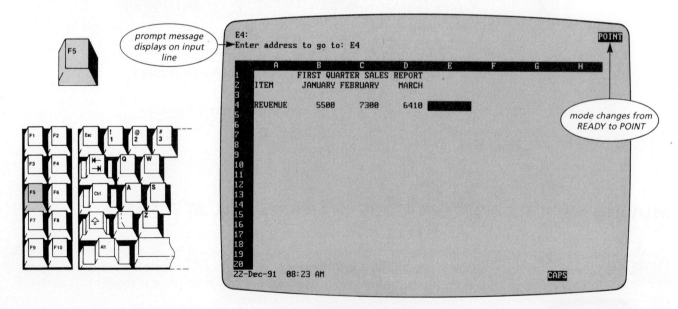

FIGURE 1-23 (Step 1 of 3) Press function key F5 to issue the GOTO command to move the cell pointer from E4 to A5.

Next, enter the cell address A5 as shown in Step 2 of Figure 1-23. Remember to enter the column letter first, followed by the row number. Now press the Enter key. The cell pointer immediately moves to cell A5 as shown in Step 3 of Figure 1-23. Note that not only does the cell pointer move, but also the current cell address on the status line in the upper left corner changes from E4 to A5.

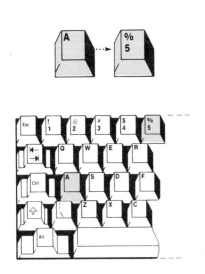

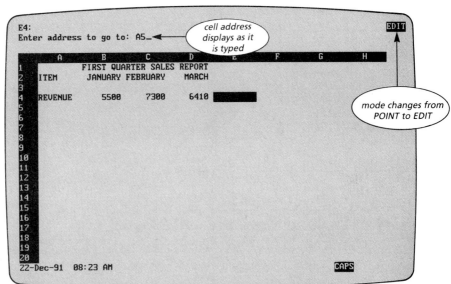

FIGURE 1-23 (Step 2 of 3) Enter the cell address A5.

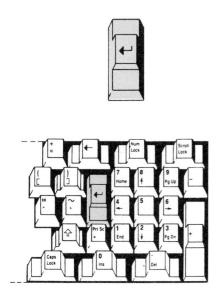

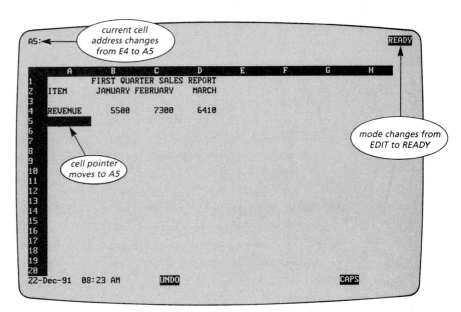

FIGURE 1-23 (Step 3 of 3) Press the Enter key and the cell pointer moves to A5.

With the cell pointer at cell A5, enter the label COSTS followed by the costs for January, February, and March in the same manner as for the revenues on the previous row. After entering the costs, enter the label PROFIT in cell A6. Figure 1-24 illustrates these entries.

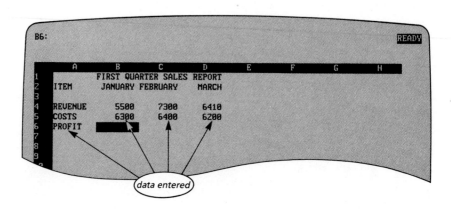

FIGURE 1-24
Costs for the three months entered into cells B5, C5, and D5 and the label PROFIT entered into cell A6.

Summary of Ways to Move the Cell Pointer

Table 1-3 summarizes the various ways you can move the cell pointer around the worksheet. As we proceed through the projects in this book, this table will be a helpful reference. Practice using each of the keys described in Table 1-3.

TABLE 1-3   **Moving the Cell Pointer Around the Worksheet**

KEY(S)	RESULT
↓	Moves the cell pointer directly down one cell.
←	Moves the cell pointer one cell to the left.
→	Moves the cell pointer one cell to the right.
↑	Moves the cell pointer directly up one cell.
Home	Moves the cell pointer to cell A1 no matter where the cell pointer is located on the worksheet.
End	Used in conjunction with the arrow keys to move to the border columns and rows of the worksheet.
F5	Moves the cell pointer to the designated cell address.
PgDn	Moves the worksheet under the cell pointer 20 rows down.
PgUp	Moves the worksheet under the cell pointer 20 rows up.
Tab	Moves the worksheet under the cell pointer one screenful of columns to the left.
Shift and Tab	Moves the worksheet under the cell pointer one screenful of columns to the right.
Scroll Lock	Causes the worksheet to move under the cell pointer when the cell pointer movement keys are used.

ENTERING FORMULAS

*T*he profit for each month is calculated by subtracting the costs for the month from the revenue for the month. Thus, the profit for January is obtained by subtracting 6300 from 5500. The result, –800, belongs in cell B6. The negative sign preceding the number indicates that the company lost money and made no profit in January.

One of the reasons why 1-2-3 is such a valuable tool is because you can assign a formula to a cell and it will be calculated automatically. In this example, the formula subtracts the value in cell B5 from the value in cell B4 and assigns the result to cell B6.

Assigning Formulas to Cells

In Figure 1-25, the cell pointer is located at cell B6. Type the formula + B4–B5 on the input line. This formula instructs 1-2-3 to subtract the value in cell B5 from the value in cell B4 and place the result in the cell to which the formula is assigned.

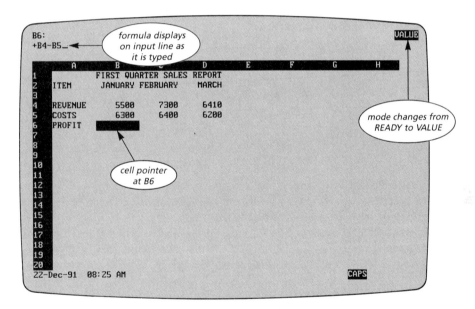

FIGURE 1-25 Entering a formula on the input line.

The plus sign (+) preceding B4 is an important part of the formula. It alerts 1-2-3 that you are entering a formula and not a label. The minus sign (–) following B4 is the **arithmetic operator**, which directs 1-2-3 to perform the subtraction operation. Other valid arithmetic operators include addition (+), multiplication (∗), division (/) and exponentiation (^).

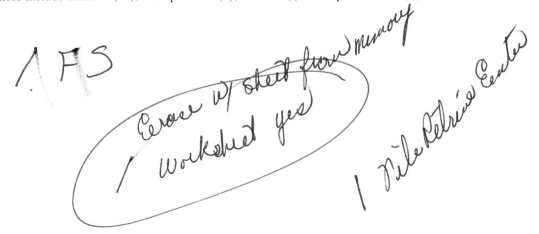

Pressing the Right Arrow key assigns the formula +B4–B5 to cell B6. Instead of displaying the formula in cell B6, however, 1-2-3 completes the arithmetic indicated by the formula and stores the result, –800, in cell B6. This is shown in Figure 1-26. Note that the negative number displays in cell B6 with the minus sign on the left side of the number. Positive numbers display without any sign.

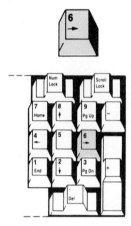

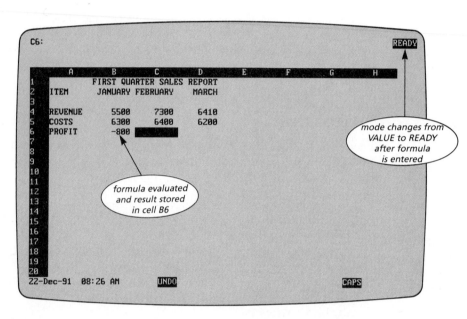

FIGURE 1-26
Pressing the Right Arrow key assigns the formula to cell B6 and moves the cell pointer to C6.

Formulas may be entered in uppercase or lowercase. That is, +b4–b5 is the same as +B4–B5. Like a number, a valid formula begins with one of the following characters: 0 1 2 3 4 5 6 7 8 9 (@ + – . # $

Otherwise, the formula is accepted as a label. Therefore, an alternative to the formula +B4–B5 is (B4–B5). The entry B4–B5 is a label and not a formula, because it begins with the letter B.

To be sure that you understand the relationship of a formula, the associated cell, and the contents of the cell, move the cell pointer back to cell B6. This procedure is shown in Figure 1-27. In the upper left corner of the screen, the status line shows the assignment of the formula +B4–B5 to cell B6. However, in the cell itself, 1-2-3 displays the result of the formula (–800).

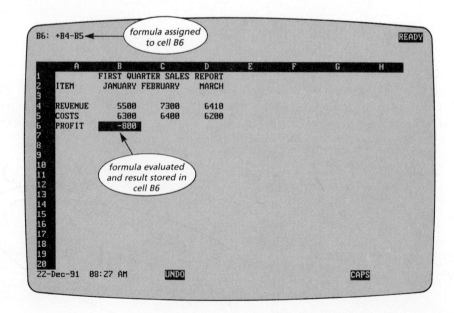

FIGURE 1-27
When the cell pointer is moved to a cell assigned a formula, the formula displays on the status line.

Next move the cell pointer to C6 and type the formula + C4–C5. As shown in Figure 1-28, the formula for determining the profit for February displays on the input line.

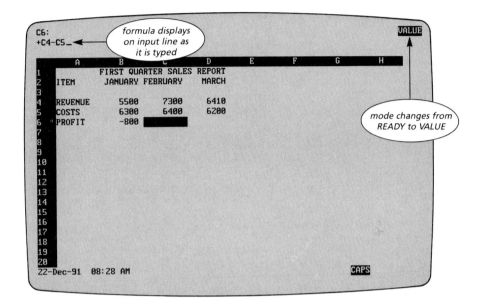

FIGURE 1-28
Entering the profit formula for
February on the input line.

Press the Right Arrow key. The value in cell C5 (February costs) is subtracted from the value in cell C4 (February revenue) and the result of the computation displays in cell C6 (February profit). The cell pointer also moves to cell D6, as shown in Figure 1-29. As you can see, the process for entering a formula into a cell is much the same as for entering labels and numbers.

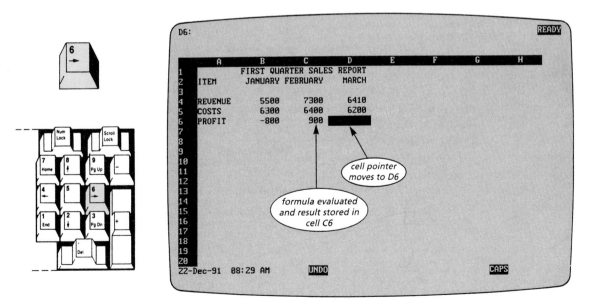

FIGURE 1-29 Pressing the Right Arrow key assigns the formula on the
input line to cell C6 and the cell pointer moves to D6.

The same technique can be used to assign the formula +D4–D5 to cell D6. After pressing the Right Arrow key to conclude the entry in D6, the worksheet is complete, as illustrated in Figure 1-30.

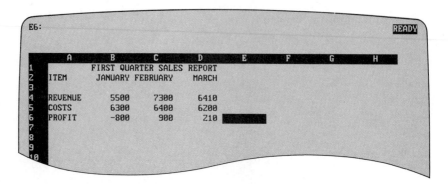

FIGURE 1-30
Worksheet for Project 1 is complete.

Order of Operations

The formulas in this project involve only one arithmetic operator, subtraction. But when more than one operator is involved in a formula, the same order of operations is used as in algebra. Moving from left to right in a formula, the **order of operations** is as follows: first all exponentiations ($\wedge$), then all multiplications ($*$) and divisions (/), and finally all additions (+) and subtractions (–). You can use parentheses to override the order of operations. Table 1-4 illustrates several examples of valid formulas.

TABLE 1-4   Valid Formula Entries

FORMULA	REMARK
+ E3 or (E3)	Assigns the value in cell E3 to the current cell.
7*F5 or +F5*7 or (7*F5)	Assigns 7 times the contents of cell F5 to the current cell.
–G44*G45	Assigns the negative value of the product of the values contained in cells G44 and G45 to the current cell.
2*(J12–F2)	Assigns the product of 2 and the difference between the values contained in cells J12 and F2 to the current cell. It is invalid to write this formula as 2(J12–F2). The multiplication sign ($*$) between the 2 and the left parenthesis is required.
+ A1/A1–A3*A4 + A5 $\wedge$ A6	From left to right: exponentiation ($\wedge$) first, followed by multiplication ($*$) or division (/), and finally addition (+) or subtraction (–).

SAVING A WORKSHEET

You use 1-2-3 either to enter data into the worksheet, as we did in the last section, or to execute a command. In this section we discuss the first of a series of commands that allows you to instruct 1-2-3 to save, load, modify, and print worksheets.

When a worksheet is created, it is stored in main computer memory. If the computer is turned off or if you quit 1-2-3, the worksheet is lost. Hence, it is mandatory to save to disk any worksheet that will be used later.

The MENU Mode

To save a worksheet, place 1-2-3 in **MENU mode**. Do this by pressing the **Slash key** (/) as illustrated in Figure 1-31. First note in Figure 1-31 that the mode at the top right side of the screen is MENU. This means that 1-2-3 is now in MENU mode. Next, notice the menus on the input line and menu line in the control panel. A **menu** is a list from which you can choose. The **command menu** appears on the input line. A second-level menu appears immediately below the input line on the menu line.

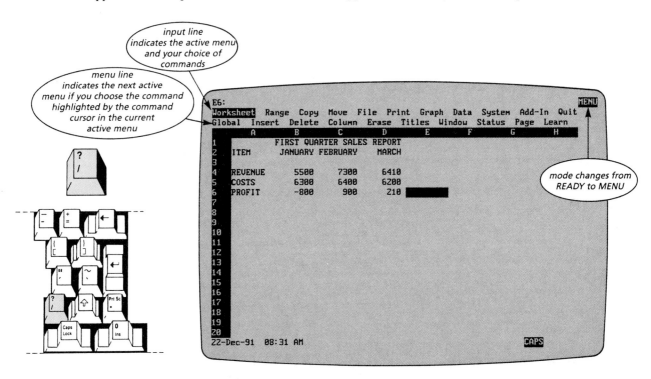

FIGURE 1-31 To save a worksheet to disk, first press the Slash key (/) to switch 1-2-3 to MENU mode.

The second-level menu lists the secondary commands that are available if you select the command highlighted by the command cursor in the command menu. The **command cursor** is a reverse video rectangle that can be moved from command to command in the active menu on the input line, using the Right Arrow and Left Arrow keys. Although there are two menus on the screen, only the one on the input line is active. The command menu is always the active one when you first press the Slash key. If you press the Right Arrow key four times, the command cursor rests on the File command. This procedure is shown in Figure 1-32. Now compare Figure 1-31 to Figure 1-32. Note that the second level of commands on the menu line has changed in Figure 1-32 to show the list of secondary commands that are available if you select the File command.

For a list of all the 1-2-3 commands, see the command structure charts in the Appendix at the back of this book.

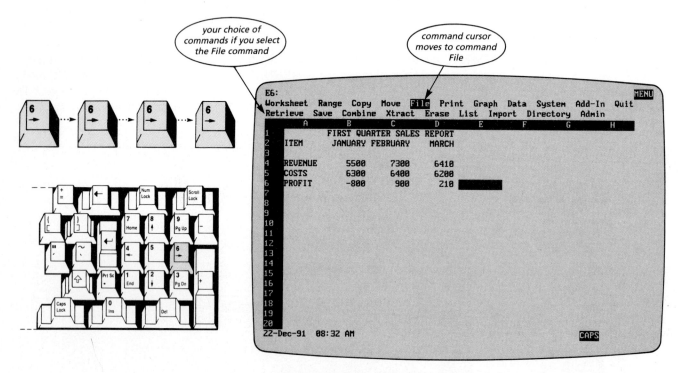

FIGURE 1-32 As you move the command cursor to each command on the input line, the menu line indicates what the command can do.

Backing Out of the MENU Mode

If you decide that you do not want to issue a command, press the **Esc key** until the mode of operation changes to READY. The Esc key, located on the top left side of the keyboard next to the digit 1 key, instructs 1-2-3 to exit MENU mode and return to READY mode.

Press the Esc key and the control panel changes from the one in Figure 1-32 to the one in Figure 1-30. Press the Slash key once and the Right Arrow key four times and the command menu in Figure 1-32 reappears in the control panel.

The Esc key allows you to *back out* of any command or entry on the input line. So if you become confused while making any kind of entry (command or data), use the Esc key to reset the current entry. When in doubt, press the Esc key.

The File Save Command

To save a file, select the File command from the command menu. There are two ways to select the File command.

1. Press the F key for File. Each command in the command menu begins with a different letter. Therefore, the first letter uniquely identifies each command.
2. Use the Right Arrow key to move the command cursor to the word File (Figure 1-32). With the command cursor on the word File, press the Enter key.

Use the first method and press the F key as shown in Figure 1-33. This causes the **File menu** to replace the command menu on the input line. The command cursor is now active in the File menu.

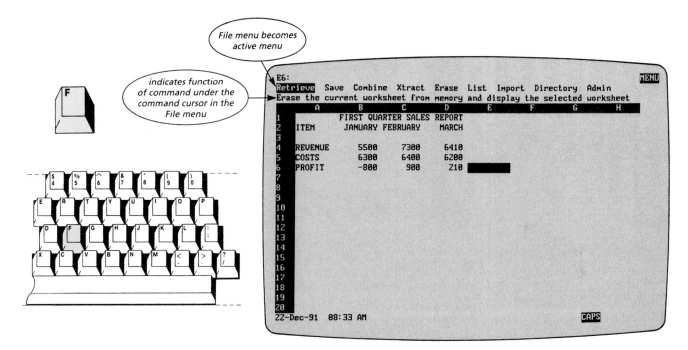

FIGURE 1-33 Typing the letter F moves the File menu from the menu line to the input line.

Pressing the S key for Save causes the message "Enter name of file to save: A:\" followed by the blinking edit cursor to appear on the input line at the top of the screen. The mode also changes from MENU to EDIT. This procedure is shown in Figure 1-34.

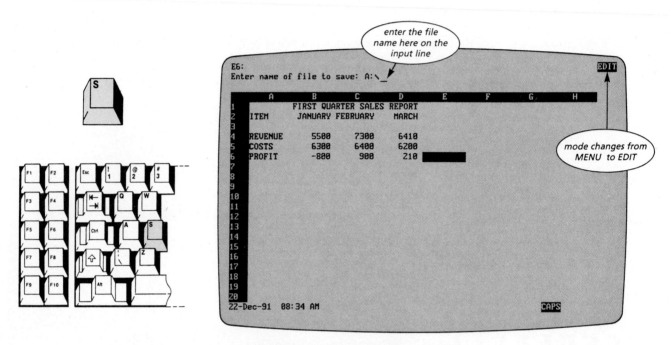

FIGURE 1-34 Typing the letter S for Save causes 1-2-3 to display the prompt message on the input line.

The next step is to select a file name. Any file name will do, so long as it is eight or fewer characters in length and includes only the characters A–Z (uppercase or lowercase), 0–9, and the special characters described earlier in the Introduction to DOS. 1-2-3 automatically adds the file extension .WK1 to the file name. The file extension .WK1 stands for worksheet.

In this example, let's choose the file name PROJS-1. Type the file name PROJS-1 as shown in Figure 1-35. Next, press the Enter key. The file is stored on the A drive with the file name PROJS-1.WK1. Remember, 1-2-3 does not distinguish between uppercase and lowercase letters. Therefore, you can type PROJS-1 or projs-1 or ProJS-1. All three file names are the same.

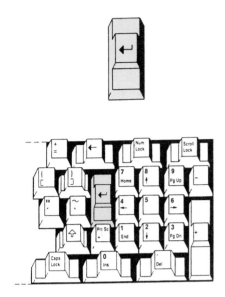

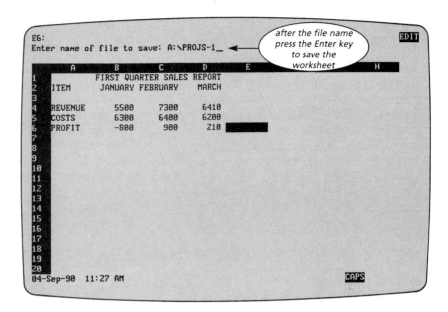

FIGURE 1-35 After you enter the file name on the input line, press the Enter key to complete the /FS command.

While 1-2-3 writes the worksheet on the disk, the mode changes from EDIT to WAIT. The red light on the A drive also lights up to show it is in use. As soon as the writing is complete, the red light goes off and 1-2-3 returns to the READY mode. This is shown in Figure 1-36.

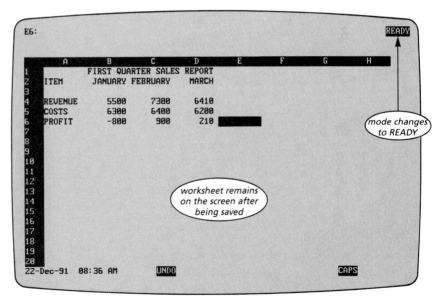

FIGURE 1-36
When the computer is finished saving the worksheet to disk, 1-2-3 returns to READY mode.

Saving Worksheets to a Different Disk Drive

If you want to save the worksheet to a different drive, enter the command /**F**ile **S**ave (/FS). Next, press the Esc key twice to delete the "A:*.wk1" from the prompt message "Enter name of file to save: A:*.wk1". Enter the drive of your choice followed by the file name. For example, to save the worksheet on the disk in drive B, enter B:PROJS-1 in response to the prompt "Enter name of file to save:". Do not attempt to save a worksheet to the B drive if it is unavailable.

To change the default drive permanently from A to B, enter the command /**W**orksheet **G**lobal **D**efault **D**irectory (/WGDD). That is, press the Slash key, then type the letters WGDD. Press the Esc key to delete the current default drive and type B: for drive B. Press the Enter key. Next, enter the commands Update and Quit (UQ). The Update command permanently changes the default drive in the 1-2-3 program. The Quit command quits the Default menu. The examples in the remainder of this book use the B drive as the default drive.

PRINTING A SCREEN IMAGE OF THE WORKSHEET

*T*he **screen image** of the worksheet is exactly what you see on the screen, including the window borders and control panel. A printed version of the worksheet is called a **hard copy**.

Anytime you use the printer, you must be sure that it is ready. To make the printer ready, turn it off and use the platen knob to align the perforated edge of the paper with the top of the print head mechanism. Then turn the printer on.

With the printer in READY mode, hold down one of the Shift keys and then press the PrtSc key (Shift-PrtSc). The screen image of the worksheet immediately prints on the printer. When the printer stops, eject the paper from the printer and carefully tear off the printed version of the worksheet (Figure 1-37).

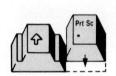
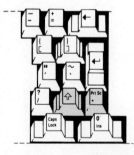

```
⌣  E6:                                                            READY  ⌣

⌣         A         B         C         D       E     F     G     H      ⌣
    1               FIRST QUARTER SALES REPORT
⌣   2    ITEM       JANUARY  FEBRUARY    MARCH                            ⌣
    3
⌣   4    REVENUE      5500      7300      6410                            ⌣
    5    COSTS        6300      6400      6200
    6    PROFIT       -800       900       210
⌣   7                                                                    ⌣
    8
    9
⌣  10                                                                    ⌣
   11
⌣  12                                                                    ⌣
   13
   14
⌣  15                                                                    ⌣
   16
   17
⌣  18                                                                    ⌣
   19
⌣  20                                                                    ⌣
   22-Dec-91   08:37 AM        UNDO                           CAPS
```

FIGURE 1-37 Hold down the Shift key and then press the PrtSc key to obtain a hard copy of the worksheet.

CORRECTING ERRORS

*T*here are several methods for correcting errors in a worksheet. The one you choose will depend on the severity of the error, and whether you notice it while typing the data on the input line or after the data is in the cell.

The error-correcting examples that follow are not part of the worksheet we are building in Project 1. However, you should carefully step through them since they are essential to building and maintaining worksheets.

Correcting Errors While the Data Is on the Input Line

Move the cell pointer to cell A5 and type the label COTTS, rather than COSTS, on the input line. This error is shown in Figure 1-38.

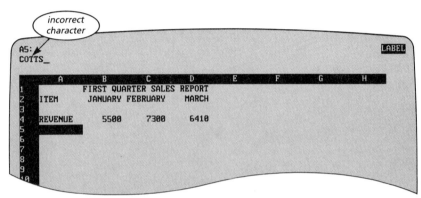

FIGURE 1-38
Incorrect data spotted on the input line.

To correct the error, move the edit cursor back to position 3 on the input line by pressing the Backspace key three times (Figure 1-39). Each time you press the Backspace key, the character immediately to the left of the edit cursor is erased.

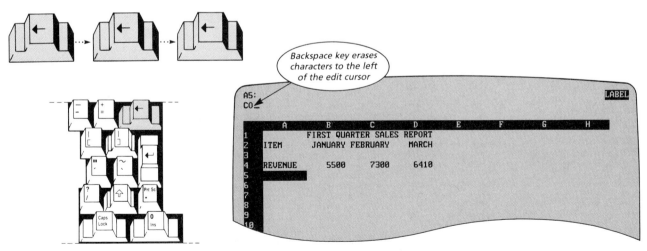

FIGURE 1-39 Press the Backspace key three times to erase the characters up to and including the first T in COTTS.

F2 Key
allows
Corrections

Then, as in Figure 1-40, type the correct letters STS. Now the entry is correct. Press the Right Arrow key to enter the label COSTS into cell A5.

A5:
COSTS_ ◄ *label is now correct*   **LABEL**

	A	B	C	D	E	F	G	H
1		FIRST QUARTER SALES REPORT						
2	ITEM	JANUARY	FEBRUARY	MARCH				
3								
4	REVENUE	5500	7300	6410				
5								
6								
7								
8								
9								

FIGURE 1-40
Enter the correct characters and press the Enter key or one of the arrow keys.

In summary, if you notice an error while the label, number, or formula is on the input line, you can do one of two things. You can use the Backspace key to erase the portion in error and then type the correct characters. Or, if the error is too severe, you can press the Esc key to erase the entire entry on the input line and reenter the data item from the beginning.

Editing Data in a Cell

If you spot an error in the worksheet, move the cell pointer to the cell with the error. You then have two ways to correct the error. If the entry is short, simply type it and press the Enter key. The new entry will replace the old entry. Remember, the cell pointer must be on the cell with the error before you begin typing the correct entry.

If the entry in the cell is long and the errors are minor, using the EDIT mode may be a better choice, rather than retyping. Move the cell pointer to cell A4 and enter the label GROSS PAY incorrectly as GRSS PSY. Figure 1-41 shows the label GRSS PSY in cell A4. You will have to insert the letter O between the letters R and S in GRSS and change the letter S in PSY to the letter A.

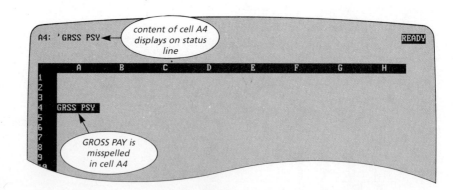

FIGURE 1-41
Error spotted in cell.

The six steps in Figure 1-42 illustrate how to use the EDIT mode to correct the entry in cell A4. As shown in Step 1, first press function key F2 to switch 1-2-3 to EDIT mode. The contents of cell A4 immediately display on the input line, followed by the edit cursor. The contents of the cell can now be corrected. Table 1-5 on page L 33 lists the edit keys available in EDIT mode and their functions.

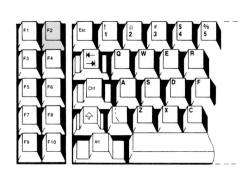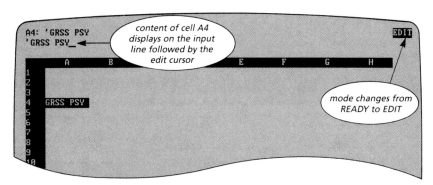

FIGURE 1-42 (Step 1 of 6) Press function key F2 to switch 1-2-3 to EDIT mode.

With 1-2-3 in EDIT mode, the next step in changing GRSS PSY to GROSS PAY is to move the edit cursor on the input line to the leftmost S in GRSS PSY. Press the Left Arrow key six times as shown in Step 2 of Figure 1-42.

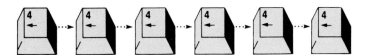

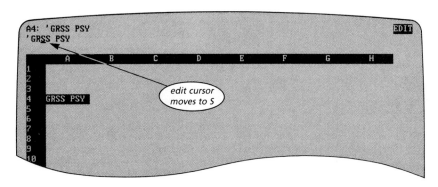

FIGURE 1-42 (Step 2 of 6) Press the Left Arrow key six times to move the edit cursor on the input line to the first S in GRSS PSY.

Next, type the letter O. Typing the letter O "pushes" the leftmost letter S and all the letters to the right of it to the right. The O is inserted as shown in Step 3 of Figure 1-42.

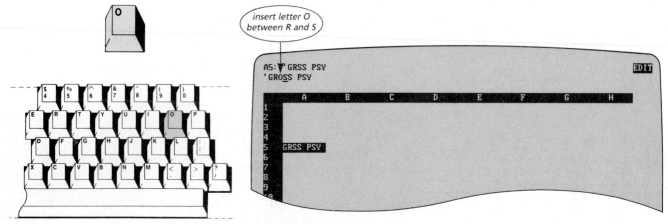

FIGURE 1-42 (Step 3 of 6) With the edit cursor on the first letter S in GRSS PSY, type the letter O.

The next step calls for moving the edit cursor to the S in PSY and changing it to the letter A. Use the Right Arrow key as shown in Step 4 of Figure 1-42. After moving the edit cursor, press the **Ins key** (Insert key) to switch from inserting characters to overtyping characters.

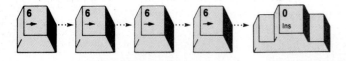

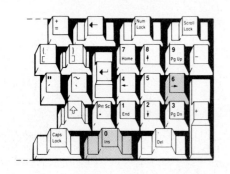

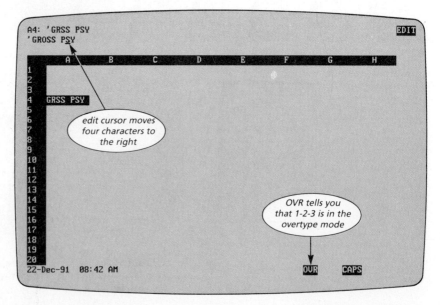

FIGURE 1-42 (Step 4 of 6) Press the Right Arrow key four times to move the edit cursor to the letter S in PSY. Press the Ins (Insert) key to switch to overtype.

Type the letter A. The correct label GROSS PAY now resides on the input line (Step 5 of Figure 1-42). Press the Enter key to replace GRSS PSY in cell A4 with GROSS PAY. This is illustrated in Step 6 of Figure 1-42.

Pay careful attention to the six steps in Figure 1-42. It is easy to make keyboard and grammatical errors. Understanding how to use the EDIT mode will make it easier to correct mistakes.

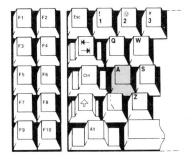

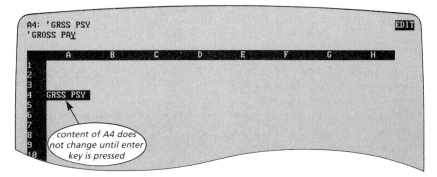

FIGURE 1-42 (Step 5 of 6) With the edit cursor on the letter S in PSY, type the letter A.

FIGURE 1-42 (Step 6 of 6) Press the Enter key to assign the edited value to cell A4.

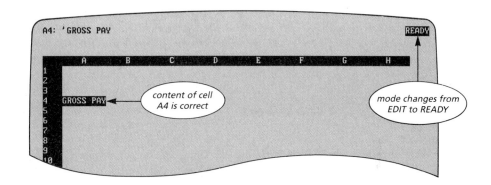

TABLE 1-5   Keys for Editing Cell Entries

KEY	FUNCTION
F2	Switches 1-2-3 to EDIT mode.
Enter	Completes entry. Up Arrow key or Down Arrow key also completes an entry. Either key also moves the cell pointer in the corresponding direction.
Backspace	Erases the character immediately to the left of the edit cursor.
Del	Deletes the character the edit cursor is on.
Ins	Used to switch between inserting characters and overtyping characters. In EDIT mode, characters are inserted when the status indicator OVR does not display at the bottom of the screen. Characters are overtyped when the status indicator OVR displays at the bottom of the screen.
Right Arrow	Moves the edit cursor one character to the right on the input line.
Left Arrow	Moves the edit cursor one character to the left on the input line.
End	Moves the edit cursor to the end of the entry on the input line.
Home	Moves the edit cursor to the first character in the entry on the input line.

Undoing the Last Entry — The UNDO command

As long as the UNDO indicator displays at the bottom of the screen (Figure 1-36), you can enter the UNDO command to erase the most recent cell entry. You enter the UNDO command by holding down the Alt key and pressing the function key F4 (Alt-F4).

Try the UNDO command by entering the value 7345.48 in cell B4. Before entering any other value into the worksheet, press Alt-F4. 1-2-3 erases the value 7345.48 from cell B4. To restore the value 7345.48 in B4, press Alt-F4 again. The second UNDO command "undoes" the first UNDO command.

UNDO is a time-saving command. It can be used to undo much more complicated worksheet activities than a single cell entry. For example, most commands issued from the command menu can be undone if you enter the UNDO command before making any other entry after 1-2-3 returns from MENU mode to READY mode. The general rule is that the UNDO command can restore the worksheet data and settings to what they were the last time 1-2-3 was in READY mode.

Erasing the Contents of Any Cell in the Worksheet

It is not unusual to enter data into the wrong cell. In such a case, to correct the error, you may want to erase the contents of the cell. Let's erase the label GROSS PAY in cell A4. Make sure the cell pointer is on cell A4. Enter the command /**R**ange **E**rase (/RE). That is, press the Slash key to display the command menu. Then press the R key for Range and the E key for Erase. When the message "Enter range to erase: A4..A4" appears on the input line at the top of the screen, press the Enter key. 1-2-3 immediately erases the entry GROSS PAY in cell A4.

Erasing the Entire Worksheet

Sometimes, everything goes wrong. If the worksheet is such a mess that you don't know where to begin to correct it, you may want to erase it entirely and start over. To do this, enter the command /**W**orksheet **E**rase **Y**es (/WEY). That is, first type the Slash key to display the command menu. Next, type the letters W for Worksheet, E for Erase and Y for Yes.

The /**W**orksheet **E**rase **Y**es (/WEY) command does not erase the worksheet PROJS-1 from disk. This command only affects the worksheet in main computer memory. Remember that the /**W**orksheet **E**rase **Y**es (/WEY) command can also be a method for clearing the worksheet on the screen of its contents after you have saved it. This is especially useful when you no longer want the current worksheet displayed because you want to begin a new one.

ONLINE HELP FACILITY

At any time while you are using 1-2-3, you can press function key F1 to gain access to the online help facility. When you press F1, 1-2-3 temporarily suspends the current activity and displays valuable information about the current mode or command. If you have a one-disk or two-disk system and no fixed disk drive, make sure the 1-2-3 system disk is in drive A before pressing the F1 key.

With 1-2-3 in READY mode, press the F1 key. The 1-2-3 Help Index screen shown in Figure 1-43 displays. Directions are given at the bottom of the help screen for accessing information on any 1-2-3 program subject. With the Help Index on the screen, use the arrow keys to select any one of the many 1-2-3 topics. To exit the help facility and return to the worksheet, press the Esc key.

If you press the F1 key while in any mode other than READY, 1-2-3 displays the appropriate help screen, rather than the 1-2-3 Help Index screen shown in Figure 1-43.

The best way to familiarize yourself with the online help facility is to use it. When you have a question about how a command works in 1-2-3, press F1. You may want to consider printing a hard copy of the information displayed on the screen. To print a hard copy, ready the printer and press Shift-PrtSc.

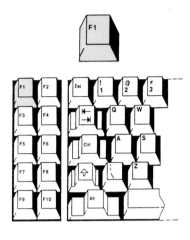

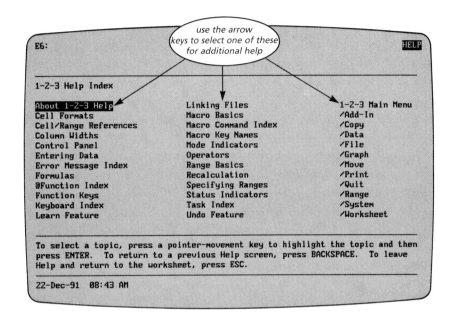

FIGURE 1-43
Press function key F1 to use the online help facility of 1-2-3.

QUITTING 1-2-3

*T*o exit 1-2-3 and return control to DOS, do the following:

1. Save the current worksheet if you made any changes to it since the last save.
2. If you loaded 1-2-3 from drive A, place the DOS disk in drive A.
3. Enter the **Q**uit command (/Q). First, press the Slash key to display the command menu. Next, type the letter Q for Quit.
4. When the message shown at the top of the screen in Figure 1-44 displays, type the letter Y to confirm your exit from 1-2-3.

If you made changes to the worksheet since the last time you saved it to disk, 1-2-3 displays the message "WORKSHEET CHANGES NOT SAVED! End 1-2-3 anyway?". Type Y to quit 1-2-3 without saving the latest changes to the worksheet to disk. Type N to return to READY mode.

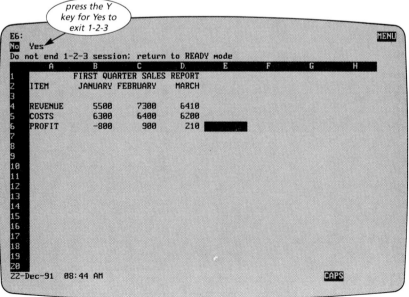

FIGURE 1-44
To quit 1-2-3 and return control to DOS, enter the command /Q and type the letter Y.

PROJECT SUMMARY

n Project 1 you learned how to move the cell pointer around the worksheet, enter data into the worksheet, and save a worksheet. Each of the steps required to build the worksheet in this project is listed in the following table. Review the steps in detail to make sure you understand them.

SUMMARY OF KEYSTROKES—Project 1

STEPS	KEY(S) PRESSED	RESULTS
1	Caps Lock	Set Caps Lock on
2	→	Move the cell pointer to B1
3	FIRST QUARTER SALES REPORT ↵	Enter report heading
4	↓ ←	Move the cell pointer to A2
5	ITEM →	Enter column heading
6	"JANUARY →	Enter column heading
7	"FEBRUARY →	Enter column heading
8	"MARCH →	Enter column heading
9	↓ ↓ ← ← ← ←	Move the cell pointer to A4
10	REVENUE →	Enter row identifier
11	5500 →	Enter January revenue
12	7300 →	Enter February revenue
13	6410 →	Enter March revenue
14	F5 A5 ↵	Move the cell pointer to A5
15	COSTS →	Enter row identifier
16	6300 →	Enter January costs
17	6400 →	Enter February costs
18	6200 →	Enter March costs
19	F5 A6 ↵	Move the cell pointer to A6
20	PROFIT →	Enter row identifier
21	+ B4–B5 →	Enter January profit formula
22	+ C4–C5 →	Enter February profit formula
23	+ D4–D5 →	Enter March profit formula
24	/FS PROJS–1 ↵	Save the worksheet as PROJS-1
25	Shift - PrtSc	Print the screen image of the worksheet

The following list summarizes the material covered in Project 1.

1. The worksheet is organized in two dimensions—columns (vertical) and rows (horizontal).
2. In the border at the top of the screen, each **column** is identified by a column letter. In the border on the left side, each **row** is identified by a row number.
3. A **cell** is the intersection of a row and a column. A cell is referred to by its **cell address**, the coordinates of the intersection of a column and row.
4. The **current cell** is the cell in which data (labels, numbers, and formulas) can be entered. The current cell is identified in two ways. A reverse video rectangle called the **cell pointer** is displayed over the current cell, and the current cell address displays on the status line at the top of the screen.
5. The area between the borders on the screen is called a **window**.
6. The three lines immediately above the window—status line, input line, and menu line—are collectively called the **control panel**.
7. The **status line** is the first line in the control panel. It indicates the current cell address and displays the mode of operation. If a value is already in the cell, the status line also shows the type of entry and its contents.
8. The second line in the control panel is the **input line**. Depending on the mode of operation, it shows the characters you type as you enter data or edit cell contents; the command menu; or input prompts asking for additional command specifications.
9. The third line in the control panel is the **menu line**. It displays information about the menu item highlighted on the input line when 1-2-3 is in the MENU mode.
10. The line at the bottom of the screen is the **indicator line**. It displays three items: the date and time of day as maintained by DOS and status indicators.
11. To move the cell pointer one cell at a time use the arrow keys found on the right side of the keyboard.
12. No matter where the cell pointer is on the worksheet, if you press the Home key, the cell pointer always moves to cell A1.
13. You may use the **GOTO command** (function key F5) to move the cell pointer to any cell in the worksheet.
14. Three types of entries may be made in a cell: labels, numbers, and formulas.
15. A cell entry is a **number** or a **formula** if the first character typed is one of the following: 0 1 2 3 4 5 6 7 8 9 (@ + − . # $
16. A number or formula is also called a **value**.
17. A cell entry is a **label** if the first character is any character other than one that identifies it as a number or formula.
18. If a label begins with a letter or apostrophe, it is positioned in the cell left-justified. If a label begins with a quotation mark ("), it is positioned right-justified. If a label begins with a circumflex (^), it is centered in the cell.
19. One of the most powerful features of 1-2-3 is the ability to assign a formula to a cell and calculate it automatically. The result of the calculation is displayed in the cell.
20. 1-2-3 uses the same order of operations as in algebra. Moving from left to right in a formula, the order of operations is as follows: all exponentiations (^) are completed first, then all multiplications (∗) and divisions (/), and finally all additions (+) and subtractions (−). Parentheses may be used to override the order of operations.
21. To put 1-2-3 in MENU mode, press the **Slash key (/)**. To leave command mode, press the Esc key.
22. There are two different cursors: edit cursor and command cursor. The **edit cursor** shows where the next character will be placed on the input line. The **command cursor** moves from command to command in the command menu.
23. If you get confused while making any kind of entry (command or data), press the **Esc key** to reset the current entry. When in doubt, press the Esc key.
24. In order to save a worksheet, enter the command /File Save (/FS) and the file name that you plan to call the worksheet.
25. 1-2-3 automatically appends the file extension .WK1 (worksheet) to the file name.
26. To print the screen image of the worksheet, make sure the printer is ready. Next, hold down one of the Shift keys and press the PrtSc key (Shift-PrtSc). After the worksheet has printed, eject the paper from the printer and carefully tear off the printed worksheet. A printed version of the worksheet is called a **hard copy**.
27. To edit the contents of a cell, press function key F2.
28. If the most recent entry into a cell is in error, use the UNDO command to erase it. You enter the UNDO command by holding down the Alt key and pressing the function key F4 (Alt-F4).
29. To erase the contents of a cell, move the cell pointer to the cell in question, enter the command /Range Erase (/RE), and press the Enter key.
30. To erase the entire worksheet, enter the command /Worksheet Erase Yes (/WEY).
31. At any time while you are using 1-2-3, you may press function key F1 to gain access to the online help facility.
32. To exit 1-2-3 and return control to DOS, enter the command /Quit (/Q). Press the Y key to confirm your exit. Before entering the Quit command, be sure that the DOS program COMMAND.COM is available to the system.

STUDENT ASSIGNMENTS

STUDENT ASSIGNMENT 1: True/False

Instructions: Circle T if the statement is true or F if the statement is false.

(T) F   1. The current cell address on the status line identifies the cell that the cell pointer is on in the worksheet.

T (F)   2. With 1-2-3, each column is identified by a number and each row by a letter of the alphabet.

(T) F   3. A cell is identified by specifying its cell address, the coordinates of the intersection of a column and a row.

(T) F   4. When 1-2-3 first begins execution, the column width is nine characters.

(T) F   5. One method of moving the worksheet cell pointer is by using the arrow keys on the right side of the keyboard.

(T) F   6. A cell entry that consists of just words or letters of the alphabet is called a label.

T (F)   7. When text data is entered that contains more characters than the width of the column, an error message displays.

T (F)   8. If a cell entry begins with a circumflex (^), the data is right-justified in the cell.

T (F)   9. To move the cell pointer from cell C1 to cell A2, press the Down Arrow key one time and the Left Arrow key one time.

(T) F   10. Numeric data entered into a worksheet is stored right-justified in a cell.

(T) F   11. The GOTO command moves the cell pointer directly to a designated cell.

T F   12. Typing GOTO A1 causes the worksheet cell pointer to be positioned in cell A1.

T F   13. The UNDO command erases the entire worksheet.

(T) F   14. When you enter a formula in a cell, the formula is evaluated and the result is displayed in the same cell on the worksheet.

T (F)   15. The cell pointer is at C6. The formula +C4–C5 causes the value in cell C5 to be subtracted from the value in cell C4. The answer is displayed in cell C5.

STUDENT ASSIGNMENT 2: Multiple Choice

Instructions: Circle the correct response.

1. In the border at the top of the screen, each column is identified by a _____ .
   a. number
   (b.) letter
   c. pointer
   d. none of the above

2. If the first character typed on the input line is the letter F, the mode on the status line changes from READY to _____ .
   a. VALUE
   (b.) LABEL
   c. MENU
   d. EDIT

3. A cell is identified by a cell _____ .
   a. pointer
   (b.) address
   c. entry
   d. none of the above

4. The command /File Save (/FS) is used to _____ .
   a. load a new worksheet
   (b.) save a worksheet on disk
   c. suspend work on the current worksheet and return to the operating system
   d. make corrections in the current entry

5. To enter the UNDO command, hold down the Alt key and press _____ .
   a. function key F4
   b. function key F5
   c. function key F6
   d. function key F7
6. Which one of the following should you press to put 1-2-3 in EDIT mode?
   a. function key F1
   b. function key F2
   c. function key F3
   d. function key F5
7. Which one of the following best describes the function of the Backspace key?
   a. deletes the value in the current cell
   b. deletes the character on the input line under which the edit cursor is located
   c. deletes the character to the right of the edit cursor on the input line
   d. deletes the character to the left of the edit cursor on the input line
8. Which one of the following should you press to activate the online help facility of 1-2-3?
   a. function key F1
   b. function key F2
   c. function key F3
   d. function key F4

STUDENT ASSIGNMENT 3: Understanding the Worksheet

Instructions: Answer the following questions.

1. In Figure 1-45, a series of arrows points to the major components of a worksheet. Identify the various parts of the worksheet in the space provided in the figure.

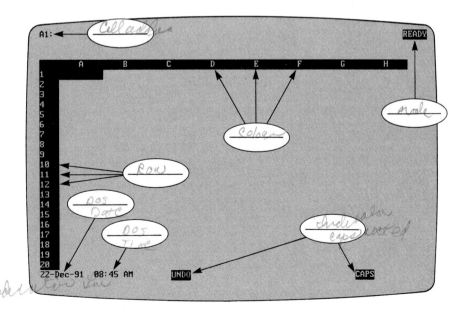

FIGURE 1-45
Problem 1 of Student Assignment 3

Student Assignment 3 (continued)

2. Explain the following entries that may be contained on the indicator line at the bottom of the screen.

   a. OVR _____

   _____

   b. 13:15 _Dos Time_ _____

   _____

   c. UNDO _Indicator_ _____

   _____

   d. CAPS _all letter capital_ _____

   _____

STUDENT ASSIGNMENT 4: Understanding 1-2-3 Commands

Instructions: Answer the following questions.

1. Use Figure 1-46 to answer the following two questions. Where is the cell pointer located in the worksheet? Which keystroke causes the display on the input line?

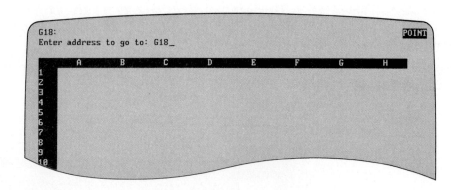

FIGURE 1-46
Problem 1 of Student Assignment 4

Cell pointer location: _G18_
Keystroke: _/ F S G P_

2. Indicate the sequence of keystrokes for saving a worksheet that causes the display shown on the input line in Figure 1-47. Assume that the first letter of each command is entered to issue the commands that cause the display.

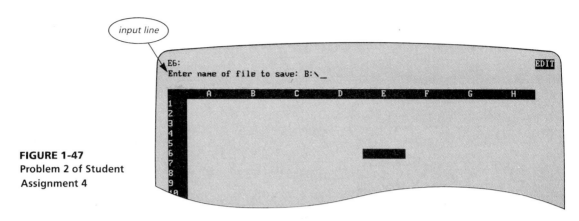

FIGURE 1-47
Problem 2 of Student
Assignment 4

Keystroke sequence: _____/ F S_____

3. Indicate the value assigned to the current cell caused by the entry on the input line in Figure 1-48. Assume that cell I23 contains the value 6 and cell I24 contains the value 7.

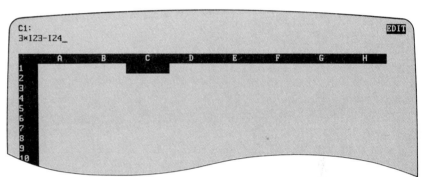

FIGURE 1-48
Problem 3 of Student
Assignment 4

Value: _Goto C-1_____

4. Which keystroke causes 1-2-3 to display the current mode shown in Figure 1-48?

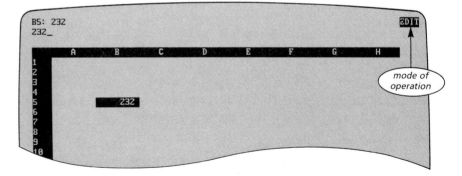

FIGURE 1-49
Problem 4 of Student
Assignment 4

Keystroke: _Goto B5_____

STUDENT ASSIGNMENT 5: Correcting Formulas in a Worksheet

Instructions: The worksheet illustrated in Figure 1-50 contains an error in the PROFIT row for January. Analyze the entries displayed on the worksheet. Explain the cause of the error and the method of correction in the space provided below.

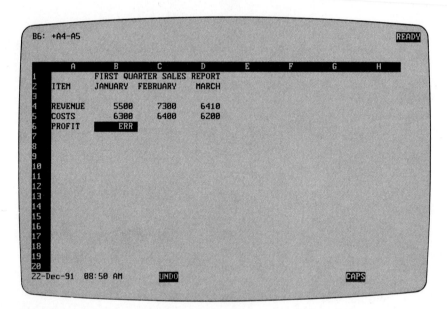

FIGURE 1-50
Student Assignment 5

Cause of error: _____

_____

Method of correction: _____

_____

STUDENT ASSIGNMENT 6: Correcting Worksheet Entries

Instructions: The worksheet illustrated in Figure 1-51 contains errors in the PROFIT row for February (cell C6) and March (cell D6). Analyze the entries displayed on the worksheet. Explain the cause of the errors for the two months and the methods of correction in the space provided on page 43.

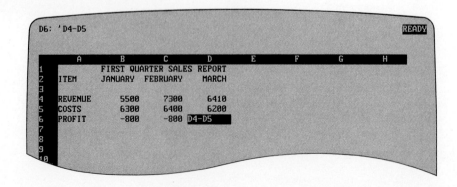

FIGURE 1-51
Student Assignment 6

Cause of error in C6: _____

_____

Method of correction for C6: _____

_____

Cause of error in D6: _____

_____

Method of correction for D6: _____

_____

STUDENT ASSIGNMENT 7: Entering Formulas

Instructions: For each worksheet below, write the formula that accomplishes the specified task and manually compute the value assigned to the specified cell.

1. Use Figure 1-52. Assign to cell A4 the product of cell A2 and cell A3.

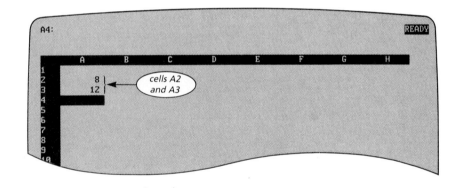

FIGURE 1-52
Problem 1 of Student
Assignment 7

Formula: _____ $+ A2+A3$ _____

Result assigned to cell A4: _____ 20 _____

2. Use Figure 1-53. Assign to cell B5 the sum of cells B2, B3, and B4, minus cell A5.

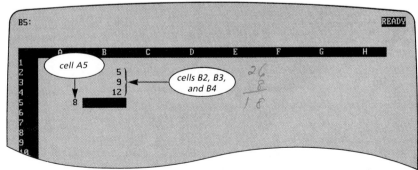

FIGURE 1-53
Problem 2 of Student
Assignment 7

Formula: _____ $@ + (B2 + B4) - A5$ _____

Result assigned to cell B5: _____ 18 _____

Student Assignment 7 (continued)

3. Use Figure 1-54. Assign to cell C3 two times the quotient of cell D2 divided by cell C2.

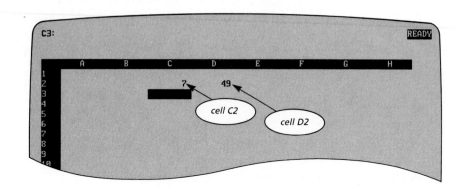

FIGURE 1-54
Problem 3 of Student
Assignment 7

Formula: _____

Result assigned to cell C3: _____

4. Use Figure 1-55. Assign to cell D5 the sum of cells D2 through D4 minus the sum of cells C3 and C4.

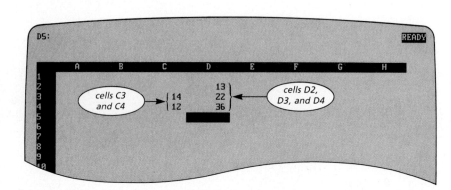

FIGURE 1-55
Problem 4 of Student
Assignment 7

Formula: _____

Result assigned to cell D5: _____

STUDENT ASSIGNMENT 8: Building an Inventory Listing Worksheet

Instructions: Perform the following tasks using a personal computer.

1. Boot the computer.
2. Load 1-2-3 into main computer memory.
3. Build the worksheet illustrated in Figure 1-56. The TOTAL line in row 7 contains the totals for Part A, Part B, and Part C for each of the plants (Seattle, Omaha, and Flint). For example, the total in cell B7 is the sum of the values in cells B4, B5, and B6.
4. Save the worksheet. Use the file name STUS1-8.
5. Print the screen image of the worksheet.

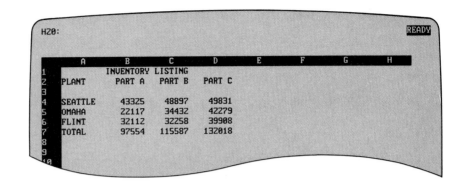

FIGURE 1-56
Student Assignment 8

STUDENT ASSIGNMENT 9: Building a Yearly Personal Expenses Comparison Worksheet

Instructions: Load 1-2-3 and perform the following tasks.

1. Build the worksheet illustrated in Figure 1-57. Calculate the total expenses for THIS YEAR in column C and LAST YEAR in column E by adding the values in the cells representing the rent, food, utilities, auto, insurance, and entertainment expenses.
2. Save the worksheet. Use the file name STUS1-9.
3. Print the screen image of the worksheet.

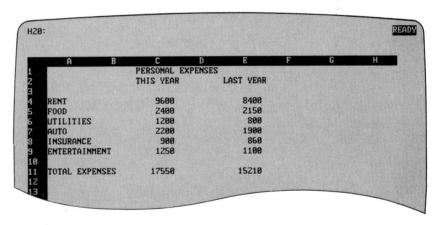

FIGURE 1-57
Student Assignment 9

STUDENT ASSIGNMENT 10: Building a Quarterly Income and Expense Worksheet

Instructions: Load 1-2-3 and perform the following tasks.

1. Build the worksheet illustrated in Figure 1-58. Calculate the total income in row 10 by adding the income for gas and oil, labor, and parts. Calculate the total expenses in row 17 by adding salaries, rent, and cost of goods. Calculate the net profit in row 19 by subtracting the total expenses from the total income.
2. Save the worksheet. Use the file name STUS1-10.
3. Print the screen image of the worksheet.

Student Assignment 10 (continued)

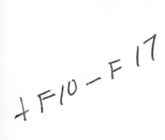

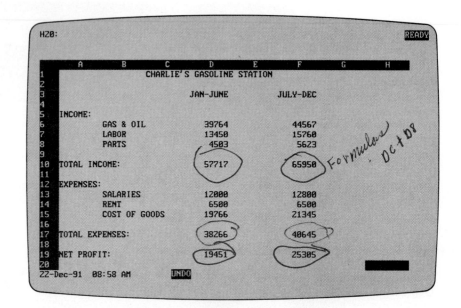

FIGURE 1-58
Student Assignment 10

STUDENT ASSIGNMENT 11: Using the Online Help Facility

Instructions: Load 1-2-3 and perform the following tasks.

1. With 1-2-3 in READY mode, press function key F1. Print the screen image.
2. Select the topic "About 1-2-3 Help". Press the Enter key. Read and print the image of the screen.
3. Select the following help screens: Status Indicators; Control Panel; Mode Indicators; and Entering Data. Read and print the image of each help screen.
4. Press the Esc key to quit the online help facility.

STUDENT ASSIGNMENT 12: Changing Data in the Quarterly Income and Expense Worksheet

Instructions: If you did not do Student Assignment 10, do it before you begin this assignment. With the worksheet in Student Assignment 10 stored on the disk, load 1-2-3 and perform the following tasks.

1. Retrieve the worksheet STUS1-10 (Figure 1-58) from disk. Use the command /**F**ile **R**etrieve (/FR). When the list of worksheet names displays on the menu line, use the arrow keys to move the command cursor to the worksheet name STUS1-10. Press the Enter key. The worksheet illustrated in Figure 1-58 will display on the screen.
2. Make the changes to the worksheet described in Table 1-6. Use the EDIT mode of 1-2-3. Recall that to use EDIT mode to change an entry in a cell, move the cell pointer to the cell and then press function key F2.

Erase work sheet
/ W E Y

TABLE 1-6   List of Corrections to the Quarterly Income and Expense Worksheet

CELL	CURRENT CELL CONTENTS	CHANGE THE CELL CONTENTS TO
C1	CHARLIE'S GASOLINE STATION	CHUCK'S GAS STATION
D6	39764	39564
F6	44567	40592
D8	4503	45003
F8	5623	45623
D13	12000	22000
F13	12800	19765

$$
\begin{array}{r}
44567 \\
15\ 6\ 8 \\
\hline
60\ 3\ 5 \\
5\ 623
\end{array}
$$

   As you edit the values in the cells containing numeric data, keep an eye on the total income, total expenses, and net profit cells. The values in these cells are based on formulas that reference the cells you are editing. You will see that each time a new value is entered into a cell referenced by a formula, 1-2-3 automatically recalculates a new value for the formula. It then stores the new value in the cell assigned the formula. This automatic recalculation of formulas is one of the more powerful aspects of 1-2-3. After you have successfully made the changes listed in Table 1-6, the net profit for Jan–June in cell D19 should equal 49751 and the net profit for July–Dec should equal 54365.

3. Save the worksheet. Use the file name STUS1-12.
4. Print the screen image of the worksheet on the printer.

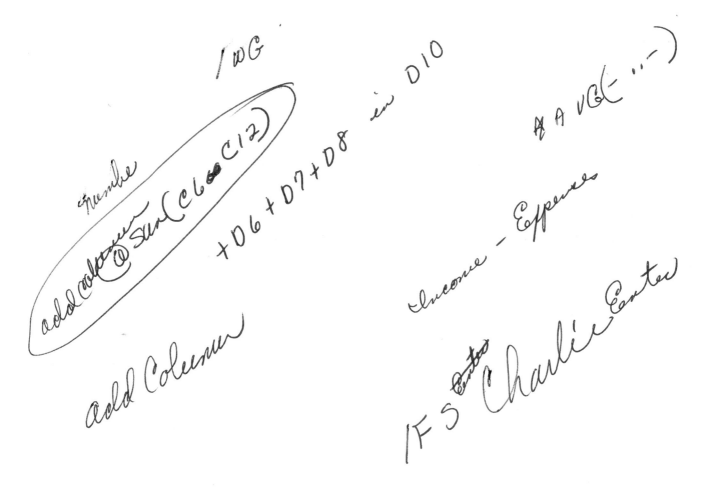

Project 2

Formatting and Printing a Worksheet

Objectives

You will have mastered the material in this project when you can:

- Retrieve a worksheet from disk
- Increase the width of the columns in a worksheet
- Define a range of cells
- Format a worksheet
- Enter repeating characters into a cell using the Backslash key
- Copy one range of cells to another range of cells
- Add the contents of a range using the SUM function
- Determine a percentage
- Print a partial or complete worksheet without window borders
- Print the cell-formulas version of a worksheet
- Display the formulas assigned to cells, rather than their numeric results

 he Sales Report worksheet created in Project 1 contains the revenue, costs, and profit for each of the three months of the first quarter, but it is not presented in the most readable manner. For example, as you can see in Figure 2-1, the columns are too close together and the numbers are displayed as whole numbers, even though they are dollar figures.

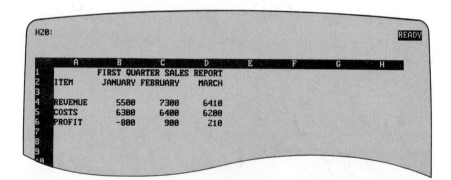

FIGURE 2-1
The worksheet we completed
in Project 1.

In this project we will use the formatting capabilities of 1-2-3 to make the worksheet more presentable and easier to read. We will also add summary totals for the quarter, using formulas. As shown in Figure 2-2, the total revenue in cell B12 is the sum of the revenue values for January, February, and March. The total cost in cell B13 is the sum of the cost values for January, February, and March; and the total profit in cell B14 is the sum of the profit values for January, February, and March. The percent profit in cell B15 is determined by dividing the total profit by the total revenue. After the worksheet is complete, we will print it without the window borders.

```
E20:                                                              READY

              A           B           C           D           E
 1              FIRST QUARTER SALES REPORT
 2    ITEM            JANUARY     FEBRUARY      MARCH
 3
 4    REVENUE          5500.00     7300.00     6410.00
 5    COSTS            6300.00     6400.00     6200.00
 6    PROFIT           -800.00      900.00      210.00
 7
 8    ------------------------------------------------------------
 9
10    QUARTER RESULTS
11
12    TOTAL REVENUE   $19,210.00
13    TOTAL COSTS     $18,900.00
14    TOTAL PROFIT      $310.00
15    % PROFIT            1.6%
16
```

FIGURE 2-2
The worksheet we will complete in Project 2.

RETRIEVING A WORKSHEET FROM DISK

Recall that at the end of Project 1, we used the Save command to store the worksheet in Figure 2-1 on disk under the name PROJS-1.WK1. Since Project 2 involves making modifications to this stored worksheet, we can eliminate retyping the whole worksheet and save a lot of time by retrieving it from disk and placing it into main memory.

After booting the computer and loading the 1-2-3 program, retrieve the worksheet PROJS-1 from the data disk. To retrieve the worksheet, enter the command /File Retrieve (/FR). First, press the Slash key (/) as illustrated in Figure 2-3. This causes 1-2-3 to display the command menu on the input line at the top of the screen. Next, use the Right Arrow key to move the command cursor to the word File. The result of this activity is shown in Figure 2-4 on the next page. With the command cursor on the word File, the File menu displays on the menu line, immediately below the command menu. To select the File menu, press the Enter key or type the letter F.

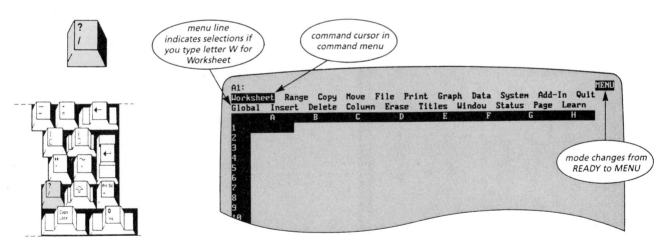

FIGURE 2-3 Step 1 of retrieving a worksheet from disk—press the Slash key (/).

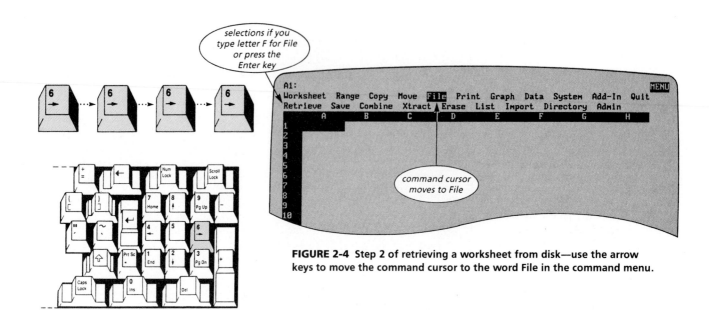

FIGURE 2-4 Step 2 of retrieving a worksheet from disk—use the arrow keys to move the command cursor to the word File in the command menu.

Let's press the Enter key. The command cursor is now active in the File menu as illustrated in Figure 2-5. The Retrieve command is the first command in the list. The message on the menu line indicates the function of this command. With the command cursor on the Retrieve command, type the letter R for Retrieve.

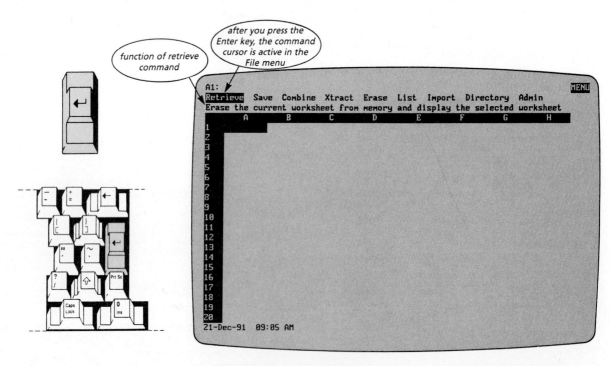

FIGURE 2-5 Step 3 of retrieving a worksheet from disk—press the Enter key to select the File command.

As illustrated in Figure 2-6, 1-2-3 displays on the menu line an alphabetized list of the file names on the default drive that have the extension .WK1. This helps you remember the names of the worksheets stored on the data disk. The list includes all the worksheets you were told to save in Project 1, including PROJS-1.WK1.

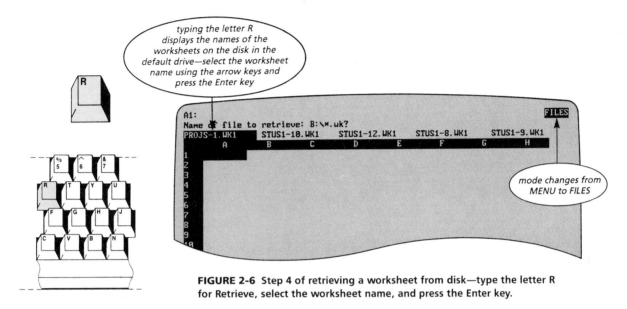

FIGURE 2-6 Step 4 of retrieving a worksheet from disk—type the letter R for Retrieve, select the worksheet name, and press the Enter key.

One way to select the worksheet you want to retrieve is to type PROJS-1 on the input line and press the Enter key. Better yet, because the command cursor is on the file name PROJS-1.WK1 in the list in Figure 2-6, press the Enter key. This method saves keying time. While 1-2-3 is accessing the worksheet, the mode indicator in the upper right corner of the screen changes to WAIT and the red light flashes on the default drive. After the worksheet is retrieved, the screen appears as shown in Figure 2-1.

According to Figure 2-2, all the new labels are in capitals. Therefore, before modifying the worksheet, press the Caps Lock key.

The tasks in this project are to widen the columns, format the dollar amounts, and add the quarter results. The tasks may be completed in any sequence. Let's complete them in the following sequence:

1. Widen the columns from 9 characters to 13 characters to allow the quarter results titles and other numeric data to fit in the columns.
2. Change the numeric representations for the three months to dollars and cents—two digits to the right of the decimal place.
3. Determine the quarter results.
4. Change the percent profit to a number in percent.
5. Change the numeric representations of the quarter results to dollars and cents with a leading dollar sign.

CHANGING THE WIDTH OF THE COLUMNS

When 1-2-3 first executes and the blank worksheet appears on the screen, all the columns have a default width of nine characters. But you might want to change the width of the columns to make the worksheet easier to read or to ensure that entries will display properly in the cells to which they are assigned.

There are three ways to change the width of the columns in a worksheet. First, make a global change, which uniformly increases or decreases the width of all the columns in the worksheet. **Global** means the entire worksheet. Second, change the width of a series of adjacent columns. Third, make a change in the width of one column at a time. Let's use the first method and change the width of all the columns

Changing the Width of All the Columns

To change the width of all the columns, enter the command /**W**orksheet **G**lobal **C**olumn-Width (/WGC). When you press the Slash key, the command menu displays at the top of the screen with the first command, Worksheet, highlighted as shown earlier in Figure 2-3. The **Worksheet menu** displays immediately below the command menu. Note that the first command in the Worksheet menu is Global. This command makes the changes to the entire worksheet. Therefore, type the letter W for Worksheet to move the command cursor to the Worksheet menu, as shown in Figure 2-7.

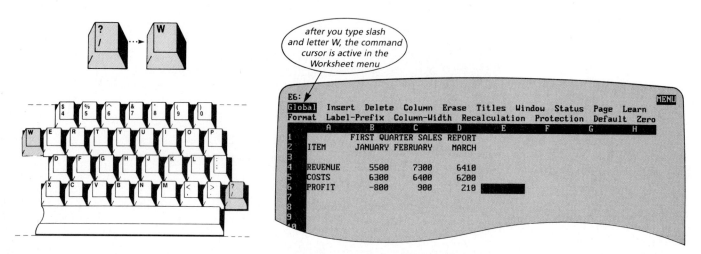

FIGURE 2-7 Step 1 of increasing the width of the columns—press the Slash key (/) and type the letter W.

Type the letter G for Global. This causes the **Global menu** to display on the input line and the **global settings sheet** to display in place of the worksheet. Press F6 if you want to view the worksheet, rather than the global settings sheet, when the Global menu is active. Press F6 again and the global settings sheet displays in place of the worksheet.

With the Global menu active, use the Right Arrow key to move the command cursor to Column-Width. Now the menu line explains the purpose of the Column-Width command. This procedure is illustrated in Figure 2-8.

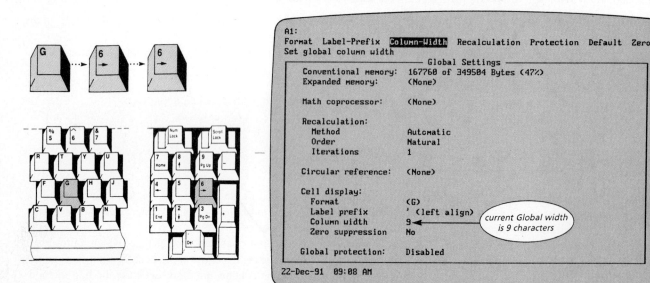

FIGURE 2-8 Step 2 of increasing the width of the columns—type the letter G and use the Right Arrow key to move the command cursor to Column-Width in the Global menu.

Before typing the letter C for Column-Width, if you decided that you did not want to increase the width of the columns, how many times would you have to press the Esc key to *back out* of the command mode in Figure 2-8 and return to READY mode? If your answer is three, you're right—once for the Global command, once for the Worksheet command, and once for the Slash key (/).

Now type the letter C for Column-Width. The prompt message "Enter global column width (1..240): 9" displays on the input line at the top of the screen. This message is illustrated on the screen in Figure 2-9. The numbers 1–240 define the range of valid entries. The number 9 following the colon indicates the current global (default) column width.

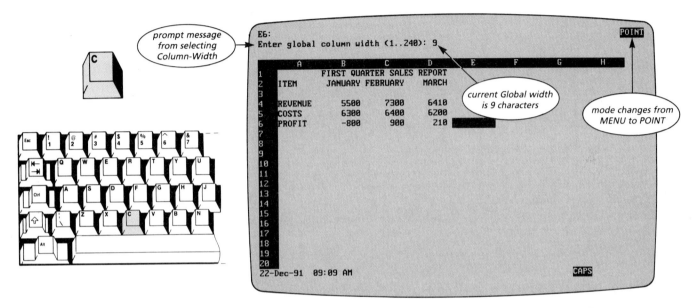

FIGURE 2-9 Step 3 of increasing the width of the columns—type the letter C for Column-Width.

Type the number 13 as shown in Figure 2-10, then press the Enter key. An alternative to typing the number 13 is to use the Right and Left Arrow keys to increase or decrease the number on the input line.

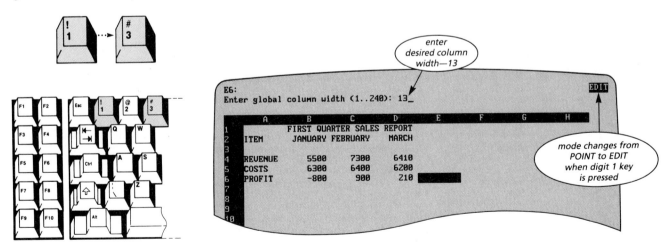

FIGURE 2-10 Step 4 of increasing the width of the columns—enter the number 13.

Figure 2-11 illustrates the worksheet with the new column width of 13 characters. Compare Figure 2-11 to Figure 2-1. Because the columns in Figure 2-11 are wider, the worksheet is easier to read. But because the columns are wider, fewer show on the screen.

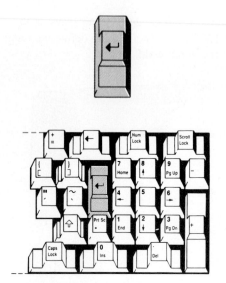

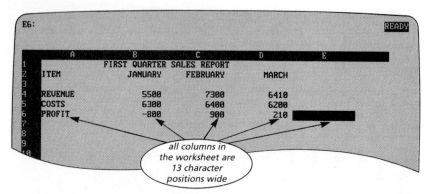

all columns in the worksheet are 13 character positions wide

FIGURE 2-11 Step 5 of increasing the width of the columns—press the Enter key.

Changing the Width of a Series of Adjacent Columns

In Figures 2-7 through 2-11, we used the /Worksheet Global Column-Width (/WGC) command to uniformly change the width of all the columns. Since we were interested in changing only the width of columns A through E to 13 characters, we could have also used the command /Worksheet Column Column-Range Set-Width (/WCCS). This command works the same as the /Worksheet Global Column-Width (/WGC) command, except that you must enter the range of columns that will be affected by the change.

Changing the Width of One Column at a Time

You can change the width of one column at a time in the worksheet. Let's change the width of column A to 20 characters while leaving the width of the other columns at 13 characters. To change the width of column A to 20 characters, do the following:

1. Press the Home key to move the cell pointer into column A.
2. Type the command /Worksheet Column Set-Width (/WCS). The Slash key (/) switches 1-2-3 to the command mode. The letter W selects the Worksheet command. The letter C selects the command Column and the letter S selects the command Set-Width.
3. In response to the prompt message "Enter column width (1..240): 13" on the input line, type the number 20 and press the Enter key.

Now column A is 20 characters wide while the other columns in the worksheet are 13 characters wide. Let's change column A back to the default width of 13 characters. With the cell pointer in column A, enter the command /Worksheet Column Reset-Width (/WCR). This command changes column A back to the default width—13 characters. The UNDO command may also be used to reset the width of column A to the default width. You must be sure, however, that no other entry has been made into the worksheet, since the width was changed from 13 characters to 20 characters.

Use the GOTO command to move the cell pointer back to cell E6, where it was before we set and then reset the width of column A.

DEFINING A RANGE

Our next step is to format the monthly dollar amounts. The Format command requires you to specify the cells you want to format. For this reason, you need to understand the term *range* before using the Format command.

A **range** in 1-2-3 means one or more cells on which an operation can take place. A range may be a single cell, a series of adjacent cells in a row or column, or a rectangular group of adjacent cells. Hence, a range may consist of one cell or many cells. However, a range cannot be made up of cells that only run diagonally or are separated. Figure 2-12 illustrates several valid and invalid ranges of cells.

When you are asked by 1-2-3 to specify a range, you simply type the cell address for the first cell in the range, followed by a **period** (.), followed by the cell address for the last cell in the range. If a range defines a rectangular group of cells, any pair of diagonally opposite corner cells may be used to identify it. For example, the upper left cell and the lower right cell of the rectangular group of cells identify the range. Table 2-1 summarizes the ranges described in Figure 2-12.

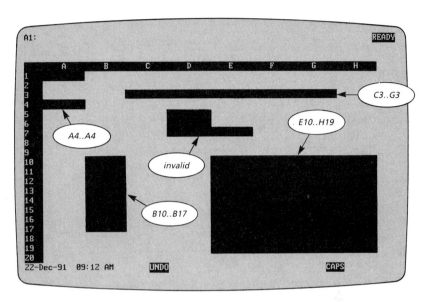

FIGURE 2-12 Valid and invalid ranges.

TABLE 2-1 A Summary of the Ranges Specified in Figure 2-12

RANGE	COMMENT
A4..A4	The range is made up of one cell, A4.
C3..G3	The range is made up of five adjacent cells in row 3. The five cells are C3, D3, E3, F3, and G3.
B10..B17	The range is made up of eight adjacent cells in column B. The eight cells are B10, B11, B12, B13, B14, B15, B16, and B17.
E10..H19	The range is made up of a rectangular group of cells. The upper left cell (E10) and the lower right cell (H19) define the rectangle. The ranges H19..E10, H10..E19, and E19..H10 define the same range as E10..H19.

Now that you know how to define a range, we can move on to the next step in Project 2: formatting the numeric values in the worksheet.

FORMATTING NUMERIC VALUES

The Format command is used to control the manner in which numeric values appear in the worksheet. As shown in Figure 2-2, we want to change the numeric values in the range B4 through D6 to display as dollars and cents with two digits to the right of the decimal point.

Invoking the Format Command

There are two ways to invoke the Format command. First, you can use the series of commands /**W**orksheet **G**lobal **F**ormat (/WGF) to format all the cells in the worksheet the same way. Second, you can use the commands /**R**ange **F**ormat (/RF) to format just a particular range of cells. Since this project involves formatting a range rather than all the cells in the worksheet, type /RF to activate the command cursor in the Format menu as shown in Figure 2-13. The **Format menu** on the input line lists the different ways to format a range. As indicated on the third line of the control panel, the first format type in the menu, Fixed, formats cells to a fixed number of decimal places. This is the format we want to use to display the monthly amounts to two decimal places. Therefore, type the letter F for Fixed.

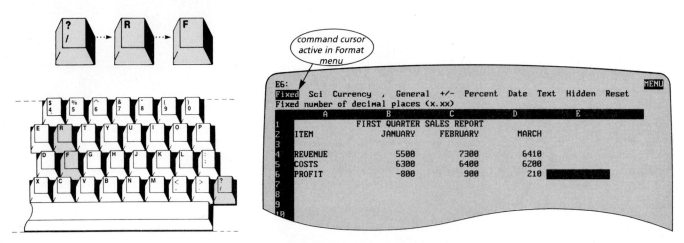

FIGURE 2-13 Step 1 of formatting a range of cells—press the Slash key (/) and type the letters R for Range and F for Format.

As shown in Figure 2-14, 1-2-3 displays the message "Enter number of decimal places (0..15): 2" on the input line at the top of the screen. Since most spreadsheet applications require two decimal positions, 1-2-3 displays 2 as the entry to save you time. Press the Enter key to enter two decimal positions. Next, 1-2-3 changes to POINT mode and displays the message "Enter range to format: E6..E6" (Figure 2-15). The range E6..E6 displays at the end of the input line because the cell pointer is at cell E6. Enter the range by typing B4.D6, or use the arrow keys to select the range. (Don't be concerned that 1-2-3 displays two periods between the cell address when you press the Period key once. It is the program's way of displaying a range.) Using the arrow keys to select a range is called **pointing**. Let's use the pointing method, as described on the next page, because it requires less effort.

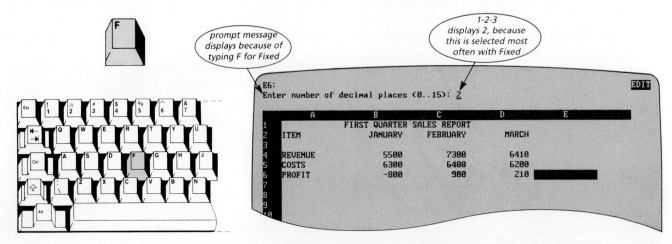

FIGURE 2-14 Step 2 of formatting a range of cells—type the letter F for Fixed and 1-2-3 displays a prompt message on the input line.

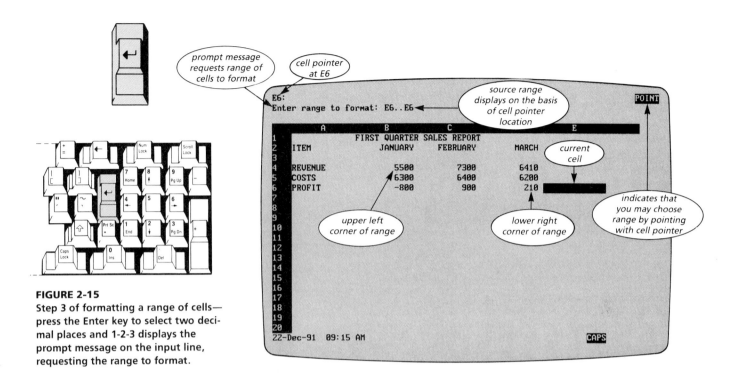

FIGURE 2-15
Step 3 of formatting a range of cells—
press the Enter key to select two decimal places and 1-2-3 displays the
prompt message on the input line,
requesting the range to format.

Selecting a Range by Pointing

To select a range by pointing, first press the Backspace key (or Esc key) to change the default entry on the input line in Figure 2-15 from E6..E6 to E6. Next, use the arrow keys to move the cell pointer to B4, the upper left corner cell of the desired range. This procedure is shown in Figure 2-16.

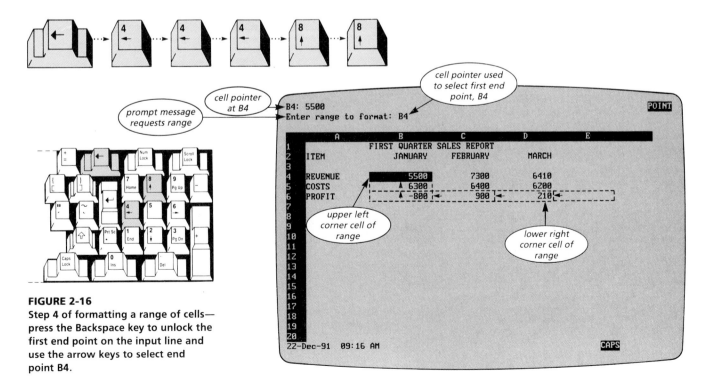

FIGURE 2-16
Step 4 of formatting a range of cells—
press the Backspace key to unlock the
first end point on the input line and
use the arrow keys to select end
point B4.

With the cell pointer at B4, press the Period key to *lock in* or *anchor* the first end point, B4. The B4 on the input line changes to B4..B4.

Now use the arrow keys to move the cell pointer to cell D6, the lower right corner of the desired range. Press the Down Arrow key twice and the Right Arrow key twice. As the cell pointer moves, a reverse video rectangle forms over the range covered. The range on the input line changes from B4..B4 to B4..D6 (Figure 2-17). Press the Enter key. 1-2-3 immediately displays the monthly values in cells B4, C4, D4, B5, C5, D5, B6, C6, and D6 with two decimal places (dollars and cents). Everything else in the worksheet remains the same as shown in Figure 2-18.

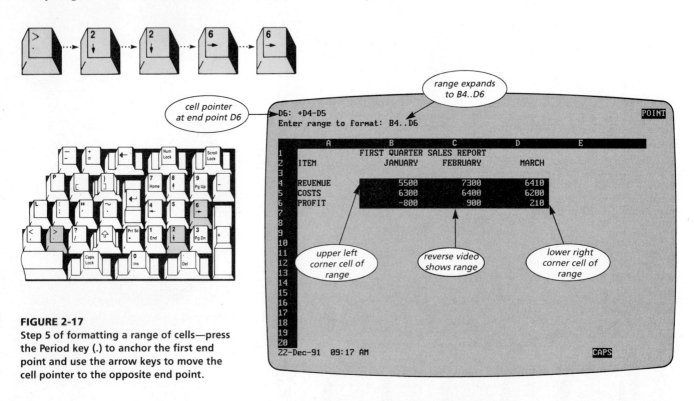

FIGURE 2-17
Step 5 of formatting a range of cells—press the Period key (.) to anchor the first end point and use the arrow keys to move the cell pointer to the opposite end point.

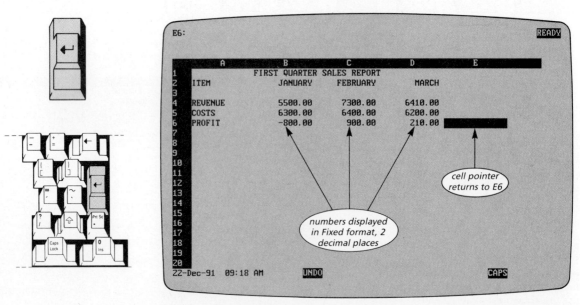

FIGURE 2-18 Step 6 of formatting a range of cells—press the Enter key and the numbers in the range B4..D6 display in Fixed format.

Don't forget that the UNDO command is available when 1-2-3 returns to READY mode after the worksheet is formatted. Thus, if you want to reset the worksheet to what it was before formatting it, issue the UNDO command (Alt-F4).

We could have used three other ways to describe the rectangular group of cells B4..D6 to 1-2-3. B6..D4 and D4..B6 are two other ways. Can you identify the third way?

Summary of Format Commands

You can format numbers in cells in a variety of ways using the /**W**orksheet **G**lobal **F**ormat (/WGF) or /**R**ange **F**ormat (/RF) commands. Table 2-2 summarizes the various format options. You will find Table 2-2 helpful when you begin formatting your own worksheets. Also, remember that 1-2-3 rounds a number to the rightmost position if any digits are lost because of the format or number of decimal positions chosen.

TABLE 2-2   Format Types for Numeric Values in the Format Menu

MENU ITEM	DESCRIPTION
Fixed	Displays numbers to a specified number of decimal places. Negative values are displayed with a leading minus sign. Examples: 38; 0.912; –45.67.
Sci	Displays numbers in a form called **scientific notation**. The letter E stands for "times 10 to the power." Examples: 3.7E + 01; –2.357E–30.
Currency	Displays numbers preceded by a dollar sign next to the leftmost digit, with a specified number of decimal places (0–15), and uses commas to group the integer portion of the number by thousands. Negative numbers display in parentheses. Examples: $1,234.56; $0.98; $23,934,876.15; ($48.34).
,	The , (comma) is the same as the Currency format, except the dollar sign does not display. Examples: 2,123.00; 5,456,023.34; (22,000).
General	This is the default format in which a number is stored when it is entered into a cell. Trailing zeros are suppressed and leading integer zeros display. Negative numbers display with a leading minus sign. Examples: 23.981; 0.563; 23401; –500.45.
+ /–	Displays a single horizontal bar graph composed of plus (+) or minus (–) signs that indicate the sign of the number and the magnitude of the number. One plus or minus sign displays for each unit value. Only the integer portion of the number is used. Examples: + + + + + + for 6; ––– for –3.8.
Percent	Displays numbers in percent form. Examples: 34% for 0.34; .11% for 0.0011; –13.245% for –0.13245.
Date	Used to format cells that contain a date or time.
Text	Displays formulas rather than their values. Numbers appear in General format. Examples: + B4–B5; 2*(F5 – G3).
Hidden	Prevents the display of the cell contents on the screen and when printed. To see what's in a hidden cell, move the pointer to that cell. The contents will display on the status line.
Reset	Resets cells back to Global format.

Determining the Format Assigned to a Cell

You can determine the format assigned to a cell by the Range Format command by moving the cell pointer to that cell. The format displays on the status line in the upper left corner of the screen, next to the cell address. In Figure 2-19, the cell pointer is at cell D6. Format F2 displays on the status line in parentheses next to the cell address. F2 is an abbreviation for the format "Fixed, 2 decimal places." Recall that we assigned this format to cell D4 in Figures 2-13 through 2-18.

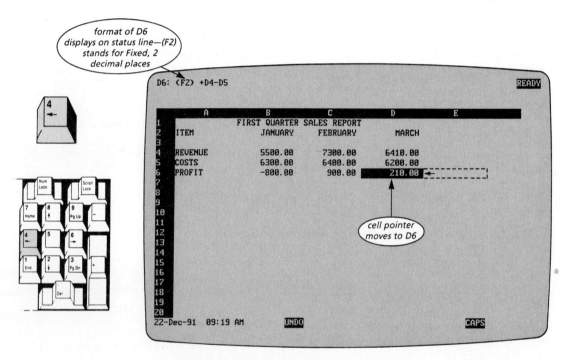

FIGURE 2-19 The format assigned to a cell displays on the status line when the cell pointer is on the cell.

REPEATING CHARACTERS IN A CELL

In Figure 2-2, row 8 contains a dashed line. We will add the dashed line to the worksheet using **repeating characters**—characters that are repeated throughout a cell.

To enter the dashed line, move the cell pointer to cell A8 using the GOTO command. Recall that function key F5 invokes the GOTO command. Next, enter the cell address A8 and press the Enter key. The cell pointer immediately moves to cell A8 as shown in Figure 2-20.

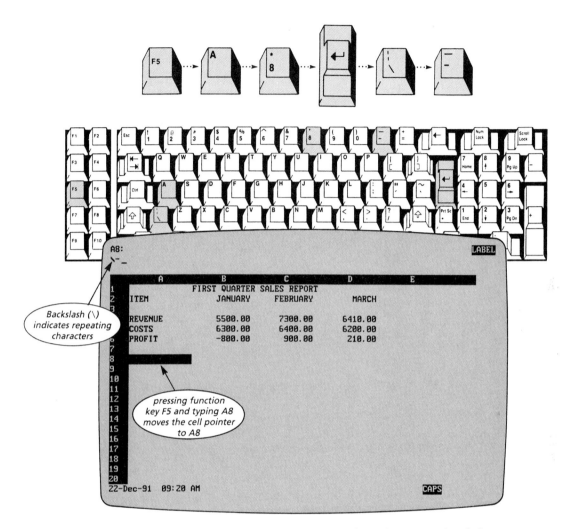

FIGURE 2-20 Moving the cell pointer to A8 and entering a repeating dash on the input line.

With the cell pointer at A8, press the Backslash key (\). The **Backslash key** signals 1-2-3 that the character or sequence of characters that follow it on the input line are to be repeated throughout the cell. Repeating the minus sign (–) creates the dashed line shown in Figure 2-2. Therefore, immediately after the Backslash key, press the Minus Sign key once as illustrated at the top of the screen in Figure 2-20.

To enter the repeating dash, press the Enter key. The dash repeats throughout cell A8 as shown in Figure 2-21. Note that the Backslash key is not included as part of the cell entry. Like the quotation mark ("), circumflex (^), and apostrophe ('), the backslash (\) is used as the first character that instructs 1-2-3 what to do with the characters that follow on the input line.

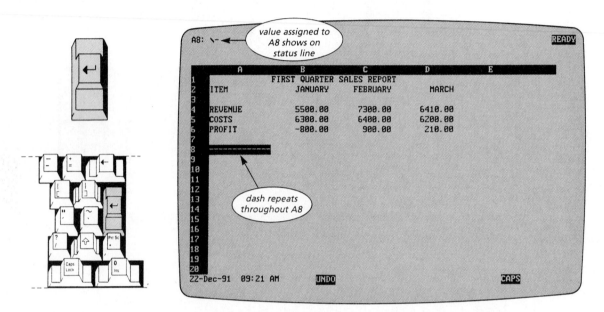

FIGURE 2-21 Press the Enter key to assign the repeating dash to cell A8.

We still need to extend the dashed line through cells B8, C8, and D8. We can move the cell pointer to each individual cell and make the same entry we made in cell A8, or we can use the Copy command. Let's use the Copy command.

REPLICATION—THE COPY COMMAND

*T*he /Copy command (/C) is used to copy or replicate the contents of one group of cells to another group of cells. This command is one of the most useful because it can save you both time and keystrokes when you build a worksheet. We will use the Copy command to copy the dashes in cell A8 to cells B8 through D8. Type the Slash key (/) to place 1-2-3 in the command mode. In the command menu list, the Copy command is the third one. Type the letter C to invoke the Copy command.

Source Range

When the Copy command is selected, the prompt message "Enter range to copy FROM: A8..A8" displays on the input line as shown in Figure 2-22. The **source range** is the range we want to copy. Since A8 is the cell that we want to copy to B8 through D8, press the Enter key.

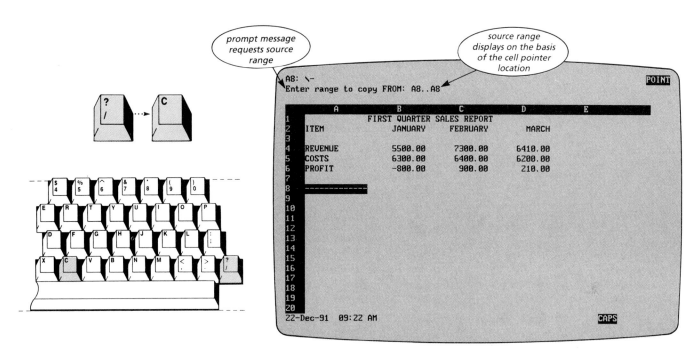

FIGURE 2-22 Step 1 of copying a range of cells—press the Slash key (/) and type the letter C for Copy.

Destination Range

After you press the Enter key, the prompt message "Enter range to copy TO: A8" displays on the input line as shown in Figure 2-23. The **destination range** is the range to which we want to copy the source range.

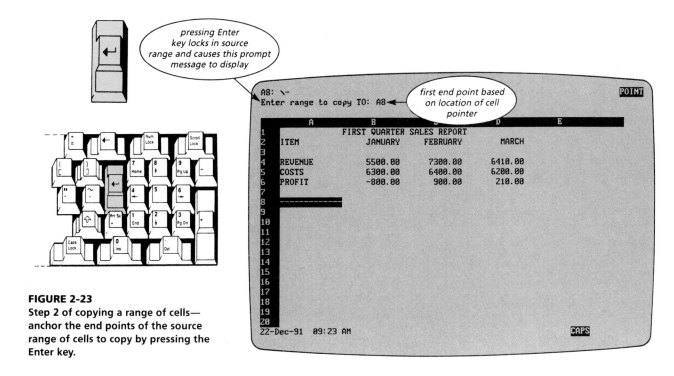

FIGURE 2-23
Step 2 of copying a range of cells—anchor the end points of the source range of cells to copy by pressing the Enter key.

Move the cell pointer to B8, the left end point of the range to copy to (Figure 2-24). Note that following the prompt message on the input line, the cell address is now B8, the location of the cell pointer.

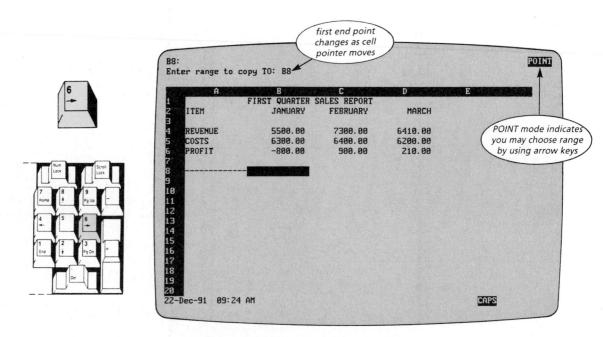

FIGURE 2-24 Step 3 of copying a range of cells—move the cell pointer to one of the end points of the destination range.

Press the Period key to anchor end point B8 and move the cell pointer to D8 as shown in Figure 2-25. Finally, press the Enter key to copy cell A8 to cells B8 through D8 (Figure 2-26).

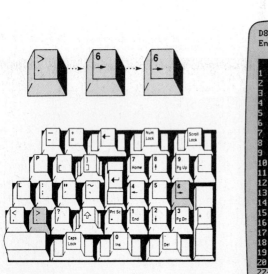

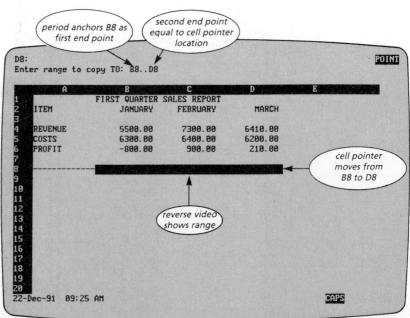

FIGURE 2-25 Step 4 of copying a range of cells—press the Period key and move the cell pointer to the opposite end point of the destination range.

As illustrated in Figure 2-26, the dashed line is complete and the cell pointer is back at cell A8, where it was before invoking the Copy command.

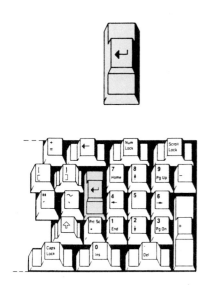

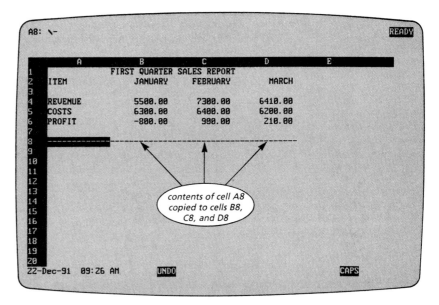

FIGURE 2-26 Step 5 of copying a range of cells—press the Enter key to anchor the end points of the destination range and complete the copy.

With the dashed line complete, move the cell pointer to A10 and begin entering the labels that identify the quarter results. First enter the label QUARTER RESULTS and press the Down Arrow key twice as shown in Figure 2-27.

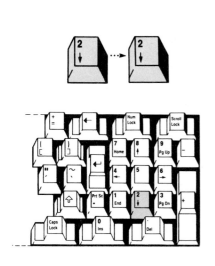

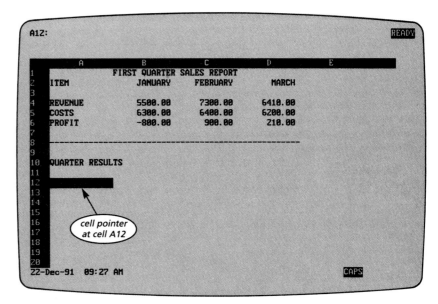

FIGURE 2-27 Step 1 of entering the total labels.

Enter the remaining labels that identify the quarter results in cells A12 through A15. Use the Down Arrow key to enter each one. After the label entries are complete, the cell pointer ends up at cell A16 as illustrated in Figure 2-28. Use the GOTO command to move the cell pointer to cell B12, the location of the next entry.

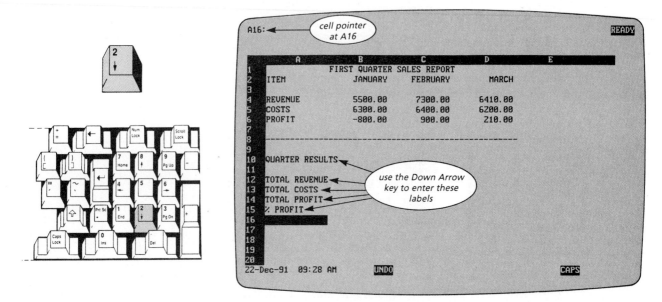

FIGURE 2-28 Step 2 of entering the total labels.

SAVING AN INTERMEDIATE COPY OF THE WORKSHEET

It's good practice to save intermediate copies of your worksheet. That way, if the computer loses power or you make a serious mistake, you can always retrieve the latest copy on disk. We recommend that you save an intermediate copy of the worksheet every 50 to 75 keystrokes. It makes sense to use the Save command often, because it saves keying time later if the unexpected happens.

Before we continue with Project 2, let's save the current worksheet as PROJS-2. Recall that to save the worksheet displayed on the screen you must do the following:

1. Enter the command /File Save (/FS).
2. In response to the prompt message on the input line, type the new file name, PROJS-2. As soon as you type the letter P in PROJS-2, the old file name, PROJS-1, disappears from the input line. File name PROJS-1 is on the input line because we retrieved it to begin this project and 1-2-3 assumes we want to save the revised worksheet under the same name.
3. Press the Enter key.

After 1-2-3 completes the save, the worksheet remains on the screen. You can immediately continue with the next entry.

USING BUILT-IN FUNCTIONS

1-2-3 has many **built-in functions** that automatically handle calculations. These built-in functions save you a lot of time and effort because they eliminate the need to enter complex formulas. The first built-in function we will discuss is the SUM function, since it is one of the most widely used. For the remainder of the projects in this book, the term *function* will mean built-in function.

Save Sales
/ F S. Sales

The SUM Function

In the worksheet for Project 2, the total revenue is calculated by adding the values in cells B4, C4, and D4. While the calculation can be written in cell B12 as + B4 + C4 + D4, an easier and more general method to produce the same result is to use the SUM function. The **SUM function** adds the values in the specified range.

With the cell pointer at B12, enter @SUM(B4.D4) as illustrated on the input line at the top of the screen in Figure 2-29. Note that the SUM function begins with the **at symbol** (@). Beginning an entry with the @ symbol indicates to 1-2-3 that the entry is a function.

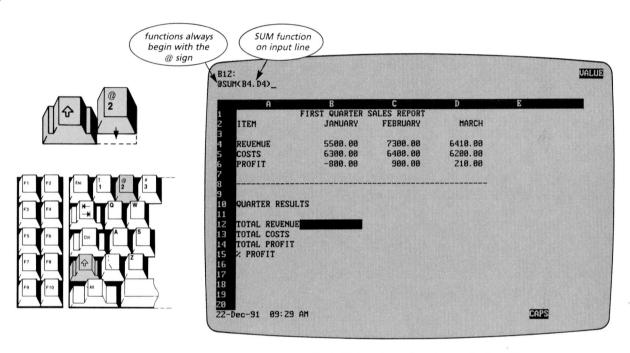

FIGURE 2-29 Entering a function on the input line.

After the @ symbol, type the function name SUM (or sum) followed by a left parenthesis. Next, enter B4.D4, the range to be added. The range can be specified either by typing the beginning and ending cells or by using the pointing feature described earlier. In this case, type the two end points of the range separated by a period (.). Finally, type the right parenthesis.

Press the Enter key as shown in Figure 2-30 on the next page. As a result, 1-2-3 evaluates the sum of the entries in cells B4, C4, and D4 and displays the result in cell B12. Functions belong to the broader category called *formulas*. Therefore, 1-2-3 handles functions the same way it handles formulas—it evaluates the function and places a number in the cell. For example, in Figure 2-30, you can see on the status line that the formula @SUM(B4..D4) is assigned to cell B12. However, the value 19210 displays in cell B12 of the worksheet. The value 19210 is the sum of the numbers in cells B4, C4, and D4.

F o/o/ enter

+B14 / B12

/ Range / .doe

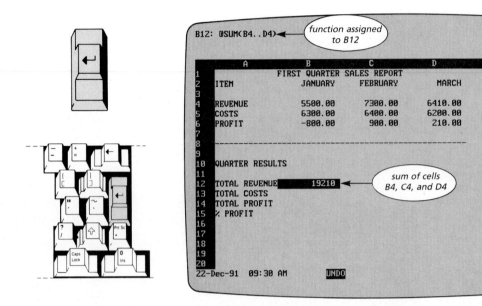

FIGURE 2-30 Press the Enter key to assign the function to B12. When a function is assigned to a cell, it is evaluated and the value displays in the cell.

Copying Functions

According to Figure 2-2, the two cells B13 and B14 require the identical function and similar ranges that we assigned to cell B12 in Figure 2-30. That is, cell B13 should contain the total costs for the quarter, or the sum of cells B5, C5, and D5. Cell B14 should contain the total profit for the quarter, or the sum of cells B6, C6, and D6. Table 2-3 illustrates the similarity between the entry in cell B12 and the entries required in cells B13 and B14.

TABLE 2-3   Three Function Entries for Cells B12, B13, and B14

CELL	FUNCTION ENTRIES
B12	@SUM(B4..D4)
B13	@SUM(B5..D5)
B14	@SUM(B6..D6)

There are two methods for entering the functions in cells B13 and B14. The first method involves moving the cell pointer to B13, entering the function @SUM(B5..D5), then moving the cell pointer to B14 and entering the function @SUM(B6..D6).

The second method, the one we are going to use, involves using the Copy command. That is, copy cell B12 to cells B13 and B14. Note in Table 2-3, however, that the ranges do not agree exactly. Each cell below B12 has a range that is one row below the previous one. Fortunately, when the Copy command copies cell addresses, it adjusts them for the new position. This cell-address adjustment used by the Copy command is called **relative addressing**. In other words, after cell B12 is copied to cells B13 and B14, the contents of B13 and B14 are identical to the entries shown in Table 2-3.

Let's complete the copy from cell B12 to cells B13 and B14. With the cell pointer at B12 as shown in Figure 2-30, enter the command /Copy (/C). The prompt message "Enter range to copy FROM: B12..B12" displays on the input line as shown in Figure 2-31. Since B12 is the cell that we want to copy to cells B13 and B14, press the Enter key.

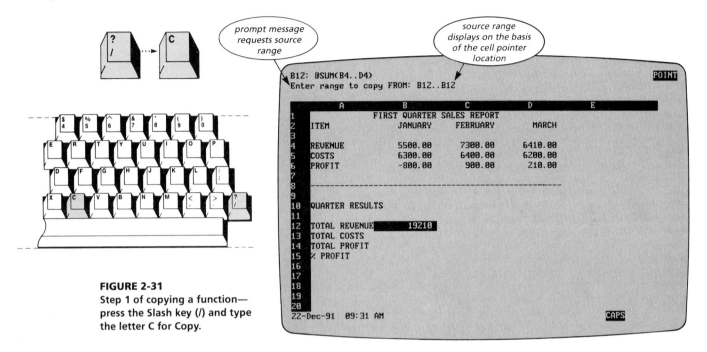

FIGURE 2-31
Step 1 of copying a function—
press the Slash key (/) and type
the letter C for Copy.

When we press the Enter key, the prompt message "Enter range to copy TO: B12" displays on the input line. This message is shown in Figure 2-32. Use the Down Arrow key to move the cell pointer to B13, the topmost end point of the destination range.

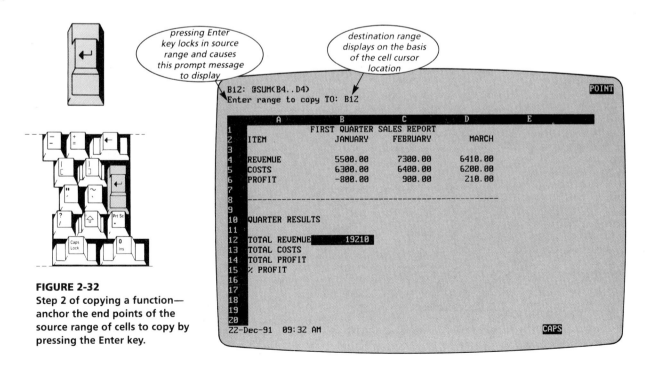

FIGURE 2-32
Step 2 of copying a function—
anchor the end points of the
source range of cells to copy by
pressing the Enter key.

As shown in Figure 2-33, the cell address following the prompt message on the input line has changed from B12 to B13.

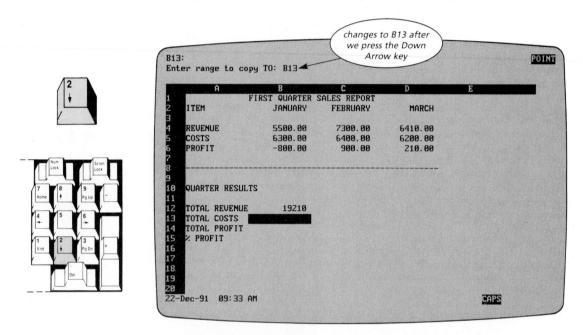

FIGURE 2-33 Step 3 of copying a function—move the cell pointer to one of the end points of the destination range.

Press the Period key to anchor the topmost end point, B13. Next, move the cell pointer to B14 as shown in Figure 2-34. Finally, press the Enter key to copy the function in cell B12 to cells B13 and B14. As illustrated in Figure 2-35 on the next page, cell B13 contains the total costs for the quarter and cell B14 contains the total profit for the quarter. The cell pointer remains at cell B12, where it was before invoking the Copy command.

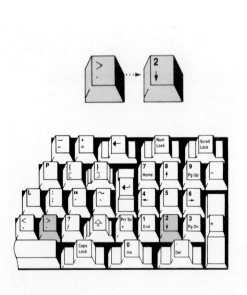

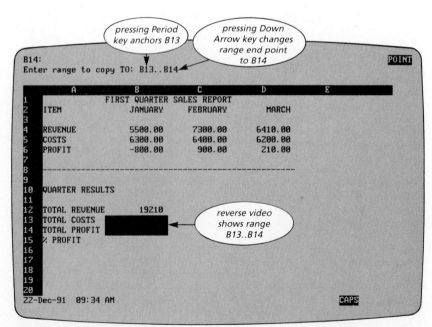

FIGURE 2-34 Step 4 of copying a function—move the cell pointer to the opposite end point of the destination range.

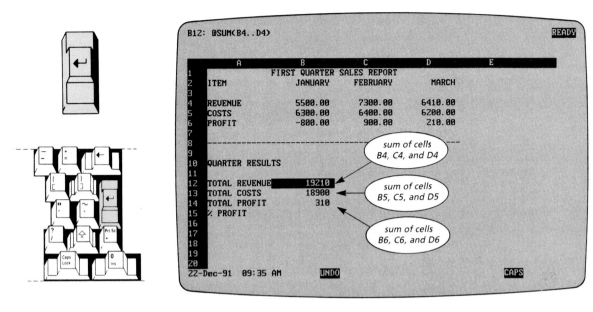

FIGURE 2-35 Step 5 of copying a function—press the Enter key to anchor the end points of the destination range and complete the copy.

Here again, you can undo the Copy command by entering the UNDO command (Alt-F4) after 1-2-3 completes the copy and returns to READY Mode.

DETERMINING A PERCENT VALUE

According to Figure 2-2, the percent profit appears in cell B15. The percent profit is determined by assigning a formula that divides the total profit (cell B14) by the total revenue (cell B12). Recall that the Slash key (/) represents the operation of division, provided it is not the first key typed in the READY mode and the entry is not a label.

Move the cell pointer to cell B15 and enter the formula +B14/B12 as shown on the input line in Step 1 of Figure 2-36 on the next page. Next, press the Enter key. 1-2-3 determines the quotient of +B14/B12 and stores the result, 0.0161374284, in cell B15. This is shown in Step 2 of Figure 2-36.

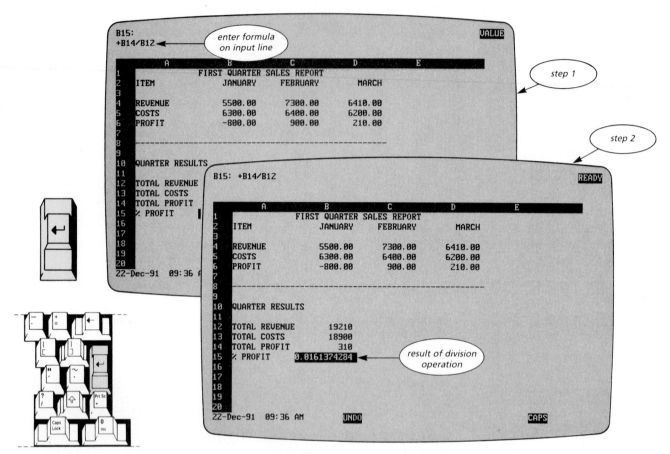

FIGURE 2-36 Entering a percentage. Step 1, enter the formula + B14/B12. Step 2, press the Enter key.

FORMATTING TO PERCENT AND CURRENCY

Although the quarter totals displayed on the worksheet in Figure 2-36 are correct, they are not in an easy-to-read format. The dollar values are displayed as whole numbers and the percentage value is displayed as a decimal number carried out to 10 places. In Figure 2-2, the dollar figures in the quarter results are displayed as dollars and cents with a leading dollar sign. Furthermore, the quotient in cell B15 is displayed as a percent with one decimal place. Let's complete the formatting for this project.

The Percentage Format

Since the cell pointer is at B15, first format the decimal value to a percentage value. With the pointer on cell B15, enter the command /Range Format (/RF) as illustrated in Figure 2-37. With the command cursor active in the Format menu, type the letter P to select the Percent format. Remember, you can also select the command Percent by moving the command cursor to highlight the word Percent and pressing the Enter key.

When you type the letter P, 1-2-3 displays the prompt message "Enter number of decimal places (0..15): 2" on the input line. Type the digit 1 for one decimal position. This procedure is shown in Figure 2-38.

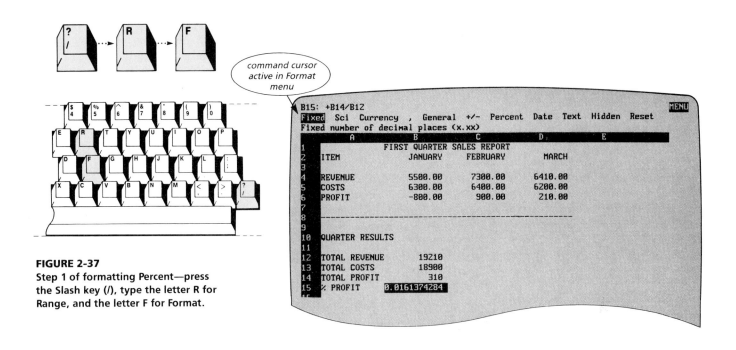

FIGURE 2-37
Step 1 of formatting Percent—press
the Slash key (/), type the letter R for
Range, and the letter F for Format.

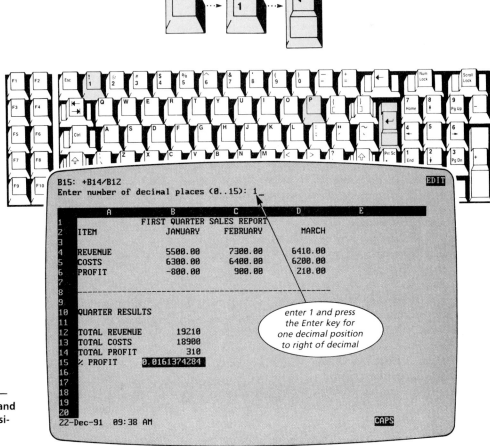

FIGURE 2-38
Step 2 of formatting Percent—
type the letter P for Percent and
the number 1 for decimal positions desired.

Next, press the Enter key. 1-2-3 displays the prompt message "Enter range to format: B15..B15" on the input line. Press the Enter key, since we want to assign this format only to cell B15. The decimal number 0.0161374284, assigned to cell B15 by the formula +B14/B12, now displays as 1.6%. This result is shown in Figure 2-39.

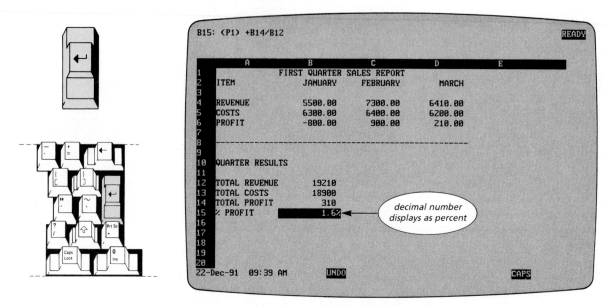

FIGURE 2-39 Step 3 of formatting Percent—press the Enter key, because the range of cells to be affected is only the cell where the cell pointer is.

The Currency Format

The next step is to format the quarter results in cells B12, B13, and B14 to dollars and cents with a leading dollar sign. Scanning the list of available formats in Table 2-2 reveals that the Currency format is the one that displays monetary amounts with a leading dollar sign. Move the cell pointer to cell B12 and type the command **/R**ange **F**ormat **C**urrency (/RFC). This activity is shown in Figure 2-40.

Press the Enter key in response to the prompt message "Enter number of decimal places (0..15): 2" because the desired number of decimal positions is 2. As shown on the input line in Figure 2-41, 1-2-3 wants to know the range to assign the Currency format. Use the pointing method to enter the range.

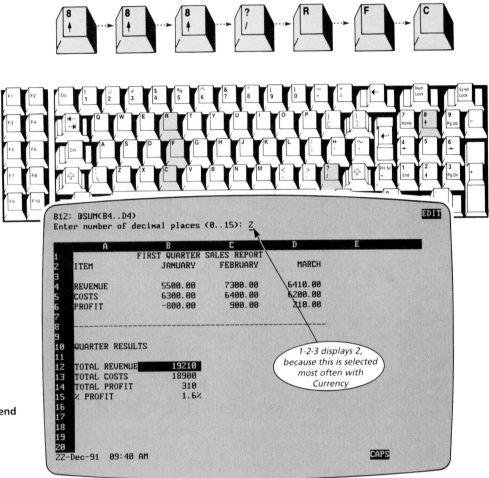

FIGURE 2-40
Step 1 of formatting Currency—move the cell pointer to one of the end points of the range of cells to be affected, press the Slash key (/), R for Range, F for Format, and C for Currency.

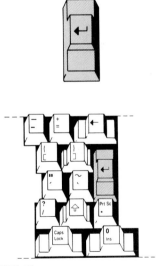

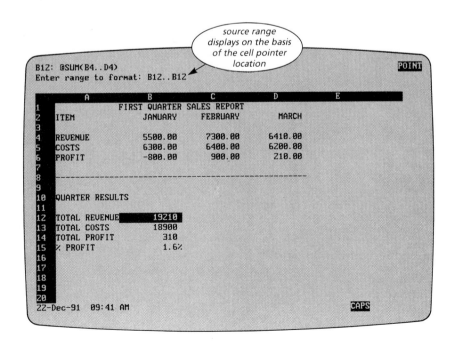

FIGURE 2-41
Step 2 of formatting Currency—press the Enter key. This sets decimal places to 2 and displays the prompt message on the input line.

The first cell address, B12, on the input line is correct. Therefore, move the cell pointer down to B14. As the cell pointer moves, 1-2-3 displays the range in reverse video. Also, the second cell address on the input line changes to agree with the location of the cell pointer. With the cell pointer on B14, the range we want to assign the Currency format is now correct (Figure 2-42).

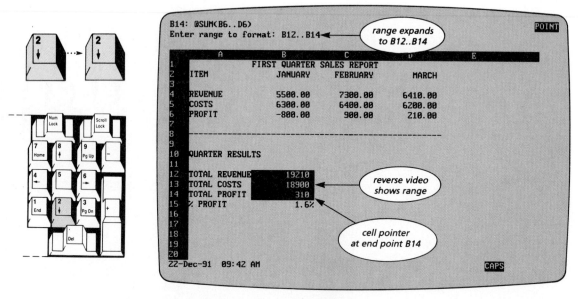

FIGURE 2-42 Step 3 of formatting Currency—use the arrow keys to select the range of cells to be affected.

Next, press the Enter key to assign the Currency format to the designated range in Figure 2-42, cells B12 through B14. Finally, press the Home key to move the cell pointer from cell B12 to cell A1 to prepare for the final step, printing the worksheet. Recall from Project 1 that no matter where the cell pointer is in the worksheet, it immediately moves to cell A1 when you press the Home key. The complete worksheet is shown in Figure 2-43.

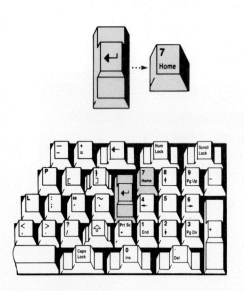

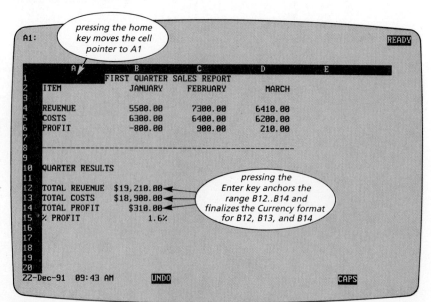

FIGURE 2-43 Step 4 of formatting Currency—press the Enter key to lock in the range B12..B14. The worksheet is complete. Press the Home key to move the cell pointer to A1.

SAVING THE WORKSHEET A SECOND TIME

e already saved an intermediate version of the worksheet as PROJS-2.
To save the worksheet again, do the following:

1. Enter the command **/F**ile **S**ave (/FS).
2. Since we saved this worksheet earlier in the session, 1-2-3 assumes we want to save it under the same file name. Therefore, it displays the name PROJS-2.WK1 on the input line at the top of the screen as shown in the first screen in Figure 2-44. This saves keying time. Press the Enter key.
3. The menu at the top of the lower screen in Figure 2-44 gives three choices—Cancel, Replace, or Backup. Type the letter R for Replace. 1-2-3 replaces the worksheet we saved earlier on disk with the worksheet on the screen.

If we type the letter C for Cancel, rather than R for Replace, the Save command is terminated, and 1-2-3 returns to READY mode. If we type the letter B for Backup, the worksheet on disk with the same name is saved under the file name PROJS-2.BAK, and the worksheet on the screen is saved under the name PROJS-2.WK1. A worksheet stored with the extension .BAK is referred to as a **backup**. Saving a backup copy of the worksheet is another form of protection against losing all your work.

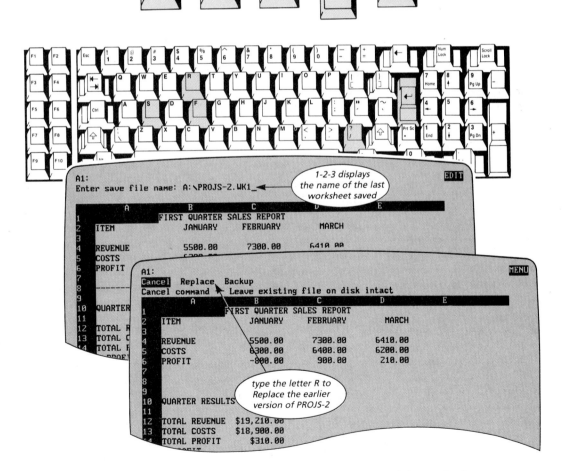

FIGURE 2-44 When a worksheet is saved a second time under the same file name, type the letter R to replace the previous version on disk.

PRINTING THE WORKSHEET

*I*n Project 1, we printed the worksheet by pressing Shift-PrtSc. The printed report included the window borders as well as the control panel and indicator line. However, window borders clutter the report and make it more difficult to read. In this section, we will discuss how to print the worksheet without the window borders, how to print sections of the worksheet, and how to print the actual entries assigned to the cells in a worksheet.

The Print Printer Command

To print the worksheet without window borders, type the command /**P**rint **P**rinter (/PP). This activates the command cursor in the **Print menu** at the top of the screen as shown in Figure 2-45. Below the Print menu, 1-2-3 displays the **print settings sheet**. Press F6 if you want to view the worksheet, rather than the print settings sheet, while the Print menu is active. Press F6 again to view the print settings sheet.

Since this is the first time we are printing this report using the Print command, we must enter the range to print. Therefore, type the letter R to select Range from the Print menu. The entire worksheet is in the range A1..D15. With the cell pointer at cell A1, press the Period key to anchor A1. Next, use the arrow keys to move the cell pointer to D15. As the cell pointer moves, the reverse video enlarges to encompass the entire range (Figure 2-46). Press the Enter key to anchor end point D15. The Print menu reappears as shown in Figure 2-47.

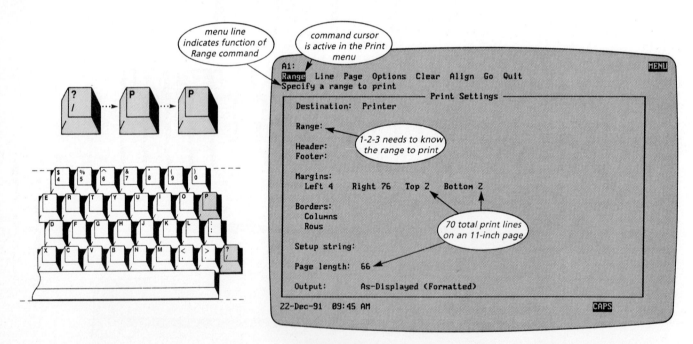

FIGURE 2-45 Step 1 of printing a worksheet using the Print command—press the Slash key (/) and type the letter P twice, once for Print and once for Printer.

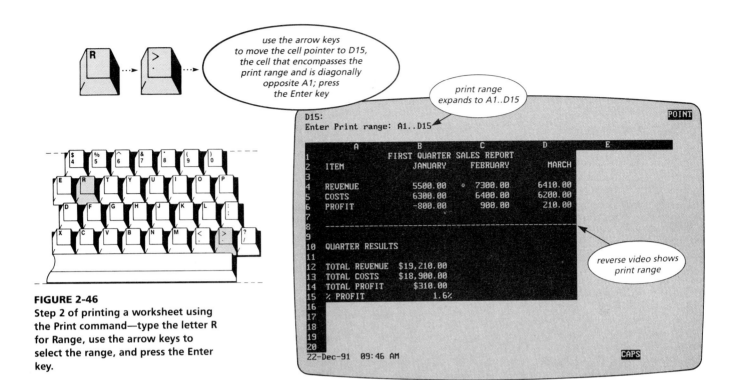

FIGURE 2-46
Step 2 of printing a worksheet using the Print command—type the letter R for Range, use the arrow keys to select the range, and press the Enter key.

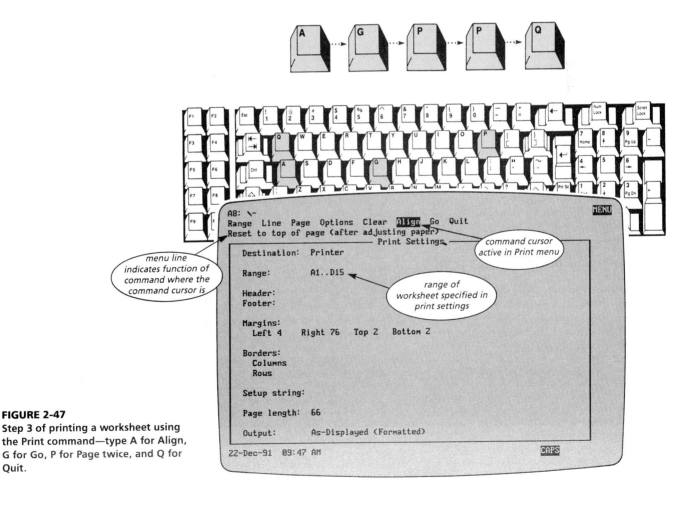

FIGURE 2-47
Step 3 of printing a worksheet using the Print command—type A for Align, G for Go, P for Page twice, and Q for Quit.

With the printer turned off, use the platen knob on the printer to align the perforated edge of the paper with the top of the print-head mechanism. Turn the printer on.

Type the letter A for Align. 1-2-3 has its own line counter. Invoking the Align command ensures that the program's line counter is the same as the printer's line counter; that is, that both counters are equal to zero after you turn the printer on and enter the Align command. If the two counters do not agree, the printed version of the worksheet may end up with a few inches of white space in the middle.

Next, type the letter G for Go. The printer immediately begins to print the worksheet. When the printer stops printing, type the letter P twice. Typing the letter P once invokes the Page command, which causes the paper in the printer to move to the top of the next page. Typing the letter P a second time moves the page with the printed worksheet completely out of the printer. Carefully tear the paper just below the report at the perforated edge. The printed results are shown in Figure 2-48(a).

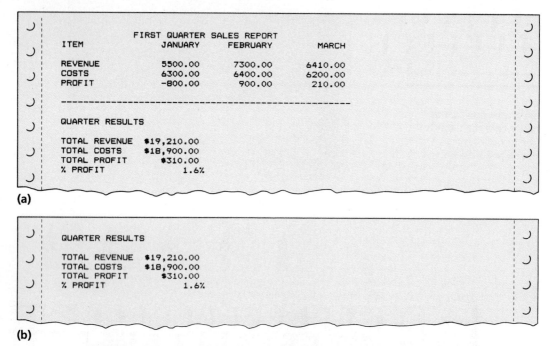

(a)

(b)

FIGURE 2-48 Complete (a) and partial (b) printed versions of the worksheet.

Quitting the Print Command

The Print command is one of the few commands that does not immediately return 1-2-3 to READY mode when the command is finished executing. To return to READY mode after the Print command is complete, type the letter Q for Quit. This Quit command clears the menu from the control panel and returns 1-2-3 to READY mode with the worksheet displayed on the screen.

Printing a Section of the Worksheet

You may not always want to print the entire worksheet. Portions of the worksheet can be printed by entering the selected range in response to the Range command. Let's assume that you want to print only the quarter results as shown in Figure 2-48(b). From Figure 2-43, you can see that the quarter results are in the range A10..B15.

To print the quarter results, enter the command /**P**rint **P**rinter (/PP) as shown in Figure 2-45. Next, type the letter R for Range. The screen in Figure 2-46 displays because 1-2-3 always remembers the last range entered for the Print command. Recall that we entered the range A1..D15 when we printed the complete worksheet earlier.

To change the range, press the Backspace key to free the end points A1 and D15 on the input line. Use the arrow keys to move the cell pointer to A10. Press the Period key (.) to anchor the upper left end point of the range containing the quarter results. Move the cell pointer to B15. At this point, the screen appears as shown in Figure 2-49. Press the Enter key to anchor the lower right end point.

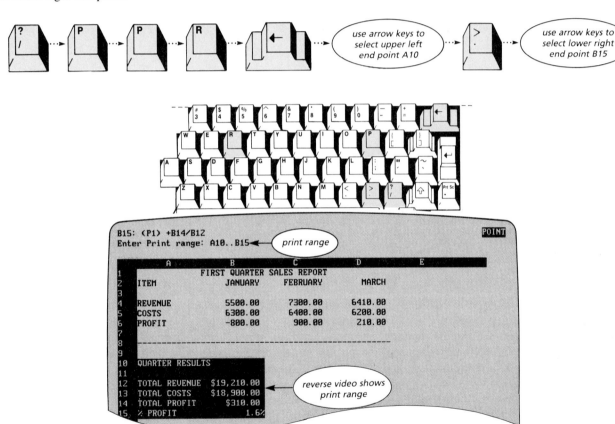

FIGURE 2-49 Printing a portion of the worksheet.

Next, make sure the paper is aligned and the printer is ready. As described in Figure 2-47, type the letter A for Align and the letter G for Go to print the partial report. The partial report shown in Figure 2-48(b) prints on the printer. When the report is complete, type the letter P twice to eject the paper from the printer. Finally, type the letter Q for Quit to complete the Print command. The Print menu disappears from the control panel and 1-2-3 returns to the READY mode with the worksheet displayed on the screen. At this point, if you enter the UNDO command (Alt-F4), 1-2-3 will reset the print settings to the ones shown in Figure 2-47.

Printing the Cell-Formulas Version of the Worksheet

Thus far, we have printed the worksheet exactly as it is on the screen. This is called the **as-displayed** version of the worksheet. Another variation that we print is called the cell-formulas version. The **cell-formulas** version prints what was assigned to the cells, rather than what's in the cells. It is useful for debugging a worksheet because the formulas and functions print out, rather than the numeric results.

Figure 2-50 illustrates the printed cell-formulas version of this worksheet. Each filled cell in the selected range is printed on a separate line. The cell address is printed in the left column, followed by any special formatting that was assigned to the cell, and the actual contents. The information displayed in the report is identical to the display on the status line for the current cell.

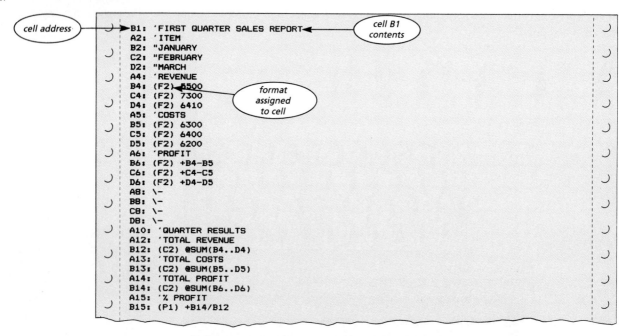

FIGURE 2-50 Cell-formulas version of the worksheet.

To print the cell-formulas version of the worksheet, type the command /**P**rint **P**rinter **R**ange (/PPR). Enter the range A1..D15 and press the Enter key. (If we had not printed a portion of the worksheet in the previous step, the range already would have been set to A1..D15. In this case we would have skipped the Range command.) With the command cursor still active in the Print menu, enter the command **O**ptions **O**ther **C**ell-formulas **Q**uit **A**lign **G**o **P**age **P**age (OOCQAGPP). With the printer in Ready mode, 1-2-3 will print the cell-formulas version of Project 2 as shown in Figure 2-50.

Once the Print command option has been set to print the cell-formulas version, 1-2-3 will continue to print this variation each time you use the /**P**rint **P**rinter (/PP) command until you change the print option back to as-displayed. Therefore, after printing the cell-formulas version, but before quitting the Print command, enter the command **O**ptions **O**ther **A**s-displayed **Q**uit **Q**uit (OOAQQ). The last Quit in the chain of commands causes 1-2-3 to return to READY mode. The next time the Print command is used, 1-2-3 will print the as-displayed version. Another way to switch back to the as-displayed version is to use the UNDO command after the cell-formulas version is printed and after 1-2-3 has returned to READY mode.

Printing a Worksheet to a File

You can instruct 1-2-3 to transmit the printed version of a worksheet to a file. This can be useful if your printer is not functioning or if you prefer to print the worksheet at a later time. Use the command /**P**rint **F**ile (/PF), rather than /**P**rint **P**rinter (/PP). When you enter the command /PF, 1-2-3 requests a file name. After you enter the file name, the Print menu in Figure 2-47 displays with the file name as the destination, rather than printer. From this point on, you can select commands from the Print menu as if you were printing the worksheet directly to the printer.

Later, after quitting 1-2-3, you can use the DOS command Type to display the worksheet on the screen or the DOS command Print to print the worksheet on the printer. The file extension .PRN, which stands for printer file, automatically appends to the file name you select.

Summary of Commands in the Print Menu

Table 2-4 summarizes the commands available in the Print menu.

TABLE 2-4   A Summary of Commands in the Print Menu

COMMAND	FUNCTION
Range	Allows you to specify what part of the worksheet is printed.
Line	Moves the paper in the printer one line.
Page	Advances the paper in the printer to the top of the next page on the basis of the program's page-length setting.
Options	Sets header, footer, margins, page length, borders, and special printer commands.
Clear	Sets Print command settings to their default and clears the current print-range setting.
Align	Resets the line counter for the printer.
Go	Starts printing the worksheet on the printer.
Quit	Returns 1-2-3 to READY mode.

DEBUGGING THE FORMULAS IN A WORKSHEET USING THE TEXT FORMAT

Debugging is the process of finding and correcting errors in a worksheet. When formulas are assigned to the cells in a worksheet, the cell-formulas version is a handy tool for debugging it. Recall that the cell-formulas version shows the formulas associated with a worksheet (Figure 2-50). An alternative to printing the cell-formulas version of the worksheet is to format the worksheet to the Text type. This format allows you to see the formulas in the cells on the screen, instead of their numeric result. When the worksheet is formatted to the Text type, it is called the **text version**.

To view the text version of the worksheet, do the following:

1. Save the worksheet to disk so that you don't lose the formats currently assigned to the cells in the worksheet.
2. Enter the command /**R**ange Format Text (/RFT) and enter the range A1..D15.

As shown in Figure 2-51, the formulas display in the cells instead of their numeric results. One problem with this procedure is that if a formula is longer than the width of the cell, a portion of it is hidden.

When you are finished viewing or printing the worksheet formatted to the Text type, retrieve from disk the original version—the one that contains the properly formatted cells.

Instead of saving the worksheet before changing the format to text, you can use the UNDO command (Alt-F4) after viewing the formulas in the cells and before making any new entries.

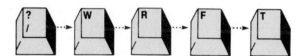

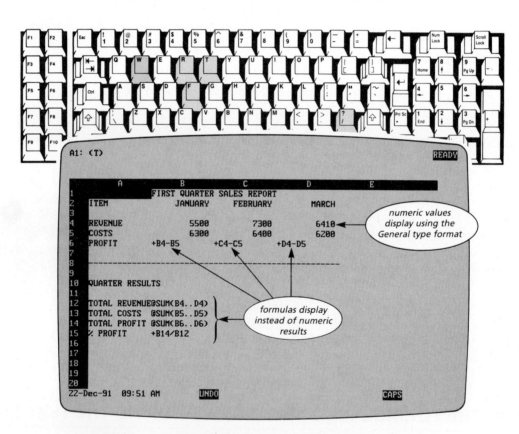

FIGURE 2-51 Display of the formulas in the cells instead of the numeric results. Use the command /Range Format Text (/RFT) and enter the range A1..D15.

PROJECT SUMMARY

*I*n Project 2 we formatted the numeric values entered in Project 1, added summaries, and formatted the summaries. Although this sequence of performing operations works well in many applications, it is not mandatory. For example, it may be more economical in terms of time and effort to enter portions of the data and then format it immediately, or it might be advisable to format the cells before entering the data into the worksheet. You will learn which sequence to choose as you gain experience with 1-2-3.

In Project 2 you learned how to load a worksheet, increase the size of columns, specify a range, copy cells, format a worksheet, and print a worksheet without window borders. The steps for Project 2 are summarized in the following table. Review each step in the table in detail to make sure you fully understand the commands and concepts.

SUMMARY OF KEYSTROKES—Project 2

STEPS	KEY(S) PRESSED	RESULTS
1	/FR ↵	Retrieve PROJS-1 from disk
2	Caps Lock	Set Caps Lock on
3	/WGC13 ↵	Set column width to 13
4	/RFF ↵ Backspace ← ← ← ↑↑.↓↓ → → ↵	Set monthly revenue, costs, and profit to a fixed format with two decimal places
5	F5 A8 ↵	Move the cell pointer to A8
6	\-↵	Repeat dashes in cell A8
7	/C ↵ → . → → ↵	Copy dashes in cell A8 to cells B8, C8, and D8
8	↓↓QUARTER RESULTS↓↓	Enter title
9	TOTAL REVENUE↓	Enter title
10	TOTAL COSTS↓	Enter title
11	TOTAL PROFIT↓	Enter title
12	% PROFIT↓	Enter title
13	F5 B12 ↵	Move the cell pointer to B12
14	/FSPROJS-2 ↵	Save worksheet as PROJS-2
15	@SUM(B4.D4) ↵	Enter SUM function for total revenue
16	/C ↵ ↓.↓ ↵	Copy SUM function from cell B12 to B13 and B14
17	↓↓↓ +B14/B12 ↵	Enter % profit formula
18	/RFP1 ↵ ↵	Format decimal number in cell B15 to percent
19	↑↑↑/RFC ↵ ↓↓ ↵	Format the total revenue, costs, and profit to the Currency type
20	Home	Move the cell pointer to A1
21	/FS ↵ R	Save worksheet as PROJS-2
22	/PPRA1.D15 ↵ AGPPQ	Print the as-displayed version of the worksheet
23	/PPRA10.B15 ↵ AGPPQ	Print a portion of the worksheet
24	/PPRA1.D15 ↵ OOCQAGPP	Print the cell-formulas version of the worksheet
25	OOAQQ	Change the print option to as-displayed
26	/RFTA1.D15 ↵	Format the worksheet to the Text type

The following list summarizes the material covered in Project 2.

1. To retrieve a worksheet from disk, enter the command /**F**ile **R**etrieve (/FR). Use the Left and Right Arrow keys to move the command cursor in the alphabetized list on the menu line to the worksheet name you wish to retrieve and then press the Enter key.

2. To change the width of all the columns in the worksheet, type the command /**W**orksheet **G**lobal **C**olumn-Width (/WGC). Enter the desired column width (1–240) on the input line and press the Enter key.

3. To change the width of a range of columns, enter the command /**W**orksheet **C**olumn **C**olumn **S**et-Width (/WCCS). Enter the range of columns and the desired column width. Press the Enter key to complete the command.

4. To change the width of a specific column in the worksheet, move the cell pointer to the column in question and type the command /**W**orksheet **C**olumn **S**et-Width (/WCS). Enter the new width and press the Enter key.

5. A **range** is one or more cells upon which you want to complete an operation. A range may be a single cell, a series of adjacent cells in a column or row, or a rectangular group of adjacent cells. A range cannot be made up of cells that only run diagonally or are separated.

Project Summary (continued)

6. To enter a range, type the cell address at one end point of the range, followed by a period (.) to anchor the first end point, followed by the cell address at the opposite end point of the range. If it is necessary to change the first end point after it is *anchored*, press the Backspace key.

7. If a range defines a rectangular group of cells, the two end points must be diagonally opposite corner cells of the rectangle.

8. To format a range, type the command /**R**ange **F**ormat (/RF). Select the type of format you wish to use from the menu. Enter the number of decimal places if required. Enter the range to be affected and press the Enter key.

9. To format the entire worksheet, type the command /**W**orksheet **G**lobal **F**ormat (/WGF). Follow the same steps described for formatting a range.

10. You can also enter a range by **pointing**. Pointing involves using the arrow keys to move the cell pointer to select the end points.

11. When you use pointing to select the range, use the Backspace key to *unlock* the end points of the range on the input line.

12. 1-2-3 displays the range with the end points separated by two periods (..), even though you enter only a single period (.) to anchor the first end point.

13. There are several ways to format numeric values (Table 2-2).

14. Move the cell pointer to a cell to determine the format assigned to it. The format displays in parentheses next to the cell address on the status line at the top of the screen.

15. To repeat a series of characters throughout a cell, begin the entry by typing the Backslash key (\).

16. To copy a range to another range, type the command /**C**opy (/C). Enter the source range and then the destination range.

17. It is good practice to save a worksheet to disk after every 50 to 75 keystrokes.

18. A **built-in function** automatically handles calculations.

19. All built-in functions begin with the @ symbol.

20. The SUM function adds the contents of the range specified in parentheses.

21. When you copy a function, the Copy command adjusts the range for the new position.

22. If the Slash key (/) is the first key pressed, 1-2-3 switches to command mode. If the Slash key follows any character in a nonlabel entry on the input line, it represents division.

23. When you save a worksheet the second time using the same file name, 1-2-3 requires that you type the letter R for Replace.

24. To print the **as-displayed** version of the worksheet without borders, type the command /**P**rint **P**rinter (/PP). If the range has not yet been established from a previous printout of the worksheet, you must enter the range to print. With the printer off, use the platen knob to align the perforated edge of the paper with the top of the print head mechanism. Turn the printer on. Type the letter A for Align and the letter G for Go. After the worksheet is printed, type the letter P (for Page) twice. Carefully remove the printed version of the worksheet from the printer. Finally, type the letter Q for Quit.

25. To print a section of the worksheet, enter the command /**P**rint **P**rinter **R**ange (/PPR). Use the Backspace key to *unlock* the range. Enter the desired range and continue with the steps just outlined.

26. To print the **cell-formulas** version of the worksheet, type the command /**P**rint **P**rinter **O**ptions **O**ther **C**ell-formulas **Q**uit **A**lign **G**o **P**age **P**age (/PPOOCQAGPP). It is important to change the print option back to as-displayed, so that future printouts will print the as-displayed version rather than the cell-formulas version. One way to change the printout back to as-displayed is to use the UNDO command after the cell-formulas version prints and 1-2-3 returns to READY mode.

27. To print the worksheet to a file, use the command /**P**rint **F**ile (/PF). Later, after you have quit 1-2-3, you may use the DOS command Type to display the worksheet on the screen or the DOS command Print to print the worksheet on the printer.

28. To display formulas assigned to cells rather than their numeric result, assign the Text type format to the cells in the worksheet.

STUDENT ASSIGNMENTS

STUDENT ASSIGNMENT 1: True/False

Instructions: Circle T if the statement is true or F if the statement is false.

T F   1. With the /**File R**etrieve (/FR) command, you are required to type the name of the worksheet you want loaded into main computer memory on the input line.

T F   2. The command /**W**orksheet **G**lobal **C**olumn-Width (/WGC) is used to set the width of all the columns in the worksheet.

T F   3. If you want to *back out* of the command /FR, press the Esc key three times.

T F   4. When using the command /**R**ange **F**ormat (/RF), entire columns can be formatted; however, entire rows cannot be formatted.

T F   5. For a rectangular group of cells, you must enter the cell addresses of two opposite corners to define the range.

T F   6. A range can be made up of one cell.

T F   7. If you decide to use the pointing method when 1-2-3 requests a range, press the Tab key to *unlock* the first end point, if necessary.

T F   8. A range can be referenced by an entry such as B4..D6.

T F   9. With the format Fixed, negative numbers display in parentheses.

T F 10. When in POINT mode, anchor the first cell end point by moving the cell pointer to it and pressing the Period key.

T F 11. The type of format assigned to a cell displays on the indicator line at the bottom of the screen when the cell pointer is on the cell.

T F 12. If the Backslash key (\) is the first character typed on the input line, the characters that follow will repeat throughout the cell when you press the Enter key or one of the arrow keys.

T F 13. The command /**C**opy (/C) is used to copy the contents of a range to another range of cells.

T F 14. If the function @SUM(B4..D4) is assigned to cell A20, A20 will be equal to the sum of the contents of cells B4, C4, and D4.

T F 15. It is not possible to copy a single cell to a group of cells.

T F 16. If the function @SUM(B4..B8) assigns a value of 10 to cell B9, and B9 is copied to C9, C9 will be equal to 10.

T F 17. If you save a worksheet a second time, you cannot use the same file name originally assigned to the worksheet.

T F 18. The Align command on the Print menu is used to align the cells on the screen.

STUDENT ASSIGNMENT 2: Multiple Choice

Instructions: Circle the correct response.

1. Which of the following is the correct command for retrieving the worksheet PROJS-1.WK1 stored on the disk in the default drive?
   a. /FRPROJS-1 ↵
   b. /WRPROJS-1 ↵
   c. /CPROJS-1 ↵
   d. none of these

2. When the command /**W**orksheet **G**lobal (/WG) is used, it means that _____ .
   a. only a single cell will be affected
   b. only a single column will be affected
   c. only a single row will be affected
   d. the entire worksheet will be affected

3. Which one of the following is a valid range of cells?
   a. B2,D2
   b. B2:D2
   c. B2.D2
   d. both b and c are correct

4. The format Currency with two decimal places causes 5000 to display as:
   a. $5,000.00
   b. 5000.00
   c. 5,000.00
   d. $5000.00

Student Assignment 2 (continued)

5. Which one of the following causes the data in cells B4, C4, and D4 to be added together?
   a. @SUM(B4.D4) c. @SUM(B4:D4)
   b. @ADD(B4.D4) d. @SUM(B4 C4 D4)

6. Which one of the following correctly identifies the range of the rectangular group of cells with corner cells at A10, A18, D10, and D18?
   a. A10.D18 c. D18.A10
   b. A18.D10 d. all of these

7. Which one of the following instructs 1-2-3 to repeat characters in the current cell?
   a. circumflex (^) c. apostrophe (')
   b. quotation mark (") d. backslash (\)

8. A listing on the printer of what was entered into each cell of a worksheet is called the _____ version of the worksheet.
   a. cell-formulas c. formatted
   b. as-displayed d. content

STUDENT ASSIGNMENT 3: Understanding Ranges

Instructions: List all the possible ranges for each of the designated areas in Figure 2-52. For example, one range that identifies the first group of cells is A1..B3. There are three other ways to identify this first group of cells.

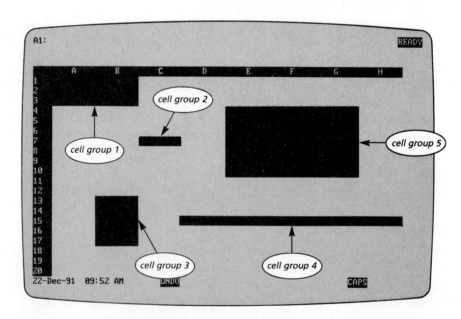

FIGURE 2-52
Student Assignment 3

Cell group 1: _____ _____ _____ _____

Cell group 2: _____

Cell group 3: _____ _____

Cell group 4: _____ _____

Cell group 5: _____ _____ _____ _____

STUDENT ASSIGNMENT 4: Understanding Formats

Instructions: Using Table 2-2, fill in the *Results In* column of Table 2-5 below. Assume that the column width of each cell is 10 characters. Use the character b to indicate positions containing the blank character. As examples, the first two problems in Table 2-5 are complete.

TABLE 2-5 Determining the Value of a Number Based on a Given Format

PROBLEM	CELL CONTENTS	FORMAT TO	DECIMAL PLACES	RESULTS IN
1	25	Fixed	1	bbbbb25.0b
2	1.26	Currency	2	bbbb$1.26b
3	5000	,(comma)	2	_____
4	3.87	Fixed	0	_____
5	.137	Percent	2	_____
6	5	+/–	Not reqd.	_____
7	–45.87	, (comma)	3	_____
8	9523.6	General	Not reqd.	_____
9	25	Percent	2	_____
10	.16	Fixed	2	_____
11	109234	Currency	0	_____
12	2357.85	Scientific	1	_____
13	1903.4	Currency	2	_____
14	23.56	Scientific	0	_____
15	–34.95	Currency	2	_____

STUDENT ASSIGNMENT 5: Correcting the Range in a Worksheet

Instructions: The worksheet illustrated in Figure 2-53 contains errors in cells B12 through B15. Analyze the entries displayed in the worksheet. Explain the cause of the errors and the method of correction in the space provided below.

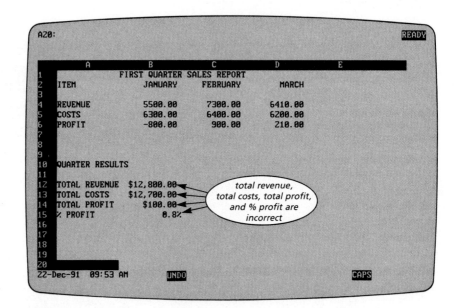

FIGURE 2-53
Student Assignment 5

Cause of error: _____

_____

Method of correction for cell B12: _____

_____

Method of correction for cells B13, B14, and B15: _____

_____

_____

STUDENT ASSIGNMENT 6: Correcting Functions in a Worksheet

Instructions: The worksheet ~~in~~ in Figure 2-54 contains invalid function entries in cells B12, B13, and B14. The invalid entries in these cells cause ~~~~ostic message ERR to display in cell B15. Analyze the entries displayed in the worksheet. Explain the cause of th~~~~ ~~and~~ the method of correction in the space provided below.

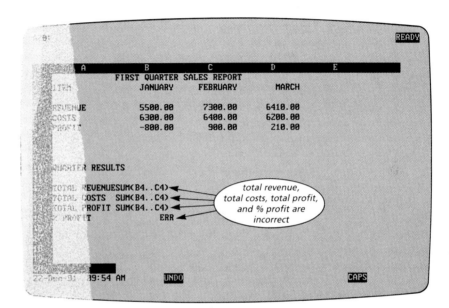

FIGURE 2-54
Student Assignment 6

Cause of error: _____

_____

Method of correction for cell B12: _____

_____

Method of correction for cells B13, B14, and B15: _____

_____

STUDENT ASSIGNMENT 7: Modifying an Inventory Worksheet

Instructions: Load 1-2-3 and perform the following tasks.

1. Load the worksheet that was created in Project 1, Student Assignment 8. This worksheet is illustrated in Figure 2-55(a).
2. Perform the following modifications:
   a. Use the Comma (,) format with zero decimal places for the numbers in rows 4, 5, 6, and 7.
   b. Include the inventory total in the worksheet, as illustrated in Figure 2-55(b). The inventory total consists of a total for each plant (B13..B16). For example, the total for Seattle is the sum of cells B4 through D4. Separate the inventory total from the other values by a double line in row 9 (use the equal sign).
   c. Use the Comma (,) format with zero decimal places for the inventory totals.
3. Save the modified worksheet. Use the file name STUS2-7.
4. Print the entire worksheet on the printer using the /**P**rint **P**rinter (/PP) command.
5. Print only the inventory totals in the range A11..B16.
6. Print the worksheet after formatting all the cells to the Text type.

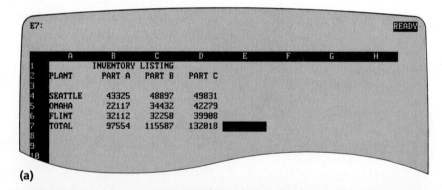

(a)

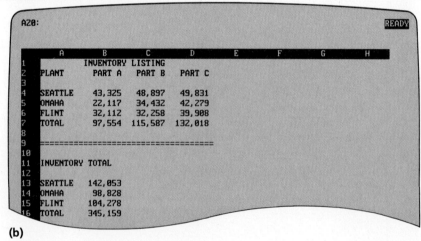

FIGURE 2-55 (a) and (b)
Student Assignment 7
Worksheet (a) before and
(b) after modification

(b)

STUDENT ASSIGNMENT 8: Building an Employee Payroll Comparison Worksheet

Instructions: Load 1-2-3 and perform the following tasks.

1. Build the worksheet illustrated in Figure 2-56. Change the width of all the columns to 14 characters. The totals displayed in row 9 of the worksheet are the sum of the salaried personnel in column B and the hourly personnel in column C. The store totals (B15..B18) are the sum of the salaried personnel and the hourly personnel for each store. The total in B20 is the sum of the store totals.
2. Save the worksheet. Use the file name STUS2-8.
3. Print the as-displayed and cell-formulas versions of this worksheet.
4. Print the portion of the worksheet in the range A1..C9.

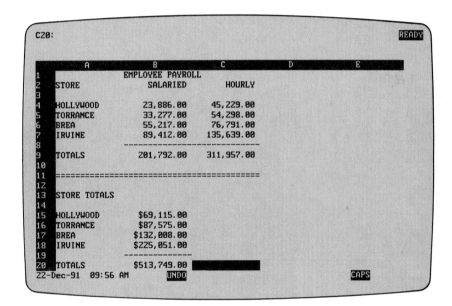

FIGURE 2-56
Student Assignment 8

STUDENT ASSIGNMENT 9: Building a Monthly Expense Worksheet

Instructions: Load 1-2-3 and perform the following tasks.

1. Build the worksheet illustrated in Figure 2-57. Change the width of all the columns to 15 character positions. The variances in column D of the worksheet are obtained by subtracting the actual expenses from the budgeted expenses. In the summary portion of the worksheet, the percentage of budget used (C17) is obtained by dividing the total actual amount (C15) by the total budgeted amount (C14).
2. Save the worksheet. Use the file name STUS2-9.
3. Print the as-displayed and cell-formulas versions of this worksheet.
4. Print the portion of the worksheet in the range A3..B8.
5. Print the worksheet after formatting all the cells to the Text type.

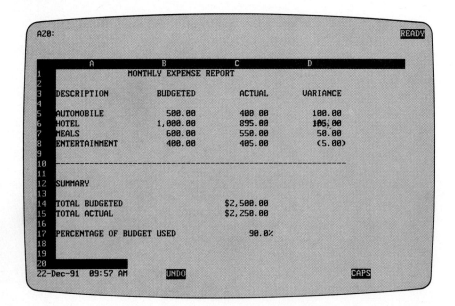

FIGURE 2-57
Student Assignment 9

Monthly

STUDENT ASSIGNMENT 10: Building a Monthly Sales Analysis Worksheet

Instructions: Load 1-2-3 and perform the following tasks.

1. Build the worksheet illustrated in Figure 2-58. Change the width of all the columns to 12 characters. Then change the width of column A to 14 positions. Center all the column headings using the circumflex (^). The net sales in column D of the worksheet is determined by subtracting the sales returns in column C from the sales amount in column B. The above/below quota amount in column F is obtained by subtracting the sales quota in column E from the net sales in column D. In the summary section of the worksheet, the totals for each group are obtained by adding the values for each salesperson. The percent of quota sold in cell C20 is obtained by dividing the total net sales amount in C17 by the total sales quota amount in C18.
2. Save the worksheet. Use the file name STUS2-10.
3. Print the as-displayed and cell-formulas versions of this worksheet.
4. Print the portion of the worksheet in the range A1..F9.
5. Print the worksheet after formatting all the cells to the Text type.

```
D20:                                                               READY

            A           B           C           D           E           F
1                              MONTHLY SALES REPORT
2
3      SALESPERSON      SALES       SALES         NET        SALES    ABOVE/BELOW
4         NAME         AMOUNT      RETURNS       SALES        QUOTA       QUOTA
5
6    HARLEY TRAPP     15,789.00      245.00    15,544.00    12,000.00    3,544.00
7    VANCE LANE        8,500.00      500.00     8,000.00    10,000.00   (2,000.00)
8    MARY CICERO      17,895.00    1,376.00    16,519.00    12,000.00    4,519.00
9    TOM COLLINS      12,843.00      843.00    12,000.00    11,000.00    1,000.00
10
11   ============================================================================
12
13   SUMMARY
14
15   TOTAL SALES AMOUNT        $55,027.00
16   TOTAL SALES RETURNS        $2,964.00
17   TOTAL NET SALES           $52,063.00
18   TOTAL SALES QUOTA         $45,000.00
19
20   % OF QUOTA SOLD              115.70%
22-Dec-91  09:58 AM      UNDO                                           CAPS
```

FIGURE 2-58
Student Assignment 10

+C17/C18

CW   14

/ RF P .. Enter

STUDENT ASSIGNMENT 11: Changing Data in the Monthly Expense Worksheet

Instructions: Load 1-2-3 and perform the following tasks.

1. Retrieve the worksheet STUS2-9 from disk. The worksheet is illustrated in Figure 2-57.
2. Decrement each of the four values in the ACTUAL column by $30.00 until the percentage of budget used in C17 is as close as possible to 80%. All four values in column C must be decremented the same number of times. You should end up with a percentage of budget used in C17 equal to 80.4%.
3. After successfully modifying the worksheet, print it on the printer.
4. Save the modified worksheet. Use the file name STUS2-11.

STUDENT ASSIGNMENT 12: Changing Data in the Monthly Sales Analysis Worksheet

Instructions: Load 1-2-3 and perform the following tasks.

1. Retrieve the worksheet STUS2-10 from disk. The worksheet is illustrated in Figure 2-58.
2. Increment each of the four values in the sales quota column by $1000.00 until the percent of quota sold in cell C20 is below, yet as close as possible to 100%. All four values in column E must be incremented the same number of times. The percent of quota sold in C20 should be equal to 98.23%.
3. Decrement each of the four values in the sales returns column by $100.00 until the percent of quota sold in cell C20 is below, yet as close as possible to 100%. All four values in column C must be decremented the same number of times. Your worksheet is correct when the percent of quota sold in C20 is equal to 99.74%.
4. After successfully modifying the worksheet, print it on the printer.
5. Save the modified worksheet. Use the file name STUS2-12.

PROJECT 3

Enhancing Your Worksheet

Objectives

You will have mastered the material in this project when you can:

- Display today's date and time in a worksheet using the NOW function
- Move a group of rows or columns to another area of the worksheet
- Insert and delete rows and columns
- Freeze the horizontal and vertical titles
- Enter percentage values using the percent sign (%)
- Copy absolute cell addresses
- Employ the pointing method to enter a range to be summed

- Print a worksheet in condensed mode
- Print selected nonadjacent columns
- Answer what-if questions
- Switch between manual and automatic recalculation of a worksheet
- Change the default settings
- Temporarily exit 1-2-3 and return control to DOS
- Produce presentation-quality printouts using the add-in program Allways

  n the first two projects you learned to build, save, retrieve, format, copy, and print worksheets. In this project we continue to emphasize these topics and discuss some new ones. We especially want to examine the Copy command in greater detail. The ability to copy one range to another range is one of the most powerful features of 1-2-3.

The new topics in this project teach you to insert and delete rows and columns in a worksheet, move the contents of a range to another range, and use the add-in program Allways to produce presentation-quality printouts. In general, they make the job of creating, saving, and printing a worksheet easier.

Finally, this project illustrates using 1-2-3 to answer **what-if questions**, like "What if the marketing expenses decrease 3%—how would the decrease affect net income for the first quarter of the year?" This capability of quickly analyzing the effect of changing values in a worksheet is important in making business decisions. To illustrate answering what-if questions, we will prepare the quarterly budget report shown in Figure 3-1.

	A	B	C	D	E
1	Quarterly Report – January through March				12/22/91
2	Prepared by SAS				10:01 AM
3					
4					
5	ITEM	JANUARY	FEBRUARY	MARCH	QUARTER TOTAL
6	==				
7					
8	REVENUE				
9	Sales Revenue	232,897.95	432,989.76	765,998.61	1,431,886.32
10	Other Revenue	1,232.93	3,265.81	2,145.99	6,644.73
11					
12	Total Revenue	234,130.88	436,255.57	768,144.60	1,438,531.05
13					
14	EXPENSES				
15	Manufacturing	88,969.73	165,777.12	291,894.95	546,641.80
16	Research	25,754.40	47,988.11	84,495.91	158,238.42
17	Marketing	37,460.94	69,800.89	122,903.14	230,164.97
18	Administrative	39,802.25	74,163.45	130,584.58	244,550.28
19	Fulfillment	18,730.47	34,900.45	61,451.57	115,082.48
20					
21	Total Expenses	210,717.79	392,630.01	691,330.14	1,294,677.95
22					
23	NET INCOME	23,413.09	43,625.56	76,814.46	143,853.10
24					
25	Budget % Values				
26					
27	Manufacturing	38%			
28	Research	11%			
29	Marketing	16%			
30	Administrative	17%			
31	Fulfillment	8%			

FIGURE 3-1 A printout of the worksheet we will build in Project 3.

The worksheet in Figure 3-1 contains a company's budgeted revenue and expenses for the quarterly period of January through March. In addition, this worksheet includes the quarter total for all revenues and budgeted expenses. The total revenues for each month and the quarter total in row 12 are determined by adding the corresponding sales revenue and other revenue.

Each of the budgeted expenses—manufacturing, research, marketing, administrative, and fulfillment—is determined by taking a percentage of the total revenue. The budget percent values located in rows 27–31 are as follows:

1. The manufacturing expense is 38% of the total revenue.
2. The research expense is 11% of the total revenue.
3. The marketing expense is 16% of the total revenue.
4. The administrative expense is 17% of the total revenue.
5. The fulfillment expense is 8% of the total revenue.

The total expenses for each month in row 21 of Figure 3-1 are determined by adding all the corresponding budgeted expenses together. The net income for each month in row 23 is determined by subtracting the corresponding total expenses from the total revenue. Finally, the quarter totals in the far right column are determined by summing the monthly values in each row.

Begin this project by booting the computer and loading 1-2-3. A few seconds after the copyright message displays, an empty worksheet appears on the screen. All the columns in the empty worksheet are nine characters wide. This default width is not enough to hold some of the larger numbers in the worksheet we plan to build. Therefore, let's change the width of the columns.

VARYING THE WIDTH OF THE COLUMNS

n the worksheet shown in Figure 3-1, column A is 17 characters wide, columns B through D are 13 characters wide, and column E is 16 characters wide. You select a column width setting on the basis of the longest column entry and the general appearance of the worksheet. Change the widths of the columns in the following manner:

1. Enter the command /**W**orksheet **G**lobal **C**olumn-Width (/WGC) to change the width of all the columns to 13 characters. Change the number on the input line from 9 to 13 by pressing the Right Arrow key four times followed by the Enter key as shown in Figure 3-2. We can also enter the number 13 in response to the prompt message on the input line and press the Enter key. The Global command is used to change the width of all the cells in the worksheet to 13 characters because that is the desired width of most of the columns for this project.

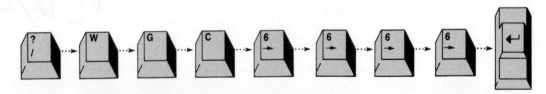

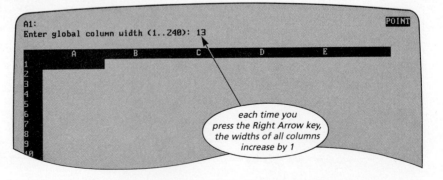

FIGURE 3-2
Using the command /WGC and the Right Arrow key to increase the width of all the columns in the worksheet to 13 characters.

/ w GfT

2. With the cell pointer at A1, enter the command /**W**orksheet **C**olumn **S**et-Width (/WCS) to change the width of column A to 17 characters. Again, press the Right Arrow key four times to change the number 13 to 17 on the input line. To complete the command, press the Enter key as shown in Figure 3-3.

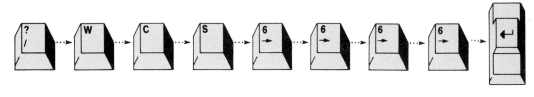

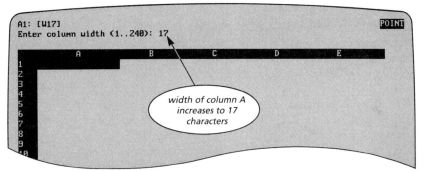

FIGURE 3-3
Using the command /WCS and the Right Arrow key to increase the width of column A to 17 characters.

3. Move the cell pointer to E1 and enter the command /**W**orksheet **C**olumn **S**et-Width (/WCS) to change the width of column E to 16 characters. This is shown in Figure 3-4.

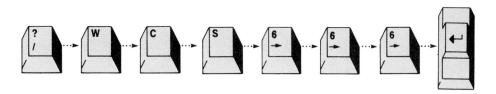

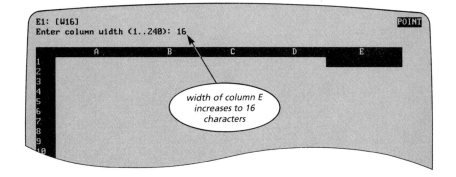

FIGURE 3-4
Using the command /WCS and the Right Arrow key to increase the width of column E to 16 characters.

As mentioned in Project 2, we could have set columns B, C, and D to 13 characters by using the command /**W**orksheet **C**olumn **C**olumn-Range **S**et-Width (/WCCS), rather than changing the width globally as we did in Figure 3-2. This command works the same as the /**W**orksheet **G**lobal **C**olumn-Width (/WGC), except that you must enter the range of columns involved in the change.

With the columns set to their designated widths, we can move on to the next step, formatting the worksheet globally.

j w"

FORMATTING THE WORKSHEET GLOBALLY

*I*n Project 2, we formatted the numbers after we entered the data. In some cases, especially when developing a large worksheet, you should consider issuing a global format before entering any data. This formats the numbers as you enter them, which makes them easier to read. The way to do this is to choose the format that is common to most of the cells. In choosing the format, don't count the empty cells or the ones with labels, because a numeric format does not affect them.

You can see from Figure 3-1 that, except for the budget percent values and the date and time, all the numbers appear as decimal numbers with two places of accuracy. These numbers also use the comma to group the integer portion by thousands. If you refer to Table 2-2 in Project 2, you will see that the required format corresponds to the Comma (,) type. Therefore, use this format for all the cells in the worksheet.

To invoke the global format command, enter the command /**W**orksheet **G**lobal **F**ormat (/WGF). This is shown in Figure 3-5. With the command cursor active in the Format menu, press the Comma key (,). The prompt message "Enter number of decimal places (0..15): 2" displays on the input line (Figure 3-6). Since we are working with dollars and cents, we want two decimal places to display. Therefore, press the Enter key.

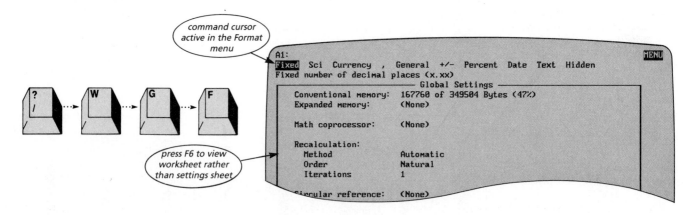

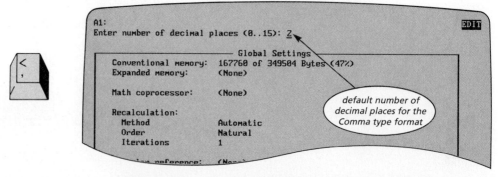

FIGURE 3-6 Step 2 of using the /WGF command to format all the cells in the worksheet to the Comma (,) type—press the Comma key (,).

The empty worksheet shown in Figure 3-7 displays. You can see that the columns are wider than nine characters. However, there is no indication of the Comma format we assigned to all the cells. The format will appear as we enter data, because 1-2-3 will automatically use the Comma format for any number entered into a cell.

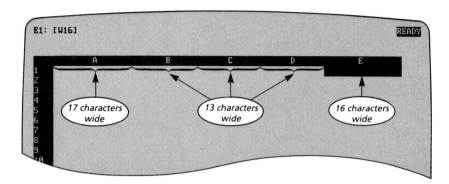

FIGURE 3-7
Step 3 of using the /WGF command to format all the cells in the worksheet to the Comma (,) type—press the Enter key.

DISPLAYING THE DATE AND TIME

W ith the column widths and the global format set, the next step is to enter the data into the worksheet. Enter the titles in cells A1 and A2 as you learned in Project 1 (Figure 3-8). Cells E1 and E2 require today's date and time. Both values can be displayed by assigning each cell the NOW function.

The NOW Function

The NOW function uses the current DOS date and time to determine the number of days since December 31, 1899. It displays the value in the assigned cell as a decimal number. For this project assume that the DOS date is December 22, 1991 and the time is approximately 10:08 AM. For the NOW function to display the correct value, it is important that you check the accuracy of the system date and system time. Recall that in the Introduction to DOS, you learned how to set the system time and system date.

To complete the time and date entries in the worksheet, move the cell pointer to E1 and enter the NOW function on the input line as illustrated in Figure 3-8.

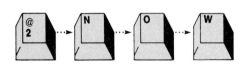

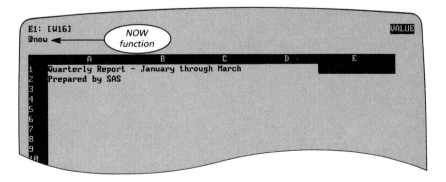

FIGURE 3-8
Entering the NOW function on the input line with the cell pointer at E1.

Next, press the Down Arrow key and enter the same function in E2. Use the Up Arrow key to enter the function in E2. This places the cell pointer in E1 as shown in Figure 3-9. The value 33,594.42 in cells E1 and E2 represents the number of days since December 31, 1899. The integer portion of the number (33,594) represents the number of complete days, and the decimal portion (.42) represents the first 10 hours of December 22, 1991. Note that the two entries are displayed in the Comma (,) format, the one we assigned earlier to the entire worksheet. The next step is to format the date and time so that they display in a more meaningful way.

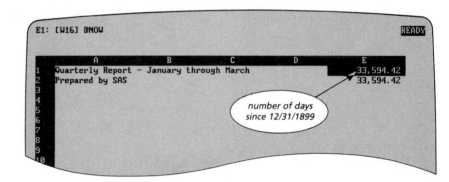

FIGURE 3-9
The NOW function assigned to cells E1 and E2.

Formatting the Date

In Figure 3-9, the cell pointer is at E1. To format the date, enter the command /**R**ange **F**ormat **D**ate (/RFD) as shown in Figure 3-10. With the command cursor active in the **Date menu**, select the fourth date format Long Intn'l (MM/DD/YY).

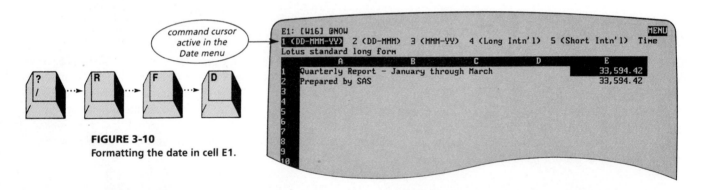

FIGURE 3-10
Formatting the date in cell E1.

To select the desired format, move the command cursor to the fourth one in the menu and press the Enter key. 1-2-3 responds by displaying the prompt message "Enter range to format: E1..E1" on the input line. E1 is the only cell we want to format, so press the Enter key. The date immediately changes in cell E1 to 12/22/91 as shown in Figure 3-11.

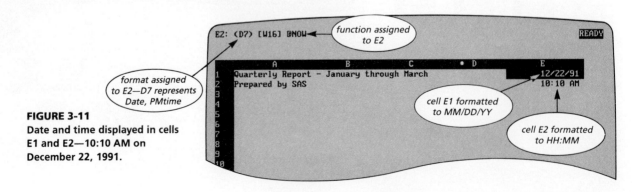

FIGURE 3-11
Date and time displayed in cells E1 and E2—10:10 AM on December 22, 1991.

Formatting the Time

Move the cell pointer to E2. To format the time, enter the same command as for the date—/**R**ange **F**ormat **D**ate (/RFD). This is shown in Figure 3-10. With the command cursor active in the Date menu, type the letter T for Time. The **Time menu** replaces the Date menu at the top of the screen. Select the second Time format (HH:MM AM/PM) by pressing the 2 key. Next, press the Enter key and the time in E2 displays as 10:10 AM (Figure 3-11).

Updating the Time—Recalculation

The time displayed on the indicator line at the bottom of the screen updates every minute. However, the time displayed in a cell, as in E2, only updates when you enter a value into a cell in the worksheet. Any entry causes 1-2-3 to recalculate all the formulas and functions in the worksheet automatically.

If you are not entering any numeric values and want to instruct 1-2-3 to recalculate all formulas and functions, press function key F9. Pressing F9 updates the time as illustrated in Figure 3-12.

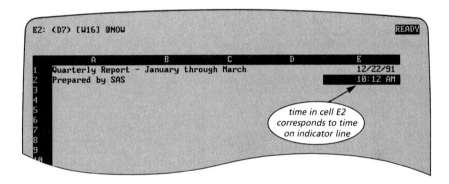

FIGURE 3-12
Press function key F9 to manually update the time in cell E2.

Date and Time Formats

Table 3-1 summarizes the date and time formats available in 1-2-3. Use this table to select formats when you want to display the date and time in a worksheet.

TABLE 3-1   Date and Time Formats
(Assume the DOS date is December 22, 1991 and the time is 3:12 PM)

FORMAT NUMBER	FORMAT TYPE	FORMAT CODE ON STATUS LINE	DATE OR TIME DISPLAYED
1	DD-MMM-YY	D1	22-Dec-91
2	DD-MMM	D2	22-Dec
3	MMM-YY	D3	Dec-91
4	Long Intn'l (MM/DD/YY)	D4	12/22/91
5	Short Intn'l (MM/DD)	D5	12/22
1	HH:MM:SS AM/PM	D6	3:12:00 PM
2	HH:MM AM/PM	D7	3:12 PM
3	Long Intn'l	D8	15:12:00
4	Short Intn'l	D9	15:12

ENTERING THE QUARTERLY BUDGET LABELS

With the date and time formatted, we can enter the column headings, group titles, and row titles. Move the cell pointer to A5. Since the column headings consist of capital letters, press the Caps Lock key before entering them. Left-justify the first column heading and right-justify the rest. Recall that to right-justify a label, you begin the label with a quotation mark ("). The worksheet with the column headings is shown in Figure 3-13.

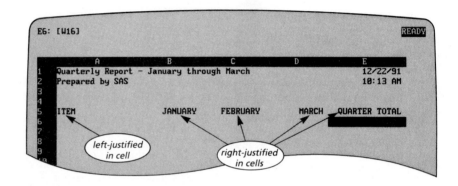

FIGURE 3-13
Column headings entered into row 5.

After completing the column headings, move the cell pointer to A6. Use the Backslash key (\) to repeat the equal sign (=) throughout cell A6. Next, use the command /Copy (/C) to copy the contents of cell A6 to cells B6 through E6. The result is a double-dashed line in row 6 as illustrated in Figure 3-14.

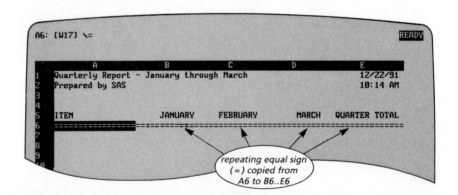

FIGURE 3-14
Column headings underlined.

Once the column headings are complete, begin entering the group titles and row titles that are shown on the left side of Figure 3-1. All the labels are left-justified. The group subtitles are indented by two spaces to make the worksheet easier to read. Since most of the remaining labels are in lowercase letters, press the Caps Lock key to toggle off capital letters after entering the group title REVENUE in cell A8.

Do not enter the two subtitles Marketing and Administrative under the group title EXPENSES. We will add these subtitles shortly.

Figure 3-15 shows the group titles and row identifiers up to row 24. Note in Figure 3-15 that with the cell pointer at A24 the window has moved down four rows, displaying rows 5 through 24 rather than rows 1 through 20. Once the cell pointer moves past row 20, the window begins to move down. The same applies when the cell pointer moves beyond the last column on the screen.

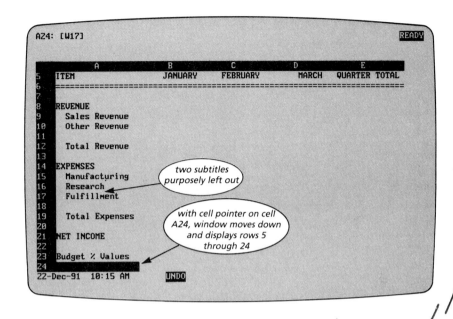

FIGURE 3-15
Group titles and subtitles entered.

INSERTING AND DELETING ROWS AND COLUMNS

t is not unusual to forget to include rows or columns of data when building a worksheet, or to include too many rows or columns. 1-2-3 is forgiving. It has commands to insert or delete as many rows or columns as required. Furthermore, you can do this at any time, even after a worksheet is well under way.

The Insert Command

The command /**Worksheet Insert** (/WI) is used to insert empty rows or columns anywhere in the worksheet. To make room for the new rows, 1-2-3 simply opens up the worksheet by *pushing down* the rows below the insertion point. If you are inserting columns, those to the right of the insertion point are *pushed* to the right. More importantly, if the *pushed* rows or columns include any formulas, 1-2-3 adjusts the cell references to the new locations.

Remember that we purposely left out the two subtitles Marketing and Administrative from the group title EXPENSES (compare Figure 3-15 to Figure 3-1). Let's insert—open up—two blank rows in the worksheet so that we can add the two subtitles. According to Figure 3-1, the two subtitles belong immediately before Fulfillment in cell A17. Therefore, move the cell pointer to A17. To complete a row insert, always position the cell pointer on the first row you want *pushed* down. This is shown in Figure 3-16. For a row insert, the column location of the cell pointer is not important.

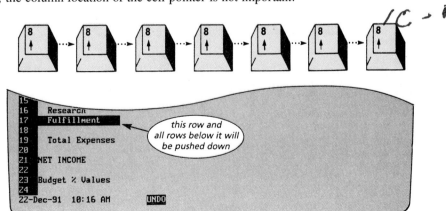

FIGURE 3-16
Step 1 of using the /WI command to insert rows—move the cell pointer to A17, the first row we want *pushed* down.

Enter the command /**W**orksheet **I**nsert (/WI) as shown in Figure 3-17.

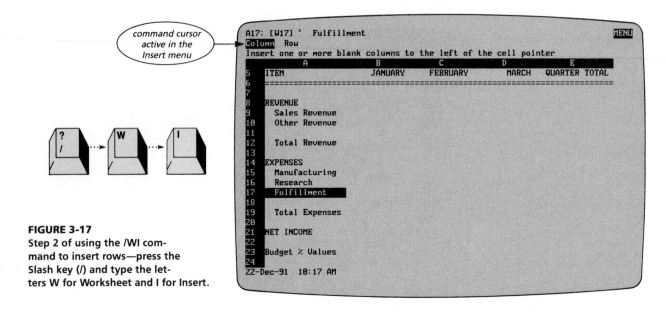

FIGURE 3-17
Step 2 of using the /WI command to insert rows—press the Slash key (/) and type the letters W for Worksheet and I for Insert.

With the command cursor active in the **Insert menu**, type the letter R for Row. 1-2-3 immediately responds on the input line at the top of the screen with the prompt message, "Enter row insert range: A17..A17". We want to add two new rows, A17 and A18. Therefore, use the Down Arrow key to increase the range on the input line from A17..A17 to A17..A18. This is illustrated in Figure 3-18.

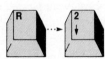

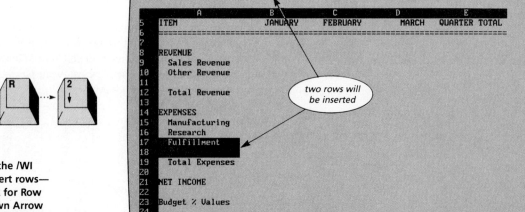

FIGURE 3-18
Step 3 of using the /WI command to insert rows—type the letter R for Row and use the Down Arrow key to select the number of rows you want to insert.

Press the Enter key and the worksheet *pushes down* all the rows beginning with row 17—the first row in the range A17..A18. This leaves rows 17 and 18 empty as shown in Figure 3-19.

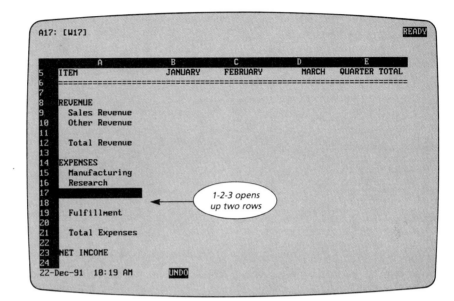

FIGURE 3-19
Step 4 of using the /WI command to insert rows—press the Enter key.

Enter the subtitle Marketing in cell A17 and the subtitle Administrative in cell A18 (Figure 3-20).

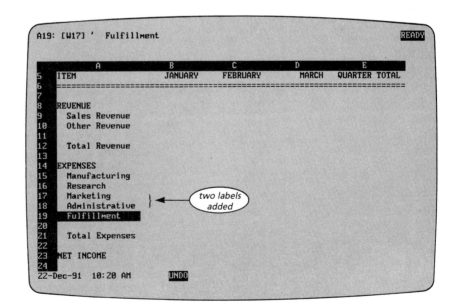

FIGURE 3-20
The two subtitles inserted into the worksheet.

The Delete Command

You can delete unwanted rows or columns from a worksheet by using the command /**W**orksheet **D**elete (/WD). Let's delete rows 17 and 18 in Figure 3-20. After deleting these two rows, we will reinsert them using the command /**W**orksheet **I**nsert (/WI).

With the cell pointer at cell A17, enter the command /**W**orksheet **D**elete (/WD). Next, type the letter R to instruct 1-2-3 to delete rows rather than columns. To delete columns you would type the letter C. When 1-2-3 requests the range to delete, press the Down Arrow key to change the range from A17..A17 to A17..A18. Press the Enter key. 1-2-3 immediately *closes up* the worksheet—rows 17 and 18 disappear. The worksheet appears as it did earlier in Figure 3-16. Note, if we had decided to close up rows 17 and 18 immediately after inserting them, we could have used the UNDO command (Alt-F4), rather than the /WD command.

Be careful when you use the /Worksheet Delete command. You do not want to delete rows or columns that are part of a range used in a formula or function elsewhere in the worksheet without carefully weighing the consequences. If any formula references a cell in a deleted row or column, 1-2-3 displays the diagnostic message ERR in the cell assigned the formula. ERR means that it was impossible for 1-2-3 to complete the computation.

Before moving on, reinsert the two rows above row 17 and enter the row titles (Marketing and Administrative). Follow the keystroke sequence just described and shown in Figures 3-17 through 3-20.

COPYING CELLS WITH EQUAL SOURCE AND DESTINATION RANGES

We are not yet finished with the labels. We need to enter the subtitles in cells A27 through A31 (Figure 3-1). These subtitles are the same as the ones entered earlier in cells A15 through A19. Therefore, we can use the Copy command to copy the contents of cells A15 through A19 to A27 through A31.

As shown in Figure 3-20, the cell pointer is at cell A19, one of the end points of the source range. Enter the command /Copy (/C). On the input line, the first end point of the source cell range (A19) is already anchored. Use the Up Arrow key to select the range A19..A15. Press the Enter key. Next, select the destination range by moving the cell pointer to A27 as shown in Figure 3-21. Press the Enter key to conclude the Copy command (Figure 3-22).

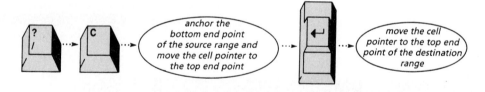

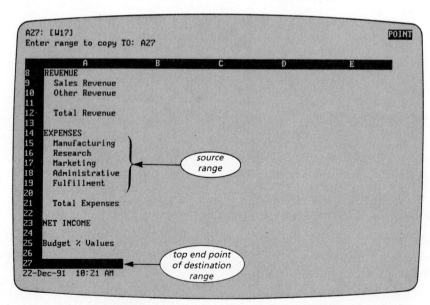

FIGURE 3-21
Step 1 of using the /C command to copy—press the Slash key (/), type the letter C for Copy, select the source range, press the Enter key, and move the cell pointer to A27.

As shown in Figure 3-22, the source range (A15..A19) and the destination range (A27..A31) are identical.

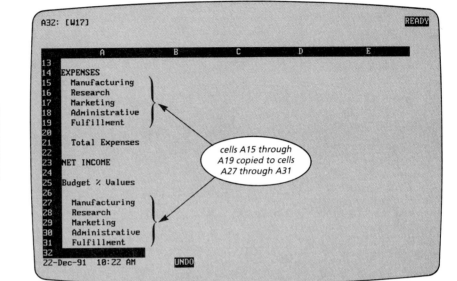

FIGURE 3-22
Step 2 of using the /C command to copy—press the Enter key. The source range (A15..A19) is copied to the destination range (A27..A31).

Two important points to note about copying the range A15..A19:

1. We selected the source range by entering A19..A15. Remember that the range A19..A15 is the same as A15..A19.
2. When both the source and destination ranges are the same size, it is not necessary to anchor the second end point of the destination range. 1-2-3 only needs to know the upper left end point, in this case A27. 1-2-3 copies the five cells in the source range beginning at cell A27. It always copies below the upper left end point of the destination range.

ENTERING NUMBERS WITH A PERCENT SIGN

Next we will enter the five budget percent values that begin in cell B27 and extend through cell B31. Use the arrow keys to move the cell pointer from its present location to B27. Rather than entering the percent value as a decimal number (.38), as we did in Project 2, enter it as a whole number followed immediately by a percent sign (%). 1-2-3 accepts the number (38%) as a percent and displays it in the cell using the global format assigned earlier to the worksheet. After entering the five budget percent values, the worksheet appears as shown in Figure 3-23.

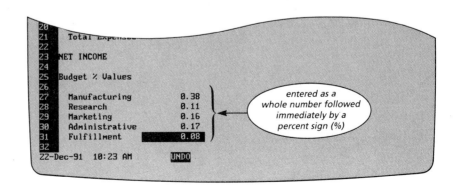

FIGURE 3-23
The five budget percent values in cells B27 through B31.

To format the five budget percent values to the Percent format, enter the command /**R**ange **F**ormat **P**ercent (/RFP). When 1-2-3 displays the prompt message "Enter number of decimal places (0..15): 2" on the input line, type the digit zero and press the Enter key. The prompt message "Enter range to format: B31..B31" displays on the input line. Enter the range B31..B27. The first end point (B31) is anchored. Use the Up Arrow key to move the cell pointer to B27. The range on the input line now reads B31..B27. Press the Enter key. The five budget percent values display in percent form as shown in Figure 3-24.

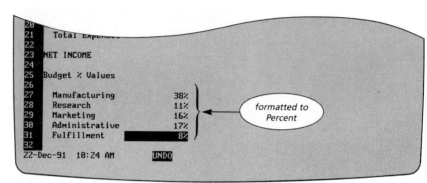

FIGURE 3-24
The five budget percent values in cells B27 through B31 formatted to the Percent type.

FREEZING THE TITLES

*T*he worksheet for this project extends beyond the size of the window. When you move the cell pointer down or to the right, the column and row titles disappear off the screen. This makes it difficult to remember where to enter the data. To alleviate this problem, 1-2-3 allows you to "freeze the titles" so that they remain on the screen no matter where you move the cell pointer. The title and column headings in rows 1 through 6 are called the **horizontal titles** and the row titles in column A are called the **vertical titles**.

The Titles Command

To freeze the titles in this worksheet, press the Home key so that most of the titles are visible on the screen. Next, use the GOTO command to move the cell pointer to B7. The horizontal titles are just above cell B7 and the vertical titles are just to the left of cell B7. Enter the command /**W**orksheet **T**itles (/WT) as shown in Figure 3-25.

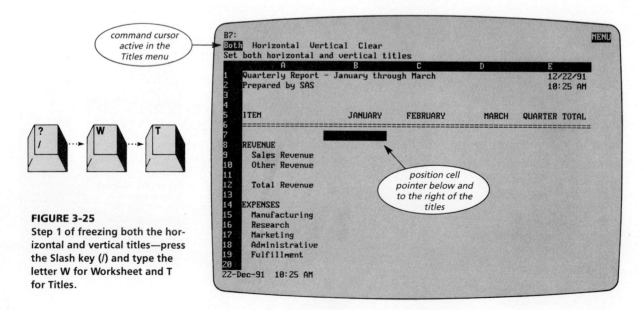

FIGURE 3-25
Step 1 of freezing both the horizontal and vertical titles—press the Slash key (/) and type the letter W for Worksheet and T for Titles.

With the command cursor active in the **Titles menu**, type the letter B for Both. This keeps the titles visible regardless of where you move the cell pointer, as shown in Figure 3-26.

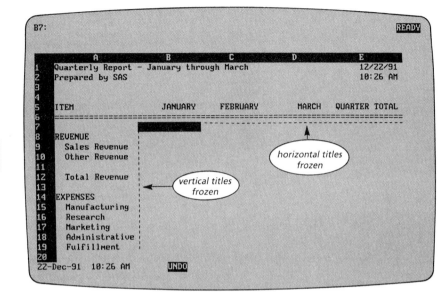

FIGURE 3-26
Step 2 of freezing both the horizontal and vertical titles— type the letter B to freeze both.

Unfreezing the Titles

Once you specify a title area, you cannot move the cell pointer into this area of the worksheet using the keys on the numeric keypad. If you want to make a change to the titles after freezing them, you must "unfreeze" them. To unfreeze the titles, enter the command /**W**orksheet **T**itles **C**lear (/WTC). Once the titles are unfrozen, you can move the cell pointer anywhere on the worksheet, including the title area, to make your desired changes. To refreeze the titles, move the cell pointer to the cell (B7) just below the horizontal titles and just to the right of the vertical titles. Next, enter the command /**W**orksheet **T**itles **B**oth (/WTB).

MOVING THE CONTENTS OF CELLS

*T*he command /**M**ove (/M) moves the contents of a cell or range of cells to a different location in the worksheet. To illustrate the use of this command, let's make a mistake by entering the sales revenue (232897.95, 432989.76, and 765998.61) that belongs in cells B9 through E9 into cells B7 through E7—two rows above its location according to Figure 3-1. This type of error is common, especially when you're not careful about cell pointer placement.

The sales revenues for January, February, and March are 232,897.95, 432,989.76, and 765,998.61. The quarter total in column E is the sum of the sales revenue for the three months. Enter the three numbers in cells B7, C7, and D7. Use the Right Arrow key after typing each number on the input line. With the cell pointer at E7, enter the function @SUM(B7..D7). 1-2-3 evaluates the function and stores the number 1,431,886.32 in E7 (232,897.95 + 432,989.76 + 765,998.61).

The values in cells C7, D7, and E7 are shown in Figure 3-27. Note that with the cell pointer at F7, the row identifiers in column A display along with columns C, D, E, and F. However, column B does not display because the titles in column A are frozen.

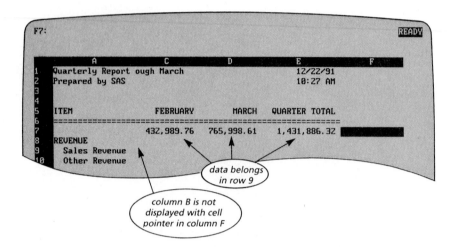

FIGURE 3-27
The sales revenue data entered into the wrong row.

As indicated earlier, the data we just entered in row 7 belongs in row 9. Let's correct the mistake and move the data from row 7 to row 9. With the cell pointer at F7, enter the command /**Move** (/M). 1-2-3 displays the message "Enter range to move FROM: F7..F7" on the input line. Press the Backspace key to *unlock* the first end point. Move the cell pointer to E7 and press the Period key. Next, move the cell pointer to B7. The range to be moved is shown in Figure 3-28. Press the Enter key to lock in the range to be moved.

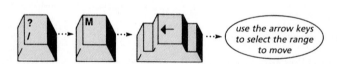

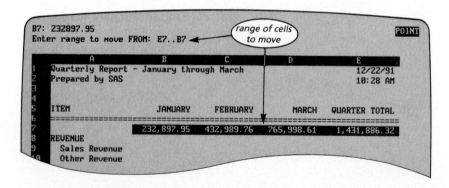

FIGURE 3-28
Step 1 of using the /M command to move data from one range to another—press the Slash key (/), type the letter M, and select the range of cells to move.

Next, 1-2-3 displays the message "Enter range to move TO: F7" on the input line. Move the cell pointer to E9. Press the Period key to anchor the first end point. Move the cell pointer to B9 as shown in Figure 3-29. To complete the command, press the Enter key and move the cell pointer to B10. Figure 3-30 illustrates the result of moving the contents of cells B7 through E7 to B9 through E9.

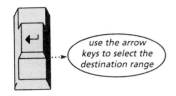

use the arrow keys to select the destination range

FIGURE 3-29
Step 2 of using the /M command to move data from one range to another—press the Enter key to lock in the range to move. Next, select the destination range.

```
B9:                                                                POINT
Enter range to move TO: E9..B9

          A              B            C            D            E
1  Quarterly Report - January through March                   12/22/91
2  Prepared by SAS                                            10:29 AM
3                                              destination
4                                                range
5  ITEM                JANUARY      FEBRUARY        MARCH   QUARTER TOTAL
6  ===================================================================
7                     232,897.95   432,989.76   765,998.61   1,431,886.32
8  REVENUE
9     Sales Revenue
10    Other Revenue
```

FIGURE 3-30
Step 3 of using the /M command to move data from one range to another—press the Enter key.

```
B10:                                                               READY

          A              B            C            D            E
1  Quarterly Report - January through March                   12/22/91
2  Prepared by SAS                                            10:30 AM
3
4
5  ITEM                JANUARY      FEBRUARY        MARCH   QUARTER TOTAL
6  ===================================================================
7
8  REVENUE
9     Sales Revenue   232,897.95   432,989.76   765,998.61   1,431,886.32
10    Other Revenue
11
12    Total Revenue
13
14 EXPENSES                              data moved from
15    Manufacturing                        row 7 to row 9
16    Research
17    Marketing
18    Administrative
19    Fulfillment
20
22-Dec-91  10:30 AM        UNDO
```

Here are some points regarding the Move command:

1. The Move and Copy commands are not the same. Where the Copy command copies one range to another, the Move command moves the contents of one range to another. Use the Move command to rearrange your worksheet. Use the Copy command to duplicate a range.

2. When you move a range containing a formula or function that references cell addresses, the referenced cell addresses are not changed relative to the new position, unless they refer to cells within the moved range. This was the case with the function in cell E7. Recall that we assigned the function @SUM(B7..D7) to cell E7. Following the Move command, the function assigned to cell E9 reads @SUM(B9..D9).

3. You can undo a Move command by entering the UNDO command, provided you do so prior to entering any other value or command.

DISPLAYING FORMULAS AND FUNCTIONS IN THE CELLS

*T*he next step in this project is to enter the other revenue in cells B10 through D10. Enter the three values for January, February, and March as described in Figure 3-1. Leave the quarter total in column E alone for now.

The monthly total revenue in row 12 is equal to the sum of the corresponding monthly revenues in rows 9 and 10. Therefore, assign cell B12 the function @SUM(B9..B10). This is illustrated in Figure 3-31.

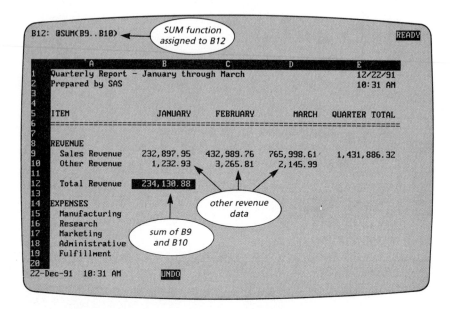

FIGURE 3-31 Other revenue and formula for January total revenue entered into worksheet.

Use the /Copy (/C) command to copy the SUM function in cell B12 to cells C12 and D12. Remember, the Copy command adjusts the cell references in the function so that it adds the contents of the cells above the cell the SUM function is copied to. Once the Copy command has been entered, 1-2-3 requests the source cell range and the destination cell range. In this case the source cell range is B12 and the destination cell range is C12..D12 (Figure 3-32).

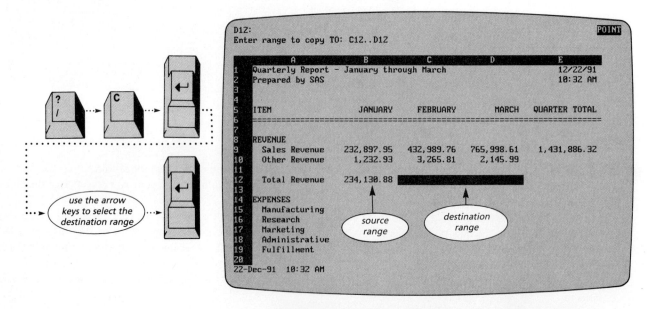

FIGURE 3-32 Using the /C command to copy cell B12 to C12 and D12—press the Slash key (/), type the letter C, press the Enter key to select the source range, use the arrow keys to select the destination range, and press the Enter key.

After entering each range, press the Enter key. The result of the copy is shown in cells C12 and D12 in Figure 3-33.

When entering or copying formulas, it is often useful to view them in the cells, instead of their numeric result. Therefore, to illustrate what is actually copied, let's change the format from Comma (,) to Text for the range B9..E19 in the worksheet. Remember from Project 2 that the Text format instructs 1-2-3 to display the formula assigned to a cell, rather than the numeric result.

Enter the command /**R**ange **F**ormat **T**ext (/RFT). 1-2-3 responds with the prompt message "Enter range to format: B12..B12" on the input line. Enter the range B9..E19 as shown in Figure 3-33 and press the Enter key.

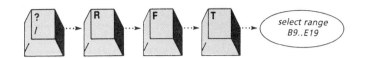

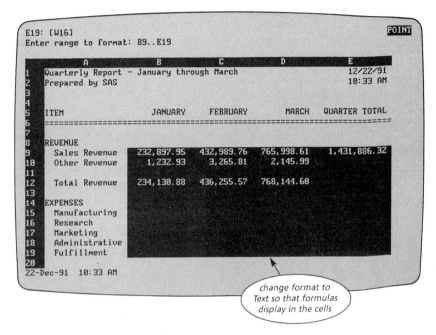

FIGURE 3-33 Step 1 of using the /RFT command to format cells B9..E19 to the Text type—press the Slash key (/), type the letters R for Range, F for Format and T for Text, and select the range B9..E19.

The functions in the worksheet (cells E9, B12, C12, and D12) now display in their respective cells and the numeric entries display using the General type format. This is shown in Figure 3-34. Later, we will reassign the Comma (,) format to the range B9..E19.

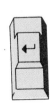

FIGURE 3-34
Step 2 of using the /RFT command to format cells B9..E19 to the Text type—press the Enter key.

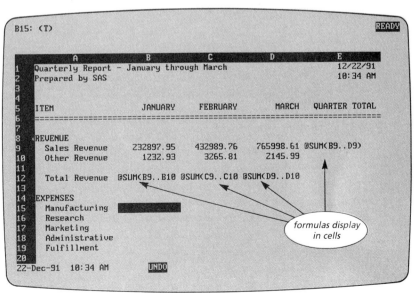

ABSOLUTE VERSUS RELATIVE ADDRESSING

The next step is to determine the five monthly budgeted expenses in the rectangular group of cells B15 through D19. Each of these budgeted expenses is equal to the corresponding budgeted percent (cells B27 through B31) times the monthly total revenue (cells B12 through D12). The formulas for each of the cells in this range are similar. They differ in that the total revenue varies by the month (column) and the budgeted percent value varies by the type of expense (row).

Relative Addressing

It would be great if we could enter the formula + B27*B12 once in cell B15 (January budgeted manufacturing expense) and then copy this formula to the remaining cells in the rectangular group B15 through D19. However, we know that when a formula with relative addresses, like B27 and B12, is copied across a row or down a column, 1-2-3 automatically adjusts the cell references in the formula as it copies to reflect its new location.

Specifying cells in a formula using relative addressing has worked well in the previous examples of copying formulas, but it won't work here because the five budgeted percent values are all located in one column and the monthly total revenues are all located in one row. For example, if we copy + B27*B12 in cell B15 to cell C15, then cell C15 equals + C27*C12. This adjustment by the Copy command is because B27 and B12 are relative addresses. The C12 is okay, because it represents the total revenue for February, but cell C27 is blank. What we need here is for 1-2-3 to maintain cell B27 as it copies across the first row.

Absolute and Mixed Cell Addressing

1-2-3 has the ability to keep a cell, a column, or a row constant when it copies a formula or function by using a technique called **absolute addressing**. To specify an absolute address in a formula, add a dollar sign ($) to the beginning of the column name, row name, or both.

For example, $B$27 is an absolute address and B27 is a relative address. Both reference the same cell. The difference shows when they are copied. A formula using $B$27 instructs 1-2-3 to use the same cell (B27) as it copies the formula to a new location. A formula using B27 instructs 1-2-3 to adjust the cell reference as it copies. Table 3-2 gives some additional examples of absolute addressing. A cell address with one dollar sign before either the column or the row is called a **mixed cell address**—one is relative, the other is absolute.

TABLE 3-2   Absolute Addressing

CELL ADDRESS	MEANING
$A$22	Both column and row references remain the same when this cell address is copied.
A$22	The column reference changes when you copy this cell address to another column. The row reference does not change—it is absolute.
$A22	The row reference changes when you copy this cell address to another row. The column reference does not change—it is absolute.
A22	Both column and row references are relative. When copied to another row and column, both the row and column in the cell address are adjusted to reflect the new location.

Copying Formulas with Mixed Cell Addresses

With the cell pointer at B15, enter the formula $B27*B$12 as shown in Figure 3-35. Because B15 was in the range we formatted to Text earlier, the formula displays in the cell, rather than the value. Note that it is not necessary to enter the formula $B27*B$12 with a leading plus sign because, in this case, the $ indicates that the entry is a formula or a number. The cell reference $B27 (budgeted manufacturing % value) means that the row reference (27) changes when you copy it to a new row, but the column reference (B) remains constant through all columns in the destination range. The cell reference B$12 (January expenses) in the formula means that the column reference (B) changes when you copy it to a new column, but the row reference (12) remains constant through all rows in the destination range. Let's copy the formula $B27*B$12 in cell B15 to the rectangular group of cells B15 through D19.

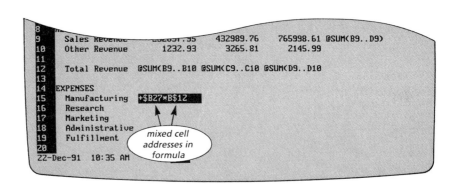

FIGURE 3-35
Formula with mixed cell addresses entered into cell B15.

The cell pointer is at B15 as shown in Figure 3-35. Enter the command /Copy (/C). When the prompt message "Enter range to copy FROM: B15..B15" displays on the input line, press the Enter key. When the message "Enter range to copy TO: B15" displays on the input line, use the arrow keys to select the range B15..D19. This is shown in Figure 3-36. Note that cell B15 is copied on top of itself, because B15 is one of the end points of the destination range.

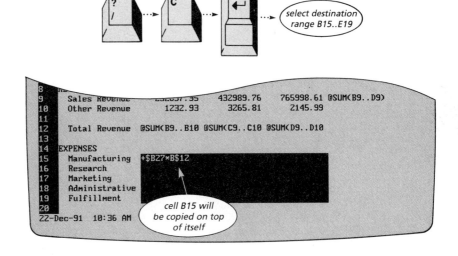

FIGURE 3-36
Step 1 of using the /C command to copy cell B15 to the range B15..D19—press the Slash key (/), type the letter C for Copy, press the Enter key, and select the destination range.

Press the Enter key. The Copy command copies the formula in cell B15 to the rectangular group of cells B15 through D19 as shown in Figure 3-37. Take a few minutes to study the formulas in Figure 3-37. You should begin to see the significance of mixed cell addressing. For example, every aspect of the five formulas in cells B15 through B19 is identical, except for the row in the first cell reference (budgeted % value). Also note, in columns C and D, that the column in the second cell reference (monthly total revenue) changes based on the column the formula is in.

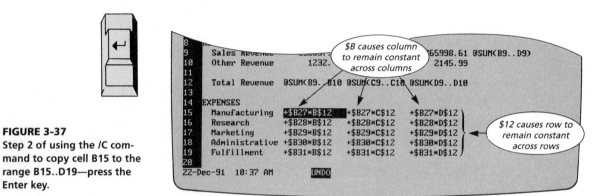

FIGURE 3-37
Step 2 of using the /C command to copy cell B15 to the range B15..D19—press the Enter key.

Switching from Text Format to the Comma Format

Let's change cells B9 through E19 from the Text format back to the Comma format. Recall that we switched the format of these cells from Comma to Text so that we could view the formulas in the cells. To change the format, move the cell pointer to the lower left end point (B19) of the range B19..E9. Enter the command /Range Format , (/RF,).

Press the Enter key when the prompt message "Enter number of decimal places (0..15): 2" displays on the input line. Finally, when 1-2-3 requests the range, use the arrow keys to select the rectangular group of cells B19..E9. Press the Enter key. The results of the formulas, rather than the formulas themselves, display in the cells (Figure 3-38).

```
B19: (,2) +$B31*B$12                                                    READY

           A              B            C            D            E
1  Quarterly Report - January through March                    12/22/91
2  Prepared by SAS                                             10:38 AM
3
4
5  ITEM               JANUARY     FEBRUARY        MARCH   QUARTER TOTAL
6
7
8  REVENUE
9    Sales Revenue   232,897.95   432,989.76   765,998.61   1,431,886.32
10   Other Revenue     1,232.93     3,265.81     2,145.99
11
12   Total Revenue   234,130.88   436,255.57   768,144.60
13
14 EXPENSES
15   Manufacturing    88,969.73   165,777.12   291,894.95
16   Research         25,754.40    47,988.11    84,495.91
17   Marketing        37,460.94    69,800.89   122,903.14
18   Administrative   39,802.25    74,163.45   130,584.58
19   Fulfillment      18,730.47    34,900.45    61,451.57
20
22-Dec-91  10:38 AM          UNDO
```

FIGURE 3-38
Range B9..E19 reformatted to the Comma (,) type.

POINTING TO A RANGE OF CELLS TO SUM

*T*he total expenses for January (cell B21) are determined by adding the five monthly budgeted expenses in cells B15 through B19. The total expenses for February (C21) and March (D21) are found in the same way.

To sum the five monthly budgeted expenses for January, move the cell pointer to B21 and begin entering the SUM function. For this entry, let's apply the pointing method to enter the range to sum. Enter @sum(on the input line. Remember that function names can be entered in lowercase. After typing the open parenthesis, use the Up Arrow key to move the cell pointer to B15, the topmost end point of the range to sum. As the cell pointer moves upward, 1-2-3 changes the cell address following the open parenthesis on the input line. Move the cell pointer until it reaches B15 (Figure 3-39).

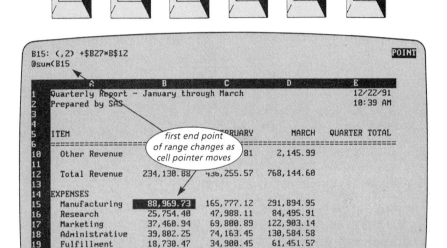

FIGURE 3-39 Step 1 of entering the SUM function using the pointing method—after the open parenthesis, use the arrow keys to select the first end point of the range.

Press the Period key (.) to lock in the first end point of the range to sum. Next, use the Down Arrow key to move the cell pointer to B19 (Figure 3-40). To complete the entry, press the Close Parenthesis key and the Enter key.

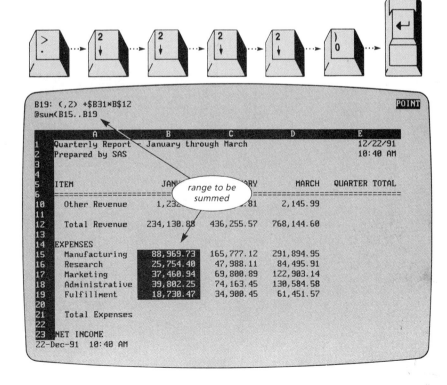

FIGURE 3-40
Step 2 of entering the SUM function using the pointing method—press the Period key (.), use the arrow keys to select the second end point of the range, type the Close Parenthesis key, and press the Enter key.

As shown in cell B21 of Figure 3-41, 1-2-3 displays the sum (210,717.79) of the five January budgeted expenses stored in cells B15 through B19.

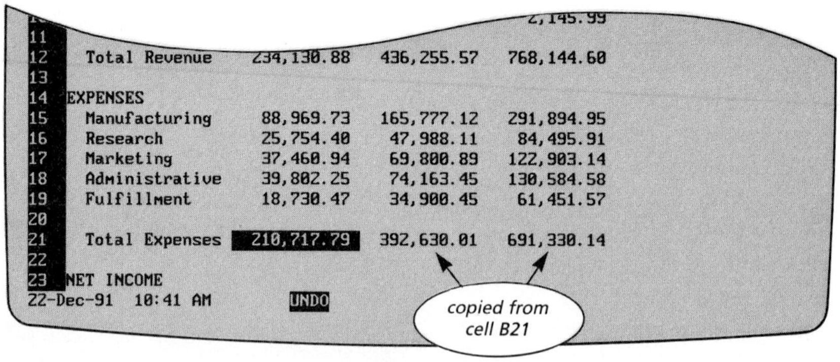

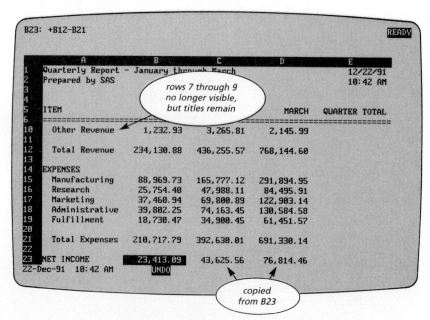

FIGURE 3-41
SUM function in cell B21 copied to cells C21 and D21.

Pointing versus Entering a Range of Cells

The pointing method used to enter the range for the SUM function in cell B21 saves keying time. Anytime you need to enter a range, you may use the arrow keys to point to it. Alternatively, you may type the cell addresses. Once you begin typing a cell address, 1-2-3 is no longer in POINT mode.

Copying the Total Expenses and Net Income for Each Month

The next step in this project is to determine the total expenses for February and March. To accomplish this task, copy the function in cell B21 to cells C21 and D21. Enter the command /Copy (/C). After entering the source range (B21), press the Enter key. Next, select the destination range (C21..D21) and press the Enter key. Figure 3-41 shows the result of copying cell B21 to cells C21 and D21.

We can now determine the net income for each month in row 23 by subtracting the total expenses for each month in row 21 from the total revenue for each month in row 12. Move the cell pointer to B23 and enter the formula +B12−B21. Copy this formula to cells C23 and D23. The result of entering the formula in cell B23 and copying it to C23 and D23 is shown in Figure 3-42.

FIGURE 3-42
Formula in cell B23 copied to cells C23 and D23.

Summing Empty Cells and Labels

One more step and the worksheet is complete. We need to determine the quarter totals in column E. Use the GOTO command to move the cell pointer to the quarter total in cell E9. Since cell E9 is not on the screen (Figure 3-42), the GOTO command causes the window to move so that cell E9 is positioned in the upper left corner, just below and to the right of the titles.

Recall that we determined the quarter total for the sales revenue after we entered the monthly sales revenue (Figure 3-30). The functions required for all the row entries (E10, E12, E15 through E19, E21, and E23) are identical to the function in cell E9. Therefore, let's copy the function in cell E9 to these cells.

Unfortunately, the cells in the destination range are not contiguous, that is, connected. For example, in the range E10 through E23, the function is not needed in E11, E13, E14, E20, and E22. We have three choices here: (1) use the copy command several times and copy the function in E9 to E10, E12, E15 through E19, E21, and E23; (2) enter the function manually in each required cell; or (3) copy the function to the range E10 through E23. If we select the third method, we have to use the command /Range Erase (/RE) to erase the function from E11, E13, E14, E20, and E22, the cells in which the function is not required. Let's use the third method.

With the cell pointer at E9, enter the command /Copy (/C). When 1-2-3 displays the prompt message "Enter range to copy FROM: E9..E9", press the Enter key. For the destination range, leave E9 anchored as the first end point and use the Down Arrow key to move the cell pointer to E23. This is shown in Figure 3-43.

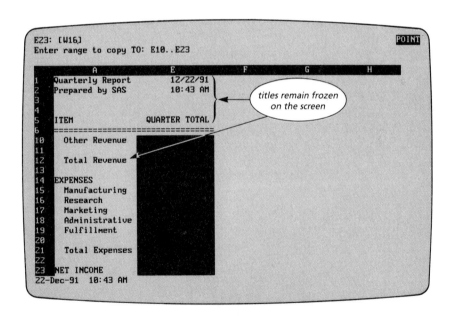

FIGURE 3-43
Step 1 of using the /C command to copy cell E9 to the range E9..E23—press the Slash key (/), type the letter C for Copy, press the Enter key, and select the destination range.

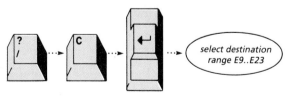

Press the Enter key and the function in cell E9 is copied to the cells in the range E9..E23 (Figure 3-44).

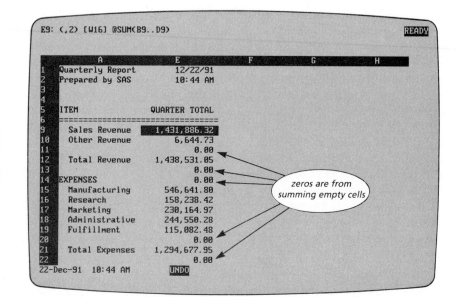

FIGURE 3-44
Step 2 of using the /C command to copy cell E9 to the range E9..E23—press the Enter key.

Notice the zeros in cells E11, E13, E14, E20, and E22. The formula in cell E11 reads @SUM(B11..D11). 1-2-3 considers empty cells and cells with labels to be equal to zero when they are referenced in a formula or function. Since cells B11, C11, and D11 are empty, the SUM function assigned to E11 produces the zero display. We need to erase the functions in the cells displaying zero. Recall from Project 1 that the command **/R**ange **E**rase (/RE) erases the contents of a cell. Use this command to erase the zeros in cells E11, E13, E14, E20, and E22.

After the zeros in column E are erased, use the command **/W**orksheet **T**itles **C**lear (/WTC) to unfreeze the titles. Finally, press the Home key to move the cell pointer to A1. The worksheet is complete as shown in Figure 3-45.

```
A1: [W17] 'Quarterly Report - January through March                    READY

           A           B            C            D            E
 1  Quarterly Report - January through March              12/22/91
 2  Prepared by SAS                                        10:45 AM
 3
 4
 5  ITEM            JANUARY      FEBRUARY       MARCH   QUARTER TOTAL
 6  ================================================================
 7
 8  REVENUE
 9    Sales Revenue 232,897.95   432,989.76   765,998.61  1,431,886.32
10    Other Revenue   1,232.93     3,265.81     2,145.99      6,644.73
11
12    Total Revenue 234,130.88   436,255.57   768,144.60  1,438,531.05
13
14  EXPENSES
15    Manufacturing  88,969.73   165,777.12   291,894.95    546,641.80
16    Research       25,754.40    47,988.11    84,495.91    158,238.42
17    Marketing      37,460.94    69,800.89   122,903.14    230,164.97
18    Administrative 39,802.25    74,163.45   130,584.58    244,550.28
19    Fulfillment    18,730.47    34,900.45    61,451.57    115,082.48
20
22-Dec-91  10:45 AM      UNDO
```

zeros removed with the /Range Erase command

FIGURE 3-45
The completed worksheet.

SAVING AND PRINTING THE WORKSHEET

Save the worksheet on disk for later use. Use the command /File Save (/FS) and the file name PROJS-3. As we discussed in Project 2, when you create a large worksheet such as this one, it is prudent to save the worksheet periodically—every 50 to 75 keystrokes. Then, if there should be an inadvertent loss of power to the computer or other unforeseen mishap, you will not lose the whole worksheet.

Printing the Worksheet

After saving the worksheet as PROJS-3, obtain a hard copy by printing the worksheet on the printer. Recall from Project 2, that to print the worksheet you use the command /**Print Printer** (/PP). This command activates the command cursor in the Printer menu and displays the printsheet settings (Figure 3-46). Type the letter R for Range. The cell pointer is at one end point of the range we wish to print, A1. Use the arrow keys to move the cell pointer to E31. Press the Enter key to anchor the second end point.

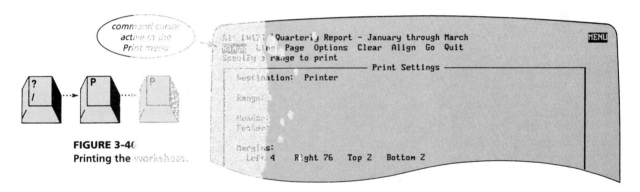

FIGURE 3-46
Printing the worksheet.

Next, check the printer to be sure it is in READY mode. Type the letter A for Align and the letter G for Go. The worksheet prints on the printer as shown in Figure 3-47. Finally, type the letter P for Page twice to move the paper through the printer so that you can tear the paper at the perforated edge below the printed version of the worksheet.

```
Quarterly Report - January through March                 12/22/91
Prepared by SAS                                          10:47 AM


ITEM                  JANUARY      FEBRUARY        MARCH    QUARTER TOTAL
===============================================================================

REVENUE
   Sales Revenue     232,897.95    432,989.76   765,998.61    1,431,886.32
   Other Revenue       1,232.93      3,265.81     2,145.99        6,644.73

   Total Revenue     234,130.88    436,255.57   768,144.60    1,438,531.05

EXPENSES
   Manufacturing      80,969.73    165,777.12   291,894.95      546,641.80
   Research           25,754.40     47,988.11    84,495.91      158,238.42
   Marketing          37,460.94     69,800.89   122,903.14      230,164.97
   Administrative     39,802.25     74,163.45   130,584.58      244,550.28
   Fulfillment        18,730.47     34,900.45    61,451.57      115,082.48

   Total Expenses    210,717.79    392,630.01   691,330.14    1,294,677.95

NET INCOME            23,413.09     43,625.56    76,814.46      143,853.10

Budget % Values


   Manufacturing         38%
   Research              11%
   Marketing             16%
   Administrative        17%
   Fulfillment            8%
```

FIGURE 3-47 The printed version of the worksheet in Project 3.

Printing the Worksheet in Condensed Mode

If you have a graphics printer, you can print more than 80 characters per line by printing the worksheet in condensed mode. This mode can be helpful if the worksheet is wider than the screen. The **condensed mode** allows nearly twice as many characters to fit across the page. To print a worksheet in the condensed mode, do the following:

1. Enter the command /**P**rint **P**rinter **O**ptions **S**etup (/PPOS). Enter the code \015 and press the Enter key.
2. With the Printer Options menu at the top of the screen, enter the command **M**argins **R**ight. Type in a right margin of 132. Press the Enter key and type the letter Q to quit the Printer Options menu.
3. Select the range to print and follow the usual steps for printing the worksheet. The condensed printed version of the worksheet prints on the printer as shown in Figure 3-48.

```
Quarterly Report - January through March              12/22/91
Prepared by SAS                                       10:48 AM


ITEM              JANUARY    FEBRUARY      MARCH   QUARTER TOTAL
===============================================================

REVENUE
  Sales Revenue  232,897.95  432,989.76  765,998.61  1,431,886.32
  Other Revenue    1,232.93    3,265.81    2,145.99      6,644.73


  Total Revenue  234,130.88  436,255.57  768,144.60  1,438,531.05

EXPENSES
  Manufacturing   88,969.73  165,777.12  291,894.95    546,641.80
  Research        25,754.40   47,988.11   84,495.91    158,238.42
  Marketing       37,460.94   69,800.89  122,903.14    230,164.97
  Administrative  39,802.25   74,163.45  130,584.58    244,550.28
  Fulfillment     18,730.47   34,900.45   61,451.57    115,082.48


  Total Expenses 210,717.79  392,630.01  691,330.14  1,294,677.95

NET INCOME        23,413.09   43,625.56   76,814.46    143,853.10


Budget % Values

  Manufacturing       38%
  Research            11%
  Marketing           16%
  Administrative      17%
  Fulfillment          8%
```

FIGURE 3-48 A printout of the worksheet in the condensed mode.

If the printer does not print in condensed mode, check the printer manual to be sure the current dip switch settings on the printer allow for it. You may have to change these settings. If you continue to experience problems, check the printer manual to be sure that code \015 instructs the printer to print in condensed mode. This code works for most printers.

To change 1-2-3 back to the normal print mode, do the following:

1. Enter the command /**P**rint **P**rinter **O**ptions **S**etup (/PPOS). Enter the code \018 and press the Enter key.
2. With the Printer Options menu at the top of the screen, enter the command Margins Right. Type in a right margin of 76. Press the Enter key and type the letter Q to quit the Printer Options menu.
3. With the command cursor in the Print menu, follow the steps outlined earlier for printing the worksheet in the normal mode.

Using Borders to Print Nonadjacent Columns

Up to this point, we have printed only columns that are side by side in the worksheet. Consider Figure 3-49. This partial printout is called a summary report, since only the row titles in column A and the corresponding totals in column E are printed.

We can print such a report through the use of the Borders command in the Printer Options menu. The Borders command prints specified columns to the left of the selected range or it prints specified rows above the selected range.

To print the summary report in Figure 3-49, do the following:

1. Move the cell pointer to column A and enter the command /**P**rint **P**rinter **O**ptions **B**orders (/PPOB). Type C for Column and press the Enter key to select column A as the border. Type Q to quit the Printer Options menu.
2. With the Print menu at the top of the screen, select E1..E23 as the range to print.
3. Press A for Align and G for Go.

In Figure 3-49, column A prints as the border and column E prints because it was selected as the range to print.

To clear column A as the border, select the Clear command in the Print menu. When the Clear menu displays at the top of the screen, type B for Borders.

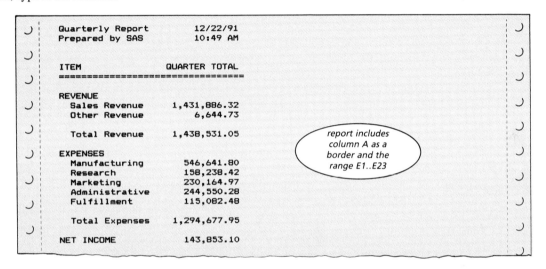

FIGURE 3-49 A summary report made up of nonadjacent columns.

Other Printer Options

There are other printer options that can enhance your worksheet. Table 3-3 summarizes the commands found in the **P**rinter **O**ptions menu.

TABLE 3-3   A Summary of Commands in the Printer Options Menu

COMMAND	DEFAULT SETTING	FUNCTION
Header	none	Prints a line of text at the top of every page of the worksheet.
Footer	none	Prints a line of text at the bottom of every page of the worksheet.
Margins	Left 4 Right 76 Top 2 Bottom 2	Sets the margins.
Borders	none	Prints specified columns or rows on every page.
Setup	none	Sends commands to the printer, for example, to print the worksheet in condensed mode.
Pg-Length	66	Sets printed lines per page.
Other		Selects the As-Displayed or Cell-Formulas version to print.
Quit		Returns to the Print menu.

Many of the options you set with the /**P**rint **P**rinter **O**ptions (/PPO) command are saved with the worksheet and stay in effect when you retrieve it. So remember, if you change any of the printer options and you want the changes to stay with the worksheet, be sure to save the worksheet after you finish printing it. That way you won't have to change the options the next time you retrieve the worksheet.

If you use the command /**W**orksheet **E**rase (/WE) to clear the worksheet on the screen or restart 1-2-3, the printer options revert back to the default settings shown in Table 3.3.

WHAT-IF QUESTIONS

 powerful feature of 1-2-3 is the ability to answer what-if questions. Quick responses to these questions are invaluable when making business decisions. Using 1-2-3 to answer what-if questions is called performing **what-if analyses** or **sensitivity analyses**.

A what-if question for the worksheet in Project 3 might be, "What if the manufacturing budgeted percentage is decreased from 38% to 35%—how would this affect the total expenses and net income?" To answer questions like this, you need only change a single value in the worksheet. The recalculation feature of 1-2-3 answers the question immediately by displaying new values in any cells with formulas or functions that reference the changed cell.

Let's change the manufacturing budgeted percentage from 38% to 35% (Figure 3-50). In the *before change* screen in Figure 3-50, the manufacturing budgeted percentage is 38%. After the change is made, the manufacturing budgeted percentage is 35%. When we make the change, all the formulas are immediately recalculated. This process generally requires less than one second, depending on how many calculations must be performed.

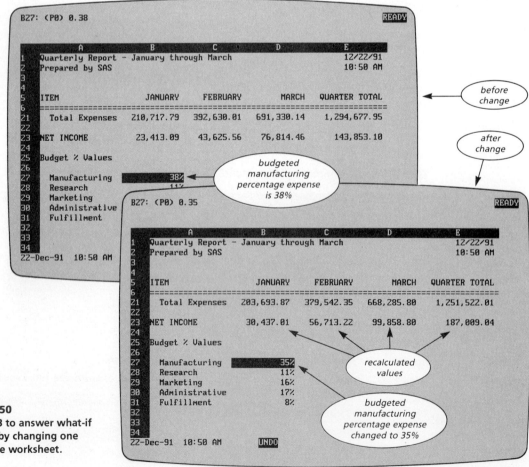

FIGURE 3-50
Using 1-2-3 to answer what-if questions by changing one value in the worksheet.

As soon as the 35% replaces the 38% in cell B27, the new expenses and new net income values can be examined (bottom screen of Figure 3-50). By changing the value in B27 from 38% to 35%, the total January expenses decrease from 210,717.79 to 203,693.87, and the January net income increases from 23,413.09 to 30,437.01. The February and March figures change the same way. The quarter total expenses decrease from 1,294,677.95 to 1,251,522.01, and the quarter net income increases from 143,853.11 to 187,009.04. Thus, if the budgeted manufacturing expenses are reduced, it is clear that net income increases.

As shown in the *after change* screen of Figure 3-51, you can change more than one percentage. Let's change all the percentages. The new calculations display immediately.

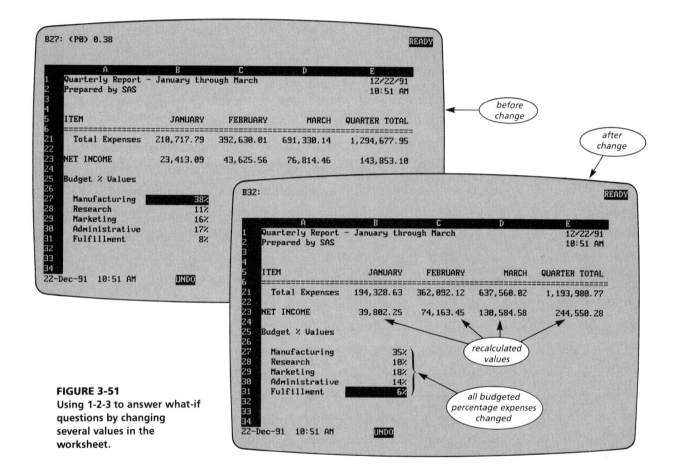

FIGURE 3-51
Using 1-2-3 to answer what-if questions by changing several values in the worksheet.

In Figure 3-51, we ask the question, "What if we change all the budgeted percent values to the following: Manufacturing (35%); Research (10%); Marketing (18%); Administrative (14%); Fulfillment (6%)—how would these changes affect the total expenses and the net income?" By merely changing the five values on the worksheet, all formulas are automatically recalculated to provide the answer to this question.

Manual versus Automatic Recalculation

Each time you enter a value in the worksheet, 1-2-3 automatically recalculates all formulas and functions in those cells that changed since the worksheet was last recalculated, and in the cells that depend on those cells. This feature is called **automatic recalculation**.

An alternative to automatic recalculation is manual recalculation. With **manual recalculation**, 1-2-3 only recalculates after you tell it to do so. To change recalculation from automatic to manual, enter the command /**W**orksheet **G**lobal **R**ecalculate (/WGR). With the command cursor active in the **Recalculate menu**, type the letter M for Manual. Then recalculation of formulas takes place *only* after you press function key F9. To change back to automatic recalculation, use the same command but type the letter A for Automatic rather than M for Manual.

When you save a worksheet, the current recalculation mode is saved along with it. For an explanation of the other types of recalculation available with 1-2-3, enter the command /WGR and press function key F1. When you are finished with the online help facility, press the Esc key to return to your worksheet.

CHANGING THE WORKSHEET DEFAULT SETTINGS

1-2-3 comes with default settings. We have already discussed some of the more obvious ones—column width is nine characters, format is General, and recalculation of formulas is Automatic. Some of the default settings, like the format, can be changed for a range or for the entire worksheet. When you make a change to the entire worksheet using the command /**W**orksheet **G**lobal (/WG), the change is saved with the worksheet when you issue the /**F**ile **S**ave (/FS) command.

There is another group of default settings that affect all worksheets created or retrieved during the current session, until you quit 1-2-3. To view or change these settings, type the command /**W**orksheet **G**lobal **D**efault (/WGD). This command displays the **Global Default menu** and **default settings sheet** as shown in Figure 3-52. Then use the arrow keys or first letters of the commands in the Global Default menu to select features to change. Remember, when you are in the MENU mode, you can display the worksheets, rather than the settings sheet, by pressing F6.

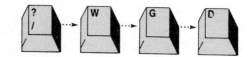

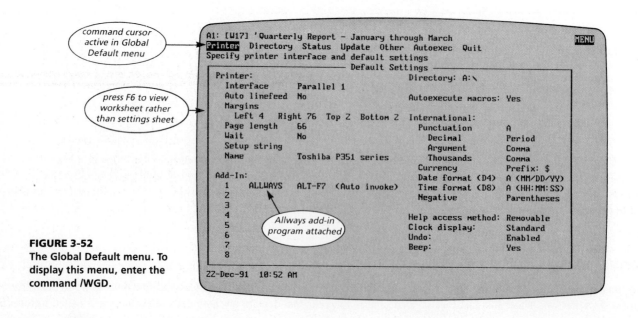

FIGURE 3-52
The Global Default menu. To display this menu, enter the command /WGD.

Once you pick the desired settings, you have the choice of saving the changes for the current session or saving them permanently. To save the changes for the current session, type the letter Q to quit the Global Default menu. To save the changes permanently, type the letters U for Update and then Q for Quit. If you typed the letter U for update, the new settings become the defaults for the current and future 1-2-3 sessions. Table 3-4 describes the features you can change by typing the command /WGD.

TABLE 3-4   A Summary of Commands in the Global Defaults Menu

COMMAND	FUNCTION
Printer	Specifies printer interface and default settings.
Directory	Changes the default directory.
Status	Displays default settings.
Update	Permanently changes default settings in configuration file.
Other	Changes international, help, add-in programs, and clock settings.
Autoexec	Instructs 1-2-3 whether to run autoexecute macros named \0 (zero).
Quit	Quits Global Default menu.

INTERACTING WITH DOS

*U*p to this point, we have used the File command to save and retrieve worksheets from disk. This command may also be used to carry out several other file management functions normally done at the DOS level. Table 3-5 summarizes the major file management commands available in 1-2-3.

TABLE 3-5   File Management Commands

COMMAND	FUNCTION	DUPLICATE DOS COMMAND
/FE	Erases a file from disk.	ERASE or DEL
/FL	Displays the names of the files of a particular type.	DIR
/FD	Changes the current directory to a new one.	CHDIR or CD

Other DOS commands and programs can be executed by placing 1-2-3 and your worksheet in a wait state. A **wait state** means that 1-2-3 has given up control to another program, like DOS, but still resides in main computer memory. To leave 1-2-3 temporarily, enter the command /System (/S). (If you do not have a fixed disk, place the DOS disk in the A drive before entering the /S command.)

You can use the System command to leave 1-2-3 to format a disk. Once the disk is formatted, you can return to 1-2-3 and the worksheet by typing the command Exit in response to the DOS prompt. One word of advice—save your worksheet before using the System command, especially if you plan to execute an external DOS command.

PRINTING THE WORKSHEET USING ALLWAYS

Allways is a spreadsheet publishing add-in program that comes with Release 2.2 of 1-2-3. **Add-in** means the program is started while 1-2-3 is running. Allways allows you to produce presentation-quality printouts as shown in Figure 3-53.

To use Allways, you must be running 1-2-3 on a hard-disk or network system with at least 512K main memory. Furthermore, Allways must be attached, that is, available to 123 as an add-in program. To check if it is attached and ready to use, enter the command **/W**orksheet **G**lobal **D**efault (/WGD). If Allways is attached, "ALLWAYS" displays in the add-in program list as shown in the lower left corner of the default settings sheet in Figure 3-52. The Alt-F7 that you see to the right of ALLWAYS in Figure 3-52 means that you can start this program while 1-2-3 is on the screen by holding down the Alt key and then pressing the F7 key.

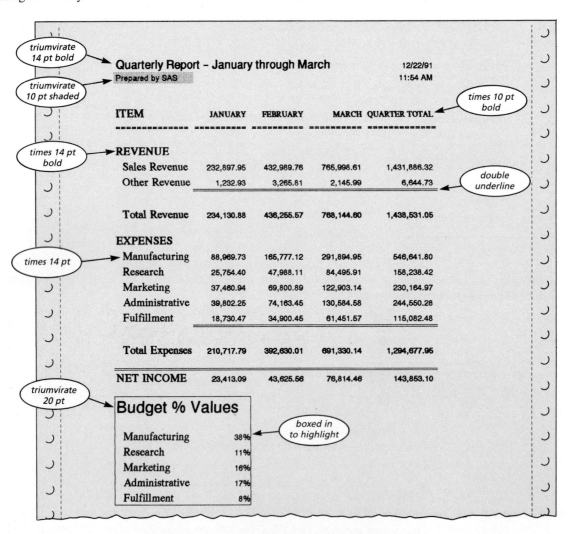

FIGURE 3-53 The worksheet in Project 3 printed using the spreadsheet publishing add-in program Allways.

As shown in Figure 3-53, Allways allows you to improve the appearance of a report significantly. With Allways you can:

- Change the font (typeface and size).
- Boldface and underline text and numbers.
- Adjust the height of rows and width of columns.
- Shade cells.
- Draw horizontal and vertical lines.
- Outline a cell or range of cells.
- Display the worksheet at 60% to 140% of its normal size.
- Include a 1-2-3 graph in the same report as the worksheet (see Project 5).
- Print in color if you have a color printer attached to your system.

Another nice feature of Allways is that if you have a graphics monitor, you get a "what you see is what you get" (**WYSIWYG**) display on the screen that is nearly identical to what will print.

Starting and Quitting Allways

With 1-2-3 running, there are two ways to invoke Allways: (1) enter the command /**A**dd-In **I**nvoke (/AI) and select Allways; or (2) press Alt-F7. The latter method is only available if the F7 key was assigned the Allways program when it was initially attached to 1-2-3. Once control passes from 1-2-3 to Allways, the screen in Figure 3-54 appears. Note that the characters in the worksheet display in **graphics form**, rather than **text form**, as they do in 1-2-3.

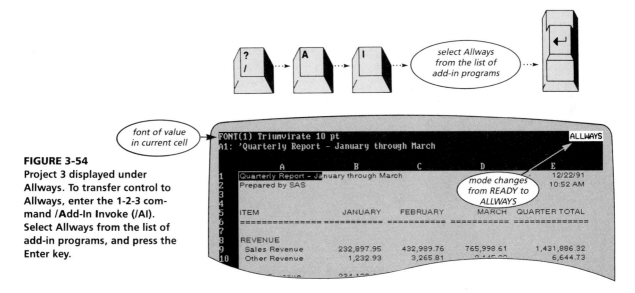

FIGURE 3-54
Project 3 displayed under Allways. To transfer control to Allways, enter the 1-2-3 command /**A**dd-In **I**nvoke (/AI). Select Allways from the list of add-in programs, and press the Enter key.

You would normally invoke Allways after you have completed the entries in the worksheet; but you can switch back and forth between Allways and 1-2-3 at any time.

There are three ways to quit Allways and return control to 1-2-3: (1) press the Esc key until 1-2-3 and the original worksheet reappear on the screen as shown in Figure 3-45; (2) enter the Allways command /**Q**uit (/Q); or (3) hold down the Alt key and press the function key assigned to Allways.

With the worksheet for Project 3 (Figure 3-45) on the screen, practice switching back and forth between 1-2-3 and Allways. As you move from 1-2-3 to Allways and back again to 1-2-3, the display on the screen switches between the one shown in Figure 3-45 (text display) and the one shown in Figure 3-54 (graphics display). Once you get a feel for how easy it is to transfer control between the two programs, switch to Allways to continue with this project.

The Allways Online Help Facility

To view Allways help screens, press the F1 key just as you do in 1-2-3. Allways displays a help screen that describes the activity you are currently performing in the program. For example, if you want information on the command /Layout Options, enter /LO and press the F1 key.

The Allways Control Panel

The control panel in Allways is similar to the one in 1-2-3. The first line displays the format of the current cell: the font, color of data, boldface, underline, lines, or shading. The mode of operation also displays on the first line. The ALLWAYS mode means that you are in Allways (Figure 3-54). This mode is the same as READY mode in 1-2-3.

The second line of the control panel shows the address and contents of the current cell. As with 1-2-3, when you press the Slash key (/), the command menu appears on the second line. If you press the Slash key in the middle of any command sequence, the command menu will reappear. The third line in the control panel displays information about the menu item highlighted when Allways is in MENU mode.

The line at the bottom of the Allways screen displays the date, time, and status indicators, as does the line at the bottom of the 1-2-3 screen.

Type Styles and Cell Formats

When you initially enter Allways, all values in the cells are assigned the same font — Triumvirate 10 point (Figure 3-54). The **font** is a typeface (Triumvirate) of a particular size (10 point). A **point** is equal to 1/72 of an inch. Thus, 10 point is equal to about 1/7 of an inch. Figures 3-55 and 3-56 illustrate a variety of typefaces and point sizes.

Allways makes available two typefaces and four different point sizes for a total of eight different fonts (bottom screen of Figure 3-57). These eight *active* fonts can be changed as described in the 1-2-3 reference manual. The most important font is Font 1 — Triumvirate 10 point — because it is the one that is assigned to all the values in the worksheet when you first enter Allways.

This is Triumvirate
This is Times
This is Courier

FIGURE 3-55 Different typefaces.

This is Times 10 point
This is Times 12 point
This is Times 14 point
This is Times 17 point
This is Times 20 point
This is Times 24 point

FIGURE 3-56 The Times typeface shown in different point sizes.

Additional publishing terms with which you should be familiar are shading, bold, double underline, outlining a range of cells, and grid. **Shading** is the darkening of a range of cells and is useful for creating contrast (line 2 of Figure 3-53).

If a range of cells is **bold** or **boldface**, then the characters are darkened to make them stand out (line 1 of Figure 3-53). A **double underline** results in a double bar at the base of a range of cells. This is shown in Figure 3-53 below the row entitled Other Revenue.

You can request Allways to outline a range of cells. When we say a range **outlined**, we mean that a box has been drawn around it. The box highlights the range of cells as shown at the bottom of Figure 3-53.

Grid lines are dotted lines that surround each cell. The dotted lines run along the rows and columns of the worksheet. You can instruct Allways to display and print your worksheet with a grid by using the command /Layout Options Grid (/LOG). You can also toggle the grid on and off by pressing Alt-G. With Project 3 on the screen, press Alt-G to create a grid on the worksheet. After the grid appears, press Alt-G again. The grid disappears. Since a grid is not called for in this project, make sure the grid is off before continuing.

Saving and Synchronizing Format Changes

To preserve the format changes made with Allways, return control to 1-2-3 and save the worksheet to disk. A separate Allways file with the same file name as the worksheet, but with an extension of .ALL, is saved along with the worksheet. The next time you load the worksheet and invoke Allways, the format changes will be the same as they were when you saved it earlier.

Allways automatically synchronizes the formats assigned to cells that are changed with 1-2-3. That is, after formatting with Allways, you can return to 1-2-3 and make any changes you want to the worksheet, such as moving cells, inserting columns or rows, or deleting columns or rows. Allways will automatically adjust the cell formats to agree with the most recent worksheet modifications.

Allways Command Menu

When you press the Slash key (/) in ALLWAYS mode, the command menu displays. Table 3-6 summarizes the functions of these commands.

TABLE 3-6   A Summary of Commands in the Allways Command Menu

COMMAND	FUNCTION
Worksheet	Sets column widths, row heights, and page breaks.
Format	Changes font, boldface, underline, color, lines, or shading of a range of cells.
Graph	Inserts or deletes a graph from the current worksheet.
Layout	Changes page size, margins, headers, footers, prints borders, and grid lines.
Print	Prints worksheet on printer or file and configures printer.
Display	Enlarges or reduces worksheet display, displays worksheet in text or graphics, turns graphs on or off, and sets colors.
Special	Copy, move, or import formats. Justifies labels in a range.
Quit	Returns control to 1-2-3.

For the remainder of this project we will use Allways to format and print the worksheet so that it looks like Figure 3-53. Just as in 1-2-3, Allways allows you to make the format changes to the worksheet in any order you want. We will make the format changes in the following order:

1. Change A1 to Triumvirate 14-point font.
2. Change A5 and A8..31 to Times 14-point font.
3. Change A25 to Triumvirate 20-point font.
4. Shade A2.
5. Bold cells A1, A5..E5, A8, A12..E12, A14, A21..E21, and A23..E23.
6. Double underline B10..E10, B19..E19, and A22..E22.
7. Outline in the range A25..B31.
8. Change the width of column A from 17 to 18 characters.
9. Print the worksheet.
10. Preserve the format changes by returning to 1-2-3 and saving the worksheet.

Changing The Font

With the Allways program in control of the computer and the cell pointer at A1, change the font of the worksheet title. Enter the command /Format Font (/FF). The Slash key (/) instructs Allways to display the command menu shown in the top screen of Figure 3-57. When you press the first F for Format, Allways displays the Format menu as shown in the middle screen of Figure 3-57. Typing the second letter F for Font, instructs Allways to display the Font menu. With the Font menu on the screen, highlight Triumvirate 14 point by pressing the Down Arrow key twice. This procedure is shown in the bottom screen of Figure 3-57.

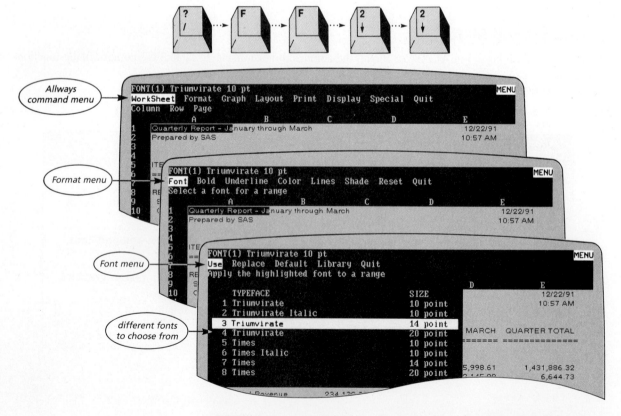

FIGURE 3-57 Step 1 of changing the font — press the Slash key (/), type the letter F for Format, type the letter F for Font, and use the Down Arrow key to select Triumvirate 14 point.

To assign the highlighted Triumvirate 14-point font to the worksheet title in A1, press the Enter key. Allways responds by prompting you to enter the range of cells to which the new font will be assigned. This procedure is shown in the top screen of Figure 3-58. Since we want to assign the font only to A1, press the Enter key. The contents of cell A1 display using the Triumvirate 14-point font as shown in the bottom screen of Figure 3-58.

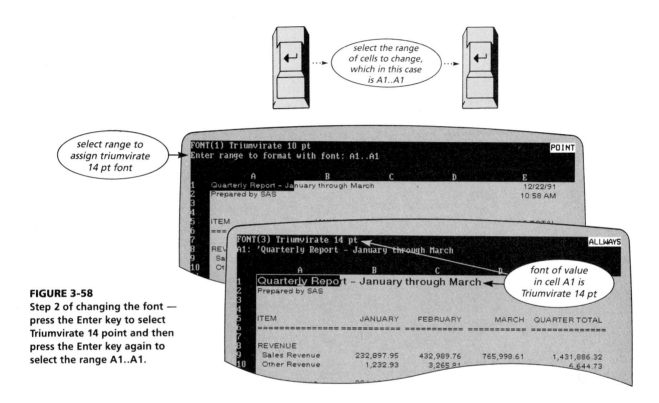

FIGURE 3-58
**Step 2 of changing the font —
press the Enter key to select
Triumvirate 14 point and then
press the Enter key again to
select the range A1..A1.**

Our next step is to change the font in cell A5 to Times 14 point. Move the cell pointer to A5 and enter the command /Format Font (/FF). Use the arrow keys to select Times 14 point from the font menu (bottom screen of Figure 3-57) and press the Enter key. When Allways displays the prompt message "Enter range to format with font: A5..A5", press the Enter key. The characters in cell A5 display in Times 14-point font as shown in Figure 3-59.

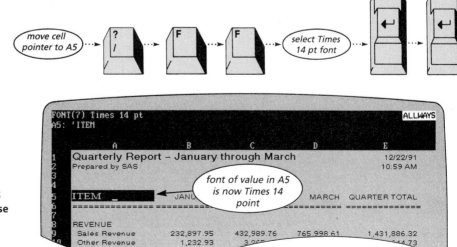

FIGURE 3-59
**Triumvirate 10 point in cell A5
changed to Times 14 point. Use
the command /Format Font
(/FF).**

Move the cell pointer to cell A8 to change the font in the range A8..A31 to Times 14 point. Enter the command /Format Font (/FF). The font menu in the bottom screen of Figure 3-57 displays. Select Times 14 point and press the Enter key. When the prompt message "Enter range to format with font: A8..A8" displays on the second line, use the Down Arrow key to expand the range to A8..A31. Press the Enter key. Allways assigns Times 14-point font to the range A8..A31 as shown in Figure 3-60.

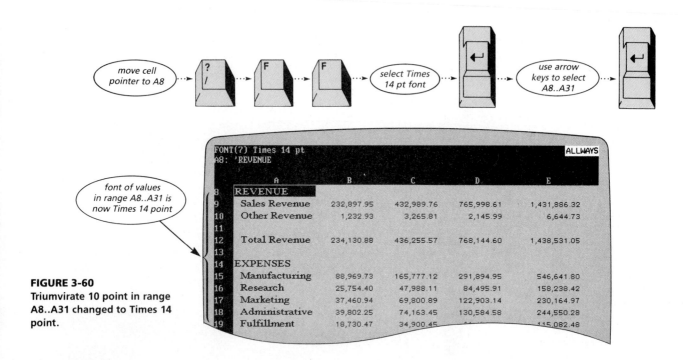

FIGURE 3-60
Triumvirate 10 point in range A8..A31 changed to Times 14 point.

In Figure 3-53, the title Budget % Values shown in cell A25 is printed using Triumvirate 20-point font. Therefore, use the GOTO command to move the cell pointer from A8 to A25. Here again, enter the command /Format Font (/FF). When the Font menu shown in the bottom screen of Figure 3-57 displays, select Triumvirate 20-point font. Press the Enter key. Respond to the prompt message asking for the range by pressing the Enter key, as we want to assign the new font only to cell A25. The screen shown in Figure 3-61 displays.

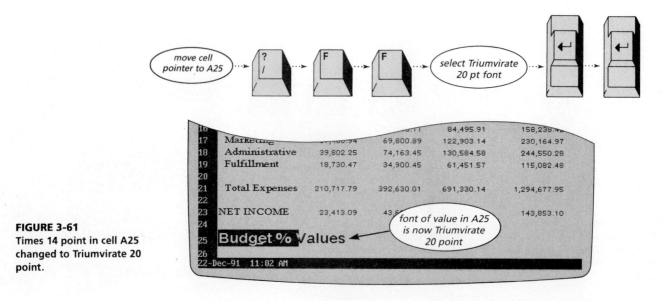

FIGURE 3-61
Times 14 point in cell A25 changed to Triumvirate 20 point.

Shading Cells

In the top left corner of the formatted report in Figure 3-53, the label "Prepared by SAS" is shaded. This label is located in cell A2. To move the cell pointer from A25 to A2, press Home and then press the Down Arrow key. Next, enter the command /Format Shade (/FS). As shown in the top screen of Figure 3-62, the Shade menu has four options: Light, Dark, Solid, and Clear. Type the L key for Light. Allways displays the prompt message "Enter range to shade: A2..A2". Since we want to shade only A2, press the Enter key. Allways shades A2 as shown in the bottom screen of Figure 3-62.

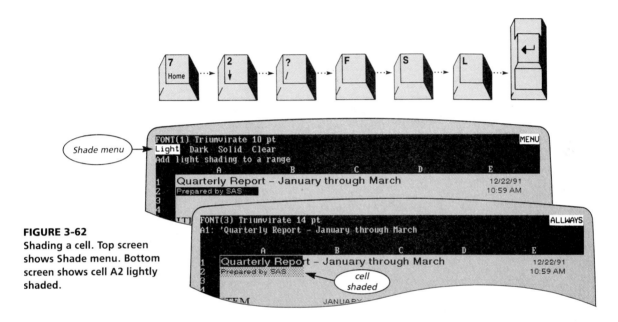

FIGURE 3-62
Shading a cell. Top screen shows Shade menu. Bottom screen shows cell A2 lightly shaded.

An alternative to using the command /Format Shade (/FS) to shade an individual cell is to position the cell pointer on the cell and press Alt-S. Each time you press this combination of keys, the shade changes from clear to light to dark to solid and back to clear. To use the Alt and S keys to shade a range of cells, first press the Period key (.) to anchor the cell pointer and use the arrow keys to highlight the range. With the range highlighted, enter Alt-S. To complete the command, press one of the arrow keys to move the highlight off the selected range.

Boldfacing Cells

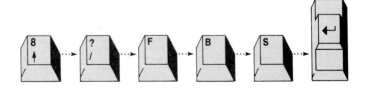

The worksheet in Figure 3-53 calls for boldfacing a number of cells. Let's start by boldfacing the worksheet title in A1. Use the Up Arrow key to move the cell pointer to A1. Enter the command /Format Bold Set (/FBS). Allways displays the prompt message "Enter range to bold: A1..A1". Press the Enter key. The worksheet title in cell A1 changes to bold as shown in Figure 3-63.

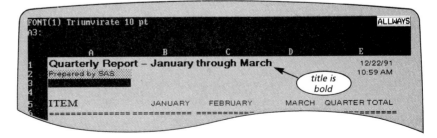

FIGURE 3-63 Boldfacing the title of the worksheet in A1 by using the command /Format Bold Set (/FBS).

You can also bold an individual cell by positioning the cell pointer on the cell and pressing Alt-B. If you press this combination of keys again, Allways clears the boldface from the cell. Hence, Alt-B turns bold on or off in the current cell. Alt-B can also be used to bold a range of cells. Before pressing the combination of keys, press the Period key to select the range. Once the range is highlighted, press Alt-B. To complete the command, press one of the arrow keys to move the highlight off the selected range.

Use Alt-B to complete the boldfacing in this project as follows:

1. Move the cell pointer to A5. Press the Period key. Use the Right Arrow key to highlight the range A5..E5. Press Alt-B.
2. Move the cell pointer to A8. Press Alt-B.
3. Move the cell pointer to A12. Press the Period key. Use the Right Arrow key to highlight the range A12..E12. Press Alt-B. Press the Down Arrow key one time.
4. Move the cell pointer to A14. Press Alt-B.
5. Move the cell pointer to A21. Press the Period key. Use the Right Arrow key to highlight the range A21..E21. Press Alt-B. Press the Down Arrow key one time.
6. Move the cell pointer to A23. Press the Period key. Use the Right Arrow key to highlight the range A23..E23. Press Alt-B. Press the Down Arrow key one time.

After completing step 6, the range A9..E23 displays as shown in Figure 3-64.

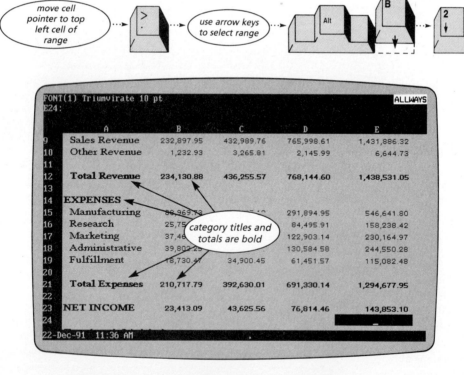

FIGURE 3-64 Boldfacing a range of cells. Use the Period key (.) to select the range, and then press Alt-B.

Underlining Cells

As shown in Figure 3-53, the rows designated Other Revenue (cells B10..E10) and Fulfillment (cells B19..E19), and the empty cells A22..E22, are double underlined. Let's double underline the range B10..E10 first.

Use the GOTO command to move the cell pointer to B10. Enter the command /Format Underline (/FU). As shown in the top screen of Figure 3-65, the Underline menu has three options: Single, Double, and Clear. Type the letter D for Double. Allways displays the prompt message "Enter range to double underline: B10..B10". Use the Right Arrow key to highlight the range B10..E10. Press the Enter key. The range B10..E10 is double underlined as shown in the bottom screen of Figure 3-65.

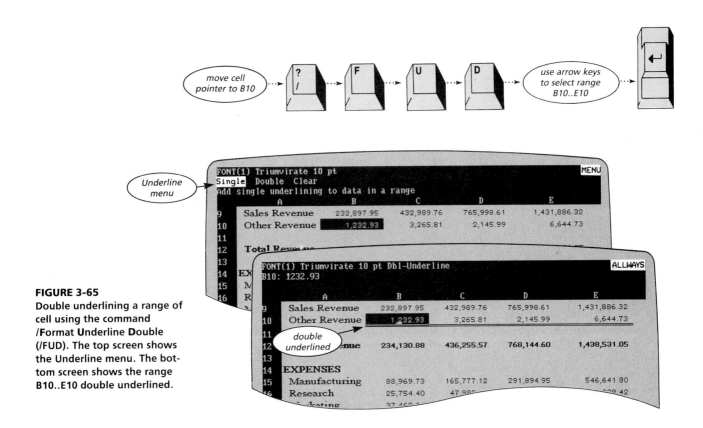

FIGURE 3-65
Double underlining a range of cell using the command /Format Underline Double (/FUD). The top screen shows the Underline menu. The bottom screen shows the range B10..E10 double underlined.

You can also use the Alt-U to underline an individual cell or range of cells. Each time you press Alt-U, the underlining changes from single to double to clear (no underline). To use Alt-U to underline a range of cells, first press the Period key to anchor the cell pointer; then use the arrow keys to highlight the range you want to underline. With the range highlighted, press Alt-U. To complete the command, press any one of the arrow keys to move the highlight off the selected range.

Use Alt-U to complete the required double underlining as described in Figure 3-53. Issue the GOTO command to move the cell pointer to B19. Press the Period key to activate range selection. Use the Right Arrow key to highlight the range B19..E19. Press Alt-U twice. Press the Down Arrow key to move the highlight off the range B19..E19.

Next, issue the GOTO command to move the cell pointer to A22. Press the Period key. Use the Right Arrow key to highlight the range A22..E22. Press Alt-U twice. Press the Down Arrow key. The worksheet displays as shown in Figure 3-66 on the next page.

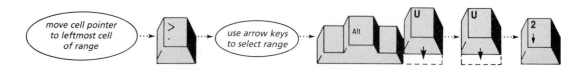

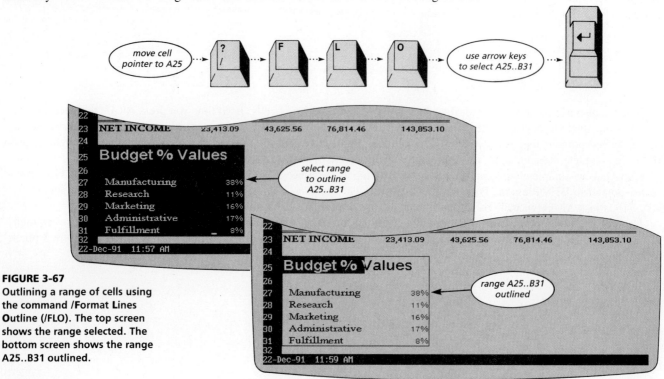

FIGURE 3-66
Double underlining a range of
cells. Use the Period key (.) to
select the range and then press
Alt-U twice.

Outlining a Range of Cells

To outline the title Budget % Values at the bottom of the worksheet (Figure 3-53), use the GOTO command to move the cell pointer to A25. Enter the command /Format Lines Outline (/FLO). When Allways displays the prompt message "Enter range to outline: A25..A25", use the arrow keys to select the range A25..B31 as shown in the top screen of Figure 3-67. Press the Enter key. A box outlines the range A25..B31 as shown in the bottom screen of Figure 3-67.

FIGURE 3-67
Outlining a range of cells using
the command /Format Lines
Outline (/FLO). The top screen
shows the range selected. The
bottom screen shows the range
A25..B31 outlined.

Note that you can also outline a range of cells by first selecting the range using the Period key and then pressing Alt-L.

In addition to outlining a range of cells, the /Format Lines (/FL) command can be used to draw vertical lines along the right or left edge of a range of cells or to draw horizontal lines along the top or bottom of a range of cells. You can also use /FL to draw a grid over a range of cells. For more information on drawing lines, enter /Format Lines (/FL), and press F1 to use the Allways online help facility.

Summary of Shortcut Keys for Invoking Commands

Shortcut keys allow you to execute a command sequence by holding down the Alt key and pressing a typewriter key. Table 3-7 summarizes the shortcut keys that invoke Allways commands. Use this table to speed the entry of your commands.

TABLE 3-7   Shortcut Keys for Invoking Allways Commands

KEYS	DESCRIPTION
Alt-B	Boldface (Set/Clear)
Alt-G	Grid lines (On/Off)
Alt-L	Lines (Outline/All/None)
Alt-S	Shade (Light/Dark/Solid/None)
Alt-U	Underline (Single/Double/None)
Alt-1	Set font 1
Alt-2	Set font 2
Alt-3	Set font 3
Alt-4	Set font 4
Alt-5	Set font 5
Alt-6	Set font 6
Alt-7	Set font 7
Alt-8	Set font 8

Changing the Widths of Columns and Heights of Rows Using Allways

When you use Allways to increase the point size in a range of cells, some characters may be truncated (chopped off) in those cells. You can overcome this problem by instructing Allways to increase the column width of the range of cells. Changing the column width in Allways does not affect the column width in 1-2-3.

Sometimes a value just fits into the cell, such as Total Expenses in cell A21 (Figure 3-68). In such cases, chances are that when the worksheet is sent to the printer, the last character will be partially or completely truncated. Therefore, we need to increase the width of column A from 17 characters to 18 characters.

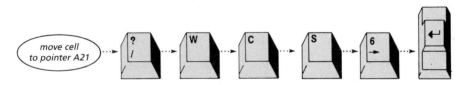

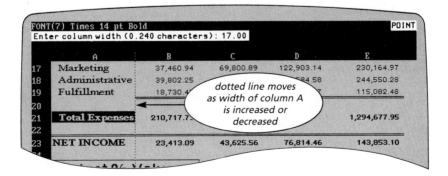

FIGURE 3-68 Increasing the width of column A. Use the command /Worksheet Column Set-Width (/WCS). Use the Right on Left Arrow keys to increase or decrease the column width.

To change the width of column A, move the cell pointer to A21. (Actually, the cell pointer can be in any cell in column A.) Enter the command /Worksheet Column Set-Width (/WCS). The screen shown in Figure 3-68 appears. Note the prompt message at the top of the screen and the vertical dotted line along the right edge of column A. Press the Right Arrow key to increase the width by 1, and the vertical line on the screen moves to the right to show the new column width. With the column width at 18.00, press the Enter key. Column A is now 18 characters wide. Press the Home key to move the cursor to A1. The completed worksheet is shown in Figure 3-69.

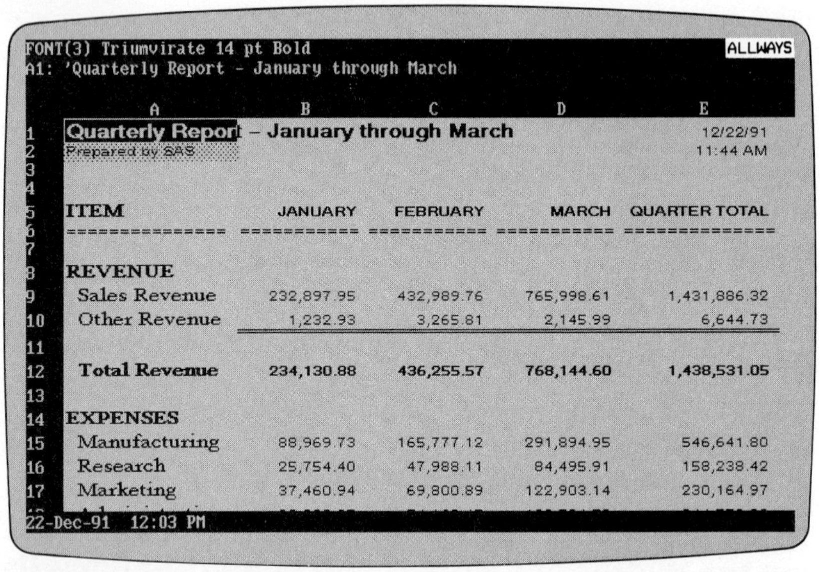

FIGURE 3-69
Format modifications to Project 3 completed.

Note one last point regarding the column width. As the prompt message indicates in Figure 3-68, Allways allows you to enter a column width to the nearest hundredths (two decimal places). You can type in the width you desire or you can increase or decrease the width by 1/10 of a character by holding down the Ctrl key and pressing the Right or Left Arrow keys. Pressing the Right or Left Arrow keys by themselves increases or decreases the column width by 1 character.

Allways automatically adjusts the height of a row on the basis of the greatest point size assigned to the cells in the row. You can manually adjust the height of a row by moving the cell pointer into the row and entering the /Worksheet Row Set-Height (/WRS) command. You can also adjust the height of several adjacent rows by using the Period key to select the rows prior to issuing the /WRS command.

Printing the Worksheet

To print the worksheet using Allways, enter the command /Print (/P). This command activates the command cursor in the Print menu (Figure 3-70). Type the letters R for Range and S for Set. Use the arrow keys to move the cell pointer to E31. Press the Enter key to anchor the second end point. The Print menu shown in Figure 3-70 reappears.

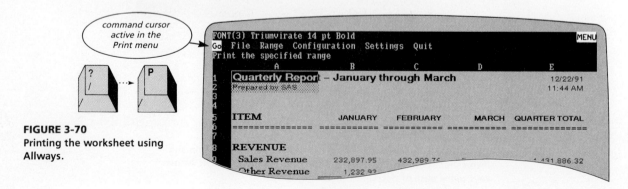

command cursor active in the Print menu

FIGURE 3-70
Printing the worksheet using Allways.

Check to be sure the printer is ready. Type the letter G for Go. The worksheet prints on the printer as shown earlier in Figure 3-53. Move the paper through the printer so that you can tear the paper at the perforated edge below the printed version of the worksheet.

If the worksheet fails to print when you type the letter G for Go and you get an "Out of Memory" message on the indicator line at the bottom of the screen, return control to 1-2-3 and save the worksheet. After the worksheet is saved, return control to Allways and issue the print command again.

Note one last point regarding the Print command. Once you establish a print range, Allways displays a dotted outline that defines the range whenever you switch from 1-2-3 to Allways.

Saving the Worksheet with Allways Format Changes

To preserve the format changes we have made to Project 3 using Allways, we need to save the worksheet to disk. To do this, return control to 1-2-3, and enter the command /File Save Replace (/FSR). 1-2-3 saves the worksheet as PROJS-3.WK1 and the corresponding Allways format changes as PROJS-3.ALL.

The Display Command

The /Display (/D) command in Allways allows you to control how the worksheet displays on the screen. Table 3-8 summarizes the functions of the commands in the Display menu.

TABLE 3-8   A Summary of Commands in the Allways Display Menu

COMMAND	FUNCTION
Colors	Sets color for background, foreground, and cell pointer.
Graphs	Turns the display of integrated graphs on or off. (Press F10 to issue this command.)
Mode	Switches display between text and graphics.
Quit	Quits Display menu and returns to ALLWAYS mode.
Zoom	Reduces or enlarges the display of the worksheet. (Use Alt-F4 to enlarge the worksheet. Press Alt-F4 repeatedly to enlarge the worksheet up to 140% of its normal size. Use F4 to reduce the size of the worksheet down to 60% of its normal size.)

The two screens in Figure 3-71 show Project 3 reduced to 60% and enlarged to 140%.

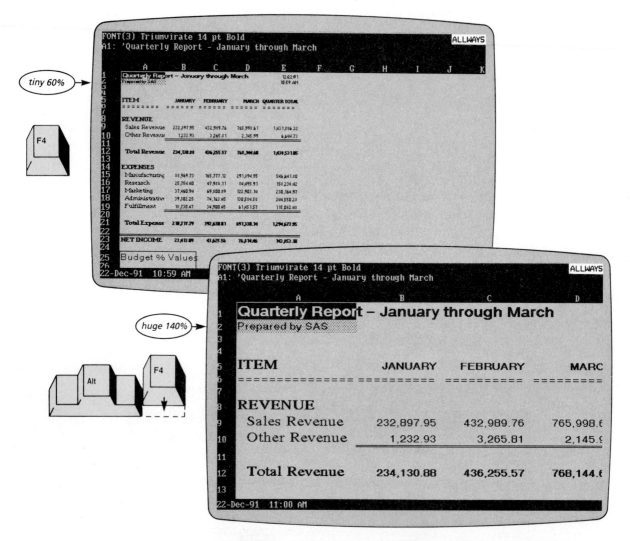

FIGURE 3-71 Minimizing and maximizing the display of the worksheet.
Use the command **/Display Zoom (/DZ)** or use **Alt-F4** to enlarge the display
and **F4** to reduce it.

PROJECT SUMMARY

*I*n this project you learned a variety of ways to enhance a worksheet and simplify the steps of building, formatting, and printing large worksheets. You were introduced to the capabilities of 1-2-3 to answer what-if questions. Finally, you learned how to change the default settings, interact with DOS through 1-2-3, and produce presentation-quality printouts through Allways.

Each of the steps required to build the worksheet in Project 3 is listed in the following tables.

SUMMARY OF KEYSTROKES—Project 3

STEPS	KEY(S) PRESSED	STEPS	KEY(S) PRESSED
1	/WGC → → → → ←	30	/RFP0 ← ↑ ↑ ↑ ↑ ←
2	/WCS17 ←	31	(Home) (F5) B7 ←
3	→ → → → /WCS16 ←	32	/WTB
4	/WGF, ←	33	232897.95 → 432989.76 → 765998.61 →
5	← ← ← ← Quarterly Report – January through March ↓	34	@SUM(B7.D7) →
6	Prepared by SAS ←	35	/M (Backspace) ← . ← ← ← ← ↓ ↓ ← . ← ← ← ←
7	(F5) E1 ← @now ↓	36	↓ ↓ ↓ ← ← ← ←
8	@now ↑	37	1232.93 → 3265.81 → 2145.99 ↓ ↓ ← ←
9	/RFD → → → ← ←	38	@SUM(B9.B10) ←
10	↓ /RFDT → ← ←	39	/C ← → . → ←
11	(F5) A5 ← (Caps Lock)	40	/RFTB9.E19 ←
12	ITEM → "JANUARY →	41	↓ ↓ ↓ $B27*B$12 ←
13	"FEBRUARY → "MARCH →	42	/C ← . ↓ ↓ ↓ ↓ → → ←
14	"QUARTER TOTAL ←	43	(F5) B19 ← /RF, ← B19.E9 ←
15	(F5) A6 ← \ = ←	44	↓ ↓ @SUM(↑ ↑ ↑ ↑ ↑ ↑ . ↓ ↓ ↓ ↓) ←
16	/C ← → . → → → ←	45	/C ← → . → ←
17	↓ ↓ REVENUE ↓ (Caps Lock)	46	↓ ↓ + B12–B21 ←
18	' Sales Revenue ↓ ' Other Revenue ↓ ↓	47	/C ← → . → ←
19	' Total Revenue ↓ ↓	48	(F5) E9 ←
20	EXPENSES ↓ ' Manufacturing ↓	49	/C ← E9.E23 ←
21	' Research ↓ ' Fulfillment ↓ ↓	50	↓ ↓ /RE ←
22	' Total Expenses ↓ ↓ NET INCOME ↓ ↓	51	↓ ↓ /RE ↓ ←
23	Budget % Values ↓	52	↓ ↓ ↓ ↓ ↓ ↓ /RE ←
24	(F5) A17 ←	53	↓ ↓ /RE ←
25	/WIR ↓ ←	54	/WTC (Home)
26	' Marketing ↓ ' Administrative ↓	55	/FSPROJS-3 ←
27	/CA15.A19 ← A27 ←	56	/PPRA1.E31 ←
28	(F5) B27 ←	57	AGPPQ
29	38% ↓ 11% ↓ 16% ↓ 17% ↓ 8% ←		

SUMMARY OF KEYSTROKES — Project 3   Using Allways

STEPS	KEY(S) PRESSED
1	/AIALLWAYS ←
2	/FF↓↓ ← ←
3	[F5] A5 ←/FF↓↓↓↓↓↓ ← ←
4	↓↓↓/FF↓↓↓↓↓↓↓ ←A8.A31←
5	[F5] A25 ←/FF↑↑↑ ← ←
6	[Home] ↓/FSL ←
7	↑/FBS ←
8	[F5] A5 ←.→ → → → [Alt-B] ↓
9	[F5] A8 ← [Alt-B]
10	[F5] A12 ←.→ → → → [Alt-B] ↓
11	[F5] A14 ← [Alt-B]
12	[F5] A21 ←.→ → → → [Alt-B] ↓
13	[F5] A23 ←.→ → → → [Alt-B] ↓
14	[F5] B10 ←/FUD → → → ←
15	[F5] B19 ←.→ → → [Alt-U] [Alt-U] ↓
16	[F5] A22 ←.→ → → → [Alt-U] [Alt-U] ↓
17	[F5] A25 ←/FLO → ↓↓↓↓↓↓ ←
18	[F5] A21 ←/WCS → ← [Home]
19	/PRSA1.E31←G
20	/Q
21	/FSR

The following list summarizes the material covered in Project 3.

1. After setting the column width for the entire worksheet, use the command /**W**orksheet **C**olumn **S**et-Width (/WCS) to set the width of individual columns requiring a different width.
2. Use the command /**W**orksheet **G**lobal **F**ormat (/WGF) to format all the cells in the worksheet to the same type.
3. To display the date and time as a decimal number, use the NOW function. The whole number portion is the number of complete days since December 31, 1899. The decimal portion represents today's time.
4. Use the command /**R**ange **F**ormat **D**ate (/RFD) to format today's date and time. Use Table 3-1 for a summary of the date and time formats.
5. The time stored in a cell is updated only after you make an entry into the worksheet or after you press function key F9.
6. To insert rows or columns into a worksheet, move the cell pointer to the point of insertion and enter the command /**W**orksheet **I**nsert (/WI). Type the letter R to insert rows or the letter C to insert columns. Use the arrow keys to select how many rows or columns you want to insert.
7. To delete rows or columns from a worksheet, move the cell pointer to one of the end points of the range you plan to delete. Enter the command /**W**orksheet **D**elete (/WD). Type the letter R to delete rows or the letter C to delete columns. Use the arrow keys to select how many rows or columns you want to delete.

8. Enter a percentage value in percent form by appending a percent sign (%) to the right of the number.
9. To freeze the titles so that they remain on the screen as you move the cell pointer around the worksheet, use the command /Worksheet Titles (/WT). You then have the choice of freezing vertical (row) titles, horizontal (column) titles, or both. Use the same command to unfreeze the titles.
10. To move a range to another range, use the command /**M**ove (/M).
11. With respect to the Copy command, a cell address with no dollar sign ($) is a **relative address**. A cell address with a dollar sign appended to the front of both the column name and row number is an **absolute address**. A cell address with a dollar sign added to the front of the column name or to the front of the row number is a **mixed cell address**.
12. When entering a formula or function, you may use the arrow keys to point to the range.
13. It is valid to copy a cell to itself. This is necessary when you copy the end point of the destination range.
14. An empty cell or a cell with a label has a numeric value of zero.
15. Use the command /**P**rint **P**rinter **O**ption (/PPO) to change the printer default settings.
16. The ability to answer what-if questions is a powerful and important feature of 1-2-3.
17. Once a worksheet is complete, you can enter new values into cells. Formulas and functions that reference the modified cells are immediately recalculated, thus giving new results.
18. Use the command /**W**orksheet **G**lobal **R**ecalculation (/WGR) to change from automatic to manual recalculation.
19. To change the default settings for the worksheet, use the command /**W**orksheet **G**lobal **D**efault (/WGD).
20. Default settings changed with the command /WGD remain in force for the entire session, until you quit 1-2-3.
21. To permanently change the default settings, type the letter U for Update before quitting the Global Default menu.
22. The File command may be used to list the names of the files on disk, delete files, and change the current directory.
23. The System command allows you to temporarily place 1-2-3 in a wait state and return control to DOS. Once control returns to DOS, you may execute DOS commands. To return to 1-2-3, enter the command Exit.
24. Allways is a spreadsheet publishing add-in program that comes with Release 2.2 of 1-2-3. **Add-in** means the program is started while 1-2-3 is running.
25. There are two ways to invoke Allways: (1) enter the command /**A**dd-**I**n Invoke (/AI) and select Allways; or (2) hold down the Alt key and press F7. The latter method is available only if the F7 key was assigned the Allways program when it was initially attached to 1-2-3.
26. The **font** is a typeface of a particular size.
27. To preserve the format changes made with Allways, return control to 1-2-3 and save the worksheet to disk.
28. To change the font of a cell or range of cells, enter the command /**F**ormat **F**ont (/FF).
29. Shade a cell or range of cells by entering the command /**F**ormat **S**hade (/FS). The Shade menu has four options: Light, Dark, Solid, and Clear.
30. Bold a cell or range of cells by entering the command /**F**ormat **B**old **S**et (/FBS).
31. To underline a cell or range of cells, enter the command /**F**ormat **U**nderline (/FU). The Underline menu has three options: Single, Double, and Clear.
32. To outline a range of cells, enter the command /**F**ormat **L**ines **O**utline (/FLO).
33. **Shortcut keys** allow you to execute an Allways command sequence by holding down the Alt key and pressing a typewriter key. Some of the more important shortcut keys are: Alt-B for bold; Alt-S for shade; Alt-U for underline; and Alt-L for lines.
34. To use the shortcut keys on a range of cells, use the Period key to select the range and then press the shortcut key. To conclude the command, use one of the arrow keys to move the highlight off the range.
35. To change the column width in Allways, enter the command /**W**orksheet **C**olumn **S**et-Width (/WCS).
36. To change the height of rows, enter the /**W**orksheet **R**ow **S**et-Height (/WRS) command.
37. To print the worksheet using Allways, enter the command /**P**rint (/P). Select the range and then press G for Go.
38. The /**D**isplay (/D) command in Allways allows you to control how the worksheet displays on the screen.

STUDENT ASSIGNMENTS

STUDENT ASSIGNMENT 1: True/False

Instructions: Circle T if the statement is true or F if the statement is false.

T F 1. The /**W**orksheet **G**lobal **F**ormat (/WGF) command requires that you enter a range in the worksheet to be affected.

T F 2. Use the NOW function to display the date and time as a decimal number.

T F 3. The time displayed in a cell is automatically updated every minute.

T F 4. You can format the cell assigned the NOW function to display today's name (i.e., Sunday, Monday, etc.).

T F 5. When you insert rows in a worksheet, 1-2-3 *pushes up* the rows above the point of insertion to open up the worksheet.

T F 6. A percentage value, like 5.3%, can be entered exactly as 5.3% on the input line.

T F 7. The range B10..B15 is the same as B15..B10.

T F 8. When using the /**W**orksheet **T**itles (/WT) command, the title and column headings are called vertical titles.

T F 9. Use the command /**W**orksheet **T**itles **R**eset (/WTR) to unfreeze the titles.

T F 10. Use the /**M**ove (/M) command to move the contents of a cell or range of cells to a different location in the worksheet.

T F 11. When numbers are displayed using the Text format, they display left-justified in the cells.

T F 12. D23 is a relative address and $D$23 is an absolute address.

T F 13. You cannot use the arrow keys to select the range for the SUM function.

T F 14. If a cell within the range summed by the SUM function contains a label, 1-2-3 displays an error message.

T F 15. When you start Allways, the default font is designated font 1 in the Font menu.

T F 16. Press Alt-B to bold the current cell.

T F 17. ALLWAYS mode in Allways is similar to READY mode in 1-2-3.

T F 18. To double underline a cell in Allways, move the cell pointer to the cell you want to double underline, and press Alt-D.

T F 19. The format changes made with Allways are preserved as part of the .WK1 file when the worksheet is saved.

T F 20. The /**D**isplay (/D) command allows you to reduce the display of the worksheet to a maximum of 25% of its normal display.

STUDENT ASSIGNMENT 2: Multiple Choice

Instructions: Circle the correct response.

1. Which one of the following functions is used to display the time?
   a. TODAY   b. TIME   c. NOW   d. CLOCK
2. Which one of the following commands is used to delete rows or columns from a worksheet?
   a. /**W**orksheet **D**elete (/WD)   c. /**W**orksheet **L**abel (/WL)
   b. /**W**orksheet **E**rase (/WE)   d. /**W**orksheet **U**nprotect (/WU)
3. Which one of the following is an absolute address?
   a. G45   b. !G!45   c. $B$45   d. #G#45
4. If cell B14 is assigned the label TEN, then the function @SUM(B10.B14) in cell C25 considers B14 to be equal to _____ .
   a. 10   b. 0   c. an undefined value   d. 3
5. The command /**P**rint **P**rinter **O**ptions (/PPO) may be used to change _____ .
   a. the margins   c. from normal mode to condensed mode
   b. the page-length   d. all of these
6. The /**F**ile (/F) command can be used to _____ .
   a. format disks   c. erase worksheets from disk
   b. change the current directory   d. both b and c

7. The command /Worksheet Global Default (/WGD) can be used to _____ .
   a. delete files
   b. select a format for the worksheet
   c. return control to DOS
   d. display default settings
8. The command /Move (/M) results in the same change to the worksheet as _____ .
   a. /Worksheet Erase (/WE)
   b. /Copy (/C)
   c. /Worksheet Insert (/WI)
   d. none of these
9. Which of the following are the initial commands in the command sequence to instruct Allways to outline a range of cells?
   a. /Format Underline (/FU)
   b. /Format Lines (/FL)
   c. /Format Display (/FD)
   d. /Format Font (/FF)
   e. /Format Shade (/FS)
10. Which one of the following keys is used with Allways to select a range of cells before a shortcut key command is entered?
    a. Slash (/)
    b. Comma (,)
    c. Period (.)
    d. Circumflex (˜)
    e. Number sign (#)

STUDENT ASSIGNMENT 3: Understanding Absolute, Mixed, and Relative Addressing

Instructions: Fill in the correct answers.

1. Write cell B1 as a relative address, absolute address, mixed address with the row varying, and mixed address with the column varying.

Relative address: _____   Mixed, row varying: _____

Absolute address: _____   Mixed, column varying: _____

2. In Figure 3-72, write the formula for cell B8 that multiplies cell B1 times the sum of cells B4, B5, and B6. Write the formula so that when it is copied to cells C8 and D8, cell B1 remains absolute. Verify your formula by checking it with the values found in cells B8, C8, and D8 in Figure 3-72.

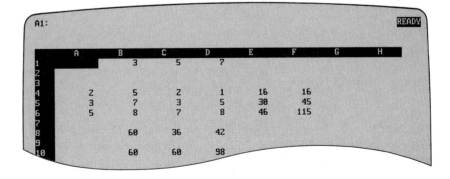

FIGURE 3-72
Student Assignment 3

Formula for cell B8: _____

3. In Figure 3-72, write the formula for cell E4 that multiplies cell A4 times the sum of cells B4, C4, and D4. Write the formula so that when it is copied to cells E5 and E6, cell A4 remains absolute. Verify your formula by checking it with the values found in cells E4, E5, and E6 in Figure 3-72.

Formula for cell E4: _____

Student Assignment 3 (continued)

4. In Figure 3-72, write the formula for cell B10 that multiplies cell B1 times the sum of cells B4, B5, and B6. Write the formula so that when it is copied to cells C10 and D10, 1-2-3 adjusts all the cell addresses according to the new location. Verify your formula by checking it with the values found in cells B10, C10, and D10 in Figure 3-72.

Formula for cell B10: _____

5. In Figure 3-72, write the formula for cell F4 that multiplies cell A4 times the sum of cells B4, C4, and D4. Write the formula so that when it is copied to cells F5 and F6, 1-2-3 adjusts all the cell addresses according to the new location. Verify your formula by checking it with the values found in cells F4, F5, and F6 in Figure 3-72.

Formula for cell F4: _____

STUDENT ASSIGNMENT 4: Writing 1-2-3 Commands

Instructions: Write the 1-2-3 command to accomplish the task in each of the problems below. Write the command up to the point where you enter the range or type the letter Q to quit the command.

1. Delete columns A, B, and C. Assume the cell pointer is at A1.

   Command: _____

2. Insert three rows between rows 5 and 6. Assume the cell pointer is at A6.

   Command: _____

3. Move the range of cells A12..C15 to F14..H17. Assume the cell pointer is at A12.

   Command: _____

4. Freeze the vertical and horizontal titles. Assume that the cell pointer is immediately below and to the right of the titles.

   Command: _____

5. Return control to DOS temporarily.

   Command: _____

6. List the worksheet names on the default drive.

   Command: _____

7. Set columns A and B as borders. Assume the cell pointer is at B1.

   Command: _____

8. Change the left print margin to 1 and the right print margin to 79 for the current worksheet only.

   Command: _____

9. Change to print in condensed mode with a right margin of 132.

   Command: _____

10. Change 1-2-3 from automatic to manual recalculation.

    Command: _____

11. Switch control to the add-in program Allways.

    Command: _____

12. List the shortcut key commands to minimize and maximize the display of a worksheet using Allways.

    Command: Minimize _____   Maximize _____

13. List the Allways command sequence for assigning bold to the range A10..E25 using the shortcut key.

    Command: _____

STUDENT ASSIGNMENT 5: Correcting the Range in a Worksheet

Instructions: The worksheet illustrated in Figure 3-73 contains errors in cells E9 through E21. Analyze the entries displayed on the worksheet, especially the formula assigned to E9 and displayed at the top of the screen. Explain the cause of the errors and the method of correction in the space provided below.

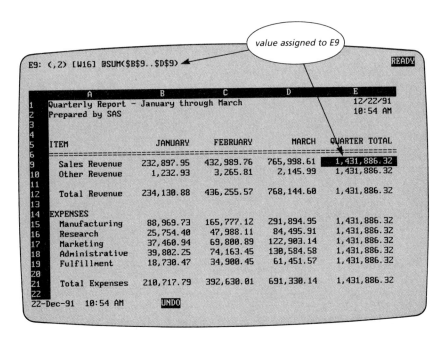

FIGURE 3-73 Student Assignment 5

Cause of errors: _____

_____

Method of correction for cell E9: _____

_____

Method of correction for cells E10 through E21: _____

_____

_____

STUDENT ASSIGNMENT 6: Correcting Errors in a Worksheet

Instructions: The worksheet illustrated in Figure 3-74 contains errors in the range B15..E23. This worksheet contains the same formulas as the worksheet in Project 3. Analyze the entries displayed on the worksheet. Explain the cause of the errors and the method of correction in the space provided below. (Hint: Check the cells that are referenced in the range B15..E23.)

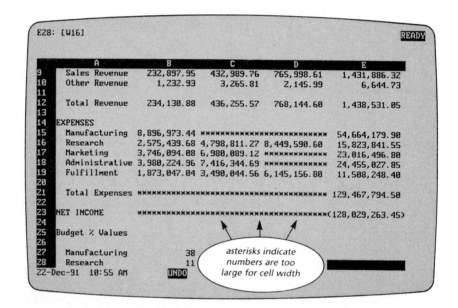

FIGURE 3-74
Student Assignment 6

Cause of errors: _____

_____

Method of correction: _____

_____

STUDENT ASSIGNMENT 7: Building a Projected Price Increase Worksheet

Instructions: Load 1-2-3 and perform the following tasks.

1. Build the worksheet illustrated in Figure 3-75. Increase the width of columns B through E to 13 characters. Enter the title, column headings, model numbers in column A, and corresponding current prices in column B. The entries in the columns labeled 10% INCREASE, 15% INCREASE, and 20% INCREASE are determined from formulas. Multiply one plus the percent specified in the column heading by the current price. For example, assign C8 the formula 1.10*B8. To determine the total current price in cell B18, enter a formula that adds the products of the on-hand column and the corresponding current price. Copy this total formula in cell B18 to cells C18 through E18 to determine the totals in the remaining columns.

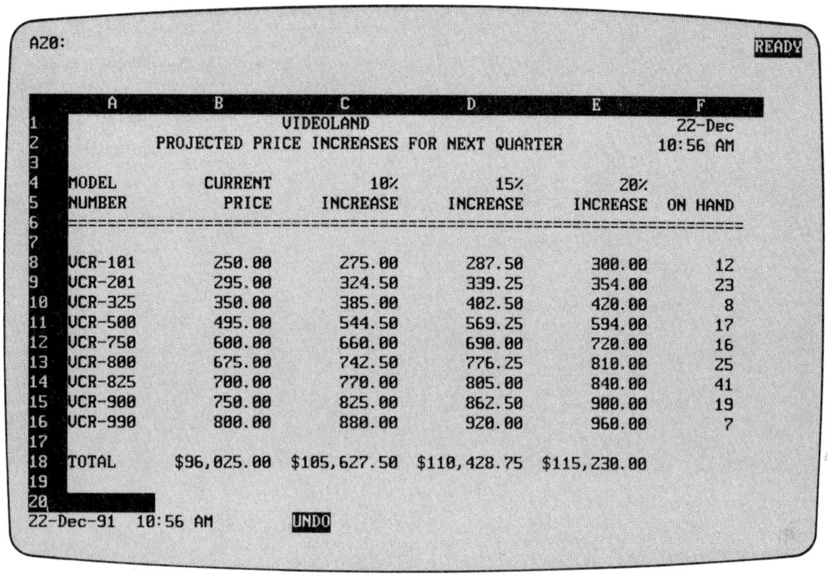

```
A20:                                                          READY

       A         B          C          D          E          F
1                        VIDEOLAND                        22-Dec
2          PROJECTED PRICE INCREASES FOR NEXT QUARTER     10:56 AM
3
4  MODEL      CURRENT       10%        15%        20%
5  NUMBER      PRICE      INCREASE   INCREASE   INCREASE   ON HAND
6  ======================================================================
7
8  VCR-101     250.00     275.00     287.50     300.00        12
9  VCR-201     295.00     324.50     339.25     354.00        23
10 VCR-325     350.00     385.00     402.50     420.00         8
11 VCR-500     495.00     544.50     569.25     594.00        17
12 VCR-750     600.00     660.00     690.00     720.00        16
13 VCR-800     675.00     742.50     776.25     810.00        25
14 VCR-825     700.00     770.00     805.00     840.00        41
15 VCR-900     750.00     825.00     862.50     900.00        19
16 VCR-990     800.00     880.00     920.00     960.00         7
17
18 TOTAL     $96,025.00 $105,627.50 $110,428.75 $115,230.00
19
20
22-Dec-91   10:56 AM          UNDO
```

FIGURE 3-75
Student Assignment 7

2. Save the worksheet as STUS3-7.
3. Print the worksheet in the condensed mode. Reset 1-2-3 back to the normal print mode.
4. Print the cell-formulas version of the worksheet.
5. Print only the first 18 rows of the model number and current price columns.
6. Print the worksheet after formatting all the cells to the Text type.

STUDENT ASSIGNMENT 8: Building a Payroll Analysis Worksheet

Instructions: Load 1-2-3 and perform the following tasks.

1. Build the worksheet illustrated in Figure 3-76. Change the global width to 13 characters. Change the width of column A to 19 characters. Enter the title, column headings, row titles, employee names in column A, and corresponding current hourly pay rate in column B. Use the NOW function to display the date and time in cells E18 and E19. Finally, enter the proposed percent increase in cell B15 and hours per week in cell B16.

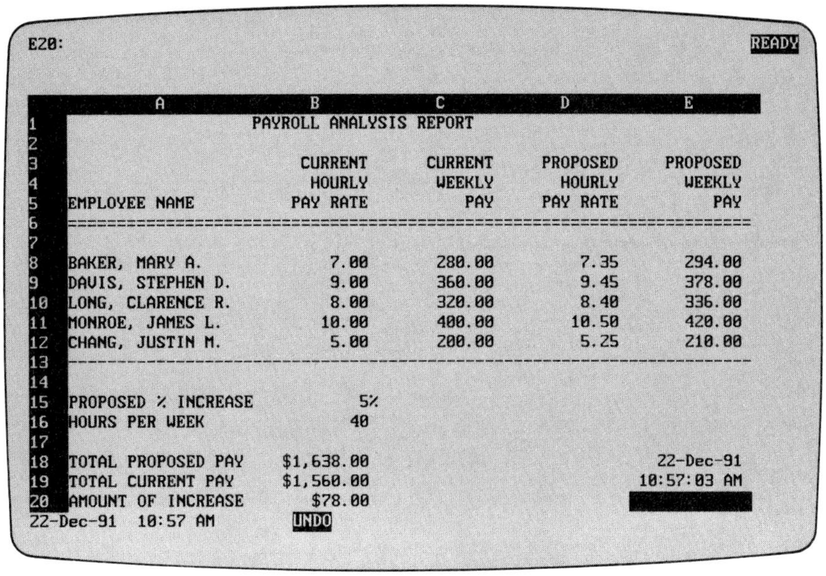

```
E20:                                                          READY

          A              B          C          D          E
1                  PAYROLL ANALYSIS REPORT
2
3                    CURRENT    CURRENT    PROPOSED   PROPOSED
4                    HOURLY     WEEKLY     HOURLY     WEEKLY
5  EMPLOYEE NAME     PAY RATE     PAY      PAY RATE     PAY
6  ======================================================================
7
8  BAKER, MARY A.      7.00      280.00      7.35      294.00
9  DAVIS, STEPHEN D.   9.00      360.00      9.45      378.00
10 LONG, CLARENCE R.   8.00      320.00      8.40      336.00
11 MONROE, JAMES L.   10.00      400.00     10.50      420.00
12 CHANG, JUSTIN M.    5.00      200.00      5.25      210.00
13
14 -------------------------------------------------------------------
15 PROPOSED % INCREASE    5%
16 HOURS PER WEEK         40
17
18 TOTAL PROPOSED PAY  $1,638.00                     22-Dec-91
19 TOTAL CURRENT PAY   $1,560.00                     10:57:03 AM
20 AMOUNT OF INCREASE    $78.00
22-Dec-91   10:57 AM          UNDO
```

FIGURE 3-76
Student Assignment 8

Student Assignment 8 (continued)

Enter the following formulas once and copy them to complete the remainder of the worksheet:

   a. Cell C8—current weekly pay = hours per week × current hourly pay rate
   b. Cell D8—proposed hourly pay rate = current hourly pay rate × (1 + proposed percent increase in B15)
   c. Cell E8—proposed weekly pay = hours per week × proposed hourly pay rate

Format the numbers in rows 8 through 12 to the Fixed type with two decimal places. Format the totals in rows 18 through 20 to the Currency type with two decimal places.

2. Save the worksheet as STUS3-8.
3. Print the worksheet in condensed mode. Reset 1-2-3 back to the normal print mode.
4. Print only the range A1..C13.
5. Answer the following what-if questions. Print the worksheet for each question.
   a. What is the total proposed pay if the proposed percent increase is changed to 10%?
   b. What is the total proposed pay if the proposed percent increase is changed to 7.5%?
6. Use Allways to print the worksheet as shown in Figure 3-77. Incorporate the following format changes:
   a. Change the font in B1 to Times 14 point.
   b. Change the font over the range A15..B20 to Times 10 point.
   c. Bold A1, A3..E5, and A15..B20.
   d. Shade dark E8..E12.
   e. Outline A15..B16.
   f. Double underline A20..B20.

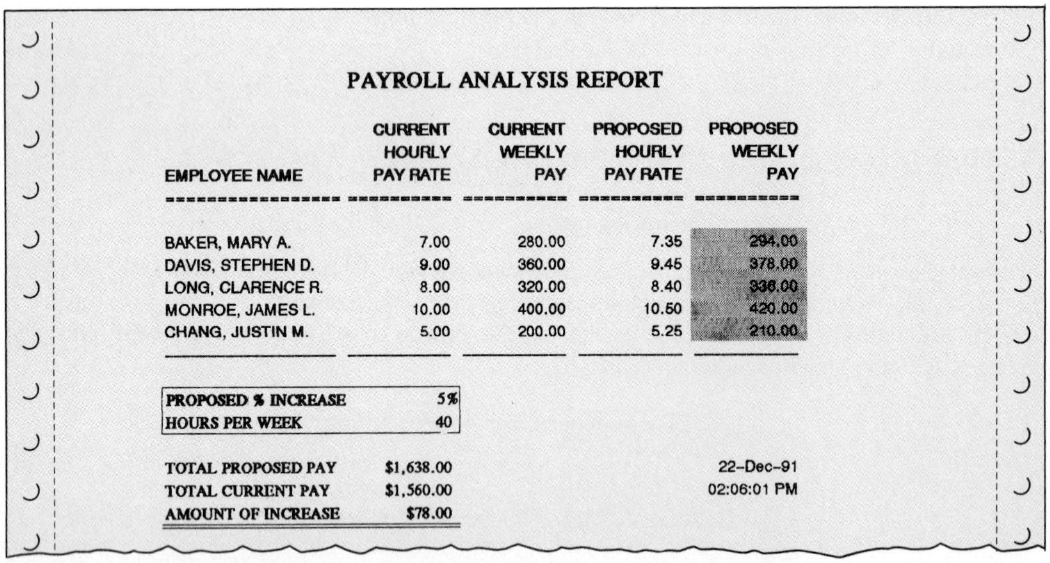

PAYROLL ANALYSIS REPORT

EMPLOYEE NAME	CURRENT HOURLY PAY RATE	CURRENT WEEKLY PAY	PROPOSED HOURLY PAY RATE	PROPOSED WEEKLY PAY
BAKER, MARY A.	7.00	280.00	7.35	294.00
DAVIS, STEPHEN D.	9.00	360.00	9.45	378.00
LONG, CLARENCE R.	8.00	320.00	8.40	336.00
MONROE, JAMES L.	10.00	400.00	10.50	420.00
CHANG, JUSTIN M.	5.00	200.00	5.25	210.00

| PROPOSED % INCREASE | 5% |
| HOURS PER WEEK | 40 |

TOTAL PROPOSED PAY	$1,638.00			22–Dec–91
TOTAL CURRENT PAY	$1,560.00			02:06:01 PM
AMOUNT OF INCREASE	$78.00

FIGURE 3-77 Student Assignment 8 printed using Allways

7. Save the worksheet with the Allways format characteristics as STUS3-8.

STUDENT ASSIGNMENT 9: Building a Book Income Worksheet

Instructions: Load 1-2-3 and perform the following tasks.

1. Build the worksheet illustrated in Figure 3-78. Set column A to a width of 18 characters and columns B through E to a width of 13 characters. The calculations for each author are determined as follows:

   a. The royalty in column C is the net sales of the book multiplied by the author's royalty percentage in cell B30 or B31.

   b. The manufacturing costs in column D are the net sales of the book multiplied by the manufacturing budgeted percent in cell B35.

   c. The net income in column E for each book is determined by subtracting the royalty and manufacturing costs from the net sales.

   d. The report totals in rows 25 and 26 are the sum of the individual book titles for each author.

```
                A              B            C           D           E
        1                          BOOK INCOME REPORT
        2 ----------------------------------------------------------------------
        3 AUTHOR:         HANSEN
        4
        5 BOOK TITLE          NET SALES      ROYALTY   MANU. COSTS   NET INCOME
        6
        7 Fury in the Sky    122,356.61    15,906.36    32,179.79    74,270.46
        8 Night Crawler      543,667.92    70,676.83   142,984.66   330,006.43
        9 White Feathers     885,443.91   115,107.71   232,871.75   537,464.45
       10
       11 ----------------------------------------------------------------------
       12 AUTHOR:         MERRIT
       13
       14 BOOK TITLE          NET SALES      ROYALTY   MANU. COSTS   NET INCOME
       15
       16 The Sharp Beak     553,889.04    74,775.02   145,672.82   333,441.20
       17 Webbed Intrique    657,443.25    88,754.84   172,907.57   395,780.84
       18 Information Blight 956,441.89   129,119.66   251,544.22   575,778.02
       19
       20 ----------------------------------------------------------------------
       21 REPORT TOTALS
       22
       23 AUTHOR              NET SALES      ROYALTY   MANU. COSTS   NET INCOME
       24
       25 Hansen           1,551,468.44   201,690.90   408,036.20   941,741.34
       26 Merrit           2,167,774.18   292,649.51   570,124.61 1,305,000.06
       27
       28 ======================================================================
       29 Royalty:
       30 Hansen                13.0%
       31 Merrit                13.5%
       32
       33
       34 Manufacturing Cost                                          Dec-91
       35 All Books             26.3%                                10:58 AM
       36
```

FIGURE 3-78 Student Assignment 9

2. Save the worksheet. Use the file name STUS3-9.
3. Print the worksheet.
4. Print only the range A3..E9.
5. Print the worksheet after formatting all the cells to the Text type.

STUDENT ASSIGNMENT 10: Building a Salary Budget Worksheet

Instructions: Load 1-2-3 and perform the following tasks.

1. Build the worksheet illustrated in Figure 3-79. Change the width of all the columns in the worksheet to 15 characters. Then change the width of column A to 20 characters. Enter the title, column headings, row titles, date, time, and current salary for full- and part-time employees. Determine the projected salaries in column C by using the salary increase in cell B27 and the current salaries in column B. Determine the salaries by department by multiplying the total salaries in row 12 by the corresponding sales allocation percent value in the range B21..B24. Use the SUM function to determine the annual totals in column D.

```
                     A               B               C               D
  1    SALARY BUDGET - CURRENT AND PROJECTED SALARIES          12/22/91
  2    PREPARED BY ACCOUNTING                                  10:59 AM
  3
  4
  5                            CURRENT         PROJECTED
  6    SALARY TYPE             JAN - JUNE      JULY - DEC      ANNUAL TOTAL
  7    =================================================================
  8
  9    FULL TIME               1,250,500.00    1,313,025.00    2,563,525.00
 10    PART TIME                 750,500.00      788,025.00    1,538,525.00
 11
 12    TOTAL SALARIES          2,001,000.00    2,101,050.00    4,102,050.00
 13
 14    SALARIES BY DEPARTMENT
 15        Accounting            200,100.00      210,105.00      410,205.00
 16        Production            600,300.00      630,315.00    1,230,615.00
 17        Sales                 500,250.00      525,262.50    1,025,512.50
 18        Distribution          700,350.00      735,367.50    1,435,717.50
 19
 20    SALES ALLOCATION % VALUES
 21        Accounting                            10%
 22        Production                            30%
 23        Sales                                 25%
 24        Distribution                          35%
 25
 26
 27    SALARY INCREASE %                          5%
 28
```

FIGURE 3-79 Student Assignment 10

2. Save the worksheet using the file name STUS3-10.
3. Print the worksheet.
4. Print the portion of the worksheet in the range A14..D18.
5. Use Allways to print the worksheet as shown in Figure 3-80. Incorporate the following format changes:
   a. Bold A1, A5..D7, and A9..A27.
   b. Double underline B10..D10, A18..D18, A27..B27.
   c. Outline A20..B24.
   d. Shade dark D9..D10.
6. Minimize the display to 60%. Maximize the display to 140%.
7. Save the worksheet with the Allways format characteristics as STUS3-10.

```
SALARY BUDGET - CURRENT AND PROJECTED SALARIE!      12/22/91
PREPARED BY ACCOUNTING                              02:20 PM


                      CURRENT      PROJECTED
SALARY TYPE           JAN - JUNE   JULY - DEC   ANNUAL TOTAL
================      ==========   ==========   ============

FULL TIME             1,250,500.00  1,313,025.00   2,563,525.00
PART TIME               750,500.00    788,025.00   1,538,525.00

TOTAL SALARIES        2,001,000.00  2,101,050.00   4,102,050.00

SALARIES BY DEPARTMENT
  Accounting            200,100.00    210,105.00     410,205.00
  Production            600,300.00    630,315.00   1,230,615.00
  Sales                 500,250.00    525,262.50   1,025,512.50
  Distribution          700,350.00    735,367.50   1,435,717.50

SALES ALLOCATION % VALUES
  Accounting                  10%
  Production                  30%
  Sales                       25%
  Distribution                35%


SALARY INCREASE %                5%
```

FIGURE 3-80 Student Assignment 10 printed using Allways

STUDENT ASSIGNMENT 11: Changing Manufacturing Costs and Royalty Rates in the Book Income Worksheet

Instructions: Load 1-2-3 and perform the following tasks.

1. Retrieve the worksheet STUS3-9 from disk. The worksheet is illustrated in Figure 3-78.
2. Answer the following what-if questions. Print the worksheet for each question. Each question is independent of the others.
   a. If the manufacturing percentage cost in cell B35 is reduced from 26.3% to 24.7%, what is the net income from all of Hansen's books?
   b. If Merrit's royalty percentage in cell B31 is changed from 13.5% to 14.8%, what would be the royalty amount for the book *Webbed Intrigue*?
   c. If Hansen's royalty percentage in cell B30 is reduced from 13% to 12.5%, Merrit's royalty percentage is increased from 13.5% to 14.1%, and the manufacturing percentage costs are reduced from 26.3% to 25%, what would be the net incomes for Hansen and Merrit?

STUDENT ASSIGNMENT 12: Changing Sales Allocation Percent Values and Salary Increase Percent in the Salary Budget Worksheet

Instructions: Load 1-2-3 and perform the following tasks.

1. Retrieve the worksheet STUS3-10 from disk. The worksheet is illustrated in Figure 3-79.
2. Answer the following what-if questions. Print the worksheet for each question. Each question is independent of the other.
   a. If the four sales allocation percent values in the range B21..B24 are each decreased by 1% and the salary increase in cell B27 is changed from 5% to 4%, what are the annual totals in the Salary Budget worksheet?
   b. If the salary increase percent is cut in half, what would be the total projected salaries?

PROJECT 4

Building Worksheets with Functions and Macros

Objectives

You will have mastered the material in this project when you can:

- Assign a name to a range and refer to the range in a formula using the assigned name
- Apply the elementary statistical functions AVG, COUNT, MAX, MIN, STD, and VAR
- Determine the monthly payment of a loan using the financial function PMT
- Enter a series of numbers into a range using the Data Fill command
- Employ the IF function to enter one value or another in a cell on the basis of a condition
- Determine the present value of an annuity using the financial function PV
- Determine the future value of an investment using the financial function FV
- Build a data table to perform what-if analyses
- Store keystrokes as a macro and execute the macro
- Use the learn feature of 1-2-3 to enter macros into the worksheet
- Write program-like macros to automate your worksheet
- Divide the screen into multiple windows
- Protect and unprotect cells

*I*n this project we will develop two worksheets, Project 4A and Project 4B. The worksheet for Project 4A, shown in Figure 4-1, is a grading report that displays a row of information for each student enrolled in DP 101. The student information includes a student identification number, three test scores, a test score total, and total percent correct. At the bottom of the worksheet is summary information for each test and all three tests grouped together. The summary includes the number of students that took the test, the highest and lowest test scores, the average test score, standard deviation, and variance. The **standard deviation** is a statistic used to measure the dispersion of test scores. The **variance** is used to make additional statistical inferences about the test scores.

```
 DP 101                    Grading Report                22-Dec-91

                 Test 1      Test 2      Test 3      Total     Percent
    Student        139         142         150         431     Correct
    =====================================================================
    1035           121         127         142         390       90.5
    1074           114         113         132         359       83.3
    1265            79          97         101         277       64.3
    1345            85         106          95         286       66.4
    1392           127         124         120         371       86.1
    3167           101         120         109         330       76.6
    3382           110         104         120         334       77.5
    3597            92         104         100         296       68.7
    4126           105         100          96         301       69.8
    5619           125         135         143         403       93.5
    7561           112         130         123         365       84.7
    ---------------------------------------------------------------------
    Count           11          11          11          11
    Lowest Grade    79          97          95         277
    Highest Grade  127         135         143         403
    Average Grade 106.5       114.5       116.5       337.5
    Std Deviation  15.2        12.6        16.8        41.4
    Variance      230.2       159.0       282.8      1711.2
```

FIGURE 4-1 The grading report we will build in Project 4A.

Project 4B has three parts. The first part is shown in Figure 4-2. This worksheet determines the monthly payment and an amortization table for a car loan. An **amortization table** shows the beginning and ending balances and the amount of payment that applies to the principal and interest for each period. This type of worksheet can be very useful if you are planning to take out a loan and want to see the effects of increasing the down payment, changing the interest rate, or changing the length of time it takes to pay off the loan.

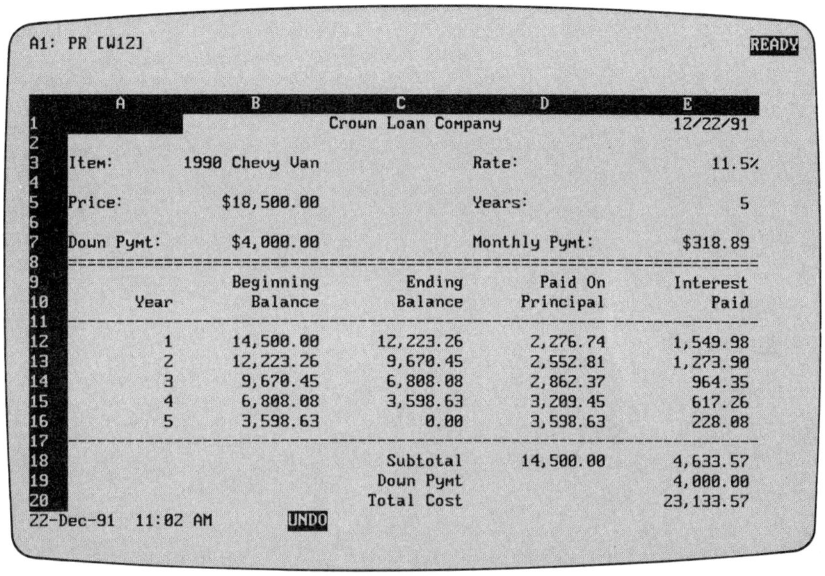

FIGURE 4-2
The monthly payment and amortization table we will build for the Crown Loan Company in Part 1 of Project 4B.

The second part of this worksheet is shown in Figure 4-3. Here we use a data table to analyze the effect of different interest rates on the monthly payment and total amount paid for the car loan. A **data table** is an area of the worksheet set up to contain answers to what-if questions. By using a data table you can automate your what-if questions and organize the answers returned by 1-2-3 into a table. For example, the data table in Figure 4-3 displays the monthly payments and total cost of the loan for interest rates that vary between 8.5% and 15% in increments of 0.5%.

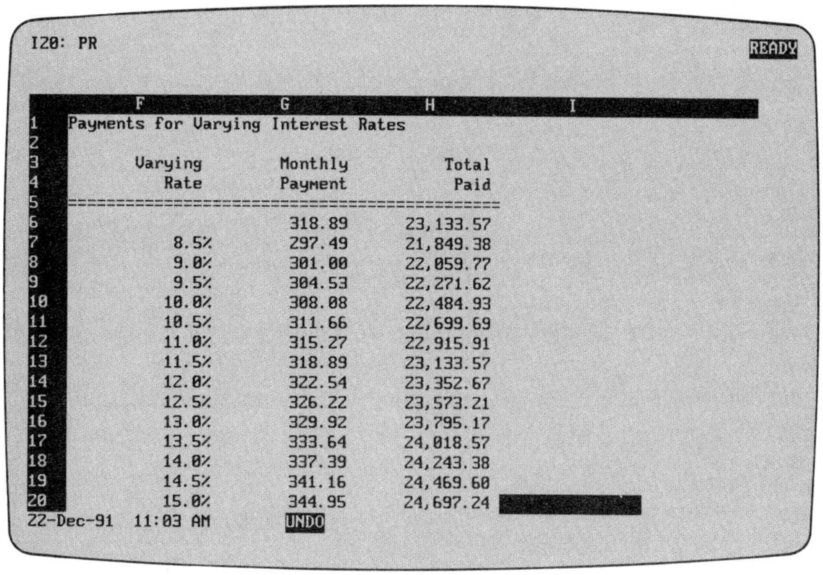

FIGURE 4-3
The data table we will build for the Crown Loan Company in Part 2 of Project 4B.

The third part of Project 4B involves writing the four macros shown in Figure 4-4. A **macro** is a series of keystrokes or instructions that are stored in a cell or a range of cells associated with that particular worksheet. They are executed by pressing only two keys: the Alt key and the single letter macro name. Macros save you time and effort. For example, they allow you to store a complex sequence of commands in a cell. Later you can execute the macro (stored commands) as often as you want by simply typing its name.

```
        A              B            C          D                    E
22                  Crown Loan Company Worksheet Macros
23
24   Macro                        Macro Name    Function
25   ============                 ==========    ================================
26   /FS~R                        \S            Saves worksheet
27
28   /PPAGPPQ                     \P            Prints worksheet
29
30   /PPOOCQAGOOAQPPQ             \C            Prints cell-formulas version
31
32
33   {HOME}                       \D            Accept loan information
34   {GOTO}B3~/RE~                              --Clear cell B3
35   {DOWN}{DOWN}/RE~                           --Clear cell B5
36   {DOWN}{DOWN}/RE~                           --Clear cell B7
37   {GOTO}E3~/RE~                              --Clear cell E3
38   {DOWN}{DOWN}/RE~                           --Clear cell E5
39   {HOME}                                     --Move to cell A1
40   /XLPurchase Item:~B3~                      --Accept item
41   /XNPurchase Price:~B5~                     --Accept price
42   /XNDown Payment:~B7~                       --Accept down payment
43   /XNInterest Rate in %:~E3~                 --Accept interest rate
44   /XNTime in Years:~E5~                      --Accept time in years
45   {HOME}                                     --Move to cell A1
46   /XQ                                        --End of macro
47
```

FIGURE 4-4 The four macros we will build for the Crown Loan Company in Part 3 of Project 4B.

When executed, the macro in cell A26 of Figure 4-4 saves the worksheet. The one in cell A28 prints the worksheet on the basis of the previously defined range. The macro in cell A30 prints the cell-formulas version of the worksheet on the basis of the previously defined range. The multicell macro in the range A33..A46 is a type of computer program. When it executes, it automatically clears the cells containing the loan information in Figure 4-2, requests new loan data on the input line, and displays the new loan information.

PROJECT 4A—ANALYZING STUDENT TEST SCORES

Begin Project 4A with an empty worksheet and the cell pointer at A1, the home position. The first step is to change the widths of the columns in the worksheet. Set the width of column A to 13 characters, so that the row identifier "Std Deviation" fits in cell A22 (Figure 4-1). Change the width of the rest of the columns in the worksheet from 9 to 11 characters so that all the student information fits across the screen. To change the columns to the desired widths, do the following:

1. Enter the command /Worksheet Global Column-Width (/WGC). Change the default width on the input line from 9 to 11 and press the Enter key.
2. With the cell pointer at A1, enter the command /Worksheet Column Set-Width (/WCS). Change the number 11 on the input line to 13 and press the Enter key.

If you reverse steps 1 and 2, the results will still be the same. That is, you can change the width of column A first and then change the width of the rest of the columns. The command /WGC affects only those columns that were not previously changed by the /WCS command.

The next step is to add the titles and student data to the worksheet. Enter the course number, worksheet title, date, column headings, maximum possible points for each test, student number, test scores, and summary identifiers as specified in Figure 4-1. Note that the numbers in column A identify the students in the class and are not used in any computations. Therefore, enter these numbers with a leading apostrophe ('). After entering the last row identifier in cell A23, press the Home key. The first 20 rows display as shown in Figure 4-5.

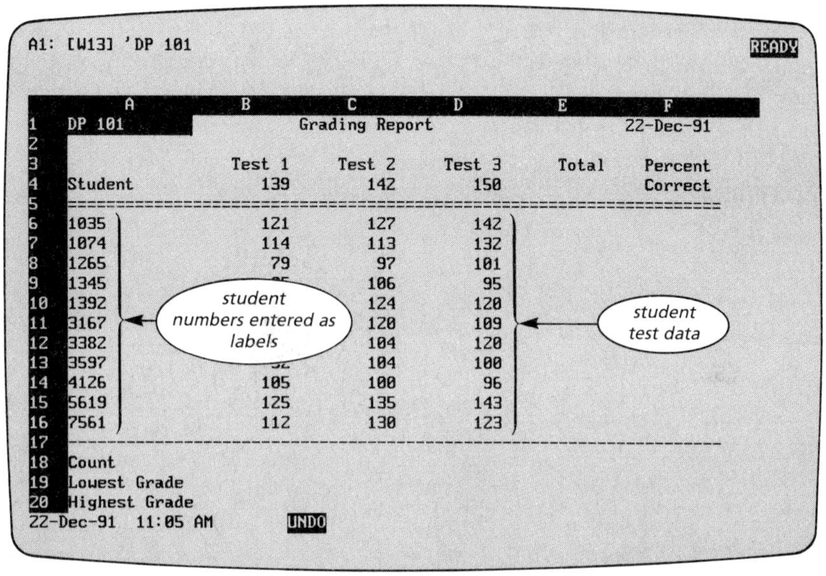

FIGURE 4-5
Labels and student data
entered into the grading report.

With the student data in the worksheet, we can determine the totals and summaries. Let's start with the maximum number of points for all three tests in cell E4. Use the GOTO command to move the cell pointer from cell A1 to cell E4 and enter the function @SUM(B4..D4). The range B4..D4 contains the maximum possible points for each test.

The SUM function in cell E4 is the same one required in the range E6..E16 to determine the total number of points received by each student. Hence, use the Copy command to copy cell E4 to the range E6..E16. With the cell pointer at E4, enter the command /Copy (/C), press the Enter key to lock in the source range, and use the Down Arrow key and Period key to select the destination range E6..E16. Press the Enter key. The total number of points received by each student displays in the range E6..E16 (Figure 4-6).

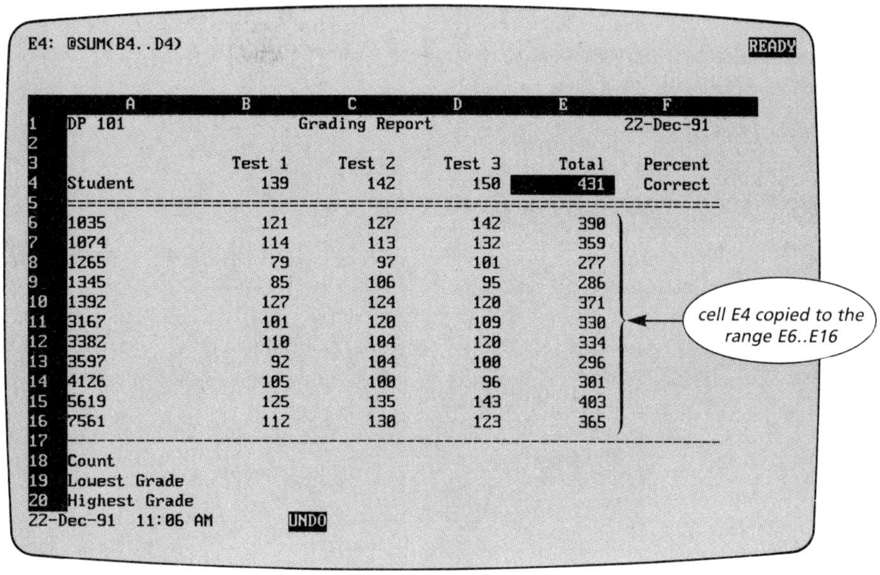

FIGURE 4-6
Student test totals entered into
column E of the grading report.

Once the total number of points received by each student is part of the worksheet, we can determine the total percent correct in column F. Move the cell pointer to F6 and enter the formula + E6/$E$4*100. The numerator in this formula, cell E6, is equal to the total number of points for the first student. The denominator, cell E4, is equal to the maximum number of points for the three tests. Multiplying the quotient + E6/$E$4 by 100 converts the ratio to a percent value. We use this procedure to display a percent value rather than formatting it in the Percent type because the column heading already indicates that the values in column E are in percent. Recall that the Percent type adds a percent sign (%) to the right side of the number.

Copy cell F6 to the range F7..F16. Note that we use the dollar sign ($) character in the denominator of the formula in cell E6 to make cell E4 an absolute cell address. Therefore, when we copy the formula in cell F6, the relative address E6 in the numerator changes based on the new location and the absolute address $E$4 in the denominator stays the same.

Format the percent correct in column F to the Fixed type with one decimal place. Enter the command /**R**ange Format **F**ixed (/RFF). Select one decimal position and press the Enter key. Enter the range F6..F16 and press the Enter key. The worksheet with each student's percent correct formatted to the Fixed type with one decimal place is illustrated in Figure 4-7.

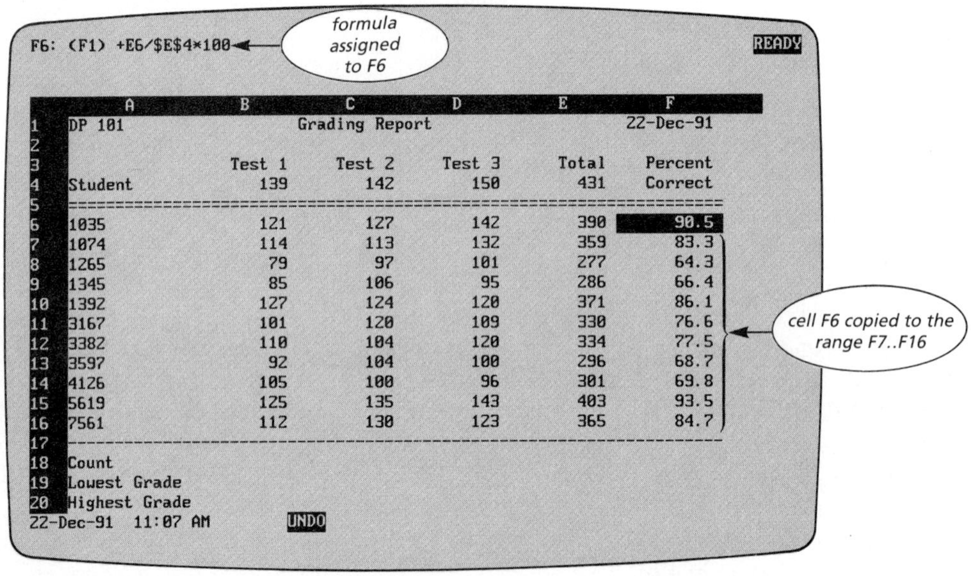

FIGURE 4-7
Total percent correct for each student formatted to the Fixed type with one decimal position.

The next step is to determine the summaries in rows 18 through 23. To make the job of entering these summaries easier, we need to discuss range names.

Assigning a Name to a Range of Cells

One of the problems with using a range is remembering the end points that define it. The problem becomes more difficult as worksheets grow in size and the same range is referred to repeatedly. This is the situation in the summary rows at the bottom of the grading report. For example, each summary item for Test 1 in cells B18 through B23 reference the same range, B6..B16. To make it easier to refer to the range, 1-2-3 allows you to assign a name to it. You may then use the name to reference the range, rather than the cell addresses of the end points. A range name can consist of up to 15 characters. Let's assign the name TEST1 to the range B6..B16.

Move the cell pointer to B6, one of the end points of the range B6..B16. Enter the command /**R**ange **N**ame (/RN). With the command cursor active in the **Range Name** menu (Figure 4-8), type the letter C for Create.

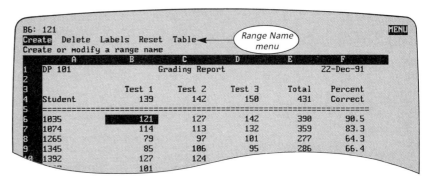

FIGURE 4-8 The display after entering the command /**R**ange **N**ame (/RN).

1-2-3 responds with the prompt message "Enter name:" on the input line (Figure 4-9). Enter the name TEST1 and press the Enter key. The prompt message "Enter range: B6..B6" immediately displays on the input line. Use the arrow keys to select the range B6..B16 as shown in Figure 4-9. Press the Enter key. The range name TEST1 can now be used in place of B6..B16.

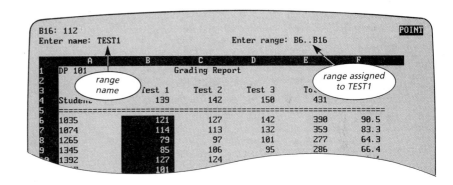

FIGURE 4-9
Range name TEST1 assigned to the range B6..B16.

As shown in the Range Name menu in Figure 4-8, there are several Range Name commands. These commands are summarized in Table 4-1. When 1-2-3 is in POINT mode, you can display a list of all the range names associated with the current worksheet by pressing function key F3.

TABLE 4-1   A Summary of Commands in the Range Name Menu

COMMAND	FUNCTION
Create	Assigns a name to a range. The name can be no longer than 15 characters.
Delete	Deletes the specified range name.
Labels	Assigns the label in the current cell as a name to the cell above, below, to the right, or to the left of the current cell.
Reset	Deletes range names associated with the worksheet.
Table	Places an alphabetized list of range names in the worksheet beginning at the upper left corner cell of the specified range.

Statistical Functions—AVG, COUNT, MIN, MAX, STD, and VAR

1-2-3 has several statistical functions that return values that are handy for evaluating a group of numbers, like the test scores in the grading report. The statistical functions are summarized in Table 4-2.

TABLE 4-2   **Statistical Functions**

FUNCTION	FUNCTION VALUE
AVG(R)	Returns the average of the numbers in range R by summing the nonempty cells and dividing by the number of nonempty cells. Labels are treated as zeros.
COUNT(R)	Returns the number of cells that are not empty in range R.
MAX(R)	Returns the largest number in range R.
MIN(R)	Returns the smallest number in range R.
STD(R)	Returns the standard deviation of the numbers in range R.
SUM(R)	Returns the sum of the numbers in range R.
VAR(R)	Returns the variance of the numbers in range R.

In the grading report, cell B18 displays the number of students that received a grade for Test 1. This value can be obtained by using the COUNT function. With the cell pointer at B18, enter the function @COUNT(TEST1). 1-2-3 immediately displays the value 11—the number of students that received a grade for Test 1. This is shown in Figure 4-10. Remember, the range name TEST1 is equal to the range B6..B16.

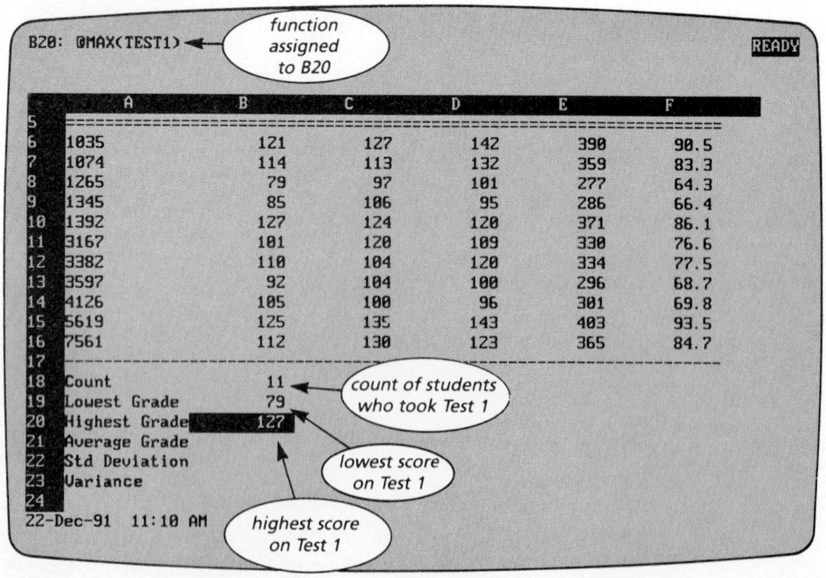

FIGURE 4-10
COUNT, MIN, and MAX functions entered into the grading report for Test 1.

In cells B19 and B20, the grading report contains the lowest score and the highest score received on Test 1. Student 1265 received the lowest score—79. Student 1392 received the highest score—127. To display the lowest score obtained on Test 1, enter the function @MIN(TEST1) in cell B19. To display the highest score, enter the function @MAX(TEST1) in cell B20. The results of entering these functions are shown in cells B19 and B20 in Figure 4-10.

The next step is to determine the average of the scores received on Test 1. Enter the function @AVG(TEST1) in cell B21. As illustrated in Figure 4-11, the average score for Test 1 in cell B21 is 106.454545. 1-2-3 arrives at this value by summing the scores for Test 1 and dividing by the number of non-empty cells in the range B6..B16.

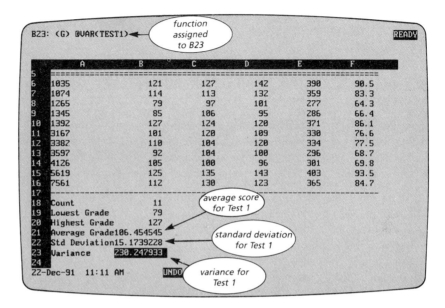

FIGURE 4-11
AVG, STD, and VAR functions entered into the grading report for Test 1.

The last two summary lines require we use the functions STD and VAR. As indicated in Table 4-2, the STD function returns the standard deviation and the VAR function returns the variance. To complete the summary lines for Test 1, enter the functions @STD(TEST1) in cell B22 and @VAR(TEST1) in cell B23. The results are shown in Figure 4-11.

The same six functions that are used to summarize the results for Test 1 are required for Test 2, Test 3, and the sum of the test scores for each student in column E. With the cell pointer at B23, enter the command /Copy (/C). Copy the source range B23..B18 to the destination range C23..E18.

As the functions in column B are copied to the new locations in columns C, D, and E, 1-2-3 adjusts the range TEST1 (B6..B16) to C6..C16 for Test 2, D6..D16 for Test 3, and E6..E16 for the sum of the test scores in column E.

To complete the worksheet, format the last three rows in the worksheet to the Fixed type with one decimal place. With the cell pointer at B23, enter the command /Range Format Fixed (/RFF). In response to the prompt message "Enter number of decimal places (0..15):2" on the input line, type the digit 1 and press the Enter key. Next, 1-2-3 displays the prompt message "Enter range to format: B23..B23". Use the arrow keys to select the range B23..E21 and press the Enter key. The complete grading report is shown in Figure 4-1.

Saving and Printing the Worksheet

To save the grading report worksheet to disk, enter the command /File Save (/FS). In response to the prompt message on the input line, enter the file name PROJS-4A and press the Enter key.

To obtain a printed version of the worksheet, follow these steps:

1. Make sure the printer is in READY mode.
2. Press the Home key to move the cell pointer to A1.
3. Enter the command /Print Printer Range (/PPR) and select the range A1..F23.
4. Type the letters A for Align and G for Go.
5. After the worksheet prints on the printer, type the letter P for Page twice. Recall that the Page command moves the paper through the printer to the top of the next page.
6. Type the letter Q to quit the /PP command and carefully remove the grading report from the printer.

Erasing the Worksheet from Main Memory

After saving and printing the grading report, we can erase it from main memory so that we can begin Project 4B. Recall from Project 1, that to erase the current worksheet, enter the command /Worksheet Erase (/WE). Finally, type the letter Y for Yes. 1-2-3 responds by clearing all the cells in the worksheet and changing all the settings to their default values.

PROJECT 4B—DETERMINING THE MONTHLY PAYMENT FOR A CAR LOAN

With the grading report worksheet cleared from main computer memory, we can begin entering Project 4B. The car loan payment worksheet is shown in Figures 4-2, 4-3, and 4-4. It is by far the most complex worksheet undertaken thus far. For this reason, use the divide and conquer strategy to build it. This strategy involves completing a section of the worksheet and testing it before moving on to the next section. Let's divide the worksheet into five sections:

1. Determine the monthly payment on a five-year loan for a 1990 Chevy Van with a sticker price of $18,500.00, down payment of $4,000.00, at an interest rate of 11.5%—range A1..E7 in Figure 4-2.
2. Display the amortization schedule—range A8..E20 in Figure 4-2.
3. Generate the data table—range F1..H20 in Figure 4-3.
4. Create the simple macros—range A22..E30 in Figure 4-4.
5. Create the multicell macro—range A33..E46 in Figure 4-4.

The first step in determining the car loan payment is to change the column widths. Set the width of column A to 12 characters and set the global width of the columns in the worksheet to 15 characters. To change the widths of the columns, do the following:

1. With the cell pointer at A1, enter the command /Worksheet Column Set-Width (/WCS) to change the width of column A to 12 characters.
2. Enter the command /Worksheet Global Column-Width (/WGC). Change the default value 9 on the input line to 15 and press the Enter key.

With the column widths set, enter the worksheet title, date, the six cell titles and the five data items in the range A1..E7 (Figure 4-12). Assign cell E1 the NOW function.

Use the command /Range Format (/RF) to change the format of the cells assigned numeric data in the range A1..E7 as follows:

1. Cell E1 to the Long Intn'l (MM/DD/YY) type.
2. Cells B5, B7, and E7 to the Currency type with two decimal positions.
3. Cell E3 to the Percent type with one decimal position.

The formatted worksheet with the cell pointer at A5 is shown in Figure 4-12.

FIGURE 4-12
Labels and data entered into the Crown Loan Company worksheet.

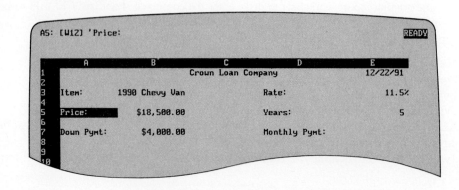

```
A5: [W12] 'Price:                                                    READY

          A              B              C              D              E
1                                  Crown Loan Company              12/22/91
2
3    Item:       1990 Chevy Van              Rate:                    11.5%
4
5    Price:          $18,500.00              Years:                       5
6
7    Down Pymt:       $4,000.00              Monthly Pymt:
8
9
10
```

Assigning a Label Name to an Adjacent Cell

In Project 4A we used the command /**R**ange **N**ame **C**reate (/RNC) to assign the name TEST1 to the range B6..B16. Later, when we built the summary lines, we used the name TEST1 several times in functions to reference the range B6..B16, because the name TEST1 is easier to remember than the range B6..B16. Another advantage of using range names is that they make it easier to remember what the range represents in the worksheet. This is especially helpful when working with complex formulas or functions.

The function for determining the monthly payment in cell E7 uses the purchase price (B5), down payment (B7), rate (E3), and years (E5). Let's name each of these cells. In this case, we'll use a second technique for assigning names to the individual cells. Rather than typing in a new name for each cell, use the adjacent cell title—the label located immediately to the left of each cell we want to name. For example, use the label Price: in cell A5 to name cell B5.

With the cell pointer at A5, enter the command /**R**ange **N**ame **L**abel (/RNL). By entering the command Label, we instruct 1-2-3 to use a label in the worksheet as the name, rather than to create a new name. With the command cursor active in the **Range Name Label menu** (Figure 4-13), type the letter R for Right. Note that this command allows us to assign any adjacent cell to the label name. Typing the letter R tells 1-2-3 that we want to assign the cell to the right of the label name.

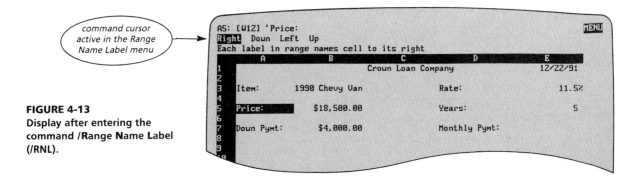

command cursor active in the Range Name Label menu

FIGURE 4-13
Display after entering the command /Range Name Label (/RNL).

Next, 1-2-3 requests that we enter the range containing the labels that we wish to assign to the cells to the right. Use the Down Arrow key to select the range A5..A7. Press the Enter key. We can now use the name Price: to refer to cell B5 and Down Pymt: to refer to cell B7.

Name cells E3, E5, and E7 in a similar fashion. Move the cell pointer to D3. Enter the command /**R**ange **N**ame **L**abel (/RNL). Type the letter R for Right, select the range D3..D7, and press the Enter key. We can now use Rate: to refer to cell E3, Years: to refer to cell E5, and Monthly Pymt: to refer to cell E7.

Three points to remember about the /RNL command: first, if a label in a cell is subsequently changed, the old label remains the name of the range; second, numbers cannot be used as range names; and third, 1-2-3 uses only the first 15 characters of the label as the name.

Determining the Loan Payment—PMT

1-2-3 has several financial functions that save you from writing out long, complicated formulas. One of the most important of these is the PMT function. This function determines the payment of a loan on the basis of the amount of the loan (principal), the interest rate (interest), and the length of time required to pay the loan back (term). If the term is in months, the PMT function returns the monthly payment. The PMT function is written in the following form:

@PMT(principal,interest,term)

To display the monthly payment of the car loan in cell E7, move the cell pointer to E7 and enter the following function:

@PMT($Price:−$Down Pymt:,$Rate:/12,$Years:*12)

The first argument ($Price:–$Down Pymt:) is the principal. The second argument ($Rate:/12) is the interest rate charged by the Crown Loan Company compounded monthly. The third argument ($Years:*12) is the number of months required to pay back the loan. As illustrated in cell E7 of Figure 4-14, it will cost $318.89 per month for 5 years to purchase the 1990 Chevy Van with a sticker price of $18,500.00, down payment of $4,000.00, at an annual interest rate of 11.5%.

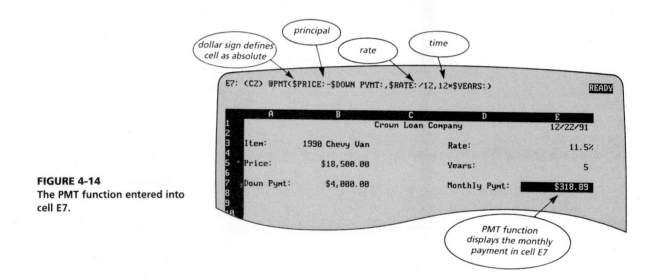

FIGURE 4-14
The PMT function entered into cell E7.

Note that we preceded all the names in the function arguments with a dollar sign ($). This is necessary because the function will be copied to another part of the worksheet later, and we want the cell references to remain the same.

Remember, 1-2-3 automatically recalculates the formula in E7 when a new entry is made into a cell referenced in the formula assigned to E7. If we change the purchase price, the amount of the down payment, the interest rate, the number of years, or any combination of these, 1-2-3 immediately adjusts the monthly payment displayed in cell E7.

The Data Fill Feature

The next step is to add the amortization table in cells A8..E16 (Figure 4-2). Enter the double underline in row 8, the column headings in rows 9 and 10, and the single underline in row 11 as shown in Figure 4.15.

In the range A12..A16, the series of numbers 1 though 5 represent the years. We can enter these numbers one at a time or we can use the Data Fill command. The Data Fill command allows you to quickly enter a series of numbers into a range using a specified increment or decrement. In this case, we want to enter a series of numbers in the range A12..A16 that begins with 1, increments by 1, and ends with 5.

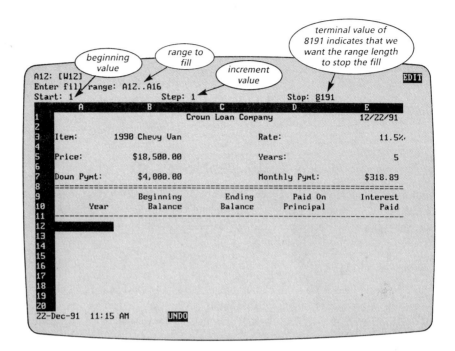

FIGURE 4-15
The display due to entering the command /**D**ata **F**ill (/DF).

With the cell pointer at A12, enter the command /**D**ata **F**ill (/DF). In response to the prompt message "Enter Fill range: A12" on the input line, press the Period key to anchor the first end point, A12. Use the Down Arrow key to move the cell pointer to the second end point (A16) and press the Enter key. Next, 1-2-3 requests that we enter the start, increment, and stop values. In response to the prompt messages on the input line, enter a start value of 1, an increment value of 1, and a stop value of 8191. The length of the range (five cells) will terminate the Data Fill command before it reaches the stop value 8191. The three entries are shown on the input line in Figure 4-15. Press the Enter key and the range A12..A16 is filled with the series of numbers 1 through 5 (Figure 4-16).

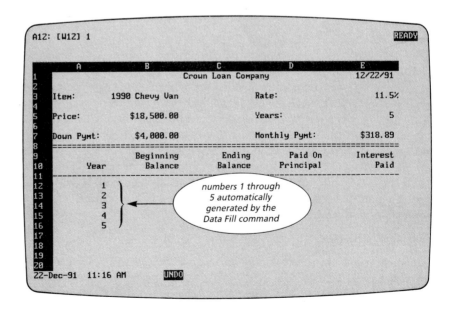

FIGURE 4-16
The display after using the Data Fill command.

Move the cell pointer to B12 and enter the beginning balance for year 1. This value is equal to the amount of the loan—+ Price:−Down Pymt: or (+ B5−B7).

Before we enter any more values in the amortization table, format cells B12 through E20 to the Comma (,) type with two decimal positions. The Comma (,) type with two decimal positions displays the numbers in the form of dollar and cents. Although labels will be part of the range (B12..E20), recall that a numeric format is only used if a numeric value is stored in the cell. Enter the command /**R**ange Format **,** (/RF,). Press the Enter key to select two decimal positions. Enter the range B12..E20 and press the Enter key.

Determining the Yearly Ending Balance—PV

Another important financial function is the PV function. This function returns the present value of an annuity. An **annuity** is a series of fixed payments made at the end of each of a fixed number of terms at a fixed interest rate. This function can be used to determine how much the borrower of the car loan still owes at the end of each year (C12..C16).

The general form of the PV function is:

@PV(payment,interest,term)

Use this function to determine the ending balance after the first year (C12) by using a term equal to the number of months the borrower must still make payments. For example, if the loan is for five years (60 months, therefore 60 payments), as it is in Figure 4-16, then the borrower still owes 48 payments after the first year. After the second year, the number of payments remaining is 36, and so on.

The entry for cell C12 that determines the ending balance reads as follows:

@PV($Monthly Pymt:, $Rate:/12, 12∗($Years:−A12))

The first argument, $Monthly Pymt:, refers to cell E7, the monthly payment. The second argument, $Rate:/12, refers to the interest rate in cell E3. The third argument, 12∗($Years:−A12), indicates the number of monthly payments that still must be made—48 after the first year. Note that each name in the three arguments of the PV function for cell C12 is preceded by a dollar sign ($). This tells 1-2-3 to treat these cell references as absolute. That is, when we copy the PV function in cell C12 to cells C13 through C16, the cell references in the arguments will not be adjusted.

Making Decisions—The IF Function

If we assign the PV function just described to cell C12 and copy it to cells C13 through C16, the ending balances for each year of a five-year loan will display properly as illustrated in Figure 4-2. If the loan is for a period of time less than five years, the ending balances displayed for the years beyond the time the loan is due are invalid. For example, if a loan is taken out for three years, the ending balance for years four and five in the amortization table should be zero. However, the PV function will display negative values even though the loan has already been paid off.

What we need here is a way to assign the PV function to the range C12..C16 as long as the corresponding year in the range A12..A16 is less than or equal to the number of years in cell E5, which contains the number of years of the loan. If the corresponding year in column A is greater than the number of years in cell E5, we need to assign C12 through C16 the value zero. 1-2-3 has a function that can handle this type of decision making. It is called the IF function.

The IF function is useful when the value you want assigned to a cell is dependent on a condition. A **condition** is made up of two expressions and a relation. Each **expression** may be a cell, a number, a label, a function, or a formula.

The general form of the IF function is:

@IF(condition,true,false)

The argument **true** is the value you want to assign to the cell when the condition is true. The argument **false** is the value you want to assign to the cell when the condition is false. For example, assume @IF(A1 = A2,C3 + D4,C3−D4) is assigned to cell B12. If the value assigned to A1 is equal to the value assigned to A2, then the sum of the values in C3 and D4 is assigned to B12. If the value assigned to A1 does not equal the value assigned to A2, then B12 is assigned the difference between the values in C3 and D4.

Valid relations and examples of their use in IF functions are shown in Table 4-3.

TABLE 4-3   Valid Relational Operators and Their Use in Conditions

RELATIONAL OPERATOR	MEANING	EXAMPLE
=	Equal to	@IF(A5 = B7,A22–A3,G5^E3)
<	Less than	@IF(E12/D5 < 6,A15,B13–5)
>	Greater than	@IF(@SUM(A1..A5) > 100,1,0)
< =	Less than or equal to	@IF(A12 < = $YEARS,A4∗D5,1)
> =	Greater than or equal to	@IF(@NOW > = 30000,H15,J12)
< >	Not equal to	@IF(5 < > F6,"Valid","Invalid")

Logical operators like NOT, AND, and OR may also be used to write a **compound condition**—two or more conditions in the same IF function. A summary of the logical operators is given in Table 4-4. Multiple logical operators in the same compound condition are evaluated from left to right.

TABLE 4-4   Valid Logical Operators and Their Use in Conditions

LOGICAL OPERATOR	MEANING	EXAMPLE
#NOT#	The compound condition is true if, and only if, the simple condition is false.	@IF(#NOT#($A$2 = A6),2,4)
#AND#	The compound condition is true if, and only if, both simple conditions are true.	@IF($J6 = R$4#AND#G5–S2 > D2, D4∗D6,T3/D2)
#OR#	The compound condition is true if, and only if, either simple condition is true, or both simple conditions are true.	@IF(A1 > $PRINCIPAL#OR#B7 = E4, "Contact","OK")

By using the IF function, we can assign the PV function or zero as the ending balance to cells C12 through C16. Enter the following IF function in cell C12:

@IF(A12 < = $Years:,@PV($Monthly Pymt:,$Rate:/12,12∗($Years:–A12)),0)

    condition   *true task*   *false task*

If the condition A12 < = $Years: is true, then C12 is assigned the PV function. If the condition is false, then C12 is assigned the value zero.

Use the command /Copy (/C) to copy cell C12 to the range C13..C16. The results of this copy are shown in Figure 4-17.

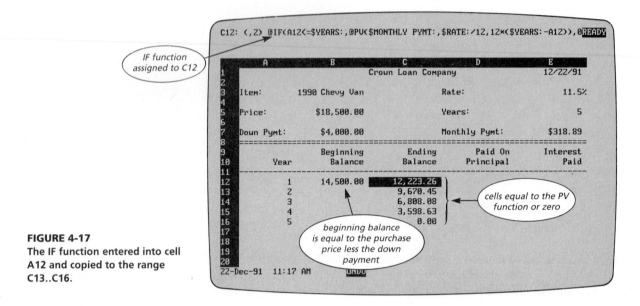

FIGURE 4-17
The IF function entered into cell A12 and copied to the range C13..C16.

Let's go back now and complete the entries in the beginning balance column, cells B13 through B16. The beginning balance in B13 is equal to the ending balance in cell C12. Therefore, enter +C12 in cell B13 and copy this cell to B14 through B16. The beginning balance for each year in cells B12 through B16 displays as shown in Figure 4-18.

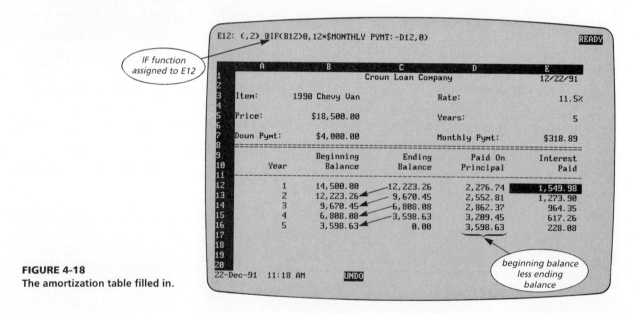

FIGURE 4-18
The amortization table filled in.

The total amount paid on the principal each year in column D is determined by subtracting the ending balance from the beginning balance. Enter the formula +B12–C12 in cell D12. Copy cell D12 to cells D13 through D16 (see Figure 4-18).

The total amount of interest paid each year by the borrower to the lender in column E is equal to 12 times the monthly payment in cell E7 less the amount paid on the principal. Here again, use the IF function because the loan may be for less than five years. Interest is paid in any year in which the beginning balance is greater than zero. Therefore, in cell E12, enter the IF function @IF(B12>0,12*$Monthly Pymt:–D12,0). Copy cell E12 to cells E13 through E16. The interest paid each year for a loan of $14,500.00 at 11.5% for 5 years is shown in column E of the worksheet in Figure 4-18.

To complete the amortization table, add the single underline in row 17 and the labels that identify the totals in cells C18 through C20. In cell D18, enter the SUM function @SUM(D12..D16). Note that this agrees with the original amount of the loan, $14,500.00. In cell E18, enter the SUM function @SUM(E12..E16). Cell E18 displays the total interest paid for the loan, $4,633.57. In cell E19, enter the name +Down Pymt:. Cell E19 displays $4,000.00, the amount in cell B7. Finally, in cell E20, enter the formula +D18+E18+E19. Cell E20 displays the total cost of the 1990 Chevy Van (Figure 4-19).

FIGURE 4-19
Part 1 of Project 4B complete.

```
E20: (,2) +D18+E18+E19                                          READY

              A              B              C              D              E
 1                                  Crown Loan Company                  12/22/91
 2
 3    Item:      1990 Chevy Van              Rate:                        11.5%
 4
 5    Price:        $18,500.00               Years:                           5
 6
 7    Down Pymt:     $4,000.00               Monthly Pymt:            $318.89
 8    ==================================================================
 9                      Beginning       Ending       Paid On      Interest
10          Year         Balance        Balance      Principal      Paid
11    ------------------------------------------------------------------
12            1         14,500.00      12,223.26      2,276.74      1,549.98
13            2         12,223.26       9,670.45      2,552.81      1,273.90
14            3          9,670.45       6,808.08      2,862.37        964.35
15            4          6,808.08       3,598.63      3,209.45        617.26
16            5          3,598.63          0.00      3,598.63        228.08
17    ------------------------------------------------------------------
18                                      Subtotal     14,500.00      4,633.57
19                                      Down Pymt                   4,000.00
20                                      Total Cost                 23,133.57
22-Dec-91  11:19 AM        UNDO
```
total cost
of car

With the amortization table complete, try various combinations of loan data to evaluate the what-if capabilities of 1-2-3. If we change the purchase price (B5), down payment (B7), interest rate (E3), time (E5) or any combination of these values, 1-2-3 will immediately change the monthly payment and the numbers in the amortization table.

Saving the Worksheet

Before we continue with Project 4B, save the worksheet as PROJS-4B. Enter the command /File Save (/FS). Enter the file name PROJS-4B and press the Enter key. The worksheet is saved on the default drive.

Using a Data Table to Answer What-If Questions

The next step is to build the data table at the right side of the amortization table (Figure 4-3). As described earlier, a data table has one purpose—it organizes the answers to what-if questions into a table. We have already seen that if a value is changed in a cell referenced elsewhere in a formula, 1-2-3 immediately recalculates and stores the new value in the cell assigned the formula. You may want to compare the results of the formula for several different values, but it would be unwieldy to write down or remember all the answers to the what-if questions. This is where a data table comes in handy.

Data tables are built in an unused area of the worksheet. You may vary one or two values and display the results of the specified formulas in table form. Figure 4-20 illustrates the makeup of a data table.

In Project 4B, the data table shows the impact of changing interest rates on the monthly payment and the total cost of the loan. The interest rates range from 8.5% to 15% in increments of 0.5%. Therefore, in this data table we are varying one value, the interest rate (E3). We are interested in its impact on two formulas: the monthly payment (E7) and the total cost (E20).

To construct the data table, enter the headings in the range F1..H5 as described in Figure 4-3. Next, move the cell pointer to F7 and use the command /**D**ata **F**ill (/DF) to enter the varying interest rates. Select the range F7..F20. Use a start value of 8.5%, an increment value of 0.5%, and a stop value of 8191. After we press the Enter key, the range F7..F20 contains the varying interest rates. Format the interest rates to the Percent type with one decimal position (Figure 4-21).

THIS CELL MUST BE EMPTY	FORMULA-1 FORMULA-2 . . . FORMULA-k
Value-1	
Value-2	
Value-3	1-2-3 places results of formulas here on the basis of the values in the left-hand column.
Value-4	
· · ·	
Value-n	

(a) Data table with one value varying

ASSIGN FORMULA TO THIS CELL	VALUE-2a VALUE-2b . . . VALUE-2k
Value-1a	
Value-1b	
Value-1c	1-2-3 places results of the formula in the upper left corner cell here on the basis of the two corresponding values.
Value-1d	
· · ·	
Value-1n	

(b) Data table with two values varying

FIGURE 4-20
General forms of a data table with one value varying (a) and two values varying (b).

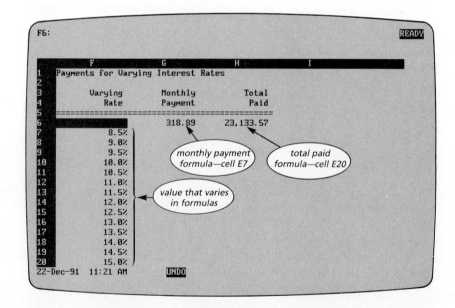

FIGURE 4-21
Monthly payment formula, total paid formula, and varying interest rates entered into the worksheet in preparation for applying a data table in the range F6..H20.

In cell G6 enter +E7, the cell with the monthly payment formula. In cell H6 enter +E20, the cell with the total cost of the loan formula. Format the range G6..H20 to the Comma (,) type with two decimal positions. Move the cell pointer to F6. The range F1..H20 of the worksheet is shown in Figure 4-21.

To define the data table, enter the command /**D**ata **T**able **1** (/DT1). 1-2-3 responds by displaying the prompt message "Enter Table range: F6" on the input line. Press the Period key to anchor F6 as one of the end points. Use the arrow keys to move the cell pointer to H20 and press the Enter key. (Note that the data table itself does not include the headings above F6.) 1-2-3 responds with the prompt message "Enter Input cell 1: F6" on the input line. The **input cell** is defined as the cell in the worksheet that contains the value we want to vary. For this data table, we want to vary the interest rate in cell E3 (also called Rate:). Therefore, enter the name Rate: in response to the prompt message on the input line and press the Enter key.

The data table, in the range F6..H20, immediately fills with monthly payments and total loan costs for the corresponding varying interest rates, as shown in Figure 4-22. Look over the table. Note how it allows you to compare the monthly payments and total loan costs for different interest rates. For example, at 10%, the monthly payment on the loan of $14,500.00 for 5 years is $308.08. At 10.5%, the monthly payment is $311.66 for the same loan. The two numbers at the top of the table, in cells G6 and H6, are the same as the monthly payment and total cost displayed in cells E7 and E20.

FIGURE 4-22
Data table in the range F6..H20 filled with answers to what-if questions regarding varying interest rates.

Here are some important points to remember about data tables:

1. You can have only one active data table in a worksheet. If you want to move or establish a new data table, use the command /**D**ata **T**able **R**eset (/DTR) to deactivate the current data table.
2. For a data table with one varying value, the cell in the upper left corner of the table (F6) must be empty. With two values varying, assign the formula you want to analyze to the upper left corner cell of the table (Figure 4-20b).
3. If you change any value in a cell referenced by the formula that is part of the data table but does not vary in the data table, you must press function key F8 to instruct 1-2-3 to recalculate the data table values.

MACROS

 A **macro** is a series of keystrokes entered into a cell or a range of cells. The macro is assigned a name using the command /**R**ange **N**ame **C**reate (/RNC). Later, when you enter the macro name, the keystrokes stored in the cell or range of cells execute one after another, as if you entered each keystroke manually at the keyboard. A macro can be as simple as the series of keystrokes required to save a worksheet or as complex as a sophisticated computer program.

Whether simple or complex, macros save time and help remove the drudgery associated with building and using a worksheet. You should consider using a macro when you find yourself typing the same keystrokes over and over again; when the series of keystrokes required is difficult to remember; or if you want to automate the use of the worksheet.

Designing a Simple Macro

In Project 2, we suggested that you save your worksheet every 50 to 75 keystrokes. If you follow this suggestion, you will be entering the series of keystrokes shown in Table 4-5 often. This is an excellent example of how a macro can save you time and effort.

TABLE 4-5   Series of Keystrokes for Saving a Worksheet Under the Same File Name

KEYSTROKE	PURPOSE
/	Switch 1-2-3 to command mode.
F	Select File command.
S	Select Save command.
←	Save worksheet under the same file name.
R	Replace the worksheet on disk.

One of the keystrokes in Table 4-5 is the Enter key(←). In a macro, we use the **tilde character** (˜) to represent the Enter key. Therefore, /FS˜R represents the series of keystrokes in Table 4-5.

After determining the makeup of the macro, the next step is to move the cell pointer to a cell in an unused area of the worksheet. According to Figure 4-4, the macros for this project are to be placed below the amortization table. Hence, use the GOTO command and move the cell pointer to A22.

Documenting Macros

We recommend that all macros be documented, even the simple ones. *Documenting* a macro means writing a comment off to the side of the cell or range containing the macro. The comment explains the purpose of the macro, and if it is complex, how it works. To document this macro, as well as the other macros in this worksheet, first enter the macro title and column headings in cells A22 through E25 (Figure 4-23).

FIGURE 4-23
The macro \S entered into cell A26 and documented in cells C26 and D26.

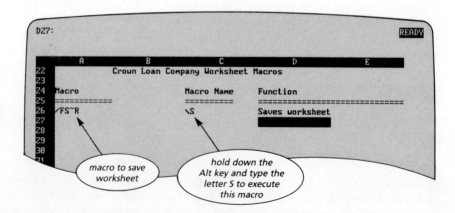

Entering and Naming a Macro

Move the cell pointer to A26 and enter the macro '/FS˜R. It is important that you begin the macro with an apostrophe or one of the other characters that defines the entry as a label (^, "). If you don't begin the macro with an apostrophe, 1-2-3 immediately switches to the command mode because the Slash key (/) is the first character entered.

With the macro in cell A26, enter the command /**R**ange **N**ame **C**reate (/RNC) and assign the macro name \S to cell A26. A macro name can consist of up to 15 characters. It is to your advantage, however, to use a name made up of only two characters in which the first character is the backslash (\) and the second character is a letter. In this way you can invoke the macro by holding down the Alt key and pressing the second letter in the macro name.

Complete the documentation in cells C26 and D26. Figure 4-23 illustrates the \S macro in cell A26 and the corresponding documentation.

The macro name \0 (zero) has special meaning to 1-2-3. If you name a macro \0, then 1-2-3 automatically executes the macro whenever you first load the worksheet from disk into main memory.

Invoking a Macro

After entering the macro '/FS˜R in cell A26 and naming it \S, execute it by pressing Alt-S. 1-2-3 automatically executes the series of keystrokes in cell A26 and saves the worksheet. Note that the \S macro is part of the worksheet that is saved. Hence, the macro will be available the next time you load the worksheet into main computer memory.

An alternative method of executing macros is to press Alt-F3. Alt-F3 displays a menu of range names at the top of the screen. Select the macro name, in this case, \S, from the menu, and press the Enter key. 1-2-3 immediately executes the \S macro. This second method of invoking a macro *must be used* to execute macros whose names are longer than two characters or begin with a character other than the backslash (\).

Adding More Macros to the Worksheet

When 1-2-3 executes a macro, it starts at the specified cell. After executing the keystrokes in this cell, it inspects the adjacent cells. First it checks the cell below, then the cell to the right. If they are empty, the macro terminates. If they are not empty, 1-2-3 considers the nonempty cell to be part of the macro and executes its contents. Hence, 1-2-3 is finished executing a macro when the cells below and to the right are empty. It is for this reason that when you add additional macros to a worksheet, make sure that there is at least one empty cell between each macro.

With this rule in mind, enter the macro /PPAGPPQ in cell A28 and /PPOOCQAGOOAQPPQ in cell A30. Also enter the corresponding documentation in cells C28 through D30 (Figure 4-24). Use the command /**R**ange **N**ame **C**reate (/RNC) and assign the names \P to cell A28 and \C to cell A30.

FIGURE 4-24
The macros \P and \C entered into cells A28 and A30 and documented in the range C28..D30.

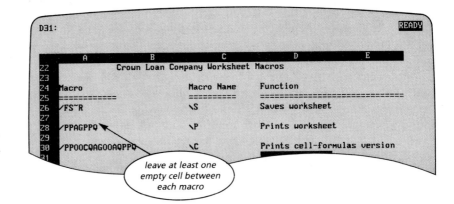

The \P macro in cell A28 prints the worksheet on the basis of the previous printer range setting. It also ejects the paper in the printer and quits the Print command. Build a print macro like this one when you expect to print the worksheet often. To prepare to execute the \P macro, use the /**P**rint **P**rinter **R**ange (/PPR) command to set the range to A1..E20. Invoke the \S macro again to save the print range permanently.

Now, imagine you are the loan officer for the Crown Loan Company. A customer comes in and requests information on the 1990 Chevy Van we discussed earlier. With the monthly payment and the amortization table on the screen, you can print a copy of the loan information and pass it to the customer. First, make sure the printer is ready. Next, hold down the Alt key and press the letter P. The monthly payment and amortization table shown in Figure 4-19 prints on the printer.

The \C macro in cell A30 prints the cell-formulas version of the worksheet according to the previously defined printer range. After printing the as-displayed version of the range A1..E20, hold down the Alt key and press the C key. This invokes the \C macro. Note that after the printer is done printing the cell-formulas version, the macro resets the print setting to the as-displayed version.

Creating Macros Using the Learn Feature of 1-2-3

1-2-3 has a macro learn feature that automatically records your keystrokes and allows you to test the command sequence at the same time. You enter the keystrokes, such as /PPAGPPQ, and 1-2-3 saves the command sequence in a specified cell as a macro. To illustrate the learn feature, let's erase the macro /PPAGPPQ in cell A28 by using the command /**R**ange **E**rase (/RE). With cell A28 blank, do the following:

1. Enter the command/**W**orksheet **L**earn **R**ange (/WLR). Specify the range A28..A28.
2. Turn on the learn feature by pressing Alt-F5. The LEARN status indicator displays at the bottom of the screen to inform you that the learn feature is active.
3. Enter the command /PPAGPPQ. 1-2-3 carries out the command sequence and prints the range A1..E20 on the printer. (Recall that the range A1..E20 was established earlier.) More importantly, 1-2-3 records the command sequence.
4. Turn off the learn feature by pressing Alt-F5.
5. Press F9 to recalculate the worksheet.

After step 5, the command sequence entered in step 3 is assigned to cell A28. Since we named cell A28 earlier, the macro recorded by 1-2-3 already has a name (\P). If we hadn't already assigned the name \P to A28, then after step 5 we would name the macro by using the /**R**ange **N**ame **C**reate (/RNC) command.

Guarding Against Macro Catastrophes

Take care when applying macros to a worksheet. If you enter the wrong letter, forget the tilde (˜) when required, place macros in adjacent cells, or transpose characters in a macro, serious damage in the form of lost data can occur. For this reason we recommend you save the worksheet before executing a macro for the first time.

You should also use the **STEP mode** of 1-2-3 to test the macro. The STEP mode allows you to watch 1-2-3 execute the macro keystroke by keystroke just as if you entered the keystrokes one at a time at the keyboard. Let's execute the \S macro again using the STEP mode. To place 1-2-3 in STEP mode, hold down the Alt key and press function key F2. The indicator STEP appears on the indicator line at the bottom of the screen. Next, invoke the \S macro by holding down the Alt key and pressing the S key. With the STEP mode active, 1-2-3 displays two items on the left side of the indicator screen: the cell address of the macro being executed and the contents of that cell. Also, the keystroke that corresponds to the command being executed within the macro is highlighted. Now press any key on the keyboard to execute the next keystroke in the macro.

If you encounter an error while in STEP mode, you could terminate the macro by holding down the Ctrl key and pressing the Break key. Next, press the Esc or Enter key and the macro terminates execution. Edit the macro and execute it once again using STEP mode. Continue in this fashion until the macro is doing exactly what you intend it to do. To quit the STEP mode, press Alt-F2. This process of finding and correcting errors in a macro is called **debugging**.

/X Macro Commands and Macro Words

The final step in Project 4B is to enter the macro that extends from cell A33 through A46. Before entering this macro, we need to discuss macro commands and macro words. **Macro commands** are used to write programs that can guide you or another user of the worksheet through complex tasks, like accepting data into various cells. Some of the macro commands are listed in Table 4-6. For a complete list of the macro commands, press function key F1 and go to the Help Index of the online help facility. Select the title Macro Command Index from the Help Index. After reading or printing the screens, press the Esc key to return to the worksheet.

TABLE 4-6 Macro Commands

COMMAND	EXAMPLE	EXPLANATION
/XC	/XCBONUS˜	Executes the macro beginning at the cell named BONUS. Saves the return cell address—the one below the cell containing /XCBONUS˜. The return cell address is used by the /XR command.
/XG	/XGB10˜	Executes the macro beginning at a specified cell.
/XI	/XIB10< =40˜/XCREG˜	Executes the macro at the cell named REG if B10 contains a value less than or equal to 40; otherwise it executes the macro in the cell below.
/XL	/XLPurchase Item:˜B3˜	Displays a prompt message on the input line, accepts a label, and assigns it to cell B3.
/XN	/XNPurchase Price:˜B5˜	Displays a prompt message on the input line, accepts a number, and assigns it to cell B5.
/XQ	/XQ	Ends the execution of a macro.
/XR	/XR	Returns control to the cell below the corresponding /XC.

Macro words are used to handle special circumstances in a macro, like moving the cell pointer from one cell to another. Except for the tilde (˜), which represents the Enter key, all macro words are enclosed in curly braces { }. The important macro words are listed in Table 4-7. For a complete list of the macro words, load 1-2-3, press function key F1, and select Macro Key Names from the Help Index. After reading or printing the screens, press the Esc key to return to the worksheet.

TABLE 4-7 Macro Words That Represent Special Keys on the Keyboard

CATEGORY	MACRO WORD
Cell pointer	{UP} {DOWN} {RIGHT} {LEFT} {PGUP} {PGDN} {HOME} {END} {BACKSPACE}
Function keys	{EDIT} {NAME} {ABS} {GOTO} {WINDOW} {QUERY} {TABLE} {CALC} {GRAPH}
Special keys	{ESC} {DEL} {INS} {MENU}
Enter key	˜
Interaction	{?}

The cell pointer movement macro words in Table 4-7 move the pointer, as if you pressed the key named within the curly braces. The function key macro words operate the same as pressing one of the function keys. The macro word {?} makes the macro pause and wait for keyboard input from the user. For example, the macro /FR{?}˜ may be used to retrieve a worksheet from disk. The macro word {?} following /FR tells the macro to pause and wait for the user to select a file name. When you press the Enter key after entering the file name, the macro resumes execution and accepts the name entered on the input line.

Interactive Macros

The macro defined in cells A33 through A46 in Figure 4-4 automates the entry of the loan data in cells B3, B5, B7, E3, and E5. The instructions in cells A34 through A39 clear the cells that contain the loan data. The instructions in cells A40 through A44 prompts the user to enter the loan data. Each /XL and /XN command displays a prompt message and halts the execution of the macro until the user responds by entering a value on the input line. /XQ in cell A46 terminates the macro.

Enter the macro and documentation in the range A33..D46 as shown in Figure 4-4. Use the command /**R**ange **N**ame **C**reate (/RNC) and assign cell A33 the macro name \D. Note that it is not necessary to assign the range A33..A46 to the macro name \D, since a macro executes downward until it comes across an empty cell. Invoke the \D macro and reenter the loan data for the 1990 Chevy Van shown in Figure 4-19. In a step-by-step fashion, Table 4-8 explains how the \D macro works. Use Table 4-8 to step through the macro activity when you execute it.

TABLE 4-8   **Step-by-Step Explanation of the \D Macro in the Range A33..A46**

STEP	CELL	ENTRY	FUNCTION
1	A33	{HOME}	Move the cell pointer to A1.
2	A34	{GOTO}B3~/RE~	Move the cell pointer to B3 and erase the contents.
3	A35	{DOWN}{DOWN}/RE~	Move the cell pointer to B5 and erase the contents.
4	A36	{DOWN}{DOWN}/RE~	Move the cell pointer to B7 and erase the contents.
5	A37	{GOTO}E3~/RE~	Move the cell pointer to E3 and erase the contents.
6	A38	{DOWN}{DOWN}/RE~	Move the cell pointer to E5 and erase the contents.
7	A39	{HOME}	Move the cell pointer to A1.
8	A40	/XLPurchase Item:~B3~	Accept the purchase item (1990 Chevy Van) and assign it to cell B3.
9	A41	/XNPurchase Price:~B5~	Accept the purchase price (18500) and assign it to cell B5.
10	A42	/XNDown Payment :~B7~	Accept the down payment (4000) and assign it to cell B7.
11	A43	/XNInterest Rate in %: ~E3~	Accept the interest rate (11.5) and assign it to cell E3.
12	A44	/XNTime in Years:~E5~	Accept the time (5) and assign it to cell E5.
13	A45	{HOME}	Move the cell pointer to A1.
14	A46	/XQ	Quit the macro.

WINDOWS

When you have a large worksheet like the one in Project 4B, it is helpful to view two parts of the worksheet at one time. 1-2-3 lets you divide the screen into two horizontal windows or two vertical windows. For example, by dividing the screen into two horizontal windows, you can view the \D macro in cells A33..A46 and the cells (A1..E7) that are affected by this macro at the same time.

To show two windows, press the Home key and use the arrow keys to move the cell pointer to A8. Enter the command /**W**orksheet **W**indow **H**orizontal (/WWH). The rows above row 8 display in the top window and rows 8 through 19 display in the lower window.

Immediately after a window split, the cell pointer is active in the window above or to the right of the split. You can move the cell pointer from window to window by pressing function key F6. Press function key F6 and use the PgDn and Down Arrow keys to move the cell pointer to A44. As shown in Figure 4-25, the top window shows the cells that are modified by the \D macro in the lower window.

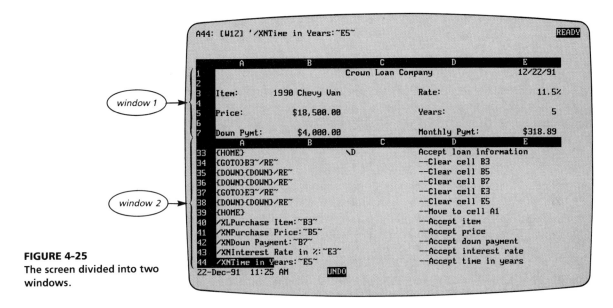

FIGURE 4-25
The screen divided into two windows.

Press function key F6 to move the cell pointer to the top window. Execute the \D macro a second time. Step through the macro in the lower window and watch the cells change in the top window.

It is important to understand that the entire worksheet is available through any window. If you make a change to a cell in one window, the change will show up in any other window. Table 4-9 summarizes the window commands available when you enter the command /**W**orksheet **W**indow (/WW).

TABLE 4-9   A Summary of Commands in the Worksheet Window Menu

COMMAND	FUNCTION
Horizontal	Splits the screen from side to side.
Vertical	Splits the screen from top to bottom.
Sync	Causes windows that are aligned horizontally or vertically to scroll together.
Unsync	Causes each window to scroll independently.
Clear	Returns the screen to a single window.

Synchronizing Windows

If you look closely at the two windows in Figure 4-25, you'll notice that they are **synchronized**, that is, the same column letters are aligned in both windows. The windows scroll together. They are **synchronized**. You can unsynchronize the windows so that they scroll independent of one another. To unsynchronize the windows, enter the command /**W**orksheet **W**indow **U**nsync (/WWU). To synchronize the windows after unsynchronizing them, enter the command /**W**orksheet **W**indow **S**ync (/WWS).

Clearing the Windows

To return to the normal worksheet display with one window, enter the command /**W**orksheet **W**indow **C**lear (/WWC). This command switches the screen from two windows back to one window.

CELL PROTECTION

Cells are either protected or unprotected. When you create a new worksheet, all cells are unprotected. **Unprotected cells** are cells whose values may be changed at any time, but **protected cells** cannot be changed. If a cell is protected and the user attempts to change its value, the computer beeps and 1-2-3 displays the error message "Protected cell" on the indicator line at the bottom of the screen.

Once the worksheet has been fully tested and displays the correct results, you should protect the cells that you don't want changed by mistake. You should protect cells that contain information that will not change or is unlikely to change, cells that contain macros, and cells whose values are determined by formulas. In the case of Project 4B, we want to protect all the cells in the worksheet except for B3, B5, B7, E3, E5, and the data table in the range F6..H20.

The first step in protecting cells is to protect all the cells in the worksheet. Once all the cells are protected, we can be selective and "unprotect" those that we want to change. To protect all the cells in the worksheet, enter the command /**W**orksheet **G**lobal **P**rotection **E**nable (/WGPE).

Next, move the cell pointer to B3. Enter the command /**R**ange **U**nprotect (/RU). Press the Enter key when 1-2-3 requests the range to unprotect. Do the same for cells B5, B7, E3, and E5. Finally, move the cell pointer to F6 and unprotect the range F6..H20, which contains the data table information.

You can check whether a cell is unprotected by moving the cell pointer to the cell in question. The letter U displays on the status line at the top of the screen if the cell is unprotected. The letters PR display if the cell is protected. If you mistakenly unprotect the wrong cell, you may protect it by using the command /**R**ange **P**rotect (/RP). This command is meaningless unless global protection has been enabled (turned on).

If for some reason you need to modify the cells that are in a protected area, such as the macros, disable (turn off) global protection by using the command /**W**orksheet **G**lobal **P**rotection **D**isable (/WGPD). Once you are finished modifying the cells, enable (turn on) global protection. The worksheet will be protected exactly as it was before you disabled (turned off) global protection.

Saving and Printing the Worksheet

To save the Crown Loan Company worksheet to disk with the cells protected, invoke the \S macro by holding down the Alt key and pressing the S key.

To obtain a printed version of the worksheet, do the following:

1. Enter the command /**P**rint **P**rinter **R**ange (/PPR) and select the range A1..H46.
2. Type the letter Q to quit the Print menu.
3. Invoke the \P macro by holding down the Alt key and pressing the P key.

1-2-3 prints the three parts of the worksheet on multiple pages. After the printer stops, carefully remove the Crown Loan Company worksheet from the printer. The complete worksheet is shown in Figures 4-2, 4-3, and 4-4.

OBTAINING A SUMMARY OF ALL THE 1-2-3 FUNCTIONS

1-2-3 has over 100 useful functions. We have discussed the most widely used ones. You may find the others to be useful in certain situations. For a complete listing and description of the functions available, load 1-2-3, press function key F1, and go to the Help Index screen. Select the title @Function Index. Press the Up Arrow key once when the @Function Index displays. Select @Function by Categories at the bottom of the screen. Print the screen for each category of functions by pressing Shift-PrtSc. After you are finished, press the Esc key to return to the worksheet.

PROJECT SUMMARY

*I*n Project 4 we developed two worksheets. Project 4A introduced you to statistical functions and range names. Project 4B taught you how to use the IF, PMT, and PV functions, the data fill feature, data tables, and macros. You also learned how to protect cells in the worksheet and how to use multiple windows to see different parts of the worksheet at the same time.

Each of the steps required to build the worksheets in Projects 4A and 4B is listed in the following tables.

SUMMARY OF KEYSTROKES—Project 4A

STEPS	KEY(S) PRESSED	STEPS	KEY(S) PRESSED
1	/WGC → → ↵	18	F5 A16 ↵ '7561 → 112 → 130 → 123 ↵
2	/WCS → → ↵	19	F5 A17 ↵ \- ↵ /C ↵ . → → → → → → ↵
3	DP 101 → → Grading Report → → →	20	↓ Count ↓ Lowest Grade ↓ Highest Grade ↓ Average Score ↓ Std Deviation ↓ Variance ↵ Home
4	@NOW ↵ /RFD1 ↵	21	F5 E4 ↵ @SUM(B4.D4) ↵
5	F5 B3 ↵ "Test 1 → "Test 2 → "Test 3 → "Total → "Percent ↵	22	/C ↵ E6.E16 ↵
6	F5 A4 ↵ Student → 139 → 142 → 150 → → "Correct ↵	23	F5 F6 ↵ + E6/$E$4∗100 ↵
7	F5 A5 ↵ \ = ↵ /C ↵ . → → → → → → ↵	24	/C ↵ F6.F16 ↵
8	↓ '1035 → 121 → 127 → 142 ↵	25	/RFF1 ↵ F6.F16 ↵
9	F5 A7 ↵ '1074 → 114 → 113 → 132 ↵	26	F5 B6 ↵ /RNCTEST1 ↵ B6.B16 ↵
10	F5 A8 ↵ '1265 → 79 → 97 → 101 ↵	27	F5 B18 ↵ @COUNT(TEST1) ↓ @MIN(TEST1) ↓ @MAX(TEST1) ↓
11	F5 A9 ↵ '1345 → 85 → 106 → 95 ↵	28	@AVG(TEST1) ↓ @STD(TEST1) ↓ @VAR(TEST1) ↵
12	F5 A10 ↵ '1392 → 127 → 124 → 120 ↵	29	/CB18.B23 ↵ C18.E23 ↵
13	F5 A11 ↵ '3167 → 101 → 120 → 109 ↵	30	/RFF1 ↵ ↑ ↑ → → → ↵
14	F5 A12 ↵ '3382 → 110 → 104 → 120 ↵	31	/FSPROJS-4A ↵
15	F5 A13 ↵ '3597 → 92 → 104 → 100 ↵	32	Home /PPRA1.F23 ↵
16	F5 A14 ↵ '4126 → 105 → 100 → 96 ↵	33	AGPPQ
17	F5 A15 ↵ '5619 → 125 → 135 → 143 ↵	34	/WEY

SUMMARY OF KEYSTROKES—Project 4B

STEPS	KEY(S) PRESSED	STEPS	KEY(S) PRESSED
1	/WCS12←	40	[F5]A22← → Crown Loan Company Worksheet Macros←
2	/WGC15←	41	[F5]A24←Macro→ → Macro Name→Function↓
3	→ →Crown Loan Company→ →	42	\ = →\ = ← ← ========== ← ←\ =↓
4	@NOW←/RFD4←	43	'/FS~R→ →'\S→Saves worksheet under same name←
5	[F5]A3←Item:↓↓Price:↓↓Down Pymt:←	44	← ←/RNC\S← ←
6	[F5]D3←Rate:↓↓Years:↓↓Monthly Pymt:←	45	[Alt]-S
7	[F5]B3←'1990 Chevy Van↓↓18500↓↓4000← /RFC←.↑↑←	46	↓↓'/PPAGPPQ→ →'\P→Prints worksheet←
8	[F5]E3←11.5%←/RFP1← ← ↓↓5↓↓/RFC← ←	47	← ← ←/RNC\P← ←
9	[F5]A5←/RNLR.↓↓←	48	↓↓'/PPOOCQAGOOAQPPQ→ →'\C→Prints cell-formulas version←
10	[F5]D3←/RNLR.↓↓↓↓←	49	← ← ←/RNC\C← ←
11	[F5]E7←@PMT($Price:–$Down Pymt:, $Rate:/12,$Years:*12)←	50	/PPRA1.E20←Q
12	[F5]A8←\ = ←/C←.→ → → →←	51	[Alt]-P
13	[F5]B9←''Beginning→''Ending→''Paid On→ ''Interest↓	52	[Alt]-C
14	''Paid←''Principal←''Balance←''Balance←''Year↓	53	↓↓↓{HOME}→ →'\D→Accept loan information←
15	\-←/C←.→ → → →←	54	← ← ←/RNC\D← ←
16	↓/DF.↓↓↓↓←1← ← ←	55	↓{GOTO}B3~/RE~→ → →'--Clear cell B3←
17	→ +Price:–Down Pymt:←	56	[F5]A35←{DOWN}{DOWN}/RE~→ → →'--Clear cell B5←
18	/RF,←B12.E20←	57	[F5]A36←/CA35←A36← → → →'--Clear cell B7←
19	→ @IF(A12< = $YEARS:,@PV($Monthly Pymt:,$Rate:/12,12*($Years:–A12)),0)←	58	[F5]A37←{GOTO}E3~/RE~→ → →'--Clear cell E3←
20	/C←.↓↓↓↓←	59	[F5]A38←{DOWN}{DOWN}/RE~→ → →'--Clear cell E5←
21	↓←+C12←/C←.↓↓↓←	60	[F5]A39←{HOME}→ → →'--Move to cell A1←
22	[F5]D12←+B12–C12←/C←.↓↓↓↓←	61	[F5]A40←'/XLPurchase Item:~B3~→ → →'--Accept purchase item←
23	→ @IF(B12>0,12*$Monthly Pymt:–D12,0) ←/C←.↓↓↓↓←	62	[F5]A41←'/XNPurchase Price:~B5~→ → →'--Accept purchase price←
24	[F5]A17←\-←/C←.→ → → →←	63	[F5]A42←'/XNDown Payment:~B7~→ → →'--Accept down payment←
25	[F5]C18←''Subtotal↓''Down Pymt↓''Total Cost←	64	[F5]A43←'/XNInterest Rate in %:~E3~→ → →' --Accept interest rate←
26	[F5]D18←@SUM(D12.D16)→	65	[F5]A44←'/XNTime in Years:~E5~→ → →'--Accept time in years←
27	@SUM(E12.E16)↓	66	[F5]A45←{HOME}→ → →'--Move to cell A1←
28	+Down Pymt:↓	67	[F5]A46←'/XQ→ → →'--End of macro←
29	+D18+E18+E19←	68	[Alt]-D1990 Chevy Van←18500←4000←11.5%←5←
30	/FSPROJS-4B←	69	/WGPE
31	[F5]F1←Payments for Varying Interest Rates↓↓	70	→ ↓↓/RU←
32	''Varying→''Monthly→''Total↓	71	↓↓/RU←
33	''Paid←''Payment←''Rate↓	72	↓↓/RU←
34	\ = →\ = →\ =↓	73	[F5]E3←/RU←
35	[F5]F7←/DFF7.F20←8.5%←0.5%← ←	74	↓↓/RU←
36	/RFP1←F7.F20←	75	[F5]F6←/RUF6.H20← [Home]
37	↑→ +E7← +E20←	76	[Alt]-S
38	/RF,←G6.H20←	77	/PPRA1.H46←Q
39	/DT1H6.F20←Rate:←	78	[Alt]-P

The following list summarizes the material covered in Project 4:

1. If you plan to reference a range often, assign a name to it. To name a range, use the command /**R**ange **N**ame **C**reate (/RNC).
2. The Range Name command allows you to create range names, delete range names, assign labels as range names, clear all range names, and insert the list of range names in the worksheet. Refer to Table 4-1.
3. 1-2-3 has several statistical functions, like AVG, COUNT, MAX, MIN, STD, and VAR. Refer to Table 4-2.
4. The command /**R**ange **N**ame **L**abel (/RNL) allows you to assign a label in a cell as the name of the cell immediately above, below, to the right, or to the left.
5. The PMT function determines the payment of a loan on the basis of the amount of the loan (principal), the interest rate (interest), and the length of time required to pay the loan back (term). The general form of the PMT function is @PMT(principal,interest,term).
6. The command /**D**ata **F**ill (/DF) allows you to quickly enter a series of numbers into a range using a specified increment or decrement.
7. The PV function can be used to return the amount the borrower still owes at the end of a period at any time during the life of a loan. The general form of the PV function is @PV(payment,interest,term).
8. The general form of the IF function is @IF(condition,true,false). When the IF function is assigned to a cell, the value displayed will depend on the condition. If the condition is true, the cell is assigned the true value. If the condition is false, the cell is assigned the false value.
9. The true and false values in an IF function may be a number, label (in quotation marks), function, or formula.
10. A condition is made up of two expressions and a relation. Each expression may be a number, label (in quotation marks), function, or formula. Refer to Table 4-3 for a list of the valid relations.
11. A compound condition is one that includes a logical operator like #AND#, #OR#, and #NOT#. Refer to Table 4-4 for examples. Multiple logical operators in the same compound condition are evaluated from left to right.
12. A data table is used to automate asking what-if questions and organize the values returned by 1-2-3.
13. A data table may have one value or two varying values (Figure 4-20).
14. A **macro** is a series of keystrokes entered into a cell or range of cells. The macro is assigned a name using the command /**R**ange **N**ame **C**reate (/RNC).
15. A macro name can consist of 15 characters. Execute a macro by pressing Alt-F3. Select the desired macro from the list displayed.
16. If the macro name is two characters long with the first character the backslash (\) and the second character a letter, then you can execute the macro by holding down the Alt key and pressing the key that corresponds to the second letter in the macro name. If you name a macro \0 (zero), then 1-2-3 automatically executes the macro whenever the worksheet is first loaded from disk into main memory.
17. If you have more than one macro associated with a worksheet, each macro should be separated by an empty cell.
18. The tilde character (˜) is used to represent the Enter key in a macro.
19. All macros should be documented.
20. Use the learn feature of 1-2-3 to enter and test macros at the same time.
21. A poorly designed macro can damage a worksheet. Before you execute a new macro, save the worksheet. To test a macro, place 1-2-3 in STEP mode, hold down the Alt key, and press function key F2. When you are finished testing the macro, hold down the Alt key and press function key F2 to toggle the STEP mode off.
22. If you encounter an error in a macro while in STEP mode, hold down the Ctrl key and press the Break key to stop the macro followed by the Esc or Enter key.
23. /X macro commands are used to write programs. Refer to Table 4-6.
24. Macro words represent special keys, like the pointer movement and function keys. Refer to Table 4-7.
25. 1-2-3 allows you to divide the screen into two windows for viewing different parts of the worksheet at the same time. Use the command /**W**orksheet **W**indow (/WW). Refer to Table 4-9.
26. To protect cells in a worksheet that you do not want the user to change, enter the command /**W**orksheet **G**lobal **P**rotection **E**nable (/WGPE). Once all the cells in the worksheet are protected, use the command /**R**ange **U**nprotect (/RU) to unprotect the cells you want the user to be able to change. If you unprotect the wrong cell, use the command /**R**ange **P**rotect (/RP) to protect it.
27. To correct the values in protected cells, enter the command /**W**orksheet **G**lobal **P**rotection **D**isable (/WGPD). After the cells are corrected, enable (turn on) global protection. 1-2-3 remembers the cells you unprotected earlier.

STUDENT ASSIGNMENTS

STUDENT ASSIGNMENT 1: True/False

Instructions: Circle T if the statement is true or F if the statement is false.

T   F   1.   A data table allows you to automate what-if questions.

T   F   2.   The @COUNT(R) function returns the largest number in the range R.

T   F   3.   You may assign a single cell to a name using the /**R**ange **N**ame **C**reate (/RNC) command.

T   F   4.   If there are seven cells in range R and five of the cells have a value of 10 and two of the cells are empty, then the
function @AVG(R) returns a value of 50.

T   F   5.   The command /**W**orksheet **E**rase (/WE) may be used to erase the contents of a single cell without affecting the
remaining cells in the worksheet.

T   F   6.   The learn feature of 1-2-3 is used to enter macros.

T   F   7.   The command /**R**ange **N**ame **L**abel (/RNL) is used to name a cell that contains a label.

T   F   8.   The PMT function may be used to determine the monthly payment on a loan.

T   F   9.   To fill a range from top to bottom with the sequence of numbers 5, 4, 3, 2, and 1, use the /**D**ata **F**ill (/DF) command with a start value of 5, a step value of 1, and a stop value of 1.

T   F   10.   The IF function is used to assign one value or another to a cell on the basis of a condition that may be true, false,
or both true and false.

T   F   11.   The logical operator #AND# requires both conditions to be true for the compound condition to be true.

T   F   12.   You may vary one or two values in a data table.

T   F   13.   1-2-3 recalculates the values in a data table when you press function key F9.

T   F   14.   To invoke a macro, hold down the Ctrl key and type the letter that names the macro.

T   F   15.   To name a macro, use the /**R**ange **N**ame **C**reate (/RNC) command.

T   F   16.   The STEP mode is used to enter a macro into a cell.

T   F   17.   Each macro should be separated by at least one empty cell.

T   F   18.   To protect cells in the worksheet, global protection must be enabled (turned on).

T   F   19.   The /**W**orksheet **W**indow (/WW) command allows you to divide the screen into two to six windows.

T   F   20.   The /X macro commands allow you to write programs.

STUDENT ASSIGNMENT 2: Multiple Choice

Instructions: Circle the correct response.

1.   Which one of the following allows you to assign a name to one or more adjacent cells?
     a. /**R**ange **N**ame **C**reate (/RNC)   c. /**R**ange **N**ame **L**abel (/RNL)
     b. /**W**orksheet **N**ame **C**reate (/WNC)   d. /**R**ange **N**ame **T**able (/RNT)

2.   Which one of the following functions returns the average of the numbers in a range?
     a. AVG   b. COUNT   c. MAX   d. MIN

3.   Which one of the following functions returns the payment on a loan?
     a. TERM   b. PMT   c. PV   d. RATE

4.   Which one of the following functions is used to assign one value or another value to a cell on the basis of a condition?
     a. CHOOSE   b. FALSE   c. IF   d. TRUE

5.   Which one of the following is used to instruct 1-2-3 to terminate the Data Fill command?
     a. The last cell in the selected range terminates the command.
     b. The STOP parameter terminates the command.
     c. Either a or b can terminate the command.
     d. None of the above.

6. Which one of the following relations is used to represent not equal to?
   a. <   b. >   c. < >   d. none of these
7. Which one of the following turns the learn feature of 1-2-3 on and off?
   a. Alt-F2   b. Alt-F5   c. Alt-F7   d. Alt-F9
8. Which one of the following characters represents the Enter key in a macro?
   a. backslash (\)   b. curly braces ({ })   c. circumflex (^)   d. tilde (˜)

STUDENT ASSIGNMENT 3: Understanding Functions

Instructions: Fill in the correct answers.

1. Write a function that will count the nonempty cells in the range B10..B50.

Function: _____

2. Write a function that will find the average of the nonempty cells in the range A12..E12.

Function: _____

3. Write a function that will display the largest value in the range D1..D13.

Function: _____

4. Write a function that will determine the monthly payment on a loan of $85,000, over a period of 30 years, at an interest rate of 9.9% compounded monthly.

Function: _____

5. The cell pointer is at F15. Write a function that assigns the value zero or 1 to cell F15. Assign zero to cell F15 if the value in cell A12 is less than the value in cell B15. Assign 1 to cell F15 if the value in A12 is not less than the value in cell B15.

Function: _____

6. The cell pointer is at F15. Write a function that assigns the value Credit OK or Credit Not OK to cell F15. Assign the label Credit OK if the value in cell A1 is equal to the value in cell B1 or the value of cell C12 is greater than 500. If both conditions are false, assign the label Credit Not OK.

Function: _____

7. When there are multiple logical operators in a compound condition, 1-2-3 determines the truth value of each simple condition. It then evaluates the logical operators left to right. Determine the truth value of the compound conditions below, given the following: E1 = 300   F1 = 500   G1 = 1   H1 = 50   I1 = 40
   a. E1<400#OR#G1=1   Truth value: _____
   b. F1<300#AND#I1<50#OR#G1=2   Truth value: _____
   c. #NOT#(F1>600)#OR#G1=0#AND#I1=40   Truth value: _____
   d. E1+F1=800#AND#H1*4/10=30   Truth value: _____

STUDENT ASSIGNMENT 4: Understanding Macros

Instructions: Fill in the correct answers.

1. Describe the function of each of the following macros.
   a. /FS˜R/QY

   Function of macro: _____

   b. /RE˜

   Function of macro: _____

   c. /RFC2˜{?}˜

   Function of macro: _____

   d. /C˜{?}˜

   Function of macro: _____

   e. /PPOML2˜MR78˜Q

   Function of macro: _____

   f. /PPR{?}˜AGPPQ

   Function of macro: _____

   g. {DOWN}{DOWN}/RE˜

   Function of macro: _____

   h. /DF{?}˜1˜2˜˜

   Function of macro: _____

2. Describe the function of each of the following macro commands and macro words.

   a. tilde (˜)   Function: _____   g. {UP}   Function: _____

   b. curly braces ({}) Function: _____   h. /XQ   Function: _____

   c. /XN   Function: _____   i. /XI   Function: _____

   d. {?}   Function: _____   j. Alt-F2   Function: _____

   e. {HOME}   Function: _____   k. Alt-F3   Function: _____

   f. {GOTO}   Function: _____   l. Alt-F5   Function: _____

STUDENT ASSIGNMENT 5: Using the Data Fill Command

Instructions: Enter the worksheet illustrated in Figure 4-26. The worksheet is a multiplication table. Change the global width of the columns to 6 characters. Use the Data Fill command twice, once to enter the numbers 1 to 18 in column A, and once to enter the numbers 2 to 22 by 2 in row 1. Enter the formula $A3*B$1 in cell B3. Copy the formula to the range B3..L20. Save the worksheet as STUS4-5. Print the as-displayed version of the worksheet. Format all the cells in the worksheet to the Text type and print the worksheet.

A1: "x   READY

	A	B	C	D	E	F	G	H	I	J	K	L
1	x	2	4	6	8	10	12	14	16	18	20	22
2												
3	1	2	4	6	8	10	12	14	16	18	20	22
4	2	4	8	12	16	20	24	28	32	36	40	44
5	3	6	12	18	24	30	36	42	48	54	60	66
6	4	8	16	24	32	40	48	56	64	72	80	88
7	5	10	20	30	40	50	60	70	80	90	100	110
8	6	12	24	36	48	60	72	84	96	108	120	132
9	7	14	28	42	56	70	84	98	112	126	140	154
10	8	16	32	48	64	80	96	112	128	144	160	176
11	9	18	36	54	72	90	108	126	144	162	180	198
12	10	20	40	60	80	100	120	140	160	180	200	220
13	11	22	44	66	88	110	132	154	176	198	220	242
14	12	24	48	72	96	120	144	168	192	216	240	264
15	13	26	52	78	104	130	156	182	208	234	260	286
16	14	28	56	84	112	140	168	196	224	252	280	308
17	15	30	60	90	120	150	180	210	240	270	300	330
18	16	32	64	96	128	160	192	224	256	288	320	352
19	17	34	68	102	136	170	204	238	272	306	340	374
20	18	36	72	108	144	180	216	252	288	324	360	396

22-Dec-91 11:26 AM   UNDO

FIGURE 4-26 Student Assignment 5

STUDENT ASSIGNMENT 6: Using the Data Table Command

Instructions: Create the following worksheets.

1. The worksheet illustrated in Figure 4-27 contains a data table with one value (time) varying. At the top of the worksheet, the PMT function is used to determine the monthly mortgage payment for a loan of $85,000.00 at 9.9% annual interest for 30 years. The data table indicates the monthly payment for the same loan for different terms (5 years, 10 years, 15 years, etc.).

B7: @PMT(PRINCIPAL:,INTEREST RATE:/12,TIME IN YEARS:*12)   READY

	A	B	C	D
1	Determining the Monthly Mortgage Payment			
2				
3	Principal:	85,000.00		
4	Interest rate:	9.9%		
5	Time in years:	30	*input cell*	
6				
7	Monthly payment:	739.66		*monthly payment for $85,000 loan at 9.9% for 30 years*
8				
9		Time	Monthly	
10		in Years	Payment	
11			739.66	*+B7*
12		5	1,801.82	
13		10	1,118.58	
		15	908.22	
		20	814.64	
		25	766.41	*monthly payment for $85,000 loan at 9.9% for varying years*
		30	739.66	
		35	724.22	
19		40	715.11	
20		45	709.65	

replace time in PMT function with these values

22-Dec-91 11:27 AM   UNDO

FIGURE 4-27
Student Assignment 6A

Do the following to create the worksheet in Figure 4-27:

a. Increase the global column width to 17.
b. Format the entire worksheet to the Comma (,) type with two decimal places.
c. Enter the labels and numeric values in the range A1 through B5 and in cell A7. Format cell B4 to the Percent type with one decimal position. Format cell B5 to the Fixed type with zero decimal positions.

Student Assignment 6 (continued)

d. Use the Range Name Label command to assign the labels in cells A3 through A7 to B3 through B7.

e. Assign the PMT function shown on the input line in Figure 4-27 to cell B7.

f. Enter the labels in the range A9..B10.

g. Use the Data Fill command to enter the multiples of five shown in the range A12..A20. Format A12..A20 to the Fixed type with zero decimal positions.

h. Assign cell B11 the formula +B7.

i. Use the command /**D**ata **T**able 1 (/DT1) to create a data table in the range A11..B20. Use B5 (time in years) as the input cell.

j. After the data table displays, save the worksheet using the file name STUS4-6A.

k. Print the worksheet.

l. Select and enter several other sets of numbers into cells B3, B4, and B5. When necessary, use function key F8 to reset the data table.

2. The worksheet illustrated in Figure 4-28 contains a data table with two values varying. It also uses the FV function in cell B7 to determine the future value of a fund. The FV function tells you how much money you will have in a fund if you pay a fixed payment and earn a fixed interest rate over a period of time.

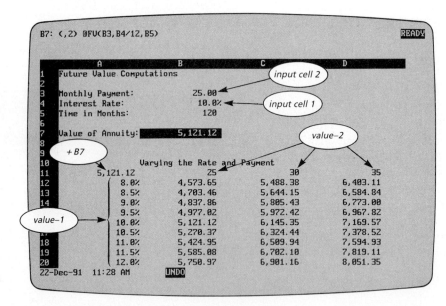

FIGURE 4-28
Student Assignment 6B

The data table describes the future values for varying interest rates and varying monthly payments. For example, if you invest $35.00 per month instead of $25.00 per month and if the interest rate is 11.5%, then you will have $7,819.11 rather than $5,585.08 at the end of 10 years.

Do the following to create the worksheet in Figure 4-28:

a. Increase the global column width to 17.

b. Enter the labels and numeric values in the range A1 through B5 and in cell A7.

c. Assign the FV function @FV(B3,B4/12,B5) to cell B7 to determine the future value of a fund in which you invest $25.00 per month at 10% interest, compounded monthly, for 10 years (120 months).

d. Use the Data Fill command to build the percent values in the range A12..A20. Assign +B7 to cell A11.

e. With the cell pointer at A11, enter the command /**D**ata **T**able 2 (/DT2). Enter the data table range A11..D20.

f. Enter an input cell-1 value of B4 and an input cell-2 value of B3. Press the Enter key. The data table should fill as shown in Figure 4-28.

g. Format the worksheet according to Figure 4-28.
h. Save the worksheet using the file name STUS4-6B.
i. Print the worksheet.
j. Try several different investment combinations in cells B3, B4, and B5. Use function key F8 to instruct 1-2-3 to recalculate the data table if you change the value in cell B5.

STUDENT ASSIGNMENT 7: Building a Weekly Payroll Worksheet

Instructions: Load 1-2-3 and perform the following tasks.

1. Build the worksheet illustrated in Figure 4-29. For each employee, use the following formulas to determine the gross pay in column E, federal tax in column F, state tax in column G, and net pay in column H:
   a. If Hours ≤ 40, then Gross Pay = Rate * Hours, otherwise Gross Pay = Rate * Hours + 0.5 * Rate * (Hours – 40).
   b. If (Gross Pay – Dependents * 38.46) > 0, then Federal Tax = 20% * (Gross Pay – Dependents * 38.46), otherwise Federal Tax = 0.
   c. State Tax = 3.2% * Gross Pay.
   d. Net Pay = Gross Pay – (Federal Tax + State Tax).

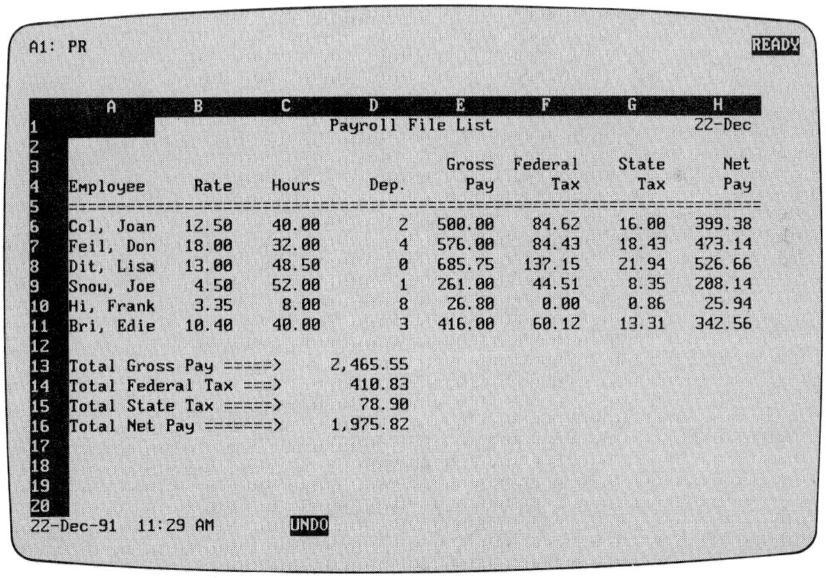
A1: PR READY

	A	B	C	D	E	F	G	H
1				Payroll File List				22-Dec
2								
3					Gross	Federal	State	Net
4	Employee	Rate	Hours	Dep.	Pay	Tax	Tax	Pay
5	==========	=======	=======	=======	=======	=======	=======	=======
6	Col, Joan	12.50	40.00	2	500.00	84.62	16.00	399.38
7	Feil, Don	18.00	32.00	4	576.00	84.43	18.43	473.14
8	Dit, Lisa	13.00	48.50	0	685.75	137.15	21.94	526.66
9	Snow, Joe	4.50	52.00	1	261.00	44.51	8.35	208.14
10	Hi, Frank	3.35	8.00	8	26.80	0.00	0.86	25.94
11	Bri, Edie	10.40	40.00	3	416.00	60.12	13.31	342.56
12								
13	Total Gross Pay =====>			2,465.55				
14	Total Federal Tax ===>			410.83				
15	Total State Tax =====>			78.90				
16	Total Net Pay =======>			1,975.82				
17								
18								
19								
20								

22-Dec-91 11:29 AM UNDO

FIGURE 4-29
Student Assignment 7

2. Use the Range Name Create command to name cells B6, C6, and D6 so that you can use the variable names described in step 1 when you enter the formulas in cells E6, F6, G6, and H6.
3. Protect all the cells in the worksheet except those in the range C6..C11. Try to enter values into the protected cells.
4. Save the worksheet as STUS4-7.
5. Print the worksheet.
6. Print the cell-formulas version of the worksheet.
7. Print the worksheet after formatting all the cells to the Text type.
8. Increase the number of hours worked for each employee by 7.5 hours. Print the worksheet with the new values.

STUDENT ASSIGNMENT 8: Building a Future Value Worksheet

Instructions: Load 1-2-3 and perform the following tasks.

1. Build the worksheet illustrated in Figure 4-30. Set column A to a width of 16 characters and the rest of the columns to a width of 14 characters. Use the Range Name Label command to name B3, B5, E3, and E5. Use the label to the right of each cell in Figure 4-30 as the label name. Determine the future value in cell E5 from the function @FV($Monthly Pymt:, $Rate:/12,12*$Time:). The FV function tells you how much money you will have in a fund if you pay a fixed payment and earn a fixed interest rate over a period of time.

```
E5: (,2) @FV($MONTHLY PYMT:,$RATE:/12,12*$TIME:)                    READY

           A              B              C              D              E
 1                                Crown Annuity Company              22-Dec-91
 2
 3   Monthly Pymt:        200.00                    Time:                 10
 4
 5   Rate:                10.0%                      Future Value:    40,969.00
 6   ======================================================================
 7                        Future         Amount         Interest
 8                Year      Value          Paid           Earned
 9   --------------------------------------------------------------------
10                  1     2,513.11       2,400.00          113.11
11                  2     5,289.38       4,800.00          489.38
12                  3     8,356.36       7,200.00        1,156.36
13                  4    11,744.50       9,600.00        2,144.50
14                  5    15,487.41      12,000.00        3,487.41
15                  6    19,622.26      14,400.00        5,222.26
16                  7    24,190.08      16,800.00        7,390.08
17                  8    29,236.22      19,200.00       10,036.22
18                  9    34,810.74      21,600.00       13,210.74
19                 10    40,969.00      24,000.00       16,969.00
20
22-Dec-91  11:30 AM        UNDO
```

FIGURE 4-30
Student Assignment 8

Determine the values in the table in rows 10 through 19 as follows:

   a. Use the Data Fill command to create the series of numbers in the range A10..A19.
   b. Assign the function @IF(A10< = $Time:,@FV($Monthly Pymt:,$Rate:/12,12*A10),0) to B10 and copy B10 to B11..B19.
   c. Assign the function @IF(A10< = $Time:,12*A10*$Monthly Pymt:,0) to C10 and copy C10 to C11..C19.
   d. Assign the formula +B10–C10 to D10 and copy D10 to D11..D19.
   e. Format the cells in the worksheet as shown in Figure 4-30.

2. Save the worksheet. Use the file name STUS4-8.
3. Determine the future value for the following: monthly payment, 500; rate of interest, 11.5%; time in years, 10.
4. Print the worksheet with the future value for the data described in step 3.
5. Print only the range A1..E5 with the future value for the data described in step 3.

STUDENT ASSIGNMENT 9: Building a Data Table for the Future Value Worksheet

Instructions: Load 1-2-3 and perform the following tasks.

1. Load STUS4-8, the future value worksheet, which you created in Student Assignment 8. This worksheet is illustrated in Figure 4-30. Determine the future value for the following: monthly payment, 1000; rate of interest, 10.5%; time in years, 8.
2. Do the following to create the data table shown in Figure 4-31.
   a. Use the Data Fill command to enter the series of numbers 8.5% to 14.5% in increments of 0.5% in the range F8..F20.
   b. Assign +E5 (future value) to cell G7.
   c. Assign the formula +Future Value:−Time:*12*Monthly Pymt: to cell H7.
   d. Use the command /Data Table 1 (/DT1) to establish the range F7..H20 as a data table.
   e. Enter an input cell value of B5, the interest rate.
   f. Format the data table as shown in Figure 4-31.

```
I20:                                                          READY

        F          G          H          I          J
1 Future Values for Varying Interest Rates
2
3
4          Varying      Future     Interest
5           Rate        Value       Earned
6 ========================================
7                    149,476.47   53,476.47
8           8.5%     136,821.45   40,821.45
9           9.0%     139,856.16   43,856.16
10          9.5%     142,975.19   46,975.19
11         10.0%     146,181.08   50,181.08
12         10.5%     149,476.47   53,476.47
13         11.0%     152,864.08   56,864.08
14         11.5%     156,346.73   60,346.73
15         12.0%     159,927.29   63,927.29
16         12.5%     163,608.76   67,608.76
17         13.0%     167,394.23   71,394.23
18         13.5%     171,286.85   75,286.85
19         14.0%     175,289.93   79,289.93
20         14.5%     179,406.83   83,406.83
22-Dec-91  11:31 AM     UNDO
```

FIGURE 4-31
Student Assignment 9

3. Save the worksheet using the file name STUS4-9.
4. Print the complete worksheet (A1..H20) with the future value for the data described in step 1.

STUDENT ASSIGNMENT 10: Building Macros for the Future Value Worksheet

Instructions: Load 1-2-3 and perform the following tasks.

1. Load STUS4-9, the future value worksheet, which was created in Student Assignments 8 and 9. This worksheet is illustrated in Figures 4-30 and 4-31.
2. Enter the three macros shown in Figure 4-32.

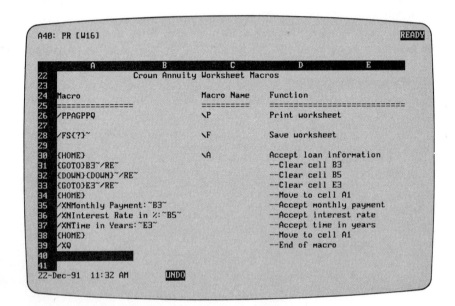

FIGURE 4-32
Student Assignment 10

3. Change the printer range to A1..E19.
4. Use the STEP mode to test each macro. For the \F macro, use the file name STUS4-10. For the \A macro, use the following data: monthly payment, 350; rate of interest, 8%; time in years, 7.
5. Enable cell protection for the worksheet. Unprotect cells B3, B5, E3, and the range F7..H20.
6. Press function key F8 to recalculate the data table.
7. Use the \F command to save the worksheet a second time.
8. Print the complete worksheet (A1..H39) with the future value for the data described in step 4.

STUDENT ASSIGNMENT 11: Building Macros for the Weekly Payroll Worksheet

Instructions: Load 1-2-3 and perform the following tasks.

1. Load STUS4-7, the weekly payroll worksheet, which was created in Student Assignment 7. This worksheet is illustrated in Figure 4-29.
2. Disable cell protection and add macros that will do the following:

   a. Save the worksheet under the file name entered by the user (\S).
   b. Print the range A1..H16 (\P).
   c. Erase the current hours worked and accept the new hours worked (\A).

3. Enable cell protection for the worksheet. Cells C6..C11 should be left unprotected.
4. Use the STEP mode to test each macro. For the save macro, use the file name STUS4-11. For the accept hours worked macro, enter the following hours worked: Col, Joan—36.5; Fiel, Don—42.5; Dit, Lisa—53.5; Snow, Joe—40; Hi, Frank—40; Bri, Edie—61.5.
5. Use the save macro to save the worksheet a second time. Use the file name STUS4-11.
6. Print the worksheet (A1..H16) for the data described in step 4.
7. Print the macros entered in step 2.

PROJECT 5

Graphing with 1-2-3 and Allways

Objectives

You will have mastered the material in this project when you can:

- Create a pie chart
- Create a line graph
- Create a multiple-line graph
- Create a scatter graph
- Create a simple bar graph
- Create a side-by-side bar graph
- Create a stack-bar graph
- Create an XY graph
- Assign multiple graphs to the same worksheet
- Dress up a graph by adding titles and legends
- Save a graph as a PIC file
- Save a worksheet with the graph settings
- Print a graph
- View the current graph and graphs saved on disk
- Use Allways to place a graph alongside the data in a worksheet

As we have seen in the previous four projects, a worksheet is a powerful tool for analyzing data. Sometimes, however, the message you are trying to convey gets lost in the rows and columns of numbers. This is where the graphics capability of 1-2-3 comes in handy. With only a little effort, you can have 1-2-3 create, display, and print a graph of the data in your worksheet and get your message across in a dramatic pictorial fashion. With the Graph command, you can select a pie chart, a line graph, a variety of bar graphs, an XY graph, or a scatter graph. We will study these types of graphs in this project.

We will use the year-end sales analysis worksheet shown in Figure 5-1 to illustrate all the graphs except the XY graph. The worksheet in Figure 5-1 includes the quarter sales for each of six cities in which King's Computer Outlet has a store. Total sales for each quarter and the year are displayed in row 13. The total sales for each of the six cities are displayed in column F.

A1: [W12]					READY
	A	B	C	D	E	F
1		King's Computer Outlet				12/22/91
2		Year-End Sales Analysis				
3						Total
4	City	Quarter 1	Quarter 2	Quarter 3	Quarter 4	Sales
5	=========	=========	=========	=========	=========	=========
6	Chicago	40,135	52,345	38,764	22,908	154,152
7	Tampa	48,812	42,761	34,499	56,123	182,195
8	Atlanta	12,769	15,278	19,265	17,326	64,638
9	Dallas	38,713	29,023	34,786	23,417	125,939
10	Boston	34,215	42,864	38,142	45,375	160,596
11	Oakland	52,912	63,182	57,505	55,832	229,431
12						
13	Total	227,556	245,453	222,961	220,981	916,951
14						
15						

FIGURE 5-1
The year-end sales analysis report we will use to illustrate graphing with 1-2-3.

Before going any further, let's build the worksheet shown in Figure 5-1. As a guide, we will follow the first 23 steps in the list of keystrokes given in the Project Summary section at the end of this project.

THE GRAPH COMMAND

With the worksheet in Figure 5-1 in main memory, the first step in drawing a graph is to enter the command /Graph (/G). The **Graph menu** and the **graph settings sheet** display as shown in Figure 5-2.

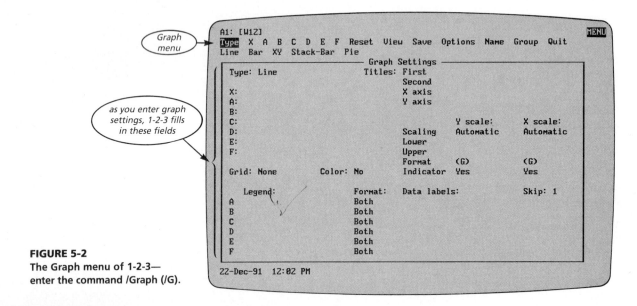

FIGURE 5-2
The Graph menu of 1-2-3—
enter the command /Graph (/G).

The functions of the commands listed in the Graph menu are described in Table 5-1.

TABLE 5-1   A Summary of Commands in the Graph Menu

COMMAND	FUNCTION
Type	Allows you to select the type of graph you want to display—Line, Bar, XY, Stack-bar, Pie.
X	Defines a range of labels for the X axis for a line or bar graph. Defines a range of labels to describe each piece of a pie chart. In an XY graph the X range is assigned the X coordinates.
ABCDEF	Allows you to define up to six Y-axis data ranges. For example, in a multiple-line graph each data range is represented by a line.
Reset	Clears the current graph specifications.
View	Displays the current graph.
Save	Saves the current graph to disk. 1-2-3 automatically adds the extension .PIC to the graph file.
Options	Allows you to define titles or labels for the X and Y axes and for the top of the graph.
Name	Allows you to save a set of graph settings by name. In this way you can have several different graphs associated with the same worksheet.
Group	Allows you to define multiple graph data ranges when the ranges are located in consecutive columns or rows.
Quit	Quits the Graph command.

PIE CHARTS

A pie chart is used to show how 100% of an amount is divided. Let's create the pie chart in Figure 5-3. This pie chart shows the percentage of total annual sales for each of the six cities where King's Computer Outlet has a store.

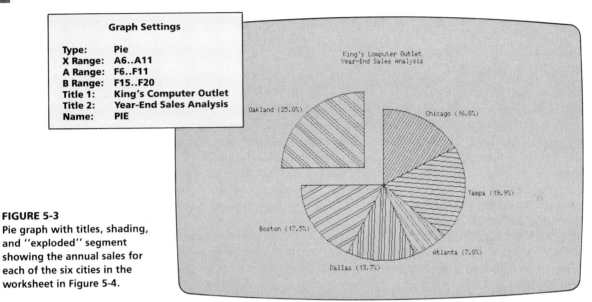

Graph Settings	
Type:	**Pie**
X Range:	**A6..A11**
A Range:	**F6..F11**
B Range:	**F15..F20**
Title 1:	**King's Computer Outlet**
Title 2:	**Year-End Sales Analysis**
Name:	**PIE**

FIGURE 5-3
Pie graph with titles, shading, and "exploded" segment showing the annual sales for each of the six cities in the worksheet in Figure 5-4.

The total annual sales for each of the six stores are in the range F6..F11 of the worksheet in Figure 5-4.

FIGURE 5-4
Ranges specified in the worksheet for the pie graph in Figure 5-3.

To create any graph using 1-2-3, we need to enter the type of graph, the ranges in the worksheet to graph, graph titles, and graph options. Collectively, these are called the **graph settings** and they display on the graph settings sheet when the Graph menu is active. Remember, function key F6 toggles the display between the graph settings sheet and the worksheet when the Graph menu is active.

With the Graph menu on the screen (Figure 5-2), enter the command **T**ype **P**ie (TP). This command tells 1-2-3 that we want to create a pie chart as the current graph. The **current graph** is the one that displays when we enter the command **/G**raph **V**iew (/GV).

Selecting the A Range

After we type the letter P for Pie, the command cursor returns to the Graph menu, the menu that begins with the command Type in Figure 5-2. For a pie chart, we can select only one data range to graph, and it must be assigned as the A range. As shown in Figure 5-4, assign the annual sales for each city (F6..F11) as the A range. Type the letter A. 1-2-3 responds by displaying the prompt message "Enter first data range: A1" on the input line. Enter the range F6..F11 and press the Enter key.

Selecting the X Range

The X range is used to identify each "slice" or segment of the pie. We must select a range that can identify the cells in the A range. Since the A range is equal to the annual sales for each of the six cities, select the names of the cities (A6..A11) to identify each segment of the pie. With the command cursor in the Graph menu, type the letter X. 1-2-3 responds by displaying the prompt message "Enter x-axis range: A1" on the input line. Enter the range A6..A11 and press the Enter key.

After we define the A range and X range, 1-2-3 has enough information to draw a *primitive* pie chart, one that shows the characteristics assigned thus far. With the command cursor in the Graph menu, type the letter V for View and the primitive pie chart in Figure 5-5 displays on the screen. After viewing it, press any key on the keyboard to redisplay the Graph menu and graph settings. Once a range has been assigned you may view the pie chart at any time and make changes if you feel the pie chart is not being drawn the way you want it.

It is the A range that causes the pie in Figure 5-5 to be divided into segments. Each segment is proportionate to the annual sales for each city. The A range is also responsible for the percentage value displayed within parentheses outside each segment. The city names outside each segment of the pie are the labels assigned as the X range.

In certain instances, you may want to assign the same group of cells to both the A and X ranges. When both ranges are assigned the same group of cells, the values in the A range that determine the size of each segment of the pie are also used to identify (label) each segment.

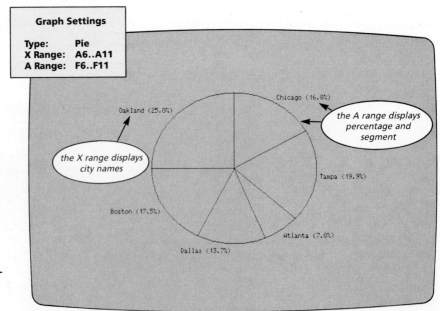

FIGURE 5-5
Primitive pie chart with no titles or shading. Shows the proportion of annual sales contributed by each city in the form of a "slice of the pie."

Selecting the B Range

The B range is used to "dress up" the pie chart and make it more presentable and easier to read. Through the use of the B range, you can create segment shading and *explode* a pie chart. An **exploded pie chart** is one in which one or more segments are offset or slightly removed from the main portion of the pie so that they stand out (Figure 5-3).

The B range is usually set up off to the side or below the worksheet. To shade and explode the pie chart in Figure 5-5 so that it looks more like Figure 5-3, we need to choose six adjacent cells for the B range, one for each pie segment. In each cell, enter a code number between 0 and 7. Each code represents a different type of shading. A code of zero instructs 1-2-3 to leave the corresponding segment of the pie chart unshaded.

Let's use the range F15..F20 to enter the code numbers. The first of the six cells, F15, will refer to the first entry in the A range, Chicago. The last of the six cells will refer to the last entry in the A range, Oakland.

To enter the shading codes, first quit the Graph menu by typing the letter Q. Use function key F5 to move the cell pointer to F15. Enter the shading codes 1 through 5 in the range F15..F19. To explode one or more segments of the pie chart, add 100 to the shading values. Explode the segment representing Oakland by entering the number 106, rather than 6, in cell F20. The six shading codes are shown in the range F15..F20 in Figure 5-4.

Select the range F15..F20 by entering the command /Graph **B** (/GB). Enter the range F15..F20 and press the Enter key. Press the V key to view the pie chart. The pie chart (without titles) displays as shown earlier in Figure 5-3. The pie chart is complete. However, we still have to add graph titles. After viewing the pie chart, press any key to redisplay the Graph menu and graph settings.

Adding a Title to the Pie Chart

To add graph titles above the pie chart, type the letter O for Options. This causes the **Graph Options menu** to display at the top of the screen. With the Graph Options menu on the screen, type the letter T for Titles. We are allowed two title lines—First Line and Second Line—of up to 39 characters each. Type the letter F for First Line. Enter the title—King's Computer Outlet—and press the Enter key. Type the letters T for Titles and S for Second Line. Enter the second line of the title—Year-End Sales Analysis—and press the Enter key.

To quit the Graph Options menu, type the letter Q for Quit. 1-2-3 returns to the Graph menu. The graph settings for the pie chart are complete as shown in Figure 5-6. Type the letter V for View and 1-2-3 displays the pie chart with titles as shown earlier in Figure 5-3. To terminate the View command, press any key on the keyboard and the Graph menu redisplays on the screen.

If the title you plan to use for a graph is identical to one in the worksheet, you can press the Backslash (\) key followed by the cell address in place of the title. For example, we could have entered \C1 for the first title and \C2 for the second title, since the titles are identical to the worksheet titles in cells C1 and C2 (Figure 5-4).

Naming the Pie Chart

With the command cursor in the Graph menu and the pie chart complete, our next step is to name the graph settings. That way we can develop a new graph from the same worksheet and still have the pie chart settings stored away to view and modify at a later time. To assign a name to the graph settings, type the letter N for Name. The **Graph Name menu** displays at the top of the screen as shown in Figure 5-6. Type the letter C for Create. 1-2-3 displays the prompt message "Enter graph name:" on the input line. Enter the name PIE for pie chart and press the Enter key. After assigning the name, 1-2-3 returns control to the Graph menu.

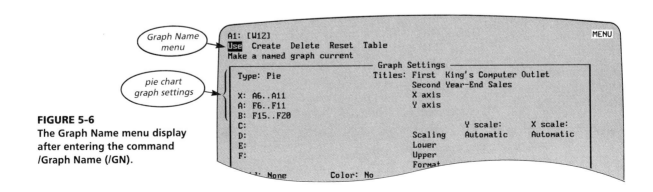

FIGURE 5-6
The Graph Name menu display after entering the command /Graph Name (/GN).

The graph settings shown in Figure 5-6 are now stored under the name PIE. Graph names, like PIE, can be up to 15 characters long and should be as descriptive as possible. Table 5-2 summarizes the commands available in the Graph Name menu.

TABLE 5-2   A Summary of Commands in the Graph Name Menu

COMMAND	FUNCTION
Use	Lists the directory of graph names associated with the current worksheet. Assigns the selected named set of graph settings as the current graph and displays the graph.
Create	Saves the current graph settings as a part of the worksheet so that another graph can be built. This command does not save the graph settings to disk.
Delete	Deletes the named set of graph settings.
Reset	Deletes all graph names and their settings.
Table	Creates a table of named graphs in the worksheet.

The Effect of What-If Analyses on the Pie Chart

Once you have assigned the pie chart settings to the worksheet, any values changed in the worksheet will show up in the pie chart the next time it is drawn. For example, quit the Graph menu and change the sales amount for Quarter 1 for Chicago in cell B6 from 40,135 to 45,550.

With the worksheet on the screen, press Function key F10 to view the pie chart. When the worksheet is displayed on the screen, it is quicker to press the F10 key to display the current graph than it is to enter the command /GV. Compare the displayed pie chart to the one in Figure 5-3. Note that the segments representing all six cities have changed because of the change in the first quarter sales for Chicago. After viewing the pie chart, press any key on the keyboard to return to the worksheet. Before continuing with this project, change the sales amount for Chicago in cell B6 back to 40,135.

Saving the Worksheet with the Pie Chart Graph Settings

When you assign a name, like PIE, to the current set of graph settings using the /GNC command, they are not saved to disk. To save the named graph settings, you must save the worksheet itself using the File Save command. When the /FS command is used, both the current graph settings and any named graph settings are saved with the worksheet. To complete the save, first type the letter Q to quit the Graph menu. When the worksheet reappears on the screen, enter the command /File Save (/FS). When the file name PROJS-5A appears on the input line, press the Enter key. Finally, type the letter R for Replace.

Later, when you retrieve the worksheet, the pie chart settings will be available and you can display or print the pie chart at any time. If you retrieve the worksheet and decide to change any of the pie chart settings, you must save the worksheet again or the latest changes will be lost.

Printing the Pie Chart

Printing a graph is a three-step process: first, save the graph to disk using the command /Graph Save (/GS); second, quit 1-2-3; and third, load the PrintGraph program (PGRAPH) into main computer memory and print the graph. The PrintGraph program allows you to print graphs that have been saved with the /Graph Save (/GS) command.

Let's print the pie chart by following the three steps described in the previous paragraph. With 1-2-3 in READY mode, enter the command /Graph Save (/GS). In response to the prompt message on the input line, enter the file name PIE-5A and press the Enter key. The pie chart (not the worksheet) is saved to disk under the name PIE-5A with an extension of .PIC (picture). We call a graph file, like PIE-5A.PIC, a **PIC file**. With a snapshot of the graph saved, quit the Graph menu and quit 1-2-3.

Our next step is to load the PrintGraph program into main memory. If you have a computer with a fixed disk, then at the DOS prompt enter PGRAPH and press the Enter key. If you have a computer with no fixed disk, replace the 1-2-3 system disk in the A drive with the PrintGraph disk and make sure the disk with PIE-5A.PIC is in the B drive. At the DOS prompt, enter PGRAPH and press the Enter key. After several seconds the **PrintGraph menu** displays on the screen (Figure 5-7). Table 5-3 describes the commands available in the PrintGraph menu.

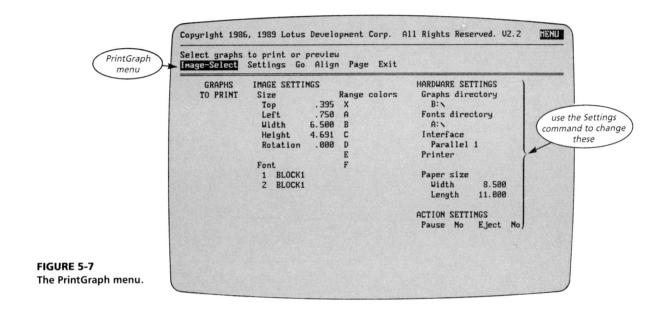

FIGURE 5-7
The PrintGraph menu.

TABLE 5-3 A Summary of Commands in the PrintGraph Menu

COMMAND	FUNCTION
Image-Select	Allows you to specify the graph to print.
Settings	Lets you set the default drive; adjust the size of the graph; select colors, fonts, and the hardware.
Go	Starts printing the graph.
Align	Resets the PrintGraph line counter.
Page	Ejects the paper in the printer to the top of the next page.
Exit	Ends the PrintGraph session.

With the PrintGraph menu on the screen, type the letter I for Image-Select. PrintGraph displays the **Image-Select menu** (Figure 5-8). This menu includes a list of all the PIC files on the default drive. Use the Up Arrow and Down Arrow keys to highlight the one to print. In our case, there is only one PIC file and it is highlighted. Press the Enter key to select PIE-5A. The PrintGraph menu shown in Figure 5-7 redisplays on the screen.

Check the printer to be sure it is in the READY mode. Type the letters A for Align and G for Go. The pie chart prints on the printer. Type the letter P for Page to advance the paper to the top of the next page. If the graph fails to print properly, refer to the section entitled "Solving PrintGraph Problems" in the Lotus 1-2-3 Release 2.2 reference manual.

To the right of the list of PIC files in the Image-Select menu in Figure 5-8 are instructions explaining how to select a graph from the list. The Space bar is used to mark or unmark the highlighted graph in the list. A graph name that is marked has a number sign (#) displayed to the left of the name. All marked graph names print when you use the Go command in the PrintGraph menu. Hence, when you print a second graph, you should unmark the previous one or it will print also.

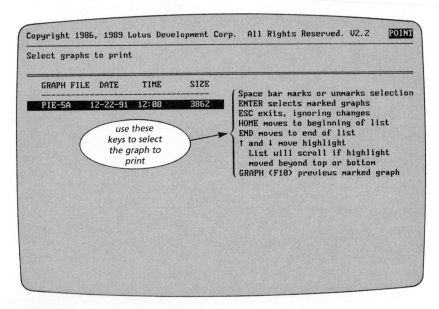

FIGURE 5-8 The Image-Select menu.

The GRAPH key is the function key F10. You may press this key to display the highlighted graph on the screen. When you are finished viewing the graph, press any key to return to the Image-Select menu.

To quit PrintGraph, type the letter E for Exit and Y for Yes to confirm your exit from the PrintGraph program. At the DOS prompt, type 123 to reenter the spreadsheet program.

LINE GRAPHS

Line graphs are used to show changes in data over time. For example, a line graph can show pictorially whether sales increased or decreased during quarters of the year. The lines are drawn on X and Y axes. You can have from one to six lines in the graph. Each line represents a different data range in the worksheet. We will create two line graphs, one with a single data range and another with six data ranges.

First we will create a line graph with a single data range that shows the trend of the total sales for the four quarters (Figure 5-9). Begin by resetting the current graph settings associated with PROJS-5A. That is, clear the pie chart—the current graph—to begin the line graph because the settings are different.

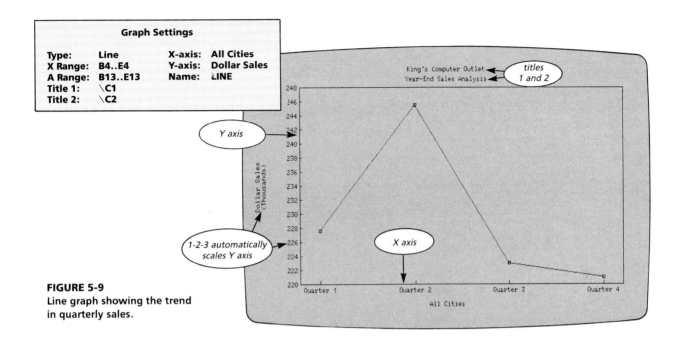

FIGURE 5-9
Line graph showing the trend in quarterly sales.

With the Graph menu on the screen, type the letter R for Reset. The **Graph Reset menu** displays at the top of the screen as shown in Figure 5-10. Note that the graph settings can be reset on an individual basis (X, A, B, C, D, E, F) or for the entire graph (Graph). In this case, reset all the graph settings. With the command cursor in the Graph Reset menu, type the letter G for Graph. The pie chart settings disappear from the screen since it is no longer the current graph. Remember, however, that the pie chart settings are stored under the name PIE and can be accessed at any time using the /**G**raph **N**ame **U**se (/GNU) command (Table 5-2).

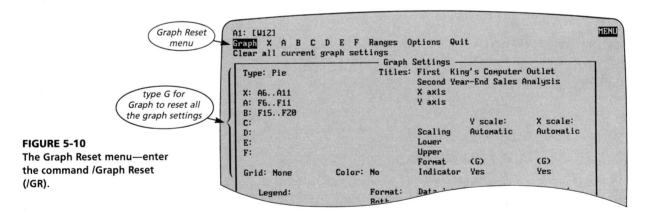

FIGURE 5-10
The Graph Reset menu—enter the command /Graph Reset (/GR).

The command cursor returns to the Graph menu after erasing the pie chart settings. We can now proceed to build the line graph in Figure 5-9. There are four steps involved:

1. With the Graph menu on the screen, enter the command **T**ype **L**ine (TL).
2. Define the X range—the cells that contain the desired labels for the X axis.
3. Define the A range—the cells that include the values that the line graph will represent.
4. Enter the title of the line graph and titles for the X and Y axes.

Selecting the X Range

With the command cursor in the Graph menu, type the letter X and assign the range B4..E4 to the X range. As shown in Figure 5-11, cells B4 through E4 contain the labels Quarter 1, Quarter 2, Quarter 3, and Quarter 4. These labels display along the X axis in the line graph (Figure 5-9).

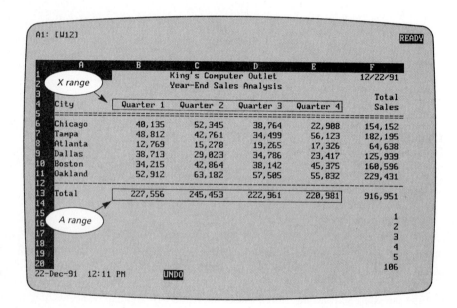

FIGURE 5-11
Range settings for line graph in
Figure 5-9.

Selecting the A Range

The next step is to select the A range. Assign to the A range the cells that include the values we want the line graph to represent. This is also called the **Y-axis data range**. With the command cursor in the Graph menu, type the letter A and enter the range B13..E13. The desired A range is shown in the worksheet in Figure 5-11.

Adding Titles to the Line Graph

We can add three different titles to the line graph: (1) line graph title (we are allowed two of these); (2) X-axis title; (3) Y-axis title. Let's add the same line graph title used for the pie chart. For the X axis use the title "All Cities". For the Y axis use the title "Dollar Sales".

To add these titles, type the letter O for Options while the Graph menu is on the screen. The Graph Options menu shown in Figure 5-12 displays. Type the letters T for Titles and F for First. Enter \C1 and press the Enter key. \C1 instructs 1-2-3 to use the label assigned to cell C1 in the worksheet as the first title. Next, type the letters T and S to enter the second title. Enter \C2 and press the Enter key. The label in cell C2 serves as the second title.

Enter the X-axis title by typing the letters T and X and the label "All Cities". Press the Enter key. Enter the Y-axis title by typing the letters T and Y and the label "Dollar Sales". Press the Enter key. Finally, type the letter Q to quit the Graph Options menu.

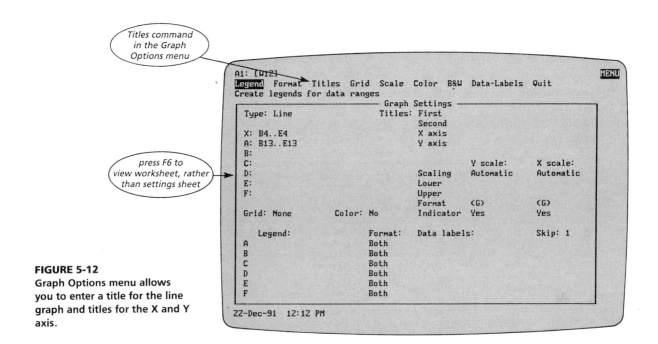

FIGURE 5-12
Graph Options menu allows
you to enter a title for the line
graph and titles for the X and Y
axis.

Viewing the Line Graph

With the command cursor in the Graph menu, type the letter V for View. The line graph previously shown in Figure 5-9 displays. Note that 1-2-3 automatically scales the numeric labels along the Y axis on the basis of the numbers in the A range. The small squares that the line graph passes through represent the points whose coordinates are the corresponding values in the X and A ranges.

You can see from Figure 5-9 that the line graph is useful for showing a trend. The line graph clearly shows that sales for King's Computer Outlet increased significantly during the second quarter and then fell sharply in the third quarter. Finally, there was a slight drop in sales during the fourth quarter. Here again, if we change any numeric values in the worksheet, the line graph will show the latest values the next time we invoke the View command.

After viewing the graph, press any key to redisplay the Graph menu.

Naming the Line Graph

With the line graph complete and the command cursor active in the Graph menu, type the letters N for Name and C for Create. When 1-2-3 requests the graph name, enter the name LINE and press the Enter key. The line graph settings are stored under the name LINE.

Saving and Printing the Line Graph

To save the named graph settings (LINE) with the worksheet to disk, type the letter Q to quit the Graph menu. Enter the command /File Save (/FS). Press the Enter key when the file name PROJS-5A appears on the input line. Type the letter R for Replace to rewrite the file to disk. Now there are two sets of graph settings associated with PROJS-5A—PIE and LINE. The line graph continues to be the current graph.

Make a hard copy of the line graph in the same manner described for the pie chart. That is, with the command cursor in the Graph menu, type the letter S for Save and name the graph LINE-5A. Quit the Graph menu and quit 1-2-3. At the DOS prompt, enter PGRAPH. When the PrintGraph menu displays, type the letter I for Image-Select and select the PIC file LINE-5A. Turn the printer on, type A for Align, G for Go, and P for Page. When the printing activity is complete, quit PrintGraph, load 1-2-3, and retrieve PROJS-5A.

Multiple-Line Graphs

1-2-3 allows up to six Y-axis data ranges (A–F) and the range of corresponding labels (X) to be assigned to a line graph. When more than one data range is assigned to a line graph, it is called a **multiple-line graph**. The multiple-line graph in Figure 5-13 includes six lines, each representing the four quarterly sales for one of the six cities in the worksheet. Multiple-line graphs like this one are used not only to show trends, but also to compare one range of data to another.

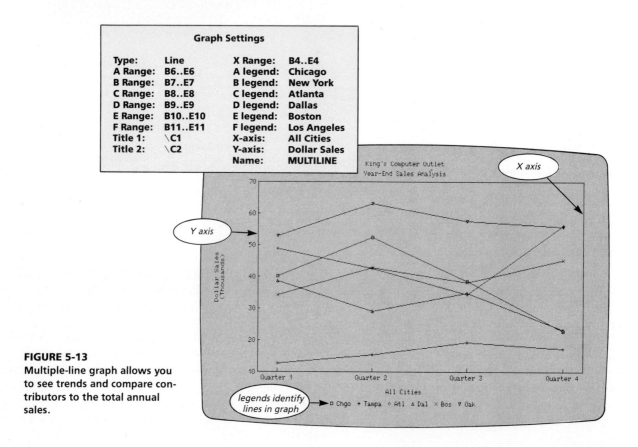

FIGURE 5-13
Multiple-line graph allows you to see trends and compare contributors to the total annual sales.

The multiple-line graph in Figure 5-13 uses the same titles, X range, and graph type as the line graph in Figure 5-9, the current graph associated with the worksheet. Therefore, rather than resetting the current graph settings, modify them.

Selecting the Data Ranges One at a Time

With the command cursor active in the Graph menu, assign to the six data ranges A through F the quarterly sales of the six cities shown in Figure 5-14. Type the letter A for the A range. Enter the range B6..E6 and press the Enter key. Follow the same procedure for the other five ranges—assign the B range B7..E7, the C range B8..E8, the D range B9..E9, the E range B10..E10, and the F range B11..E11.

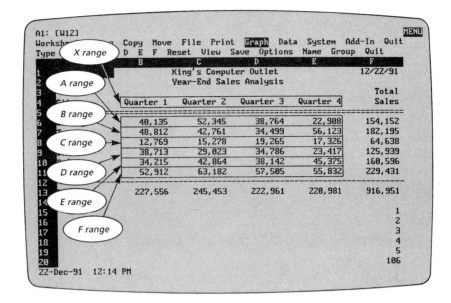

FIGURE 5-14
Multiple-line graph range settings.

Selecting the Data Ranges as a Group

If the majority of the data ranges are in adjacent rows or adjacent columns, you can use the Group command in the Graph menu (Figure 5-2) to select all the data ranges at once, rather than one by one, as we did in the previous section. In Figure 5-14, the data ranges A through F are in adjacent rows, and the X range is separated from the rest of the data ranges by row 5. Let's use the Group command to assign the range B5..E11 to X through F, and then let's change the X range to B4..E4.

With the Graph menu active, type the letter G for Group. 1-2-3 responds by prompting you to enter the range. Enter B5..E11 and press the Enter key. 1-2-3 then asks if the selected range should be assigned by columns or rows to the data ranges. Since Figure 5-14 shows that the data ranges are in rows, type the letter R. 1-2-3 responds by assigning X range B5..E5, A range B6..E6, B range B7..E7, C range B8..E8, D range B9..E9, E range B10..E10, and F range B11..E11. To complete the selection, we need to change the X range. With the Graph menu still on the screen, type the letter X. Change the X range to B4..E4.

This alternative method for selecting the data ranges saves time because we can assign all the data ranges with two commands, instead of seven.

Assigning Legends to the Data Ranges

Before quiting the Graph menu, we need to enter **legends** that help identify each of the six lines that are drawn in the multiple-line graph. Without legends, the multiple-line graph is useless because we cannot identify the lines.

To enter the legend that identifies the A range, type the letters O for Options, L for Legend, and A for A range. From Figure 5-14 we can determine that the A range was assigned the quarterly sales for Chicago (B6..E6). Therefore, enter the label Chgo in response to the prompt message "Enter legend for A range:" on the input line. Assign the abbreviated city names as the legends for the B through F ranges as described at the top of Figure 5-13.

Viewing the Multiple-Line Graph

Next, type the letter V for View and the multiple-line graph illustrated in Figure 5-13 displays on the screen. The six lines in the graph show the trend in quarterly sales for each of the six cities. The graph also allows us to compare the sales for the six cities. To identify the line that represents a particular city, scan the legends at the bottom of the graph in Figure 5-13. Before each abbreviated city name is a special character called a **symbol**, like the square for Chicago. The line that passes through the square in the graph represents Chicago's four quarterly sales. After viewing the multiple-line graph, press any key to return control to the Graph menu.

Naming the Multiple-Line Graph

To assign a name to the multiple-line graph specifications, type the letters N for Name and C for Create. When 1-2-3 requests the graph name, enter the name MULTLINE and press the Enter key. The multiple-line graph settings are stored under the name MULTLINE.

There are now three graphs associated with the worksheet—PIE, LINE, and MULTLINE. However, there is only one current graph. At this point, the current graph is the multiple-line graph, because it was the last one created.

Saving and Printing the Multiple-Line Graph

Type Q to quit the Graph menu. The worksheet in Figure 5-1 reappears on the screen. Save the worksheet. This ensures that the graph settings under the name MULTLINE are saved with the worksheet on disk. Enter the command /**F**ile **S**ave (/FS). When the file name PROJS-5A appears on the input line, press the Enter key. Type the letter R to replace the old version of PROJS-5A with the new one.

After saving the worksheet, enter the command /**G**raph **S**ave (/GS) to save the multiple-line graph as a PIC file using the name MLINE-5A. Quit the graph menu and quit 1-2-3. At the DOS prompt enter PGRAPH. Follow the steps for printing a graph outlined earlier.

Scatter Graphs

A **scatter graph** displays the points (symbols) in a graph without any connecting lines. Sometimes a scatter graph is better able to illustrate what a multiple-line graph is attempting to show. To create the scatter graph shown in Figure 5-15, we need only instruct 1-2-3 not to connect the symbols with lines in the multiple-line graph. Remember, the multiple-line graph is still the current graph.

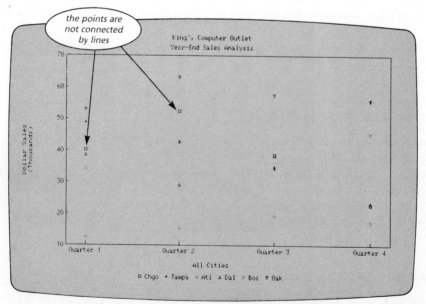

FIGURE 5-15 The scatter graph is an alternative to the multiple-line graph.

Changing the Multiple-Line Graph to a Scatter Graph   With the Graph menu on the screen, type the letter O for Options, F for Format, and G for Graph. The default setting for the Format Graph command is Both. This means that both lines and symbols are displayed for the current multiple-line graph. Change this to Symbols so that only the symbols are displayed. Type the letter S for Symbols. Finally, type the letter Q twice, once to quit the Format section of the Graph Options menu and once to quit the Graph Options menu.

Viewing the Scatter Graph   Type the letter V and the original multiple-line graph (Figure 5-13) displays as a scatter graph (Figure 5-15). Here again, the symbols are identified by the legends displayed below the scatter graph. Press any key to redisplay the Graph menu.

Naming, Saving, and Printing the Scatter Graph   To assign a name to the scatter graph settings, type the letters N for Name and C for Create. When 1-2-3 requests the graph name, enter the name SCATTER and press the Enter key. Type the letter Q to quit the Graph menu and save the worksheet to disk using the File Save command. Now there are four graphs associated with the worksheet—PIE, LINE, MULTLINE, and SCATTER.

  To print the scatter graph, first save it as a PIC file using the /Graph Save (/GS) command and the filename SCAT-5A. Next, quit 1-2-3 and use PGRAPH to print the PIC file SCAT-5A.

BAR GRAPHS

Т he **bar graph** is the most popular business graphic. It is used to show trends and comparisons. The bar graph is similar to a line graph, except that a bar rather than a point on a line represents the Y-axis value for each X-axis value. Unlike the line graph that shows a continuous transition from one point to the next, the bar graph emphasizes the magnitude of the value it represents.

  We will discuss three types of bar graphs: simple bar graphs, side-by-side bar graphs, and stack-bar graphs. The following examples change the preceding line graphs to bar graphs. The range settings, titles, and legends remain the same.

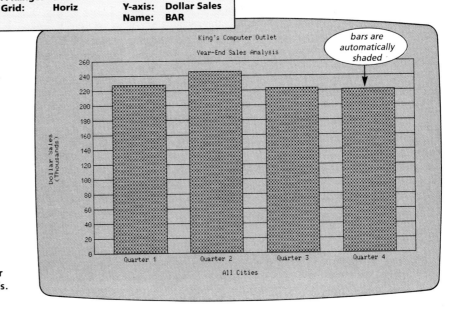

Graph Settings			
Type:	Bar	**Title 1:**	\C1
X Range:	B4..E4	**Title 2:**	\C2
A Range:	B13..E13	**X-axis:**	**All Cities**
Grid:	Horiz	**Y-axis:**	**Dollar Sales**
		Name:	**BAR**

Simple Bar Graphs

A **simple bar graph** has a single bar for each value in the X range. The graph settings for a bar graph are similar to those for a line graph. Let's create the bar graph in Figure 5-16. It is a bar graph of the same data used earlier for the line graph shown in Figure 5-9. Recall that the line graph showed the trend in total sales for the four quarters.

FIGURE 5-16
A simple bar chart is useful for comparing and showing trends.

Using a Named Graph   The first step in creating the bar graph is to assign the line graph settings stored under the graph name LINE as the current graph. Therefore, with the Graph menu on the screen, type the letters N for Name and U for Use. 1-2-3 displays an alphabetized list of all the graph names associated with worksheet PROJS-5A—LINE, MULTLINE, PIE, and SCATTER. With the command cursor on the name LINE, press the Enter key. The line graph shown earlier in Figure 5-9 immediately displays on the screen. Press any key on the keyboard and the Graph menu reappears. The graph settings for the line graph (LINE) now represent the current graph.

Changing the Line Graph to a Bar Graph   With the Graph menu on the screen, type the letters T for Type and B for Bar. The current graph is now a bar graph, rather than a line graph. To improve the appearance of the bar graph and make it easier to read, add a horizontal grid. Type the letter O for Options. With the Graph Options menu displayed, type the letters G for Grid and H for Horizontal. Quit the Graph Options menu by typing the letter Q for Quit.

Viewing the Simple Bar Graph   Type the letter V for View. The simple bar graph shown in Figure 5-16 displays on the screen. Note that it gives a more static view of the total sales for each quarter as compared to the line graph in Figure 5-9. The horizontal grid in the simple bar graph makes it easier to recognize the magnitude of the bars that are not adjacent to the Y axis. When you are finished viewing the graph, press any key on the keyboard. The Graph menu reappears on the screen.

Naming, Saving, and Printing the Simple Bar Graph   To name the simple bar graph, type the letters N for Name and C for Create. Enter the graph name BAR and press the Enter key. Type the letter Q to quit the Graph menu. Use the command /File Save (/FS) to save the worksheet to disk. Press the Enter key when the file name PROJS-5A appears on the input line. Next, press the letter R to replace PROJS-5A on disk with the latest version. Now there are five graphs associated with the worksheet—PIE, LINE, MULTLINE, SCATTER, and BAR.

Save the simple bar graph as a PIC file by entering the command /Graph Save (/GS). When 1-2-3 requests a file name, enter BAR-5A and press the Enter key. Use PrintGraph to print the bar graph.

Side-by-Side Bar Graphs

Like a line graph, a bar graph can have from one to six independent bars (data ranges) for each value in the X range. When a bar graph has more than one bar per X value, we call it a **side-by-side bar graph** (Figure 5-17). This type of graph is primarily used to compare data. For example, you might want to compare the sales in each quarter for Oakland to the sales of the rest of the cities.

Using a Named Graph   To create a side-by-side bar graph, let's assign the graph name MULTLINE as the current graph. With the command cursor in the Graph menu, type the letters N for Name and U for Use. When the list of named graphs display on the screen, select the name MULTLINE and press the Enter key. The multiple-line graph displays on the screen and is assigned to the worksheet as the current graph. Press any key to redisplay the Graph menu.

Changing the Multiple-Line Graph to a Side-by-Side Bar Graph   Change the current graph from a multiple-line graph to a side-by-side bar graph by typing the letters T for Type and B for Bar. All the other graph settings (A–F ranges, titles, and legends) remain the same. Add the horizontal grid, as we did earlier with the simple bar graph, by typing the letters O for Options, G for Grid, and H for Horizontal. Quit the Graph Options menu by typing the letter Q.

Viewing the Side-by-Side Bar Graph   Type the letter V for View. The side-by-side bar graph shown in Figure 5-17 displays on the screen. The different shading that you see for each bar (data range) is automatically done by 1-2-3. The legends below the graph indicate which shaded bar corresponds to which city. Compare Figure 5-17 to Figure 5-13. The side-by-side bar graph is much easier to interpret than the multiple-line graph. For example, it is clear that Oakland had the greatest sales during the first three quarters. For the fourth quarter, Oakland had about the same sales as Tampa. After viewing the graph, press any key to redisplay the Graph menu.

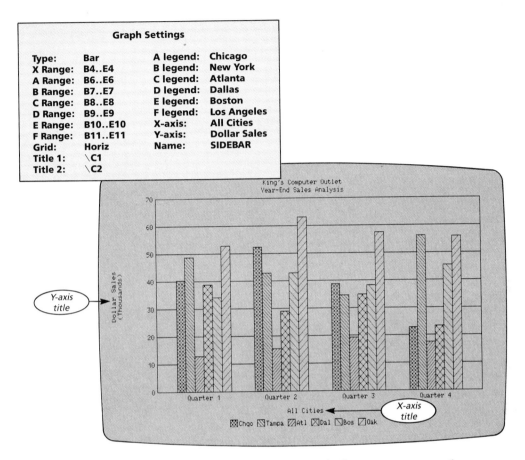

Graph Settings

Type:	Bar	A legend:	Chicago
X Range:	B4..E4	B legend:	New York
A Range:	B6..E6	C legend:	Atlanta
B Range:	B7..E7	D legend:	Dallas
C Range:	B8..E8	E legend:	Boston
D Range:	B9..E9	F legend:	Los Angeles
E Range:	B10..E10	X-axis:	All Cities
F Range:	B11..E11	Y-axis:	Dollar Sales
Grid:	Horiz	Name:	SIDEBAR
Title 1:	\C1		
Title 2:	\C2		

FIGURE 5-17 A side-by-side bar graph allows you to compare the sales in each city on a quarterly basis.

Naming, Saving, and Printing the Side-by-Side Bar Graph   With the Graph menu on the screen, type the letters N for Name and C for Create to name the side-by-side bar graph. Enter the graph name SIDEBAR and press the Enter key. Next, type the letter Q to quit the Graph menu.

Use the command /**F**ile **S**ave (/FS) to save the worksheet to disk. Press the Enter key when the file name PROJS-5A appears on the input line. Finally, type the letter R for Replace. Now there are six graphs associated with the worksheet—PIE, LINE, MULTLINE, SCATTER, BAR, and SIDEBAR.

With the worksheet on the screen, enter the command /**G**raph **S**ave (/GS) to save the side-by-side bar graph as a PIC file. Use the file name MBAR-5A. Quit 1-2-3 and load PrintGraph into main memory. Type the letter I for Image-Select and highlight MBAR-5A. Press the Enter key and the PrintGraph menu redisplays. Type the letters A for Align and G for Go. The side-by-side bar graph shown in Figure 5-17 prints on the printer.

Stack-Bar Graphs

One of the problems with the side-by-side bar graph in Figure 5-17 is that it does not show the combined total sales for the six cities for any quarter. An alternative graph to consider is the stack-bar graph. A **stack-bar graph** has a single bar for every value in the X range (Figure 5-18). Each bar is made up of shaded segments. Each segment or piece of the total bar represents an element (city) as a distinct contributor. Together, the stacked segments make up a single bar that shows the cumulative amount (total quarterly sales) of all elements for each value in the X range (quarter).

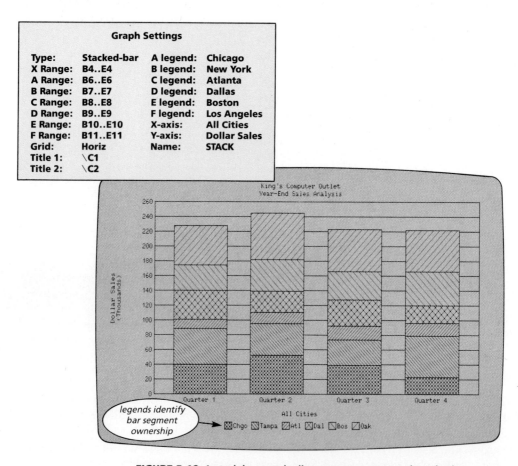

FIGURE 5-18 A stack-bar graph allows you to compare the sales in each city on a quarterly basis. It also shows the total sales for each quarter.

Changing the Side-by-Side Bar Graph to a Stack-Bar Graph   The side-by-side bar graph is still the current graph associated with the worksheet. Therefore, let's modify it to display the stack-bar graph shown in Figure 5-18. With the Graph menu on the screen, enter the command **T**ype **S**tack-bar (TS). This command changes the side-by-side bar graph (Figure 5-17) to a stack-bar graph (Figure 5-18). All the other side-by-side bar graph settings (A–F ranges, titles, horizontal grid, and legends) remain the same for the stack-bar graph.

Viewing the Stack-Bar Graph   Type the letter V for View. The stack-bar graph shown in Figure 5-18 displays on the screen. Compare Figure 5-18 to Figure 5-17. Notice how the stack-bar graph shows both the quarterly contributions of each city and the total sales for each quarter. The stack-bar graph is an effective way of showing trends and contributions from all segments, while still showing a total for each quarter.

Naming, Saving, and Printing the Stack-Bar Graph   With the stack-bar graph still on the screen, press any key to redisplay the Graph menu. Type the letters N for Name and C for Create to name the stack-bar graph. Enter the graph name STACK and press the Enter key. Quit the Graph menu by typing the letter Q.

Save the worksheet to disk. Enter the command /**F**ile **S**ave (/FS). Press the Enter key when the file name PROJS-5A appears on the input line. Press the letter R for Replace. Now there are seven graphs associated with the worksheet—PIE, LINE, MULTLINE, SCATTER, BAR, SIDEBAR, and STACK.

Save the stack-bar graph as a PIC file by entering the command /**G**raph **S**ave (/GS). Use the file name SBAR-5A. Finally, use PrintGraph to print the stack-bar graph.

ADDITIONAL GRAPH OPTIONS

hree graph options that we did not cover in this project are the Data-Labels, Scale, and Color/B&W commands.

Data-Labels

Data-labels are used to explicitly label a bar or a point in a graph. Select the actual values in the range that the bar or point represents. 1-2-3 then positions the labels near the corresponding points or bars in the graph (Figure 5-19).

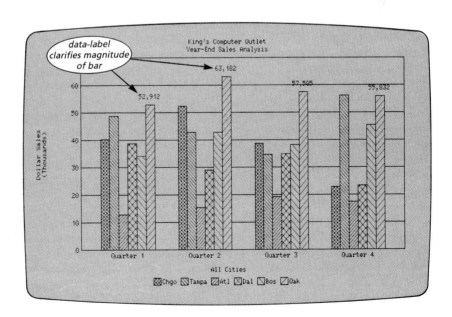

FIGURE 5-19
Data-labels are useful for clarifying and emphasizing various segments of the graph.

To illustrate the use of data-labels, make the SIDEBAR graph settings the current graph by entering the command **/Graph Name Use (/GNU)**. When the alphabetized list of named graphs display on the screen (Figure 5-20), use the Down Arrow key to select SIDEBAR and press the Enter key. 1-2-3 immediately displays the side-by-side bar graph shown in Figure 5-17. Press any key on the keyboard and the Graph menu reappears on the screen.

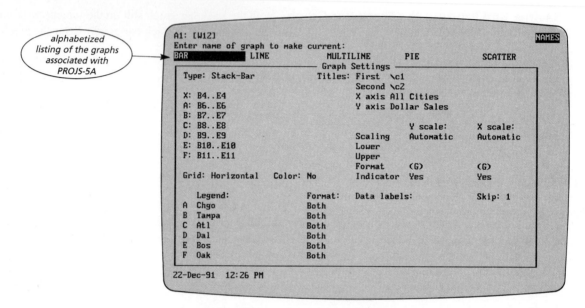

FIGURE 5-20 Directory of named graphs associated with the worksheet PROJS-5A—enter the command /Graph Name Use (/GNU).

Let's emphasize the four bars in Figure 5-17 that represent the quarterly sales for Oakland by displaying the actual quarterly sales above each corresponding bar. Enter the command **Options Data-Labels (OD)**. This command causes the **Data Labels menu** to display.

Type the letter F to select the F range because it was assigned the range representing the four quarterly sales for Oakland. The worksheet reappears on the screen and 1-2-3 responds with the prompt message "Enter data label for F range data: A1". Type the range B11..E11 and press the Enter key. The range B11..E11 contains the four quarterly sales for Oakland. Therefore, we are selecting the same range for the F data-label that we selected earlier for the F range.

After we press the Enter key, 1-2-3 prompts us to enter the desired position of the data-labels in the graph. A response to this prompt is only possible for line and XY graphs. For simple and side-by-side bar graphs, 1-2-3 automatically positions data-labels above each bar. Hence, press the Enter key. Next, type the letter Q twice, once to quit the Data-Labels section of the Graph Options menu and once to quit the Graph Options menu. Finally, type the letter V for View. The modified side-by-side bar graph in Figure 5-19 displays on the screen. Notice how the data-labels above the four bars representing Oakland emphasize and clarify them in the graph.

Press any key to redisplay the Graph menu. Type the letter Q to quit the Graph menu. The worksheet shown earlier in Figure 5-1 displays again on the screen.

Scale Command

When you build a graph, 1-2-3 automatically adjusts the graph to include all points in each data range. The Scale command in the Graph Options menu may be used to override 1-2-3 and manually set the scale on the X or Y axis or both. This command may also be used to specify the display of labels on the X axis and to format the numbers that mark the X and Y axis.

Color/B&W Commands

If your monitor can display colors, the Color command in the Graph Options menu causes bars, lines, and symbols to display in contrasting colors. Alternatively, the B&W command causes the bar and stack-bar graphs to have crosshatched patterns. The Color and B&W commands are mutually exclusive.

XY GRAPHS

X Y graphs differ from the graphs we have discussed thus far. Rather than graphing the magnitude of a value at a fixed point on the X axis, an XY graph plots points of the form (x,y), where x is the X-axis coordinate and y is the Y-axis coordinate. Adjacent points are connected by a line to form the graph (Figure 5-21). The XY graph is the type of graph used to plot mathematical functions.

In an XY graph, both the X and Y axes are automatically scaled relative to the low and high values, so that all (x,y) points display and the graph fits on the screen. You can switch to manual scaling and scale either the X or Y axis yourself (use the Scale command).

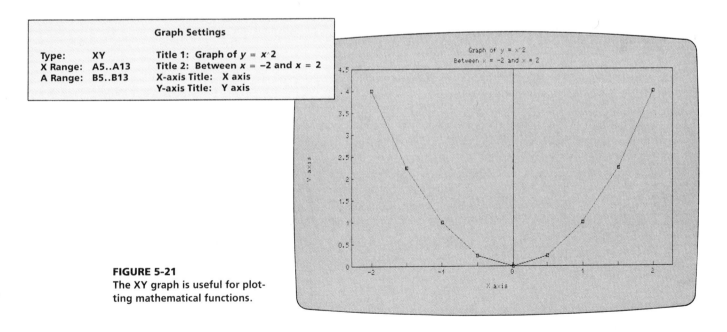

Graph Settings

Type:	XY	Title 1: Graph of $y = x^2$
X Range:	A5..A13	Title 2: Between $x = -2$ and $x = 2$
A Range:	B5..B13	X-axis Title: X axis
		Y-axis Title: Y axis

FIGURE 5-21
The XY graph is useful for plotting mathematical functions.

To illustrate an XY graph, we will use the worksheet in Figure 5-22. As the title indicates, this worksheet includes a table of x and y coordinates for the function $y = x^2$. The x coordinates are in the range A5..A13. They begin at –2 and end at 2 in increments of 0.5. The x coordinates are formed in the worksheet by using the Data Fill command. The y coordinates are determined by assigning the formula $+A5^2$ to cell B5 and then copying B5 to the range B6..B13. Enter the worksheet in Figure 5-22 by following the first seven steps in the second list of keystrokes in the Project Summary section.

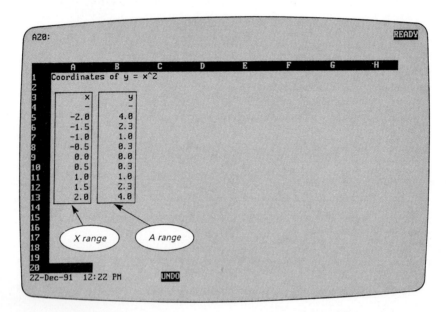

FIGURE 5-22 The worksheet we will use to plot the function $y = x^2$.

To plot the function $y = x^2$ in the form of an XY graph, enter the command /Graph **T**ype **XY** (/GTX). Next, type the letter X to define the X range. Assign the X range the x coordinates (cells A5 through A13). Type the letter A to define the A range. Assign the A range the y coordinates (cells B5 through B13).

To complete the XY graph, let's dress it up using the Graph Options menu. Assign "Graph of $y = x^2$" to the first line of the title and assign "Between x = –2 and x = 2" to the second line. Label the X axis as "X axis" and the Y axis as "Y axis". Type the letter Q to quit the Graph Options menu.

With the command cursor in the Graph menu, type the letter V for View. The XY graph shown on the previous page in Figure 5-21 displays on the screen. To return to the Graph menu after viewing the graph, press any key on the keyboard.

Quit the Graph menu and save the worksheet shown in Figure 5-22 as PROJS-5B. Print the XY graph in Figure 5-21 by saving it as a PIC file using the file name XYGRAPH.PIC. Finally, quit 1-2-3 and use PrintGraph to print the XY graph.

ADDING A GRAPH TO THE WORKSHEET USING ALLWAYS

In the previous sections, we printed the graph independent of the worksheet by using PrintGraph. In this section we will demonstrate how to use the add-in program Allways to place a graph alongside the data in a worksheet, and how to print the graph and data in the same report. Allways allows you to add up to 20 graphs in a worksheet and you can place them wherever you like. Once a graph is part of the worksheet, you can enhance its appearance by resizing it, shading its background, changing the graph title to a larger font, or drawing a box around the graph. To illustrate how to add a graph to the worksheet, we will place the graph of $y = x^2$ next to the table of coordinates in the worksheet as shown in Figure 5-23.

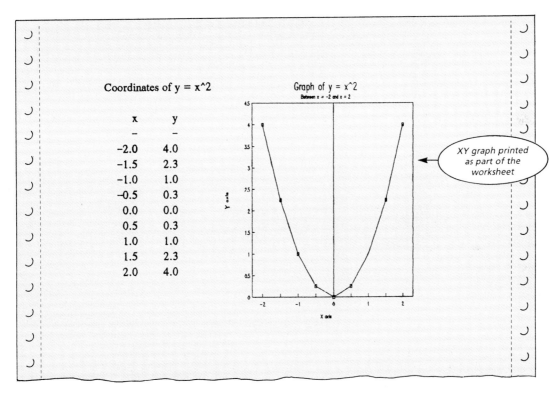

FIGURE 5-23 The XY graph included in the worksheet through the use of the Allways command **/Graph Add (/GA)**.

Starting Allways

With the worksheet in Figure 5-22 on the screen and the XY graph saved under the name XYGRAPH.PIC, enter the command **/Add-In Invoke (/AI)**. Select the add-in program Allways and press the Enter key. The worksheet with the table of coordinates shown earlier in Figure 5-21 displays on the screen in graphics form, rather than in text form.

Adding the Graph to the Worksheet

Enter the Allways command /**G**raph (/G). The Graph menu displays as shown in the top screen of Figure 5-24. Type the letter A for Add. Allways displays a list of the PIC files on the default drive. Select XYGRAPH and press the Enter key. Allways prompts you to enter the range of cells where you want the graph to appear in the worksheet. Enter the range D1..H13 and press the Enter key. Allways responds by crosshatching the range to indicate where the graph will display (bottom screen of Figure 5-24).

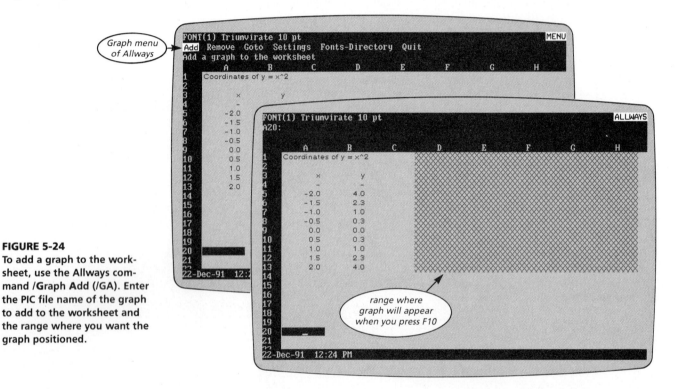

FIGURE 5-24
To add a graph to the worksheet, use the Allways command /**G**raph **A**dd (/GA). Enter the PIC file name of the graph to add to the worksheet and the range where you want the graph positioned.

Press the F10 key to display the graph (Figure 5-25), rather than the crosshatched design. The F10 key serves as a toggle key. Press it once and the graph appears in the specified range. Press it again and the crosshatched design appears in place of the graph. The advantage of displaying the crosshatched design in the range is that Allways redisplays the worksheet faster when you are enhancing it because Allways does not have to continually redraw the graph.

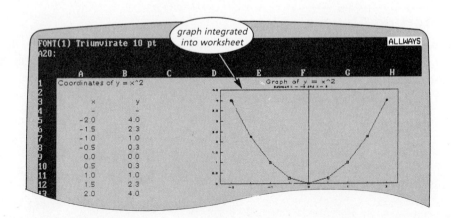

FIGURE 5-25
Press the F10 key to display the XYGRAPH.PIC graph in the specified range of the worksheet.

Compare the graph in Figure 5-25 to the one in Figure 5-21. Note that Allways automatically sizes the graph in Figure 5-25 so that it fits in the specified range.

Before we print the worksheet, let's change the table of coordinates font to Times 14 point and resize the graph.

Changing the Font

Press the Home key to move the cell pointer to A1. Enter the Allways command /**F**ormat **F**ont (/FF). Select Times 14 point from the menu of fonts. Press the Enter key. Next, select the entire table of coordinates (A1..B13) and press the Enter key. The table of coordinates display in Times 14-point font as shown in Figure 5-26.

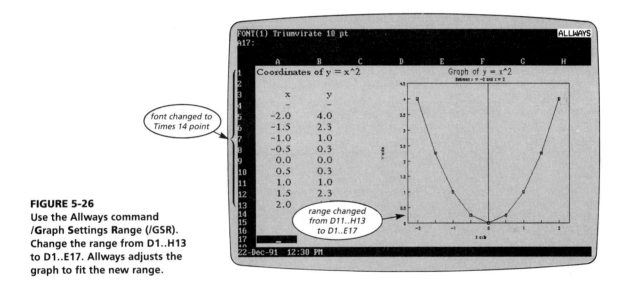

FIGURE 5-26
Use the Allways command
/Graph Settings Range (/GSR).
Change the range from D1..H13
to D1..E17. Allways adjusts the
graph to fit the new range.

Resizing the Graph

Once the graph displays in the worksheet, you can resize it by increasing or decreasing the graph range. Enter the command /**G**raph **S**ettings (/GS). Allways prompts you to enter the name of the graph you want to adjust. Select XYGRAPH from the list. Next, type the letter R for Range. Allways highlights the old range (D1..H13) and prompts you to enter the new range. Enter the range D1..H17 and press the Enter key. Finally, type the letter Q to return to ALLWAYS mode. Allways immediately adjusts the graph to fit the new range as shown in Figure 5-26. Compare Figure 5-26 to Figure 5-25 and note the difference in the graph sizes.

Printing the Worksheet with the Graph

To print the worksheet (table of coordinates and graph), enter the Allways command /**P**rint **R**ange **S**et (/PRS). Select the range A1..H17 and press the Enter key.

Check to be sure the printer is ready. Type the letter G for Go. The worksheet containing both the table of coordinates and the graph prints on the printer as shown earlier in Figure 5-23.

If an "Out of Memory" message appears on the indicator line at the bottom of the screen, return control to 1-2-3 and save the worksheet. After the worksheet is saved, return control to Allways and issue the print command again.

Saving the Worksheet

To preserve the graph in the worksheet, use 1-2-3 to save it to disk. Use the Allways command /Quit (/Q). Enter the 1-2-3 command /File Save Replace (/FSR). 1-2-3 saves the worksheet as PROJS-5B.WK1 and the corresponding Allways format changes as PROJS-5B.ALL.

The next time the worksheet is loaded into main memory and displayed using Allways, the graph will appear as part of the worksheet.

The Graph Commands

To add or modify a graph in a worksheet, enter the Allways command /Graph (/G). The Graph menu shown in the top screen of Figure 5-24 displays. Table 5-4 summarizes the function of each of the commands in the Graph menu.

TABLE 5-4   A Summary of Commands in the Allways Graph Menu

COMMAND	FUNCTION
Add	Adds a graph to the worksheet.
Remove	Erases a graph from the worksheet.
Goto	Moves the cell pointer to the specified graph.
Settings	Specifies fonts, scaling, colors, margins, and graph replacement.
Fonts-Directory	Defines the directory where the graph fonts are located.
Quit	Quits the Graph command.

The command /Graph Settings (/GS) displays the **Graph Settings menu**. This menu is primarily used to enhance the appearance of the graph in the worksheet. Table 5-5 summarizes the commands available in the Graph Settings menu.

TABLE 5-5   A Summary of Commands in the Allways Graph Settings Menu

COMMAND	FUNCTION
PIC-File	Replaces a graph in the worksheet with another graph.
Fonts	Sets fonts for text in graphs.
Scale	Sets the scaling factor for fonts.
Colors	Sets colors for the graph data ranges.
Range	Resizes the graph or moves it to another area of the worksheet.
Margins	Sets margins for the graph.
Default	Restores the default graph settings.
Quit	Returns control to ALLWAYS mode.

PROJECT SUMMARY

n this project we created several graphs. Each of the steps required to build the worksheets and graphs is listed in the following two tables.

SUMMARY OF KEYSTROKES—PROJS-5A (Figure 5-1 and Associated Graphs)

STEPS	KEY(S) PRESSED	STEPS	KEY(S) PRESSED
1	/WGC12 ↵ (Build worksheet)	42	V
2	→ → King's Computer Outlet ↓	43	← NCLINE ← Q
3	Year-End Sales Analysis → → → ↑	44	/FS ← R
4	@NOW ↵	45	/GSLINE-5A ↵
5	/RFD1 ↵	46	AB6.E6 ↵ (Build multiple-line graph)
6	↓ ↓ "Total ↵	47	BB7.E7 ↵
7	F5 A4 ← City → "Quarter 1 → "Quarter 2 →	48	CB8.E8 ↵
8	"Quarter 3 → "Quarter 4 → "Sales ↵	49	DB9.E9 ↵
9	F5 A5 ← \ = ← /C ← . → → → → → ↵	50	EB10.E10 ↵
10	↓ Chicago → 40135 → 52345 → 38764 → 22908 ↵	51	FB11.E11 ↵
11	F5 A7 ← Tampa → 48812 → 42761 → 34499 → 56123 ↵	52	OLAChgo ← LBTampa ← LCAtl ←
12	F5 A8 ← Atlanta → 12769 → 15278 → 19265 → 17326 ↵	53	LDDallas ← LEBos ← LFOak ← Q
13	F5 A9 ← Dallas → 38713 → 29023 → 34786 → 23417 ↵	54	V
14	F5 A10 ← Boston → 34215 → 42864 → 38142 → 45375 ↵	55	← NCMULTLINE ← Q
15	F5 A11 ← Oakland → 52912 → 63182 → 57505 → 55832 ↵	56	/FS ← R
16	F5 A12 ← \ - ← /C ← . → → → → → ↵	57	/GSMLINE-5A ↵
17	F5 F6 ← @SUM(B6.E6) ↵	58	OFGSQQ (Build scatter graph)
18	/C ← . ↓ ↓ ↓ ↓ ↓ ↵	59	V
19	F5 A13 ← Total →	60	← NCSCATTER ← Q
20	@SUM(B6.B11) ↵	61	/FS ← R
21	/C ← . → → → → → ↵	62	/GSSCAT-5A ↵
22	/RF,0 ← A6.F13 ← HOME	63	NU → ← (Build simple bar graph)
23	/FSPROJS-5A ↵	64	← TB
24	/GTP (Build pie chart)	65	OGHQ
25	AF6.F11 ↵	66	V
26	XA6.A11 ← Q	67	← NCBAR ← Q
27	F5 F15 ← 1 ↓ 2 ↓ 3 ↓ 4 ↓ 5 ↓ 106 ↵	68	/FS ← R
28	/GBF15.F20 ↵	69	/GSBAR-5A ↵
29	OTFKing's Computer Outlet ↵	70	NUMULTLINE ↵ (Build side-by-side bar graph)
30	TSYear-End Sales Analysis ↵ Q	71	← TB
31	V	72	OGHQ
32	← NCPIE ← Q	73	V
33	/FS ← R	74	← NCSIDEBAR ← Q
34	/GS	75	/FS ← R
35	PIE-5A ↵	76	/GSMBAR-5A ↵
36	RG (Build line graph)	77	TS (Build stack-bar graph)
37	TL	78	V
38	XB4.E4 ↵	79	← NCSTACK ← Q
39	AB13.E13 ↵	80	/FS ← R
40	OTF\C1 ← TS\C2 ↵	81	/GSSBAR-5A ↵
41	TXAll Cities ← TYDollar Sales ← Q		

SUMMARY OF KEYSTROKES—PROJS-5B (Figures 5-21 through 5-26)

STEPS	KEY(S) PRESSED	STEPS	KEY(S) PRESSED
1	/WEY	13	TYY axis ↵ Q
2	Coordinates of y = x^2↓↓	14	V
3	"x→"y↓"–←"–↓	15	↵Q/FSPROJS-5B ↵
4	/DFA5.A13↵–2↵0.5↵ ↵	16	/GSXYGRAPH ↵Q
5	→+A5^2↵/C↵B6.B13↵	17	/AIALLWAYS ↵
6	/RFF1↵A5.B13↵	18	/GAXYGRAPH ↵D1.H13↵Q F10
7	/GTX (Start XY graph)	19	/FF↓↓↓↓↓↓↵A1.B13↵
8	XA5.A13↵	20	/GS↵RD1.H17↵Q
9	AB5.B13↵	21	/PRSA1.H17↵G
10	OTFGraph of y = x^2↵	22	/Q
11	TSBetween x = –2 and x = 2↵	23	/FSR
12	TXX axis ↵	24	/Q

The following list summarizes the material covered in Project 5:

1. 1-2-3 allows you to create, display, and print a graph of the data in your worksheet and get your message across in a dramatic pictorial fashion.
2. The first step in drawing a graph is to enter the command /**G**raph (/G). This command activates the command cursor in the **Graph menu**.
3. A **pie chart** is used to show how 100% of an amount is divided.
4. With a pie chart, you are allowed only three ranges. The A range specifies the data that is used to segment the pie. The X range is assigned the range of labels that identify the segments. The B range is used to shade and explode segments of the pie chart.
5. Through the Graph Options menu, you can assign two title lines of 39 characters each to identify the graph. Except on the pie chart, you may also add titles of up to 39 characters each for the X axis and Y axis. Titles may be entered by keying in the title or by keying in a cell address preceded by a backslash (\).
6. When numbers are changed in a worksheet, the current graph will reflect the changes the next time it is displayed.
7. The command /**G**raph **N**ame **C**reate (/GNC) can be used to store the current graph settings under a name. This allows you to have more than one set of graph settings associated with a worksheet. To assign a named set of graph settings as the current graph, use the command /**G**raph **N**ame **U**se (/GNU).
8. To save any named graph settings to disk, you must save the worksheet. Use the /**F**ile **S**ave (/FS) command.
9. The command /**G**raph **R**eset (/GR) allows you to reset all the current graph settings or any individual ones.
10. Printing a graph is a three-step process: first, save the graph to disk as a PIC file; second, quit 1-2-3; and third, use the PrintGraph program (PGRAPH) to print the graph.
11. **Line graphs** are used to show trends. You may have from one to six lines drawn in the graph. Each line represents a different data range (A through F) in the worksheet.
12. In a line graph, assign the labels for the X axis to the X range and assign the data ranges to the A through F ranges.
13. When more than one line is assigned to a line graph, it is called a **multiple-line graph**. Multiple-line graphs are used to show trends and comparisons.
14. The Group command in the Graph menu allows you to assign multiple data ranges when the ranges are located in consecutive rows or columns.
15. To identify the lines in a multiple-line graph, use the Legends command in the Graph Options menu.
16. A **scatter graph** displays the points in a graph without any connecting lines.
17. To create a scatter graph, follow the steps for a multiple-line graph. Next, through the Graph Options menu, use the Format Graph Symbols command to draw the symbols and delete the connecting lines.

18. A **bar graph** is used to show trends and comparisons.
19. A **simple bar graph** has a single bar (A range) for each value in the X range.
20. To add a horizontal grid to a graph, display the Graph Options menu and type the letters G for Grid and H for Horizontal.
21. A **side-by-side bar graph** is used to compare multiple data ranges. A side-by-side bar graph may have up to six bars per X-range value.
22. A **stack-bar** graph shows one bar per X-range value. However, the bar shows both the sum of the parts and the individual contributors.
23. 1-2-3 automatically scales the Y axis for bar and line graphs and the X and Y axes for XY graphs. If you prefer to set the scales manually, use the Scale command in the Graph Options menu.
24. The Color and B&W commands in the Graph Options menu are used to display graphs in color or in black and white.
25. Data-labels are used to explicitly label a bar or point in a graph. You may label any of the six data ranges A through F.
26. **XY graphs** are used to plot mathematical functions. In an XY graph the X range is assigned the X-axis values and the A range is assigned the Y-axis values.
27. The add-in program Allways allows you to place a graph alongside the data in a worksheet and to print the graph and data in the same report.
28. Allways allows you to add up to 20 graphs to a worksheet.
29. To add a graph to the worksheet, first use the 1-2-3 command /Graph Save (/GS) to save the graph as a PIC file. Next, use the Allways command /Graph Add (/GA) to add the graph to the worksheet.
30. Once the graph is part of the worksheet, use the F10 key to toggle between displaying the graph and the crosshatched design in the range.
31. To resize the graph in the worksheet, use the command /Graph Settings Range (/GSR).

STUDENT ASSIGNMENTS

STUDENT ASSIGNMENT 1: True/False

Instructions: Circle T if the statement is true or F if the statement is false.

T F 1. A pie chart is used to show a trend.
T F 2. The Save command in the Graph Options menu saves the worksheet.
T F 3. A PIC file contains a worksheet.
T F 4. The PrintGraph program is used to print PIC files.
T F 5. A pie chart can have from one to six data ranges.
T F 6. The B range is used to shade the segments of a pie chart.
T F 7. A line graph can have from one to six lines.
T F 8. To store the graph settings assigned to a worksheet under a name, save the worksheet using the Save command in the Graph menu.
T F 9. Multiple-line graphs are used to show trends and comparisons.
T F 10. If the title for a graph is the same as a label in a cell of the corresponding worksheet, enter the cell address preceded by a circumflex (^) for the title.
T F 11. Legends are used to identify the bars and lines in a graph.
T F 12. Data-labels are used to clarify a bar or a point in a graph.
T F 13. A scatter graph shows a random sample of points in the graph.
T F 14. Side-by-side bar graphs are used to compare data ranges for the same period.
T F 15. A stack-bar graph differs from a side-by-side bar graph in that it shows the combined total of the contributors.
T F 16. 1-2-3 automatically scales the axes in a graph unless you use the Scale command in the Graph Options menu.
T F 17. The XY command in the Graph Type menu is used to display a bar graph.
T F 18. The Reset command in the Graph Options menu allows you to reset individual graph specifications, like the ranges A through F.
T F 19. A graph must be saved as a PIC file before it can be added to the worksheet using the add-in program Allways.
T F 20. Once a graph is part of a worksheet, it can be moved to another range, resized, or deleted from the worksheet.

STUDENT ASSIGNMENT 2: Multiple Choice

Instructions: Circle the correct response.

1. Which of the following types of graphs can you draw with 1-2-3?
   a. line b. bar c. pie d. XY e. all of these
2. Which of the following ranges are meaningless for a pie chart?
   a. X b. A c. B d. C through F
3. A pie chart is used to show _____ .
   a. how 100% of an amount is divided   c. how two or more data ranges compare
   b. trends   d. none of these
4. A side-by-side bar graph can have up to _____ bars per value in the X range.
   a. 3 b. 5 c. 6 d. 8
5. Data-labels are used to _____ .
   a. assign a title to the graph   c. clarify points and bars in a graph
   b. define which bar or line belongs to which data range   d. scale the X and Y axes
6. To explode a segment of a pie chart, add _____ to the corresponding cell in the _____ range.
   a. 10, C b. 100, B c. 1000, A d. none of these
7. In a stack-bar graph each bar shows _____ .
   a. the total amount for a label in the X range   c. none of these
   b. the contribution of each participant   d. both a and b
8. Which one of the following commands in the Graph menu displays the current graph?
   a. View b. Type c. Save d. both a and b

STUDENT ASSIGNMENT 3: Understanding Graph Commands

Instructions: Describe the function of each of the following 1-2-3 commands.

a. /G _____   i. /GS _____
b. /GRG _____   j. /GV _____
c. /GNU _____   k. /GQ _____
d. /GO _____   l. /GND _____
e. /GTB _____   m. /GTS _____
f. /GTP _____   n. /GNC _____
g. /GOTF _____ o. /GOL _____
h. /GRXQ _____ p. /GG _____

STUDENT ASSIGNMENT 4: Understanding the Graph Options

Instructions: Describe the purpose of the following titled sections in the Graph Options menu.

a. DATA-LABELS

   Purpose: _____

b. TITLES

   Purpose: _____

c. LEGEND

   Purpose: _____

d. SCALE

Purpose: _____

e. FORMAT

Purpose: _____

f. GRID

Purpose: _____

g. COLOR

Purpose: _____

h. B&W

Purpose: _____

i. QUIT

Purpose: _____

STUDENT ASSIGNMENT 5: Drawing a Pie Chart

Instructions: Load 1-2-3. Retrieve the worksheet PROJS-2 built in Project 2 (Figure 2-2).

Draw a pie chart that shows the revenue contribution for each month to the total quarterly revenue in the first quarter sales report. The pie chart should resemble the one shown in Figure 5-27. Use the following graph settings:

Type = Pie   A range = B4..D4   Title 1 = \B1
X range = B2..D2   B range = E4..E6   Title 2 = TOTAL REVENUE
                          (explode the February revenue)

Save the worksheet with the graph settings as STUS5-5. Save the graph as STUSP5-5.PIC. Use PrintGraph to print the pie chart.

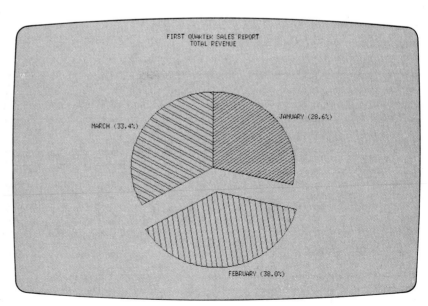

FIGURE 5-27
Student Assignment 5

STUDENT ASSIGNMENT 6: Drawing a Multiple-Line Graph and Side-by-Side Bar Graph

Instructions: Load 1-2-3. Retrieve the worksheet PROJS-2 built in Project 2 (Figure 2-2). In this assignment we will draw a multiple-line graph and a side-by-side bar graph that show the trends in the revenue, costs, and profit of the first quarter sales report. We will also use Allways to add graphs to the worksheet and enhance the worksheet's appearance.

First, we will draw the multiple-line graph. This graph should resemble the one shown in Figure 5-28. Use the following graph settings, and name the multiple-line graph MULTLINE. Save the Multiple-line graph as STUSM5-6.PIC.

Type = Line
X range = B2..D2
A range = B4..D4
B range = B5..D5
C range = B6..D6
Title 1 = \B1
Y-axis title = Dollars
A legend = \A4
B legend = \A5
C legend = \A6

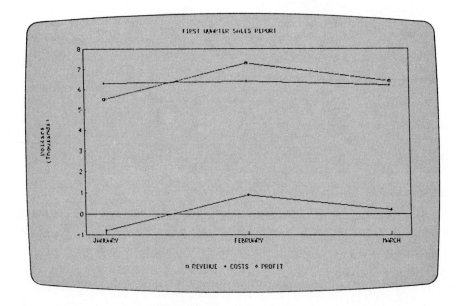

FIGURE 5-28
Student Assignment 6

Next, draw a side-by-side bar graph to show the same trends for the first quarter. This graph should resemble the one shown in Figure 5-29. Use the same graph settings given above for the multiple-line graph, and name the graph SIDEBAR. For the side-by-side bar graph, change the Type to Bar. Save the side-by-side bar graph as STUSS5-6.PIC.

Save the worksheet as STUS5-6, and use PrintGraph to print both graphs.

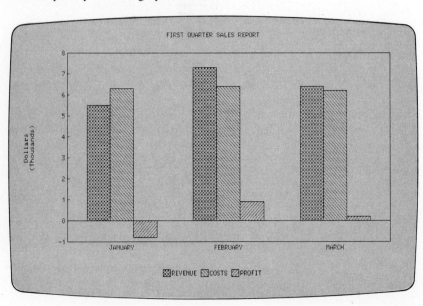

FIGURE 5-29
Student Assignment 6

Finally, add the multiple-line graph (Figure 5-28) and side-by-side graph (Figure 5-29) to the worksheet STUS5-6 as shown in Figure 5-30. Use Allways to modify the worksheet in the following ways:

1. Increase the width of column A to 15 characters.
2. Change the report title in cell B1 and the totals title in cell A10 to Times 14-point font.
3. Add the multiple-line graph in the range A17..C34.
4. Add the side-by-side graph in the range D17..F34.
5. Print the range A1..F34.

Return control to 1-2-3 and save the worksheet as STUS5-6.

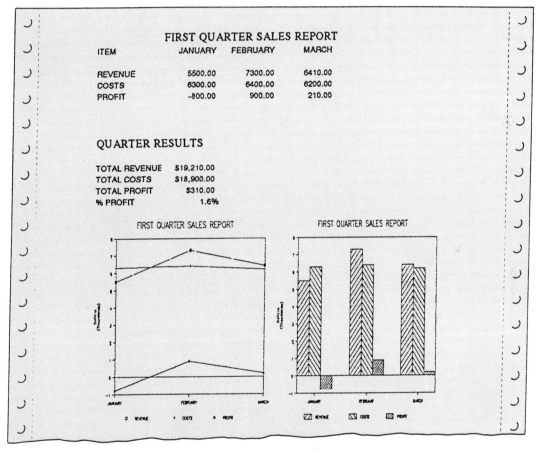

FIGURE 5-30 Student Assignment 6

STUDENT ASSIGNMENT 7: Drawing a Stack-Bar Graph

Instructions: Load 1-2-3. Retrieve the worksheet PROJS-3 built in Project 3 (Figure 3-1).

Draw a stack-bar graph that shows the individual contributions of each expense category and the total estimated expenses for each of the three months. The stack-bar graph should resemble the one shown in Figure 5-31.

Use the following graph settings:

Type = Stack-bar   Title 2 = Estimated Expenses
X range = B5..D5   Y-axis title = Dollars
A range = B15..D15   A legend = Mfg.
B range = B16..D16   B legend = Res.
C range = B17..D17   C legend = Mktg.
D range = B18..D18   D legend = Adm.
E range = B19..D19   E legend = Fulfill.
Title 1 = \A1   Grid = Horizontal

Save the worksheet with the stack-bar graph settings as STUS5-7. Save the stack-bar graph as STUSS5-7.PIC. Use Print-Graph to print the stack-bar graph.

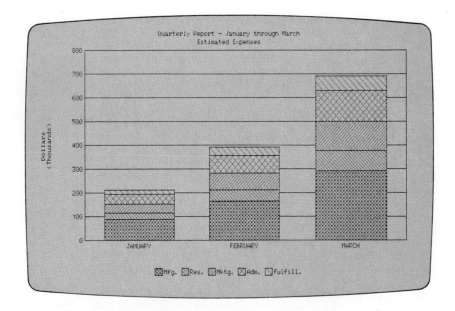

STUDENT ASSIGNMENT 8: Building a Table of Coordinates and Drawing the Corresponding XY Graph

Instructions:　Load 1-2-3. Complete Parts 1 and 2 below.

Part 1: Build the table of coordinates for the function $y = 2x^3 + 6x^2 - 18x + 6$ shown in the top screen of Figure 5-32 and draw the corresponding XY graph shown in the bottom screen of Figure 5-32

For the worksheet, use the Data Fill command to build the column of X coordinates in the range A6..A20. Start with –5, increment by 0.5, and stop at 8191. Assign to B6 the formula $2*A6\wedge3 + 6*A6\wedge2 - 18*A6 + 6$. Copy B6 to the range B7..B20. Format the range A6..B20 to the Fixed type with 1 decimal position.

For the XY graph in Figure 5-32, use the following graph settings:

Type = XY
X range = A6..A20
A range = B6..B20
Title 1 = Graph of y = 2x^3 + 6x^2 – 18x + 6
X-axis title = X axis
Y-axis title = Y axis

Save the worksheet with XY graph settings as STUS5-8. Save the graph as STUSX5-8.PIC. Use PrintGraph to print the XY graph.

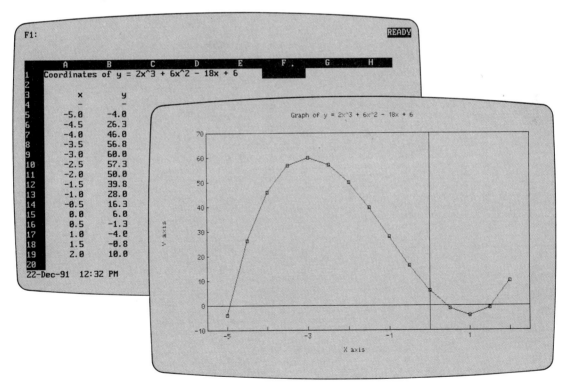

Part 2: Add the XY graph in the bottom screen of Figure 5-32 to the worksheet STUS5-8 as shown in Figure 5-33. Use Allways to modify the worksheet in the following ways:

1. Change the report title in A1 to Times 14-point font.
2. Add the XY graph in the range D3..H20.
3. Print the range A1..H20.

Return control to 1-2-3 and save the worksheet as STUS5-8.

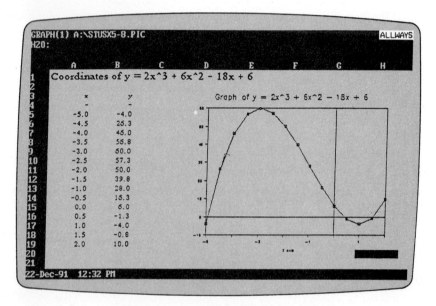

FIGURE 5-33   Student Assignment 8 Part 2

PROJECT 6

Sorting and Querying a Worksheet Database

Objectives

You will have mastered the material in this project when you can:

- Define the terms database, DBMS, field, field name, and record
- Differentiate between records in ascending and descending sequence
- Sort a database on the basis of a primary key
- Sort a database on the basis of both primary and secondary keys
- Establish criteria for selecting records in a database
- Find records in a database that match specified criteria
- Extract records from a database that match specified criteria
- Apply the database functions to generate information about the database
- Utilize the lookup functions to select values from a list or a table
- Search for strings in the worksheet
- Replace strings in the worksheet

*I*n this project we will discuss some of the database capabilities of 1-2-3. A **database** is an organized collection of data. For example, a telephone book, a grade book, and a list of company employees are databases. In these cases, the data related to a person is called a **record**, and the data items that make up a record are called **fields**. In a telephone book database, the fields are name, address, and telephone number.

A worksheet's row and column structure can easily be used to organize and store a database (Figure 6-1). Each row of a worksheet can be used to store a record and each column can store a field. Furthermore, a row of column headings at the top of the worksheet can be used as **field names** to identify each field.

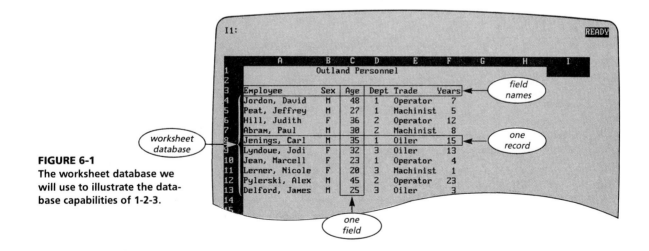

FIGURE 6-1
The worksheet database we will use to illustrate the database capabilities of 1-2-3.

A **database management system (DBMS)** is a software package that is used to create a database and store, access, sort, and make additions, deletions, and changes to that database. Although somewhat limited by the number of records that can be stored, 1-2-3 is capable of carrying out many of the DBMS functions. We have already used 1-2-3 as a database management system when we built, formatted, and enhanced our worksheets in the earlier projects.

In this project, we will focus on the two functions of a DBMS that we have not yet discussed—sorting and accessing records. We also discuss the special database and table lookup functions and the Search command available with 1-2-3. For the remainder of this project, the term *database* will mean *worksheet database*.

The database for this project is illustrated in Figure 6-1. It consists of 10 personnel records. Each record represents an employee for the Outland Company. The names, columns, types, and sizes of the fields are described in Table 6-1. Since the database is visible on the screen, it is important that it be readable. Therefore, most of the field sizes (column widths) in Table 6-1 are determined from the column headings (field names) and not the maximum length of the data as is the case with most database management systems. For example, column E represents the Trade field, which has a width of nine characters because the longest trade designation is machinist (nine characters). Column F, which represents the years of seniority, is five characters wide because the field name Years is five letters long. The column headings in the row immediately above the first record (row 3) play an important role in the database commands issued to 1-2-3.

TABLE 6-1   Field Descriptions for the Outland Personnel Database

FIELD NAME	COLUMN	TYPE OF DATA	SIZE
Employee	A	Label	16
Sex	B	Label	5
Age	C	Numeric	5
Dept	D	Label	6
Trade	E	Label	9
Years	F	Numeric	5

Build the database shown in Figure 6-1 by following the steps listed in the first table of the Project Summary section at the end of this project.

SORTING A DATABASE

*T*he information derived from a database is easier to work with and more meaningful if the records are arranged in sequence on the basis of one or more fields. Arranging the records in sequence is called **sorting**. Figure 6-2 illustrates the difference between unsorted data and the same data in ascending and descending sequence. Data that is in sequence from lowest to highest in value is in **ascending sequence**. Data that is in sequence from highest to lowest in value is in **descending sequence**.

Data in No Particular Sequence	Data in Ascending Sequence	Data in Descending Sequence
7	1	9
5	3	7
9	5	5
1	7	3
3	9	1

FIGURE 6-2 Data in various sequences.

The Sort Menu

To sort a database, enter the command /**D**ata **S**ort (/DS). The **Sort menu** displays in the control panel at the top of the screen, and the **sort settings sheet** displays in place of rows 1 through 10 in the worksheet (Figure 6-3). The commands available in the Sort menu are described in Table 6-2.

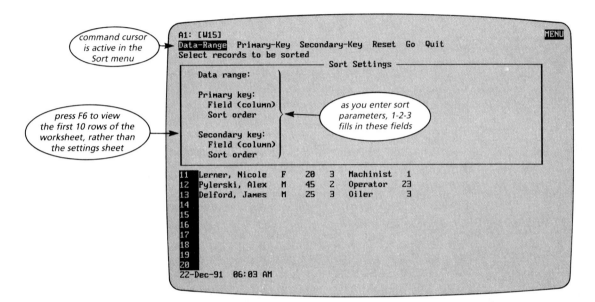

FIGURE 6-3 Step 1 of using the Sort command—enter the command /Data Sort (/DS) and the sort menu displays at the top of the screen.

TABLE 6-2   A Summary of Commands in the Sort Menu

COMMAND	FUNCTION
Data-Range	Prompts you to specify the range of the database to sort.
Primary-Key	Prompts you to enter the field (column) you wish to sort the records on and the sequence.
Secondary-Key	Prompts you to enter a second field (column) you wish to sort on within the primary-key field, and the sequence for the secondary-key field. Used to "break ties" on the primary-key field.
Reset	Clears all sort settings.
Go	Causes the database to be sorted on the basis of the sort settings.
Quit	Quits the Data command and returns control to READY mode.

To illustrate the use of the Data Sort command, we will first sort the database in Figure 6-1 into ascending sequence on the basis of the employee name field (column A). Next, we will sort the same database on years of seniority (column F) within the sex code (column B). That is, the sex code will be the primary-key field and years of seniority will be the secondary-key field.

Sorting the Records by Employee Name

With the command cursor active in the Sort menu (Figure 6-3), do the following:

1. Enter the data range.
2. Enter the primary-key field.
3. Enter the Go command.

To enter the data range, type the letter D for Data-Range. The **data range** defines the fields and records to be sorted in the database. The data range almost always encompasses *all* the fields in *all* the records below the column headings, although it can be made up of fewer records or fewer fields. Be aware, however, that if you do not select all the fields (columns) in the database, the unselected fields will not remain with the records they belong to and the data will get mixed up.

When you type the letter D for Data-Range, 1-2-3 responds by displaying the "Enter data range: A1" prompt message on the input line. Use the arrow keys and Period key to select the range A4..F13 as shown in Figure 6-4. Press the Enter key and the Sort menu shown at the top of the screen in Figure 6-3 reappears on the screen.

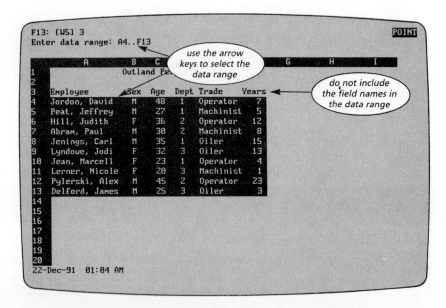

FIGURE 6-4 Step 2 of using the Sort command—enter the data range. The data range usually encompasses all the fields in all the records of the database.

The next step is to enter the primary-key field. With the Sort menu on the screen and the cell pointer at A4, type the letter P for Primary-Key. 1-2-3 responds by displaying the prompt message "Primary sort key: A4" on the input line. Since column A is the employee name field and the cell pointer is in column A, press the Enter key. As shown in Figure 6-5, 1-2-3 responds with a second prompt message requesting the desired sequence of the sort. Type the letter A for ascending sequence and press the Enter key.

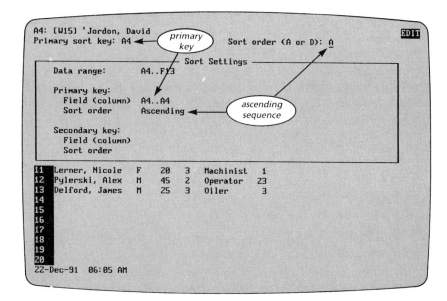

FIGURE 6-5
Step 3 of using the Sort command—enter the primary key and desired sequence for sorting the database by employee name.

To complete the sort, type the letter G for Go. 1-2-3 sorts the records and displays them in ascending sequence according to employee name. Following the completion of the Go command, control returns to READY mode as shown in Figure 6-6. Whereas the records in Figure 6-1 are in no particular sequence, the same records in Figure 6-6 are now in ascending sequence by employee name.

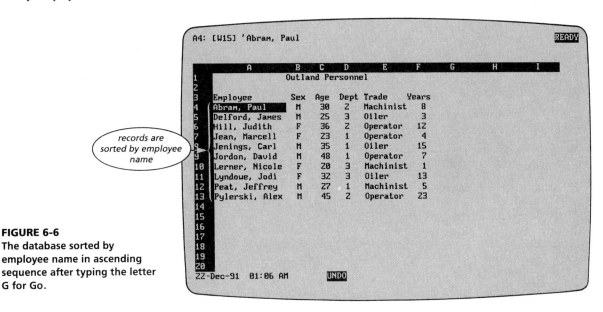

FIGURE 6-6
The database sorted by employee name in ascending sequence after typing the letter G for Go.

To complete this portion of the project, save and print a hard copy of the sorted database. Save the database using the file name PROJS-6A. Print the database using the same procedures we used in the previous projects.

Sorting the Records by Years of Seniority within Sex Code

In this example, we will use two sort keys. Our goal is to order the records so that the secondary-key field, years of seniority (column F), is ordered in descending sequence within the primary-key field, sex code (column B). We will sort the primary-key field into ascending sequence. Therefore, the female with the most years of seniority will be at the top of the list, and the male with the least seniority will be at the bottom of the list. This nested sorting always assumes that the primary-key field contains duplicate values.

To start this portion of the project, load the original database PROJS-6 (Figure 6-1) into main memory and enter the command **/Data Sort (/DS)**. With the command cursor active in the Sort menu (Figure 6-3), type the letter D for Data-Range. Next, select all the records in the database (A4..F13) as shown in Figure 6-4. Press the Enter key and the Sort menu shown earlier in Figure 6-3 reappears on the screen.

After the data range is set, enter the primary-key field. To accomplish this, type the letter P for Primary-Key. Move the cell pointer to column B (sex code) and press the Enter key. Type the letter A for ascending sequence. The primary-key field selections are shown on the input line in Figure 6-7. Press the Enter key to finalize the primary-key selections.

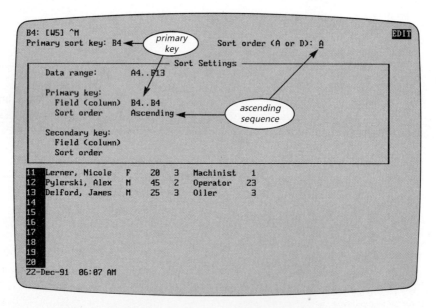

FIGURE 6-7 Entering the primary key and desired sequence for sorting the database by years of seniority within sex code.

Type the letter S for Secondary-Key. 1-2-3 responds by displaying a prompt message on the input line requesting the secondary key. Move the cell pointer to column F, the one that contains the years of seniority, and press the Enter key. In response to the second prompt message on the input line, leave the D for descending sequence.

The secondary-key field selections are shown in Figure 6-8. Press the Enter key to return control to the Sort menu.

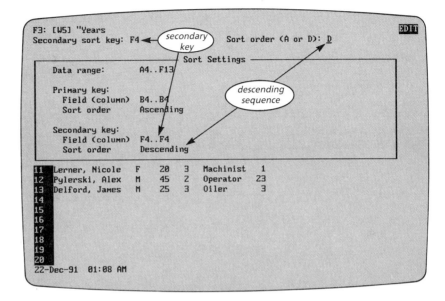

FIGURE 6-8
Entering the secondary key and desired sequence for sorting the database by years of seniority within sex code.

To complete the sort, type the letter G for Go. 1-2-3 sorts the records and places them in ascending sequence according to the sex-code field in column B. Within the sex code, the records are in descending sequence according to the years of seniority in column F. This is shown in Figure 6-9. Following the completion of the Go command, 1-2-3 displays the sorted records and returns to READY mode.

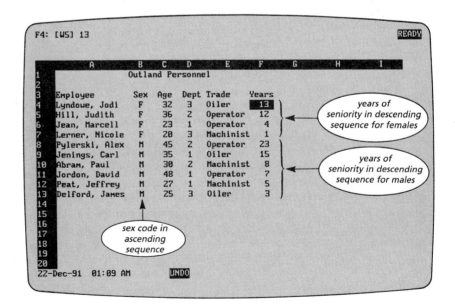

FIGURE 6-9
The database sorted by years of seniority within sex code.

Save and print a hard copy of the sorted database. Use the file name PROJS-6B.

QUERYING A DATABASE

 ne of the most powerful aspects of a DBMS is its ability to select records from a database that match specified criteria. This activity is called **querying a database**. Records that match the criteria can be highlighted, copied to another part of the worksheet, or deleted.

The Query Menu

To query a database, enter the command /**D**ata **Q**uery (/DQ). The **Query menu** displays in the control panel at the top of the screen, and the **query settings sheet** displays in place of rows 1 through 6 in the worksheet (Figure 6-10). The function of each of the Query commands is described in Table 6-3.

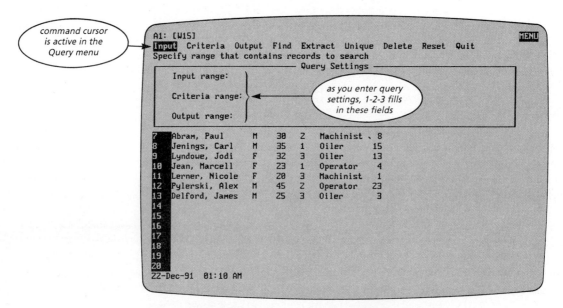

FIGURE 6-10 The Query menu displays when you enter the command /Data Query (/DQ).

TABLE 6-3 A Summary of Commands in the Query Menu

COMMAND	FUNCTION
Input	Prompts you to enter the range of the database to be queried. Usually the entire database is selected.
Criteria	Prompts you to enter the range of cells that includes the conditions for record selection. The conditions are entered into the worksheet off to the side or below the database.
Output	Prompts you to enter a range of cells to which records can be copied. The Output range is defined in the worksheet off to the side or below the database.
Find	Moves the cell pointer to the first record in the database that passes the test. The cell pointer moves one record at a time as you press the Up Arrow or Down Arrow keys. When you invoke the Find command, the cell pointer extends to include the entire record. Pressing the Esc key or Enter key cancels the search.
Extract	Copies all selected records from the database to the Output range. The records that pass the test are selected from the database. Records that flunk the test are not copied to the Output range.
Unique	Same as the Extract command, except that it copies only the first of any duplicate records.
Delete	Deletes all records from the database that pass the test.
Reset	Resets the Input, Output, and Criteria settings.
Quit	Quits the Data command and returns control to READY mode.

The Find Command

The Find command is used to search for records in the database that meet certain criteria. The command highlights the first record in the database that passes the test and continues to highlight records that pass the test as you press the Up and Down Arrow keys. If no more records pass the test in the direction you are searching, the computer beeps at you and the last record meeting the criteria remains highlighted.

With the database (PROJS-6) in Figure 6-10 in main memory, let's search for records representing males who work in department 2 (Sex = M AND Dept = 2). To complete the search, do the following:

1. Choose an unused area off to the side of the database and set up the criteria.
2. Type the command /**D**ata **Q**uery (/DQ) and enter the Input range.
3. Enter the Criteria range.
4. Type the letter F for Find.

The first step in setting up the Criteria range is to select an unused area of the worksheet. Let's begin the Criteria range at cell H3. Next, copy the names of those fields (column headings) that we are basing the search on to this area. That is, copy cell B3 (Sex) to cell H3 and cell D3 (Dept) to cell I3. You can bypass the Copy command and enter the field names through the keyboard, but the field names in the Criteria range must agree exactly with the field names in the database, or the search won't work properly. To ensure that they are the same, it's best to use the Copy command.

An alternative to using the Copy command to set up the field names in the Criteria range is to assign cell H3 the formula +B3 and cell I3 the formula +D3. However, be aware that when you use formulas to assign a label to a cell, you lose right-justification and centering. Even so, the labels are considered to be identical. A positive result of using the formula method instead of the Copy command is that if you change a field name in the database, the corresponding field name in the Criteria range will change automatically.

Under each field name in the Criteria range, enter the value for which you want to search. In our example, we want to search for males who work in department 2. Therefore, enter the letter M in cell H4. (1-2-3 considers lowercase m and upper-case M to be the same in a Criteria range.) In cell I4, enter the label 2 (^2 or "2 or '2). These entries for the Criteria range are shown in Figure 6-11. Note that the Criteria range must contain at least two rows—the field names in the first row and the criteria in the second row.

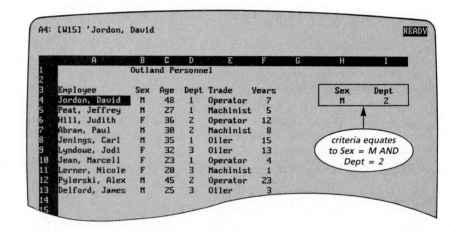

FIGURE 6-11
Step 1 of using the Find command—enter the criteria in unused cells off to the side of the database before issuing the Data Query command.

After building the Criteria range, enter the command /**D**ata **Q**uery (/DQ). The Query menu displays as shown in Figure 6-10. Type the letter I for Input and use the arrow keys to select the entire database (A3..F13). This is shown in Figure 6-12. Note that the field names in row 3 must be included in the Input range. Press the Enter key.

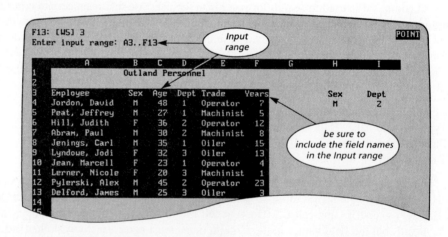

FIGURE 6-12
Step 2 of using the Find command—enter the command /Data Query Input (/DQI). Enter the Input range, which should encompass all the fields in all the records of the database, including the field names at the top.

Earlier, we set up the Criteria range (H3..I4). Now we must select it. Therefore, type the letter C for Criteria. Select the range H3..I4 as illustrated in Figure 6-13 and press the Enter key.

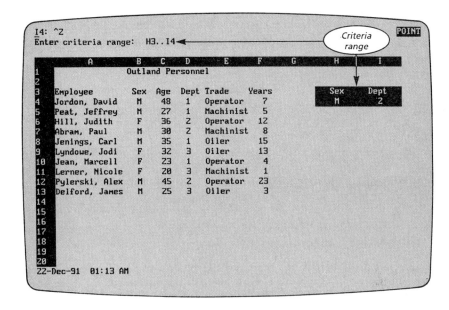

FIGURE 6-13
Step 3 of using the Find command—select the Criteria range.

Next, type the letter F for Find. As shown in the top screen of Figure 6-14, the first record that passes the test (Sex = M AND Dept = 2) is highlighted. Press the Down Arrow key and the next record that passes the test is highlighted. This is shown in the bottom screen of Figure 6-14. If we press the Down Arrow key again, the computer will beep at us because there are no more records that pass the test below the highlighted one. If we press the Up Arrow key, the previous record that passed the test is highlighted again.

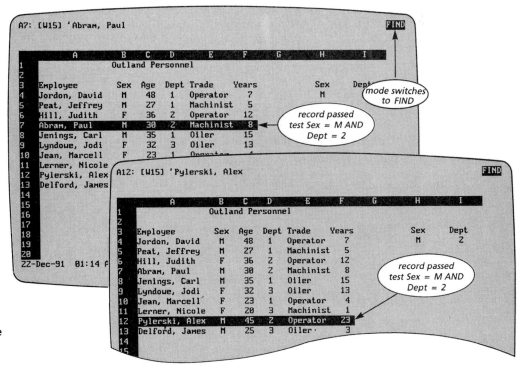

FIGURE 6-14
Step 4 of using the Find command—use the Up and Down Arrow keys to highlight the next record that passes the criteria.

After typing the letter F to invoke the Find command, we can move the elongated cursor to the very first record by pressing the Home key. We can move it to the last record by pressing the End key. These two keys allow us to start the search at the top or the bottom of the database. To terminate the Find command, press the Enter key or the Esc key to return to the Data Query menu.

While the Find command is still active, we can edit the record that is highlighted. Use the Right Arrow and Left Arrow keys to move from one field to another. Because the entire record is highlighted, the cell pointer does not move to the different fields when we use the arrow keys. However, we can determine the field location of the cell pointer because the cell address displays at the top of the screen on the status line. The blinking underline cursor that is active in the current cell also indicates the location of the cell pointer. When the cell address of the field we want to change displays on the status line, we can retype the contents or use function key F2 to edit them. If we decide the original values were correct before pressing the Enter key to complete the change, we can press the Esc key to discard the change.

To complete this portion of this project, save and print the database and criteria. Use the file name PROJS-6C.

More About the Criteria Range

The way you set up the Criteria range determines which records pass the test when you use the Find command. The following paragraphs describe several different examples of valid field names and logical expressions within a Criteria range.

No Conditions   If the Criteria range contains no values below the field names, all the records pass the test. For example, if you use the Criteria range at the right, then all the records in the Input range pass the test and the Find command highlights every record in the Input range, one at a time.

Sex	Trade

Conditions with Labels   The values below the field names in the Criteria range can be labels, numbers, or formulas. For example, if you want to select all the records in the database that represent employees who are operators, use the criteria at the right. In this example Operator is a label. If you use the Find command, this Criteria range causes 1-2-3 to use the condition Trade = Operator to evaluate each record. If the condition is true, the record passes the test and it is highlighted. If Trade does not equal Operator, the record fails the test and it is bypassed.

Trade
Operator

More than one type of trade can be listed in the Criteria range. For example, if you want to select records that represent employees who are operators or employees who are oilers (Trade = Operator OR Trade = Oiler), you can set up a Criteria range with the entries at the right. In this example, the Criteria range is three rows long.

Trade
Operator
Oiler

The global characters question mark (?) and asterisk (*) can be used within labels. The asterisk (*) means "any characters at this position and all remaining positions." The question mark (?) means "any character at this position." These global characters are also called **wild-card characters**. For example, the Criteria range at the right causes all records whose trade begins with the letter O to be selected. In our database, records with the trade of oiler or operator pass the test. The remaining records fail the test.

Trade
O*

The Criteria range at the right causes all records to be selected that represent employees whose trade is five characters long, begins with the letter O, and ends with the letters er. With regard to the placement of wild-card characters in a label, the question mark (?) can be used in any character position. The asterisk (*) can only be used at the end of a label.

Trade
O??er

Labels can also be preceded by the tilde (˜) to exclude a match. To select the records representing employees that work in any department other than department 3, you may use the criteria at the right. Note that the department numbers in our database are labels, not numbers. The tilde (˜) can only precede labels. Table 6-4 summarizes the special symbols that may be used with labels in a Criteria range.

Dept
˜3

TABLE 6-4   A Summary of Special Symbols That Can Be Used with Labels in a Criteria Range

SYMBOL	MEANING	EXAMPLE
*	Any characters at this position and all remaining positions	Tr*
?	Any character at this position	M??T
˜	Not	˜F

Conditions with Numbers   If you want to select records that represent employees who are 30 years old, enter the criteria in the entry at the right. In this example, 1-2-3 uses the expression Age = 30 to determine if each record passes the test when the Find command is used. It is invalid to begin a number with any of the special characters described earlier for labels, like *, ?, and ˜.

Age
30

Conditions with Formulas   Formula criteria are entered into the Criteria range beginning with a plus sign (+). The plus sign is followed by the address of the cell of the first record immediately below the specified field name in the Input range. The cell address is followed by a relational operator and the value to which to compare the field name. (Table 4-3 in Project 4 contains a list of the valid relational operators.) If you want to select all records that represent employees who are older than 25, use the criteria at the right.

Age
+C4>25

The cell address C4 is the first cell in the database below the field name Age (Figure 6-15 on the next page). Since C4 is a relative cell address, 1-2-3 adjusts the row as it goes through the database, passing and flunking records. Hence, when you invoke the Find command, cell address C4 is only used to evaluate the first record. Thereafter, the 4 in C4 is adjusted to 5, 6, and so on, as each record in the database is evaluated.

In the previous example, the formula +C4>25 was shown in the cell below the field name Age. Actually, when a condition containing a formula is assigned to the cell, 0 or 1 displays. The number displayed in the cell assigned the formula +C4>25 depends on the value in cell C4. If it is greater than 25, then 1 (true) displays. If C4 contains a value less than or equal to 25, then 0 (false) displays. You can use the command /**R**ange **F**ormat **T**ext (/RFT) to display the formula in the Criteria range, rather than the numeric value 0 or 1.

Compound conditions may be formed by using the logical operators #AND#, #OR#, and #NOT#. (Table 4-4 in Project 4 provides an explanation of their meaning.) In the following example, all records are selected that meet the criteria Age < 37 AND Years ≥ 10.

Age
+C4<37#AND#+F4>=10

Note that the compound condition may include numeric fields that are not directly under the field name. In this case, C4 refers to the Age field and F4 refers to the Years field.

Mixing Conditions with Formulas and Labels   If the criteria require both a label and a formula, use multiple field names. For example, if you wanted to find all records in the employee database that represent operators with more than 10 years of seniority (Trade = Operator AND Years > 10), use the criteria at the right.

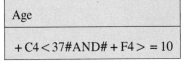

Trade	Years
Operator	+F4>10

To select records that meet the criteria Trade = Operator OR Years > 10, use the entry at the right. Because the expressions Operator and +F4>10 are in different rows, 1-2-3 selects records that represent employees who are operators or have more than 10 years of seniority.

Trade	Years
Operator	
	+F4 > 10

The Extract Command

The Extract command copies data from the records that pass the test to the designated fields in the Output range. The Output range is a group of cells off to the side or below the database. The first row of the Output range includes duplicates of the field names in the Input range that you want to extract. This command is very powerful because it allows you to build a database that is a subset of the original one. The subset database can be printed, saved as a new database, or queried like any other database.

Again, consider the employee database in Figure 6-1. Assume that your manager wants you to generate a list of all those employees who meet the following criteria:

Age ≥ 27 AND NOT(Dept = 3) AND Years < 10

In the list, include the employee name, department, and sex code of all the records that pass the test.

To complete the extract, do the following:

1. Choose an area off to the side of the database and set up the criteria.
2. Choose an area below the database and set up an area to receive the extracted results.
3. Invoke the command **/Data Query** (/DQ) and enter the Input range.
4. Enter the Criteria range.
5. Enter the Output range.
6. Type the letter E for Extract.

The criteria for this query involve three fields—Age, Dept, and Years. Use the cells in the range G3 through I4 for the Criteria range. Copy the three field names Age, Dept, and Years from the database in row 3 to cells G3, H3, and I3. The first condition in the previously stated criteria is Age ≥ 27. Therefore, in cell G4, enter the formula +C4> = 27. This is shown in Figure 6-15. (Cells G4 through I4 have been formatted to the Text type so that the formulas display, rather than the numeric values 0 or 1.) The second condition is NOT(Dept = 3). Therefore, in cell H4, enter ~3. The condition for the third field is Years < 10. In cell I4, enter +F4<10.

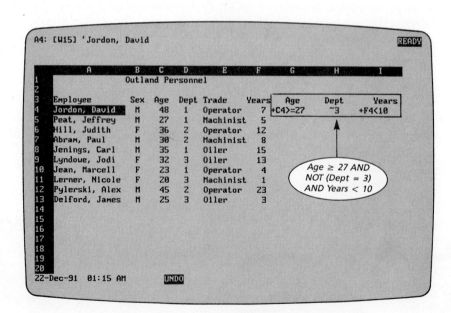

FIGURE 6-15

Step 1 of using the Extract command—enter the criteria in unused cells off to the side of the database.

The next step is to set up the Output range. This involves copying the names of the fields at the top of the database (row 3) to an area below the database. Since we want to extract the employee name, department, and sex code, copy the three field names to row 16 as illustrated in Figure 6-16.

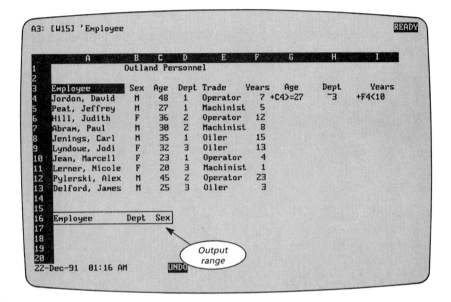

FIGURE 6-16
Step 2 of using the Extract command—copy the field names for the Output range below the database.

Enter the command /Data Query (/DQ). The Query menu shown at the top of the screen in Figure 6-10 displays. Type the letter I for Input. Use the arrow keys to select the entire database, including the field names in row 3 (A3..F13). The Input range is shown in Figure 6-17. Press the Enter key.

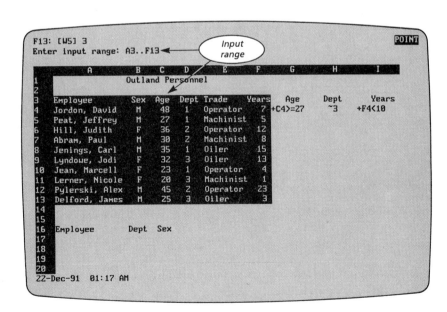

FIGURE 6-17
Step 3 of using the Extract command—enter the command /Data Query (/DQ) and enter the Input range. The Input range usually encompasses all the fields in all the records of the database, including the field names.

With the command cursor in the Query menu, type the letter C for Criteria. Select the Criteria range G3..I4 as shown in Figure 6-18. Press the Enter key.

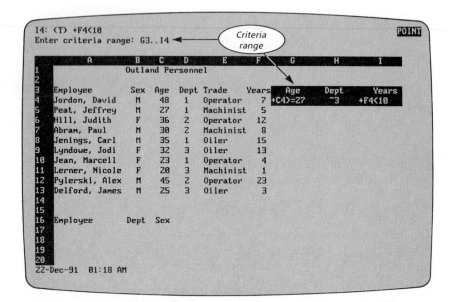

FIGURE 6-18
Step 4 of using the Extract command—enter the Criteria range.

Now type the letter O for Output. Select the range A16..C16 (Figure 6-19). Press the Enter key.

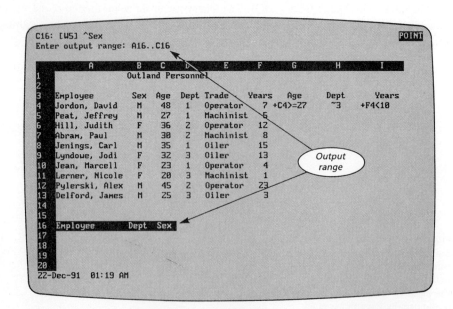

FIGURE 6-19
Step 5 of using the Extract command—enter the Output range.

After the Input, Criteria, and Output ranges are set, type the letter E for Extract. This causes 1-2-3 to select the records that meet the criteria specified in the range A3..I4. For each record selected, it copies the employee name, department, and sex code to the next available row beneath the field names in the Output range. Type the letter Q to Quit the Data Query command. The results of the extract display below the database as shown in Figure 6-20. Save and print the database, criteria, and records extracted. To save the database, use the file name PROJS-6D.

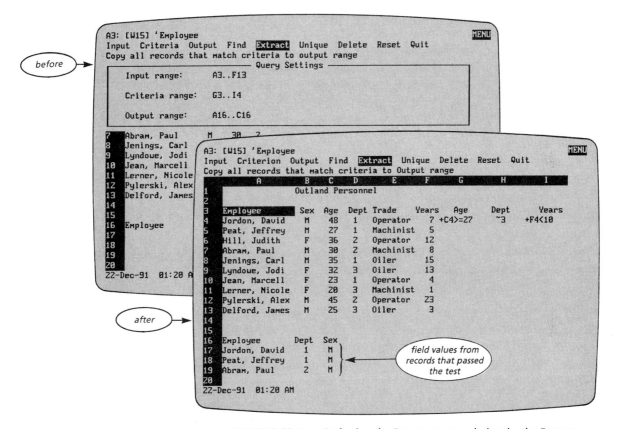

FIGURE 6-20 Step 6 of using the Extract command—invoke the Extract command. Specified fields are displayed in the Output range from the records that pass the test Age > = 27 AND NOT(Dept = 3) AND Years > 10.

In the previous example, we defined the Output range to be the row containing the field names (A16..C16). When the Output range is defined in this fashion, any number of records can be extracted from the database. The alternative is to define a rectangular Output range. In this case, if more records are extracted than rows in the Output range, 1-2-3 displays the diagnostic message "Too many records for Output range".

THE DATABASE FUNCTIONS

-2-3 has seven functions for evaluating numeric data in the database. The functions, which are similar to the statistical functions discussed in Project 4, are described in Table 6-5.

TABLE 6-5 Database Statistical Functions

FUNCTION	FUNCTION VALUE
DAVG(I,O,C)	Returns the average of the numbers in the Offset column (O) of the Input range (I) that meet the criteria (C).
DCOUNT(I,O,C)	Returns the number of nonempty cells in the Offset column (O) of the Input range (I) that meet the criteria (C).
DMAX(I,O,C)	Returns the largest number in the Offset column (O) of the Input range (I) that meet the criteria (C).
DMIN(I,O,C)	Returns the smallest number in the Offset column (O) of the Input range (I) that meet the criteria (C).
DSTD(I,O,C)	Returns the standard deviation of the numbers in the Offset column (O) of the Input range (I) that meet the criteria (C).
DSUM(I,O,C)	Returns the sum of the numbers in the Offset column (O) of the Input range (I) that meet the criteria (C).
DVAR(I,O,C)	Returns the variance of the numbers in the Offset column (O) of the Input range (I) that meet the criteria (C).

The purpose of these functions is to return a statistic, like the average, on the values in the column of the records that meet the specified criteria. For example, with the database in Figure 6-1 in main memory, let's compute the average age of the male employees and the average age of the female employees.

The first step is to set up the criteria for each average. For the average age of females, use the criteria shown in cells H3 and H4 in Figure 6-21. Likewise, for the average age of males, use the criteria shown in cells I3 and I4. Next, enter the labels that identify the averages. This is shown in cells A16 and A17 in Figure 6-21.

FIGURE 6-21
Using the DAVG function to display the average age of the male employees and the average age of the female employees.

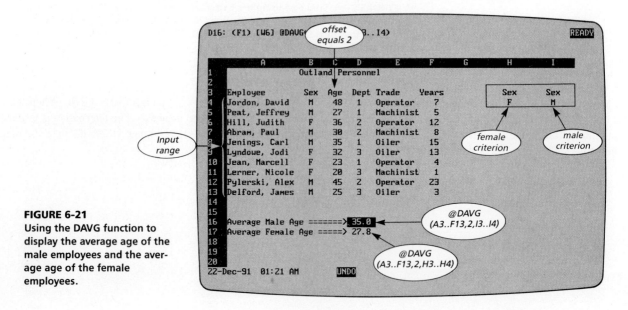

We can now assign the DAVG function to cells D16 and D17. This function has three arguments—Input range, offset, and Criteria range. Since the arguments in the function define the ranges, this function does not require that the ranges be defined through the Data Query command.

Set the Input range to the entire database (A3..F13). The **offset** argument defines the field in the database to be used in the computation. The offset of the leftmost field (Employee) is 0. The offset of the Sex field is 1. The offset of the Age field is 2, and so on. Hence, use the value 2 for the offset argument in the DAVG function. The third argument is the range of cells that make up the criteria—H3..H4 for females and I3..I4 for the males.

With the cell pointer at D16, enter the function @DAVG(A3..F13,2,I3..I4). This causes the average age of the male employees to display in cell D16. Press the Down Arrow key and enter the function @DAVG(A3..F13,2,H3..H4). This function causes the average age of the female employees to display in cell D17. Format cells D16 and D17 to the Fixed type with one decimal position. The effect of entering these two functions and formatting the results is shown in Figure 6-21. To complete this portion of the project, save and print the database, criteria, and averages. Save the database using the file name PROJS-6E.

THE LOOKUP FUNCTIONS

hree functions that we have not discussed are the CHOOSE, VLOOKUP, and HLOOKUP functions. These three functions are called **lookup functions** because they allow you to look up values in a list or a table that is part of the worksheet.

The CHOOSE Function

The CHOOSE function selects a value from a list on the basis of an index. The general form of the CHOOSE function is @CHOOSE(x,y0,y1,y2,...,yn), where the value of x determines the value in the list (y0, y1, y2, ..., yn) to store in the cell. If x equals 0, the first value (y0) is stored in the cell. If x equals 1, the second value (y1) is stored in the cell, and so on. The list can contain values, quoted strings, cell addresses, formulas, range names, or a combination of these.

Consider the partial worksheet in Figure 6-22. The table in the range E1..E7 contains costs. B1 is assigned the index that determines the value in the list that the function returns. The CHOOSE function is assigned to cell B3. It is entered as follows: @CHOOSE(B1,0,E2,E3,E4,E5 + .02,E6*.95,E7,.46). Since B1 is equal to 3, the CHOOSE function returns the fourth value in the list—the value of cell E4.

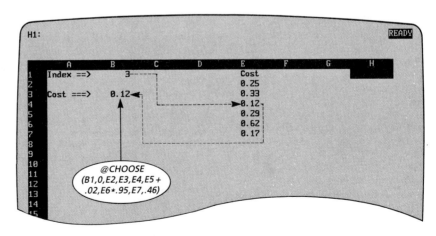

FIGURE 6-22
Using the CHOOSE function to select a value from the list of arguments following the index.

If we change the value of B1 to some other number between 0 and 7, the function will store a different value in B3. If the value in B1 exceeds the number of items in the list, the diagnostic message ERR is assigned to B3. Note that an index value of zero in cell B1 causes the CHOOSE function to assign zero to B3. If cell B1 is assigned a value of 7, the function returns the value .46 from the list and stores it in cell B3.

The VLOOKUP and HLOOKUP Functions

The VLOOKUP and HLOOKUP functions are useful for looking up values in tables, like tax tables, discount tables, and part tables. The general form of the VLOOKUP function is @VLOOKUP(x,range,offset). The first argument, x, is called the **search argument**. It is compared to values in the leftmost column of the multiple-column table defined by the second argument, range. The leftmost column of the range is called the **range column**. Offset defines the column from which a value is returned when a hit is made in the range column. A **hit** occurs when a value is found in the range column that is closest to but not greater than the search argument x.

The offset in the VLOOKUP function can be zero or positive. The offset value of the range column is zero. A positive offset causes a value to be selected from a column to the right of the range column.

While the VLOOKUP function looks up values in a table arranged vertically, the HLOOKUP function looks up values in a table arranged horizontally. Vertical tables are used more often than horizontal tables.

Consider the top screen of Figure 6-23. Column B contains a list of student test scores. A grade scale table is in the range F5..G9. Look up the corresponding letter grade in the grade scale table for each student test score and assign it to the appropriate cell in column D. For example, a test score of 78 returns the letter grade C; a test score of 99 returns the letter grade A. To look up the letter grades for the student test scores, enter the function @VLOOKUP(B5,$F$5..$G$9,1) in cell D5, the location of the letter grade for student number 1035.

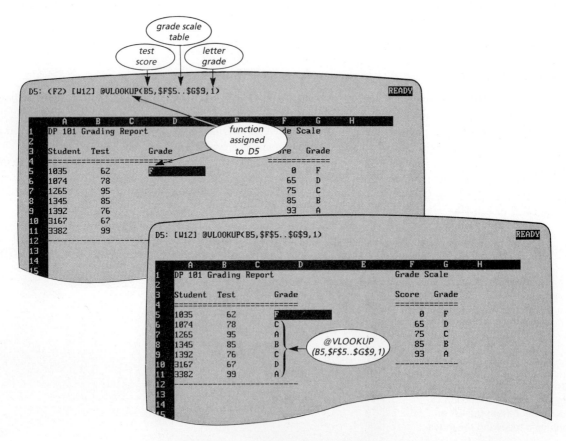

FIGURE 6-23 Top screen—enter the VLOOKUP function in cell D5 to look up the letter grade for the test score in B5. Bottom screen—copy the VLOOKUP function from D5 to the range D6..D11.

The first argument in the VLOOKUP function is cell B5, the test score for student number 1035. The second argument, $F$5..$G$9, defines the grade scale table. The third argument, 1, is the offset. It instructs 1-2-3 to assign the corresponding value in the grade scale table that is located one column to the right of the range column—column F.

Copy the VLOOKUP function in cell D5 to the range D6..D11. As the copy takes place, the first argument in the VLOOKUP function, B5, is adjusted to B6, B7, B8, and so on. The result of copying the VLOOKUP function is shown in the bottom screen of Figure 6-23. In this case, the VLOOKUP function in cells D5 through D11 returns the letter grades that correspond to the student test scores.

THE SEARCH AND REPLACE COMMANDS

he /**R**ange Search (/RS) command is used to locate a string in labels and formulas within a specified range of the worksheet. A **string** consists of a series of letters or numbers that make up a cell entry. Use the Find command to locate a string. Use the Replace command to locate and replace one string with another.

The Find Command

To illustrate the use of the Find command, let's locate the string Oiler in the Outland Personnel worksheet shown in Figure 6-1. To find the string Oiler, do the following:

1. Enter the command /**R**ange **S**earch (/RS).
2. Select the range A4..F13 to search.
3. Type the word Oiler as shown in the top screen of Figure 6-24. Note that 1-2-3 does not differentiate between uppercase and lowercase letters. Hence, Oiler and oiler are the same.
4. Type the letter L for Labels. As shown in the bottom screen of Figure 6-24, you have three selections: Formulas, Labels, and Both. The Labels command tells 1-2-3 to search only those cells containing labels in the worksheet. Formulas means 1-2-3 will search cells containing only formulas. The command Both instructs 1-2-3 to search cells that contain either labels or formulas.
5. Type the letter F for Find as shown in the top screen of Figure 6-25 on the next page.

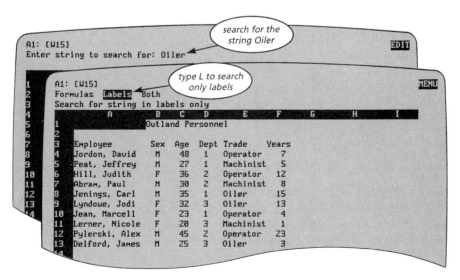

FIGURE 6-24 Initiating a search.

1-2-3 begins the search at the upper left cell of the specified range. It continues the search down and to the right. When 1-2-3 finds the word Oiler, it highlights the cell as shown in the bottom screen of Figure 6-25. Type the letter N to locate the next occurrence of Oiler. Type the letter Q to Quit the search and return 1-2-3 to READY mode.

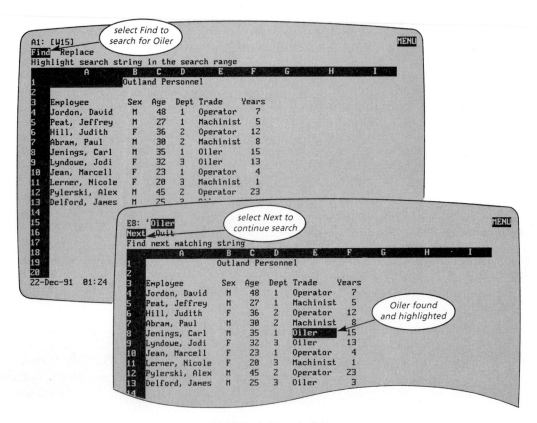

FIGURE 6-25 Completing the search.

The Replace Command

The Replace command is similar to the Find command, except that the search string is replaced by a new string. To illustrate how the Replace command works, let's replace all occurrences of the word Oiler with Boiler. To initiate this command, follow the first four steps described for the Find command in the previous section (Figure 6-24).

With the top screen of Figure 6-25 displayed, type the letter R for Replace, instead of F for Find. 1-2-3 responds by displaying the prompt message "Enter replacement string:". Type the word Boiler as shown in the top screen of Figure 6-26 and press the Enter key. When 1-2-3 displays the menu shown in the middle screen of Figure 6-26, type the letter R for Replace. The first occurrence of Oiler is replaced with Boiler and 1-2-3 continues to search the worksheet. When it finds the next occurrence of Oiler, it redisplays the menu shown in the middle screen of Figure 6-26. This next occurrence is not changed until you select one of the commands. The bottom screen of Figure 6-26 shows all occurrences of Oiler changed to Boiler.

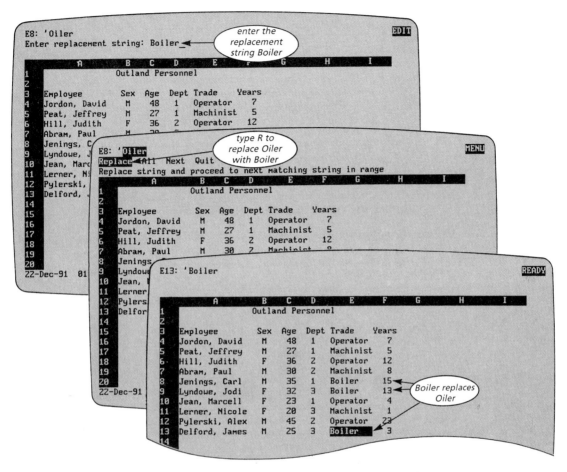

FIGURE 6-26 Completing a string replacement.

Table 6-6 describes the functions of the Replace commands available in the middle screen of Figure 6-26.

TABLE 6-6   Summary of the Commands in the
Range Search Replace Menu

COMMAND	FUNCTION
Replace	Replaces the highlighted string and highlights the next cell containing the search string.
All	Replaces all remaining occurrences of the search string.
Next	Finds the next occurrence of the search string without changing the cell that is highlighted.
Quit	Stops the search and returns 1-2-3 to READY mode.

PROJECT SUMMARY

*I*n this project you learned how to sort and query a worksheet database. You sorted the database in two different ways, first by employee name and then by years of seniority within sex code.

Querying a database involves searching for records that meet a specified criteria. The selected records can be highlighted, extracted, or deleted.

Powerful database functions can be used to generate information about the database. In this project you were introduced to the lookup functions. These functions are used to return a value from a list or table. Finally, the Search and Replace commands were discussed.

Each of the steps required to build and manipulate the worksheet database presented in Project 6 is listed in the following tables.

SUMMARY OF KEYSTROKES—PROJS-6 (Figure 6-1)

STEPS	KEY(S) PRESSED	STEPS	KEY(S) PRESSED
1	/WCS16 ↵	13	[F5]A4 ↵ Jordon, David → ^M → 48 → ^1 → Operator → 7 ↵
2	→ /WCS5 ↵	14	[F5]A5 ↵ Peat, Jeffrey → ^M → 27 → ^1 → Machinist → 5 ↵
3	→ /WCS5 ↵	15	[F5]A6 ↵ Hill, Judith → ^F → 36 → ^2 → Operator → 12 ↵
4	→ /WCS6 ↵	16	[F5]A7 ↵ Abram, Paul → ^M → 30 → ^2 → Machinist → 8 ↵
5	→ → /WCS5 ↵	17	[F5]A8 ↵ Jenings, Carl → ^M → 35 → ^1 → Oiler → 15 ↵
6	[F5]B1 ↵ Outland Personnel ↓	18	[F5]A9 ↵ Lyndowe, Jodi → ^F → 32 → ^3 → Oiler → 13 ↵
7	↓ ← Employee →	19	[F5]A10 ↵ Jean, Marcell → ^F → 23 → ^1 → Operator → 4 ↵
8	^Sex →	20	[F5]A11 ↵ Lerner, Nicole → ^F → 20 → ^3 → Machinist → 1 ↵
9	"Age →	21	[F5]A12 ↵ Pylerski, Alex → ^M → 45 → ^2 → Operator → 23 ↵
10	^Dept →	22	[F5]A13 ↵ Delford, James → ^M → 25 → ^3 → Oiler → 3 ↵
11	Trade →	23	[Home]
12	"Years ↵	24	/FSPROJS-6 ↵

SUMMARY OF KEYSTROKES—Sorting PROJS-6
by Employee Name (Figure 6-6)

STEPS	KEY(S) PRESSED
1	/FRPROJS-6 ↵
2	/DS
3	DA4.F13 ↵
4	PA4 ↵ A ↵
5	G
6	/PPRA1.F13 ↵ AGPPQ
7	/FSPROJS-6A ↵

SUMMARY OF KEYSTROKES—Sorting PROJS-6 by Years of Seniority
within Sex Code (Figure 6-9)

STEPS	KEY(S) PRESSED
1	/FRPROJS-6 ←
2	/DS
3	DA4.F13 ←
4	PB4 ← A ←
5	SF4 ← ←
6	G
7	/PPRA1.F13 ← AGPPQ
8	/FSPROJS-6B ←

SUMMARY OF KEYSTROKES—Finding Records That Meet the Criteria
Sex = M AND Dept = 2 (Figure 6-14)

STEPS	KEY(S) PRESSED	STEPS	KEY(S) PRESSED
1	/FRPROJS-6 ←	7	CH3.I4 ←
2	F5 B3 ← /C ← H3 ←	8	F ↓ ↓
3	F5 D3 ← /C ← I3 ←	9	Esc
4	F5 H4 ← ^M → ^2 ←	10	/PPRA1.I13 ← OMR77 ← QAGPPQ
5	/DQ	11	/FSPROJS-6C ←
6	IA3.F13 ←		

SUMMARY OF KEYSTROKES—Extracting Records That Meet the Criteria
Age > = 27 AND NOT (Dept = 3) AND Years < 10 (Figure 6-20)

STEPS	KEY(S) PRESSED	STEPS	KEY(S) PRESSED
1	/FRPROJS-6 ←	9	F5 B3 ← /C ← C16 ←
2	F5 C3 ← /C ← G3 ←	10	/DQ
3	→ /C ← H3 ←	11	IA3.F13 ←
4	→ → /C ← I3 ←	12	CG3.I4 ←
5	→ ↓ + C4 > = 27 → ^ ˜3 → + F4 < 10 ←	13	OA16.C16 ←
6	/RFT ← ← ←	14	EQ
7	F5 A3 ← /C ← A16 ←	15	/PPRA1.I20 ← OMR77 ← QAGPPQ
8	F5 D3 ← /C ← B16 ←	16	/FSPROJS-6D ←

SUMMARY OF KEYSTROKES—Using the Database Function DAVG (Figure 6-21)

STEPS	KEY(S) PRESSED
1	/FRPROJS-6 ↵
2	[F5] B3 ↵ /C ↵ H3.I3 ↵
3	[F5] H4 ↵ ^F → ^M ↵
4	[F5] A16 ↵ Average Male Age ======> ↓
5	Average Female Age =====> ↵
6	[F5] D16 ↵ @DAVG(A3.F13,2,I3.I4) ↓
7	@DAVG(A3.F13,2,H3.H4) ↑
8	/RFF1 ↵ ↓ ↵
9	/FSPROJS-6E ↵
10	/PPRA1.I17 ↵ AGPPQ

The following list summarizes the material covered in Project 6:

1. A **database** is an organized collection of data.
2. The data related to a person, place, or thing is called a **record**.
3. The data items that make up a record are called **fields**.
4. Each row in a worksheet can be used to store a record.
5. Each column in a worksheet can be used to store a field.
6. The row immediately above the first record contains the field names.
7. A **database management system (DBMS)** is a software package that is used to create a database and store, access, sort, and make additions, deletions, and changes to that database.
8. **Sorting** rearranges the records in a database in a particular sequence on the basis of one or more fields.
9. Data that is in sequence from lowest to highest is in **ascending sequence**.
10. Data that is in sequence from highest to lowest is in **descending sequence**.
11. To sort a database, enter the command /**D**ata **S**ort (/DS). Enter the data range and the sort keys. To complete the sort, enter the Go command.
12. The data range for a sort is usually all the records in the database. Never include the field names in the data range.
13. A sort key, like the primary key, is assigned a column and a sort sequence.
14. Selecting records in a database on the basis of a specified criteria is called **querying a database**. Records that match the criteria can be highlighted, copied to another part of the worksheet, or deleted.
15. To query a database, enter the command /**D**ata **Q**uery (/DQ).
16. Before you enter the Data Query command, the criteria should be present in the worksheet. If you use an Output range, the field names for the Output range should also be present in the worksheet.
17. The Find command highlights records that pass the criteria.
18. To apply the Find command to a database, use the Data Query command to define the Input range and Criteria range. Finally, type the letter F for Find.
19. The criteria used to pass records include the field names and the values that the field names are compared to. Field names can be compared to labels, numbers, and formulas.
20. Global or wild-card characters are allowed in labels in the criteria. The two valid wild-card characters are the asterisk (*), which means "any characters in this position and all remaining positions," and the question mark (?), which means "any character at this position." The question mark (?) can be used anywhere in the label. The asterisk (*) can only be used at the end of a label.
21. A label preceded by a tilde (˜) in the criteria range negates the condition.
22. The criteria can include the logical operators AND, OR, and NOT.
23. The Extract command is used to copy selected records from the database to the Output range.
24. 1-2-3 includes database statistical functions to generate information about the database.
25. The lookup functions, CHOOSE, VLOOKUP, and HLOOKUP allow you to look up values in a list or table that is part of the worksheet.
26. To search for a string or replace a string with another in the worksheet, use the command /**R**ange /**S**earch (/RS).

STUDENT ASSIGNMENTS

STUDENT ASSIGNMENT 1: True/False

Instructions: Circle T if the statement is true or F if the statement is false.

T F   1. A database is an organized collection of data.
T F   2. A database management system is a worksheet.
T F   3. The series of numbers 1, 3, 4, 5, 6 is in descending sequence.
T F   4. The Reset command in the Sort menu resets the database back to its original sequence.
T F   5. In a sort operation, the secondary-key field has a lower priority than the primary-key field.
T F   6. A sort key is identified by any cell in the column containing the field you wish to sort by.
T F   7. To query a database, you must first select unused cells off to the side or below the database and set up the criteria.
T F   8. The Find command copies selected records to the Output range.
T F   9. The Criteria range must contain at least two rows and two columns.
T F   10. A Criteria range consisting of field names and empty cells below the field names will cause all the records in the database to be selected.
T F   11. The wild-card character asterisk (*) may only be used at the front of a label that is part of the criteria.
T F   12. The tilde (˜) is used to negate a condition in the Criteria range.
T F   13. It is not required that the field names in the Output range be the same as the field names in the Input range.
T F   14. The database functions require that you define the Input range and Criteria range by invoking the Data Query command.
T F   15. The Offset column is relative to the rightmost field in the Input range.
T F   16. The DAVG function returns the average number of records in the database.
T F   17. The Offset column in the VLOOKUP function cannot be negative.
T F   18. An Offset column value of zero causes the VLOOKUP function to return the value in the range column that is closest to but not greater than the search argument.
T F   19. The VLOOKUP and HLOOKUP functions are the same, except that VLOOKUP verifies the search of the table and HLOOKUP does not.
T F   20. The /Range Search (/RS) command causes 1-2-3 to search for a string from left to right in the worksheet, one row at a time.

STUDENT ASSIGNMENT 2: Multiple Choice

Instructions: Circle the correct response.

1. Which one of the following series of numbers is in descending sequence?
    a. 1, 2, 3, 4, 5   b. 5, 4, 3, 2, 1   c. 1, 3, 5, 3, 1   d. none of these
2. Which one of the following commands in the Query menu is used to highlight records?
    a. Find   b. Extract   c. Unique   d. Criteria
3. To properly execute the Find command, the _____ and _____ range must be set.
    a. Input, Output   b. Input, Criteria   c. Data-Range, Output   d. Data-Range, Criteria
4. Which one of the following characters represent "any character in this position?"
    a. tilde (˜)   b. number sign (#)   c. asterisk (*)   d. question mark (?)
5. To copy all records that satisfy the criteria to the Output range, use the _____ command.
    a. Find   b. Extract   c. Delete   d. Output
6. Which one of the following database functions returns the number of nonempty cells in the Offset column (O) of the records in the Input range (I) that meet the Criteria range (C)?
    a. DMAX(I,O,C)   b. DAVG(I,O,C)   c. DCOUNT(I,O,C)   d. DVAR(I,O,C)
7. If a database has four fields, the rightmost column has an Offset value of _____ .
    a. 0   b. 3   c. 4   d. 5
8. Which one of the following functions is used to search a columnar table?
    a. CHOOSE   b. VLOOKUP   c. HLOOKUP   d. SEARCH

STUDENT ASSIGNMENT 3: Understanding Sorting

Instructions: Rewrite the order of the seven records in the database listed below on the basis of the problems that follow. Treat each problem independently.

1. Sort the database into descending sequence by division.
2. Sort the database by district within division. Both sort keys are to be in ascending sequence.
3. Sort the database by department within district within division. All three sort keys are to be in ascending sequence.
4. Sort the database into descending sequence by cost.
5. Sort the database by department within district within division. All three sort keys are to be in descending sequence.

DIVISION	DISTRICT	DEPARTMENT	COST
2	1	2	1.21
1	2	2	2.22
2	1	3	1.57
1	2	1	3.56
1	1	1	1.11
2	1	1	1.45
1	2	3	2.10

STUDENT ASSIGNMENT 4: Understanding Criteria

Instructions: Write the criteria required to select records from the database in Figure 6-1 according to the problems listed below. So that you can better understand what is required for this assignment, we have answered the first problem.

1. Select records that represent male employees who are less than 25 years old.

Criteria:

Sex	Age
M	+ C4 < 25

2. Select records that represent employees whose trade is machinist or oiler.

Criteria:

3. Select records that represent employees whose last names begin with P or who work in department 2.

Criteria:

4. Select records that represent female employees who are at least 30 years old and have at least 10 years of seniority.

Criteria:

5. Select records that represent male employees or employees who are at least 30 years old.

Criteria:

6. Select records that represent male machinist employees who are at least 28 years old and whose last names begin with P.

Criteria:

STUDENT ASSIGNMENT 5: Understanding Database and Lookup Functions

Instructions: Load 1-2-3 and perform the following tasks.

1. Consider Figure 6-21. Write a database function and the criteria that will assign to the current cell the number of years of seniority for the female employee with the maximum years of seniority. Use a Criteria range of I3..I4.
2. Consider Figure 6-21. Write a database function and the criteria that will assign to the current cell the average years of seniority of the male employees. Use a Criteria range of I3..I4.
3. Consider Figure 6-21. Write a database function and the criteria that will assign to the current cell the sum of the ages of the female employees. Use a Criteria range of I3..I4.
4. Consider Figure 6-21. Write a database function and the criteria that will assign to the current cell the average years of seniority for both the male and female employees. Use a Criteria range of I3..I4.
5. Consider Figure 6-22. Use the CHOOSE function to assign cell B3 twelve times the cost in column E. Select the cost in column E on the basis of the index value in cell B1.
6. Consider Figure 6-23. Consider the VLOOKUP function in the top screen of Figure 6-23. Complete the following problems independently and write down the results displayed in column D:
    a. Decrease all test scores in column B by 10 points.
    b. Increase all test scores in column B by 10 points.
    c. Reset the test scores in column B to their original values and change the offset argument in the VLOOKUP function to zero.

STUDENT ASSIGNMENT 6: Building and Sorting a Database of Prospective Programmers

Instructions: Load 1-2-3 and perform the following tasks.

1. Build the database illustrated in Figure 6-27. Use the field sizes listed in Table 6-7.
2. Save and print the database. Use the file name STUS6-6.
3. Sort the records in the database into ascending sequence by name. Print the sorted version.
4. Sort the records in the database by age within sex. Select descending sequence for the sex code and ascending sequence for the age. Print the sorted version.

TABLE 6-7 Field Descriptions for the Prospective Programmer Database

FIELD NAME	COLUMN	TYPE OF DATA	SIZE
Name	A	Label	16
Sex	B	Label	5
Age	C	Numeric	5
Years	D	Numeric	7
BASIC	E	Label	7
COBOL	F	Label	7
C	G	Label	5
RPG	H	Label	5
123	I	Label	5
DBASE	J	Label	7

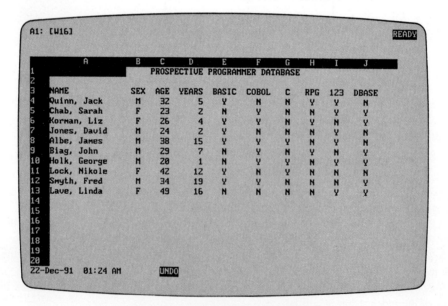

FIGURE 6-27 Student Assignment 6

STUDENT ASSIGNMENT 7: Finding Records in the Prospective Programmer Database

Instructions: Load 1-2-3 and perform the following tasks.

1. Load the database created in Student Assignment 6 (STUS6-6). This worksheet is illustrated in Figure 6-27.
2. For the Criteria range, copy row 3 (A3..J3) to row 15 (A15..J15).
3. In columns E through J of the database, the letter Y indicates that a prospective programmer knows the language or software package identified by the field name. The letter N indicates no experience with the language or software package. Find records that meet the following criteria. Treat each set of criteria in problems a through e separately.
   a. Find all records that represent prospective programmers who are female and can program in COBOL.
   b. Find all records that represent prospective programmers who can program in BASIC and RPG and use 123.
   c. Find all records that represent prospective male programmers who are at least 26 years old and can use dBASE.
   d. Find all records that represent prospective programmers who know COBOL and dBASE.
   e. Find all records that represent prospective programmers who know at least one programming language and can use 123 or dBASE.
   f. All prospective programmers who did not know dBASE were sent to a seminar on the software package. Use the Find command to locate the records of these programmers and change the entries from the letter N to the letter Y under the field name dBASE. Save and print the database and the accompanying Criteria range. Use the file name STUS6-7.

STUDENT ASSIGNMENT 8: Extracting Records from the Prospective Programmer Database

Instructions: Load 1-2-3 and perform the following tasks.

1. Load the database created in Student Assignment 6 (STUS6-6). This worksheet is illustrated in Figure 6-27.
2. For the Criteria range, copy row 3 (A3..J3) to row 15 (A15..J15). For the Output range, copy the field names NAME, SEX, and AGE (A3..C3) to K3..M3. Change the widths of column K to 16, column L to 5, and column M to 5. Extract the three fields from the records that meet the criteria in problems a through e. Treat each extraction in problems a through e separately. Print the worksheet after each extraction.
   a. Extract from records that represent prospective programmers who are female.
   b. Extract from records that represent prospective programmers who can program in COBOL and RPG.
   c. Extract from records that represent prospective male programmers who are at least 24 years old and can use 123.
   d. Extract from records that represent prospective programmers who know COBOL and dBASE.
   e. Extract from records that represent prospective programmers who do not know how to use any programming language.
3. Save the database with the Criteria range specified in 2e. Use the file name STUS6-8.

STUDENT ASSIGNMENT 9: Property Tax Rate Table Lookup

Instructions: Load 1-2-3 and perform the numbered tasks to build the worksheet shown in Figure 6-28. This worksheet uses the VLOOKUP function in cell C5 to look up the tax rate in the tax table in columns F and G. The VLOOKUP function employs cell C3 as the search argument. From the tax rate, the tax amount due in cell C7 can be determined.

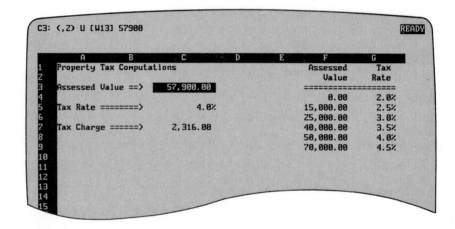

FIGURE 6-28
Student Assignment 9

1. Change the widths of column A to 11, column C to 13, and column F to 10. Leave the widths of the remaining columns at 9 characters.
2. Enter the title, column headings, and row identifiers.
3. Format cells C3 and C7 and range F4..F9 to the Comma (,) type with two decimal positions. Format cell C5 and range G4..G9 to the Percent type with one decimal position.
4. Enter the table values in the range F4..G9.
5. Assign the function @VLOOKUP(C3,F4..G9,1) to cell C5.
6. Assign the formula +C3*C5 to cell C7. This cell displays the tax amount due.
7. Test the worksheet to ensure that the VLOOKUP function is working properly.
8. Use the command /Worksheet Global Protection Enable (/WGPE) to enable (turn on) cell protection. Unprotect cell C3.
9. Save the worksheet. Use the file name STUS6-9.
10. Determine the tax rate and tax charge for the following assessed valuations: $10,980.00; $25,000.00; $350,450.00; $48,560.00; and $57,900.00. Remember that commas (,) are not allowed in a numeric entry. Print the worksheet for each assessed valuation.

APPENDIX

Command Structure Charts for Release 2.2

his appendix includes structure charts for each of the commands in the main command menu of Release 2.2. The red commands indicate features added in Release 2.2.

The Worksheet Command

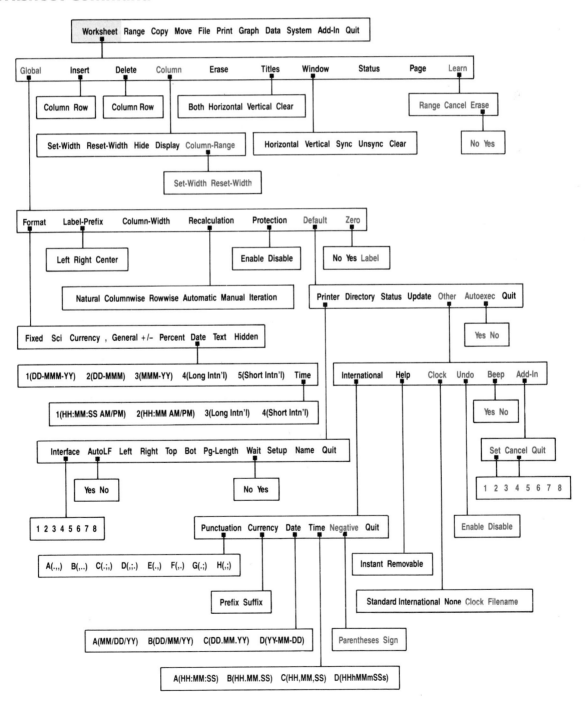

The Range Command

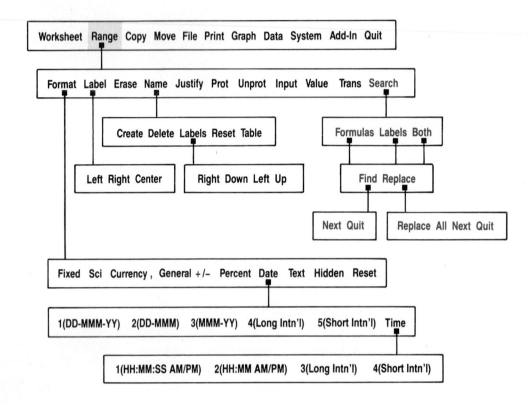

The Copy and Move Commands

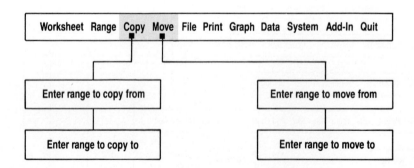

The File Command

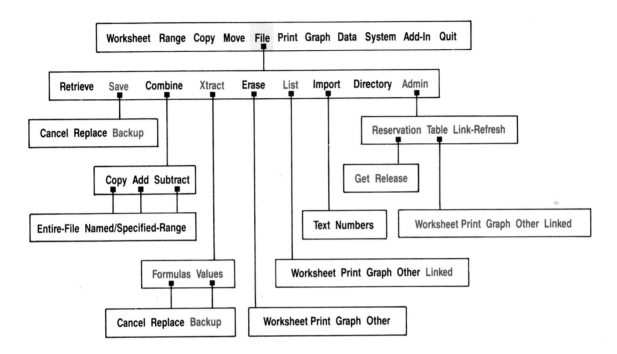

The Print Command

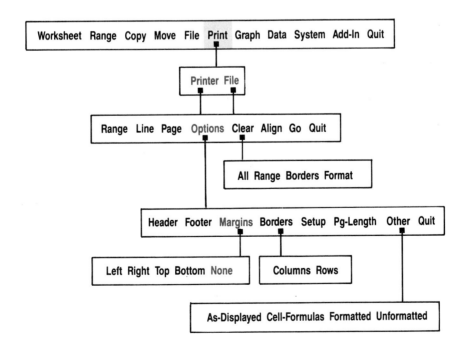

The Graph Command

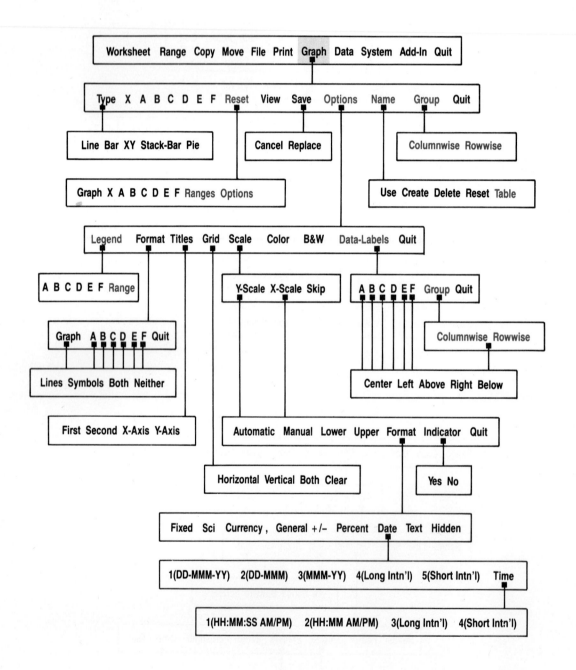

The Data Command

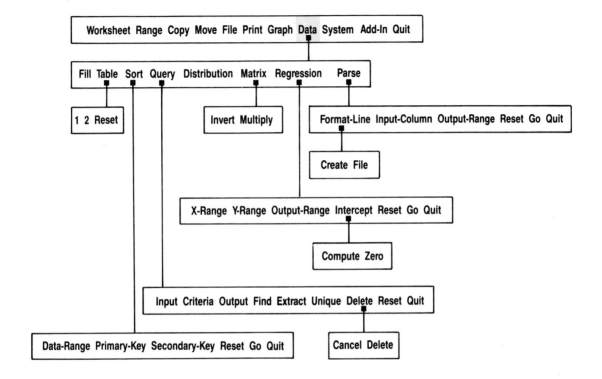

The System Command

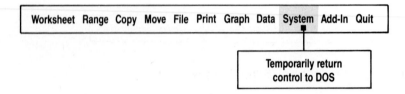

The Add-In Command

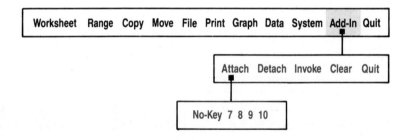

The Quit Command

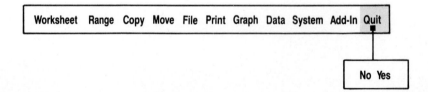

The PrintGraph Command

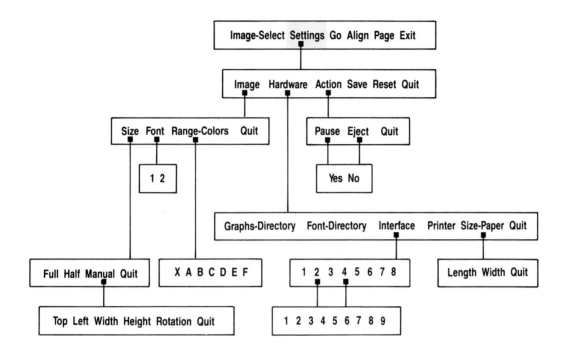

Lotus 1-2-3 Index

Database Management Using dBASE III PLUS

Creating, storing, sorting, and retrieving data are important tasks. In their personal lives, most people keep data in a variety of records such as the names, addresses, and telephone numbers of friends and business associates, records of investments, and records of expenses for income tax purposes. These records must be arranged so that the data can be accessed easily when required. In business, information must also be stored and accessed quickly and easily. Personnel and inventory records must be kept; payroll information and other types of data must be accumulated and periodically updated. Like personal records, business records must be organized so that the information they contain can be retrieved easily and rapidly.

The term **database** describes a collection of data organized in a manner that allows access, retrieval, and use of that data. A database is a structure that can hold data concerning many different types of objects (technically called **entities**) as well as relationships between these objects. For example, a company's database might hold data on such objects as sales reps and customers. In addition, the database would include the relationship between sales reps and customers; that is, we could use the data in the database to determine the sales rep who represents any particular customer, and to determine all the customers who are represented by any given sales rep.

Figure 1 gives a sample of such a database. It consists of two tables: SLSREP and CUSTOMER. The columns in the SLSREP table include the sales rep number, name, address, total commission, and commission rate. For example, the name of sales rep 3 is Mary Jones. She lives at 123 Main St. in Grant, Michigan. Her total commission is $2,150.00 and her commission rate is 5 percent.

SLSREP_ NUMBER	SLSREP_NAME	SLSREP_ADDRESS	TOTAL_ COMMISSION	COMMISSION_ RATE
3	Mary Jones	123 Main,Grant,MI	2150.00	.05
6	William Smith	102 Raymond,Ada,MI	4912.50	.07
12	Sam Brown	419 Harper,Lansing,MI	2150.00	.05

sales rep 3

CUSTOMER_ NUMBER	NAME	ADDRESS	CURRENT_ BALANCE	CREDIT_ LIMIT	SLSREP_ NUMBER
124	Sally Adams	481 Oak,Lansing,MI	418.75	500	3
256	Ann Samuels	215 Pete,Grant,MI	10.75	800	6
311	Don Charles	48 College,Ira,MI	200.10	300	12
315	Tom Daniels	914 Cherry,Kent,MI	320.75	300	6
405	Al Williams	519 Watson,Grant,MI	201.75	800	12
412	Susan Lin	16 Elm,Lansing,MI	908.75	1000	3
522	Mary Nelson	108 Pine,Ada,MI	49.50	800	12
567	Joe Baker	808 Ridge,Harper,MI	201.20	300	6
587	Judy Roberts	512 Pine,Ada,MI	57.75	500	6
622	Dan Martin	419 Chip,Grant,MI	575.50	500	3

customers of sales rep 3

FIGURE 1 Sample Database of Sales Reps and Customers

The first five columns in the customer table include the customer number, name, address, current balance, and credit limit. The name of customer 622 is Dan Martin. He lives at 419 Chip St. in Grant, Michigan. His current balance is $575.50, which happens to exceed his $500 credit limit.

The last column in the customer table, SLSREP_NUMBER, serves a special purpose. It *relates* customers and sales reps. Using this column, we can see that Dan Martin's sales rep is sales rep 3 (Mary Jones). Likewise, we can see that Mary Jones also represents customers 124 (Sally Adams) and 412 (Susan Lin). We do this by first looking up Mary's number in the SLSREP table and then looking for all rows in the CUSTOMER table that contain this number in the column labeled SLSREP_NUMBER.

In a sense, the tables shown in Figure 1 form a database even if they are simply kept on paper. But for easy and rapid access, they should be kept on a computer. All that is needed to do this is a tool that will assist users in accessing such a database. The term database management system describes this tool. A **database management system** or **DBMS** is a software product that can be used easily to create a database; make additions, deletions, and changes to data in the database; sort the data in the database; and retrieve data from the database in a variety of ways.

The most widely used DBMS available for personal computers is dBASE III PLUS, developed by Ashton-Tate. dBASE III PLUS is a powerful DBMS. Its commands let users easily create and manage databases for either personal or business needs. dBASE III PLUS is one of a general category of database management systems called **relational**. In simplest terms, this means that the data in the database can be visualized in exactly the fashion you saw in Figure 1, that is, as a collection of tables, each consisting of a series of rows and columns, which relate different pieces of data.

The dBASE III PLUS software package used in this book is an educational version of dBASE III PLUS. This version contains all the features of the original product except that the number of rows in each table is limited to 31. From this point on we will refer to dBASE III PLUS as simply dBASE.

In the first five projects, you will use a dBASE feature called the ASSISTANT. The **ASSISTANT** is a collection of menus that assist you in processing the data in a database. The menus and choices covered in this text are shown in Figure 2. Don't worry about the specifics of these options now. They will become clear as you work your way through the material in these projects. In Project 6, you will learn to type commands to access the database. The commands you will use are shown in Figure 3 on the next page. Again, don't worry about the specifics at this point.

OPTION	PURPOSE
Set Up	Activate a
Database file	database file
View	view
Quit dBASE III PLUS	leave dBASE III PLUS
Create	Create a
Database file	database file (extension DBF)
View	view (extension VUE)
Report	report (extension FRM)
Update	Change a database file by
Append	adding records at the end
Edit	changing records viewing one at a time
Browse	changing records viewing several at a time
Replace	changing the data in all records that satisfy some condition
Delete	deleting records
Recall	undeleting records
Pack	physically removing deleted records
Position	Move the record pointer by
Seek	finding a match using an index
Locate	finding the first record that satisfies some condition
Goto Record	specifying a record number
Retrieve	Retrieve data from a database file
List	show desired fields and records on the screen or printer
Display	like "List" (differences between the two are covered in the text)
Report	print a report
Sum	calculate a total
Average	calculate an average
Count	count the number of records
Organize	
Index	create an index (extension NDX)
Sort	sort a database file
Modify	Change an existing
Database file	database file
Report	report file
Tools	
List structure	show the structure of the active database file

FIGURE 2 Menus and Options within the dBASE ASSISTANT

COMMAND	PURPOSE
APPEND	Add records to a database file
AVERAGE	Calculate an Average
CLEAR	Clear the screen
COUNT	Count the number of records
DISPLAY	Show desired fields and records
DO	Run a command file (program)
EJECT	Force the printer to advance to the top of the next page
MODIFY COMMAND	Create a command file (program) (extension PRG)
SET VIEW TO	Activate a view
SORT	Sort a database file
SUM	Calculate a total
USE	Activate a database file

FIGURE 3
dBASE Commands

Each project ends with four minicases. Minicase 1 in each project involves a database of personal checks. Minicase 2 involves a music library database. Minicase 3 deals with a database for a software store. The database for Minicase 4 contains information on homes for sale. You should work on the same minicase in each project. Your instructor will probably assign you a specific minicase. If not, you can choose any of the four. Just make sure you select the same one in each project.

The material in the minicases is cumulative. That is, the assignment for Minicase 1 in Project 2 builds on the assignment for Minicase 1 from Project 1. It is very important that you work through the minicase completely before proceeding to the next project. If not, you will encounter serious difficulties later on.

As you work through these projects, you will create a number of files and select a name for each one. dBASE will automatically add a period and three characters to the name you have chosen to indicate the type of file created. This is called the file extension. It need not concern you, but if you examine the files on your disk, you will see these extensions. In the first project, for example, you will create a database file and name it EMPLOYEE. Since dBASE uses the extension DBF for database files, the file on your diskette will actually be called EMPLOYEE.DBF. You can see the file types used in these projects and their extensions in Figure 4.

FILE TYPE	EXTENSION
Database file	DBF
Index file	NDX
Report file	FRM
View file	VUE
Command file (program)	PRG

FIGURE 4
dBASE File Types and
Extensions

PROJECT 1

Creating and Displaying a Database

Objectives

You will have mastered the material in this project when you can:

- Plan a database
- Load and use dBASE
- Choose menus and options using the dBASE ASSISTANT

- Create a database file
- Add records to a database file
- Correct errors in a database file
- Display a list of all records in a database file

n Project 1, you will learn how to create a database using dBASE. You will use the menus and options in the ASSISTANT that are shown in blue in Figure 1-1. To illustrate the process, we will work through a sample problem about creating and accessing a company's employee records.

OPTION	PURPOSE
Set Up	Activate a
Database file	database file
View	view
Quit dBASE III PLUS	leave dBASE III PLUS
Create	Create a
Database file	database file (extension DBF)
View	view (extension VUE)
Report	report (extension FRM)
Update	Change a database file by
Append	adding records at the end
Edit	changing records viewing one at a time
Browse	changing records viewing several at a time
Replace	changing the data in all records that satisfy some condition
Delete	deleting records
Recall	undeleting records
Pack	physically removing deleted records
Position	Move the record pointer by
Seek	finding a match using an index
Locate	finding the first record that satisfies some condition
Goto Record	specifying a record number
Retrieve	Retrieve data from a database file
List	show desired fields and records on the screen or printer
Display	like "List" (differences between the two are covered in the text)
Report	print a report
Sum	calculate a total
Average	calculate an average
Count	count the number of records
Organize	
Index	create an index (extension NDX)
Sort	sort a database file
Modify	Change an existing
Database file	database file
Report	report file
Tools	
List structure	show the structure of the active database file

FIGURE 1-1
Menus and Options within
the dBASE ASSISTANT

The employee record form (see Figure 1-2) is the basis of the database. Each record contains an employee number, the employee name, the date hired, a department name, the employee's pay rate, and an entry indicating whether the employee is a member of the union. The forms taken as a whole comprise a **file**. Each form that contains information about a single employee is called a **record**, and the individual units of information within each record are called **fields**. In this example the date hired is a field. All the information about Anthony P. Rapoza is a record. And Anthony Rapoza's record along with the records of all the other employees in the company make up the file.

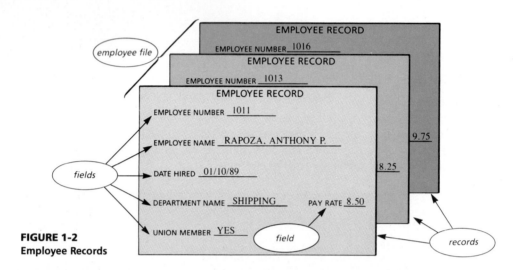

FIGURE 1-2
Employee Records

Now look at the sample table shown in Figure 1-3. Notice that it contains the same data shown in Figure 1-2, but the data is represented in a more concise fashion. The rows in this table are the records, the columns are the fields, and the whole table is a file.

EMPLOYEE NUMBER	EMPLOYEE NAME	DATE HIRED	DEPARTMENT NAME	PAY RATE	UNION MEMBER
1011	Rapoza, Anthony P.	01/10/89	Shipping	8.50	Y
1013	McCormack, Nigel L.	01/15/89	Shipping	8.25	Y
1016	Ackerman, David R.	02/04/89	Accounting	9.75	N
1017	Doi, Chan J.	02/05/89	Production	6.00	Y
1020	Castle, Mark C.	03/04/89	Shipping	7.50	Y
1022	Dunning, Lisa A.	03/12/89	Marketing	9.10	N
1025	Chaney, Joseph R.	03/23/89	Accounting	8.00	N
1026	Bender, Helen O.	04/12/89	Production	6.75	Y
1029	Anderson, Mariane L.	04/18/89	Shipping	9.00	Y
1030	Edwards, Kenneth J.	04/23/89	Production	8.60	Y
1037	Baxter, Charles W.	05/05/89	Accounting	11.00	N
1041	Evans, John T.	05/19/89	Marketing	6.00	N
1056	Andrews, Robert M.	06/03/89	Marketing	9.00	N
1057	Dugan, Mary L.	06/10/89	Production	8.75	Y
1066	Castleworth, Mary T.	07/05/89	Production	8.75	Y

FIGURE 1-3
Employee Table

records

fields

Rather than the term "file," however, dBASE uses the term "database file." Thus, in dBASE, a **database file** is a single table. Recall from the introduction that a relational database can be a single table or a collection of tables. In dBASE terminology, this means that a database is a collection of database *files*. (You don't have to worry about the distinction at this point, however. In the examples discussed in the first four projects, each database will consist of a single database file (a single table). In Project 5, you will encounter databases that contain more than one database file.

Other database management systems use the terms **table** (for file), **row** (for record), and **column** (for field). We use the dBASE terminology throughout this text.

PLANNING A DATABASE FILE

Before using dBASE to create a database file, you must perform four steps. These steps are:

1. Select a name for the database file.
2. Define the structure of the database file. This means determining the fields that will be part of the file.
3. Name the fields.
4. Determine the type and width of each field.

Naming a Database File

When using dBASE, you must assign a name to each database file. The rules for forming a name are:

1. The name can be up to eight characters long.
2. The first character must be a letter of the alphabet.
3. The remaining characters can be letters, numbers, or the underscore (_).
4. Blank spaces are not allowed.

You should select names that are as meaningful as possible. This will make it easier to identify the database file later. In the sample problem, let's use the name EMPLOYEE.

Defining the Structure of a Database File

To define the structure of the database file, you must determine the fields that will make up the file. The fields you want to include must be based upon the type of information you want to extract from the database. We have determined that we will require access to each of the fields contained on the employee form in Figure 1-2, that is, the employee number field, the employee name field, the date hired field, the department name field, the pay rate field, and the field that tells whether or not the employee is a member of the union. In dBASE, you can have a maximum of 128 fields in a record and records can be a maximum of 4000 characters long.

Naming the Fields

You must assign a unique name to each field in the database.

1. A field name can contain up to 10 characters.
2. The first character must be alphabetic.
3. The remaining characters can consist of letters of the alphabet, numbers, or the underscore (_).
4. No blank spaces are allowed.

The chart in Figure 1-4 illustrates the field names that will be used in the sample database file.

FIELD DESCRIPTION	FIELD NAME
EMPLOYEE NUMBER	NUMBER
EMPLOYEE NAME	NAME
DATE HIRED	DATE
DEPARTMENT NAME	DEPARTMENT
PAY RATE	PAY_RATE
UNION MEMBER	UNION

FIGURE 1-4
Fields in Employee File

You should select meaningful field names that are closely related to the contents of the field. Note that the field name for the pay rate field is PAY_RATE. We often use the underscore to join words together to improve readability, because blanks are not allowed within field names.

Defining Field Types

Next, you must determine the type of each field in the database. There are five field types in dBASE. They are:

1. **Character fields** These fields may be used to store any printable characters that can be entered from the keyboard. This includes letters of the alphabet, numbers, special characters, and blanks. A maximum of 254 characters may be included in a character field.
2. **Date fields** Date fields are used to store dates. Unless otherwise specified, the date is stored in the form MM/DD/YY (month/day/year). The field width is always eight characters.
3. **Numeric fields** These fields are used to store integer or decimal numbers. Integer numbers are numbers that do not contain a decimal point. Numeric fields may contain a plus (+) or minus (–) sign. Accuracy is to 15 digits. A field must be defined as numeric if it will be used in a calculation.
4. **Logical fields** Logical fields consist of a single value representing a true or false condition. The entry must be T (true), F (false), Y (yes), or N (no). Lowercase letters of the alphabet can also be used. The field width is always one character.
5. **Memo fields** Memo fields are used to store large blocks of text such as words or sentences.

Figure 1-5 illustrates the field type for the various fields used in the sample problem. Note that the employee number is specified as a character field. A field that contains all numbers but is not involved in calculations should normally be defined as a character field. The name field is defined as a character field, the date hired field as a date field, the department name field as a character field, the pay rate field as a numeric field, and the union code field as a logical field.

FIELD DESCRIPTION	FIELD NAME	FIELD TYPE	WIDTH	DECIMAL POSITIONS
EMPLOYEE NUMBER	NUMBER	CHARACTER	4	
EMPLOYEE NAME	NAME	CHARACTER	20	
DATE HIRED	DATE	DATE	8	
DEPARTMENT NAME	DEPARTMENT	CHARACTER	10	
PAY RATE	PAY_RATE	NUMERIC	5	2
UNION MEMBER	UNION	LOGICAL	1	

decimal positions only necessary for numeric fields

FIGURE 1-5
Field Characteristics for Employee File

Indicating Width and Decimal Position

The width of the field indicates the maximum number of characters that will be contained in the field. Date fields always have width 8 and logical fields always have width 1. For other types of fields, you must specify the width. In addition, for numeric fields, you must specify the decimal position, or the location of the decimal point. For example, a decimal position of 2 indicates that there are two positions to the right of the decimal point.

In Figure 1-5 the PAY_RATE field is defined as having a width of five characters. This means that the maximum value that can be stored in the PAY_RATE field is 99.99. In a numeric field, count the decimal point when specifying the field width.

USING dBASE

Loading dBASE

*T*o create a database file, you must load dBASE into main memory. First, load the operating system and enter the current date and time. You should see the A> prompt displayed on the screen. Place your first dBASE disk in drive A. Then type the word dbase in either uppercase or lowercase letters. The example in Figure 1-6 uses lowercase letters. (If you have dBASE on a hard disk drive, make that the default disk before typing the word dbase.)

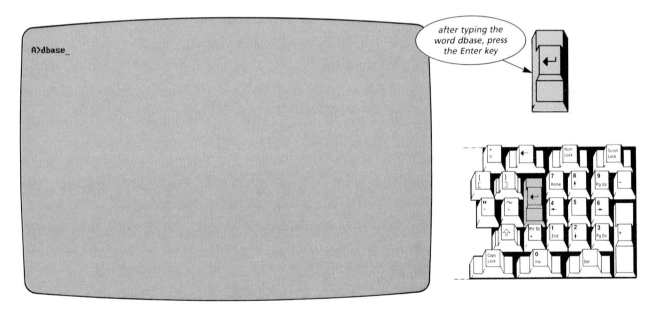

FIGURE 1-6 Loading dBASE

After typing the word dbase, press the Enter key (also called the Return key). After you have done this, dBASE will be loaded into main computer memory and the display in Figure 1-7 will appear on the screen.

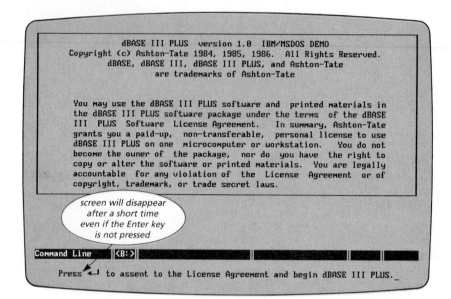

FIGURE 1-7
The License Screen for
dBASE III PLUS

The paragraph displayed in Figure 1-7 describes the licensing agreement and related information. The line at the bottom of the screen tells you to press the Enter key to begin working with dBASE. Once you have done this, the display will change. (If you wait a few seconds without pressing the Enter key, the display will change automatically.) The display will change to the screen shown in Figure 1-8 unless you are using dBASE on a hard disk, in which case you will immediately proceed to the display shown in Figure 1-9.

The message at the bottom of the display in Figure 1-8 tells you to place the second dBASE disk in drive A and a data disk in drive B. Initially, this data disk will be empty. As you create files using dBASE, you will put them on this disk. Once these diskettes have been inserted in the correct drives, press the Enter key. (If you are using dBASE on a hard disk, you should still place your data disk in drive B unless your instructor indicates differently.)

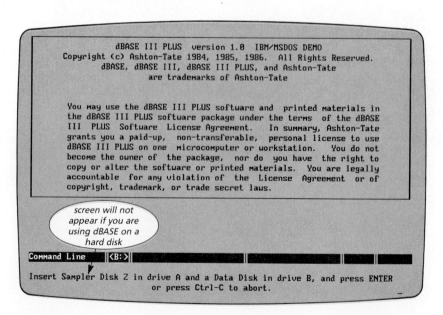

FIGURE 1-8
Ready to Insert Disks

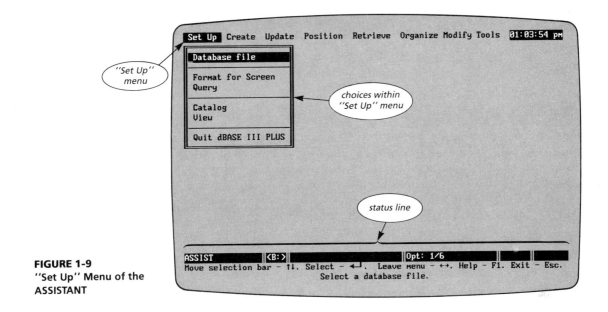

FIGURE 1-9
"Set Up" Menu of the
ASSISTANT

The ASSISTANT

At this point, the display will look like the one shown in Figure 1-9. This screen is part of the dBASE ASSISTANT. The **ASSISTANT** is a collection of menus that assist you in processing the data in a database. When you use the menus, you are in **ASSIST** mode. The names of the various menus are displayed across the top of the screen. They are "Set Up," "Create," "Update," "Position," "Retrieve," "Organize," "Modify," and "Tools." Notice that the name of one of the menus is highlighted on the screen. The highlight indicates the currently selected menu. Thus, at this point, the "Set Up" menu is the one from which you can choose. Press the Right Arrow key a few times. Notice how the highlight and the box move to the menus immediately to the right of the current menu. Press the Left Arrow key a few times and notice how the highlight and the box move to the menus immediately to the left. Notice also how the choices within the selected menu are displayed in a box on the screen.

To indicate your choice, you would use the Up or Down Arrow keys to move the highlight within the box to the desired selection and then press Enter. Try this with the choices in the "Set Up" menu. Move the highlight to your selection. Do not press Enter yet, however.

The line shown at the bottom of the screen is called the **status line** or **status bar**. This line gives information about the current status of dBASE. In Figure 1-9, for example, the status line indicates that:

1. You are currently in ASSIST mode; that is, you are using the ASSISTANT but have not yet begun to take any special action.
2. The default drive for data files is B.
3. No database file is currently active (if one were active, its name would appear in the next portion of the screen).
4. The option currently highlighted is option 1 out of 6.

Compare the status line in Figure 1-9 to the one shown in Figure 1-10 which indicates that:

1. Data in a database file is being EDITed (changed).
2. The file is located in drive B.
3. The file name is EMPLOYEE.
4. The current position in the file is record 1.
5. There are 15 records altogether.
6. The insert mode is on (Ins).

If insert mode is on, a character that you type will be inserted into a string of characters rather than replacing an existing character. Pressing Ins when insert mode is off turns it on. Pressing Ins when insert mode is on turns it off.

Two other lines, beneath the status line, give important information. The first line indicates the effect of special keys. In Figure 1-9, for example, this line indicates that the Up and Down Arrow keys are used to move the status bar, the Enter key is used to make a selection, the Right or Left Arrow keys are used to leave this menu (and move to another), and so on. The second line under the status line gives a brief description of the current option.

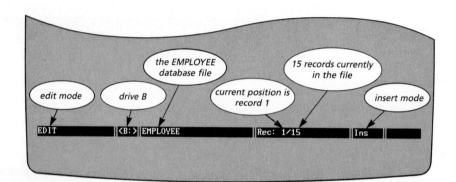

FIGURE 1-10
Status Line

The Dot Prompt

Press the Esc key with the ASSISTANT menu on the screen. Your display will change to the one shown in Figure 1-11. The period near the lower left-hand corner of the screen is called the **dot prompt** in dBASE. It puts you into the **dot prompt mode**. (In the student version, the dot is preceded by the word DEMO.)

The dot prompt indicates that dBASE is ready to accept a command. A **dBASE command** is a word or collection of words that will cause some function to be performed by dBASE, such as displaying data or calculating a total. Following the dot prompt is a blinking underscore character called a cursor. The **cursor** indicates where the characters you enter at the keyboard will be displayed.

In Project 6, you will have a chance to type commands at this dot prompt. In the rest of the projects, however, your work will be done through the ASSISTANT in what is termed the **ASSIST mode**. Even though you will be working in the ASSIST mode, you need to be aware of the dot prompt because if you press the Esc key, you may find yourself in this dot prompt mode. Fortunately, there is an easy way to return to the ASSIST mode. Simply press F2 (function key 2). The ASSISTANT menu will return to the screen and you will be back in ASSIST mode.

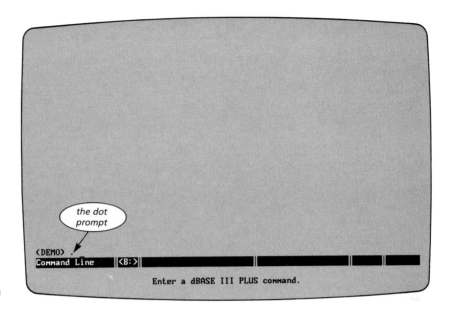

FIGURE 1-11
The Dot Prompt Screen

When you use the ASSISTANT, dBASE actually constructs the commands for you. These are the same commands that you could type at the dot prompt. They are shown immediately above the status line. As you work through the examples in the first five projects, watch these commands as they are being constructed. This will help you when you get to Project 6 and start constructing these commands on your own.

Escaping from Problems

When using the ASSISTANT, you might find that you have selected an option that you did not want and you might not be sure how to leave the option. Even if you have selected the correct option, there may be times when you are not sure how to proceed. In other cases, you may discover that you simply don't have enough time to complete the task you started. For these reasons, you will occasionally want to *escape* from a task.

Normally the Right or Left Arrow keys will allow you to leave a task. If they don't, however, there is another way to escape. Repeatedly press the Esc key. Eventually, this will bring you to the dot prompt (Figure 1-11). Once you see the dot prompt, press F2 and you will return to the "Set Up" menu of the ASSISTANT.

Quitting

You stop using dBASE by returning to the "Set Up" menu (Figure 1-12) and selecting "Quit dBASE III PLUS." First, choose the "Set Up" menu by using the Right or Left Arrow keys. Then move the highlight to "Quit dBASE III PLUS" using the Down Arrow key. After that, press the Enter key. Control will return to the operating system. Practice this now. Then restart dBASE in the same manner as before.

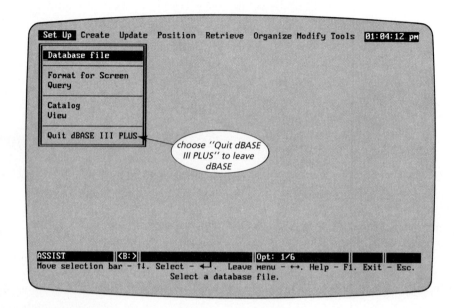

FIGURE 1-12
"Set Up" Menu

Getting Help

If you need additional information about dBASE, you can use the help feature. As indicated on the screen (Figure 1-12), press the F1 key for help. When you press this key, you will see information concerning the menu choice that is currently highlighted on the screen. Pressing the F1 key while the highlight is on the "Database file" option within the "Set Up" menu, for example (see Figure 1-13a), would display the screen shown in Figure 1-13b. Once you have viewed this information, simply press any key and the display will return to its original state.

Practicing

At this point, it's a good idea for you to practice moving through the menus. As you do, note the effect on the last two lines on the screen. Try getting help. Try pressing the Esc key to move to the dot prompt and then pressing F2 to get back to the ASSISTANT. Do this until you are comfortable moving around the menu structure.

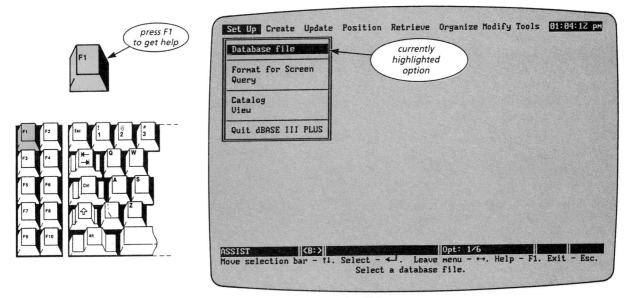

FIGURE 1-13a Getting Help

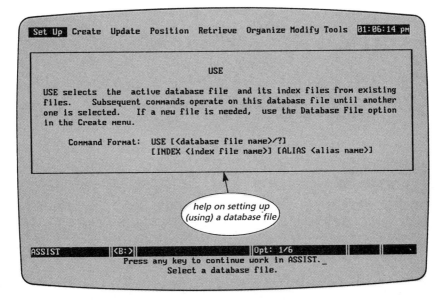

FIGURE 1-13b Sample Help Screen

CREATING THE DATABASE

To create the database, move to the "Create" menu using the Right or Left Arrow keys. If you are currently on the "Set Up" menu, you only have to press the Right Arrow key once. The highlight within the box will already be on "Database file," which is the correct option, so you will not need the Up or Down Arrow keys. Press the Enter key to indicate that "Database file" is your choice.

The display should now look like the one shown in Figure 1-14. (Note: Your display may have only A: and B: in the box. It may also have additional options besides A:, B:, and C:. Don't worry about this.) Make sure that B: in the box is highlighted. If it isn't, use the Up or Down Arrow keys to move the highlight to it, because the file created should be placed on the diskette in drive B. Then press the Enter key. It is now time to indicate the name of the database file.

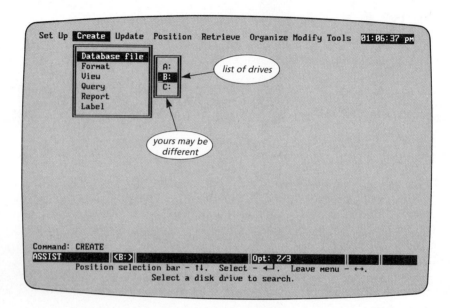

FIGURE 1-14
Creating a Database File

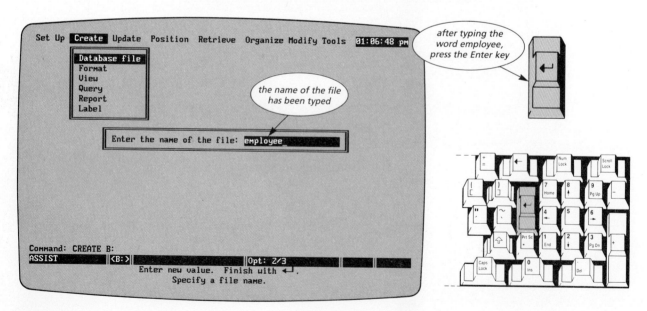

FIGURE 1-15
Entering the Name of the File

As shown in Figure 1-15, type the word employee (in either uppercase or lowercase) and press the Enter key. The screen used to define the structure of the database will appear, as shown in Figure 1-16.

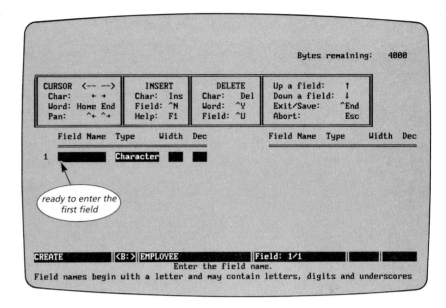

ready to enter the first field

FIGURE 1-16
Entering the First Field

Next, define the structure of the database by specifying the following information for each field: field name, field type, field width, and decimal places (if appropriate). The screen in Figure 1-16 assists you in entering this information. Near the bottom of the screen you will see the file name EMPLOYEE. In the upper right-hand portion of the screen, information specifies the bytes remaining in the record. A *byte* is a single position of main computer memory, the amount of main memory required to store a single character. Thus, you can think of "byte" and "character" as being synonymous. In dBASE, a record can contain a maximum of 4000 bytes or characters, so the number 4000 appears. Underneath the byte display is a box indicating the effect of some of the special keys.

Beneath this box are screen headings for field name, type, width, and dec (decimal position). There are two sets of these entries, one set at the left of the screen and the other set at the right. Beneath the headings at the left of the screen are reverse video blocks. These indicate where you will enter the field name, select the field type, and enter the field width and decimal positions for numeric fields. The cursor is in the first position of the area where you enter the field name. The number 1 to the left of the cursor merely indicates that this is the area in which you will define the first field.

The entry at the bottom of the screen provides information to assist you in making the appropriate entry in the field name portion of the display. This message will change as the cursor moves from one portion of the screen to the next.

Begin by typing the name of the first field you wish to define. In the example, the first field is the employee number field. Recall from Figure 1-5 that the field name is NUMBER. Therefore, enter the word NUMBER as the first field name (Figure 1-17).

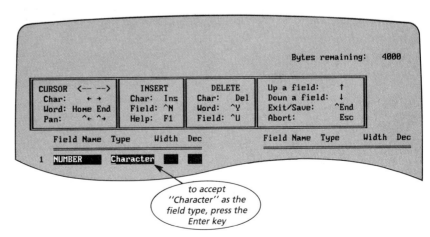

FIGURE 1-17
Selecting Field Type

to accept "Character" as the field type, press the Enter key

If the entry in the field name portion of the screen has less than 10 characters, you must press the Enter key to move the cursor to the next area on the screen. Since the word NUMBER contains only six characters, press the Enter key. When you have done so, the cursor will move to the type column on the screen. Under the type column is the word "Character" within the reverse video block (Figure 1-17).

Next you will specify the type of field being defined. To do this, simply press the space bar until the desired field type is displayed. Do this a few times. After you have pressed it once, the entry in the type column will change to the word "Numeric." A second time changes it to "Date." The next time, it changes to "Logical," and one more time changes it to "Memo." Pressing the space bar again changes it back to "Character," at which point the whole sequence would start all over again.

Because the employee number field is not used in calculations, the field should be defined as a character field. To specify that NUMBER is a character field, make sure the word "Character" is displayed on the screen and press the Enter key. The cursor will then advance to the width column (Figure 1-18).

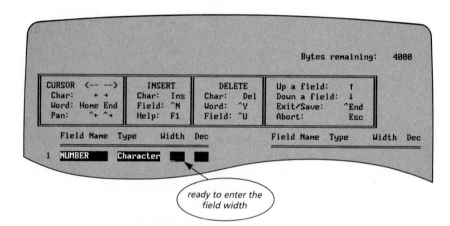

FIGURE 1-18
Entering Field Width

Now you must type the width of the field. In the example, there are a maximum of four digits in the employee number field (see Figure 1-5). Therefore, type the number 4 and press the Enter key, producing the display shown in Figure 1-19. There can be no decimal entries for a character field, so the entries for the NUMBER field are complete once you indicate the width. Thus, the cursor and the reverse video display move to the next line. Look at the upper right corner of Figure 1-19. You will see that 3996 bytes remain for this record.

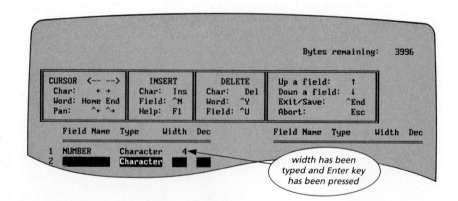

FIGURE 1-19
Ready to Enter Another Field

The entries for the NAME field are illustrated in Figure 1-20. Make these entries in the same fashion as for the NUMBER field. Figure 1-20 also shows the name of the DATE field. You should make the same entry now and then press Enter.

When you press the Enter key after typing the word DATE, the cursor will move to the type column. Because DATE is to be treated as a date field, press the space bar repeatedly until the word "Date" appears in the type column (Figure 1-21) and then press the Enter key. dBASE will automatically specify the width as 8. (Remember that the slashes in a date count as positions in the field.)

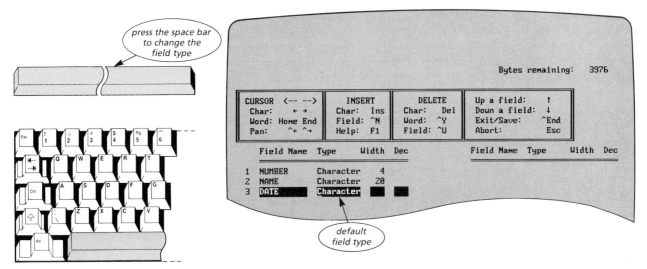

FIGURE 1-20 Changing the Type

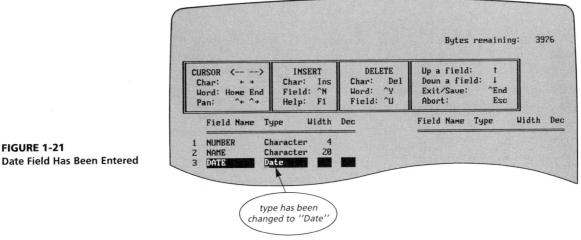

FIGURE 1-21
Date Field Has Been Entered

Make the remaining entries as shown in Figure 1-22.

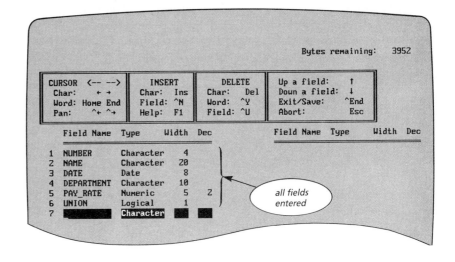

FIGURE 1-22
All Fields Have Been Entered

Because the name DEPARTMENT occupies all positions in the field name portion of the display, when you type the last character (the last T in DEPARTMENT), a beep will sound and the cursor will automatically advance to the next column.

You have now defined all the fields in the database. Press the Enter key while the cursor is in the first position of the blank row (Figure 1-23). A message will appear at the bottom of the screen directing you to press Enter to confirm that you are done or any other key to resume. Press the Enter key again.

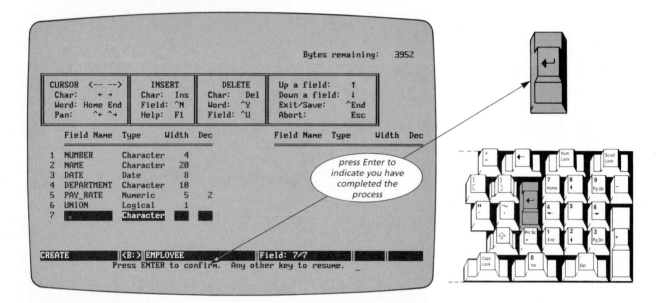

FIGURE 1-23 Completing the Creation Process

At this point, dBASE will ask if records are to be added now. If you answer with the letter Y (yes), you could begin entering records immediately. This is a special shortcut that dBASE provides for adding records. It only works immediately after you create a file. We will use the normal method for adding records, one that is appropriate whether or not the file has just been created. Type the letter N (no) to indicate that you will not use this feature to add any records. The ASSISTANT menu screen will reappear.

ENTERING DATA

Adding Data

ove the highlight to the "Update" menu (see Figure 1-24). To add records, choose the "Append" option. Make sure the word "Append" is highlighted (it should already be) and press Enter, producing the screen shown in Figure 1-25.

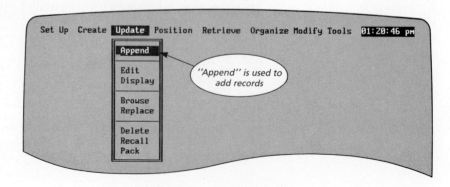

FIGURE 1-24
The "Update" Menu

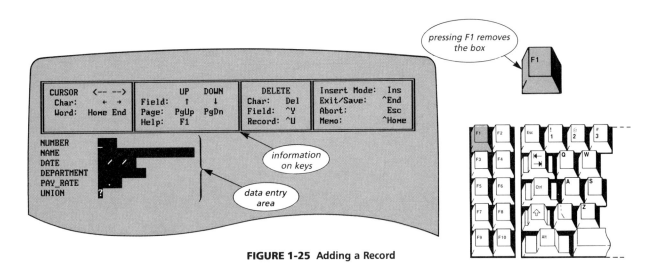

FIGURE 1-25 Adding a Record

At the top of the screen in Figure 1-25 is a box that describes various keys used during the data entry process. Pressing F1 removes the box from the screen. Pressing F1 a second time will return the box to the display. A common practice is to remove it from the screen and then bring it back whenever you need to see any of the information it contains.

The next portion of the screen is the area where you will enter data. It consists of the field names from your database file followed by reverse video blocks representing the maximum number of characters that can be entered in each field. Notice that the DATE field contains slashes. When you enter the date, type a two-digit month, a two-digit day, and a two-digit year. The date will be positioned correctly around the slashes. The PAY_RATE field contains a decimal point in the screen display because it was defined as a field with a width of 5 and two positions to the right of the decimal place. The UNION field, defined as a logical field, contains a question mark because all logical fields have a question mark in the area where you enter the letter Y, N, T, or F.

When you enter a value for UNION, it's a good idea to restrict yourself to just T (true) or F (false), even though dBASE allows you to enter Y (yes) or N (no). It is easy to get confused if you use T or F some of the time and Y or N other times. Further, when dBASE displays this data, it will display only T or F. So even if you enter the letter Y, it will be displayed as T. If you enter N, it will be displayed as F. For these reasons, it makes sense to use only T or F.

Enter the data up to the union code, as shown in Figure 1-26. Note that the name Rapoza, Anthony P. is to be entered incorrectly as Rappozi, Athony P. This will give you a chance to experiment with making corrections.

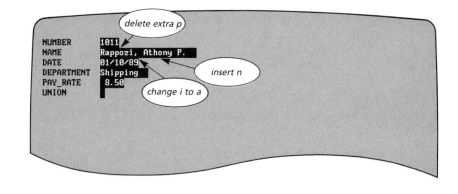

**FIGURE 1-26
Incorrectly Entered Name—
Must Be Fixed**

Enter the data one field at a time. The cursor will automatically move to the next line if the data entered occupies the entire width of the field. If not, you must press the Enter key after you have entered the data for a field. When entering the pay rate, you enter the value with the decimal point. For example, you type the amount 8.50. dBASE will properly position the value around the decimal point in the area reserved for the pay rate.

Correcting Errors During Data Entry

If you make an error when typing data, you can correct it, provided you have not yet pressed the Enter key. Merely press the Backspace key as many times as necessary to delete unwanted characters and then retype the data. The Backspace key is found in the upper right-hand portion of the keyboard (Figure 1-27).

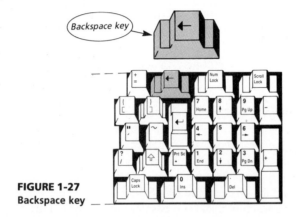

FIGURE 1-27
Backspace key

dBASE has very powerful editing capabilities for correcting errors made *after* you have pressed the Enter key. These editing capabilities are useful both when entering data on the screen that defines the field name, type, width, and decimal position, and when entering data directly into the database.

For example, let's suppose that after you entered the data for PAY_RATE in the first record, you discover that you spelled the name Rapoza, Anthony P. incorrectly as Rappozi, Athony P. (Figure 1-26).

Three errors are apparent. First, there is an extra p in the last name. Second, the last character in the last name should be a instead of i; and third, n should be inserted after the first character in the first name.

You can use the Up, Down, Right, and Left Arrow keys to move the cursor to the location where you want to make a correction. You could simply retype the whole name, this time making sure you do it correctly. Often a quicker alternative is to use the Delete and Insert keys to delete and insert data. Figure 1-28 illustrates the keys that are used for moving the cursor and inserting and deleting data. Let's correct the name by using these keys.

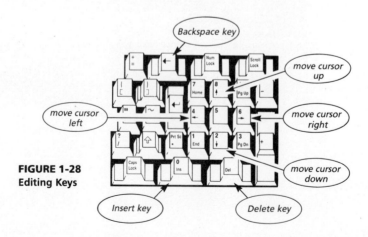

FIGURE 1-28
Editing Keys

First, use the Up and Right Arrow keys to move the cursor so that it is under the extra p in Rappozi. Once the cursor is in position, press the Delete key, found in the lower right-hand portion of the keyboard, to produce the display shown in Figure 1-29. When you press the Delete key, the extra p will be deleted. The field now reads "Rapozi, Athony P." The cursor is positioned under the letter o.

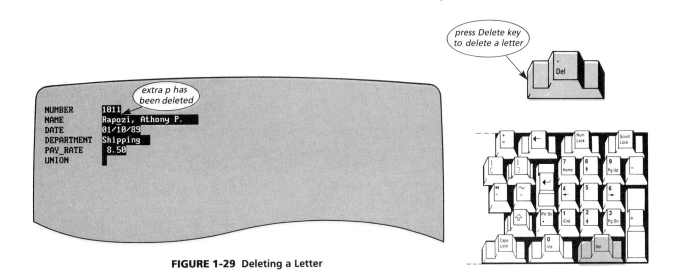

FIGURE 1-29 Deleting a Letter

To change the last character in the name Rapozi from i to a, position the cursor under the i by pressing the Right Arrow key two times. Then, with the cursor positioned under the incorrect character, type the correct letter (a). The results are shown in Figure 1-30. When you type the letter a, it replaces the i and the cursor will move one position to the right. The name now reads "Rapoza, Athony P."

FIGURE 1-30
Letter Has Been Corrected

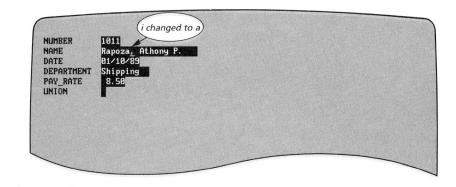

The next step is to insert an n before the letter t in the name Athony. Do this by pressing the Right Arrow key three times to place it under the letter t, pressing the Insert key to enter the insert mode (see the result in Figure 1-31), and then typing the letter n (see the result in Figure 1-32).

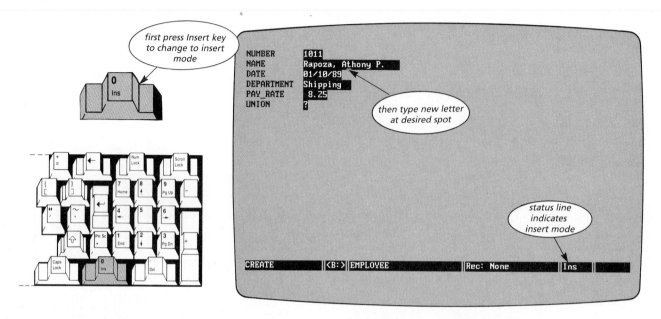

FIGURE 1-31 Inserting a Letter

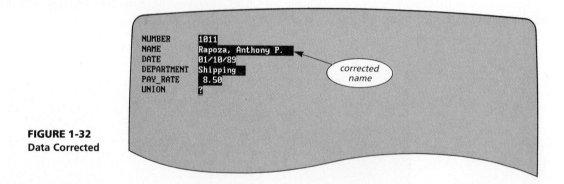

FIGURE 1-32
Data Corrected

When you press the Insert key, the letters "Ins" appear in the lower portion of the screen, indicating that the insert mode is in effect. While you are in this mode, each character you type will be inserted at the location of the cursor. The character at the cursor location and all characters to the right of it will move one position to the right. When you typed the letter n, it was inserted at the location of the cursor and the characters "thony P." were all shifted one position to the right.

After completing the insertion, press the Insert key again to exit from the insert mode. The letters "Ins" will no longer appear on the screen.

Once you have made the corrections to the name, you can resume normal data entry.

Resuming Normal Data Entry

Now enter the union code. dBASE allows you to type either T or F (true or false) or Y or N (yes or no). As mentioned earlier, it is a good idea to restrict yourself to T or F. Therefore, enter the letter T for those employees with Y in the UNION column and the letter F for those employees with N. When you have entered the union code (the letter T in this case), a new screen will appear automatically. It contains the field names and blank reverse video blocks so that you may enter the data for record 2.

Make the entries for record 2 and record 3 as illustrated in Figures 1-33 and 1-34. Note that you are to make some mistakes in the data for record 2. They will be used to illustrate how to correct errors after records have already been added to the database file. Once you have entered these records, terminate the data entry process by pressing the Enter key when the cursor is in the first position of the first field on the screen. At this point, the ASSISTANT menu screen will reappear. The data you have entered is automatically saved, so there is no need for a special save step, which you often encounter when using word processors or spreadsheet programs.

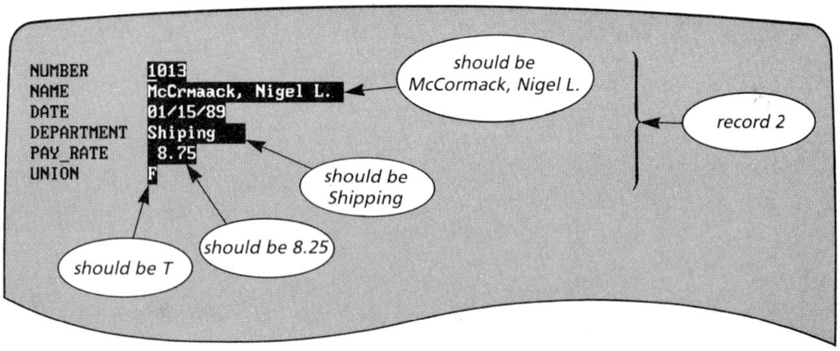

FIGURE 1-33
Second Record (Entered Incorrectly)

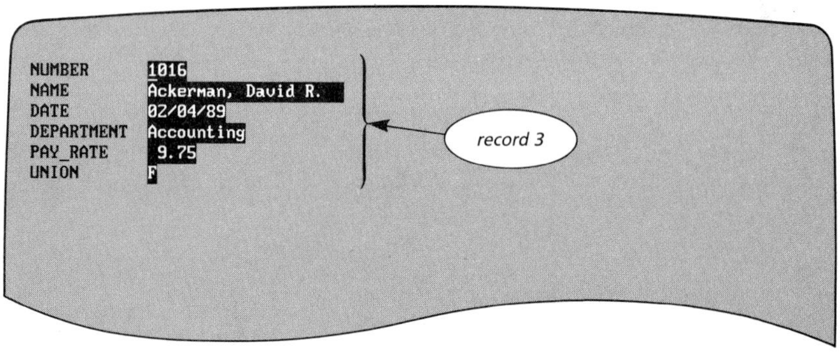

FIGURE 1-34
Third Record Entered

Activating a Database File

As long as you continue working on the EMPLOYEE database file, it remains active. If you leave dBASE, however, EMPLOYEE is no longer active. Thus, if you don't have time to add all the records in a single sitting, you must be able to reactivate the EMPLOYEE database file the next time you start dBASE.

You accomplish this with "Database file" option of the "Set Up" menu (Figure 1-35). Use the Right or Left Arrow keys to move to this menu. (If you had just started dBASE you would already be on this menu.) Make sure the highlight is on "Database file." If it isn't, use the Up or Down Arrow keys to move the highlight to this selection. Then press Enter. Your display should look like the one shown in Figure 1-36.

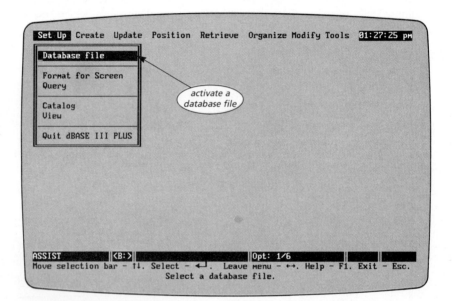

FIGURE 1-35
"Set Up" Menu

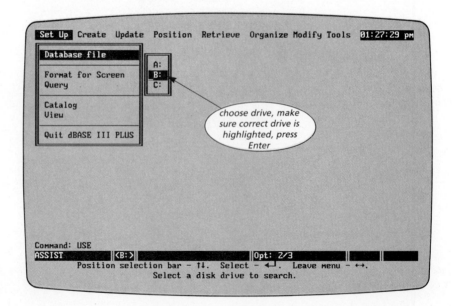

FIGURE 1-36
Selecting a Drive

This display allows you to indicate the drive on which the desired database file is located. Highlight B: and press the Enter key. This will display a list of all database files on the diskette (see Figure 1-37).

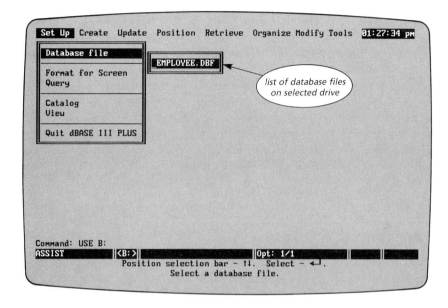

FIGURE 1-37
Selecting a Database File

At the present time, there is only one file, EMPLOYEE.DBF (remember that dBASE automatically assigns the extension DBF to database files). Because there is only one, you can simply press the Enter key. If there is more than one file, you must highlight the one you want before you press the Enter key. The final screen in this process is shown in Figure 1-38. dBASE is asking whether the file is indexed or not. At this point, no files are indexed, so you can type the letter N, which stands for no. Alternatively, you can simply press the Enter key, in which case dBASE will assume that the answer is no.

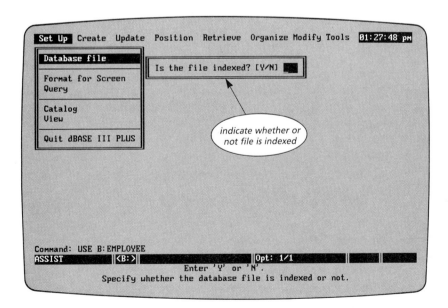

FIGURE 1-38
Is File Indexed?

Changing Existing Records

You will now correct the errors made when you entered the data for record 2. Press the Right Arrow key twice to move to the "Update" menu and press the Down Arrow key once to move to the "Edit" option (see Figure 1-39). This option is used to correct errors that you discover after you entered the data. The file containing the error must be the active file. If it is not, activate it by using the technique described in the previous section.

Once you have chosen the "Edit" option, the same data entry screen you used to enter the data will appear. In addition, data will be displayed for the record identified by the record number that appears in the status line. You can change any of the data in this record in exactly the same way you corrected the name Rappozi, Athony P. earlier.

The record you want to correct must be on the screen. If it isn't, use the PgUp and PgDn keys to bring it to the screen. Pressing PgUp moves you to the previous record and pressing PgDn moves you to the next record. By pressing PgUp or PgDn enough times, you can bring the record you want to the screen. In this case, record 1 is on the screen but you want to correct record 2, so press the PgDn key once. Then make the necessary corrections. Change the name to McCormack, Nigel L., the department to Shipping, the pay rate to 8.25, and the union to T. Once you are done, hold the Ctrl key down and press the End key.

Adding Additional Records

At this point, you should add the remaining records shown in Figure 1-3. To do so, choose the "Append" option of the "Update" menu (see Figure 1-39). If you make any mistakes, you can correct them using the same techniques you used to correct the errors in the first two records. It is not necessary to add all the records in one sitting. Just remember that if you leave dBASE, when you return you will have to reactivate the EMPLOYEE file (using the "Database file" option of the "Set Up" menu) and then choose the "Append" option of the "Update" menu to continue adding records.

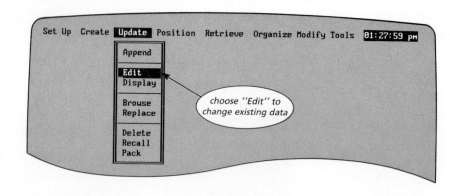

FIGURE 1-39
Changing Existing Data

DISPLAYING DATA

After you have created a database, you have a variety of ways to display its contents. We discuss one way here, the "List" option of the "Retrieve" menu.

Move to the "Retrieve" menu using the Right or Left Arrow keys. Once you have done so, your display should look like the one shown in Figure 1-40. Since "List" is already highlighted, press the Enter key, producing the screen shown in Figure 1-41. Select "Execute the command." Since this option is already highlighted, press the Enter key. Your display should now look like the one shown in Figure 1-42. If you want to print the results, type the letter Y. If not, either type the letter N or press the Enter key. The results are shown in Figure 1-43 on page dB 30.

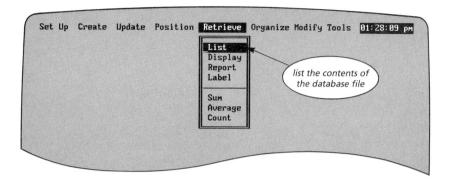

FIGURE 1-40
Retrieve Menu

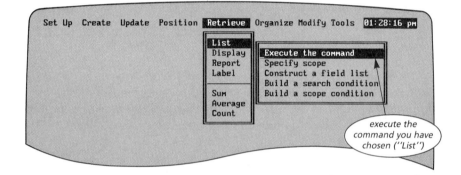

FIGURE 1-41
Option Box for Commands on
the Retrieve Menu

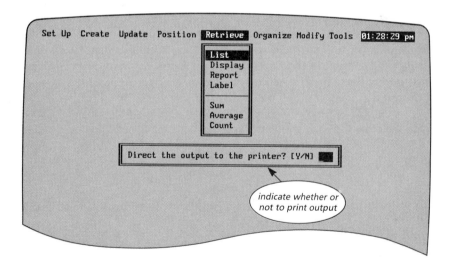

FIGURE 1-42
Output to the Printer?

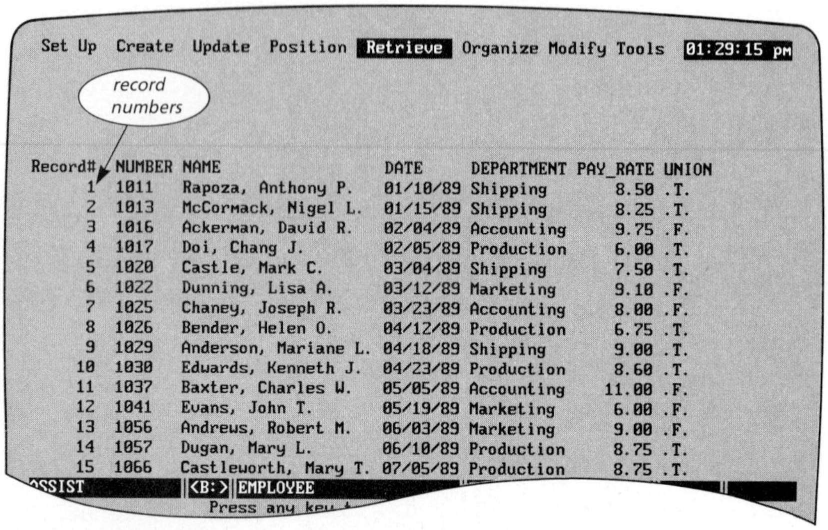

FIGURE 1-43
Results of "List" Option

In the display in Figure 1-43, the leftmost column contains a record number that was created by dBASE based on the sequence in which the records were entered. The fields are displayed with the field names that you already defined. Note that in the UNION field there is a period before and after the letters T and F. This is the way dBASE displays logical fields.

BACKING UP YOUR DATABASE FILES

To be safe, it is a good idea to periodically make a copy of your database files. This copy is called a **backup** copy and the database file itself is called the **live** copy. If you discover a problem with a database file, you can then copy the backup version over the live one. This effectively returns the database file to its original state.

While dBASE contains facilities to make such copies, there are some special issues involved in using them. You don't need to worry about them, however, since you can simply use the DOS COPY command after you have exited dBASE. For example, to copy the database file EMPLOYEE.DBF located on drive B to a backup copy named EMPLOYEE.BCK also located on drive B, you can use the command shown in Figure 1-44. The name EMPLOYEE.BCK is arbitrary. You can choose whatever name you wish. Just make sure it is something that is easy for you to recognize.

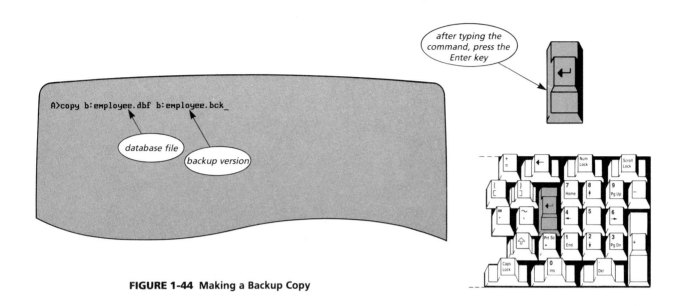

FIGURE 1-44 Making a Backup Copy

If you discover a problem, you can restore EMPLOYEE.DBF to the state it was in when the backup was made by typing the command shown in Figure 1-45.

You may wish to place the backup copy on a separate diskette. Place the other diskette in drive A and change the letter B that precedes EMPLOYEE.BCK in the command to the letter A.

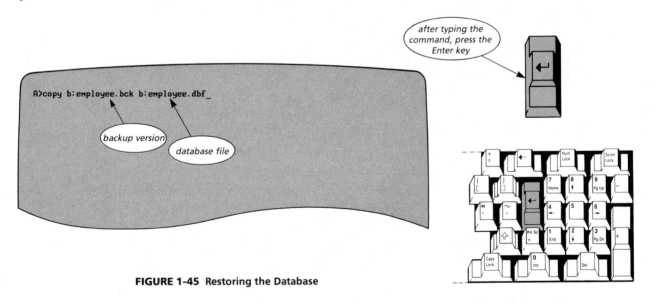

FIGURE 1-45 Restoring the Database

PROJECT SUMMARY

*I*n Project 1 you learned how to create a database file, how to add records to a database file, and how to correct any errors you might have made. You also learned one way to display the contents of a database file. Finally, you saw how to make a copy of the database file for backup purposes.

If you followed along with the steps in this project, you have created the EMPLOYEE database file. If you did not, but wish to create this file now, you can use the following keystroke sequence. Start dBASE as described in the project but do not choose any options when the ASSISTANT menu appears on the screen. Instead, type the following:

SUMMARY OF KEYSTROKES—Project 1

STEPS	KEY(S) PRESSED	RESULTS
1	→ ← ←	Create database file
2	employee ←	
3	NUMBER ← ←4←	
4	NAME ← ←20←	
5	DATE ← SPACE SPACE ←	
6	DEPARTMENT ←10←	
7	PAY_RATE ← SPACE ←5←2←	
8	UNION ← SPACE SPACE SPACE ←	
9	← ←Y	Fields specified
10	1011Rapoza, Anthony P. ←011089Shipping ←8.50T	Record entered
11	1013McCormack, Nigel L. ←011589Shipping ←8.25T	Record entered
12	1016Ackerman, David R. ←020489Accounting9.75F	Record entered
13	1017Doi, Chang J. ←020589Production6.00T	Record entered
14	1020Castle, Mark C. ←030489Shipping ←7.50T	Record entered
15	1022Dunning, Lisa A. ←031289Marketing ←9.10F	Record entered
16	1025Chaney, Joseph R. ←032389Accounting8.00F	Record entered
17	1026Bender, Helen O. ←041289Production6.75T	Record entered
18	1029Anderson, Mariane L.041889Shipping ←9.00T	Record entered
19	1030Edwards, Kenneth J. ←042389Production8.60T	Record entered
20	1037Baxter, Charles W. ←050589Accounting11.00F	Record entered
21	1041Evans, John T. ←051989Marketing ←6.00F	Record entered
22	1056Andrews, Robert M. ←060389Marketing ←9.00F	Record entered
23	1057Dugan, Mary L. ←061089Production8.75T	Record entered
24	1066Castleworth, Mary T.070589Production8.75T	Record entered
25	←	

The following list summarizes the material covered in Project 1:

1. An individual unit of information, such as an employee number or name, is called a **field**. A group of related fields is called a **record**. A collection of records is called a **file**. Sometimes, the words **table**, **row**, and **column** are used in place of file, record, and field, respectively.

2. In dBASE, each individual file (table) is called a **database file**. Thus, in dBASE, a database can actually be a collection of database files. (Throughout the first four projects, each database consists of a single database file.)

3. **Character fields** may be used to store any printable character. **Date fields** can only be used to store dates. **Numeric fields** can only be used to store numbers. Arithmetic operations can only be applied to numeric fields. **Logical fields**

consist of a single value representing a true or false condition. They can hold only T (true), F (false), Y (yes), or N (no). **Memo fields** may be used to store large blocks of text such as words or sentences.

4. The **ASSISTANT** is a collection of menus to assist you in accessing databases. When you use these menus, you are said to be working in **ASSIST mode** .

5. The **status line** or **status bar** is a line that appears near the bottom of the screen. It gives information about the current status of dBASE, including which database file is active and the current position within the file.

6. To select a different menu in the ASSISTANT, use the Right or Left Arrow keys.

7. To select an option within a menu, move the highlight to that option using the Up or Down Arrow keys and press the Enter key.

8. A **dBASE command** is a word or collection of words that will cause some function to be performed by dBASE.

9. The **dot prompt mode** is a mode of operating with dBASE in which a single dot, called the **dot prompt** appears on the screen. It prompts the user to type commands directly, rather than with the help of the menu structure of the ASSISTANT. It is followed by the blinking underscore or **cursor**, which shows where the characters you enter will be displayed. To change from the ASSISTANT to the dot prompt mode, use the Esc key. To change from the dot prompt mode to the ASSISTANT, use the F2 key.

10. To leave dBASE, select "Quit dBASE III PLUS" from the "Set Up" menu.

11. To get help, use the F1 key.

12. To create a database file, select "Database file" from the "Create" menu, then describe each of the fields that comprise the database file. After that, you will have a chance to begin entering data if you wish.

13. To add additional records, select the "Append" option of the "Update" menu. To activate a database file, select the "Database file" option of the "Set Up" menu, indicate the drive on which the desired database file is located, and then select the desired file from the list presented to you by dBASE.

14. To change records, select the "Edit" option of the "Update" menu.

15. To move between records when entering or editing data, use the PgUp and PgDn keys.

16. To display all data, select the "List" option of the "Retrieve" menu. Then select "Execute the command" and indicate whether or not the output is to be directed to the printer.

17. A **backup** copy of a database file is a copy that is made and stored as a safety measure. If problems occur in the active or **live** database file, copying the backup version over the live version returns the database file to the state it was in when the backup was made.

18. Make a backup copy of a database file by using the DOS COPY command after you have exited dBASE. In the event of a problem, you can copy the backup copy over the live version with the same COPY command.

STUDENT ASSIGNMENTS

STUDENT ASSIGNMENT 1: True/False

Instructions: Circle T if the statement is true and F if the statement is false.

T F   1. The term database is used to describe a collection of data organized in a manner that allows access, retrieval, and use of that data.

T F   2. A database can only contain a single table.

T F   3. In dBASE, there can be at most 10 fields in a record.

T F   4. In dBASE, a field name can contain a maximum of eight characters.

T F   5. WEEKLY_PAY is a valid field name.

T F   6. A field used in a calculation must be defined as a numeric field.

T F   7. A date field can be used in calculations.

T F   8. A logical field must contain either T, F, 0, or 1.

T F   9. Individual units of information within each record are called files.

T F 10. A numeric field that contains a value such as 99.99 is considered to have a width of 4.

Student Assignment 1 (continued)

T F 11. In dBASE, a file name can be up to eight characters long.
T F 12. To load dBASE into memory, type the word DBASE in either uppercase or lowercase letters when the A> prompt appears.
T F 13. To create a database file, choose the option "Database file" from the "Set Up" menu.
T F 14. The option "List" of the "Retrieve" menu can be used to list all records of a database file on the screen.
T F 15. To move back one record while adding data, press the PgDn key.
T F 16. The line on the screen that indicates the name of the database file being accessed is called the database line.

STUDENT ASSIGNMENT 2: Multiple Choice

Instructions: Circle the correct response.

1. A field that contains numbers but is not involved in calculations should normally be defined as a
   a. character field.
   b. numeric field.
   c. logical field.
   d. memo field.
2. The full name of a database file called EMPLOYEE and stored on drive B is
   a. B>EMPLOYEE
   b. EMPLOYEE
   c. B:EMPLOYEE.DBF
   d. EMPLOYEE:DBF
3. After you enter the data for all records, you can terminate the data entry process by
   a. pressing the Enter key when the cursor is in the last position of the last field entered.
   b. pressing the Esc key.
   c. pressing the Enter key when the cursor is in the first position of the first field on the screen where no entries have been made.
   d. pressing the Enter key while holding down the End key.
4. If you find an error in one of the records after entering the data and storing it on disk,
   a. you cannot correct the data.
   b. you can use the "Edit" option of the "Update" menu to correct the error.
   c. pressing F1 will allow you to correct the error.
   d. pressing Esc will allow you to correct the error.
5. To exit dBASE and return to the operating system,
   a. press Esc.
   b. choose the last option on the "Set Up" menu.
   c. choose the last option on the "Tools" menu.
   d. type the words exit dBASE.
6. "Edit" is an option on
   a. the "Set Up" menu.
   b. the "Create" menu.
   c. the "Update" menu.
   d. the "Retrieve" menu.

STUDENT ASSIGNMENT 3: Understanding dBASE Options

Instructions: Explain what will happen after you perform each of the following actions.

Problem 1. Type the word dBASE at the A> prompt and press the Enter key.

Explanation: _____

_____

_____

Problem 2. Choose the "Database file" option of the "Create" menu.

Explanation: _____

_____

_____

Problem 3. Choose the "List" option of the "Retrieve" menu.

Explanation: _____

_____

_____

Problem 4. Choose the "Edit" option of the "Update" menu.

Explanation: _____

_____

_____

STUDENT ASSIGNMENT 4: Using dBASE

Instructions: Explain how to accomplish each of the following tasks using dBASE.

Problem 1. Load dBASE into main computer memory.

Explanation: _____

_____

_____

Problem 2. Create a database file.

Explanation: _____

_____

_____

Problem 3. Move back to a previous record while adding data.

Explanation: _____

_____

_____

Student Assignment 4 (continued)

Problem 4. Indicate that a given field is a numeric field.

Explanation: _____

_____

_____

Problem 5. List the contents of a database file.

Explanation: _____

_____

_____

Problem 6. Add records to an already existing database file.

Explanation: _____

_____

_____

STUDENT ASSIGNMENT 5: Recovering from Problems

Instructions: In each of the following cases, a problem occurred. Explain the cause of the problem and how it can be corrected.

Problem 1: The dot prompt appears on the screen.

Cause of Problem: _____

_____

Method of Correction: _____

_____

Problem 2: You find yourself looking at a display that you don't recognize and that definitely does not correspond to the option you thought you selected.

Cause of Problem: _____

_____

Method of Correction: _____

_____

Problem 3: You intended to print a list of all data in a database file on your printer. The list appeared on the screen, but not on the printer. You checked your printer and it is on.

Cause of Problem: _____

_____

Method of Correction: _____

_____

MINICASES:

Creating and Displaying a Database

*E*ach project ends with four minicases. Minicase 1 in each project involves a database of personal checks. Minicase 2 involves a music library database. Minicase 3 deals with a database for a software store. The database for Minicase 4 contains information on homes for sale. You should work on the same minicase in each project. Your instructor will probably assign you a specific minicase. If not, you can choose any of the four. Just make sure you select the same one in each project.

The material in the minicases is cumulative. That is, the assignment for Minicase 1 in Project 2 builds on the assignment for Minicase 1 from Project 1. It is very important that you work through the minicase completely before proceeding to the next project. If not, you will encounter serious difficulties later on.

Minicase 1: Personal Checks

Instructions: Design and create a database file to store a list of personal checks and related information on disk using dBASE. The data and field characteristics are illustrated below.

CHECK NUMBER	DATE	PAYEE	CHECK AMOUNT	EXPENSE TYPE	TAX DEDUCTIBLE
109	01/19/90	Oak Apartments	750.00	Household	Y
102	01/05/90	Sav-Mor Groceries	85.00	Food	N
111	01/19/90	Edison Company	55.25	Household	N
106	01/12/90	Performing Arts	25.00	Charity	Y
105	01/12/90	Union Oil	22.75	Automobile	Y
101	01/05/90	American Express	45.30	Entertainment	Y
107	01/19/90	Sav-Mor Groceries	64.95	Food	N
108	01/19/90	Amber Inn	22.45	Entertainment	Y
104	01/12/90	Brady's Shoes	69.50	Personal	N
110	01/19/90	Standard Oil	33.16	Automobile	Y
103	01/05/90	Pacific Telephone	23.72	Household	N

FIELD DESCRIPTION	FIELD NAME	FIELD TYPE	WIDTH	DECIMAL POSITIONS
CHECK NUMBER	CHECKNUM	CHARACTER	4	
DATE	DATE	DATE	8	
PAYEE	PAYEE	CHARACTER	18	
CHECK AMOUNT	AMOUNT	NUMERIC	6	2
EXPENSE	EXPENSE	CHARACTER	14	
TAX DEDUCTIBLE	TAXDED	LOGICAL	1	

Minicase 1 (continued)

Perform the following tasks:

1. Load dBASE and insert your data disk in drive B.
2. Create the database file and enter the above data. Use the name CHECK for the database file.
3. After creating the database file and loading the data, use the "List" option of the "Retrieve" menu to display all the data.
4. Leave the database file that you created on this disk for use with assignments in later projects.

Minicase 2: Music Library

Instructions: Design and create a database file to store information about a music library on disk using dBASE. The music is stored on either cassette tape (CS), long-playing records (LP), or compact disk (CD), as indicated by the entry under the heading Type. The data and field characteristics are illustrated below. The date field represents the date the music was obtained.

DATE	MUSIC NAME	ARTIST	TYPE	COST	CATEGORY
02/22/90	Greatest Hits	Panache, Milo	LP	8.95	Classical
02/15/90	America	Judd, Mary	CS	5.95	Vocal
01/02/90	Rio Rio	Duran, Ralph	LP	8.95	Rock
02/15/90	Passione	Panache, Milo	LP	6.99	Classical
01/02/90	Country Hills	Lager, Ricky	CD	11.95	Country
02/22/90	Rockin'	Brady, Susan	CS	5.95	Rock
02/22/90	Pardners	Hudson, Randy	CS	5.95	Country
01/02/90	Private Love	Toner, Arlene	CD	11.95	Vocal
02/22/90	Moods	Silver, Sandy	CD	11.95	Rock

FIELD DESCRIPTION	FIELD NAME	FIELD TYPE	WIDTH	DECIMAL POSITIONS
DATE	DATE	DATE	8	
MUSIC NAME	NAME	CHARACTER	14	
ARTIST	ARTIST	CHARACTER	14	
TYPE	TYPE	CHARACTER	2	
COST	COST	NUMERIC	5	2
CATEGORY	CATEGORY	CHARACTER	9	

Perform the following tasks:

1. Load dBASE and insert your data disk in drive B.
2. Create the database file and enter the above data. Use the name MUSIC for the database file.
3. After creating the database file and loading the data, use the "List" option of the "Retrieve" menu to display all the data.
4. Leave the database file that you created on this disk for use with assignments in later projects.

Minicase 3: Computer Software Store

Instructions: Design and create a database file to store information about the inventory of a company that sells computer software. Fields in the database consist of the name of the software, the name of the company that sells the software, the software category, an entry Y (yes) or N (no) to indicate if the software is compatible with MS-DOS, the quantity of software on hand, and the cost of the software. A list of software products in inventory is illustrated in the chart below.

SOFTWARE NAME	COMPANY	CATEGORY	MS_DOS	QUANTITY	COST
Databurst	Electric Software	Database	Y	5	299.95
Type Ease	Edusoft Inc.	WP	N	22	29.95
Image Fonts	Graph Tech Inc.	WP	Y	12	49.95
Data Filer	Anchor Software	Database	Y	18	149.95
Master	Edusoft Inc.	Education	N	10	49.95
Math Tester	Learnit Software	Education	N	10	49.95
PC-Writer	Anchor Software	WP	Y	30	129.95
Print File	Graph Tech Inc.	Database	Y	16	99.95
Learning Calc	Edusoft Inc.	Spreadsheet	Y	34	69.95
Number Crunch	Anchor Software	Spreadsheet	Y	8	279.95

FIELD DESCRIPTION	FIELD NAME	FIELD TYPE	WIDTH	DECIMAL POSITIONS
SOFTWARE NAME	NAME	CHARACTER	14	
COMPANY	COMPANY	CHARACTER	17	
CATEGORY	CATEGORY	CHARACTER	12	
MS_DOS	MS_DOS	LOGICAL	1	
QUANTITY	QUANTITY	NUMERIC	2	0
COST	COST	NUMERIC	6	2

Perform the following tasks:

1. Load dBASE and insert your data disk in drive B.
2. Create the database file and enter the above data. Use the name SOFTWARE for the database file.
3. After creating the database file and loading the data, use the "List" option of the "Retrieve" menu to display all the data.
4. Leave the database file that you created on this disk for use with assignments in later projects.

Minicase 4: Home Sales

Instructions: Design and create a database file to store information about homes for sale. The records contain the date the home was listed, its address, city, zip code, number of bedrooms, number of bathrooms, an entry Y (yes) or N (no) to indicate if the home has a pool, and the selling price of the home. A list of the homes in the database is illustrated below:

DATE	ADDRESS	CITY	ZIP	BDRM	BATH	POOL	PRICE
09/15/90	9661 King Pl.	Anaheim	92644	4	2	Y	185000.00
09/19/90	1625 Brook St.	Fullerton	92633	3	1	N	95000.00
10/02/90	182 Oak Ave.	Fullerton	92634	4	2	Y	92000.00
10/09/90	145 Oak Ave.	Garden Grove	92641	5	3	Y	145000.00
10/15/90	124 Lark St.	Anaheim	92644	3	2	N	119000.00
10/22/90	926 Pine Ln.	Garden Grove	92641	3	1	N	92500.00
11/20/90	453 Adams Ave.	Costa Mesa	92688	5	3	Y	185000.00
11/23/90	1456 Kern St.	Costa Mesa	92688	4	2	Y	163900.00
12/10/90	862 Stanley St.	Garden Grove	92641	4	2	Y	189995.00
12/13/90	1552 Weldon Pl.	Garden Grove	92641	3	2	N	169500.00

FIELD DESCRIPTION	FIELD NAME	FIELD TYPE	WIDTH	DECIMAL POSITIONS
DATE	DATE	DATE	8	
ADDRESS	ADDRESS	CHARACTER	16	
CITY	CITY	CHARACTER	12	
ZIP	ZIP	CHARACTER	5	
BEDRMS	BDRM	NUMERIC	2	0
BATHRMS	BATH	NUMERIC	2	0
POOL	POOL	LOGICAL	1	
PRICE	PRICE	NUMERIC	9	2

Perform the following tasks:

1. Load dBASE and insert your data disk in drive B.
2. Create the database file and enter the data above. Use the name HOME for the database file.
3. After creating the database file and loading the data, use the "List" option of the "Retrieve" menu to display all the data.
4. Leave the database file that you created on this disk for use with assignments in later projects.

PROJECT 2

Displaying Records in a Database

Objectives

You will have mastered the material in this project when you can:

- Activate a previously created database file
- Display the structure of a database file
- Change the current active record
- Display a single record
- Display all records and all fields
- Display only selected fields
- Display only records meeting a given condition
- Use both simple and compound conditions
- Count the number of records satisfying a given condition
- Calculate sums and averages

A major benefit of a database management system is that once you have created a database, you can rapidly access its records and fields and easily display them. For example, after accessing the employee database file illustrated in Project 1, you can use dBASE options to display a single employee record or specific collections of records, such as the records of employees who work in the accounting department or the records of those who are members of the union.

As we work through this project, we explain the dBASE options that are used to display records and fields within records. We explain the options for counting various types of records and those for calculating totals and averages. You will use the menus and options within the ASSISTANT that are shown in blue in Figure 2-1.

FIGURE 2-1
Menus and Options within the dBASE ASSISTANT

OPTION	PURPOSE
Set Up	Activate a
Database file	database file
View	view
Quit dBASE III PLUS	leave dBASE III PLUS
Create	Create a
Database file	database file (extension DBF)
View	view (extension VUE)
Report	report (extension FRM)
Update	Change a database file by
Append	adding records at the end
Edit	changing records viewing one at a time
Browse	changing records viewing several at a time
Replace	changing the data in all records that satisfy some condition
Delete	deleting records
Recall	undeleting records
Pack	physically remove deleted records
Position	Move the record pointer by
Seek	finding a match using an index
Locate	finding the first record that satisfies some condition
Goto Record	specifying a record number
Retrieve	Retrieve data from a database file
List	show desired fields and records on the screen or printer
Display	like "List" (differences between the two are covered in the text)
Report	print a report
Sum	calculate a total
Average	calculate an average
Count	count the number of records
Organize	
Index	create an index (extension NDX)
Sort	sort a database file
Modify	Change an existing
Database file	database file
Report	report file
Tools	
List structure	show the structure of the active database file

ACTIVATING THE DATABASE

 fter you have loaded dBASE into main computer memory, you must activate a database file on disk so that you can access it. Recall that you do this with the "Database file" option of the "Set Up" menu (Figure 2-2).

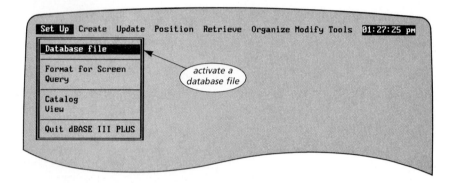

FIGURE 2-2
The "Set Up" Menu

Press Enter when the highlight is on "Database file" to produce the display shown in Figure 2-3. Make sure the drive containing your data is highlighted and press the Enter key again to display a list of all database files on the diskette (see Figure 2-4). With EMPLOYEE.DBF highlighted, press the Enter key. At this point, dBASE will ask you if the file is indexed. Either type the letter N or just press the Enter key to indicate that the file is not indexed.

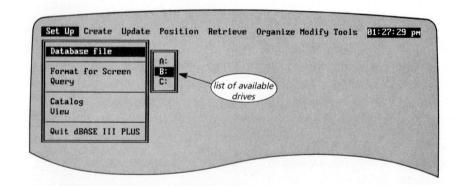

FIGURE 2-3
Selecting a Drive

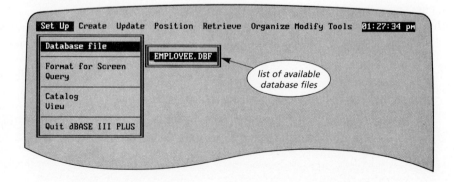

FIGURE 2-4
Selecting a Database File

In the following examples, we assume that the file with the name EMPLOYEE.DBF is the active database file.

DISPLAYING THE DATABASE STRUCTURE

*S*ometimes you might not know the precise field names and characteristics of a database file. Perhaps you don't remember the specific names you used. You have probably written this information down somewhere, but maybe you don't have it with you. It may be that the database file was created by someone else. Fortunately, there is an easy way to obtain this information. Use the "List structure" option within the "Tools" menu to review the structure of a database, that is, to review the field names and related information. Select the "Tools" menu, move the highlight to "List structure" (Figure 2-5), and press the Enter key. At this point, dBASE asks whether or not you want to print the results (see Figure 2-6). If you do, you would type the letter Y. But let's assume you don't want the results printed. Simply type the letter N or press the Enter key. Figure 2-7, on the next page, shows the results of choosing the "List structure" option.

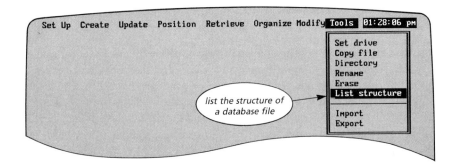

FIGURE 2-5
The "Tools" Menu

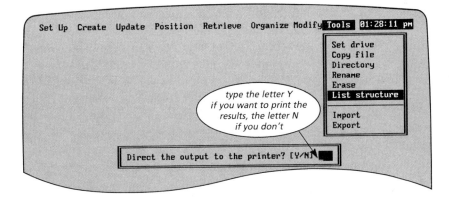

FIGURE 2-6
Print the Results?

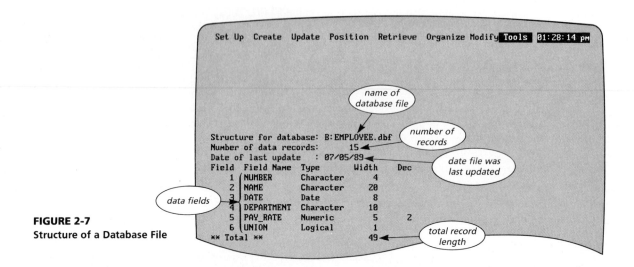

FIGURE 2-7
Structure of a Database File

In the figure, the first line of output gives the name of the active database file. It is identified by the entry B:EMPLOYEE .DBF. The next line displays the number of records in the file, and the third line gives the date of the last update. Following lines show the field number, field name, type, width, and decimal positions of any numeric fields in the database.

The last line contains the word "Total" and the total number of characters in the records in the file. If you add the field widths together the total will be 48. In the figure, however, the total number of charactures is specified as 49. This is because one position field is automatically attached to the beginning of each record. dBASE uses this field for its own internal purposes.

In this screen, as well as those throughout the remainder of the project, dBASE reminds you that you can press the Enter key as soon as you are finished with the display. This will return you to the ASSISTANT and allow you to take another action.

DISPLAY

Y ou saw in Project 1 that the "List" option within the "Retrieve" menu can be used to display the contents of a database file. The "Display" option within the same menu can also be used for the same purpose. The two options are very similar, but there are two main differences. First, if the data to be displayed does not fit on a single screen, the "Display" option will pause whenever the screen is full, but the "List" option will not. If you use the "List" option, the data seems to fly by, right before your eyes. Second, if you use the "List" option you will be given the chance to send the report to the printer, but with the "Display" option, you will not.

Changing the Current Active Record

dBASE continually maintains a position within the active database file. The current position is indicated on the status line following the word Rec:. For example, Rec: 4/15 on the status line means that the current position is the fourth record of the fifteen records currently contained in the file. The number of the current position is called the **record pointer** and the record indicated by the record pointer is called the **current active record**.

For some operations, it doesn't matter which record is the current active record. If, for example, you want to display all the records in a database file, it makes no difference whether the current active record is record 4 or record 8 or anything else. There are some operations, however, such as displaying a single record, in which it is crucial that the current active record be the one that you want. Thus, there must be a way to change the current active record or, in other words, to change the record pointer.

Actually, there are two ways. One is to use PgUp and/or PgDn during data entry. Recall that when you used these keys in Project 1, the number following Rec: changed appropriately. This approach, while handy for moving a few records one way or the other, can be very time consuming, especially if the file contains many records. Fortunately, there is an alternative.

The alternative uses the "Position" menu. Select the "Position" menu using the Right or Left Arrow keys. You should see the screen shown in Figure 2-8. The only option that you want at this time is "Goto Record," so use the Down Arrow key to move the highlight to this option. Then press the Enter key, producing the screen shown in Figure 2-9. The three possibilities are "TOP," which will move the record pointer to the first record in the file; "BOTTOM," which will move it to the last record; and "RECORD." Select "RECORD" by moving the highlight to it and pressing the Enter key. You are now asked to supply a numeric value. The record pointer will then change to this value. Enter the number 3 (see Figure 2-10) and press the Enter key. The record pointer will change to 3; that is, the third record will become the current active record (shown in Figure 2-11).

Repeat the process, but this time choose "TOP" rather than "RECORD." This will make record 1 the current active record.

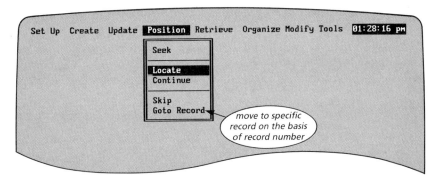

FIGURE 2-8 The "Position" Menu

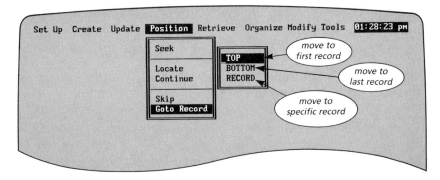

FIGURE 2-9 Indicating Record

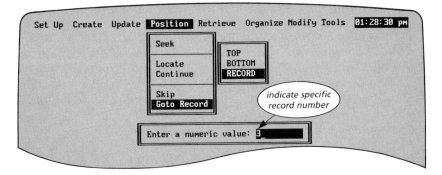

FIGURE 2-10 Giving Record Number

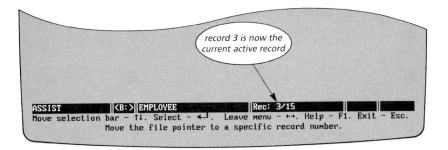

FIGURE 2-11 Record Pointer Has Been Changed

Displaying a Single Record

To display a single record, select the "Display" option from the "Retrieve" menu. To do so, use the Right and Left Arrow keys to move to the "Retrieve" menu, then the Down Arrow key to highlight the "Display" option. Once you have done so, press the Enter key. Your display should look like the one shown in Figure 2-12.

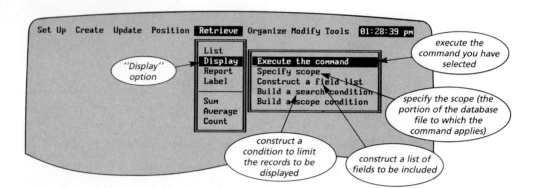

FIGURE 2-12
Using the "Display" Option

We use the right-hand box on the screen to specify precise details concerning the data we want displayed. The first choice, "Execute the command," is used once we have specified all other details concerning the fields and records we want included. To understand the second option, "Specify scope," you need to understand what dBASE means by scope. The **scope** is the portion of the database file to which the option (in this case, "Display") applies. The normal scope of the "Display" option is only a single record, namely the current active record. This means that unless special action is taken, only the current active record will be displayed. In this case, that is precisely what we want. If it is not, we use the "Specify scope" option to change it.

Normally, dBASE will display all fields. If this is not appropriate, we use the third option, "Construct a field list," to specify precisely the fields that we want. Sometimes we only want to list records that satisfy some condition (for example, all employees whose pay rate is $6.00). The fourth option, "Build a search condition," is used for this. (The fifth option, "Build a scope condition," is not often used and we will not cover it in this text.)

Since the normal scope of the "Display" option is a single record, the current active record, and dBASE normally displays all fields, you don't need to use any special options. Thus, you are ready to "Execute the command." That option is already highlighted, so you can simply press the Enter key. The results of this operation are shown in Figure 2-13. Note that only a single record was displayed. In this case it is record 1, because that is the current active record. If you wanted to display another record instead, such as record 3, you would first use the techniques of the previous section to make record 3 the current active record, then select the "Display" option.

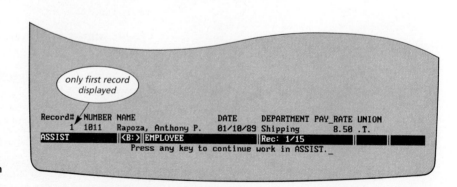

FIGURE 2-13
Results of the "Display" Option

Displaying All Records

The normal scope, often referred to as the *default scope*, is not appropriate for displaying all records using the "Display" option, because it will only display one record. It must be changed, and fortunately this is easy to do. Select the "Display" option of the "Retrieve" menu as you did previously: Right or Left Arrow keys to move to the "Retrieve" menu, Down Arrow key to move to "Display," and then the Enter key. This time, however, don't immediately choose "Execute the command." Instead, move the highlight down to "Specify scope" (see Figure 2-14). Then press the Enter key, producing the display shown in Figure 2-15.

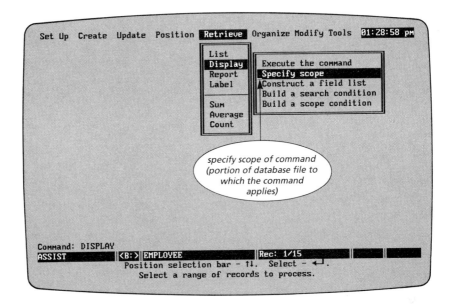

FIGURE 2-14
Specifying Scope

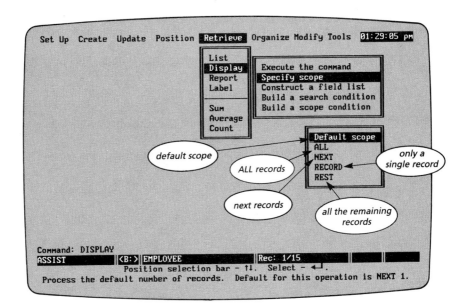

FIGURE 2-15
Selecting a Scope

The new box that has appeared contains the various possibilities of the scope. The "Default scope" for the "Display" option, as we saw earlier, is only the current active record. The second possibility, "ALL," means that the option applies to *all* records. "NEXT" means that the option only applies to records *following* the current active record. "RECORD" means the option only applies to a single record. Finally, "REST" means that the option pertains to all the records from the current active record to the end of the file, but none of the earlier records.

Instead of the default scope, you want "ALL." Move the highlight to it using the Down Arrow key. Then press the Enter key, producing the display shown in Figure 2-16. Now you can use the Up Arrow key to move the highlight to "Execute the command" and then press the Enter key. The result is shown in Figure 2-17. Note that all records are indeed included.

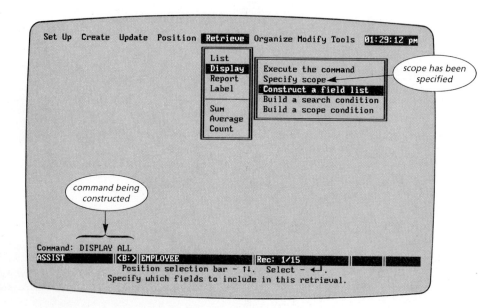

FIGURE 2-16
Scope Has Been Specified

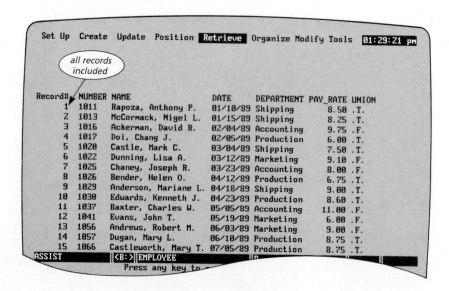

FIGURE 2-17
Results of Display

Displaying Selected Fields

Often you only care about certain fields. For example, you may only be interested in each employee's name, department, and pay rate. Fortunately, it is not necessary to view all the fields in a record. You can display selected fields using the "Display" option. To do so, begin in exactly the same fashion as before. Select "Display" from the "Retrieve" menu and change the scope to "ALL," but do not choose "Execute the command" yet. Instead, highlight "Construct a field list" (shown in Figure 2-18), and press the Enter key, producing the display in Figure 2-19.

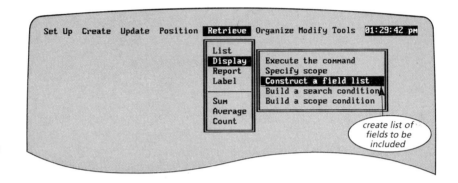

FIGURE 2-18
Selecting Fields

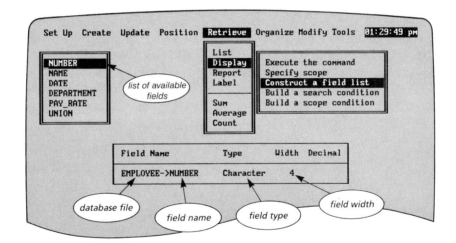

FIGURE 2-19
Selecting Fields

The box in the display gives the characteristics of the highlighted field. Within the box is an expression that may seem strange to you, EMPLOYEE->NUMBER. This is the notation used in dBASE to indicate that the NUMBER field is part of the EMPLOYEE database file. You may not see why this notation is important. After all, you are only working with a single database file at this point, so it is obvious that any field that appears on the screen must be part of the EMPLOYEE file. Later, however, when you work with more than one database file, you will find this notation to be very useful.

At this point, you can specify precisely those fields you wish to include in the display. In this case, you only want to included NAME, DEPARTMENT, and PAY_RATE. Move the highlight to the first field you want, NAME, using the Down Arrow key, and press the Enter key. Your display should now look like the one in Figure 2-20. Note that NAME is not as bright as the rest of the fields in the box. This means that it has been selected for the display. Note also that the command at the bottom now reads "DISPLAY ALL NAME," which also indicates that the NAME field has been selected.

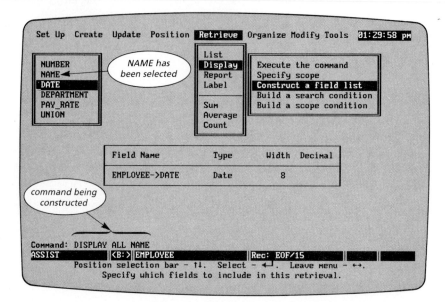

FIGURE 2-20
One Field Has Been Selected

Next move the highlight to DEPARTMENT and press the Enter key, producing the display shown in Figure 2-21. Now both NAME and DEPARTMENT are less bright than the other fields. In addition, the command at the bottom now reads "DISPLAY ALL NAME, DEPARTMENT." The highlight should now be on the PAY_RATE field, so you can simply press the Enter key to select it. After that, press the Right Arrow key to leave this menu. The command that dBASE has constructed for you, "DISPLAY ALL NAME, DEPARTMENT, PAY_RATE," will be displayed at the bottom of your screen.

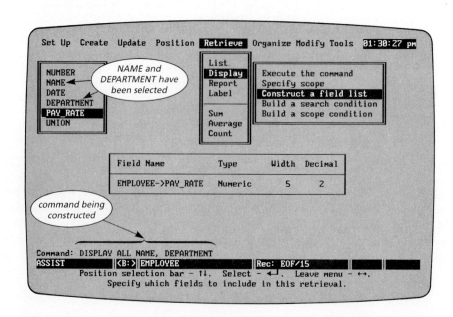

FIGURE 2-21
Two Fields Have Been Selected

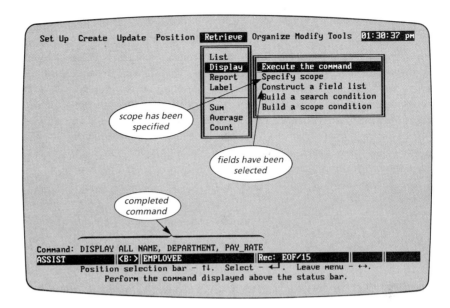

FIGURE 2-22
Desired Fields Have Been
Selected

You are now ready to choose "Execute the command," so move the highlight to it (Figure 2-22) and press the Enter key. The display produced is shown in Figure 2-23. Only the fields you selected have been included.

The order in which you select the columns is the order in which they will appear. Thus, to create a display with the same three columns in a different order, say DEPARTMENT, NAME, PAY_RATE, make sure you select them in this order. First move the highlight to DEPARTMENT and press the Enter key, then to NAME and press the Enter key, and then to PAY_RATE and press the Enter key. Then press the Right Arrow key to leave. When you choose "Execute the command," the columns will be displayed in the desired order.

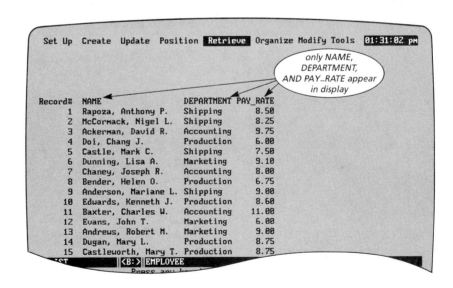

FIGURE 2-23
Results of Display

Using Conditions

One very nice feature of dBASE is its ability to display records and fields based upon certain conditions. A **condition** is an expression that evaluates to either true or false. Suppose that you only wanted information about employee 1030. You don't want to see a report of all employees and have to scan through it looking for this employee. What you really want is to display only the information about the employee for whom the condition "number is equal to 1030" is true.

Select the "Display" option from the "Retrieve" menu in the usual manner: Right or Left Arrows to move to the "Retrieve" menu, Down Arrow key to move to "Display," then press Enter. This time move the highlight in the box to "Build a search condition" (Figure 2-24) and press the Enter key. Your display should look like the one shown in Figure 2-25.

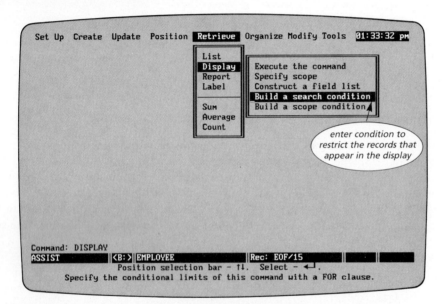

FIGURE 2-24 Building a Condition

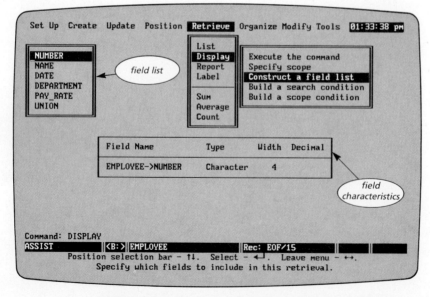

FIGURE 2-25 Selecting a Field for the Condition

At this point, move the highlight to the field that will be used in the condition. In this case the field is NUMBER, which is already highlighted, so just press the Enter key. Your display now looks like the one shown in Figure 2-26.

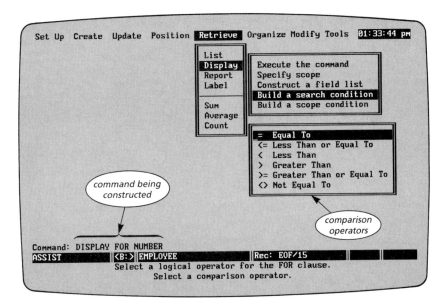

FIGURE 2-26 Selecting a Comparison Operator

You are being asked to select a comparison operator. The possibilities are shown in the box on the screen. You want NUMBER to be *equal to* 1030, so you must highlight the "Equal To" line. Since it already is highlighted, press the Enter key. To choose a different operator, you would first move the highlight to your selection using the Down Arrow key and then press the Enter key.

You are now asked to enter a character string (Figure 2-27). Enter the number 1030 and the display will look like the one shown in Figure 2-28. At this point, if you had additional conditions, you would choose either "Combine with .AND." or "Combine with .OR." But since there are no other conditions, indicate this by pressing the Enter key (the line labeled "No more conditions" is already highlighted).

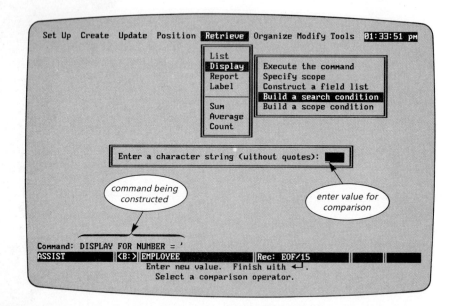

FIGURE 2-27
Completing the Condition

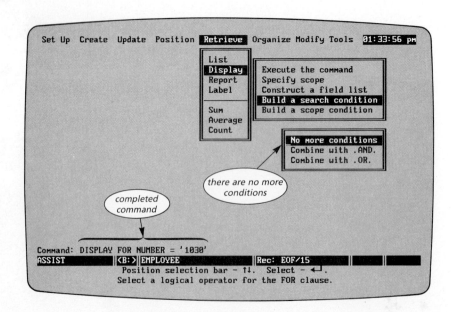

FIGURE 2-28
Completing the Search
Condition

Move the highlight to "Execute the command" (Figure 2-29) and press the Enter key. The results are shown in Figure 2-30. The screen displays only information about employee 1030.

○ RESCORE   ○ MARK ✓   ○ TOTAL ONLY/BOTH SIDES

T F

1 Ⓐ Ⓑ Ⓒ Ⓓ Ⓔ
2 Ⓐ Ⓑ Ⓒ Ⓓ Ⓔ
3 Ⓐ Ⓑ Ⓒ Ⓓ Ⓔ
4 Ⓐ Ⓑ Ⓒ Ⓓ Ⓔ
5 Ⓐ Ⓑ Ⓒ Ⓓ Ⓔ
6 Ⓐ Ⓑ Ⓒ Ⓓ Ⓔ
7 Ⓐ Ⓑ Ⓒ Ⓓ Ⓔ
8 Ⓐ Ⓑ Ⓒ Ⓓ Ⓔ
9 Ⓐ Ⓑ Ⓒ Ⓓ Ⓔ
10 Ⓐ Ⓑ Ⓒ Ⓓ Ⓔ
11 Ⓐ Ⓑ Ⓒ Ⓓ Ⓔ
12 Ⓐ Ⓑ Ⓒ Ⓓ Ⓔ
13 Ⓐ Ⓑ Ⓒ Ⓓ Ⓔ
14 Ⓐ Ⓑ Ⓒ Ⓓ Ⓔ
15 Ⓐ Ⓑ Ⓒ Ⓓ Ⓔ
16 Ⓐ Ⓑ Ⓒ Ⓓ Ⓔ
17 Ⓐ Ⓑ Ⓒ Ⓓ Ⓔ
18 Ⓐ Ⓑ Ⓒ Ⓓ Ⓔ
19 Ⓐ Ⓑ Ⓒ Ⓓ Ⓔ
20 Ⓐ Ⓑ Ⓒ Ⓓ Ⓔ
21 Ⓐ Ⓑ Ⓒ Ⓓ Ⓔ
22 Ⓐ Ⓑ Ⓒ Ⓓ Ⓔ
23 Ⓐ Ⓑ Ⓒ Ⓓ Ⓔ
24 Ⓐ Ⓑ Ⓒ Ⓓ Ⓔ
25 Ⓐ Ⓑ Ⓒ Ⓓ Ⓔ

T F

26 Ⓐ Ⓑ Ⓒ Ⓓ Ⓔ
27 Ⓐ Ⓑ Ⓒ Ⓓ Ⓔ
28 Ⓐ Ⓑ Ⓒ Ⓓ Ⓔ
29 Ⓐ Ⓑ Ⓒ Ⓓ Ⓔ
30 Ⓐ Ⓑ Ⓒ Ⓓ Ⓔ
31 Ⓐ Ⓑ Ⓒ Ⓓ Ⓔ
32 Ⓐ Ⓑ Ⓒ Ⓓ Ⓔ
33 Ⓐ Ⓑ Ⓒ Ⓓ Ⓔ
34 Ⓐ Ⓑ Ⓒ Ⓓ Ⓔ
35 Ⓐ Ⓑ Ⓒ Ⓓ Ⓔ
36 Ⓐ Ⓑ Ⓒ Ⓓ Ⓔ
37 Ⓐ Ⓑ Ⓒ Ⓓ Ⓔ
38 Ⓐ Ⓑ Ⓒ Ⓓ Ⓔ
39 Ⓐ Ⓑ Ⓒ Ⓓ Ⓔ
40 Ⓐ Ⓑ Ⓒ Ⓓ Ⓔ
41 Ⓐ Ⓑ Ⓒ Ⓓ Ⓔ
42 Ⓐ Ⓑ Ⓒ Ⓓ Ⓔ
43 Ⓐ Ⓑ Ⓒ Ⓓ Ⓔ
44 Ⓐ Ⓑ Ⓒ Ⓓ Ⓔ
45 Ⓐ Ⓑ Ⓒ Ⓓ Ⓔ
46 Ⓐ Ⓑ Ⓒ Ⓓ Ⓔ
47 Ⓐ Ⓑ Ⓒ Ⓓ Ⓔ
48 Ⓐ Ⓑ Ⓒ Ⓓ Ⓔ
49 Ⓐ Ⓑ Ⓒ Ⓓ Ⓔ
50 Ⓐ Ⓑ Ⓒ Ⓓ Ⓔ

KEY ITEM COUNT

⓪	⓪	⓪
①	①	①
②	②	
③	③	
④	④	
⑤	⑤	
⑥	⑥	
⑦	⑦	
⑧	⑧	
⑨	⑨	

FEED THIS DIRECTION ↑ 1

STUDENT ID (UPON REQUEST)

⓪⓪⓪⓪⓪⓪⓪⓪⓪⓪⓪
①①①①①①①①①①①
②②②②②②②②②②②
③③③③③③③③③③③
④④④④④④④④④④④
⑤⑤⑤⑤⑤⑤⑤⑤⑤⑤⑤
⑥⑥⑥⑥⑥⑥⑥⑥⑥⑥⑥
⑦⑦⑦⑦⑦⑦⑦⑦⑦⑦⑦
⑧⑧⑧⑧⑧⑧⑧⑧⑧⑧⑧
⑨⑨⑨⑨⑨⑨⑨⑨⑨⑨⑨

MARKING INSTRUCTIONS

USE NO. 2 PENCIL ONLY

Use a No. 2 Pencil

Ⓐ ● Ⓒ Ⓓ Ⓔ
Fill circle completely

Ⓐ Ⓑ Ⓒ Ⓓ Ⓔ
Erase cleanly

39
41
80

SCORE	39 78	# CORRECT	
		% CORRECT	
RESCORE		# CORRECT	
		% CORRECT	
ROSTER NUMBER		SCORE	
		RESCORE	

NAME _Kathryn Kraben_

SUBJECT _____

PERIOD _____ DATE _____

ROSTER NUMBER		RESCORE
		SCORE
RESCORE		% CORRECT
		# CORRECT
SCORE	82	% CORRECT
	41	# CORRECT

DO NOT WRITE IN THIS AREA

FEED THIS DIRECTION

2

KEY ITEM COUNT

0 0
1 1
2 2
3 3
4 4
5 5
6
7
8
9

SIDE 2

RESCORE ○ MARK ✓

T F

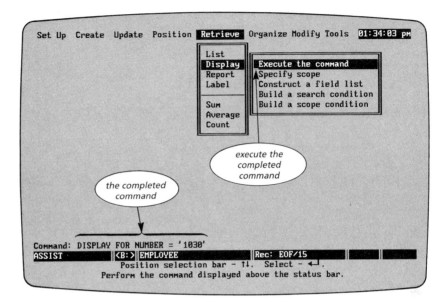

FIGURE 2-29
Executing the Command

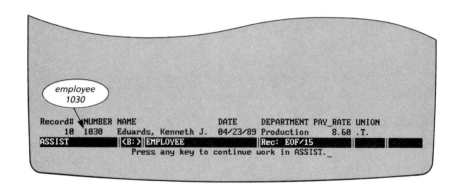

FIGURE 2-30
Results of the Display

You may have noticed that here, unlike the previous examples, you didn't specify a scope. This is because dBASE automatically uses the scope of "ALL" whenever you employ search conditions. It would not have been wrong to specify such a scope, however.

Try to produce a list of all employees whose pay rate is $6.00. You will have to select PAY_RATE instead of NUMBER when you are building a search condition. In addition, when you are entering a value, you should type the amount 6.00. Since this value does not completely fill the allocated space on the screen, you will have to press the Enter key to proceed. The correct results are shown in Figure 2-31.

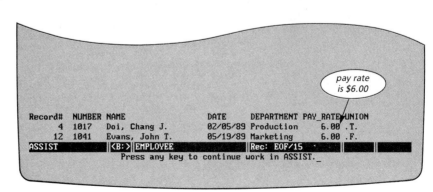

FIGURE 2-31
Employees Whose Pay Rate Is
$6.00

Next try to produce a list of all employees whose pay rate is greater than $9.00. This time you will need to select "Greater Than" rather than "Equal To" as the comparison operator. The correct results are shown in Figure 2-32.

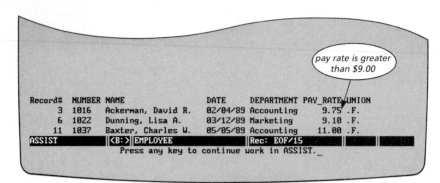

FIGURE 2-32
Employees Whose Pay Rate Is Greater Than $9.00

Now try to list the name, department, and pay rate for those employees in the shipping department. In this case, first construct a field list consisting of NAME, DEPARTMENT, and PAY_RATE in the same manner as before. Next, build a search condition that requires DEPARTMENT to be equal to Shipping. When you type the word Shipping it is important to type an uppercase S followed by lowercase hipping, because this is the way the information was entered into the database file. If you type SHIPPING, for example, no records will be found since dBASE considers SHIPPING to be different from Shipping. The correct results are shown in Figure 2-33.

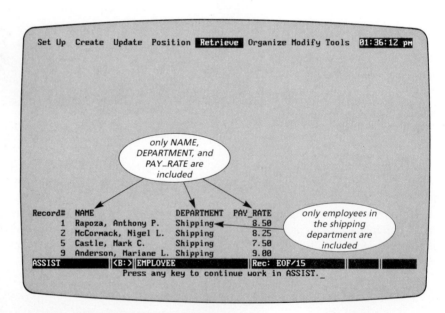

FIGURE 2-33
Restricting Fields and Records

Finally, try to produce a list of all employees whose name is the single letter A. This time the field in the condition will be NAME, the comparison operator will be "Equal To," and the character string will consist of a single uppercase A. This must seem strange. No employee has the name A. Try this anyhow. The results may surprise you.

The results are shown in Figure 2-34. Three employees are listed, none of whose names are A. Each name, however, *begins* with the letter A. This is the way dBASE handles these comparisons. If the value in the field is equal to the character string entered as far as it goes, the two are considered to be the same. If the value had been An, for example, then Ackerman would not have been listed, but Anderson and Andrews would.

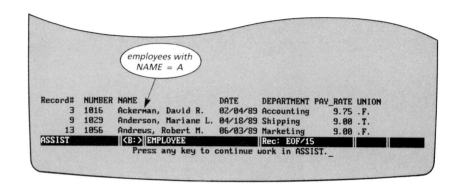

FIGURE 2-34
Results of Display

Using Logical Fields in Conditions

Choose the "Display" option of the "Retrieve" menu as you have now done many times and then choose "Build a search condition." This time choose the UNION field (Figure 2-35). Notice that you are not asked to enter a comparison operator. Why?

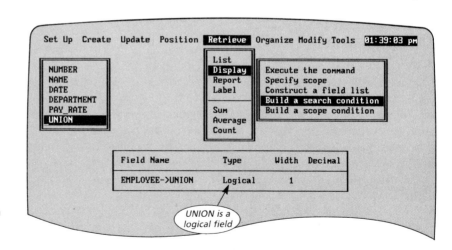

FIGURE 2-35
Building a Search Condition

Remember that a condition is simply an expression that can be either true or false. The condition "PAY_RATE = 6.00," for example, is true for some records and false for others. A logical field like UNION is either true or false *by itself*. It does not need to be compared with some value.

If you now choose "No more conditions" and "Execute the command," you will see the screen in Figure 2-36. Note that the employees listed are all those for whom the value of UNION is true (.T.).

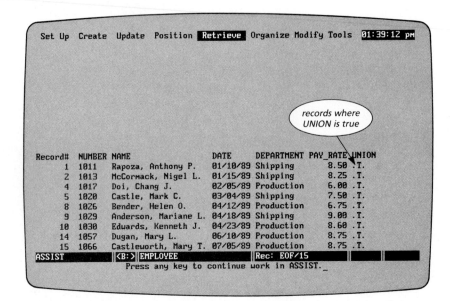

FIGURE 2-36
Results of Display

Using Compound Conditions

The conditions you have used so far are called **simple conditions**. They consist of a single field, a comparison operator, and a value. (In the special case of logical fields, they consist solely of a single field.) Simple conditions can be combined using AND or OR to form **compound conditions**.

Suppose you want to list all employees in the accounting department whose pay rate is $11.00. That is, you want all employees for whom DEPARTMENT equals Accounting *and* pay rate equals 11.00.

Begin the process as before by selecting the "Display" option of the "Retrieve" menu. Start building a search condition. Choose DEPARTMENT, "Equal to," and then enter the word Accounting. This time, choose "Combine with .AND." by moving the highlight to it and pressing the Enter key. You can now build another condition. For this condition, choose PAY_RATE, "Equal to," and then enter the amount 11.00. Note the command that dBASE has created at the bottom of the screen (in Figure 2-37). This time, choose "No more conditions" and then "Execute the command." The results are shown in Figure 2-38.

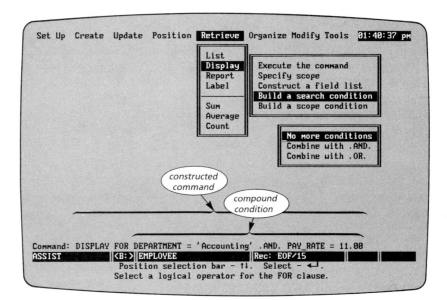

FIGURE 2-37
Display with Compound
Condition

FIGURE 2-38
Result of Display

Now suppose you want to list all employees who are in the accounting department or who belong to a union (or both). Start just as you did in the previous example. This time, however, select "Combine with .OR." after you have finished the first condition. For the second condition, select the UNION field. Since this is a logical field, you need take no further action in building the condition. Choose "No more conditions" and then "Execute the command." The results are shown in Figure 2-39.

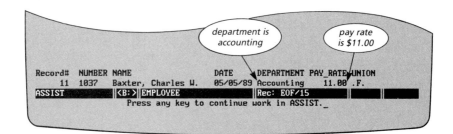

FIGURE 2-39
Results of Display

CALCULATIONS

ou can perform three types of computations in dBASE: count, sum, and average. Select the appropriate option from the "Retrieve" menu exactly as you selected "Display." We use these options in a way that is very similar to the way we use the "Display" option.

"Count"

To count the number of records in a database file that satisfy a certain condition, select the "Count" option from the "Retrieve" menu in the usual manner (see Figure 2-40). If you immediately choose "Execute the command," dBASE will count the number of records in the entire database file. Optionally, you could build a search condition, in which case dBASE will count only the records that satisfy the condition.

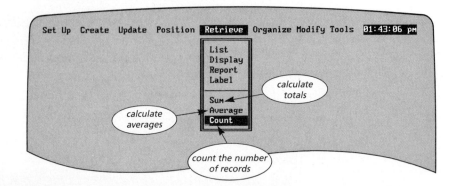

FIGURE 2-40
Counting Records

To count the number of employees in the accounting department, for example, select "Build a search condition," pick the DEPARTMENT field and the comparison operator "Equal to," and then enter "Accounting." Do this in exactly the same fashion as limiting the record to be displayed using the "Display" option. In the process dBASE creates a COUNT command for you (see Figure 2-41). Choose "Execute the command" to have the command executed and the count displayed (Figure 2-42).

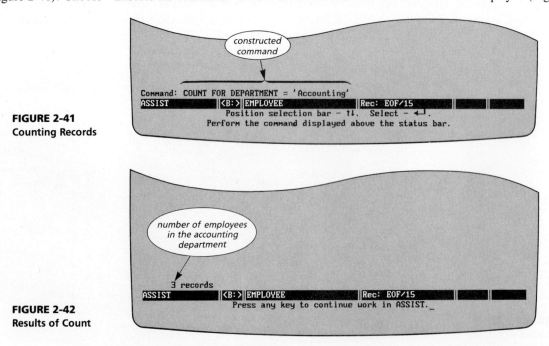

FIGURE 2-41
Counting Records

FIGURE 2-42
Results of Count

"Sum"

To calculate a sum, choose the "Sum" option from the "Retrieve" menu. Next select "Construct a field list" just as you did with the "Display" option. In this case, you will indicate the fields for which you want a sum to be calculated. Only numeric fields may be summed.

Suppose you want to calculate the sum of all the pay rates. After you choose "Construct a field list" the highlight will be on PAY_RATE (Figure 2-43), so press the Enter key. Then choose "Execute the command." The results are shown in Figure 2-44. As you see, the sum is 124.95. Note that the screen also shows the number of records summed. Thus, if you needed to know the number of employees and the total of their pay rates, you could do it all with the "Sum" option. You would not have to use *both* the "Count" *and* the "Sum" options to produce the desired results.

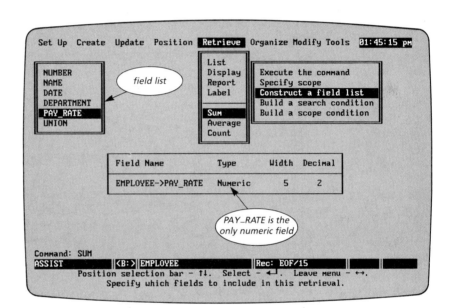

FIGURE 2-43
Calculating a Total

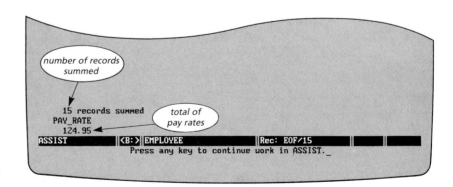

FIGURE 2-44
Results of "Sum" Option

It is also possible to employ search conditions so that only records that satisfy the conditions will be included in the total. Build these search conditions exactly as you did with the "Display" option. Try to calculate the total of the pay rates for the employees in the accounting department. If you have done it correctly, the answer should be three records summed and a total pay rate of $28.75.

"Average"

The "Average" option within the "Retrieve" menu is employed in *exactly* the same fashion as the Sum option. The only difference is that dBASE will compute an average rather than a sum. Try to calculate the average pay rate of all employees. If you have done it correctly, dBASE will indicate that 15 records were averaged and the average pay rate is $8.33. Now try to calculate the average pay rate of all the employees in the accounting department. If you have done this correctly, dBASE will indicate three records averaged with the average pay rate being $9.58.

PROJECT SUMMARY

I n Project 2 you learned how to display the structure of a database file, how to use the "Display" option to list various fields and records within a database file, and how to use the "Count," "Sum," and "Average" options of the "Retrieve" menu to count records, calculate totals, and calculate averages.

If you followed along with the steps in this project, you have created a variety of displays. If you did not but wish to see the results now, you can use the following keystroke sequence. Start dBASE as described in the project and activate the EMPLOYEE database file. Then type the following:

SUMMARY OF KEYSTROKES—Project 2

STEPS	KEY(S) PRESSED	RESULTS
1	→ → → → → → →	
2	↓↓↓↓↓ ← ← ←	Show database structure
3	← ← ← ←↓↓ ←	
4	↓↓ ←3←	Change record pointer
5	← ←	Change record pointer
6	→↓ ← ← ←	Display
7	←↓ ←↓ ←↑ ← ←	Display
8	←↓ ←↓ ← ←↓ ←	
9	↓ ← ←→↑ ← ←	Display
10	←↓↓↓ ← ← ←1030 ←	
11	↑↑↑ ← ←	Display
12	←↓↓↓ ←↓↓↓↓	
13	↓ ← ←↑↑↑ ← ←	Display
14	←↓↓↓ ←↓↓↓ ←	
15	←Accounting↓ ←↓↓↓↓	
16	← ←11.00 ←	
17	↑↑↑ ← ←	Display
18	←↓↓↓ ←↓↓↓ ←	
19	←Accounting↓↓ ←↓↓↓	
20	↓↓ ← ←↑↑↑	
21	← ←	Display
22	↓↓↓↓↓ ← ← ←	Count
23	←↓↓ ←↓↓↓ ← ←	
24	Accounting ←↑↑ ← ←	Count
25	↑↑ ←↓↓ ← ←	
26	↑↑ ← ←	Count

The following list summarizes the material covered in Project 2:

1. To display the structure of a database, use the "List structure" option within the "Tools" menu.
2. dBASE continually maintains a position within a database file. The number used to indicate this position is called the **record pointer**. The record indicated by the record pointer is called the **current active record**.
3. To change the current active record, you can use the "Goto Record" option of the "Position" menu.
4. The **scope** is the portion of a database file to which a given command or option applies. A scope of "ALL," for example, indicates the command or option is to apply to all records in the file.
5. To display the current active record, you can use the "Display" option of the "Retrieve" menu. Simply select "Execute the command" without specifying anything else and the current active record will be displayed.
6. To display all records, you can use the "Display" option of the "Retrieve" menu. Using the "Specify scope" option, change the scope to "ALL." Then select "Execute the command."
7. To display selected fields, you can use the "Display" option of the "Retrieve" menu. Using "Construct a field list," select the desired fields. Then select "Execute the command."
8. A **condition** is an expression that evaluates to either true or false. A **simple condition** consists of a single field followed by a comparison operator and a value. (The value could be replaced by another field.) A simple condition could also consist solely of a single field, if the field is a logical field. A **compound condition** is one or more simple conditions combined with .AND. or .OR.
9. To display only records meeting a certain condition, you can use the "Display" option of the "Retrieve" menu. Use the "Build a search condition" option to construct the appropriate condition. Then select "Execute the command."
10. To count the number of records, use the "Count" option of the "Retrieve" menu.
11. To calculate totals, use the "Sum" option of the "Retrieve" menu.
12. To calculate averages, use the "Average" option of the "Retrieve" menu.

STUDENT ASSIGNMENTS

STUDENT ASSIGNMENT 1: True/False

Instructions: Circle T if the statement is true and F if the statement is false.

T F   1. When you use the "Database file" option of the "Set Up" menu, dBASE will display a list of all the database files on the default drive.
T F   2. When you choose the "Database file" option of the "Set Up" menu and then request the EMPLOYEE database file, the contents of the database file are automatically displayed.
T F   3. To review field names and related information, use the "List structure" option of the "Tools" menu.
T F   4. Both the "List" and "Display" options of the "Retrieve" menu give you a chance to decide whether or not the output is to be directed to the printer.
T F   5. Selecting the "Display" option from the "Retrieve" menu followed by "Execute the command" causes all records of the database file to be displayed.
T F   6. To display the contents of record 6, select "Display" and then choose the "Record number" option.
T F   7. To change the record pointer to a specific number, use the "Goto Record" option of the "Position" menu.
T F   8. To change the record pointer to the last record in the file, select the "Goto Record" option of the "Position" menu, then choose "LAST."
T F   9. In order to select all records in a database file meeting a certain condition, use the option called "Build a search condition."
T F   10. If you have built a search condition while using the "Display" option and you want the scope to be "ALL," you don't have to use the "Specify scope" option.
T F   11. When building a search condition involving a character field, the character string must be enclosed in quotes.
T F   12. To specify a search condition to find those employees who are in a union, select "UNION," then "Equal to," and then type the letter T.
T F   13. To count the number of records, use the "Sum" option of the "Retrieve" menu.

Student Assignment 1 (continued)

T F 14. If you use the "Average" option of the "Retrieve" menu, you must build a search condition.

T F 15. You could build a search condition by choosing "NAME" and then "Equal to." Then you type the single letter B and press the Enter key. When the command is executed, the display will include any employees whose name begins with the letter B.

T F 16. The "Count" option can only be selected for numeric fields.

STUDENT ASSIGNMENT 2: Multiple Choice

Instructions: Circle the correct response.

1. dBASE will display a list of all database files on the current directory when you select
   a. the "Database file" option of the "Set Up" menu.
   b. the "Database file" option of the "Create" menu.
   c. the "Database file" option of the "Retrieve" menu.
   d. the "Display" option of the "Retrieve" menu.

2. You first select the "List" option within the "Retrieve" menu and then choose "Execute the command." Then you select the "Display" option within the "Retrieve" menu and choose "Execute the command." Which of the following would be true in both situations?
   a. all records would be displayed.
   b. the display would pause every time the screen was filled.
   c. record numbers would be displayed.
   d. you would be asked whether or not the display was to be sent to the printer.

3. You have selected the "Display" option within the "Retrieve" menu and built the search condition "PAY_RATE = 6.00." When you execute this command, dBASE will
   a. display the first record in which the pay rate field contains a value equal to $6.00.
   b. display all the records in which the pay rate field contains a value equal to $6.00.
   c. display an error message because the value $6.00 was not enclosed in quotation marks.
   d. display the active record if the value in the pay rate field is $6.00.

4. Which of the following expressions is used by dBASE to indicate the field called NUMBER that is part of the database file called EMPLOYEE?
   a. EMPLOYEE.NUMBER
   b. NUMBER IN EMPLOYEE
   c. NUMBER->EMPLOYEE
   d. EMPLOYEE->NUMBER

5. Which option can be used to change the record pointer?
   a. the "Goto record" option of the "Position" menu.
   b. the "Change pointer" option of the "Position" menu.
   c. the "Change" option of the "Update" menu.
   d. the "Change" option of the "Retrieve" menu.

6. Which calculation cannot be made using the "Retrieve" menu?
   a. the sum of all the pay rates.
   b. the largest pay rate.
   c. the average of all the pay rates.
   d. the number of employees whose pay rate is greater than $6.00.

STUDENT ASSIGNMENT 3: Understanding dBASE Options

Instructions: Explain what will happen after you perform each of the following actions.

Problem 1. Choose the "Database file" option of the "Set Up" menu.

Explanation: _____

_____

_____

Problem 2. Choose the "Display" option of the "Retrieve" menu.

Explanation: _____

_____

_____

Problem 3. Select the "Goto record" option of the "Position" menu.

Explanation: _____

_____

_____

Problem 4. Select "Build a search condition."

Explanation: _____

_____

_____

STUDENT ASSIGNMENT 4: Using dBASE

Instructions: Explain how to accomplish each of the following tasks using dBASE.

Problem 1. Activate the database file called EMPLOYEE.

Explanation: _____

_____

_____

Problem 2. Make record 3 the current active record.

Explanation: _____

_____

_____

Problem 3. Display record 6.

Explanation: _____

_____

_____

Student Assignment 4 (continued)

Problem 4. Display the NAME and DEPARTMENT fields for all records.

Explanation: _____

_____

_____

Problem 5. Display the records for those employees whose last name begins with the letter M.

Explanation: _____

_____

_____

Problem 6. Count the number of employees in the union.

Explanation: _____

_____

_____

STUDENT ASSIGNMENT 5: Recovering from Problems

Instructions: In each of the following cases, a problem occurred. Explain the cause of the problem and how it can be corrected.

Problem 1: You chose the "Display" option to list all the records in the active database file. Only one record was displayed.

Cause of Problem: _____

_____

Method of Correction: _____

_____

Problem 2: You wanted to display all fields for those employees in a union. You selected UNION when a box containing all fields was displayed. The display that was produced contained all records, but only the UNION field.

Cause of Problem: _____

_____

Method of Correction: _____

_____

Problem 3: You attempted to choose the "Display" option from the "Retrieve" menu and were unable to do so since there was no highlight in the box to move to "Display."

Cause of Problem: _____

_____

Method of Correction: _____

_____

MINICASES:

Displaying Records in a Database

Minicase 1: Personal Checks

Instructions: In Project 1 you created a database of personal checks. Now use this database and dBASE options to accomplish the following tasks. Obtain a printed copy of the output displayed after each command is executed. Do this by holding down the Shift key and pressing the PrtSc key. Write the step(s) to produce the output requested. Record the step(s) in the space provided and then execute them on the computer.

1. Activate the database file so you can access it.

STEPS: _____

_____

_____

2. Display the structure of the database file.

STEPS: _____

_____

_____

3. Display all the records in the database file.

STEPS: _____

_____

_____

4. Display the CHECK NUMBER, DATE, PAYEE, and CHECK AMOUNT fields.

STEPS: _____

_____

_____

5. Display the DATE field, then the CHECK NUMBER field, the PAYEE field, and the CHECK AMOUNT field.

STEPS: _____

_____

_____

6. Use the "Position" menu to position the record pointer at the first record. Display the first record.

STEPS: _____

_____

_____

Minicase 1 (continued)

7. Use the "Position" menu to position the record pointer at the last record in the file. Display the last record.

STEPS: _____

_____

_____

8. Display record 4.

STEPS: _____

_____

_____

9. Display the record for check 108.

STEPS: _____

_____

_____

10. Display the record that contains the check written for the amount of $69.50.

STEPS: _____

_____

_____

11. Display the records for all checks written for entertainment. Include the CHECK NUMBER, PAYEE, CHECK AMOUNT, and EXPENSE fields.

STEPS: _____

_____

_____

12. Display the records for all checks written to Sav-Mor Groceries.

STEPS: _____

_____

_____

13. Display the records for all checks written that are tax deductible.

STEPS: _____

_____

_____

14. Display the records of all checks written for entertainment for an amount of more than $25.00.

STEPS: _____

_____

_____

15. Display the records for all checks written for household expenses or checks for food expenses.

STEPS: _____

_____

_____

16. Count the number of records in the database file.

STEPS: _____

_____

_____

17. Sum the amount of checks written.

STEPS: _____

_____

_____

18. Sum the amounts of the checks written for household expenses.

STEPS: _____

_____

_____

19. Average the amount of all checks written.

STEPS: _____

_____

_____

20. Average the amount of all checks written for entertainment.

STEPS: _____

_____

_____

Minicase 2: Music Library

Instructions: In Project 1 you created a database of music library information. Now use this database and dBASE options to accomplish the following tasks. Obtain a printed copy of the output displayed after each command is executed. Do this by holding down the Shift key and pressing the PrtSc key. Write the step(s) to produce the output requested. Record the step(s) in the space provided and then execute them on the computer.

1. Activate the database file so that it can be accessed.

STEPS: _____

_____

_____

Minicase 2 (continued)

2. Display the structure of the database file.

STEPS: _____

_____

_____

3. Display all the records.

STEPS: _____

_____

_____

4. Display the MUSIC NAME, ARTIST, TYPE, and COST fields.

STEPS: _____

_____

_____

5. Display the CATEGORY first and then the other fields in the record.

STEPS: _____

_____

_____

6. Use the "Position" menu to position the record pointer at the first record in the file. Display the first record.

STEPS: _____

_____

_____

7. Use the "Position" menu to position the record pointer at the last record in the file. Display the last record.

STEPS: _____

_____

_____

8. Display record 8.

STEPS: _____

_____

_____

9. Display the records for the classical music.

STEPS: _____

_____

_____

10. Display the records for all the music that costs $5.95.

STEPS: _____

_____

_____

11. Display the records for all music on cassette tape (CS).

STEPS: _____

_____

_____

12. Display the records for all music on compact disk (CD). Include the TYPE, MUSIC NAME, ARTIST, and COST fields.

STEPS: _____

_____

_____

13. Display the records for all the music by Milo Panache.

STEPS: _____

_____

_____

14. Display the records for all classical music that costs less than $8.95.

STEPS: _____

_____

_____

15. Display the records for all rock music that costs less than $8.95.

STEPS: _____

_____

_____

16. Display the ARTIST and MUSIC NAME for all rock music that is unavailable on cassette tape.

STEPS: _____

_____

_____

17. Count the number of records in the database file.

STEPS: _____

_____

_____

Minicase 2 (continued)

18. Count the number of music selections in the vocal category.

STEPS: _____

_____

_____

19. Sum the total cost of all types of music.

STEPS: _____

_____

_____

20. Sum the total cost of the music in the country category.

STEPS: _____

_____

_____

21. Determine the average cost for all types of music.

STEPS: _____

_____

_____

Minicase 3: Computer Software Store

Instructions: In Project 1 you created a database of software information. Now use this database and dBASE options to accomplish the following tasks. Obtain a printed copy of the output displayed after each command is executed. Do this by holding down the Shift key and pressing the PrtSc key. Write the step(s) to produce the output requested. Record the step(s) in the space provided and then execute them on the computer.

1. Activate the database file so that it can be accessed

STEPS: _____

_____

_____

2. Display the structure of the database file.

STEPS: _____

_____

_____

3. Display all the records.

STEPS: _____

_____

_____

4. Display the SOFTWARE NAME field, the CATEGORY field, the MS_DOS field, the QUANTITY field, and the COST field for all records in the database.

STEPS: _____

_____

_____

5. Display the CATEGORY field, the SOFTWARE NAME field, and the COST field for all records in the database.

STEPS: _____

_____

_____

6. Use the "Position" menu to position the record pointer at the first record in the file. Display the first record.

STEPS: _____

_____

_____

7. Use the "Position" menu to position the record pointer at the last record in the file. Display the last record.

STEPS: _____

_____

_____

8. Display record 8.

STEPS: _____

_____

_____

9. Display the record for the software called Image Fonts.

STEPS: _____

_____

_____

10. Display all software produced by the company Anchor Software.

STEPS: _____

_____

_____

11. Display all software in the education category.

STEPS: _____

_____

_____

Minicase 3 (continued)

12. Display all software that is MS-DOS compatible (the entry .T. in the MS_DOS field).

STEPS: _____

_____

_____

13. Display all records with a quantity less than 10.

STEPS: _____

_____

_____

14. Display all records with a quantity greater than 25.

STEPS: _____

_____

_____

15. Display all word processing software (WP in the CATEGORY field) that costs less than $50.00.

STEPS: _____

_____

_____

16. Display all records in the database or spreadsheet categories.

STEPS: _____

_____

_____

17. Count the number of records in the database file.

STEPS: _____

_____

_____

18. Sum the QUANTITY field to determine the number of products on hand.

STEPS: _____

_____

_____

19. Average the COST field to determine the average cost of the software.

STEPS: _____

_____

_____

20. Average the cost of the software in the education category.

STEPS: _____

_____

_____

Minicase 4: Home Sales

Instructions: In Project 1 you created a database of information about homes for sale. Now use this database and dBASE options to accomplish the following tasks. Obtain a printed copy of the output displayed after each command is executed. Do this by holding down the Shift key and pressing the PrtSc key. Write the step(s) to produce the output requested. Record the step(s) in the space provided and then execute them on the computer.

1. Activate the database file so that it can be accessed.

STEPS: _____

_____

_____

2. Display the structure of the database file.

STEPS: _____

_____

_____

3. Display all the records.

STEPS: _____

_____

_____

4. Display the ADDRESS field, the CITY field, and the PRICE field for all records in the database.

STEPS: _____

_____

_____

5. Display the PRICE field, the ADDRESS field, the CITY field, and the ZIP field for all records in the database.

STEPS: _____

_____

_____

6. Use the "Position" menu to position the record pointer at the first record in the file. Display the first record.

STEPS: _____

_____

_____

Minicase 4 (continued)

7. Use the "Position" menu to position the record pointer at the last record in the file. Display the last record.

STEPS: _____

_____

_____

8. Display record 8.

STEPS: _____

_____

_____

9. Display the record that has 10/22/90 in the DATE field.

STEPS: _____

_____

_____

10. Display information about the house at 145 Oak Ave.

STEPS: _____

_____

_____

11. Display the records for all houses listed in the city of Anaheim.

STEPS: _____

_____

_____

12. Display the records for all houses in the 92641 zip code.

STEPS: _____

_____

_____

13. Display the records for all houses with a pool (the entry Y in the POOL field).

STEPS: _____

_____

_____

14. Display the records for all houses that cost less than $125,000.00.

STEPS: _____

_____

_____

15. Display the records for all houses that cost more than $150,000.00.

STEPS: _____

_____

_____

16. Display the records for all houses with four bedrooms that cost less than $100,000.00.

STEPS: _____

_____

_____

17. Count the number of records in the database file.

STEPS: _____

_____

_____

18. Find the average cost of a house in Anaheim.

STEPS: _____

_____

_____

19. Find the average cost of a four-bedroom house.

STEPS: _____

_____

_____

20. Find the average cost of a three-bedroom house in Garden Grove.

STEPS: _____

_____

_____

PROJECT 3

Sorting and Report Preparation

Objectives

You will have mastered the material in this project when you can:

- Sort the records in a database file
- Display the sorted records
- Understand the sequence in which records will be sorted
- Sort on multiple fields
- Create a report file using dBASE
- Print a report using a report file you have created
- Print a report containing only selected records
- Implement subtotals in a report

*T*he records in a database file are initially arranged in the order in which you entered the data when you created the database file. Thus, when you use the "Display" or "List" options, the records will be displayed in the order they were entered.

For some applications, you may want to rearrange the records into a different sequence. For example, you may want to list the employees alphabetically by name. You can accomplish this by sorting the records in the database file. **Sorting** simply means rearranging the records so that they are in some desired order.

In Project 1, we entered the employee records in a date-hired sequence (see Figure 3-1). But there are additional ways in which to arrange the records to display the data in a useful form. For example, we could arrange them in alphabetical order by last name, in ascending or descending order by pay rate, or in alphabetical order within various departments. If you need a list of employees in alphabetical order by last name, for example, you must sort the records in the database file using the employee name field as the basis of the sorting operation (Figure 3-2). A field used as the basis of a sorting operation is called a **key field**. Figure 3-3 illustrates a display of records that have been sorted by pay rate. In this case, the PAY_RATE field was the key field.

records are in sequence by date hired field

NUMBER	NAME	DATE	DEPARTMENT	PAY_RATE	UNION
1011	Rapoza, Anthony P.	01/10/89	Shipping	8.50	.T.
1013	McCormack, Nigel L.	01/15/89	Shipping	8.25	.T.
1016	Ackerman, David R.	02/04/89	Accounting	9.75	.F.
1017	Doi, Chang J.	02/05/89	Production	6.00	.T.
1020	Castle, Mark C.	03/04/89	Shipping	7.50	.T.
1022	Dunning, Lisa A.	03/12/89	Marketing	9.10	.F.
1025	Chaney, Joseph R.	03/23/89	Accounting	8.00	.F.
1026	Bender, Helen O.	04/12/89	Production	6.75	.T.
1029	Anderson, Mariane L.	04/18/89	Shipping	9.00	.T.
1030	Edwards, Kenneth J.	04/23/89	Production	8.60	.T.
1037	Baxter, Charles W.	05/05/89	Accounting	11.00	.F.
1041	Evans, John T.	05/19/89	Marketing	6.00	.F.
1056	Andrews, Robert M.	06/03/89	Marketing	9.00	.F.
1057	Dugan, Mary L.	06/10/89	Production	8.75	.T.
1066	Castleworth, Mary T.	07/05/89	Production	8.75	.T.

FIGURE 3-1
Records Sorted by Date

records are in alphabetical order by last name

NUMBER	NAME	DATE	DEPARTMENT	PAY_RATE	UNION
1016	Ackerman, David R.	02/04/89	Accounting	9.75	.F.
1029	Anderson, Mariane L.	04/18/89	Shipping	9.00	.T.
1056	Andrews, Robert M.	06/03/89	Marketing	9.00	.F.
1037	Baxter, Charles W.	05/05/89	Accounting	11.00	.F.
1026	Bender, Helen O.	04/12/89	Production	6.75	.T.
1075	Caine, William J.	08/16/89	Marketing	9.25	.F.
1020	Castle, Mark C.	03/04/89	Shipping	7.50	.T.
1066	Castleworth, Mary T.	07/05/89	Production	8.75	.T.
1025	Chaney, Joseph R.	03/23/89	Accounting	8.00	.F.
1017	Doi, Chang J.	02/05/89	Production	6.00	.T.
1057	Dugan, Mary L.	06/10/89	Production	8.75	.T.
1022	Dunning, Lisa A.	03/12/89	Marketing	9.10	.F.
1030	Edwards, Kenneth J.	04/23/89	Production	8.60	.T.
1041	Evans, John T.	05/19/89	Marketing	6.00	.F.
1070	Fisher, Ella C.	07/15/89	Accounting	8.00	.F.
1013	McCormack, Nigel L.	01/15/89	Shipping	8.25	.T.
1011	Rapoza, Anthony P.	01/10/89	Shipping	8.50	.T.

FIGURE 3-2
Records Sorted by Name

records are sorted by pay rate

NUMBER	NAME	DATE	DEPARTMENT	PAY_RATE	UNION
1041	Evans, John T.	05/19/89	Marketing	6.00	.F.
1017	Doi, Chang J.	02/05/89	Production	6.00	.T.
1026	Bender, Helen O.	04/12/89	Production	6.75	.T.
1020	Castle, Mark C.	03/04/89	Shipping	7.50	.T.
1025	Chaney, Joseph R.	03/23/89	Accounting	8.00	.F.
1013	McCormack, Nigel L.	01/15/89	Shipping	8.25	.T.
1011	Rapoza, Anthony P.	01/10/89	Shipping	8.50	.T.
1030	Edwards, Kenneth J.	04/23/89	Production	8.60	.T.
1066	Castleworth, Mary T.	07/05/89	Production	8.75	.T.
1057	Dugan, Mary L.	06/10/89	Production	8.75	.T.
1029	Anderson, Mariane L.	04/18/89	Shipping	9.00	.T.
1056	Andrews, Robert M.	06/03/89	Marketing	9.00	.F.
1022	Dunning, Lisa A.	03/12/89	Marketing	9.10	.F.
1016	Ackerman, David R.	02/04/89	Accounting	9.75	.F.
1037	Baxter, Charles W.	05/05/89	Accounting	11.00	.F.

FIGURE 3-3
Records Sorted by Pay Rate

You may often need to sort on more than one field. For example, you may want to prepare a list of employees in alphabetical order by last name within departments. Figure 3-4 illustrates output from a sorting operation of this type. Note that the names are in alphabetical order within each department.

records are sorted by name within each department

NUMBER	NAME	DATE	DEPARTMENT	PAY_RATE	UNION
1016	Ackerman, David R.	02/04/89	Accounting	9.75	.F.
1037	Baxter, Charles W.	05/05/89	Accounting	11.00	.F.
1025	Chaney, Joseph R.	03/23/89	Accounting	8.00	.F.
1070	Fisher, Ella C.	07/15/89	Accounting	8.00	.F.
1056	Andrews, Robert M.	06/03/89	Marketing	9.00	.F.
1075	Caine, William J.	08/16/89	Marketing	9.25	.F.
1022	Dunning, Lisa A.	03/12/89	Marketing	9.10	.F.
1041	Evans, John T.	05/19/89	Marketing	6.00	.F.
1026	Bender, Helen O.	04/12/89	Production	6.75	.T.
1066	Castleworth, Mary T.	07/05/89	Production	8.75	.T.
1017	Doi, Chang J.	02/05/89	Production	6.00	.T.
1057	Dugan, Mary L.	06/10/89	Production	8.75	.T.
1030	Edwards, Kenneth J.	04/23/89	Production	8.60	.T.
1029	Anderson, Mariane L.	04/18/89	Shipping	9.00	.T.
1020	Castle, Mark C.	03/04/89	Shipping	7.50	.T.
1013	McCormack, Nigel L.	01/15/89	Shipping	8.25	.T.
1011	Rapoza, Anthony P.	01/10/89	Shipping	8.50	.T.

FIGURE 3-4 Records Sorted on Two Fields

dBASE provides an option that can be used to perform sorting operations. In addition, dBASE provides an option for preparing report and column headings, space control, and totaling for numeric fields. We discuss sorting and report preparation in this project. You will use the menus and options within the ASSISTANT that are shown in blue in Figure 3-5.

OPTION	PURPOSE
Set Up	Activate a
Database file	database file
View	view
Quit dBASE III PLUS	leave dBASE III PLUS
Create	Create a
Database file	database file (extension DBF)
View	view (extension VUE)
Report	report (extension FRM)
Update	Change a database file by
Append	adding records at the end
Edit	changing records viewing one at a time
Browse	changing records viewing several at a time
Replace	changing the data in all records that satisfy some condition
Delete	deleting records
Recall	undeleting records
Pack	physically remove deleted records
Position	Move the record pointer by
Seek	finding a match using an index
Locate	finding the first record that satisfies some condition
Goto Record	specifying a record number
Retrieve	Retrieve data from a database file
List	show desired fields and records on the screen or printer
Display	like "List" (differences between the two are covered in the text)
Report	print a report
Sum	calculate a total
Average	calculate an average
Count	count the number of records
Organize	
Index	create an index (extension NDX)
Sort	sort a database file
Modify	Change an existing
Database file	database file
Report	report file
Tools	
List structure	show the structure of the active database file

FIGURE 3-5 Menus and Options within the dBASE ASSISTANT

SORTING

Figure 3-6 illustrates the sorting process of the records in the EMPLOYEE file. First, the records in the EMPLOYEE file are read into main computer memory. Second, the records are sorted in main computer memory. Third, the sorted records are stored on the disk. In this example, the new sorted file is stored on disk with the file name SORTFLE1. After the sorting operation is completed, there are two separate files stored on disk: the original file (EMPLOYEE) and the sorted file (SORTFLE1).

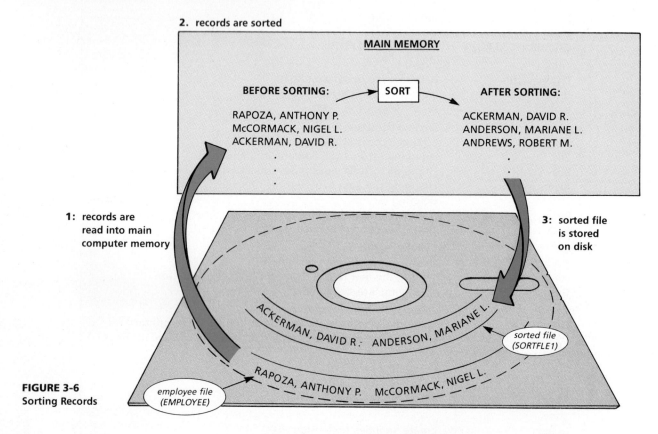

FIGURE 3-6
Sorting Records

The "Sort" Option

Before you can sort, you must load dBASE into main computer memory and activate the file to be sorted using the "Database file" option of the "Set Up" menu. You will use EMPLOYEE, the same file used in Projects 1 and 2, to learn how to sort, so this is the file you should activate.

This file is currently in sequence by date hired, but now you want the records to be sorted in alphabetical order by last name. This requires sorting using the NAME field as the key field. Character fields, numeric fields, and date fields can be sorted, but logical fields and memo fields cannot be sorted. Since NAME is a character field, there is no problem using it as the key field.

To sort records in this file, choose the "Sort" option of the "Organize" menu (Figure 3-7). Use the Right Arrow key to move to the "Organize" menu. Then press the Down Arrow key once to move the highlight to "Sort" and press the Enter key.

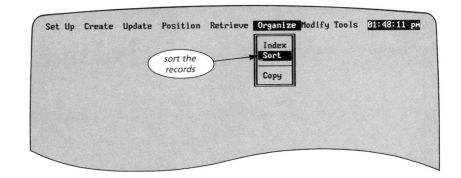

FIGURE 3-7
The Organize Menu

Next, dBASE will prompt you to indicate the key field. Note that all the fields are listed in a box on the left of the screen (Figure 3-8). Since we want to sort using NAME as the key field, move the highlight to the word NAME (in the figure, this has already been done) by pressing the Down Arrow key once. To indicate that this is the key field, press the Enter key. Then press the Right Arrow key to indicate that there are no other key fields. The display should now look like the one in Figure 3-9.

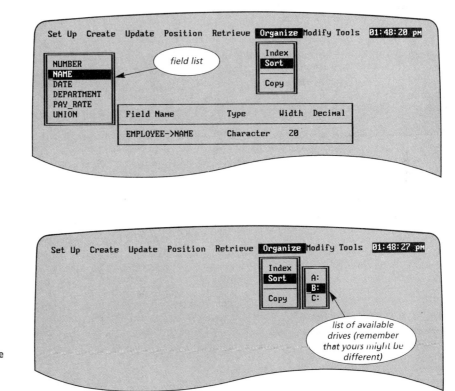

FIGURE 3-8
Selecting Sort Key

FIGURE 3-9
Selecting a Drive for the
Sorted File

At this point, you must indicate the drive on which you want to place the sorted file. To do this, make sure the B: is highlighted and press the Enter key.

The display shown in Figure 3-10 will appear. It requests you to enter a file name. Any legitimate file name is allowed, except that you cannot sort a file onto itself. Thus, you can't use EMPLOYEE as the file name. In this example, pick the file name SORTFLE1.

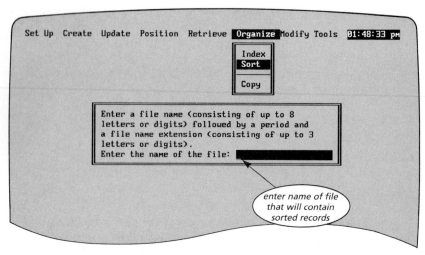

FIGURE 3-10 Entering Name of Sorted File

Once you have typed the file name, press the Enter key. At this point, the sort will take place. During the sort operation, dBASE provides messages on the screen indicating the percentage of the file that has been sorted. Once the message says that the file has been 100% sorted, the sort is done. The number of records sorted will also be displayed. Your new sorted file, named SORTFLE1, is now stored on the disk in disk drive B.

Displaying a Sorted File

You created SORTFLE1, but EMPLOYEE is still considered to be the active database file. Therefore, any option you select, such as "List" or "Display," will operate on the records in EMPLOYEE. To use the sorted version, you must first activate it. Return to the "Set Up" menu and choose "Database file" as before.

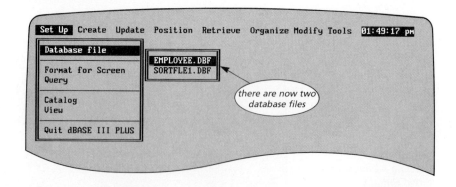

FIGURE 3-11
Selecting a Database File

Now SORTFLE1.DBF will be one of the files displayed (Figure 3-11). Activate it by moving the highlight to it and pressing the Enter key. Respond to the question "Is file indexed?" by typing the letter N. Then choose the "Display" option from the "Retrieve" menu, change the scope to "ALL," and choose "Execute the command." The results are shown in Figure 3-12. You can see that the records are now sorted alphabetically by name. Note the status line, which indicates that SORTFLE1 is the active database file. After displaying the records, SORTFLE1 is still considered the active file. If you now wanted to work on the EMPLOYEE file, you would have to reactivate it using the "Database file" option of the "Set Up" menu.

records have been sorted by NAME

```
Record#  NUMBER  NAME                DATE      DEPARTMENT  PAY_RATE  UNION
      1   1016   Ackerman, David R.   02/04/89  Accounting     9.75   .F.
      2   1029   Anderson, Mariane L. 04/18/89  Shipping       9.00   .T.
      3   1056   Andrews, Robert M.   06/03/89  Marketing      9.00   .F.
      4   1037   Baxter, Charles W.   05/05/89  Accounting    11.00   .F.
      5   1026   Bender, Helen O.     04/12/89  Production     6.75   .T.
      6   1020   Castle, Mark C.      03/04/89  Shipping       7.50   .T.
      7   1066   Castleworth, Mary T. 07/05/89  Production     8.75   .T.
      8   1025   Chaney, Joseph R.    03/23/89  Accounting     8.00   .F.
      9   1017   Doi, Chang J.        02/05/89  Production     6.00   .T.
     10   1057   Dugan, Mary L.       06/10/89  Production     8.75   .F.
     11   1022   Dunning, Lisa A.     03/12/89  Marketing      9.10   .F.
     12   1030   Edwards, Kenneth J.  04/23/89  Production     8.60   .T.
     13   1041   Evans, John T.       05/19/89  Marketing      6.00   .F.
     14   1013   McCormack, Nigel L.  01/15/89  Shipping       8.25   .T.
     15   1011   Rapoza, Anthony P.   01/10/89  Shipping       8.50   .T.
ASSIST              <B:> SORTFLE1                Rec: 1/15
              Press any key to continue work in ASSIST._
```

FIGURE 3-12
Results of Sort

SORTFLE1 is the active file

Sort Sequence   The data in numeric fields are sorted based on algebraic values. For example, if three records in a temperature field contain the values $+10$, -25, and $+90$ and the records are sorted in ascending sequence, the values would be arranged as follows: -25, $+10$, $+90$.

Character data are sorted in a sequence based on the **American Standard Code for Information Interchange**, called the **ASCII code**. This code is used when storing data. Figure 3-13 illustrates a segment of a chart of ASCII code.

ASCII VALUE	CHARACTER	ASCII VALUE	CHARACTER	ASCII VALUE	CHARACTER	ASCII VALUE	CHARACTER	ASCII VALUE	CHARACTER
032	Space	051	3	070	F	089	Y	108	l
033	!	052	4	071	G	090	Z	109	m
034	''	053	5	072	H	091	[	110	n
035	#	054	6	073	I	092	\	111	o
036	$	055	7	074	J	093	]	112	p
037	%	056	8	075	K	094	∧	113	q
038	&	057	9	076	L	095	—	114	r
039	'	058	:	077	M	096	`	115	s
040	(	059	;	078	N	097	a	116	t
041	)	060	<	079	O	098	b	117	u
042	*	061	=	080	P	099	c	118	v
043	+	062	>	081	Q	100	d	119	w
044	,	063	?	082	R	101	e	120	x
045	-	064	@	083	S	102	f	121	y
046	.	065	A	084	T	103	g	122	z
047	/	066	B	085	U	104	h		
048	0	067	C	086	V	105	i		
049	1	068	D	087	W	106	j		
050	2	069	E	088	X	107	k		

lowest value

highest value

FIGURE 3-13 ASCII Codes

It is important to understand that numbers are lower in the ASCII sequence than uppercase letters of the alphabet, and uppercase letters of the alphabet are lower than lowercase letters of the alphabet. For example, in an auto supply store a part number field contains part numbers A33, 333, and a33. When these part numbers are sorted in ascending sequence, the fields would be sorted as 333, A33, a33. Number 333 would be first, because it does not begin with a letter, followed by A33, because it begins with capital A, and then a33, because it begins with lowercase a.

Sorting on Multiple Fields   Records can be sorted on the basis of more than one field. Figure 3-4, for example, illustrated records sorted in alphabetical order by name within department.

Let's try another example and sort on more than one field. First, reactivate the EMPLOYEE database file in the usual manner, using the "Database file" option of the "Set Up" menu. Next sort the file as before. Select both key fields the same way you selected NAME in the previous example. The only special consideration is that the most significant field must be selected first. In this example, records are sorted by name *within* department; therefore, the most significant field is the DEPARTMENT field and you must select it first. After you select both fields, press the Right Arrow key. The remainder of the process is identical to the previous example, except that this time use the name SORTFLE2 for the sorted file (Figure 3-14).

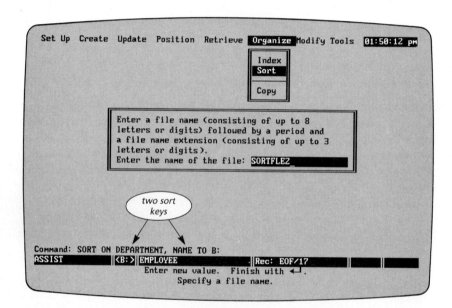

FIGURE 3-14
Sorting with Two Keys

Once the sort has been completed, activate SORTFLE2 and use "Display" to display all records. This produces the report shown in Figure 3-15. (Don't forget to specify a scope of "ALL.")

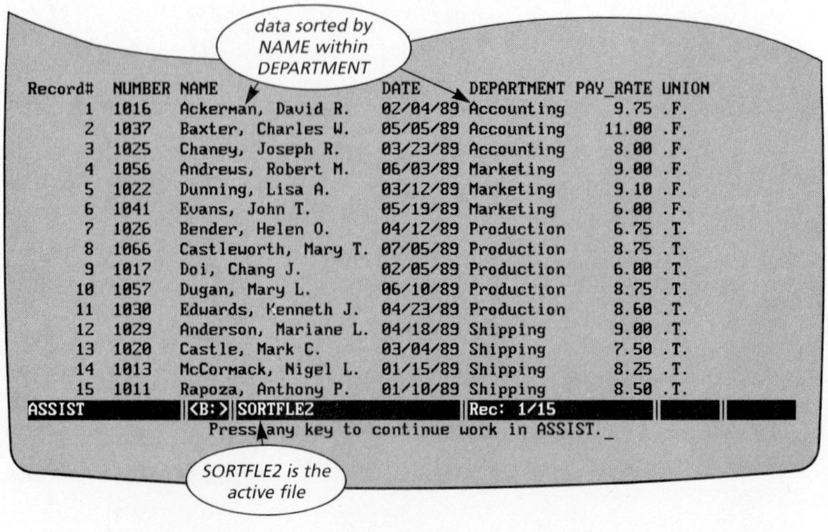

FIGURE 3-15
Results of Sort

REPORTS

In previous examples, we used the "Display" option to produce output that could be displayed on the screen or the printer. The format of this output was very restricted, listing only the field headings and one or more fields in a record or records.

You can also use dBASE to produce reports suitable for business purposes. These reports can contain such items as page numbers, dates, report and column headings, and totals. The reports may be formatted to give a professional appearance. dBASE's report-generating feature displays a series of screens prompting you in the steps necessary to produce the desired output. We explain this technique in the following paragraphs.

Designing the Output

Design your report carefully *before* entering any information into dBASE. It helps to lay out the form of the output on graph paper or on a special form such as a printer spacing chart, illustrated in Figure 3-16a. Figure 3-16b, on the next page, shows a weekly payroll report, which we will design together. Printer spacing charts are readily available. You could take a blank chart and make the entries as we go along.

As you begin thinking about your report, you decide that you want to include employee name, department name, pay rate, and weekly pay. Weekly pay is calculated by multiplying the value in the pay rate field by 40. You want the report to contain page and column headings. You also want a final total to be accumulated and printed for the weekly pay, but you do not want to include the total of all the pay rates.

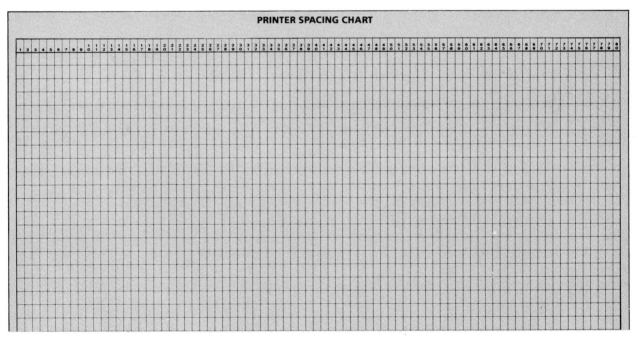

FIGURE 3-16a Printer Spacing Chart

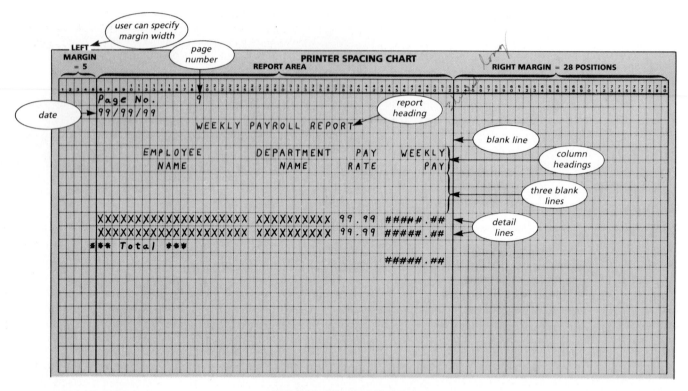

FIGURE 3-16b Report Layout

Before starting to lay out the report, let's examine the printer spacing chart in a little more detail. As you can see from Figure 3-16b, the numbers 1 to 80 are printed across the top of the form. These numbers represent the standard number of printing positions used by dBASE. Within the grid on the form you will record the location and the type of information that is to appear on the report.

The first thing to do is to specify the left margin of the report. We decide the left margin should be five and indicate this as shown in the figure.

Next, determine the report area, that is, the area occupied by the data that will appear on the report. Indicate where to place the data in this area by using the letter X for character fields, the number 9 for numeric fields for which no total will be calculated, or the symbol # for numeric fields for which a total is to be calculated. For numeric fields, place a decimal point where you want it to appear. Enter the appropriate symbols on the tenth line of the report as shown in Figure 3-16. The first data field, the employee's name, is represented by 20 X's, indicating that it is a character field 20 positions long. The second data field, the department, is represented by 10 X's. The third, pay rate, is represented by 99.99. This means that it is a numeric field occupying five positions, with the decimal point at the third position, and no total will be calculated for the field. The final field, weekly pay, is represented by #####.##. This means that it is a numeric field of eight positions, with the decimal point at the sixth position, and a total will be calculated for the field.

The unused right portion of the form, from one space past the end of the last field out to position 80, is considered to be the right margin. In this report the right margin is 28. It's important to specify the left margin, the report area, and the right margin, because dBASE will automatically center the page heading in the report area.

Now construct the top portion of the form. On the first line, place the words Page No. followed by the number 9. This does not mean page number 9. Rather, it indicates that a numeric value will be displayed in that space. The report-generating feature of dBASE will always produce the words Page No. and the actual page number on the first line of a report in the location you have indicated.

On the next line, place the entry 99/99/99, which shows where the date will be displayed. The date will always appear on the second line when you use the report-generating feature of dBASE. It is displayed in the MM/DD/YY format.

On the third line place the page heading, centered over the data fields. In our example the page heading is WEEKLY PAYROLL REPORT. Enter it as shown in Figure 3-16. Note that it is centered over the data. dBASE automatically centers this heading for you when you construct the report, but the main reason you center it here is to make sure that what you write on the printer spacing chart is an accurate reflection of the way the final report will look. Below the heading, leave a blank line and then write the column headings. Make sure the column headings are centered over the appropriate data fields.

There should be three blank lines between the column headings and the lines showing the data fields. dBASE puts these in automatically. If you have not left enough room on the chart for three blank lines, simply erase and redraw the bottom portion of the report.

You should always include two lines of the X's, 9's, and #'s to describe the vertical spacing of the report. The fact that there is no blank line between the two lines shows that the report is to be single spaced (no blank spaces between lines). To construct a double-spaced report, leave a single blank line between the two lines.

At the bottom of the display, place the entry *** Total *** on the left, and on the next line, underneath the weekly pay column at the right, place #####.##. This indicates where the total of the weekly pay amounts will appear. dBASE automatically generates the entry *** Total *** when a final total is taken. In addition, when you specify a left margin of one or more characters, dBASE places the leftmost asterisk of *** Total *** in the left margin. dBASE also controls the position of the total.

It is important to understand that dBASE automatically positions the page number, the date, the three blank lines after the column headings, the single blank space between each field, the entry *** Total ***, and the actual total at the bottom of the report. Whenever you design another report to implement in dBASE, make sure these sections of the new report are in the same positions as in this example.

Beginning the Report Creation Process

After designing the report, make sure the database file that will furnish the data for the report is the active database file. Select the file SORTFLE1, since it will furnish the data, using the "Database file" option of the "Set Up" menu. Then use the "Report" option of the "Create" menu to call the screens that allow a report to be created.

Once you have chosen the "Report" option (Figure 3-17), indicate the drive on which to place the file that contains the report description. You are probably using a data disk in drive B. If so, select B: as you have done before. If not, select the correct drive by moving the highlight to it and pressing the Enter key. The display should now look like the one in Figure 3-18. Enter the name REPORT1 for the name of the report as shown in the figure and press the Enter key. dBASE will automatically add .FRM as an extension, so the file that is created will actually be called REPORT1.FRM.

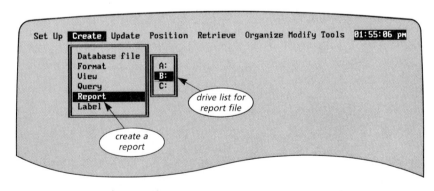

FIGURE 3-17
Creating a Report

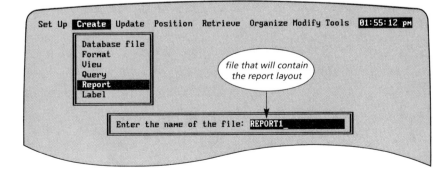

FIGURE 3-18
Entering the Name of a Report

Entering Basic Report Information

Once you have pressed the Enter key, you will see a screen on which you enter the page heading and define the page width, left and right margins, number of lines per page, and double or single spacing (Figure 3-19).

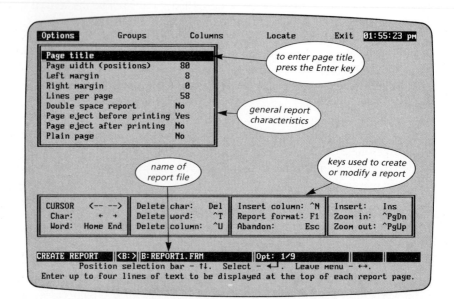

FIGURE 3-19
Entering General Report Characteristics

At the bottom of the screen appears the name of the report file. The box near the bottom of the screen describes some of the key combinations that you can use when creating or modifying a report. The box at the top of the screen indicates the various items that you can enter or change at this point.

The first step is to enter the heading, WEEKLY PAYROLL REPORT. To do so, highlight "Page title" and press the Enter key. The page heading area now appears (Figure 3-20).

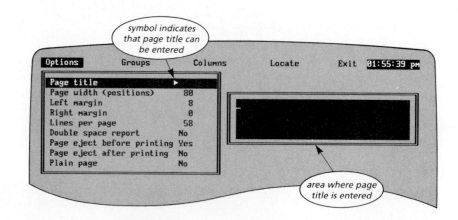

FIGURE 3-20
Entering a Page Title

Type the words WEEKLY PAYROLL REPORT in this page heading area (Figure 3-21). After you have typed the heading, press the Enter key. The cursor will move to the first position on the second line of the page heading area. There is room for four lines of headings in the page heading area. For example, the name of the company could be printed on the next line, followed by the city and state, and then the phone number. Because there are no additional headings in the example, hold the Ctrl key down and press the End key. The display now looks like the one shown in Figure 3-22. Note that a small portion of the title appears on the "Page title" line within the box.

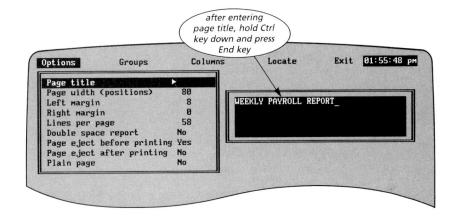

FIGURE 3-21
Page Title Is Being Entered

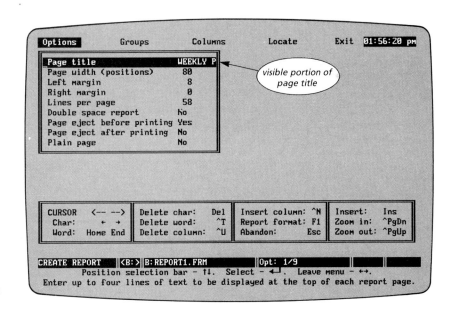

FIGURE 3-22
Page Title Has Been Entered

Move the cursor to the "Page width" line. A width of 80 is acceptable, so you don't have to take any action. Move the cursor again to the "Left margin" line. The default value for the left margin is 8, but in the example, the left margin is to be 5. To make the change, first press the Enter key, producing the screen shown in Figure 3-23. Note that a small triangle appears. This symbol acts as a prompt, indicating that you are to enter data.

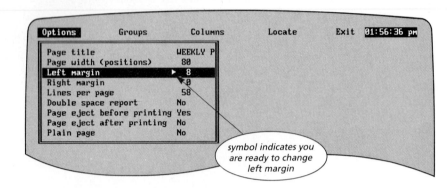

FIGURE 3-23
Changing the Left Margin

Now type the number 5 at the prompt (Figure 3-24). The 5 will be aligned to the left but the default value of 8 will still show on the screen. Press the Enter key. The number 5 will be right justified, and dBASE will now use a left margin of 5 (Figure 3-25).

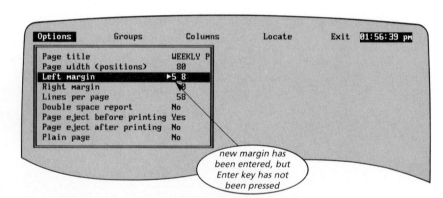

FIGURE 3-24
Changing the Left Margin

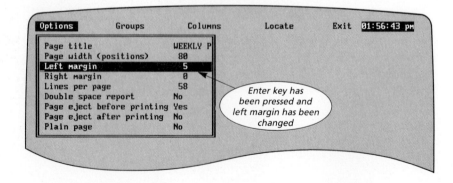

FIGURE 3-25
Left Margin Has Been Changed

Now change the right margin to 28 in exactly the same fashion. All the other values on this screen can be left as they are, so you are ready to move to the next step. To do so, press the Right Arrow key to move from "Options" to "Groups." The display will now look like the one shown in Figure 3-26.

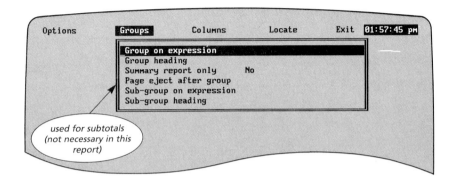

FIGURE 3-26
Specifying Groups

The box you see in the figure is used if any subtotals are required in a report. Since this report does not have subtotals, you will not use any of the options in this box. Press the Right Arrow key a second time and the display will look like Figure 3-27. This box is used to describe the body of the report.

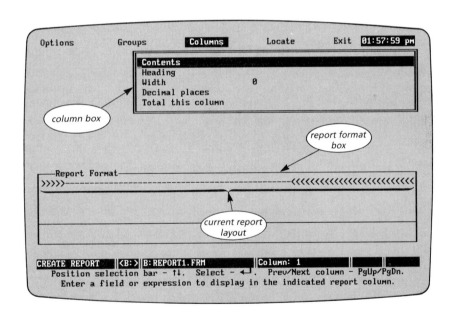

FIGURE 3-27
Specifying Columns

Entering Column Information

You must make an entry on the screen illustrated in Figure 3-27 for each column in the report. The box near the top of the screen is used to describe the required information for the columns. The box near the bottom, called the report format box, continually displays the current layout of the report. The display > > > > > refers to the five spaces specified for the left margin area. The dashes (----) represent the area where the format of the report will be displayed. Later, as we describe the fields, the fields and headings will also be displayed in this box.

It is now time to describe each of the columns. Checking back with Figure 3-16, our report design, note that the first column to appear on the report is the employee name. To define this column, make sure the highlight is on "Contents" and press the Enter key. This produces the screen shown in Figure 3-28. Notice the small triangle that appears after "Contents," which indicates that you are to enter the field or expression for this portion of the report.

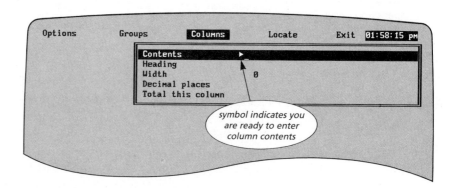

FIGURE 3-28
Specifying Column Contents

One way to specify the field is to type its name. In this case, you could type the word NAME and press the Enter key. If you know the exact name of the field, this is probably the simplest approach to take. But there are times when you might not remember the exact name. In such cases, you would like to see a list of the available fields. Fortunately, there is an easy way to do so. Press the F10 key and a field list will appear (Figure 3-29).

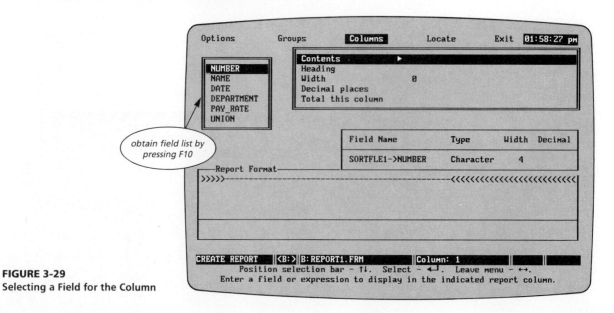

FIGURE 3-29
Selecting a Field for the Column

Use the Down Arrow key to move the highlight to the field you desire and press the Enter key. Select NAME. Your display should look like Figure 3-30. Press the Enter key again to remove the triangle symbol.

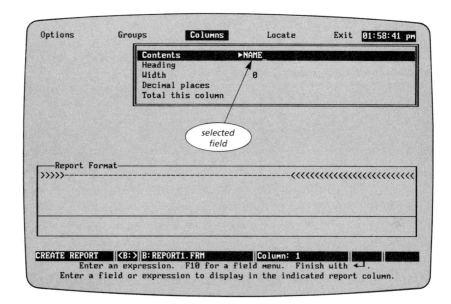

FIGURE 3-30
Field Has Been Selected

Now enter the heading that will be placed over the field. First move the highlight down to "Heading" and then press the Enter key. This produces the display shown in Figure 3-31. Note the box that is used to enter the heading. Also note the line of X's that have appeared in the report format box. These indicate the position of the first field, the NAME field, on the report.

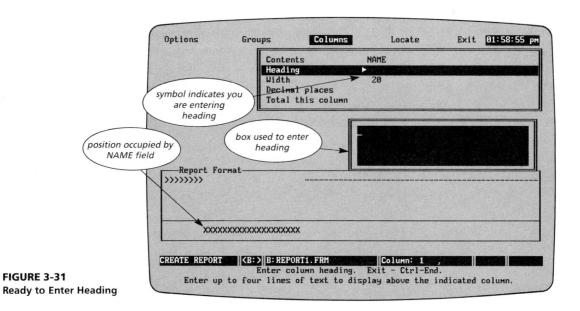

FIGURE 3-31
Ready to Enter Heading

Referring to your report design (Figure 3-16), remember that the first column heading consists of the words "EMPLOYEE NAME," which are indented and displayed on two lines. The first part of the column heading should be entered on the first available line. To accomplish this, press the space bar six times to indent and then type the word EMPLOYEE. After you have done so, press the Enter key, causing the cursor to move to the next line. Press the space bar eight times to properly position the cursor in the area where NAME must be typed, that is, to center it, and then type the word NAME (Figure 3-32).

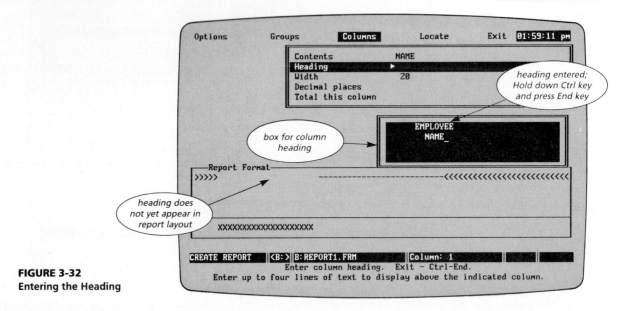

FIGURE 3-32
Entering the Heading

To complete the process, again hold down the Ctrl key and press the End key, or else repeatedly press the Enter key until you have returned to the "Heading" line in the box at the top of the screen. Now the display should look like the one in Figure 3-33. The heading is displayed in the report format box.

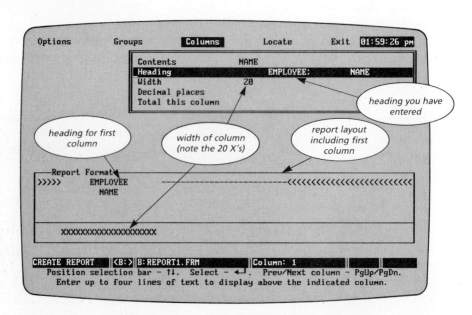

FIGURE 3-33
Heading Has Been Entered

The entry called "Width" indicates the width of the field. Initially dBASE sets this equal to the width of the NAME field. You can change it if you feel the width should be different. The other lines, "Decimal places" and "Total this column," do not apply to character fields like NAME.

Now, you are ready to proceed to the next column. Press the PgDn key, which is used to move to the next column in the report. (The PgUp key is used to move back to the previous column in the report.)

The next step is to enter the information for the second column. In the heading box, type the word DEPARTMENT, press the Enter key, press the space bar three times, type the word NAME, and then hold down the Ctrl key while pressing the End key. The results are shown in Figure 3-34.

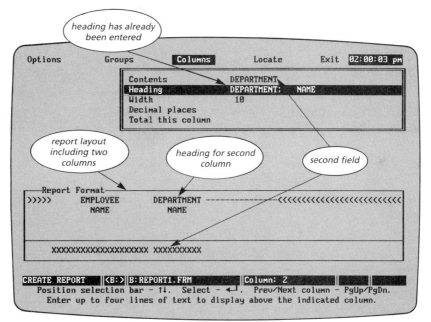

FIGURE 3-34
Second Column Has Been Entered

To create the third column, press PgDn and enter the information for PAY_RATE in the same way. In the heading box, press the space bar once, type the word PAY, press the Enter key, type the word RATE, and then hold down the Ctrl key while pressing the End key. This produces the screen shown in Figure 3-35. Do not move to the next column yet, however.

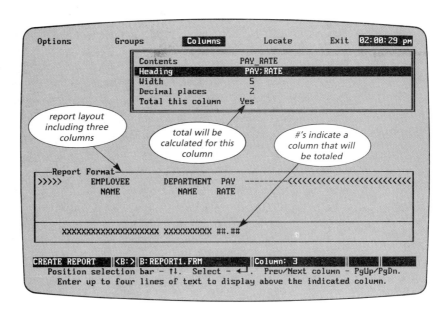

FIGURE 3-35
Specifying Totaling

This is the first numeric field that we have encountered. Two special things happen in numeric fields. First, the number of decimal places is filled in. There is no problem here, since dBASE automatically set the number of decimal places to 2 and that is exactly right. Second, there is an entry on the line labeled "Total this column." The value dBASE placed in this column is "Yes," meaning a total will be displayed automatically on the report. Since the report does not call for a total of all the pay rates, we must change this. Move the highlight to "Total this column" and press the Enter key. The word "Yes" will change to the word "No" (Figure 3-36). (Press the Enter key a few times and you will see the word change from "Yes" to "No" and back.) Note that the characters under PAY_RATE in the report format box changed from ##.##, which indicates a field that will be totaled, to 99.99, which indicates a field that will not be totaled. When this is done, press PgDn to move to the next field.

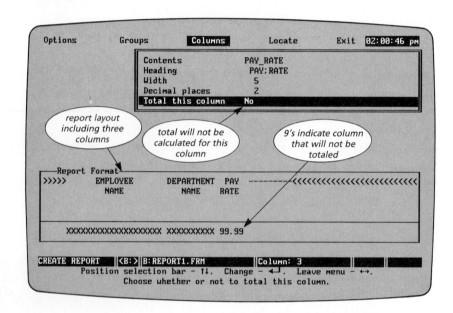

FIGURE 3-36
Column Will Not Be Totaled

The next field to be included on the report is the weekly pay field. This field is not contained in the records in the database. dBASE allows calculations to be specified as field contents, in which case the results of the calculations will be displayed on the report. To calculate the weekly pay, enter the numeric expression PAY_RATE * 40 in the contents row as shown in Figure 3-37. (Recall that you have to press the Enter key first to be able to enter the contents.) The asterisk, called an arithmetic operator, is used to specify multiplication. Other basic arithmetic operators include addition (+), subtraction (–), and division (/).

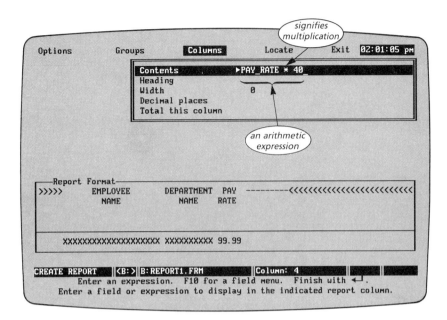

FIGURE 3-37
Using an Expression

After entering the calculation to be performed, press the Enter key. You can then enter the heading as shown in Figure 3-38. Press Enter to get the heading box. Then, in the heading box, press the space bar twice, type the word WEEKLY, press the Enter key, press the space bar five times, type the word PAY, and then hold down the Ctrl key while pressing the End key.

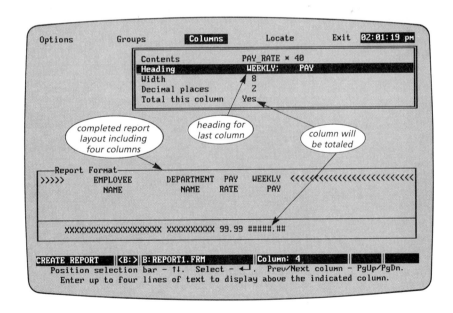

FIGURE 3-38
Last Column Specified

Because the entries for "Width," "Decimal places," and "Total this column" are appropriate (the total is to be of the weekly pay figures), you are done with this entry and, consequently, done with the report. The entire report format has been displayed in the report format box. Review it for accuracy. Any mistakes can be corrected by using the PgUp and PgDn keys to move to the column that is in error (PgUp moves you to the previous column and PgDn to the next). Then change the incorrect data in exactly the same fashion as you first entered the data.

Saving the Report

Once you have determined that the report is correct, press the Right Arrow key, producing the display shown in Figure 3-39. The box shown in this figure can be used to rapidly move to any particular column on a report. Actually, unless a report has a large number of columns, it is just as easy to use PgUp and PgDn to move through the columns, so this feature is rarely used. The only reason we present it here is that we need to pass through it to get to the next option, the one that will allow us to finish the operation. Move to the next option now by pressing the Right Arrow key. The display will look like the one shown in Figure 3-40.

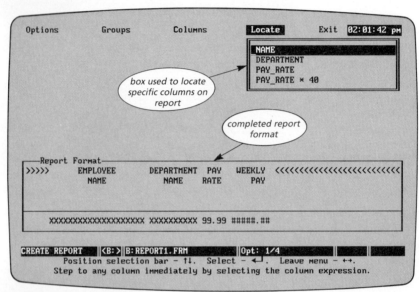

FIGURE 3-39
The "Locate" Menu

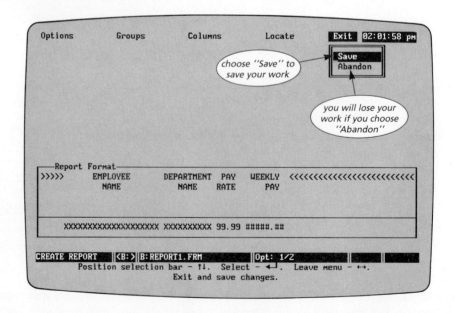

FIGURE 3-40
The "Exit" Menu

The two choices in this box are "Save" and "Abandon." "Save" is used to make the report description permanent. Assuming you like the report layout, select "Save" at this point. Make sure it is the highlighted choice and then press the Enter key. That will save the report on disk and you will return to the ASSISTANT menu.

In the event the report is not correct, you can use the Left Arrow key to return to one of the previous boxes, make the necessary corrections, and then return to this box to save your work. If you simply want to abandon the operation and start over again at some other time, choose "Abandon." Move the highlight to it and press Enter. dBASE will ask if you are sure you want to abandon the operation. If you type the letter Y (for yes) you will be returned to the ASSISTANT menu. Remember, if you choose "Abandon," none of your work will be saved.

Printing a Report

To print a report, use the "Report" option of the "Retrieve" menu (Figure 3-41). Once you have pressed the Enter key, dBASE will ask you to indicate the drive on which the report is located. Make sure the highlight is on the correct drive (B:) and press the Enter key.

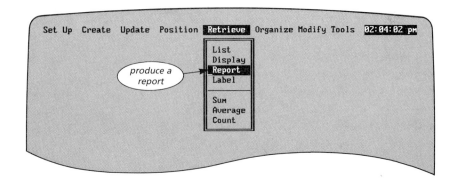

FIGURE 3-41
The "Report" Option of the "Retrieve" Menu

dBASE will now present a list of all reports on the indicated drive (Figure 3-42). In this case there is only one, so the right choice is automatically highlighted. If there were more than one, you would need to move the highlight to the correct report. Once this has been done, press the Enter key and the familiar box (the one that contains "Execute the command," "Specify scope," and so on) will appear.

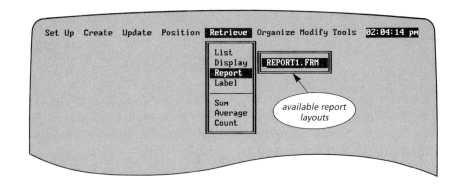

FIGURE 3-42
Selecting a Report

Assuming you simply want to produce the report and not impose any special search conditions, put the highlight on "Execute the command" and press the Enter key. dBASE will then ask if you want the report directed to the printer. If so, type the letter Y. If not, either type the letter N or press the Enter key. The report you just produced is shown in Figure 3-43.

column has not been totaled

column has been totaled

Page No.   **1**
12/19/89

WEEKLY PAYROLL REPORT

EMPLOYEE NAME	DEPARTMENT NAME	PAY RATE	WEEKLY PAY
Ackerman, David R.	Accounting	9.75	390.00
Anderson, Mariane L.	Shipping	9.00	360.00
Andrews, Robert M.	Marketing	9.00	360.00
Baxter, Charles W.	Accounting	11.00	440.00
Bender, Helen O.	Production	6.75	270.00
Castle, Mark C.	Shipping	7.50	300.00
Castleworth, Mary T.	Production	8.75	350.00
Chaney, Joseph R.	Accounting	8.00	320.00
Doi, Chang J.	Production	6.00	240.00
Dugan, Mary L.	Production	8.75	350.00
Dunning, Lisa A.	Marketing	9.10	364.00
Edwards, Kenneth J.	Production	8.60	344.00
Evans, John T.	Marketing	6.00	240.00
McCormack, Nigel L.	Shipping	8.25	330.00
Rapoza, Anthony P.	Shipping	8.50	340.00
*** Total ***			
			4998.00

FIGURE 3-43
Weekly Payroll Report

Reporting Only Selected Records

You can use the REPORT1 format to display selected records from a file. For example, you want a weekly payroll report that contains information only about those individuals working in the shipping department. The report must be alphabetical by employee name. Since a file exists with the records sorted in alphabetical sequence by name and the REPORT1 file contains the format for a weekly payroll report, we can use existing files to produce this output. In fact, the only difference between producing this report and the previous one is that before choosing "Execute the command" you must choose "Build a search condition," in exactly the same fashion as before. In this case, you will select the field called DEPARTMENT and the comparison operator "Equal to," and then enter the word Shipping.

Reports with Subtotals

It is also possible to produce reports with subtotals. The report in Figure 3-44 contains subtotals based on a change in department name. When the department name changes, a total is displayed.

```
Page No.     1
12/19/89
                    WEEKLY PAYROLL REPORT

            EMPLOYEE      DEPARTMENT    PAY    WEEKLY
              NAME          NAME       RATE     PAY

** Accounting
 Ackerman, David R.      Accounting    9.75    390.00
 Baxter, Charles W.      Accounting   11.00    440.00
 Chaney, Joseph R.       Accounting    8.00    320.00
** Subtotal **

                                              1150.00

** Marketing
 Andrews, Robert M.      Marketing     9.00    360.00
 Dunning, Lisa A.        Marketing     9.10    364.00
 Evans, John T.          Marketing     6.00    240.00
** Subtotal **

                                               964.00

** Production
 Bender, Helen O.        Production    6.75    270.00
 Castleworth, Mary T.    Production    8.75    350.00
 Doi, Chang J.           Production    6.00    240.00
 Dugan, Mary L.          Production    8.75    350.00
 Edwards, Kenneth J.     Production    8.60    344.00
** Subtotal **

                                              1554.00

** Shipping
 Anderson, Mariane L.    Shipping      9.00    360.00
 Castle, Mark C.         Shipping      7.50    300.00
 McCormack, Nigel L.     Shipping      8.25    330.00
 Rapoza, Anthony P.      Shipping      8.50    340.00
** Subtotal **

                                              1330.00

    *** Total ***

                                              4998.00
```

FIGURE 3-44 Report with Subtotals

Two approaches can be used to produce such a report. The first approach is to create another report format called, perhaps, REPORT2. This involves calling up the report generation screens provided by dBASE and making the appropriate entries.

The second approach is to modify the REPORT1 format. If the report represents a permanent modification of the original report format, we can modify the original report format. To modify the report format for REPORT 1, choose the "Report" option from the "Modify" menu. This is illustrated in Figure 3-45.

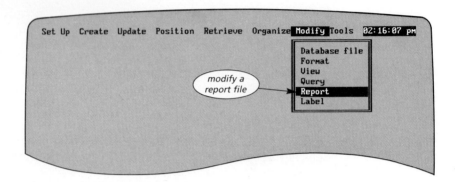

FIGURE 3-45
The "Modify" Menu

After indicating the drive on which the report file is located, you will see a list of all report files on the drive. Move the highlight to the desired report (in this case there is only one, so no movement is required) and press the Enter key. The display now looks like the screen in Figure 3-46.

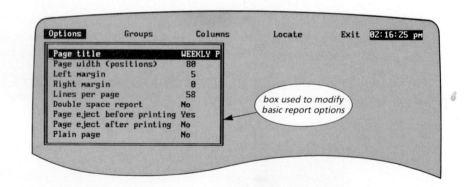

FIGURE 3-46
Modifying a Report

The process of modifying a report is similar to the process of creating a report. Just as you described the report initially, you can change the page title, margins, fields, column headings, and so on. In this case, the only change that needs to be made is to indicate the grouping that is to take place. Records are to be grouped by department.

To make this change, press the Right Arrow key to move to "Groups" (Figure 3-47). Press the Enter key and you will be able to enter the expression on which records are to be grouped. At this point, you could simply type the word DEPARTMENT. As before, you could also press F10 to get a field list (Figure 3-48), then move the highlight to DEPARTMENT and press the Enter key. In either case, the word DEPARTMENT will appear on the line labeled "Group on expression." Press Enter to complete this process. The screen should now look like the one in Figure 3-49. No further entries need be made, so press the Right Arrow key three times to move to the "Exit" box and choose "Save" in the same manner as before.

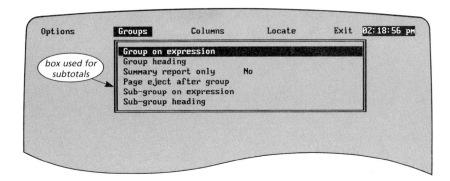

FIGURE 3-47
Indicating Subtotals

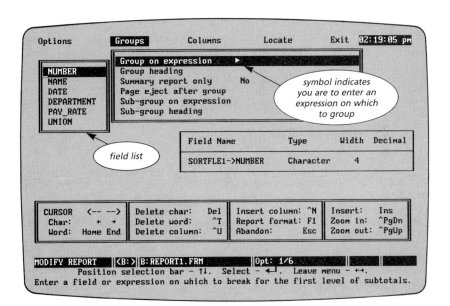

FIGURE 3-48
Entering an Expression for Grouping

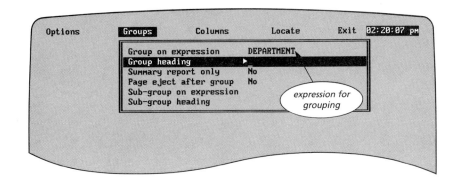

FIGURE 3-49
Expression for Grouping Has Been Entered

If you now produce the report just as you did before, you will see something interesting. Look at Figure 3-50 (to see the complete report, you should send it to the printer; it does not all fit on the screen). There is a group for accounting, followed by a group for shipping, one for marketing, and then *another* one for accounting. What's wrong? The problem is that the records are not sorted correctly. All the records for a given department must be together. This is not the case in SORTFLE1.

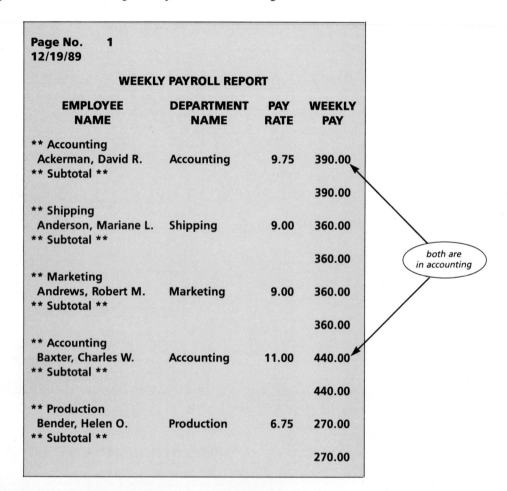

Page No.   1
12/19/89

WEEKLY PAYROLL REPORT

EMPLOYEE NAME	DEPARTMENT NAME	PAY RATE	WEEKLY PAY
** Accounting			
Ackerman, David R.	Accounting	9.75	390.00
** Subtotal **			
			390.00
** Shipping			
Anderson, Mariane L.	Shipping	9.00	360.00
** Subtotal **			
			360.00
** Marketing			
Andrews, Robert M.	Marketing	9.00	360.00
** Subtotal **			
			360.00
** Accounting			
Baxter, Charles W.	Accounting	11.00	440.00
** Subtotal **			
			440.00
** Production			
Bender, Helen O.	Production	6.75	270.00
** Subtotal **			
			270.00

both are in accounting

FIGURE 3-50
Weekly Payroll Report with Subtotals (Incorrect)

Fortunately, another file that you have already created, SORTFLE2, contains records that were sorted by NAME within DEPARTMENT, which is precisely the correct order. Activate this file in the usual manner (using the "Database file" option of the "Set Up" menu). Then produce the report again and you will see that it looks like the one shown in Figure 3-44, which you were trying to get.

What if SORTFLE2 did not exist? All you would have to do now would be to create it, in exactly the fashion described earlier in this project.

PROJECT SUMMARY

In Project 3 you learned how to sort a database file, producing a file containing the same records in a different order. You also learned how to design a report and use the dBASE report facility to create a report file containing the report layout. You used this report file to produced a report with the desired layout. Finally, you saw how to use subtotals in reports.

If you followed along with the steps in this chapter, you have created two sorted database files and a report. You have also modified the report. If you did not do this but you want to do so now, you can use the following keystroke sequence. Start dBASE as described in the project and activate the EMPLOYEE database file. Then type the following:

SUMMARY OF KEYSTROKES—Project 3

STEPS	KEY(S) PRESSED	RESULTS
1	→ → → → → ↓ ← ↓	
2	← → ← SORTFLE1 ← ←	File sorted
3	← ← ← ← ← ← ← ↓ ← ←	
4	→ → → → ↓ ← ↓ ← ↓	
5	← ↑ ← ←	Sorted file displayed
	(Make sure SORTFLE1 is active database file)	
	(Note: The following assumes you are at the "Set Up" Menu)	
6	→ ↓ ↓ ↓ ↓ ← ←	
7	REPORT1 ←	Report creation begun
8	← WEEKLY PAYROLL REPORT ← `Ctrl-End`	
9	↓ ↓ ← 5 ← ↓ ← 28 ←	Basic report information entered
10	→ → ← < F10 > ↓ ← ↓ ← ↓ ←	
11	`SPACE` `SPACE` `SPACE` `SPACE` `SPACE` `SPACE` EMPLOYEE ←	
12	`SPACE` `SPACE` `SPACE` `SPACE` `SPACE` `SPACE` `SPACE` `SPACE`	
13	NAME ← `Ctrl-End` `PgDn`	First column entered
14	← < F10 > ↓ ↓ ↓ ← ← ↓ ←	
15	DEPARTMENT ← `SPACE` `SPACE` `SPACE` NAME ← `Ctrl-End`	
16	`PgDn`	Second column entered
17	← < F10 > ↓ ↓ ↓ ↓ ← ← ↓ ←	
18	`SPACE` PAY ← < RATE > `Ctrl-End` ↓ ↓ ↓ ←	
19	`PgDn`	Third column entered
20	← PAY_RATE * 40 ← ↓ ← `SPACE` `SPACE` WEEKLY	
21	← `SPACE` `SPACE` `SPACE` `SPACE` `SPACE` PAY ←	
22	`Ctrl-End`	Fourth column entered
23	→ → ←	Report saved
24	→ → → ↓ ↓ ← ← ← ←	
25	← ←	Report printed
26	→ → ↓ ↓ ↓ ↓ ← ← ←	
27	→ ← DEPARTMENT ← → → → ←	Report modified

The following list summarizes the material covered in Project 3:

1. A **key field** is a field that is used as the basis of a sorting operation.
2. To sort the records in a database file, producing a new database file, use the "Sort" option of the "Organize" menu.
3. To sort on multiple keys, select the keys in order of importance.
4. To display the records in a sorted file, first activate the file using the "Database file" option of the "Set Up" menu.
5. The **American Standard Code for Information Interchange**, usually called simply the **ASCII code**, is used for storing data.
6. Numeric fields are sorted on the basis of their algebraic values. Character data are sorted on the basis of the ASCII code.
7. To create a report, use the "Report" option of the "Create" menu.
8. When creating a report, to specify such things as page title, page width, margins, and so on, use the "Options" menu.
9. To indicate the fields and column headings on a report, use the "Columns" menu.
10. To terminate the report creation process, choose either "Save" (to save your work) or "Abandon" (to exit without saving your work) from the "Exit" menu.
11. To print a report, use the "Report" option of the "Retrieve" menu.
12. To change the layout of an existing report, choose the "Report" option of the "Modify" menu.
13. To specify grouping on a report, use the "Groups" option.

STUDENT ASSIGNMENTS

STUDENT ASSIGNMENT 1: True/False Questions

Instructions: Circle T if the statement is true and F if the statement is false.

T   F   1. A field used as the basis of a sorting operation is called a key field.

T   F   2. Before a file can be sorted, it must be made active.

T   F   3. The file created as a result of the "Sort" option is automatically active.

T   F   4. After choosing the "Sort" option of the "Organize" menu, you must type the names of each of the key fields.

T   F   5. When sorting on more than one key field, the more important key must be specified last.

T   F   6. A key field must be of a character field.

T   F   7. In the ASCII code, letters of the alphabet are lower in the sorting sequence than numbers.

T   F   8. Within the "Sort" option it is possible to build a search condition so that only records meeting the condition will be sorted.

T   F   9. The "Report" option in the "Set Up" menu is used to call the screens that allow a report to be created.

T   F   10. In the report creation feature of dBASE, the first screen is the screen for changing the page heading, page width, margins, and so on.

T   F   11. To change the current entry for left margin, place the highlight on the "Left margin" line, press the Enter key, enter the new value, and press the Enter key a second time.

T   F   12. When specifying the fields to include on a report, you can obtain a field menu by pressing F1.

T   F   13. When specifying the fields to include on a report, you can use PgUp to move back to the previous field.

T   F   14. When defining the contents of a field on a report, you may use expressions.

T   F   15. To print a report, use the "Report" option of the "Retrieve" menu and then select the name of the desired report from the list of possibilities presented by dBASE.

T   F   16. To change the layout of a report, use the "Report" option of the "Modify" menu.

STUDENT ASSIGNMENT 2: Multiple Choice

Instructions: Circle the correct response.

1. To sort by name within department:
   a. First select the "Sort" option and choose the NAME field. After the sort has been completed, select the "Sort" option again and choose the DEPARTMENT field.
   b. First select the "Sort" option and choose the DEPARTMENT field. After the sort has been completed, select the "Sort" option again and choose the NAME field.
   c. First select the "Sort" option and choose the NAME field. Immediately after you have chosen the NAME field, choose the DEPARTMENT field.
   d. First select the "Sort" option and choose the DEPARTMENT field. Immediately after you have chosen the DEPARTMENT field, choose the NAME field.
2. You activated the EMPLOYEE database file, selected the "Sort" option, and chose the NAME field from the list of possible fields. You then pressed the Right Arrow key, typed the word PAY_RATE, and pressed the Enter key. Which of the following will occur?
   a. The records within EMPLOYEE will be sorted by NAME within PAY_RATE.
   b. The EMPLOYEE records will be sorted by NAME and the result will be placed in a file called PAY_RATE.
   c. The EMPLOYEE records will be sorted by NAME and the result will be placed in a file called PAY_RATE.DBF.
   d. An error will occur, since PAY_RATE is a field within the EMPLOYEE file and thus cannot be used as the name of a file.
3. The values A99, 999, and a99 are to be sorted in ascending sequence. After sorting the sequence will be:
   a. 999, A99, a99
   b. a99, A99, 999
   c. A99, a99, 999
   d. 999, a99, A99
4. When you choose the "Report" option of the "Create" menu and select the desired drive, the first thing you must do is
   a. specify the page heading.
   b. indicate a name for the report.
   c. indicate the page width for the report.
   d. indicate if any totals are to be calculated.
5. To print a report,
   a. select the "Report" option of the "Set Up" menu.
   b. select the "Report" option of the "Create" menu.
   c. select the "Report" option of the "Retrieve" menu.
   d. select the "Report" option of the "Modify" menu.
6. The "Report" option of the "Modify" menu will
   a. cause the output from a report to be displayed on the screen so that it can be modified from the keyboard.
   b. cause the report generation screen used for entering page headings and related information to appear.
   c. cause a new report file, which can be changed, to be created on disk.
   d. cause the current report format to be deleted.

STUDENT ASSIGNMENT 3: Understanding dBASE Options

Instructions: Explain what will happen after you perform each of the following actions.

Problem 1. Select the "Sort" option of the "Organize" menu.

Explanation: _____

_____

_____

Problem 2. Select the "Report" option of the "Create" menu.

Explanation: _____

_____

_____

Problem 3. Choose the "Report" option of the "Retrieve" menu.

Explanation: _____

_____

_____

Problem 4. Choose the "Report" option of the "Modify" menu.

Explanation: _____

_____

_____

STUDENT ASSIGNMENT 4: Using dBASE

Instructions: Explain how to accomplish each of the following tasks using dBASE.

Problem 1. Sort the EMPLOYEE file by pay rate within department, producing a file called SORTFL.

Explanation: _____

_____

_____

Problem 2. After sorting EMPLOYEE and producing SORTFL, display all records in SORTFL.

Explanation: _____

_____

_____

Problem 3. Create a report called REPT1.

Explanation: _____

_____

_____

Problem 4. Specify a three-line page heading for REPT1.

Explanation: _____

_____

_____

Problem 5. Cause totals to be calculated for a numeric field in a report.

Explanation: _____

_____

_____

Problem 6. Make a change to the layout of the report called REPT1.

Explanation: _____

_____

_____

STUDENT ASSIGNMENT 5: Recovering from Problems

Instructions: In each of the following cases, a problem occurred. Explain the cause of the problem and how it can be corrected.

Problem 1: You are using the "Sort" option. When you specified a name for the sorted file, dBASE rejected the name you entered.

Cause of Problem: _____

_____

Method of Correction: _____

_____

Problem 2: You described a complete report layout, exited the report creation process, and later found that the report you specified does not exist.

Cause of Problem: _____

_____

Method of Correction: _____

_____

Problem 3: You specified a report using the "Report" option of the "Create" menu. The report involved a database called STUDENT, containing student data. In the report, you indicated that records were to be grouped by MAJOR, one of the fields in each student's record. After printing the report, you notice that it starts with a group of two students in biology, then one student in physics, followed by two students in math and then another student in biology.

Cause of Problem: _____

_____

Method of Correction: _____

_____

MINICASES

Sorting Records and Report Preparation

Minicase 1: Personal Checks

Instructions: Use the personal checks database that you created in Project 1. These problems require sorting the database and preparing reports from it.

Problem 1: Sorting Records

a. Sort the records stored in the personal checks database that you created in Project 1 in ascending order by CHECK NUMBER. Use CKFLE1 as the file name for the sorted file. Record the steps you followed in the space provided below.

Steps: _____

_____

_____

b. After sorting the records, display the CHECK NUMBER, DATE, PAYEE, and CHECK AMOUNT fields using the "Display" option. Record the steps you followed in the space provided below.

Steps: _____

_____

_____

Problem 2: Sorting Records on Multiple Fields

a. Sort the records in the personal checks database file in alphabetical order by PAYEE within EXPENSE type. Use CKFLE2 as the file name for the sorted file. Record the steps you followed in the space provided below.

Steps: _____

_____

_____

b. After sorting the records, display the EXPENSE, PAYEE, CHECK AMOUNT, DATE, and CHECK NUMBER fields. Record the steps you followed in the space provided below.

Steps: _____

_____

_____

Problem 3: Creating a Report

a. Design the report using a printer spacing chart or graph paper. The report should contain a page number, date, and report and column headings. Include these fields: CHECK NUMBER, DATE, PAYEE, CHECK AMOUNT, and EXPENSE. Display a final total of the CHECK AMOUNT field.

b. After designing the report, enter the dBASE steps to create the report format.

c. After creating the report format and saving it on disk, enter the steps to print a report. Use the data contained in CKFLE1 to prepare the report.

d. Modify the report format so that a subtotal is taken when there is a change in EXPENSE. Enter the steps to display the output on the printer. Use the data contained in CKFLE2 to prepare the report.

Minicase 2: Music Library

Instructions: Use the music library database that you created in Project 1. These problems require sorting the database and preparing reports from it.

Problem 1: Sorting Records

a. Sort the records stored in the music library database that you created in Project 1 in alphabetical order by ARTIST. Use MSCFL1 as the file name for the sorted file. Record the steps you followed in the space provided below.

Steps: _____

_____

_____

b. After sorting the records, display the ARTIST, MUSIC NAME, TYPE, COST, and CATEGORY fields using the "Display" option. Record the steps you followed in the space provided below.

Steps: _____

_____

_____

Problem 2: Sorting Records on Multiple Fields

a. Sort the records in the music library database file in alphabetical order by MUSIC NAME within CATEGORY. Use MSCFL2 as the file name of the sorted file. Record the steps you followed in the space provided below.

Steps: _____

_____

_____

b. After sorting the records, display the MUSIC NAME, ARTIST, TYPE, COST, and CATEGORY fields. Record the steps you followed in the space provided below.

Steps: _____

_____

_____

Problem 3: Creating a Report

a. Design the report using a printer spacing chart or graph paper. The report should contain a page number, date, and report and column headings. Include these fields: CATEGORY, MUSIC NAME, ARTIST, TYPE, and COST. Display a final total of the COST field.

b. After designing the report, enter the dBASE steps to create the report format.

c. After creating the report format and saving it on disk, enter the steps to print a report. Use the data contained in MSCFL2 to prepare the report.

d. Modify the report format so that a subtotal is taken when there is a change in CATEGORY. Enter the steps to display the output on the printer. Use the data contained in the file named MSCFL2 to prepare the report.

Minicase 3: Computer Software Store

Instructions: Use the software inventory database that you created in Project 1. These problems require sorting the database and preparing reports from the database.

Problem 1: Sorting Records

a) Sort the records stored in the software inventory database that you created in Project 1 in ascending order by SOFTWARE NAME. Use SOFTFLE1 as the file name for the sorted file. Record the steps you followed in the space provided below.

Steps: _____

_____

_____

b. After the records have been sorted, display the SOFTWARE NAME, CATEGORY, QUANTITY, and COST fields using the "Display" option. Record the steps you followed in the space provided below.

Steps: _____

_____

_____

Problem 2: Sorting Records on Multiple Fields

a. Sort the records in the software inventory file in alphabetical order by SOFTWARE NAME within CATEGORY. Use SOFTFLE2 as the file name of the sorted file. Record the steps you followed in the space provided below.

Steps: _____

_____

_____

b. After sorting the records, display the CATEGORY, SOFTWARE NAME, COMPANY, QUANTITY, and COST fields. Record the steps you followed in the space provided below.

Steps: _____

_____

_____

Problem 3: Creating a Report

a. Design the report using a printer spacing chart or graph paper. The report should contain a page number, date, and report and column headings. Include these fields: SOFTWARE NAME, CATEGORY, COMPANY, QUANTITY, COST, and TOTAL INVENTORY VALUE. Calculate TOTAL INVENTORY VALUE by multiplying COST by QUANTITY. Display a final total of the TOTAL INVENTORY VALUE.

b. After designing the report, enter the dBASE steps to create the report format.

c. After creating the report format and saving it on disk, enter the steps to print a report. Use the data contained in SOFTFLE1 to prepare the report.

d. Modify the report format so that a subtotal is taken for TOTAL INVENTORY VALUE when there is a change in CATEGORY. Enter the steps to display the output on the printer. Use the data contained in the file named SOFTFLE2 to prepare the report.

Minicase 4: Home Sales

Instructions: Use the database of houses for sale that you created in Project 1. These problems require sorting the database and preparing reports from the database.

Problem 1: Sorting Records

a. Sort the records stored in the home sales database that you created in Project 1 in ascending order by PRICE. Use HSFLE1 as the file name for the sorted file. Record the steps you followed in the space provided below.

Steps: _____

_____

_____

b. After sorting the records, display the ADDRESS, CITY, ZIP, and PRICE fields using the "Display" option. Record the steps you followed in the space provided below.

Steps: _____

_____

_____

Problem 2: Sorting Records on Multiple Fields

a. Sort the records in the home sales database file by PRICE within CITY. Use HSFLE2 as the file name of the sorted file. Record the steps you followed in the space provided below.

Steps: _____

_____

_____

b. After sorting the records, display the ADDRESS, CITY, and PRICE fields. Record the steps you followed in the space provided below.

Steps: _____

_____

_____

Problem 3: Creating a Report

a. Design the report using a printer spacing chart or graph paper. The report should contain a page number, date, and report and column headings. Include these fields: ADDRESS, CITY, ZIP, and PRICE. Display a final total of the prices of all houses. This total lists the total value of all houses for sale in an area.

b. After designing the report, enter the dBASE steps to create the report format.

c. After creating the report format and saving it on disk, enter the steps to print a report. Use the data contained in HSFLE1 to prepare the report.

d. Modify the report format so that a subtotal is taken when there is a change in CITY. Enter the steps to display the output on the printer. Use the data contained in the file named HSFLE2 to prepare the report.

PROJECT 4

Adding, Changing, and Deleting

Objectives

You will have mastered the material in this project when you can:

- Add records to a previously created database file using "Append"
- Change records in a database file using "Edit"
- Position the record pointer using "Locate"
- Change records using "Replace"
- Change records using "Browse"
- Delete records using "Edit"
- Delete records using "Browse"
- Delete records using "Delete"
- Undelete records using "Recall"
- Physically remove deleted records using "Pack"

The examples in Projects 1, 2, and 3 illustrated many dBASE functions. You created a database file, displayed various records in the file, sorted the file, and prepared reports using the data in the file.

For your database file to be useful, however, you must keep the information in it up to date. New employees are hired; existing employees may leave the company; when employees are given pay raises, their pay rates must be changed; and so on. Thus, you must be able to perform three basic functions: add records to the file; delete records from the file; and make changes to the records in the file. In this project we explain the dBASE options that you can use to perform these functions. You will use the menus and options within the ASSISTANT that are shown in blue in Figure 4-1.

FIGURE 4-1
Menus and Options within the dBASE ASSISTANT

OPTION	PURPOSE
Set Up	Activate a
Database file	database file
View	view
Quit dBASE III PLUS	leave dBASE III PLUS
Create	Create a
Database file	database file (extension DBF)
View	view (extension VUE)
Report	report (extension FRM)
Update	Change a database file by
Append	adding records at the end
Edit	changing records viewing one at a time
Browse	changing records viewing several at a time
Replace	changing the data in all records that satisfy some condition
Delete	deleting records
Recall	undeleting records
Pack	physically remove deleted records
Position	Move the record pointer by
Seek	finding a match using an index
Locate	finding the first record that satisfies some condition
Goto Record	specifying a record number
Retrieve	Retrieve data from a database file
List	show desired fields and records on the screen or printer
Display	like "List" (differences between the two are covered in the text)
Report	print a report
Sum	calculate a total
Average	calculate an average
Count	count the number of records
Organize	
Index	create an index (extension NDX)
Sort	sort a database file
Modify	Change an existing
Database file	database file
Report	report file
Tools	
List structure	show the structure of the active database file

ADDING RECORDS

To study the commands for adding records to a file, let's use the EMPLOYEE database file created in Project 1 and assume that two new employes have been hired. The file is shown in Figure 4-2.

RECORD#	NUMBER	NAME	DATE	DEPARTMENT	PAY_RATE	UNION
1	1011	Rapoza, Anthony P.	01/10/89	Shipping	8.50	.T.
2	1013	McCormack, Nigel L.	01/15/89	Shipping	8.25	.T.
3	1016	Ackerman, David R.	02/04/89	Accounting	9.75	.F.
4	1017	Doi, Chang J.	02/05/89	Production	6.00	.T.
5	1020	Castle, Mark C.	03/04/89	Shipping	7.50	.T.
6	1022	Dunning, Lisa A.	03/12/89	Marketing	9.10	.F.
7	1025	Chaney, Joseph R.	03/23/89	Accounting	8.00	.F.
8	1026	Bender, Helen O.	04/12/89	Production	6.75	.T.
9	1029	Anderson, Mariane L.	04/18/89	Shipping	9.00	.T.
10	1030	Edwards, Kenneth J.	04/23/89	Production	8.60	.T.
11	1037	Baxter, Charles W.	05/05/89	Accounting	11.00	.F.
12	1041	Evans, John T.	05/19/89	Marketing	6.00	.F.
13	1056	Andrews, Robert M.	06/03/89	Marketing	9.00	.F.
14	1057	Dugan, Mary L.	06/10/89	Production	8.75	.T.
15	1066	Castleworth, Mary T.	07/05/89	Production	8.75	.T.

FIGURE 4-2
Employee Data

You will add the two additional employees to the EMPLOYEE file. To add records, use the "Append" option of the "Update" menu. After you have loaded dBASE, activate the EMPLOYEE file as you have done before. Choose the "Database file" option of the "Set Up" menu, select drive B and the database file named EMPLOYEE.DBF, then indicate that the file is not indexed.

After that, choose the "Append" option within the "Update" menu (Figure 4-3). Once you have done this, the display shown in Figure 4-4 (on the next page) will appear. Note that this is the same display you saw when you first created the file. You are currently positioned at the end of the file. This is indicated by the fact that the current record (Rec:) is listed as EOF/15 (EOF is an abbreviation for end of file). Recall that pressing F1 will remove the box from the top of the screen.

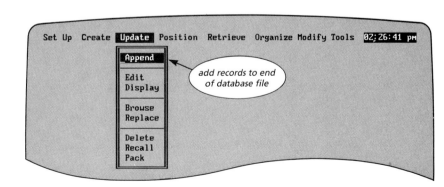

FIGURE 4-3
Adding New Records

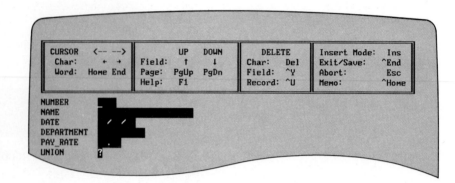

FIGURE 4-4
Form for Adding Records

After you have entered the information for the first additional record (Figure 4-5), another screen will appear and you can enter the information for the second (Figure 4-6). After you have entered the data for the second, a screen for a third additional record will appear. Because there are no more records to be added to the file, press the Enter key. The new additions will have been added to the end of the EMPLOYEE file, and you will be returned to the ASSISTANT menu screen.

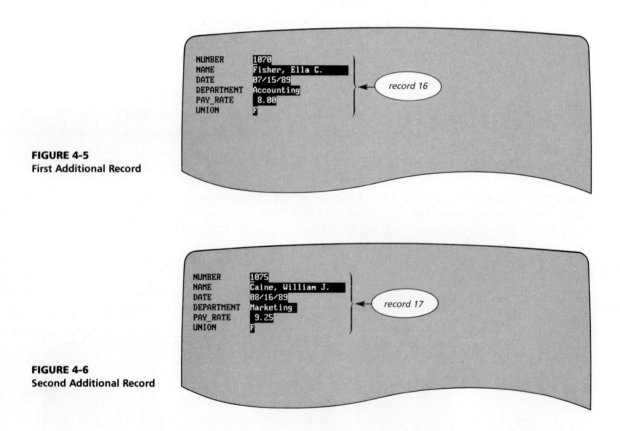

FIGURE 4-5
First Additional Record

FIGURE 4-6
Second Additional Record

Figure 4-7 illustrates the use of the "Display" option of the "Retrieve" menu to list all the records in the EMPLOYEE file after the two records have been added. Note that records 16 and 17 have indeed been added to the file.

RECORD#	NUMBER	NAME	DATE	DEPARTMENT	PAY_RATE	UNION
1	1011	Rapoza, Anthony P.	01/10/89	Shipping	8.50	.T.
2	1013	McCormack, Nigel L.	01/15/89	Shipping	8.25	.T.
3	1016	Ackerman, David R.	02/04/89	Accounting	9.75	.F.
4	1017	Doi, Chang J.	02/05/89	Production	6.00	.T.
5	1020	Castle, Mark C.	03/04/89	Shipping	7.50	.T.
6	1022	Dunning, Lisa A.	03/12/89	Marketing	9.10	.F.
7	1025	Chaney, Joseph R.	03/23/89	Accounting	8.00	.F.
8	1026	Bender, Helen O.	04/12/89	Production	6.75	.T.
9	1029	Anderson, Mariane L.	04/18/89	Shipping	9.00	.T.
10	1030	Edwards, Kenneth J.	04/23/89	Production	8.60	.T.
11	1037	Baxter, Charles W.	05/05/89	Accounting	11.00	.F.
12	1041	Evans, John T.	05/19/89	Marketing	6.00	.F.
13	1056	Andrews, Robert M.	06/03/89	Marketing	9.00	.F.
14	1057	Dugan, Mary L.	06/10/89	Production	8.75	.T.
15	1066	Castleworth, Mary T.	07/05/89	Production	8.75	.T.
16	1070	Fisher, Ella C.	07/15/89	Accounting	8.00	.F.
17	1075	Caine, William J.	08/16/89	Marketing	9.25	.F.

new records have been added

FIGURE 4-7 Updated Employee Data

CHANGING RECORDS

*I*n most database files, the data in one or more fields must be changed periodically. In the EMPLOYEE database file, for example, pay rates may need to be changed. There are three options within the "Update" menu that you can use to make changes to the records in a file. These options are "Edit," "Browse," and "Replace."

Using "Edit"

Assume that employee 1016 received a pay increase from $9.75 to $10.00 per hour. This pay rate change should be made to the PAY_RATE field in the database file. To accomplish this, choose the "Edit" option from the "Update" menu (Figure 4-8). The current active record will be displayed on the screen in the form that should now be very familiar to you (Figure 4-9). If the box describing the various keystrokes is on your screen, press F1 to remove it. Your screen will then look like the one shown in Figure 4-9.

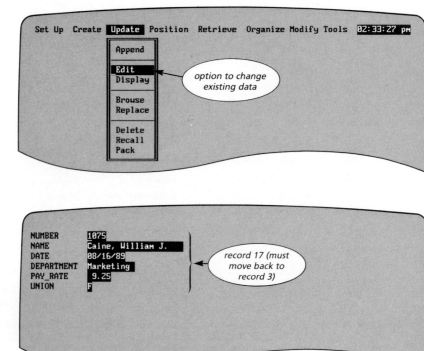

FIGURE 4-8
Changing Existing Data

FIGURE 4-9
Editing Data

If the record you want to update happens to be the one displayed on the screen, you could simply begin the updating process. In this case, it is not. So the first order of business is to bring the desired record to the screen. In a small file like this one, you can repeatedly press PgUp (to move to the previous record) or PgDn (to move to the next record) until you find the correct one.

Initially, the cursor is in the first position of the first field. Press the Down Arrow key four times to position the cursor in the PAY_RATE field (see Figure 4-10.) Then you can type the new pay rate. Type the amount 10.00. Since this is the only change, finish the process by holding down the Ctrl key while pressing the End key. The change will be saved and you will be returned to the ASSISTANT menu. Figure 4-11 shows the EMPLOYEE file with the pay rate change.

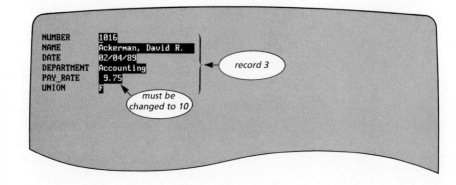

FIGURE 4-10
Editing Data

RECORD#	NUMBER	NAME	DATE	DEPARTMENT	PAY_RATE	UNION
1	1011	Rapoza, Anthony P.	01/10/89	Shipping	8.50	.T.
2	1013	McCormack, Nigel L.	01/15/89	Shipping	8.25	.T.
3	1016	Ackerman, David R.	02/04/89	Accounting	10.00	.F.
4	1017	Doi, Chang J.	02/05/89	Production	6.00	.T.
5	1020	Castle, Mark C.	03/04/89	Shipping	7.50	.T.
6	1022	Dunning, Lisa A.	03/12/89	Marketing	9.10	.F.
7	1025	Chaney, Joseph R.	03/23/89	Accounting	8.00	.F.
8	1026	Bender, Helen O.	04/12/89	Production	6.75	.T.
9	1029	Anderson, Mariane L.	04/18/89	Shipping	9.00	.T.
10	1030	Edwards, Kenneth J.	04/23/89	Production	8.60	.T.
11	1037	Baxter, Charles W.	05/05/89	Accounting	11.00	.F.
12	1041	Evans, John T.	05/19/89	Marketing	6.00	.F.
13	1056	Andrews, Robert M.	06/03/89	Marketing	9.00	.F.
14	1057	Dugan, Mary L.	06/10/89	Production	8.75	.T.
15	1066	Castleworth, Mary T.	07/05/89	Production	8.75	.T.
16	1070	Fisher, Ella C.	07/15/89	Accounting	8.00	.F.
17	1075	Caine, William J.	08/16/89	Marketing	9.25	.F.

pay rate has been changed

FIGURE 4-11 Updated Employee Data

More on Positioning the Record Pointer

Earlier, you learned how to change the record pointer using the "Position" menu. You could move it to the first record in the file or the last record in the file. You could also move it to some specific record provided you knew the number of the record. But what if you don't know the number? What if you want to move the pointer to the record for employee 1016 and you don't happen to know where in the file this employee is located? It would be cumbersome to have to move through the file one record at a time looking for this employee. Fortunately, there is an easy way to move directly to this record.

In the discussion that follows, the current record pointer is assumed to be 1; that is, the first record is the current active record. If your current record pointer is not 1, you should change it at this time. Recall that you do this by selecting the "Goto" option of the "Position" menu and then selecting "TOP."

The option that will allow you to locate employee 1016 is the "Locate" option of the "Position" menu. Use the Right or Left Arrow key to move to the "Position" menu and the Down Arrow key to move to "Locate" (Figure 4-12). Then press the Enter key. Your screen should look like the one shown in Figure 4-13. Does the box on the right look familiar? It should. You have encountered it several times already.

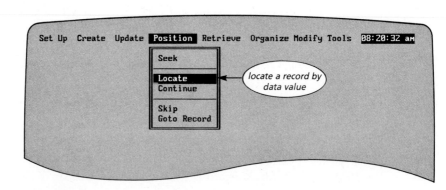

FIGURE 4-12
Finding Employee 1016

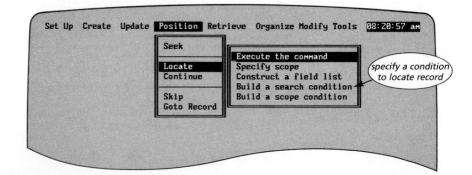

FIGURE 4-13
Finding Employee 1016

Next, build a search condition to identify the record you are looking for. In this case, select the field called NUMBER and the comparison operator "Equal to," and then enter the value 1016. Indicate that there are "No more conditions."

Notice the command that dBASE has constructed for you (see Figure 4.14). Move the highlight to "Execute the command" and press Enter. Your screen will now look like the one shown in Figure 4-15. Note that dBASE has identified the record for you, but the record pointer has not yet changed.

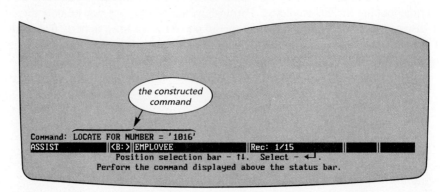

FIGURE 4-14
Finding Employee 1016

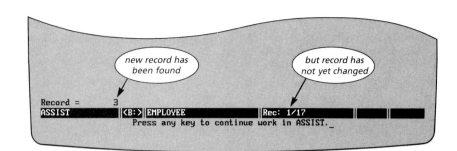

FIGURE 4-15
Finding Employee 1016

You are instructed to press any key to continue. Do so now and the screen shown in Figure 4-16 will appear. If you look at the record number in the status line, you will find that dBASE has indeed moved to the correct record.

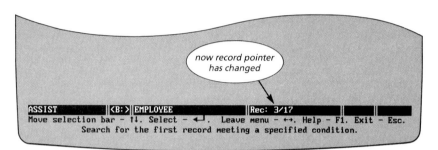

FIGURE 4-16
Finding Employee 1016

Using "Replace"

Another option that can be used to change data is the "Replace" option of the "Update" menu. Suppose you want to change the pay rate of employee 1016 from $10.00 back to $9.75, reversing the change you made earlier.

Select the option in the usual manner. Once you have done so, you will see a box containing all the field names. Move the highlight to PAY_RATE (Figure 4-17) and press the Enter key. Your display will now look like the one shown in Figure 4-18 on the next page. You are being asked to give the new value for PAY_RATE.

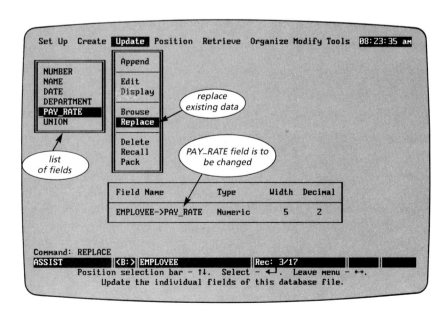

FIGURE 4-17
Replacing Data

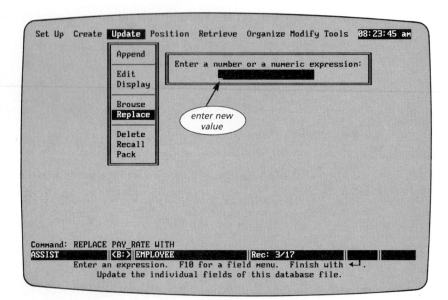

FIGURE 4-18
Entering Replacement Value

Enter the amount 9.75 and press the Enter key. The field menu reappears (Figure 4-19) and you could choose to make some other replacement, for example, changing the department to production. Since the change is only to the pay rate, press the Right Arrow key to leave this menu.

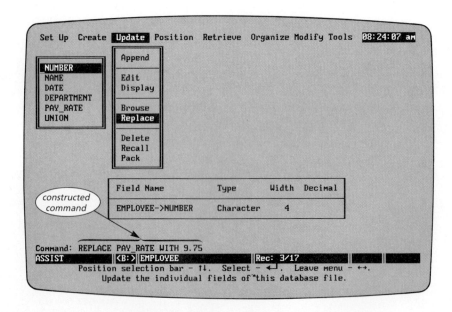

FIGURE 4-19
Replacement Value Has Been Entered

The familiar box will appear. It is now time to build a search condition to identify the record or records on which the change is to take place. For this condition, select the field NUMBER and the comparison operator "Equal to," and enter the number 1016. Indicate that there are no more conditions.

Your display should now look like the one shown in Figure 4-20. Note the command that has been constructed for you. At this point, choose "Execute the command." dBASE will make the change and display the message "1 record replaced." After you have read the message, press any key.

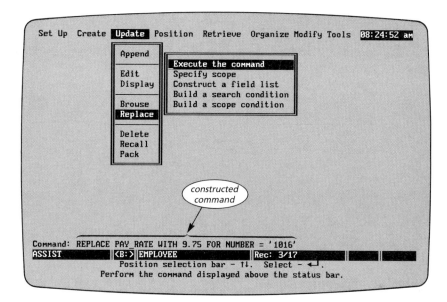

FIGURE 4-20
Completed REPLACE Command

This is a very powerful facility. You can change many records at the same time by entering a condition that will identify several records rather than just one (like DEPARTMENT, "Equal to," and Marketing). The change can also involve a computation. To give employee 1016 a 5% raise, for example, type the numeric expression PAY_RATE $* 1.05$ in the position where you typed the amount 9.75.

Using "Browse"

The "Browse" option of the "Update" menu furnishes yet another method of making changes to records in a database. The "Browse" option will display up to 17 records on the screen at one time and as many fields as will fit horizontally on the screen. This option displays records beginning with the current active record and moving toward the end of the file. To begin with the first record, you should make sure it is the current active record. If not, use the techniques you have learned to make it the current active record. After that, select "Browse" from the "Update" menu as shown in Figure 4-21.

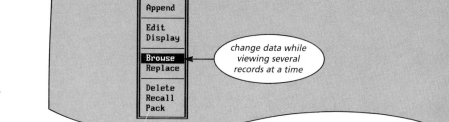

FIGURE 4-21
Using "Browse" to Change Data

The screen illustrated in Figure 4-22, will be displayed with the current active record highlighted. You can move the highlight to any other record by pressing the Down Arrow key or the Up Arrow key.

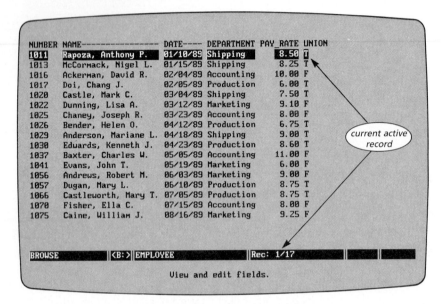

FIGURE 4-22
Using "Browse" to Edit Records

To change a field in a record, you must highlight the record to be changed. For example, to change Helen Bender's pay rate from $6.75 to $7.00, move the highlight to record 8 by pressing the Down Arrow key seven times (Figure 4-23).

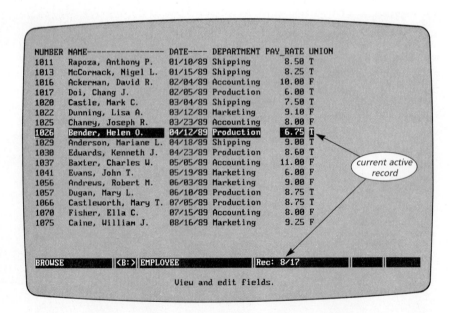

FIGURE 4-23
Using "Browse" to Edit Records

You can use the Right Arrow key to move the cursor to the PAY_RATE field (Figure 4-24) and then type the new pay rate, 7.00. (see Figure 4-25). But pressing the End key is a faster way to move the cursor from one field to the next. Pressing the End key will move the cursor one field at a time to the right. Pressing the Home key will move the cursor one field at a time to the left. The End and Home keys can be very useful with the "Browse" option.

If you only want to change Helen Bender's pay rate, hold the Ctrl key down and press the End key. The change will be saved and you will return to the ASSISTANT menu. If you want to make changes to several records, make all of them before holding down Ctrl and pressing End.

You can also add records to a file using the "Browse" option by moving the reverse video block highlighting each record past the last data record. The message "Add new record? (Y/N)" will appear on the screen. If you choose Y, spaces will be displayed at the bottom of the screen so that you can enter a new record. If you select N, the highlight will remain on the bottom row. The most common method of adding records, however, is with the "Append" option.

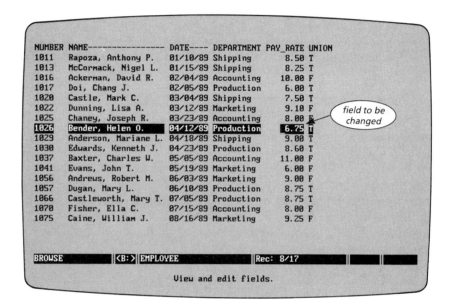

FIGURE 4-24
Using "Browse" to Edit Records

FIGURE 4-25
Using "Browse" to Edit Records

DELETING RECORDS

*I*t may be necessary to delete records from a file. For example, if an employee no longer works for the company, his or her record should be removed (deleted) from the EMPLOYEE file. This can be accomplished with the "Edit," "Browse," or "Delete" options of the "Update" menu.

When you delete records from a database file using any of these options, the records are not actually removed from the file. Instead, dBASE merely marks them with an asterisk as being deleted. It is the "Pack" option that physically removes the records from the file. Until such an operation is performed, the records are still in the file. dBASE will, however, indicate which records have been so marked. When a collection of records is displayed, an asterisk will be placed immediately before the first field of any deleted records. When records are being edited and the current active record happens to be one that has been marked for deletion, the letters "Del" will appear near the right-hand end of the status line.

Since records are only marked for deletion, dBASE provides another option, "Recall," that allows you to remove this deletion mark, that is, to "undelete" these records. This can come in handy if you ever delete the wrong records. Choosing the "Pack" option, however, physically removes such records and the "Recall" option can no longer bring them back. Always be very careful, both when choosing to delete records in the first place and also when deciding to pack your database files.

Deleting Records with "Edit"

The "Edit" option is normally used to change data in one or more records in a database file. It can also be used to delete records, however. To delete a record, simply bring it to the screen using any of the methods we discussed. When the record is on the screen, hold the Ctrl key down and type the letter U. The record will be marked for deletion and the characters "Del" will appear near the lower right-hand corner of the screen. The same process can be used to recall a record. If a deleted record is on the screen, holding the Ctrl key down and typing the letter U will recall it. The record becomes an active record in the file and the letters "Del" will disappear from the screen.

Deleting Records with "Browse"

Records can be deleted using the "Browse" option. Position the reverse video block over the record to be deleted and hold down the Ctrl key while typing the letter U. The record will be marked for deletion.

Deleting Records with "Delete"

The "Delete" option within the "Update" menu is used to delete either individual records or groups of all records satisfying certain conditions. When you choose this option, the familiar box appears (Figure 4-26). Typically, you would then specify a search condition that will be used to identify the records to be deleted. If you immediately select "Execute the command," only the current active record would be deleted. This usually is not what you want.

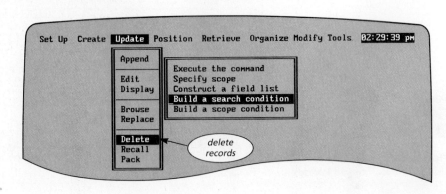

FIGURE 4-26
Using "Delete" to Delete Records

Search conditions are specified in exactly the same fashion as the "Display" option on the "Retrieve" menu. To delete the records for the employee whose name is Andrews, Robert M., for example, move the highlight to "Build a search condition" and press the Enter key. Then move the highlight to NAME (Figure 4-27) and press the Enter key. Select "Equal to" and type the name Andrews, Robert M. Press Enter and then select "No more conditions." Once this has been done, move the highlight to "Execute the command." Before pressing Enter, check the command that dBASE has constructed (DELETE FOR NAME = 'Andrews, Robert M.') to make sure you have typed everything correctly (see Figure 4-28). If so, press the Enter key. If not, press Esc and begin again.

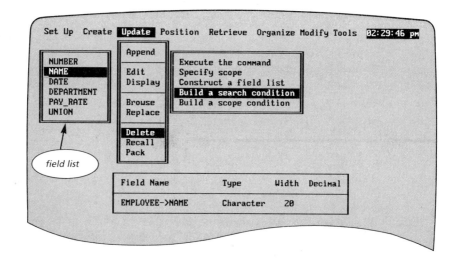

FIGURE 4-27
Using "Delete" to Delete
Records

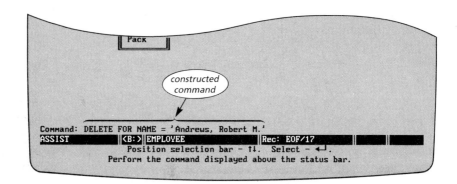

FIGURE 4-28
Using "Delete" to Delete
Records

This record will now be marked for deletion. In the display of all employee records shown in Figure 4-29, it is marked with an asterisk. If we were to use "Edit" or "Browse," the letters "Del" would appear on the screen whenever this record was the current active record.

RECORD#	NUMBER	NAME	DATE	DEPARTMENT	PAY_RATE	UNION
1	1011	Rapoza, Anthony P.	01/10/89	Shipping	8.50	.T.
2	1013	McCormack, Nigel L.	01/15/89	Shipping	8.25	.T.
3	1016	Ackerman, David R.	02/04/89	Accounting	10.00	.F.
4	1017	Doi, Chang J.	02/05/89	Production	6.00	.T.
5	1020	Castle, Mark C.	03/04/89	Shipping	7.50	.T.
6	1022	Dunning, Lisa A.	03/12/89	Marketing	9.10	.F.
7	1025	Chaney, Joseph R.	03/23/89	Accounting	8.00	.F.
8	1026	Bender, Helen O.	04/12/89	Production	7.00	.T.
9	1029	Anderson, Mariane L.	04/18/89	Shipping	9.00	.T.
10	1030	Edwards, Kenneth J.	04/23/89	Production	8.60	.T.
11	1037	Baxter, Charles W.	05/05/89	Accounting	11.00	.F.
12	1041	Evans, John T.	05/19/89	Marketing	6.00	.F.
13	*1056	Andrews, Robert M.	06/03/89	Marketing	9.00	.F.
14	1057	Dugan, Mary L.	06/10/89	Production	8.75	.T.
15	1066	Castleworth, Mary T.	07/05/89	Production	8.75	.T.
16	1070	Fisher, Ella C.	07/15/89	Accounting	8.00	.F.
17	1075	Caine, William J.	08/16/89	Marketing	9.25	.F.

indicates deleted record →

FIGURE 4-29 Current Employee Data

Using "Recall"

If you want to return a record or collection of records marked for deletion to the EMPLOYEE file once again, use the "Recall" option of the "Update" menu to reinstate the record. This option works in the same fashion as the "Delete" option except for one obvious difference. Instead of deleting records, this option *un*deletes (recalls) records. The manner in which the two options are used, however, is identical. To recall the record for Andrews, Robert M., follow the same steps as with the "Delete" option to produce the command shown in Figure 4-30. Then move the highlight to "Execute the command" and press the Enter key. Once this has been done, the record will no longer be deleted.

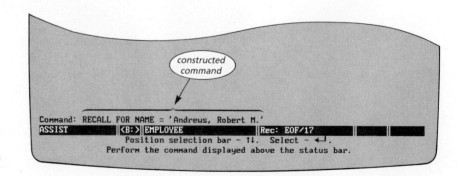

FIGURE 4-30
Using "Recall" to Undelete Records

Using "Pack"

To permanently remove a record from a file, choose the "Pack" option of the "Update" menu. There are no choices to make once you have selected this option. "Pack" removes records that are marked for deletion from the active database file. These records are *permanently* removed from the file. You will no longer be able to recall any of them. Thus, it is a good idea to review the contents of the file before you choose this option to make sure that you have marked the correct records for deletion.

PROJECT SUMMARY

*I*n Project 4 you learned how to change the data in a database file, how to add records using the "Append" option of the "Update" menu, and how to change data using the "Edit," "Browse," and "Replace" options of that menu. You also learned how to delete records using the "Edit," "Browse," and "Delete" options; how to recall records using the "Recall" option; and how to physically remove deleted records using the "Pack" option.

If you followed along with the steps in this chapter, you have made a number of updates to the EMPLOYEE database file. If you did not but wish to make these updates now, you can use the following keystroke sequence. Start dBASE as described in the project and activate the EMPLOYEE database file. Then type the following:

SUMMARY OF KEYSTROKES— Project 4

STEPS	KEY(S) PRESSED	RESULTS
1	→ → ←	
2	1070Fisher, Ella C. ←071589	
3	Accounting8.00F	
4	1075Caine, William J. ←081689	
5	Marketing ←9.25F ←	Records added
6	← ← ↓ ← PgUp PgUp PgUp (Enough times to make record 3 the current active record)	
7	↓↓↓↓10.00[Ctrl-End]	Records changed with "Edit"
8	→↓↓←←	Current active record is 1
9	↑↑←↓↓←←←1016←	
10	↑↑←←	Employee 1016 located
11	←↓↓↓↓←↓↓↓↓	
12	←9.75←→↓↓←←←	
13	1016←↑↑←←	Records changed
14	→↓↓↓←←	Current active record is 1
15	←↓↓↓←↓↓↓↓	
16	↓↓ End End End End 7.00 Ctrl-End	Records changed with "Browse"
17	↓↓←↓↓←↓←←	
18	Andrews, Robert M. ←←↑	
19	↑←←	Record deleted
20	↓←↓↓←↓←←	
21	Andrews, Robert M. ←←↑	
22	↑←←	Record recalled
23	↓←←	Database file packed

The following list summarizes the material covered in Project 4:

1. To add records, use the "Append" option of the "Update" menu.
2. To change records while viewing one record at a time, use the "Edit" option of the "Update" menu.
3. To position the record pointer to a record containing a certain value, use the "Locate" option of the "Position" menu.
4. To make the same change to all records satisfying a certain condition, use the "Replace" option of the "Update" menu.
5. To change records while viewing several records at a time, use the "Browse" option of the "Update" menu.
6. Deleting records does not remove them from a database file. Rather, such records are marked for deletion. To physically remove such records from the file, use the "Pack" option of the "Update" menu.
7. To delete records, use the "Edit" or the "Browse" options of the "Update" menu. In either case, move to the record to be deleted, hold the Ctrl key down, and type the letter U. (The letters "Del" on the status line indicate that the current active record has been deleted.)
8. To recall records, use the "Edit" or the "Browse" options of the "Update" menu. In either case, move to the deleted record, hold the Ctrl key down, and type the letter U. The letters "Del" will disappear from the screen.
9. To delete all records satisfying a certain condition, use the "Delete" option of the "Update" menu.
10. To recall all records satisfying a certain condition, use the "Recall" option of the "Update" menu.

STUDENT ASSIGNMENTS:

STUDENT ASSIGNMENT 1: True/False

Instructions: Circle T if the statement is true and F if the statement is false.

T F   1. Three basic functions which must be performed to keep a database file up to date are making additions, deletions, and changes to the database.
T F   2. Use the "Append" option of the "Update" menu to add records at the beginning of a database file.
T F   3. When you choose the "Append" option of the "Update" menu, a screen will appear asking you to define the names of the fields to be used.
T F   4. When you are done adding records using the "Append" option, press the End key.
T F   5. When you use the "Edit" option of the "Update" menu, one record at a time is displayed on the screen.
T F   6. You can delete records using the "Edit" option of the "Update" menu.
T F   7. Use the "Locate" option of the "Position" menu to find the record for employee 1234.
T F   8. To make the same change to all records satisfying a given condition, use the "Change" option of the "Update" menu.
T F   9. To change a record using the "Browse" option of the "Update" menu, highlight the record.
T F 10. Records cannot be deleted using the "Browse" option of the "Update" menu.
T F 11. The "Browse" option is used to view data in a database but should not be used to make additions, deletions, or changes to the data.
T F 12. Records marked for deletion are physically removed from the file through the "Remove" option of the "Update" menu.
T F 13. Records may be undeleted using the "Edit" option of the "Update" menu.
T F 14. Records marked for deletion will not appear on a listing of all the data in the database file.
T F 15. The "Recall" option of the "Update" menu can be used to display deleted records.
T F 16. When you edit records with the "Edit" option of the "Update" menu, holding Ctrl down while typing the letter U always deletes the current active record.

STUDENT ASSIGNMENT 2: Multiple Choice

Instructions: Circle the correct response.

1. The option to add records at the end of a database file is
   a. "Append"   c. "Add"
   b. "Insert"   d. "Change"
2. To change data while viewing several records at a time, the option is
   a. "View"   c. "Edit"
   b. "Browse"   d. "Replace"
3. Which of the following cannot be used to delete records?
   a. "Edit"   c. "Delete"
   b. "Browse"   d. "Remove"
4. Which of the following is not an option on the "Update" menu?
   a. "Append"   c. "Locate"
   b. "Recall"   d. "Replace"
5. Immediately after you select the "Browse" option of the "Update" menu, the first record shown on the screen
   a. will always be the first record in the file.   c. cannot be updated.
   b. will always be the current active record.   d. is always the last record in the file.
6. To physically remove records that have been marked for deletion, the option is
   a. "Remove"   c. "Pack"
   b. "Delete"   d. "Compress"

STUDENT ASSIGNMENT 3: Understanding dBASE Options

Instructions: Explain what will happen after you perform each of the following actions.

Problem 1. Select the "Append" option of the "Update" menu.

Explanation: _____

_____

_____

Problem 2. Select the "Edit" option of the "Update" menu.

Explanation: _____

_____

_____

Problem 3. Select the "Browse" option of the "Update" menu.

Explanation: _____

_____

_____

Problem 4. Select the "Pack" option of the "Update" menu.

Explanation: _____

_____

_____

STUDENT ASSIGNMENT 4: Using dBASE

Instructions: Explain how to accomplish each of the following tasks using dBASE.

Problem 1. Add a single record at the end of the active database file.

Explanation: _____

_____

_____

Problem 2. Use the "Edit" option to make a change to a field on the fourth record of the active database file.

Explanation: _____

_____

_____

Problem 3. Use the "Browse" option to make a change to a field on the fourth record of the active database file.

Explanation: _____

_____

_____

Problem 4. Add $1.00 to the pay rate for all employees in the shipping department.

Explanation: _____

_____

_____

Problem 5. Mark for deletion the records for all members of the marketing department.

Explanation: _____

_____

_____

Problem 6. Physically remove all records that have been marked for deletion.

Explanation: _____

_____

_____

STUDENT ASSIGNMENT 5: Recovering from Problems

Instructions: In each of the following cases, a problem occurred. Explain the cause of the problem and how it can be corrected.

Problem 1: You were certain you made a change using the "Edit" option and yet, when you later examined the data, you found that the change was not made.

Cause of Problem: _____

_____

Method of Correction: _____

_____

Problem 2: You used the "Delete" option to delete employee 1016 and yet, when you later examined the data, you found that you had deleted all employees whose numbers were greater than 1016.

Cause of Problem: _____

_____

Method of Correction: _____

_____

Problem 3: You deleted a number of records incorrectly. Before discovering this, however, you chose the "Pack" option.

Cause of Problem: _____

_____

Method of Correction: _____

_____

MINICASES:

Adding, Deleting, and Changing Records

Minicase 1: Personal Checks

Instructions: Use the personal checks database that you created in Project 1 for the following problems. These problems require adding, deleting, and changing records in the database.

Problem 1: Adding Records to a Database File

   a. Using the "Append" option, add the checks listed in the table below to the personal checks database file created in Project 1. Record the steps you followed in the space provided.

CHECK NUMBER	DATE	PAYEE	CHECK AMOUNT	EXPENSE TYPE	TAX DEDUCTIBLE
113	02/19/90	Oak Apartments	750.00	Household	N
114	02/19/90	Edison Company	45.95	Household	N
115	02/21/90	Pacific Telephone	29.85	Household	N
116	02/21/90	Standard Oil	33.98	Automobile	Y
117	02/21/90	Cable Television	45.00	Household	N

STEPS: _____

_____

_____

   b. After adding the records to the database file, obtain a listing of the records using the "Display" option. Record the steps you followed in the space provided below.

STEPS: _____

_____

_____

Minicase 1 (continued)

Problem 2: Deleting Records from a Database File

    a. Using the "Delete" option, delete the last record in the file, the record for check 117. Record the steps you followed in the space provided below.

STEPS: _____

_____

_____

    b. Display the records in the file. Record the steps you followed in the space provided below.

STEPS: _____

_____

_____

    c. The record for check 117 should remain in the file. Enter the steps that will make the record for check 117 part of the original file again and no longer marked for deletion. Record the steps you followed in the space provided below.

STEPS: _____

_____

_____

Problem 3: Changing the Records in a Database File

    a. Using the "Replace" option, change the DATE field for check 115 from 02/21/90 to 02/19/90. Record the steps you followed in the space provided below.

STEPS: _____

_____

_____

    b. Using the "Edit" option, change the CHECK AMOUNT field for check 116 from $33.98 to $39.98. Record the steps you followed in the space provided below.

STEPS: _____

_____

_____

    c. Obtain a listing of the records in the file. Record the steps you followed in the space provided below.

STEPS: _____

_____

_____

Problem 4: The "Browse" Option

    a. Delete and pack records with check numbers 113, 114, 115, 116, and 117.

    b. Return to Problems 1, 2, and 3 of this minicase and use the "Browse" option to add, delete, and change records as specified.

Minicase 2: Music Library

Instructions: Use the music library database that you created in Project 1 for the following problems. These problems require adding, deleting, and changing records in the database.

Problem 1: Adding Records to a Database File

   a. Using the "Append" option, add the following records to the music library database file created in Project 1. Record the steps you followed in the space provided below.

DATE	MUSIC NAME	ARTIST	TYPE	COST	CATEGORY
02/26/90	Summer Roses	Davis, Eva	CD	11.95	Vocal
03/02/90	What a Time	Logo, Tom	CS	8.95	Vocal
03/02/90	Camille	Rudin, Lana	LP	8.95	Classical
03/02/90	You Told Me	Lager, Ricky	CD	11.95	Country
03/05/90	Not Tomorrow	Baker, Ted	CS	5.95	Rock

STEPS: _____

_____

_____

   b. After adding the records to the database file, obtain a listing of the records using the "Display" option. Record the steps you followed in the space provided below.

STEPS: _____

_____

_____

Problem 2: Deleting Records from a Database File

   a. Using the "Delete" option, delete the record of the music called "Not Tomorrow." Record the steps you followed in the space provided below.

STEPS: _____

_____

_____

   b. Display the records in the file. Record the steps you followed in the space provided below.

STEPS: _____

_____

_____

   c. You decided that this record should remain in the file. Enter the steps that will make the record part of the original file and no longer marked for deletion. Record the steps you followed in the space provided below.

STEPS: _____

_____

_____

Minicase 2 (continued)

Problem 3: Changing the Records in a Database File

a. Using the "Replace" option, change the TYPE field for the record of the music called "America" from CS to LP. Record the steps you followed in the space provided below.

STEPS: _____

_____

_____

b. Using the "Edit" option, change the music called "Camille" to "Carmen," the TYPE from LP to CD, and the cost from $8.95 to $11.95. Record the steps you followed in the space provided below.

STEPS: _____

_____

_____

c. Obtain a listing of the records in the file. Record the steps you followed in the space provided below.

STEPS: _____

_____

_____

Problem 4: The "Browse" Option

a. Delete and pack the five records added to the database file in Problem 1. Change the TYPE field in record 2 back to CS from LP.

b. Return to Problems 1, 2, and 3 of this minicase and use the "Browse" option to add, delete, and change records.

Minicase 3: Computer Software Store

Instructions: Use the software inventory database that you created in Project 1 for the following problems. These problems require adding, deleting, and changing records in the database.

Problem 1: Adding Records to a Database File

a. Using the "Append" option, add the following records to the software inventory database file created in Project 1. Record the steps you followed in the space provided below.

SOFTWARE NAME	COMPANY	CATEGORY	MS_DOS	QUANTITY	COST
Quick File	Electric Software	Database	Y	10	99.95
Math Drill	Edusoft Inc.	Education	N	12	29.95
Script Print	Graph Tech Inc.	WP	Y	6	49.95
Laser Print	Graph Tech Inc.	WP	N	5	199.95
Speed Calc	Anchor Software	Spreadsheet	Y	20	49.95

STEPS: _____

_____

_____

b. After adding the records to the database file, obtain a listing of the records using the "Display" option. Record the steps you followed in the space provided below.

STEPS: _____

_____

_____

Problem 2: Deleting Records from a Database File

a. Using the "Delete" option, delete the Speed Calc record. Record the steps you followed in the space provided below.

STEPS: _____

_____

_____

b. Display the records in the file. Record the steps you followed in the space provided below.

STEPS: _____

_____

_____

c. You decided that this record should remain in the file. Enter the steps that will make the record part of the original file and no longer marked for deletion. Record the steps you followed in the space provided below.

STEPS: _____

_____

_____

Problem 3: Changing the Records in a Database File

a. Using the "Replace" option, change the QUANTITY field for Databurst software from 5 to 4, the QUANTITY field for Image Fonts from 12 to 10, and the QUANTITY field for Print File from 16 to 10. Record the steps you followed in the space provided below.

STEPS: _____

_____

_____

b. Using the "Edit" option, change the name of Type Ease software to Type Ease 1.0. Record the steps you followed in the space provided below.

STEPS: _____

_____

_____

c. Obtain a listing of the records in the file. Record the steps you followed in the space provided below.

STEPS: _____

_____

_____

Minicase 3 (continued)

Problem 4: The "Browse" Option

a. Delete and pack the records that you added to the database in Problem 1. Change the QUANTITY field for Databurst software back to 5, the QUANTITY field for Image Fonts to 12, and the QUANTITY field for Print File to 16. Also change the NAME field for Type Ease 1.0. back to Type Ease.

b. Return to Problems 1, 2, and 3 of this minicase. Use the "Browse" option to add, delete, and change records.

Minicase 4: Home Sales

Instructions: Use the database of houses for sale that you created in Project 1 for the following problems. These problems require adding, deleting, and changing records in the database.

Problem 1: Adding Records to a Database File

a. Using the "Append" option, add the following checks to the home sales database file created in Project 1. Record the steps you followed in the space provided below.

DATE	ADDRESS	CITY	ZIP	BDRM	BATH	POOL	PRICE
12/15/90	321 Flora St.	Fullerton	92633	4	2	Y	125000.00
12/15/90	499 Lake St.	Anaheim	92644	3	1	N	98000.00
12/18/90	512 Sun Ave.	Fullerton	92633	4	2	N	134900.00
12/18/90	221 Daisy Ln.	Garden Grove	92641	3	2	N	110000.00

STEPS: _____

_____

_____

b. After adding the records to the database file, obtain a listing of the records using the "Display" option. Record the steps you followed in the space provided below.

STEPS: _____

_____

_____

Problem 2: Deleting Records from a Database File

a. Using the "Delete" option, delete the record of the house at 221 Daisy Ln. Record the steps you followed in the space provided below.

STEPS: _____

_____

_____

b. Display the records in the file. Record the steps you followed in the space provided below.

STEPS: _____

_____

_____

c. You decided that this record should remain in the file. Enter the steps that will make the record part of the original file again and no longer marked for deletion. Record the steps you followed in the space provided below.

STEPS: _____

_____

_____

Problem 3: Changing the Records in a Database File

a. Using the "Replace" option, change the PRICE field for the house at 182 Oak Ave. from $92,000.00 to $85,000.00. Record the steps you followed in the space provided below.

STEPS: _____

_____

_____

b. Using the "Edit" option, change the address of the house at 926 Pine Ln. to 962 Pine St. Record the steps you followed in the space provided below.

STEPS: _____

_____

_____

c. Obtain a listing of the records in the file. Record the steps you followed in the space provided below.

STEPS: _____

_____

_____

Problem 4: The "Browse" Option

a. Delete and pack the records that were added in Problem 1. Change the PRICE field for the house at 182 Oak Ave. back to $92,000.00 and the address in Record 6 back to 926 Pine Ln.

b. Return to Problems 1, 2, and 3 of this minicase. Use the "Browse" option to add, delete, and change records.

PROJECT 5

Additional Topics

Objectives

You will have mastered the material in this project when you can

- Change the characteristics of fields in a database file
- Add new fields to a database file
- Delete existing fields from a database file
- Create indexes for database files
- Use indexes in place of sorting
- Use indexes for rapid retrieval
- Create a view relating two database files
- Use a view for retrieving data from two database files

OPTION	PURPOSE
Set Up	Activate a
Database file	database file
View	view
Quit dBASE III PLUS	leave dBASE III PLUS
Create	Create a
Database file	database file (extension DBF)
View	view (extension VUE)
Report	report (extension FRM)
Update	Change a database file by
Append	adding records at the end
Edit	changing records viewing one at a time
Browse	changing records viewing several at a time
Replace	changing the data in all records that satisfy some condition
Delete	deleting records
Recall	undeleting records
Pack	physically remove deleted records
Position	Move the record pointer by
Seek	finding a match using an index
Locate	finding the first record that satisfies some condition
Goto Record	specifying a record number
Retrieve	Retrieve data from a database file
List	show desired fields and records on the screen or printer
Display	like "List" (differences between the two are covered in the text)
Report	print a report
Sum	calculate a total
Average	calculate an average
Count	count the number of records
Organize	
Index	create an index (extension NDX)
Sort	sort a database file
Modify	Change an existing
Database file	database file
Report	report file
Tools	
List structure	show the structure of the active database file

FIGURE 5-1
Menus and Options within the dBASE ASSISTANT

*I*n this project, you will learn how to make changes to the structure of a database. You will be able to change the characteristics of existing fields, add additional fields, and delete fields. You will also learn about indexes and how they increase the efficiency of retrieval. Finally, you will learn about views and how they allow easy access to more than a single database file. You will use the menus and options within the ASSISTANT that are shown in blue in Figure 5-1.

Before beginning the material in this project, start dBASE and activate the EMPLOYEE database file exactly as you have done before.

CHANGING THE DATABASE STRUCTURE

Why Change the Structure?

*T*here are a variety of reasons why you might want to change the structure of a database file. Changes in users' needs might require additional fields. For example, if it is important to store the number of hours an employee has worked, we need to add such a field to the EMPLOYEE file, because it is not there already.

We might have to change the characteristics of a given field. It so happens that Mary Castleworth's name is stored incorrectly in the database. Rather than Castleworth, Mary T. it should be Castleworth, Marianne K. There is no problem changing the middle initial, but there is a big problem changing the first name from Mary to Marianne, because there isn't enough room in the NAME field to hold the correct name! To accommodate this change, we must increase the width of the NAME field.

It may turn out that a field in the database file is no longer necessary. If no one ever uses the DEPARTMENT field, for example, there is no point in having it in the database file. It is occupying space but serving no useful purpose. It would be nice to remove it.

Sometimes you discover that the structure you specified has some inherent problems. For example, you had to type a complete department name when entering each employee. Wouldn't it be easier to simply type a code number? This would make the data entry process simpler. It would also save space in the database, since storing a one- or two-character code number does not take as much space as storing a 10-character department name. Finally, it will cut down on errors during data entry. If you only have to type the number 01 rather than the name Accounting, you will be much less likely to make mistakes that can have serious consequences. If you inadvertently enter Accouning as the department for an employee, that employee will be *omitted* from any list of employees whose department is Accounting.

Thus, you might want to store the code number rather than the department number. What do you do, however, if you are supposed to print the department *name* on some crucial reports? The answer is that you create a separate table containing department numbers and names. This would mean that rather than the single table that you have been using (Figure 5-2), there will be two (Figure 5-3). Notice that the first table has no DEPARTMENT column but instead has a column for code numbers (DEPT_NUMB). The second table also has a DEPT_NUMB column as well as a column that contains the department name. Using these two tables still allows you to list the name of the department for each employee. To find the department name for Anthony Rapoza, you would first look in the DEPT_NUMB column in his row and find that he works in department 04. Then you would look for the row in the second table that contained 04 in the DEPT_NUMB column. Once you found it, you would look in the next column on the same row and see that department 04 is "Shipping." Thus, Anthony Rapoza works in the shipping department.

EMPLOYEE NUMBER	EMPLOYEE NAME	DATE HIRED	DEPARTMENT NAME	PAY RATE	UNION MEMBER
1011	Rapoza, Anthony P.	01/10/89	Shipping	8.50	Y
1013	McCormack, Nigel L.	01/15/89	Shipping	8.25	Y
1016	Ackerman, David R.	02/04/89	Accounting	9.75	N
1017	Doi, Chang J.	02/05/89	Production	6.00	Y
1020	Castle, Mark C.	03/04/89	Shipping	7.50	Y
1022	Dunning, Lisa A.	03/12/89	Marketing	9.10	N
1025	Chaney, Joseph R.	03/23/89	Accounting	8.00	N
1026	Bender, Helen O.	04/12/89	Production	7.00	Y
1029	Anderson, Mariane L.	04/18/89	Shipping	9.00	Y
1030	Edwards, Kenneth J.	04/23/89	Production	8.60	Y
1037	Baxter, Charles W.	05/05/89	Accounting	11.00	N
1041	Evans, John T.	05/19/89	Marketing	6.00	N
1056	Andrews, Robert M.	06/03/89	Marketing	9.00	N
1057	Dugan, Mary L.	06/10/89	Production	8.75	Y
1066	Castleworth, Mary T.	07/05/89	Production	8.75	Y
1070	Fisher, Ella C.	07/15/89	Accounting	8.00	N
1075	Caine, William J.	08/16/89	Marketing	9.25	N

department name

FIGURE 5-2 Employee Data in a Single File

Suppose that you also need to maintain some other information for each department, such as the department's office location, phone number, annual budget, and so on. With the approach that you have been using so far (Figure 5-2), you would have to add additional columns to the employee table: a column for location, a column for phone number, a column for annual budget, and so on. The location, phone number, and annual budget of the shipping department would appear on the first, second, fifth, and ninth rows in the employee table, since each of those rows contains employees in the shipping department. Doesn't this seem cumbersome? With the new approach (Figure 5-3), the new information would be added to the department table. In this case, the location, phone number, and annual budget of the shipping department would only appear on the fourth row, since that is the only row on which "Shipping" occurs. In this project you will focus on the two columns, DEPT_NUMB and DEPARTMENT NAME, as shown in Figure 5-3.

EMPLOYEE NUMBER	EMPLOYEE NAME	DATE HIRED	PAY RATE	UNION MEMBER	DEPT NUMB
1011	Rapoza, Anthony P.	01/10/89	8.50	Y	04
1013	McCormack, Nigel L.	01/15/89	8.25	Y	04
1016	Ackerman, David R.	02/04/89	9.75	N	01
1017	Doi, Chang J.	02/05/89	6.00	Y	03
1020	Castle, Mark C.	03/04/89	7.50	Y	04
1022	Dunning, Lisa A.	03/12/89	9.10	N	02
1025	Chaney, Joseph R.	03/23/89	8.00	N	01
1026	Bender, Helen O.	04/12/89	7.00	Y	03
1029	Anderson, Mariane L.	04/18/89	9.00	Y	04
1030	Edwards, Kenneth J.	04/23/89	8.60	Y	03
1037	Baxter, Charles W.	05/05/89	11.00	N	01
1041	Evans, John T.	05/19/89	6.00	N	02
1056	Andrews, Robert M.	06/03/89	9.00	N	02
1057	Dugan, Mary L.	06/10/89	8.75	Y	03
1066	Castleworth, Marianne K.	07/05/89	8.75	Y	03
1070	Fisher, Ella C.	07/15/89	8.00	N	01
1075	Caine, William J.	08/16/89	9.25	N	02

DEPT NUMB	DEPARTMENT NAME
01	Accounting
02	Marketing
03	Production
04	Shipping

department name

department number

FIGURE 5-3 Employee Data Stored in Two Files

You now have a database that consists of more than one table or, in dBASE jargon, more than one database file. You will need a way of relating the two tables, that is, of using information from both. This is done by using what is called a view. You will see this a little later in this project. Before you can look at views, however, you must change the structure of the database from the one represented in Figure 5-2 to the one represented in Figure 5-3. You must also look at an important concept called an index.

To change the structure, you will:

1. Create and fill in the department database file (called DEPT).
2. Change the length of the NAME field in the EMPLOYEE database file to 24.
3. Add the DEPT_NUMB field to the EMPLOYEE file.
4. Fill in the DEPT_NUMB field with appropriate values.
5. Delete the DEPARTMENT field from the EMPLOYEE database file.

Creating Additional Files

Before making changes to the EMPLOYEE file, create the file of departments mentioned in the previous section. Select "Database file" from the "Create" menu, choose drive B, and then enter the word DEPT as the name of the file. Describe the two fields shown in Figure 5-4 and then press the Enter key. Press the Enter key a second time to confirm that the information is correct.

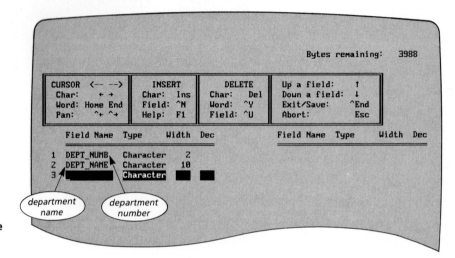

FIGURE 5-4
Creating the DEPT Database File

When asked if you wish to add data now, type the letter Y and then enter the data shown in Figure 5-5. The first record has 01 for the department number and Accounting for the department name. The second record has 02 for the number and Marketing for the name, and so on. Make sure to enter the zeros in the department number field. When you have added these four records, press Enter to complete the process.

FIGURE 5-5 Data for DEPT Database File

Activating the Database File To Be Changed

The database file whose structure is to be changed must be activated. Activate the EMPLOYEE file now, using the "Database file" option of the "Set Up" menu.

To change the structure of the active database file, choose "Database file" from the "Modify" menu (Figure 5-6). The same screen you used to create the file in the first place is displayed along with all the current fields (Figure 5-7).

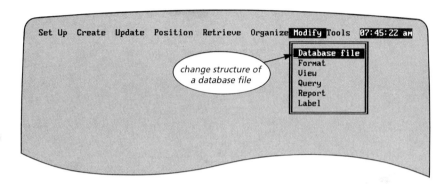

FIGURE 5-6
Changing the Structure of a
Database File

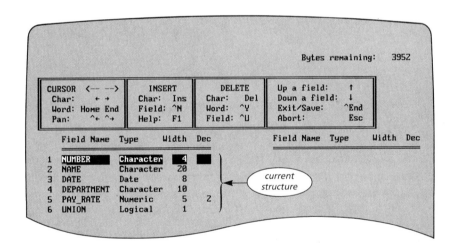

FIGURE 5-7
Change Structure of a
Database File

Changing the Characteristics of Fields

To change the characteristics of any field, repeatedly press the Enter key until the data to be changed is highlighted. In this case, move the highlight to the width column in the second row, type the number 24 (the new width for the NAME field), and press the Enter key.

Adding New Fields

Keep pressing the Enter key until you have arrived at the bottom of the current list of fields. A new line will be created for you.

Type the words DEPT_NUMB as the name of the new field, choose Character for the type and enter the number 2 as the width, as shown in Figure 5-8. Another new line has been created for you. Since there are no other fields to add, simply press the Enter key.

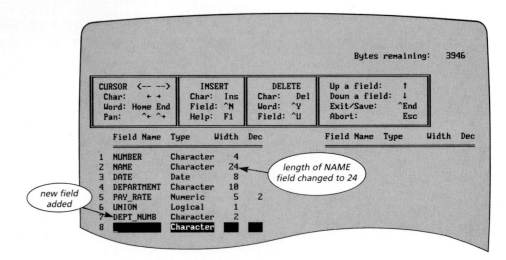

FIGURE 5-8
Change Structure of a
Database File

Press the Enter key again as dBASE instructs you to and the changes will be made. The line at the bottom of your screen will state: "Database records will be APPENDED from backup fields of the same name only!!" This simply means that if you changed the name of any field, dBASE would not be able to keep the current data. Since you did not do so, there is no problem.

Once the process is complete, display all records and fields to see the screen shown in Figure 5-9. Note the new field, DEPT_NUMB, on the right. Since the headings do not fit on one line, dBASE wraps them around to the next. This is why the characters "DEPT" appear at the end of one line and "_NUMB" at the beginning of the next. No entries have yet been filled in for DEPT_NUMB. Note also that the NAME field is wider than it was before.

```
          Record#  NUMBER  NAME                      DATE      DEPARTMENT  PAY_RATE  UNION  DEPT
          _NUMB
             1      1011    Rapoza, Anthony P.        01/10/89  Shipping       8.50    .T.
             2      1013    McCormack, Nigel L.       01/15/89  Shipping       8.25    .T.
             3      1016    Ackerman, David R.        02/04/89  Accounting     9.75    .F.
             4      1017    Doi, Chang J.             02/05/89  Production     6.00    .T.
             5      1020    Castle, Mark C.           03/04/89  Shipping       7.50    .T.
             6      1022    Dunning, Lisa A.          03/12/89  Marketing      9.10    .F.
             7      1025    Chaney, Joseph R.         03/23/89  Accounting     8.00    .T.
             8      1026    Bender, Helen O.          04/12/89  Production     7.00    .T.
             9      1029    Anderson, Mariane L.      04/18/89  Shipping       9.00    .T.
            10      1030    Edwards, Kenneth J.       04/23/89  Production     8.60    .T.
            11      1037    Baxter, Charles W.        05/05/89  Accounting    11.00    .F.
            12      1041    Evans, John T.            05/19/89  Marketing      6.00    .F.
            13      1056    Andrews, Robert M.        06/03/89  Marketing      9.00    .F.
            14      1057    Dugan, Mary L.            06/10/89  Production     8.75    .T.
            15      1066    Castleworth, Mary T.      07/05/89  Production     8.75    .T.
            16      1070    Fisher, Ella C.           07/15/89  Accounting     8.00    .F.
            17      1075    Caine, William J.         08/16/89  Marketing      9.25    .F.
```

NAME field is longer

new field

FIGURE 5-9
Database File with
New Structure

Making Entries for New Fields

To fill in the entries for DEPT_NUMB, you could use either "Edit" or "Browse" and simply proceed through each record. Whenever you encounter a record on which the value for DEPARTMENT is Accounting, set DEPT_NUMB to "01". If the value is "Marketing," set DEPT_NUMB to "02", and so on. Does this approach seem tedious to you? Even though there are only 17 records, it probably seems like a lot of busy work. What if there were several thousand records? It would take a long time to make these changes, with many chances to make errors. There must be an easier way.

Recall that the "Replace" option of the "Update" menu allowed you to make the same change to all records in a file that satisfy a given condition. This is exactly what you need. To use this option, choose "Replace" from the "Update" menu (Figure 5-10).

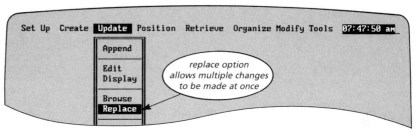

FIGURE 5-10
Changing Data Using Replace

Choose DEPT_NUMB from the field list that will be displayed by moving the cursor to it (Figure 5-11) and pressing the Enter key. You will next be asked for a character string (Figure 5-12). Enter the numbers 01. You can now choose other fields to replace. Press the Right Arrow key since this is the only field is to be changed.

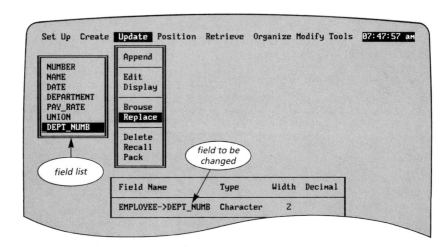

FIGURE 5-11
Changing Data Using Replace

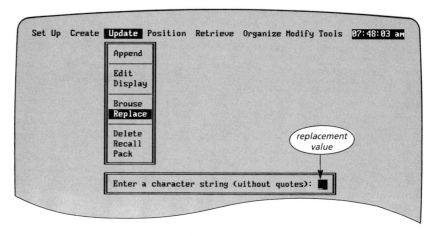

FIGURE 5-12
Changing Data with Replace

Next, select "Build a search condition" from the familiar box. Select the DEPARTMENT field in the usual manner, and then "Equal to." Enter the word Accounting as the character string and then choose "No more conditions."

Note the command dBASE has constructed for you (see Figure 5-13). Select "Execute the command." dBASE will replace the current value of DEPT_NUMB with 01 for all records in which DEPARTMENT is "Accounting." When this is done a message will appear on the screen indicating the number of records that were replaced (4).

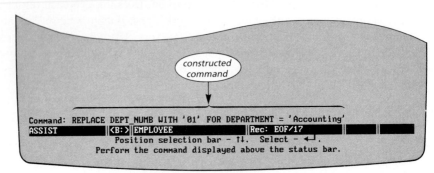

FIGURE 5-13
Changing Data with Replace

In exactly the same fashion, change the value for DEPT_NUMB to 02 for all records in which DEPARTMENT is "Marketing," 03 for all records in which DEPARTMENT is "Production," and 04 for all records in which DEPARTMENT is "Shipping." The changes are now complete and all records now contain an appropriate value in the DEPT_NUMB field.

Making Other Corrections

Next, choose "Edit" from the "Update" menu and move to record 15 (Figure 5-14). Change the name from Castleworth, Mary T. to Castleworth, Marianne K. (Figure 5-15). If you have correctly changed the length of the NAME field, there should be sufficient room to make this change. Hold down the Ctrl key and press the End key to indicate that you are done.

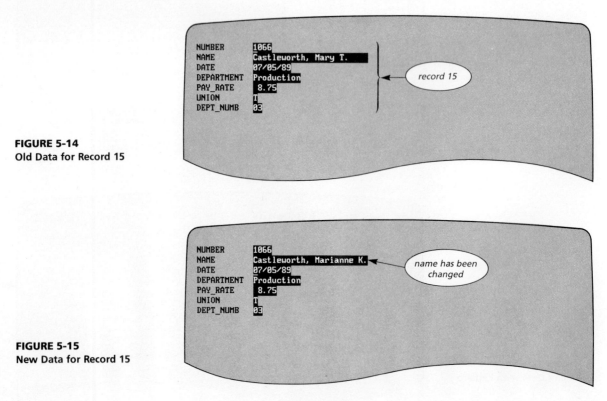

FIGURE 5-14
Old Data for Record 15

FIGURE 5-15
New Data for Record 15

At this point, display all records to produce the screen shown in Figure 5-16. Note that the DEPT_NUMB column contains the correct values and that the name of Marianne K. Castleworth is now correct.

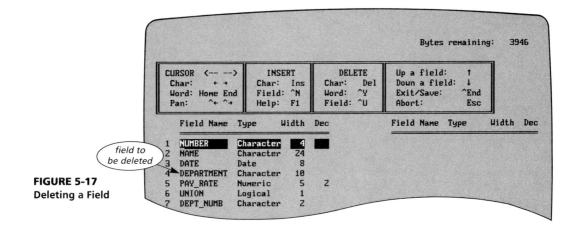

Record#	NUMBER	NAME	DATE	DEPARTMENT	PAY_RATE	UNION	DEPT_NUMB
1	1011	Rapoza, Anthony P.	01/10/89	Shipping	8.50	.T.	04
2	1013	McCormack, Nigel L.	01/15/89	Shipping	8.25	.T.	04
3	1016	Ackerman, David R.	02/04/89	Accounting	9.75	.F.	01
4	1017	Doi, Chang J.	02/05/89	Production	6.00	.T.	03
5	1020	Castle, Mark C.	03/04/89	Shipping	7.50	.T.	04
6	1022	Dunning, Lisa A.	03/12/89	Marketing	9.10	.F.	02
7	1025	Chaney, Joseph R.	03/23/89	Accounting	8.00	.F.	01
8	1026	Bender, Helen O.	04/12/89	Production	7.00	.T.	03
9	1029	Anderson, Mariane L.	04/18/89	Shipping	9.00	.T.	04
10	1030	Edwards, Kenneth J.	04/23/89	Production	8.60	.T.	03
11	1037	Baxter, Charles W.	05/05/89	Accounting	11.00	.F.	01
12	1041	Evans, John T.	05/19/89	Marketing	6.00	.F.	02
13	1056	Andrews, Robert M.	06/03/89	Marketing	9.00	.F.	02
14	1057	Dugan, Mary L.	06/10/89	Production	8.75	.T.	03
15	1066	Castleworth, Marianne K.	07/05/89	Production	8.75	.T.	03
16	1070	Fisher, Ella C.	07/15/89	Accounting	8.00	.F.	01
17	1075	Caine, William J.	08/16/89	Marketing	9.25	.F.	02

name has been lengthened

department numbers have been filled in

FIGURE 5-16 Changes Have Been Made

Deleting Fields

The DEPARTMENT field is no longer required so let's delete it. Choose "Database file" from the "Modify" menu, producing the display shown in Figure 5-17. Press the Enter key enough times to move the highlight to the fourth row (DEPARTMENT). Hold the Ctrl key down and type the letter U. Does this seem familiar to you? It is exactly the same way you delete records when using "Edit" or "Browse." Once this has been done, the field will disappear (Figure 5-18 on the next page). Since this is the only change you want to make, hold the Ctrl key down and press the End key. Press the Enter key to confirm that you want this change made.

Bytes remaining: 3946

CURSOR <-- -->	INSERT	DELETE	Up a field: ↑
Char: ← →	Char: Ins	Char: Del	Down a field: ↓
Word: Home End	Field: ^N	Word: ^Y	Exit/Save: ^End
Pan: ^← ^→	Help: F1	Field: ^U	Abort: Esc

	Field Name	Type	Width	Dec		Field Name	Type	Width	Dec
1	NUMBER	Character	4						
2	NAME	Character	24						
3	DATE	Date	8						
4	DEPARTMENT	Character	10						
5	PAY_RATE	Numeric	5	2					
6	UNION	Logical	1						
7	DEPT_NUMB	Character	2						

field to be deleted

FIGURE 5-17
Deleting a Field

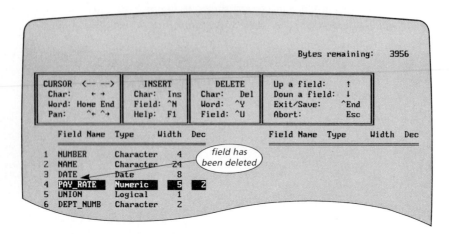

FIGURE 5-18
Deleting a Field

Now displaying all records produces the screen shown in Figure 5-19. Note that there is no DEPARTMENT column.

```
                                                            no DEPARTMENT
                                                                field

    Record#  NUMBER  NAME                      DATE      PAY_RATE UNION DEPT_NUMB
         1   1011    Rapoza, Anthony P.        01/10/89     8.50  .T.   04
         2   1013    McCormack, Nigel L.       01/15/89     8.25  .T.   04
         3   1016    Ackerman, David R.        02/04/89     9.75  .F.   01
         4   1017    Doi, Chang J.             02/05/89     6.00  .T.   03
         5   1020    Castle, Mark C.           03/04/89     7.50  .T.   04
         6   1022    Dunning, Lisa A.          03/12/89     9.10  .F.   02
         7   1025    Chaney, Joseph R.         03/23/89     8.00  .F.   01
         8   1026    Bender, Helen O.          04/12/89     7.00  .T.   03
         9   1029    Anderson, Mariane L.      04/18/89     9.00  .T.   04
        10   1030    Edwards, Kenneth J.       04/23/89     8.60  .T.   03
        11   1037    Baxter, Charles W.        05/05/89    11.00  .F.   01
        12   1041    Evans, John T.            05/19/89     6.00  .F.   02
        13   1056    Andrews, Robert M.        06/03/89     9.00  .F.   02
        14   1057    Dugan, Mary L.            06/10/89     8.75  .T.   03
        15   1066    Castleworth, Marianne K.  07/05/89     8.75  .T.   03
        16   1070    Fisher, Ella C.           07/15/89     8.00  .F.   01
        17   1075    Caine, William J.         08/16/89     9.25  .F.   02
```

FIGURE 5-19
Field Has Been Deleted

INDEXES

What Is an Index?

You are already familiar with the concept of an index. The index in the back of a book contains important words or phrases together with a list of pages on which the words or phrases can be found. An index for a database file is similar. Figure 5-20 shows the EMPLOYEE database file along with an index built on employee names. In this case, the items of interest are employee names rather than key words or phrases. Each employee name is listed along with the number of the record on which the employee name is found. If you were to use this index to find Helen Bender, for example, you would find her name in the index, look at the corresponding record number (8) and then go immediately to record 8 in the EMPLOYEE file. This is faster than looking at each employee name in turn. It is precisely what dBASE will do when using an index. Thus, indexes make the retrieval process much more efficient.

There is another benefit to indexes. They provide an efficient alternative to sorting. Look at the record numbers in the index. Suppose you need these to list all employees. That is, you simply follow down the record number column, listing the corresponding employees as you go. In this example, you would first list the employee on record 3 (David Ackerman), then the employee on record 9 (Mariane Anderson), then the employee on record 13 (Robert Andrews), and so on. You will be listing the employees in alphabetical order *without sorting the file*.

REC NUM	EMPLOYEE NUMBER	EMPLOYEE NAME	DATE HIRED	PAY RATE	UNION MEMBER	DEPT NUMB
1	1011	Rapoza, Anthony P.	01/10/89	8.50	Y	04
2	1013	McCormack, Nigel L.	01/15/89	8.25	Y	04
3	1016	Ackerman, David R.	02/04/89	9.75	N	01
4	1017	Doi, Chang J.	02/05/89	6.00	Y	03
5	1020	Castle, Mark C.	03/04/89	7.50	Y	04
6	1022	Dunning, Lisa A.	03/12/89	9.10	N	02
7	1025	Chaney, Joseph R.	03/23/89	8.00	N	01
8	1026	Bender, Helen O.	04/12/89	7.00	Y	03
9	1029	Anderson, Mariane L.	04/18/89	9.00	Y	04
10	1030	Edwards, Kenneth J.	04/23/89	8.60	Y	03
11	1037	Baxter, Charles W.	05/05/89	11.00	N	01
12	1041	Evans, John T.	05/19/89	6.00	N	02
13	1056	Andrews, Robert M.	06/03/89	9.00	N	02
14	1057	Dugan, Mary L.	06/10/89	8.75	Y	03
15	1066	Castleworth, Mary T.	07/05/89	8.75	Y	03
16	1070	Fisher, Ella C.	07/15/89	8.00	N	01
17	1075	Caine, William J.	08/16/89	9.25	N	02

INDEX ON NAME

EMPLOYEE NAME	REC NUM
Ackerman, David R.	3
Anderson, Mariane L.	9
Andrews, Robert M.	13
Baxter, Charles W.	11
Bender, Helen O.	8
Castle, Mark C.	5
Castleworth, Mary T.	15
Chaney, Joseph R.	7
Doi, Chang J.	4
Dugan, Mary L.	14
Dunning, Lisa A.	6
Edwards, Kenneth J.	10
Evans, John T.	12
McCormack, Nigel L.	2
Rapoza, Anthony P.	1

FIGURE 5-20 Use of an Index

Creating Indexes

To create an index, choose the "Index" option of the "Organize" menu (Figure 5-21). The next step is to define the **index key**, that is, the field or fields on which the index will be built (Figure 5-22).

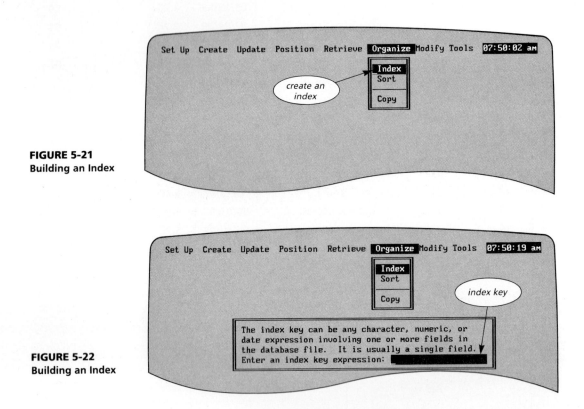

FIGURE 5-21
Building an Index

FIGURE 5-22
Building an Index

Indexing on a Single Field   You can define the index key by simply typing the name of the field. Alternatively, you could press F10 to get a field list. Once you have done this, your display will look like the one shown in Figure 5-23. In this figure, the highlight has already been moved to NAME, the field on which the index is to be built.

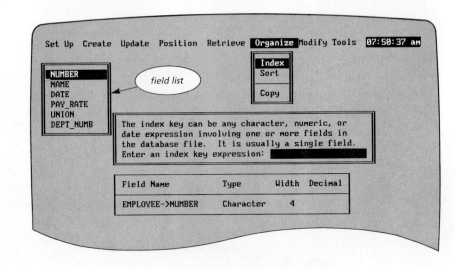

FIGURE 5-23
Building an Index

Next, press the Enter key, producing the display shown in Figure 5-24. You could specify additional fields at this point. In this case, however, the index key is only the NAME field, so press the Enter key.

Next, you must indicate the drive on which the index file is to be placed. Make sure the B: is highlighted and press the Enter key. The final step is to enter the name of the index file. Enter the word empind1 and press the Enter key. The index will be created. When the process is complete, you will see a message indicating that the file is 100% indexed and that 17 records were indexed. At this point, press any key to continue.

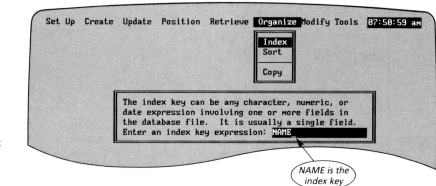

FIGURE 5-24
Building an Index

If you now display all the records, you will see the results shown in Figure 5-25. Note that the records appear to be sorted by name, even though the file itself has not been sorted.

```
         Record#  NUMBER  NAME                        DATE      PAY_RATE  UNION  DEPT_NUMB
               3    1016  Ackerman, David R.          02/04/89     9.75   .F.    01
               9    1029  Anderson, Mariane L.        04/18/89     9.00   .T.    04
              13    1056  Andrews, Robert M.          06/03/89     9.00   .F.    02
              11    1037  Baxter, Charles W.          05/05/89    11.00   .F.    01
               8    1026  Bender, Helen O.            04/12/89     7.00   .T.    03
              17    1075  Caine, William J.           08/16/89     9.25   .F.    02
               5    1020  Castle, Mark C.             03/04/89     7.50   .T.    04
              15    1066  Castleworth, Marianne K.    07/05/89     8.75   .T.    03
               7    1025  Chaney, Joseph R.           03/23/89     8.00   .F.    01
               4    1017  Doi, Chang J.               02/05/89     6.00   .T.    03
              14    1057  Dugan, Mary L.              06/10/89     8.75   .T.    03
               6    1022  Dunning, Lisa A.            03/12/89     9.10   .F.    02
              10    1030  Edwards, Kenneth J.         04/23/89     8.60   .T.    03
              12    1041  Evans, John T.              05/19/89     6.00   .F.    02
              16    1070  Fisher, Ella C.             07/15/89     8.00   .F.    01
               2    1013  McCormack, Nigel L.         01/15/89     8.25   .T.    04
               1    1011  Rapoza, Anthony P.          01/10/89     8.50   .T.    04
```

file appears to be sorted by NAME

FIGURE 5-25 Employee Data Using Index

Indexing on Multiple Fields   It is possible to build an index on a combination of fields. The process is almost identical to that for building an index on a single field. To build an index on the combination of DEPT_NUMB and NAME, for example, the only difference is that you define the index key to be DEPT_NUMB + NAME. You could simply type this expression directly. Alternatively, you could press F10 for a field menu, choose DEPT_NUMB, type the symbol + , press F10 for another field menu, and choose NAME.

In either case, once you have entered the expression, press the Enter key, choose drive B, and then type the word empind2 as the name of this index file. Now, if you display all the records, you will see the display shown in Figure 5-26. Note that the records appear to be sorted by name *within* department.

file appears to be sorted by NAME within DEPT_NUMB

Record#	NUMBER	NAME	DATE	PAY_RATE	UNION	DEPT_NUMB
3	1016	Ackerman, David R.	02/04/89	9.75	.F.	01
11	1037	Baxter, Charles W.	05/05/89	11.00	.F.	01
7	1025	Chaney, Joseph R.	03/23/89	8.00	.F.	01
16	1070	Fisher, Ella C.	07/15/89	8.00	.F.	01
13	1056	Andrews, Robert M.	06/03/89	9.00	.F.	02
17	1075	Caine, William J.	08/16/89	9.25	.F.	02
6	1022	Dunning, Lisa A.	03/12/89	9.10	.F.	02
12	1041	Evans, John T.	05/19/89	6.00	.F.	02
8	1026	Bender, Helen O.	04/12/89	7.00	.T.	03
15	1066	Castleworth, Marianne K.	07/05/89	8.75	.T.	03
4	1017	Doi, Chang J.	02/05/89	6.00	.T.	03
14	1057	Dugan, Mary L.	06/10/89	8.75	.T.	03
10	1030	Edwards, Kenneth J.	04/23/89	8.60	.T.	03
9	1029	Anderson, Mariane L.	04/18/89	9.00	.T.	04
5	1020	Castle, Mark C.	03/04/89	7.50	.T.	04
2	1013	McCormack, Nigel L.	01/15/89	8.25	.T.	04
1	1011	Rapoza, Anthony P.	01/10/89	8.50	.T.	04

FIGURE 5-26 Employee Data Using Index

Unfortunately, to build an index on a combination of fields, both fields must be of character type. This means that you couldn't use the same technique to build an index on the combination of DEPARTMENT and PAY_RATE, for example. There are ways around this problem, but they are beyond the scope of this text. Fortunately, you usually won't need to do this. If you ever find yourself in such a situation, consult the dBASE manual.

Using Indexes

One use for indexes is as an alternative to sorting. The index on the NAME field caused the database file to *appear* to be in name order. The index on the combination of the DEPARTMENT and NAME fields caused it to appear to be sorted by name within department.

The other use for indexes is to allow you to rapidly find records. Build an index on the NUMBER field and call it empind3. Use the "Index" option of the "Organize" menu, select NUMBER as the index key, press the Enter key, choose drive B, and enter the word empind3 as name of the file. If you were to list the records now, they would appear to be sorted by employee number.

Now let's suppose that you to find employee 1037. Choose "Seek" from the "Position" menu (Figure 5-27). You will then be asked to enter an expression. Enter the number 1037 as shown Figure 5-28. The quote marks are crucial, since the NUMBER field is of character type. Without them, dBASE would indicate that there is a "Data type mismatch." Once you have entered the number, press the Enter key. If there were no such employee, dBASE would display the message "No find." If, as is the case here, there is such an employee, this employee's record will become the current active record. Displaying a single record would cause the data for employee 1037 to be displayed as shown in Figure 5-29.

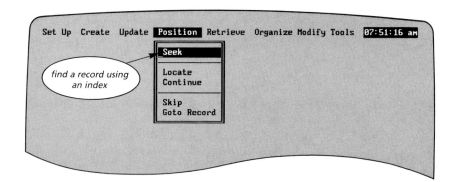

FIGURE 5-27
Using "Seek" to Find a Record

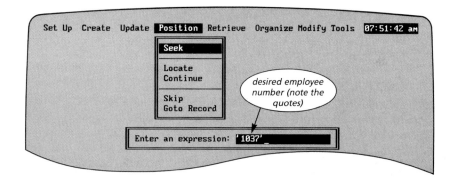

FIGURE 5-28
Using "Seek" to Find a Record

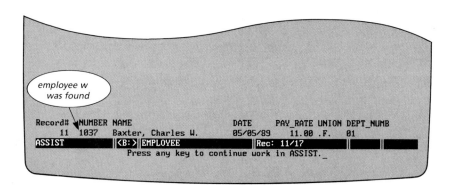

FIGURE 5-29
Desired Record

At this point, you might wonder what value this option has. You may recall that you used the "Locate" option to accomplish the same task back in Project 2. Why is this "Seek" option necessary?

The answer is that the "Seek" option, which only works if you are using an index, is *much* more efficient than the "Locate" option. The "Seek" option will use the index to go directly to the desired record. The "Locate" option steps through every record looking for one that will match the condition. In the case of a file with only a handful of records, this doesn't make much difference. But imagine a file with 50,000 records in which the record that you want happens to be record 40,176. Think about the time it will take if dBASE has to look at the first 40,175 records before finding the one you want. In such a case, the difference between "Seek" and "Locate" will be dramatic.

Activating Indexes   To activate an index, simply type the letter Y in response to the question "Is the file indexed?" dBASE will present you with a list of possible indexes (Figure 5-30). Note that each index contains the extension NDX, which was added automatically by dBASE.

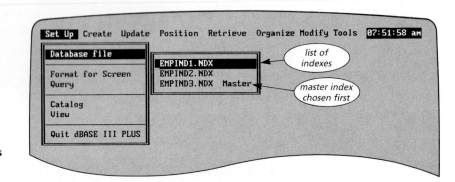

FIGURE 5-30
Activating Indexes

Simply move the highlight to the desired index and press Enter (in the figure this has already been done). In this example, EMPIND3 was chosen. Recall that this is the index built on employee number. Thus, dBASE can rapidly retrieve employees on the basis of their numbers. Also, a list of employees will automatically appear in numbered order. If you wanted one of the other orders, such as name, you would pick a different index.

You can pick more than one index. The other indexes will not affect the order. The only reason to select additional indexes is that any index selected will be kept current by dBASE; that is, if you make a change to the database that requires changing the index, dBASE will do so. Adding additional employees, for example, requires changes to all indexes. Changing the name of an employee would require a change to the index that was built on NAME but not to any others. Any index not selected will not be kept current.

To select additional indexes, simply move the highlight to them and press Enter. dBASE will indicate that these indexes have been selected by placing numbers (02, 03, and so on) after these indexes. Once all indexes have been selected, press the Left Arrow key to indicate that you are done with this step.

Keeping Indexes Current   As long as you activate all indexes associated with a database file whenever you activate the file, the indexes will be kept current. But what if you forget? If an index does not match the actual data in the database it is useless. How can you fix an index that is no longer current? The answer is simple. The "Pack" option of the "Update" menu not only physically removes records marked for deletion, it also recreates the data in all indexes that are active. If you activate a database file and all its indexes and then choose "Pack," all indexes will be valid when you are done.

VIEWS

What Is a View?

To access data from more than one database file in dBASE, you use a view. A **view** is a pseudotable or pseudodatabase file that can combine two or more existing database files. Calling it a pseudodatabase file simply means it appears to the user to be a database file. The data doesn't really exist in this fashion, however. Instead, dBASE will assemble the data for you at the time you use the view.

To see how it works, consider the two database files shown in Figure 5-31, EMPLOYEE and DEPT. There is a special kind of relationship, called a **one-to-many relationship**, between these two files. In this case *one* department is associated with *many* employees, but each employee is associated with *one* department. Department 01, for example, is associated with employees 1016, 1025, 1037, and 1070. Employee 1016, on the other hand, is associated with *only* department 01. DEPT is called the "one" database file and EMPLOYEE is called the "many" database file in this relationship.

When two database files are related in this fashion, they can become part of a view. In such a case, you work with the "many" database file and dBASE automatically keeps track of which record in the "one" file is associated with the current active in the "many" file. For example, if record 1 (employee 1011) is the current active record, dBASE knows that the related record in the DEPT file is record 4 (department 04) since the department numbers match (see the arrow in Figure 5-31). dBASE will allow you to use not only fields in the EMPLOYEE file but also any fields in the DEPT file. Thus, if you list the department name for employee 1011, you will get "Shipping," since it is the name on the related record in the DEPT file.

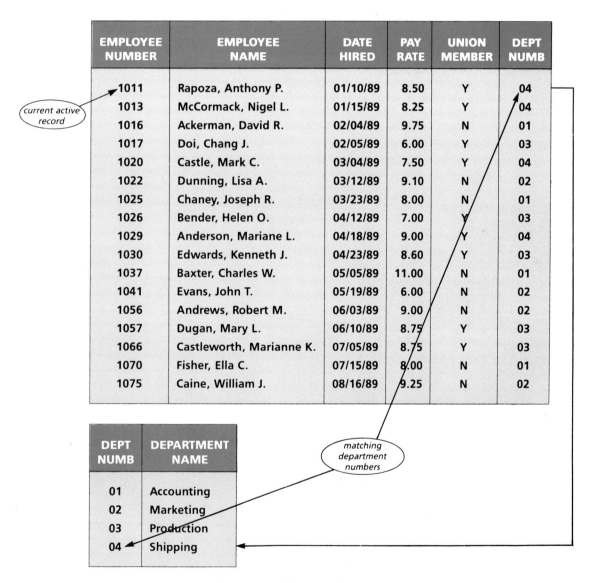

FIGURE 5-31 Relating Database Files

Suppose you make record 3 the current active record (Figure 5-32). Then the corresponding record in the DEPT file is record 1 (department 01). If you list the department name for this employee, you will get "Accounting."

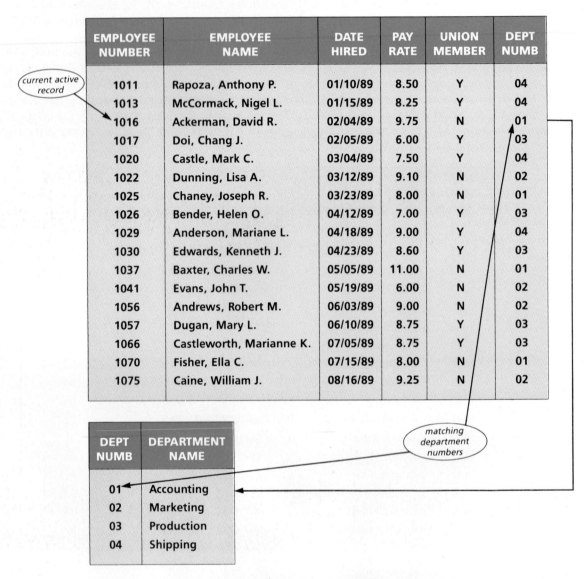

FIGURE 5-32 Relating Database Files

When accessing such a view, you don't have to be aware of these details. dBASE will handle them automatically. Simply indicate that you wish the department name included on a display or report and dBASE will ensure that it is the correct name.

Creating Views

Before beginning the process of creating the view, activate the DEPT database file and build an index on DEPT_NUMB. Call the index DEPTIND1. Once you have finished this process, activate the EMPLOYEE file in the usual manner, without indexes. Then, choose "View" from the "Create" menu (Figure 5-33). Indicate that the view will be created on drive B and that the name of the view file will be "empdept."

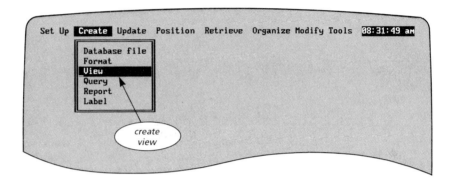

FIGURE 5-33
Creating a View

Selecting Database Files   You are now asked to select the database files that will be represented in the view (Figure 5-34). When you select one, a special mark will appear in front of its name in the list. Note that there already is such a mark in front of EMPLOYEE, the active database file. dBASE assumes that you will want to choose this one. To choose any other, move the highlight to it and press the Enter key. A similar mark will appear in front of the database file you have selected. You can remove the mark (that is, *de*select a previously selected file) by moving the highlight to it and pressing the Enter key. If you don't want the active database file included in the view, it is a simple matter to remove the mark.

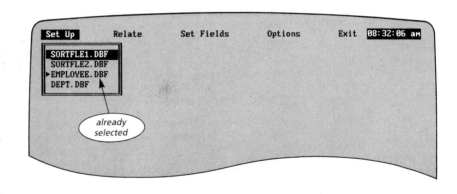

FIGURE 5-34
Selecting Database Files for a View

In your case, you want EMPLOYEE.DBF, which is already selected, and DEPT.DBF, which is not. Highlight DEPT.DBF and press the Enter key. When you do so, the display shown in Figure 5-35 will appear. You are asked to select an index file for DEPT.DBF. It is essential that you select an index built on the field that will be used to match records with EMPLOY-EE.DBF. In this case, this field is DEPT_NUMB. Fortunately, such an index already exists. It is called DEPTIND1.NDX. If it did not exist, you would have to create it using the method discussed earlier. Select this index by moving the highlight to it and pressing the Enter key. There are no other indexes to select, so use the Left Arrow key to leave this process.

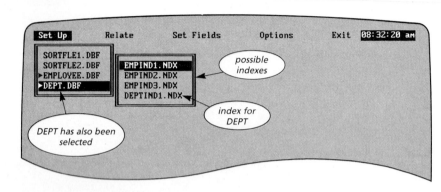

FIGURE 5-35
Selecting Database Files for a View

Relating Database Files   Next, use the Right Arrow key to move to "Relate." This option (Figure 5-36) is used to indicate the relationship between the database files. You must first select the database file that represents the "many" part of the relationship, in this case, EMPLOYEE.DBF. With the highlight on EMPLOYEE.DBF, the "many" part of the relationship, press the Enter key, producing the display shown in Figure 5-37.

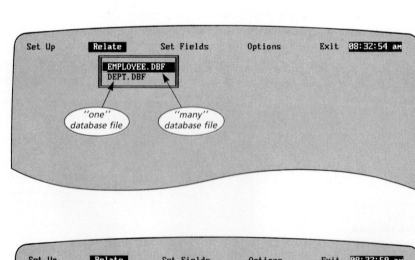

FIGURE 5-36
Relating Database Files

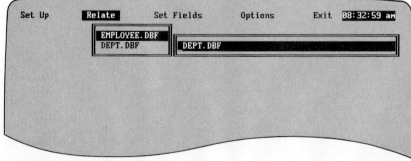

FIGURE 5-37
How Database Files Are Related

In the right-hand box, you must indicate the database file that represents the "one" part of the relationship. It might seem strange that you have to do this. It should be obvious that it must be the only other database file, namely DEPT.DBF. The reason that it must be specified is that dBASE permits more than two database files to be included in a view. In general, this step would indicate which of the other database files forms this part of the relationship.

Next you must indicate how the two files are to be related, that is, which fields in the two files must match. In the database file that is the "one" part of the relationship, dBASE automatically assumes that the field is the one on which the index was built. In your case, that means dBASE will assume that the field within the DEPT.DBF database file is DEPT_NUMB. So you only need to identify the matching field within EMPLOYEE.DBF. To do so, press the Enter key, producing the display shown in Figure 5-38. The mark that follows DEPT.DBF indicates that you must make an entry, namely, the matching field in the other database file, EMPLOYEE.DBF.

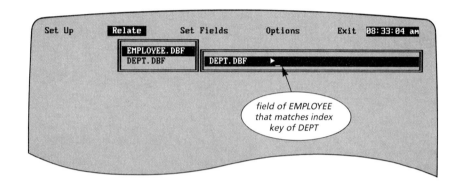

FIGURE 5-38
How Database Files Are Related

You can type the name of the field directly. Alternatively, you can press F10 to get a field menu, move the highlight to DEPT_NUMB, and press the Enter key. In either case, you produce the screen shown in Figure 5-39. Press the Enter key a final time and then the Left Arrow key to indicate you are done. The mark will be removed.

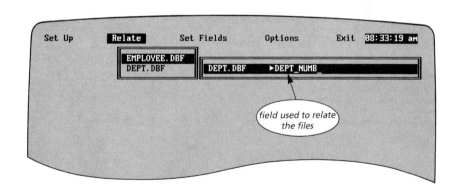

FIGURE 5-39
How Database Files Are Related

Selecting Fields The final part of the process is to indicate which fields from both tables are to be included in the view. To do so, press the Right Arrow key to move to "Set fields" (Figure 5-40). To indicate which of the fields from EMPLOY-EE.DBF you want to include, press the Enter key while the highlight is on EMPLOYEE.DBF, producing the display shown in Figure 5-41.

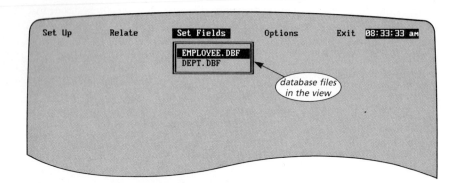

FIGURE 5-40
Selecting Fields To Be Included

FIGURE 5-41
Selecting Fields To Be Included

All fields are listed within the box at the left. The mark in front of a field signifies that it is currently selected, or currently considered to be part of the view. You can "deselect" a field by moving the highlight to it and pressing the Enter key, in which case the mark will disappear. In this case you want all of these fields included, so just press the Right Arrow key to remove this box from the screen.

Next, move the highlight to DEPT.DBF and press the Enter key. The fields from DEPT.DBF are displayed (Figure 5-42). You have chosen to include the field DEPT_NUMB from the EMPLOYEE.DBF file, so there is no need to include DEPT_NUMB from the DEPT.DBF file (remember that the two must match). Press the Enter key with the highlight on DEPT_NUMB to deselect this field. Next, press the Right Arrow key to remove the box from the screen.

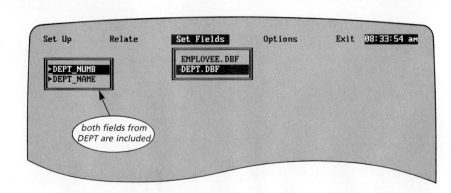

FIGURE 5-42
Selecting Fields To Be Included in the View

Press the Right Arrow key a second time to move to "Options." You will not use these options, so press the Right arrow key again to move to "Exit." With the highlight on "Save," press the Enter key to save your work.

Using Views

The display of all records shown in Figure 5-43 could be produced using either "List" or "Display." This particular one has been printed. If you display it on your screen, you will see only one screen full at a time. If you want to print it, use the "List" option and answer Y when dBASE asks you if the result is to be sent to the printer. Note that the department names listed for each employee are exactly what they should be.

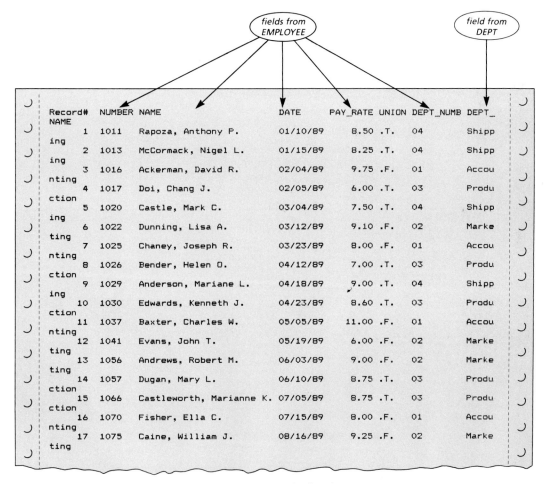

FIGURE 5-43 Data in the View

Next, use the "Display" option again, choose a scope of "ALL," and then choose "Construct a field list." In the list of fields displayed on the screen (Figure 5-44), you will see all the fields in the view, the fields from EMPLOYEE.DBF as well as those from DEPT.DBF. Simply select the ones you want in exactly the same manner as before. In this case, select NUMBER, NAME, and DEPT_NAME. When you are done, choose "Execute the command" and you will see the results shown in Figure 5-45.

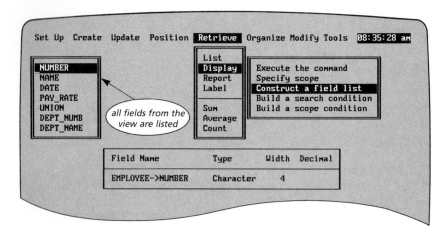

FIGURE 5-44
Selecting Fields from the View

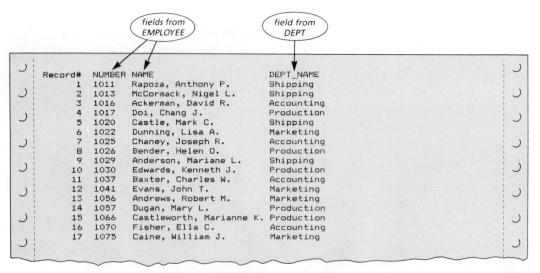

FIGURE 5-45 Selecting Fields from the View

Since you just constructed this view, it is considered to be active. Once you leave dBASE, however, it will no longer be active. To use it again, you must activate it by choosing "View" from the "Set Up" menu, indicating the drive on which the view is found, and then selecting the view from the list that is displayed (Figure 5-46). You do this *instead of* selecting a database file. Once this has been done, you can use the view exactly as you did before. You can use all the options on the "Retrieve" menu with views. You can create reports for views. You can sort views producing database files containing the sorted data. The only thing you really should not do with the view is update the data. That should be done by updating the individual database files that are part of the view.

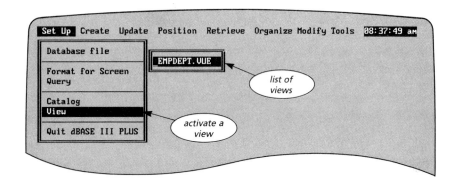

FIGURE 5-46
Activating a View

Special Considerations

There are some special considerations concerning views:

1. When you have activated a view, only the "many" database file (in the example, the EMPLOYEE database file) is displayed in the status bar. Don't worry about this. You can access all the fields that you selected for the view regardless of which database file they are in.
2. To update any of the data, update the appropriate database file. For example, to add a new employee, activate the EMPLOYEE database file and use the "Append" option of the "Update" menu to add the employee. To change the name of an employee, activate the EMPLOYEE database file and use the "Edit" option. To add a new department, though, activate the DEPT database file before using the "Append" option.
3. The data never exists in the form represented in a view. Rather, dBASE draws data from the underlying database files and assembles it in the form defined for the view *at the time you access the view*. No special action is taken beforehand. The nice thing about this arrangement is that, whenever changes are made to any of the database files included in the view, you will automatically see the results of these changes the next time you use the view. You don't need to recreate the view to access the current data.

PROJECT SUMMARY

*I*n Project 5 you learned how to change the structure of a database file using the "Database file" option of the "Modify" menu. You saw how to add new fields, change the characteristics of existing fields, and delete fields. You also learned how to create indexes, using the "Index" option of the "Organize" menu. You can use these indexes in place of sorting as well as to increase retrieval efficiency. You learned how to create a view encompassing data from two database files, using the "View" option of the "Retrieve" menu. You also saw that data could be retrieved from a view in the same manner as from an individual database file.

If you followed along with the steps in this chapter, you have changed the structure of your database file, created an additional database file, created some indexes, and created a view. If you did not do these things but wish to do so at this time, you can use the following keystroke sequence. Start dBASE in the usual manner. Then type the following:

SUMMARY OF KEYSTROKES—Project 5

STEPS	KEY(S) PRESSED	RESULTS	STEPS	KEY(S) PRESSED	RESULTS
1	→ ← ←dept ←		20	**Ctrl-End**	Name changed
2	DEPT_NUMB ← ←2 ←		21	(Move to the "Modify" menu, then do the following)	
3	DEPT_NAME ← ←12 ← ← ←Y		22	← ← ← ← ← ← ← ← **Ctrl-U** **Ctrl-End** ←	DEPARTMENT field deleted
4	01Accounting ←		23	(Move to the "Organize" menu, then do the following)	
5	02Marketing ←		24	← **F10** ↓ ← ← ←	
6	03Production ←		25	empind1 ← ←	Index built
7	04Shipping ← ←	DEPT file created	26	←DEPT_NUMB + NAME ← ←	
8	← ← ← ← ←	EMPLOYEE file activated	27	empind2 ← ←	Second index built
9	→ → → → → → ←		28	←NUMBER ← ←empind3 ← ←	Third index built
10	← ← ← ← ←24 ←		29	←'1037' ← ←	Employee found
11	← ← ← ← ← ← ← ← ← ← ←		30	(Activate DEPT using the "Database file" option of the "Set Up" menu, then do the following)	
12	DEPT_NUMB ← ←2 ← ← ←	EMPLOYEE file structure modified	31	→ → → → → ←DEPT_NUMB ← ←deptind1 ← ←	Index built for DEPT
13	(Move to the "Update" menu, then do the following) ↓ ↓ ↓ ↓ ←		32	Activate the EMPLOYEE file without any indexes using the "Database file" option of the "Set Up" menu, then do the following)	
14	↓ ↓ ↓ ↓ ↓ ↓ ←01 → ↓ ↓ ← ↓ ↓ ↓ ← ←Accounting ← ↑ ↑ ← ←		33	→ ↓ ↓ ← ←empdept ←	
15	← ↓ ↓ ↓ ↓ ↓ ↓ ←02 → ↓ ↓ ← ↓ ↓ ↓ ← ←Marketing ← ← ↑ ↑ ← ←		34	↓ ↓ ↓ ← (Note: Make sure DEPT.DBF is highlighted before pressing ENTER)	
16	← ↓ ↓ ↓ ↓ ↓ ↓ ←03 → ↓ ↓ ← ↓ ↓ ↓ ← ←Production ← ↑ ↑ ← ←		35	↓ ↓ ↓ ← (Note: Make sure DEPTIND1.NDX is highlighted before pressing ENTER)	
17	← ↓ ↓ ↓ ↓ ↓ ↓ ←04 → ↓ ↓ ← ↓ ↓ ↓ ← ←Shipping ← ← ↑ ↑ ← ←	Values entered for DEPT_NUMB	36	← → ← ← **F10** ↓ ↓ ↓ ↓ ↓ ← ← ← ← →	
18	↑ ↑ ↑ ←		37	↓ ← ← ← → → → ←	View created
19	**PgUp** **PgUp** ←Castleworth, Marianne K.				

The following list summarizes the material covered in Project 5:

1. To change the structure of a database file, activate the database file in the usual way, then choose the "Database file" option from the "Modify" menu.
2. To change the characteristics of a field, move the highlight to the data to be changed and enter the new value.
3. To add a field, move the highlight to the beginning of the first row past all the existing fields, then type in the name and characteristics of the new field.
4. To make mass changes to the new field, use the "Replace" option of the "Update" menu.
5. To delete a field, use the "Database file" option from the "Modify" menu, move the highlight to the field to be deleted, hold the Ctrl key down, and type the letter U.
6. An **index key** is the field or combination of fields on which an index is built.
7. To build an index, use the "Index" option of the "Organize" menu. Specify the index key and the name of the file to hold the index.
8. To build an index on multiple fields, the fields should be character fields. Enter the names of the fields separated by plus signs.
9. If an index is active, records in a database file appear to be sorted in the order of the index key.
10. An index may be used to allow rapid retrieval of individual records on the basis of the index key.
11. Indexes are activated when they are created. They can be activated later using the "Database file" option of the "Set Up" menu by indicating that the file is indexed and then selecting the appropriate indexes from the list presented on the screen. The first index selected is the master or controlling index. The other selected indexes will be kept up to date when changes are made to data in the database.
12. If indexes are out of date, they can be made current by activating them and then choosing "Pack" from the "Update" menu.
13. A **view** is a pseudotable or pseudodatabase file.
14. A **one-to-many** relationship between two database files occurs when one record in one of the files is related to many records in the second but each record in the second is related to only one record in the first. The first database file is called the "one" database file and the second is called the "many" database file.
15. To create a view, use the "View" option of the "Create" menu. Specify the database files to be included in the view, the relationship between these database files, and the fields from the database files that are to be included.
16. To activate a view, use the "View" option of the "Set Up" menu. The database files that comprise the view are then activated automatically.
17. Once activated, a view may be used in displays and reports just as though it were a database file. It may also be sorted, producing a database file.
18. To update any of the data in a view, update the appropriate database file.

STUDENT ASSIGNMENTS

STUDENT ASSIGNMENT 1: True/False

Instructions: Circle T if the statement is true and F if the statement is false.

T F 1. To change the structure of a database file, use the "Database file" option of the "Update" menu.
T F 2. You can change the length of an existing field in a database file.
T F 3. You can add new fields to a database file, but you can't delete existing fields.
T F 4. If you add a character field to a database file, initially the field will be blank on all records.
T F 5. The simplest way to change a given field to a specific value for all records meeting some condition is by using the "Browse" option.
T F 6. An index may be used in place of sorting.
T F 7. The field on which an index is built is called an index key.
T F 8. An index key can only be a single field.

Student Assignment 1 (continued)

T F   9. A plus sign (+) between two field names in an index key expression means that the fields are to be added together to produce the index key.

T F 10. When an index is created it is automatically active.

T F 11. Any out-of-date indexes may be brought up to date using the "Reindex" option of the "Update" menu.

T F 12. A view can involve more than one database file.

T F 13. Database files in a view need not have any relationship with each other.

T F 14. To say there is a one-to-many relationship between database file A and database file B means that each record in file A is related to many records in file B but each record in file B is related to only one record in file A.

T F 15. To indicate a relationship between two database files when creating a view, first select the "one" database file, then the "many."

T F 16. When creating a view, if you don't take special action, all fields from both database files will be included in the view.

STUDENT ASSIGNMENT 2: Multiple Choice

Instructions: Circle the correct response.

1. To change the structure of a database file, use the
   a. "Database file" option of the "Set Up" menu.
   b. "Database file" option of the "Create" menu.
   c. "Database file" option of the "Update" menu.
   d. "Database file" option of the "Modify" menu.

2. What kind of changes to the structure of a database file are possible?
   a. adding new fields.   c. deleting fields.
   b. changing the characteristics of existing fields.   d. all of the above.

3. The simplest way to change the value of DEPT_NUMB to "02" for all records on which DEPARTMENT = "Marketing" is to use the
   a. "Edit" option.   c. "Replace" option.
   b. "Browse" option.   d. "Update" option.

4. Which of the following statements about creating indexes is not true?
   a. The file on which the index is created must be active.
   b. The index that is created will automatically be active.
   c. The index key can be more than one field.
   d. The file on which the index is created cannot have any other indexes.

5. Which of the following statements is not true?
   a. The "Index" option of the "Tools" menu is used to create an index.
   b. Indexes give an alternative to sorting.
   c. Any time a change is made in a database file, dBASE automatically makes changes in corresponding indexes.
   d. Indexes may be brought up to date by using the "Pack" option.

6. To activate an existing view, use the "View" option of the
   a. "Set Up" menu.   c. "Update" menu.
   b. "Create" menu.   d. "Modify" menu.

7. Which of the following is true concerning the way two database files involved in a view are related?
   a. There need be no relationship between the files.
   b. There must be fields that have the same name in both files.
   c. A field in one file must match the value in the index key of the second file.
   d. The index key of one file must match the index key in the second.

8. Views can be used just as if they were database files when using the
   a. "Display" option.   c. "Report" option.
   b. "Edit" option.   d. "Sort" option.

STUDENT ASSIGNMENT 3: Understanding dBASE Options

Instructions: Explain what will happen after you perform each of the following actions.

Problem 1. Choose the "Database file" option of the "Modify" menu.

Explanation: _____

_____

_____

Problem 2. Choose the "Replace" option of the "Update" menu.

Explanation: _____

_____

_____

Problem 3. Choose the "Index" option of the "Tools" menu.

Explanation: _____

_____

_____

Problem 4. Choose the "View" option of the "Create" menu.

Explanation: _____

_____

_____

STUDENT ASSIGNMENT 4: Using dBASE

Instructions: Explain how to accomplish each of the following tasks using dBASE.

Problem 1. Change the length of a field in an existing database file.

Explanation: _____

_____

_____

Problem 2. Add a new field to an existing database file.

Explanation: _____

_____

_____

Problem 3. Delete a field from an existing database file.

Explanation: _____

_____

_____

Student Assignment 4 (continued)

Problem 4. Create an index.

Explanation: _____

_____

_____

Problem 5. Use an index instead of sorting.

Explanation: _____

_____

_____

Problem 6. Create a view.

Explanation: _____

_____

_____

STUDENT ASSIGNMENT 5: Recovering from Problems

Instructions: In each of the following cases, a problem occurred. Explain the cause of the problem and how it can be corrected.

Problem 1: You were changing the structure of a database file, intending to delete the fourth field. You looked up at your display and found you deleted the third field instead.

Cause of Problem: _____

_____

Method of Correction: _____

_____

Problem 2: You attempted to find a record using the "Seek" option of the "Position" menu and were told there was a data type mismatch.

Cause of Problem: _____

_____

Method of Correction: _____

_____

Problem 3: When you display the data in a view, the data seems totally wrong. None of the data from the "many" database file matches anything from the "one" database file.

Cause of Problem: _____

_____

Method of Correction: _____

_____

MINICASES:

Changing the Structure of a Database

Minicase 1: Personal Checks

Instructions: Modify the structure of the personal check database called CHECK that you created in Project 1. Change the structure from:

CHECK NUMBER	DATE	PAYEE	CHECK AMOUNT	EXPENSE	TAX DEDUCTIBLE
109	01/19/90	Oak Apartments	750.00	Household	Y
102	01/05/90	Sav-Mor Groceries	85.00	Food	N
111	01/19/90	Edison Company	55.25	Household	N
106	01/12/90	Performing Arts	25.00	Charity	Y
		.			
		.			
		.			

to:

CHECK NUMBER	DATE	PAYEE	CHECK AMOUNT	TAX DEDUCTIBLE	EXP_ CODE
109	01/19/90	Oak Apartments	750.00	Y	HH
102	01/05/90	Sav-Mor Groceries	85.00	N	FD
111	01/19/90	Edison Electric Company	55.25	N	HH
106	01/12/90	Performing Arts	25.00	Y	CH
		.			
		.			
		.			

EXP_ CODE	EXPENSE DESCRIPTION
HH	Household
FD	Food
CH	Charity
AU	Automobile
EN	Entertainment
PR	Personal

Make the following changes:

1. Expand the length of the PAYEE field to accommodate the name Edison Electric Company, the new name for the Edison Company.
2. Add a second database file. This file contains two fields, EXP_CODE and EXP_DESC, used to relate expense codes to the corresponding descriptions (for example, HH stands for household).
3. Remove the EXPENSE field from the original database file.
4. Add a new field, EXP_CODE.
5. Fill in the correct codes for each check.

To make these changes, perform the following tasks:

1. Create the new database file. Use the name EXPCATS for this file.
2. Add the indicated expense codes and descriptions to this database file.
3. Create an index on the EXP_CODE field for the EXPCATS database file. Call the index EXPIND1. Use it to list the data in the database file.

Minicase 1 (continued)

4. Change the length of the PAYEE field in the CHECK database file to accommodate the name Edison Electric Company. Change the names.
5. Add the EXP_CODE field to the CHECK database.
6. Fill in the EXP_CODE field in the CHECK database with appropriate data (HH for records where EXPENSE is household, FD for records where EXPENSE is food, and so on).
7. Delete the EXPENSE field from the CHECK database.
8. Create an index called CHECKIN1 on the Payee field in the CHECK database. Use it to list the records in CHECK in PAYEE order.
9. Create an index called CHECKIN2 on the combination of the EXP_CODE and PAYEE fields in the CHECK database. Use it to list the records in CHECK ordered by PAYEE within EMP_CODE.
10. Create an index called CHECKIN3 on the CHECK NUMBER field in the CHECK database. Use this index and the "Seek" option to locate the record containing check 107. Display the record.
11. Create a view called EXPVIEW that contains both the EXPCATS and CHECK database files. The EXP_CODE field in both files should be used to relate the two. Include all fields from the CHECK database and the EXP_DESC field from the EXPCATS database in this view. List all the data in the view.
12. Using this view, display the CHECK NUMBER, DATE, PAYEE and AMOUNT for all checks whose description is Household.
13. What do you think about the change that was made? Is it a good idea? What are the advantages? What are the disadvantages?

Minicase 2: Music Library

Instructions   Modify the structure of the database called MUSIC, that you created in Project 1. Change the structure from:

DATE	MUSIC NAME	ARTIST	TYPE	COST	CATEGORY
02/22/90	Greatest Hits	Panache, Milo	LP	8.95	Classical
02/15/90	America	Judd, Mary	CS	5.95	Vocal
01/02/90	Rio Rio	Duran, Ralph	LP	8.95	Rock
02/15/90	Passione	Panache, Milo	LP	6.99	Classical
		.			
		.			
		.			

to:

DATE	MUSIC NAME	ARTIST	TYPE	COST	CAT_CODE		CAT_CODE	CATEGORY DESCRIPTION
02/22/90	Greatest Hits #1	Panache, Milo	LP	8.95	CL		CL	Classical
02/15/90	America	Judd, Mary	CS	5.95	VO		CO	Country
01/02/90	Rio Rio	Duran, Ralph	LP	8.95	RK		VO	Vocal
02/15/90	Passione	Panache, Milo	LP	6.99	CL		RK	Rock
		.						
		.						
		.						

Make the following changes:

1. Expand the length of the MUSIC NAME field to accommodate the name "Greatest Hits #1," the correct name for the "Greatest Hits" album by Milo Panache.
2. Add a second database file. This file contains two fields, CAT_CODE and CAT_DESC, used to relate category codes to corresponding descriptions (for example, CL stands for classical).
3. Remove the CATEGORY field from the original database file.
4. Add a new field, CAT_CODE.
5. Fill in the correct codes for each record.

To make these changes, perform the following tasks:

1. Create the new database file. Use the name MUSCATS for this file.
2. Add the indicated category codes and descriptions to this database file.
3. Create an index on the CAT_CODE field for the MUSCATS database file. Call the index CATIND1. Use it to list the data in the database file.
4. Change the length of the MUSIC NAME field in the MUSIC database file to accommodate the name "Greatest Hits #1." Change the name.
5. Add the CAT_CODE field to the MUSIC database.
6. Fill in the CAT_CODE field in the MUSIC database with appropriate data (CL for records where CATEGORY is classical, CO for records where CATEGORY is country, and so on).
7. Delete the CATEGORY field from the MUSIC database.
8. Create an index called MUSICIN1 on the TYPE field in the MUSIC database. Use it to list the records in MUSIC in TYPE order.
9. Create an index called MUSICIN2 on the combination of the ARTIST and MUSIC NAME fields in the MUSIC database. Use it to list the records in MUSIC ordered by MUSIC NAME within ARTIST.
10. Create an index called MUSICIN3 on the MUSIC NAME field. Use this index and the "Seek" option to locate the record on which the music name is "Rio Rio." Display the record.
11. Create a view called MUSVIEW. This view should contain both the MUSCATS and MUSIC database files. The CAT_CODE field in both files should be used to relate the two. Include all fields from the MUSIC database and the category description field from the MUSCATS database in this view. Display the data in the view.
12. Using this view, display the DATE, MUSIC NAME, ARTIST, and COST for all classical records.
13. What do you think about the change that was made? Is it a good idea? What are the advantages? What are the disadvantages?

Minicase 3: Computer Software Store

Instructions: Modify the structure of the database called SOFTWARE that you created in Project 1. Change the structure from:

SOFTWARE NAME	COMPANY	CATEGORY	MS_DOS	QUANTITY	COST
Databurst	Electric Software	Database	Y	5	299.95
Type Ease	Edusoft Inc.	WP	N	22	29.95
Image Fonts	Graph Tech Inc.	WP	Y	12	49.95
Data Filer	Anchor Software	Database	Y	18	149.95
Master	Edusoft Inc.	Education	N	10	49.95
		.			
		.			
		.			

Minicase 3 (continued)

to:

SOFTWARE NAME	CATEGORY	MS_DOS	QUANTITY	COST	CMP_CODE
Databurst	Database	Y	5	299.95	01
Type Ease	WP	N	22	29.95	05
Image Fonts	WP	Y	12	49.95	04
Data File Manager	Database	Y	18	149.95	02
Master	Education	N	10	49.95	05
.					
.					
.					

CMP_CODE	COMPANY NAME
01	Electric Software
02	Anchor Software
03	Learnit Software
04	Graph Tech Inc.
05	Edusoft Inc.

Make the following changes:

1. Expand the length of the NAME field to accommodate the name Data File Manager, the new name for Data Filer.
2. Add a second database file. This file contains two fields, CMP_CODE and CMP_NAME, used to relate company codes to corresponding names (for example, 01 is the code for Electric Software).
3. Remove the COMPANY field from the original database file.
4. Add a new field, CMP_CODE.
5. Fill in the correct codes for each record.

To make these changes, perform the following tasks:

1. Create the new database file. Use the name SOFTCATS for this file.
2. Add the indicated company codes and names to this database file.
3. Create an index on the CMP_CODE field for the SOFTCATS database file. Call the index CMPIND1. Use it to list the data in the database file.
4. Change the length of the NAME field in the SOFTWARE database file to accommodate the name Data File Manager. Change the name.
5. Add the CMP_CODE field to the SOFTWARE database.
6. Fill in the CMP_CODE field in the SOFTWARE database with appropriate data (01 for records where COMPANY is Electric Software, 02 for records where COMPANY is Anchor Software, and so on).
7. Delete the COMPANY field from the SOFTWARE database.
8. Create an index called SOFTWIN1 on the CATEGORY field in the SOFTWARE database. Use it to list the records in SOFTWARE in CATEGORY order.
9. Create an index called SOFTWIN2 on the combination of the CATEGORY and NAME fields in the SOFTWARE database. Use it to list the records in SOFTWARE ordered by NAME within CATEGORY.
10. Create an index called SOFTWIN3 on the NAME field in the SOFTWARE database. Use this index and the "Seek" option to locate the record containing Image Fonts. Display the record.
11. Create a view called SOFTVIEW. This view should contain both the SOFTCATS and SOFTWARE database files. The CMP_CODE field in both files should be used to relate the two. Include all fields from the SOFTWARE database and the CMP_NAME field from the SOFTCATS database in this view. Display the data in the view.
12. Using this view, display the NAME, CATEGORY, and COST for all software produced by Electric Software.
13. What do you think about the change that was made? Is it a good idea? What are the advantages? What are the disadvantages?

Minicase 4: Home Sales

Instructions: Max, the user of the HOMES database file that you created in Project 1, decided to make a change. Max realized that there were only a few zip codes in which the homes for sale were likely to be located. Further, since each of these zip codes uniquely identified a city, Max decided to remove CITY from the HOMES file and create a separate database file called ZIPCODE, relating zip codes and cities. In particular, the structure is to be changed from:

DATE	ADDRESS	CITY	ZIP	BDRM	BATH	POOL	PRICE
09/15/90	9661 King Pl.	Anaheim	92644	4	2	Y	185000.00
09/19/90	1625 Brook St.	Fullerton	92633	3	1	N	95000.00
10/02/90	182 Oak Ave.	Fullerton	92634	4	2	Y	92000.00
10/09/90	145 Oak Ave.	Garden Grove	92641	5	3	Y	145000.00
10/15/90	124 Lark St.	Anaheim	92644	3	2	N	119000.00
10/22/90	926 Pine Ln.	Garden Grove	92641	3	1	N	92500.00
		.					
		.					
		.					

to:

DATE	ADDRESS	ZIP	BDRM	BATH	POOL	PRICE
09/15/90	9661 King Pl.	92644	4	2	Y	185000.00
09/19/90	1625 Brook St.	92633	3	1	N	95000.00
10/02/90	182 Oak Ave.	92634	4	2	Y	92000.00
10/09/90	145 Oak Ave.	92641	5	3	Y	145000.00
10/15/90	124 Lark St.	92644	3	2	N	119000.00
10/22/90	926 Pine Ln.	92641	3	1	N	92500.00
		.				
		.				
		.				

ZIP	CITY
92644	Anaheim
92641	Garden Grove
92688	Costa Mesa
92633	Fullerton
92634	Fullerton

Perform the following tasks:

1. Create the new database file. Use the name ZIPCODE for this file.
2. Add the indicated zip codes and cities to this database file.
3. Create an index on the ZIP field for the ZIPCODE database file. Call the index ZIPIND1. Use it to list the data in the database file.
4. Delete the CITY field from the HOMES database.
5. Create an index called HOMESIND on the ADDRESS field in the HOMES database. Use this index and the "Seek" option to locate the record for the house at 145 Oak Ave. Display the record.
6. Create a view called ZIPVIEW. This view should contain both the ZIPCODE and HOMES database files. The ZIP field in both files should be used to relate the two. Include all fields from the HOMES database and the CITY field from the ZIPCODE database in this view. Display the data in the view.
7. Using this view, display the DATE , ADDRESS, CITY, ZIP, and PRICE for all homes in Fullerton.
8. What do you think about the change that was made? Is it a good idea? What are the advantages? What are the disadvantages?

PROJECT 6

The Dot Prompt

Objectives

You will have mastered the material in this project when you can accomplish the following from the dot prompt:

- Activate a database file
- Clear the screen
- Correct errors in commands
- Send the results of DISPLAY commands to the printer
- Display individual records
- Display all records
- Display selected fields
- Display computed fields

- Use conditions
- Calculate counts, sums, and averages
- Sort database files on multiple keys, using descending order if desired
- Display the contents of a view
- Create programs (command files) and execute the programs from the dot prompt

 n this project, you will learn to use the commands shown in Figure 6-1 at the dot prompt. By now, you should have become comfortable with the ASSISTANT and the way it helps you access your database files. You might wonder why you would ever need to type commands at the dot prompt. There are two reasons.

COMMAND	PURPOSE
APPEND	Add records to a database file
AVERAGE	Calculate an average
CLEAR	Clear the screen
COUNT	Count the number of records
DISPLAY	Show desired fields and records
DO	Run a command file (program)
EJECT	Force the printer to advance to the top of the next page
MODIFY COMMAND	Create a command file (program) (extension PRG)
SET VIEW TO	Activate a view
SORT	Sort a database file
SUM	Calculate a total
USE	Activate a database file

FIGURE 6-1
dBASE commands

First, if you know a particular command, you can often type it more quickly than you can go through the appropriate menus of the ASSISTANT. Second, and more important, there are some things that can be accomplished through commands at the dot prompt that *cannot* be accomplished through the ASSISTANT. You will see examples of these operations in this project. For both of these reasons, it is important to know how to enter and use commands at the dot prompt.

To begin, press Esc to change to dot prompt mode. With the dot prompt on the screen, type the words USE EMPLOYEE. This activates the EMPLOYEE database file. It is like using the "Database file" option of the "Set Up" menu and then choosing the EMPLOYEE database file.

USEFUL TIPS

 efore we examine the commands, we will look at two special tips that can be helpful. The first is how to clear the screen and the second involves correcting errors in commands.

Clearing the Screen

There are various times when you might wish to clear the screen. To do so, simply type the word CLEAR at the dot prompt. All the material other than the dot prompt and the status line will disappear.

Correcting Errors in Commands

Occasionally, you may make a mistake when you type a command. You might, for example, type the word DSPLAY instead of DISPLAY. In such cases, dBASE responds with an error message as shown in Figure 6-2, and asks whether or not you want help. To receive help, type the letter Y. Otherwise, type the letter N or simply press the Enter key. Sometimes the information dBASE provides is indeed helpful. Usually, however, you can discover the problem yourself by carefully comparing the line you typed with examples you have used before. If you want help on a specific command, you can type the word HELP followed by the command at the dot prompt. Typing the words HELP DISPLAY, for example, would produce the screen shown in Figure 6-3.

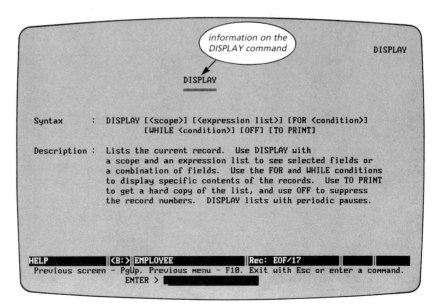

FIGURE 6-2
Incorrectly Entered Command

FIGURE 6-3
Help Screen

Once you have discovered the problem, you could simply retype the entire command correctly. There is a shortcut, however. If you press the Up Arrow key, the command containing the mistake will be displayed on the screen (Figure 6-4). At this point, use the Right and Left Arrow keys to move the cursor to the mistake, make the necessary corrections (Figure 6-5) and press the Enter key. In this example, the problem is that the letter I in DISPLAY was omitted. To correct the problem, you would move the cursor to the letter S in DSPLAY, press the Ins key to change to insert mode, type the letter I, and then press the Ins key again to leave insert mode.

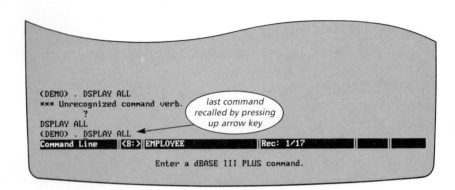

FIGURE 6-4
Displaying Incorrect Command

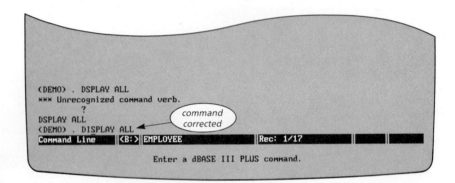

FIGURE 6-5
Command Has Been Corrected

Once you have corrected the problem and pressed the Enter key, dBASE will display the results (Figure 6-6).

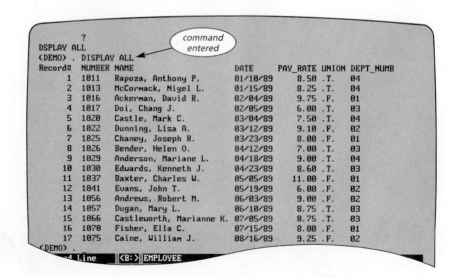

FIGURE 6-6
Results of Corrected Command

DISPLAY COMMAND

Sending the Results to the Printer

o print the results of any DISPLAY command, end the command with the words TO PRINT. We will not do so in the examples in this project, however. Make sure your printer is on before you execute a command containing this clause!

Displaying the Current Active Record

The simplest form of the DISPLAY command is just the word DISPLAY. As shown in Figure 6-7, this command will display a single record, the current active record. If the current active record does not happen to be the one you want, you can type the word GOTO followed by the number of the desired record at the dot prompt. The command GOTO 1, for example would make the first record the current active record. Once you have done this, type the DISPLAY command as shown in the figure.

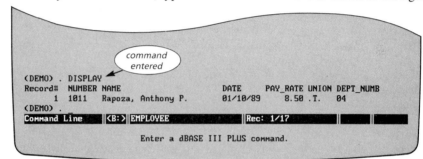

FIGURE 6-7
Displaying a Single Record

Displaying All Records

To display all the records, you need some way of changing the scope to "ALL" (remember the "Specify scope" option). You do this by including the word ALL in the DISPLAY command (shown in Figure 6-6).

Omitting Record Numbers

With the ASSISTANT, there was no way to request that record numbers *not* be displayed. This is easily accomplished at the dot prompt by including the word OFF in the DISPLAY command (Figure 6-8).

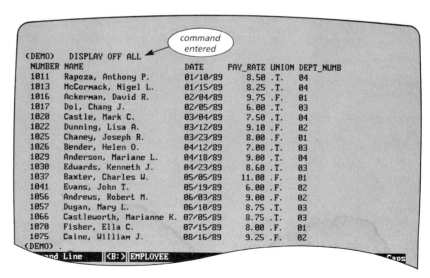

FIGURE 6-8
Omitting Record Numbers

Displaying Selected Fields

To specify a particular collection of fields to display, list the fields in the command (Figure 6-9).

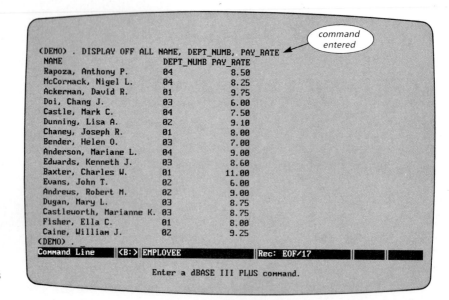

FIGURE 6-9
Displaying Selected Fields

Making Computations

Suppose you want to list the number, name, pay rate, and weekly pay (pay rate times 40) for all employees. Further, you do not wish to include record numbers. You can do so by the DISPLAY command shown in Figure 6-10.

```
<DEMO> . DISPLAY OFF ALL NUMBER, NAME, PAY_RATE, PAY_RATE * 40
NUMBER NAME                        PAY_RATE PAY_RATE * 40
1011   Rapoza, Anthony P.            8.50       340.00
1013   McCormack, Nigel L.           8.25       330.00
1016   Ackerman, David R.            9.75       390.00
1017   Doi, Chang J.                 6.00       240.00
1020   Castle, Mark C.               7.50       300.00
1022   Dunning, Lisa A.              9.10       364.00
1025   Chaney, Joseph R.             8.00       320.00
1026   Bender, Helen O.              7.00       280.00
1029   Anderson, Mariane L.          9.00       360.00
1030   Edwards, Kenneth J.           8.60       344.00
1037   Baxter, Charles W.           11.00       440.00
1041   Evans, John T.                6.00       240.00
1056   Andrews, Robert M.            9.00       360.00
1057   Dugan, Mary L.                8.75       350.00
1066   Castleworth, Marianne K.      8.75       350.00
1070   Fisher, Ella C.               8.00       320.00
1075   Caine, William J.             9.25       370.00
<DEMO> .
Command Line    <B:> EMPLOYEE                    Rec: EOF/17              Caps
               Enter a dBASE III PLUS command
```

command entered

FIGURE 6-10
Making Computations

Displaying a Specific Record

You have already seen how to change the current active record using GOTO and how to display the current active record. You can accomplish both tasks in a single step by listing the desired record number in the DISPLAY command as shown in Figure 6-11, where the desired record number is 6. This command will display record 6 and also make record 6 the current active record.

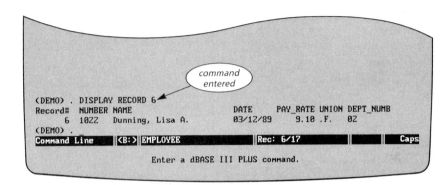

FIGURE 6-11
Displaying a Single Record

Using Conditions

Search conditions are indicated in a DISPLAY command through the FOR clause. To display the data for employee 1030, for example, you can use the DISPLAY command shown in Figure 6-12. When you used the ASSISTANT, you didn't need to enter the quote marks around the number 1030. But they are essential when you enter DISPLAY commands at the dot prompt. Whenever you are making a comparison involving a character field, you *must* use quote marks, either double quote marks (") or single quote marks (') around the character string.

You may have noticed that the command does not include the word ALL. The word is not required if a FOR clause is used. Including the word ALL would not be wrong, however.

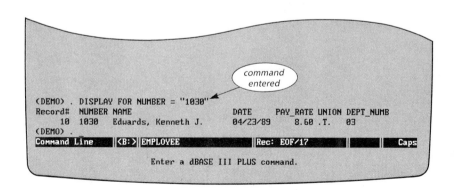

FIGURE 6-12
Using Conditions

The DISPLAY command shown in Figure 6-13 will display all employees whose pay rate is $6.00. Since PAY_RATE is a numeric field, the 6.00 *must not* be enclosed in quotes.

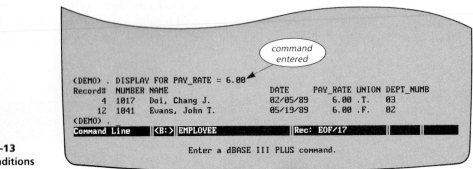

FIGURE 6-13
Using Conditions

Comparisons need not involve equality. You can use any of the normal comparison operators (= , > , < , > = , < =) as well as > < (NOT EQUAL). The DISPLAY command in Figure 6-14, for example, lists all employees whose pay rate is more than $9.00.

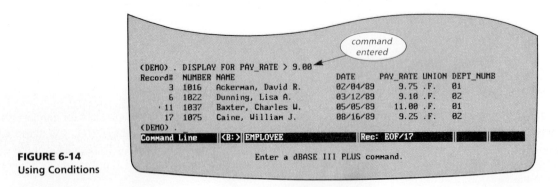

FIGURE 6-14
Using Conditions

To restrict the display to certain columns and rows meeting a given condition, list the desired columns in the DISPLAY command and include an appropriate condition. The DISPLAY command in Figure 6-15 lists the name, department number, and pay rate for all employees in department 04.

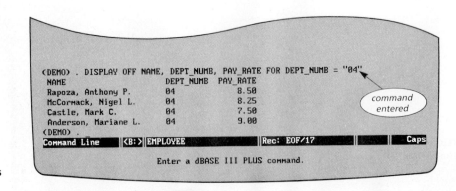

FIGURE 6-15
Using Conditions

Searching for a Name

Recall that when you search for a name, you must type the letters the same way they occur in the database. The DISPLAY command shown in Figure 6-16 would find Charles Baxter, but the DISPLAY command shown in Figure 6-17 would not, since the letters are all uppercase and that is not the way the name was entered into the database.

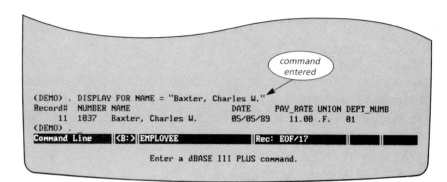

FIGURE 6-16
Searching for a Name

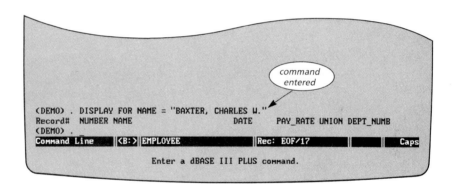

FIGURE 6-17
Searching for a Name

Fortunately, when using the DISPLAY command, there is a simple way around this problem. You use a special dBASE function called UPPER, as shown in Figure 6-18. The expression UPPER(NAME) represents the same letters that are in NAME, converted to upper case. Thus, if NAME is Baxter, Charles W., UPPER(NAME) would be BAXTER, CHARLES W. and the condition would be true.

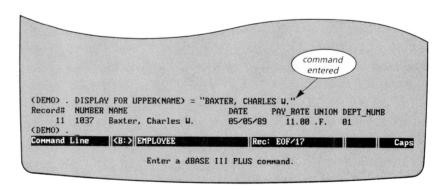

FIGURE 6-18
Using the UPPER Function

As with the ASSISTANT, if you enter the single letter A in the comparison, you will find all employees whose name *begins with* the letter A (Figure 6-19).

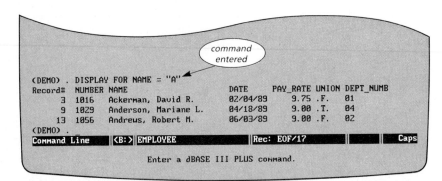

FIGURE 6-19
Searching for Names That Begin with A

With the ASSISTANT, there would be no way to find all the employees having a given first name. This can easily be done in the DISPLAY command, using the $ function, technically called the substring function. It is used to determine whether one string of characters is contained in (a "substring" of) another. Thus, to find all employees whose names contain the characters David, you could use a DISPLAY command like the one shown in Figure 6-20.

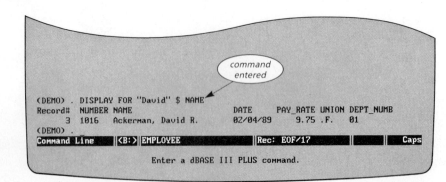

FIGURE 6-20
Searching for Names That Contain David

Using Logical Fields in Conditions

As with the ASSISTANT, you can use logical fields in comparisons by themselves. The DISPLAY command shown in Figure 6-21 is used to display all employees for whom UNION is true.

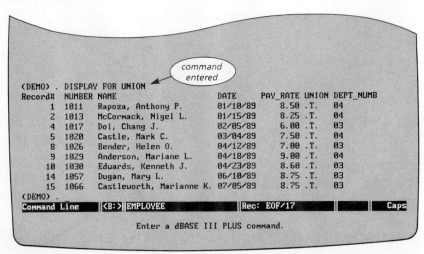

FIGURE 6-21
Using Logical Fields

One of the things you cannot do with the ASSISTANT is to DISPLAY all employees for whom UNION is false. This is easily accomplished through a DISPLAY command by preceding the word UNION with the word NOT as shown in Figure 6-22. Any condition can be preceded with the word NOT. Doing so simply reverses the truth or falsity of the condition. If UNION is true, NOT UNION is false. Likewise, if UNION is false, NOT UNION is true. When you use the word NOT, you must put periods on both sides of the word as shown in the figure.

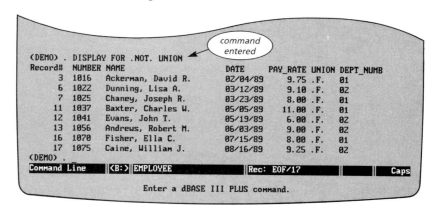

FIGURE 6-22
Using Logical Fields

Using Dates in Conditions

Date fields may be used in conditions. Dates must be entered using a special dBASE function called CTOD (it stands for convert characters to a date.) The proper way to enter 01/15/89, for example, is CTOD("01/15/89"). A FOR clause to find employees who were hired on 1/15/89 would be FOR DATE = CTOD("01/15/89") as in Figure 6-23. A FOR clause to find employees who were hired after 3/1/89 would be FOR DATE > CTOD("03/01/89") as in Figure 6-24.

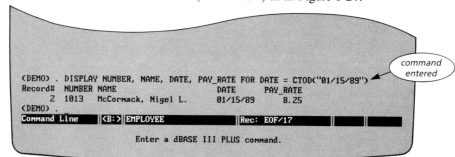

FIGURE 6-23
Using a Date

FIGURE 6-24
Using a Date

Using Compound Conditions

You can create compound conditions. To find all employees who are in department 01 and have a pay rate of $11.00, for example, you can use a condition like the one shown in Figure 6-25. Note that like the word NOT, the word AND must have periods on both sides.

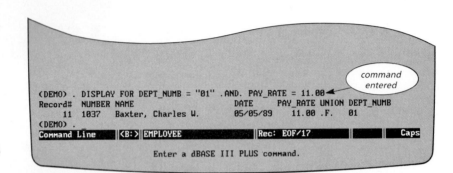

FIGURE 6-25
Using AND

You can also use conditions involving the word OR. The DISPLAY command shown in Figure 6-26, lists all employees who are in department 01 or who belong to the union.

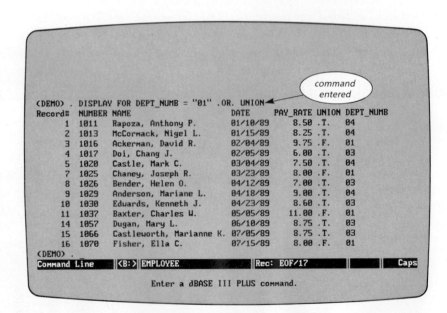

FIGURE 6-26
Using OR

CALCULATIONS

Within the ASSISTANT, you can count records and calculate sums and averages. The same calculations are available from the dot prompt using the COUNT, SUM, and AVERAGE commands.

COUNT

To count all the records in a database file, the command is simply COUNT, as shown in Figure 6-27.

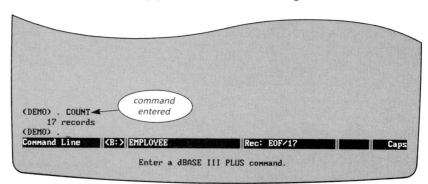

FIGURE 6-27
Counting All Records

To count all the records satisfying some condition, include an appropriate FOR clause after the word COUNT. To count the number of employees in department 01, for example, you would use the command shown in Figure 6-28.

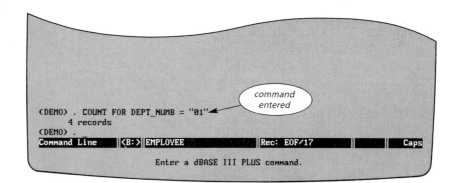

FIGURE 6-28
Counting Records with Conditions

Like conditions within the DISPLAY command, the condition could involve a logical field. The command shown in Figure 6-29 produces a count of the number of employees who are in the union.

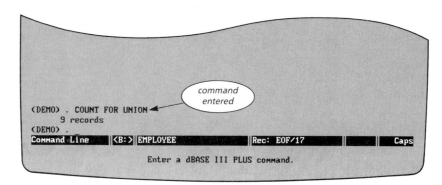

FIGURE 6-29
Counting Records with Conditions

SUM

The SUM command is used to obtain totals. The word SUM is followed by a list of the fields to be totaled. To calculate the total pay rate, for example, use the command shown in Figure 6-30.

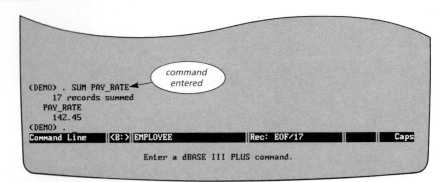

FIGURE 6-30
Calculating a Total

The command shown in Figure 6-31 calculates the total pay rate for all employees in department 01.

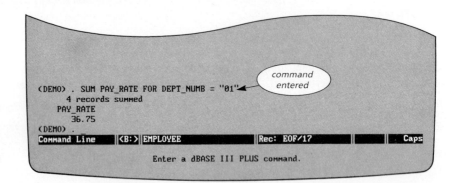

FIGURE 6-31
Calculating a Total with Conditions

The command shown in Figure 6-32 calculates the total pay rate for all employees in the union.

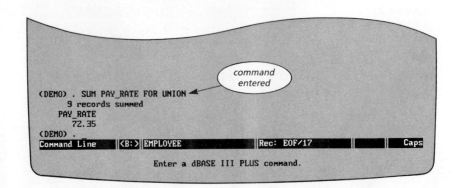

FIGURE 6-32
Calculating a Total with Conditions

AVERAGE

The AVERAGE command is almost identical to the SUM command. The only difference is that it produces an average rather than a total. The word AVERAGE is followed by a list of the fields to be averaged. To calculate the average pay rate, for example, use the command shown in Figure 6-33.

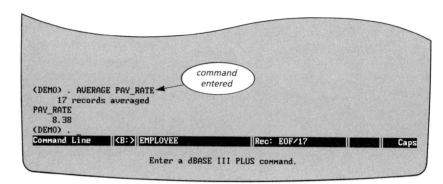

FIGURE 6-33
Calculating an Average

The command shown in Figure 6-34 calculates the average pay rate for all employees in department 01.

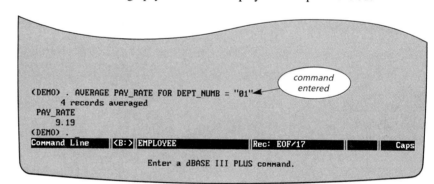

FIGURE 6-34
Calculating an Average with Conditions

The command shown in Figure 6-35 calculates the average pay rate for all employees in the union.

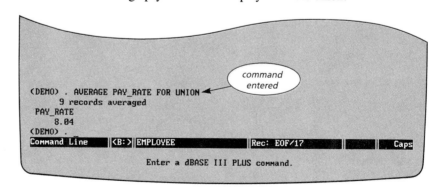

FIGURE 6-35
Calculating an Average with Conditions

ENTERING LONG COMMANDS

Suppose you want to type this DISPLAY command: DISPLAY OFF NUMBER, NAME, DATE, PAY_RATE, DEPT_NUMB FOR DEPT_NUMB = "01" .AND. PAY_RATE > 9.00. Clearly there won't be enough room to fit this command on a single line. How can you type this line?

It turns out that dBASE handles this situation in an interesting way. Start typing the command and stop when you get to the position shown in Figure 6-36.

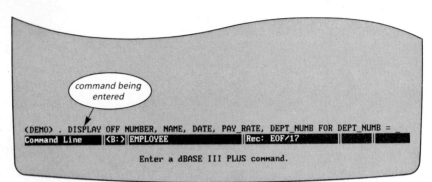

FIGURE 6-36
Typing a Long Command

Continue typing. You will see the portion you have typed move to the left to allow you to continue with the command (Figure 6-37). By the time you have completed the command, your screen will look like the one shown in Figure 6-38. If you need to corect a portion of the line that has disappeared from the screen, simply press the left arrow key enough times to move back to the desired position. As you do, dBASE will return the portion that has disappeared back to the screen.

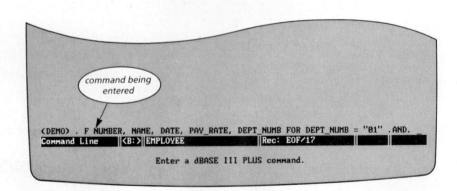

FIGURE 6-37
Typing a Long Command

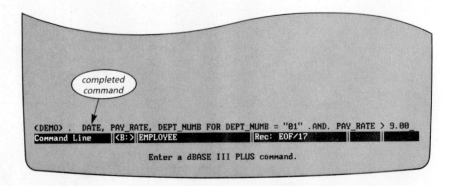

FIGURE 6-38
Command Has Been Completed

Once the command is complete, press the Enter key. The results are shown in Figure 6-39.

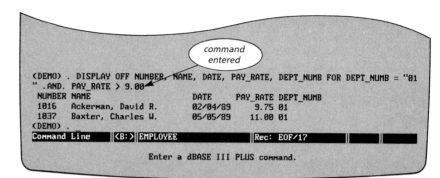

FIGURE 6-39
Results of Command

SORT

You can use the SORT command to sort a database file. The command in Figure 6-40, sorts the active database file (EMPLOYEE) on the NAME field, producing a file called SORT1 (actually SORT1.DBF). Because it is simple enough to sort using the ASSISTANT, it might seem that you would never need this command.

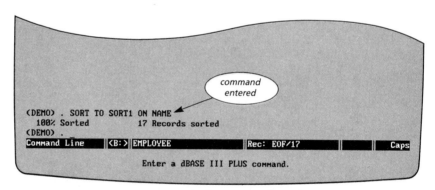

FIGURE 6-40
Sorting

There is one difficulty about sorting within the ASSISTANT, however. There is no way to sort in reverse (usually called *descending*) order. Fortunately, there is an easy way to do so using the SORT command. Simply follow the name of the key with a slash and the letter D, as shown in Figure 6-41. If there were multiple sort fields, they would all be listed after the word TO and separated by commas. Any sort field for which you want descending order would be followed by the slash and the letter D.

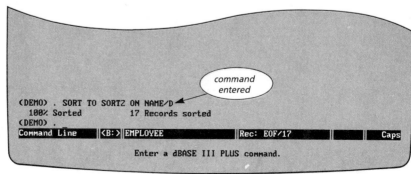

FIGURE 6-41
Sorting in Descending Order

To see the results of the sort in Figure 6-41, you could activate the file called SORT2 and then display all the records. Activating the file can be accomplished through the "Database file" option of the "Set Up" menu within the ASSISTANT. It can also be activated from the dot prompt. Type the word USE followed by the name of the file. Thus, to activate SORT2 and display all the records, you could use the commands shown in Figure 6-42. Note that the records displayed are in *reverse* alphabetical order.

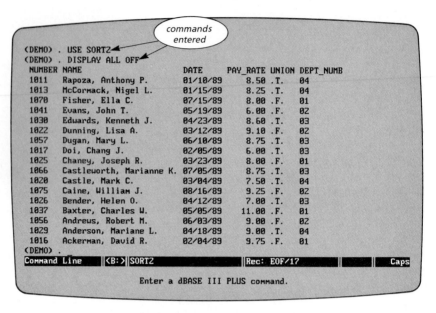

FIGURE 6-42 Results of the Sort

USING VIEWS

Activating a View

iews can be used in DISPLAY commands. Activate the view before executing any of the commands. This can be accomplished through the "View" option of the "Set Up" menu within the ASSISTANT, or from the dot prompt by typing the words SET VIEW TO followed by the name of the view.

Displaying Data in a View

To display all the data in the EMPDEPT view, for example, type the two commands shown in Figure 6-43.

Once you have activated the view you will not need to keep typing the SET VIEW TO command. From this point on, each DISPLAY command will access the data in the EMPDEPT view.

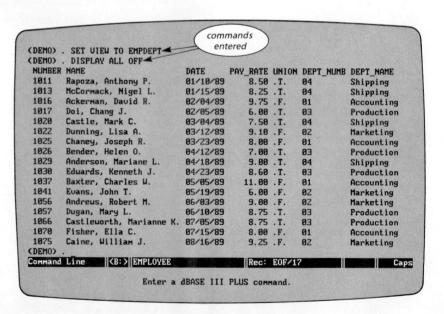

FIGURE 6-43 Using a View

PROGRAMMING

Using the ASSISTANT or typing commands at the dot prompt are both relatively simple actions once you have become comfortable with the various options. Sometimes, however, you may find that there is a command or series of commands that you use frequently. For example, once a week you may enter a DISPLAY command to display the employee number, name, hire date, pay rate, and pay amount (pay rate times 40). You have to enter a separate command for each department, one to print just the employees in department 01, another for department 02, and so on. You also need to calculate the average pay rate for the employees in the department and the total pay amount.

If you find yourself in such a situation, you will undoubtedly wish that there were a simple way to type the commands once and be able to use them from that point on. Fortunately, there is an easy way to do this. You simply create a file containing these commands. Such a file is called a **command file** or **program**. Programs can be created using a word processor that is capable of producing ASCII files or through the dBASE text editor. We will create some sample command files using the dBASE editor.

Let's create a program that will: (1) activate the EMPLOYEE database file; (2) produce a display of the employee number, name, hire date, pay rate, and pay amount for all employees in department 01; (3) calculate the average pay rate of all employees in department 01; and (4) calculate the total pay amount for all employees in department 01.

To start the dBASE editor, type the words MODIFY COMMAND followed by the name of the program. Let's call this program LISTEMP1. Then the appropriate command is MODIFY COMMAND LISTEMP1. Once this command has been executed you will see the screen shown in Figure 6-44. At the top of the screen is the name of the program. Note that dBASE has automatically added the extension "prg" to the name you entered. If you look for this file on your disk, it will appear as LISTEMP1.PRG.

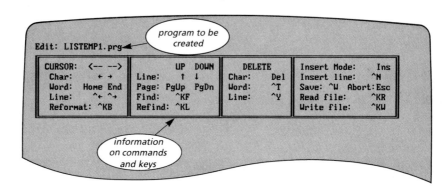

FIGURE 6-44
The dBASE Editor

The box on the screen shows the various things you can do as you create a program. The first part of the box indicates that the Left and Right Arrows will move the cursor one character to the left or right. The Home key will move the cursor one word to the left, and the End key will move it one word to the right. Holding the Ctrl key down while pressing the Left or Right Arrow key will move the cursor to the left or right end of a line. Holding the Ctrl key down and pressing the letters K and B will reformat a paragraph. (This type of reformatting, while useful for creating documents, is not used to create programs.)

The second part of the box indicates that the upward and downward arrows are used to move up or down one line, respectively. The PgUp and PgDn keys are used to move up or down a whole page. When you hold down the Ctrl key and press the letters K or F, dBASE will ask you for a string of characters to find and will then locate this string in the file. If you want to locate the next occurrence of the string of characters you just found, you can use ∧KL instead of ∧KF.

The next part of the box indicates that the Del key is used to delete a single character. Ctrl plus the letter T is used to delete a whole word. Ctrl plus the letter Y is used to delete a whole line.

The final part of the box indicates that the Ins key is used to change from insert mode to overwrite mode and back. In insert mode, typed characters are inserted into the file at the position of the cursor. In overwrite mode, typed characters at the position of the cursor replace those characters previously in the file. To insert a new line, use Ctrl plus the letter N. To save the file and terminate editing, use Ctrl plus the letter W. To terminate editing the file *but not save the changes you have made,* use Esc. (As a safety feature, dBASE will ask whether you are sure you don't want to save the changes.) To insert the contents of another file at the position of the cursor, hold down the CTRL key and type the letters KR. dBASE will request the name of the file to read. Finally, to write the contents of the current file to a different file, hold the Ctrl key down and type the letters KW. dBASE will ask you for the name of the file to write.

To create the first program, type the commands as shown in Figure 6-45. These commands accomplish the specified tasks. You should recognize the commands from the work you have done earlier in this project. There are only two new things. First, in a program, you can continue a command from one line to another by ending the line with a semicolon. Thus, the DISPLAY command is spread over three lines. Second, note the word EJECT. This is used to make the printer advance to the top of a new page. Technically, this is called a *page eject*.

If you wanted to access the EMPDEPT view rather than the single EMPLOYEE database file, the USE EMPLOYEE command would be replaced with SET VIEW TO EMPDEPT. This was not necessary here, however, since all the required data is contained within the EMPLOYEE file.

To save this program, hold the Ctrl key down and type the letter W. You can execute the commands in a program by typing the word DO followed by the name of the program at the dot prompt. Thus you may execute the commands you created by typing the words DO LISTEMP1. Try this now.

Figure 6-46 shows another useful program called ADDEMP. This program will activate the EMPLOYEE file and then put you into Append mode to allow you to add additional records to the EMPLOYEE file—the same as selecting the "Append" option from the "Update" menu of the ASSISTANT. Once you make all the additions and exit the APPEND process, the CLEAR command will clear the screen.

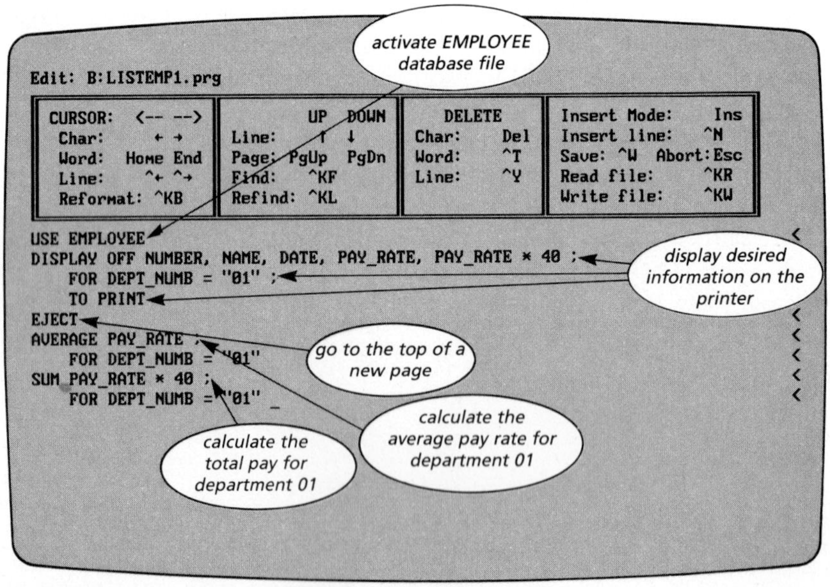

With this program in place, if you want to add records, you don't have to go through the options of the ASSISTANT or the commands at the dot prompt. You can simply type the words DO ADDEMP. You could create a similar program called EDI-TEMP that replaces the word APPEND with the word EDIT. This program could be used when you want to change existing records rather than add new ones.

This is as far as we will go with programming in dBASE in this text. dBASE does have a complete programming language. There are many textbooks about dBASE programing to consult if you are interested in pursuing this study further.

FIGURE 6-45 Program LISTEMP1

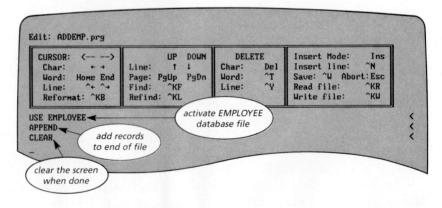

FIGURE 6-46 Program ADDEMP

PROJECT SUMMARY

*I*n Project 6 you learned how to use the DISPLAY command to display data from the dot prompt. You also learned how to use the COUNT, SUM, and AVERAGE commands to calculate statistics. You learned that you can sort from the dot prompt. You activated a view and displayed data in the view from the dot prompt. Finally, you saw how to place dBASE commands in a program (also called a command file) and how to execute the commands in these programs.

If you followed along with the steps in this chapter, you have created a variety of displays. If you did not but wish to see the results now , you can use the following keystroke sequence. Start dBASE and press Esc to change to the dot prompt mode. Then type the following:

SUMMARY OF KEYSTROKES—Project 6

STEPS	KEY(S) PRESSED	STEPS	KEY(S) PRESSED
1	USE EMPLOYEE ←	32	SUM PAY_RATE FOR DEPT_NUMB = "01" ←
2	DISPLAY ←	33	SUM PAY_RATE FOR UNION ←
3	DISPLAY ALL ←	34	AVERAGE PAY_RATE ←
4	DISPLAY OFF ALL ←	35	AVERAGE PAY_RATE FOR DEPT_NUMB = "01" ←
5	DISPLAY ALL NAME, DEPT_NUMB, PAY_RATE ←	36	AVERAGE PAY_RATE FOR UNION ←
6	DISPLAY OFF ALL NUMBER, NAME, PAY_RATE,	37	DISPLAY OFF NUMBER, NAME, DATE, PAY_RATE, DEPT_NUMB
7	PAY_RATE * 40 ←	38	FOR DEPT_NUMB = "01" .AND. PAY_RATE > 9.00 ←
8	DISPLAY RECORD 6 ←	39	SORT TO SORT1 ON NAME ←
9	DISPLAY FOR NUMBER = "1030" ←	40	SORT TO SORT2 ON NAME/D ←
10	DISPLAY FOR PAY_RATE = 6.00 ←	41	USE SORT2 ←
11	DISPLAY FOR PAY_RATE > 9.00 ←	42	DISPLAY ALL OFF ←
12	DISPLAY OFF NAME, DEPT_NUMB, PAY_RATE FOR	43	SET VIEW TO EMPDEPT ←
13	DEPT_NUMB = "04" ←	44	DISPLAY ALL OFF ←
14	DISPLAY FOR NAME = "Baxter, Charles W." ←	45	DISPLAY NUMBER, NAME, PAY_RATE, DEPT_NAME FOR
15	DISPLAY FOR NAME = "BAXTER, CHARLES W." ←	46	DEPT_NAME = "Accounting" ←
16	DISPLAY FOR UPPER(NAME) = "BAXTER, CHARLES W." ←	47	MODIFY COMMAND LISTEMP1 ←
17	DISPLAY FOR NAME = "A" ←	48	USE EMPLOYEE ←
18	DISPLAY FOR "David" $ NAME ←	49	DISPLAY OFF NUMBER, NAME, DATE, PAY_RATE,
19	DISPLAY FOR UNION ←	50	PAY_RATE * 40 ; ←
20	DISPLAY FOR .NOT. UNION ←	51	[SPACE][SPACE][SPACE][SPACE]FOR DEPT_NUMB = "01" ; ←
21	DISPLAY NUMBER, NAME, DATE, PAY_RATE FOR DATE =	52	[SPACE][SPACE][SPACE][SPACE]TO PRINT ←
22	CTOD("01/15/89") ←	53	EJECT ←
23	DISPLAY NUMBER, NAME, DATE, PAY_RATE FOR DATE >	54	AVERAGE PAY_RATE ; ←
24	CTOD("03/01/89") ←	55	[SPACE][SPACE][SPACE][SPACE]FOR DEPT_NUMB = "01" ←
25	DISPLAY FOR DEPT_NUMB = "01" .AND.	56	SUM PAY_RATE * 40 ; ←
26	PAY_RATE = 11.00 ←	57	[SPACE][SPACE][SPACE][SPACE]FOR DEPT_NUMB = "01" [Ctrl-W]
27	DISPLAY FOR DEPT_NUMB = "01" .OR. UNION ←	58	DO LISTEMP1 ←
28	COUNT ←	59	MODIFY COMMAND ADDEMP ←
29	COUNT FOR DEPT_NUMB = "01" ←	60	USE EMPLOYEE ←
30	COUNT FOR UNION ←	61	APPEND ← [SPACE][SPACE][SPACE][SPACE]
31	SUM PAY_RATE ←	62	CLEAR [Ctrl-W]

The following list summarizes the material covered in Project 6:

1. To clear the screen, type CLEAR.
2. To recall the previously entered command, press the Up Arrow key.
3. To send the results of a DISPLAY command to the printer, include the clause TO PRINT in the command.
4. To display the current active record, type DISPLAY and nothing else.
5. To change the scope to ALL, include the word ALL in the DISPLAY command.

Project Summary (continued)

6. To suppress the printing of record numbers, use the word OFF in the DISPLAY command.
7. To display only selected fields, list the fields in the desired order in the DISPLAY command.
8. To display a single record other than the current active record, use DISPLAY RECORD followed by the number of the desired record.
9. To restrict the display to those records meeting a condition, use a FOR clause in the DISPLAY command.
10. To avoid having to worry about uppercase and lowercase letters when searching for a name, use the UPPER function.
11. To search for a name containing a given string of characters, use the substring function, $.
12. To use a date field in a condition, use the CTOD function.
13. To count the number of records satisfying a given condition, use the COUNT command.
14. To calculate totals, use the SUM command.
15. To calculate averages, use the AVERAGE command.
16. To sort the records in a database file, producing another database file, use the SORT command. To sort in descending order, follow the name of the sort key with /D.
17. To activate a view, use the SET VIEW TO command. (The view could also be activated through the ASSISTANT using the "View" option of the "Set Up" menu.)
18. To enter a command that is too long to fit on the screen, simply type the command. Once you have reached the right-hand edge of the screen, dBASE will begin pushing the command to the left to allow more room for you to type.
19. A file containing dBASE commands is called a **command file** or **program**. To execute the commands in the file, type the word DO followed by the name of the program at the dot prompt. dBASE automatically assigns such files the extension "PRG."
20. The EJECT command causes the printer to advance to the top of the next page.
21. The APPEND command can be used to add records to a database file.
22. The EDIT command can be used to change records in a database file.

STUDENT ASSIGNMENTS

STUDENT ASSIGNMENT 1: True/False

Instructions: Circle T if the statement is true and F if the statement is false.

T F   1. While working at the dot prompt, pressing the up arrow key will recall the most recently entered command.
T F   2. To clear the screen from the dot prompt, type the word CLEAR.
T F   3. If no scope is entered in a DISPLAY command, a scope of "ALL" is assumed.
T F   4. To send the results of a DISPLAY command to the printer, include the clause TO PRINT in the command.
T F   5. To suppress the printing of record numbers, include the clause NOREC in a DISPLAY command.
T F   6. To display a single record, the record must be the current active record before the DISPLAY command is executed.
T F   7. To restrict the display to records meeting a certain condition, use a FOR clause.
T F   8. The command DISPLAY FOR NUMBER = "1030" is invalid because 1030 cannot be enclosed in quotes.
T F   9. The command DISPLAY PAY_RATE > 9.00 will display all records that contain a pay rate greater than 9.00.
T F 10. If the UNION field is a logical field, the command DISPLAY FOR UNION could be used to display all records for which the UNION field is true.
T F 11. The SUM command could be used to count the number of records in a database file.
T F 12. To list each employee whose name contains the characters "R.", an appropriate FOR clause would be "R." $ NAME.
T F 13. The command SORT TO XXX ON YYY will create a file called YYY.DBF.
T F 14. To sort in descending order, follow the name of the sort key with a slash and the letter D (/D).
T F 15. A DISPLAY command can be used to display data in a view.
T F 16. To execute the commands stored in the command file XXX.PRG, type the expression DO XXX at the dot prompt.

STUDENT ASSIGNMENT 2: Multiple Choice

Instructions: Circle the correct response.

1. The command DISPLAY OFF ALL will display
   a. all records but the record number will not be displayed.
   b. all records on the screen but the printer will be turned off.
   c. all records on the printer but the screen display will be turned off.
   d. only the first record in the file.
2. The command DISPLAY FOR PAY_RATE = 6.00, when the PAY_RATE field is a numeric field, will display
   a. the first record in the database file where the pay rate field contains a value equal to 6.00.
   b. all the records in the database file where the pay rate field contains a value equal to 6.00.
   c. the current active record if the value of the pay rate field on that record is equal to 6.00. If not, no records will be displayed.
   d. an error message, since 6.00 is not enclosed in quotes.
3. The command DISPLAY FOR UPPER(NAME) = "BAXTER, CHARLES W." will display
   a. all names in uppercase letters of the alphabet.
   b. the name Baxter, Charles W. if it is in the NAME field of the active record in uppercase letters of the alphabet.
   c. all records in the database containing the name following the equal sign regardless of whether the characters were entered in uppercase or lowercase letters of the alphabet.
   d. all records in the database containing the name Baxter, Charles W. in uppercase letters of the alphabet.
4. Which of the following commands can be used to display all records in a logical field called UNION that contain the entry .F.?
   a. DISPLAY FOR UNION   c. DISPLAY FOR .NOT. UNION
   b. DISPLAY FOR UNION = F   d. DISPLAY FOR NOT UNION
5. The command to count all the records in a file is:
   a. SUM   c. COUNT ALL RECORDS
   b. SUM ALL RECORDS   d. COUNT
6. The clause that can be used to test whether the characters "Mary" are contained within the NAME field is:
   a. NAME CONTAINS "Mary"   c. "MARY" ISIN NAME
   b. "MARY" $ NAME   d. NAME $ "MARY"
7. The command to sort the EMPLOYEE file by descending pay rate, producing the file called SORTEMP, is:
   a. SORT TO SORTEMP on PAY_RATE/D
   b. SORT TO SORTEMP ON DESCENDING PAY_RATE
   c. SORT ON SORTEMP, PAY_RATE/D
   d. SORT DESCENDING PAY_RATE TO SORTEMP
8. When typing a command at the dot prompt that is too long to fit on a single line,
   a. type what will fit on one line, press Enter, and continue typing.
   b. type what will fit on one line, type an ampersand (&), press Enter, and then continue typing.
   c. just keep typing.
   d. such a command cannot be entered from the dot prompt. You must use the ASSISTANT.

STUDENT ASSIGNMENT 3: Understanding dBASE Options

Instructions: Explain what will happen after you have typed each of the following lines at the dot prompt and pressed the Enter key.

Problem 1. DISPLAAY

Explanation: _____

Problem 2. DISPLAY OFF ALL TO PRINT

Explanation: _____

Student Assignment 3 (continued)

Problem 3. DISPLAY FOR UNION

Explanation: _____

Problem 4. SORT TO DEPARTMENT ON NAME

Explanation: _____

STUDENT ASSIGNMENT 4: Using dBASE

Instructions: Explain how to accomplish each of the following tasks using dBASE.

Problem 1. Recall the most recently entered command.

Explanation: _____

Problem 2. Display all records without record numbers.

Explanation: _____

Problem 3. Send the results of a DISPLAY command to the printer.

Explanation: _____

Problem 4. Find all employees with a first name of Mary.

Explanation: _____

Problem 5. Find the average pay rate for those employees who are not in the union.

Explanation: _____

Problem 6. Sort the EMPLOYEE file by descending pay rate within department, producing a file called SORTPAY.

Explanation: _____

STUDENT ASSIGNMENT 5: Recovering from Problems

Instructions: In each of the following cases, a problem occurred. Explain the cause of the problem and how it can be corrected.

Problem 1: You type the expression DISPLAY FOR NUMBER = 1030 and dBASE responds with the message "Data type mismatch."

Cause of Problem: _____

Method of Correction: _____

Problem 2: You attempt to display all data for members of the union by typing the words DISPLAY ALL UNION. Instead, you see a column of T's and F's.

Cause of Problem: _____

Method of Correction: _____

Problem 3: You attempt to display the record for an employee with a specific name. No record is displayed even though you know such an employee exists in the database.

Cause of Problem: _____

Method of Correction: _____

MINICASES

Working from the Dot Prompt

Minicase 1: Personal Checks

Instructions: Use the database of personal checks that you created in Minicase 1 of Project 1 and modified in Minicase 1 of Project 5. You should use the view, EXPVIEW, that you created in Project 5. Activate the view by typing the words SET VIEW TO EXPVIEW at the dot prompt. Once you have done this, use dBASE commands to accomplish the following tasks.

For each problem, write the command that you use to accomplish the task in the space provided. Execute the command on the computer. Obtain a printed copy of the output by holding down the Shift key and pressing the PrtSc key, or by ending the command with the clause TO PRINT.

1. Display the first record.

   COMMAND: _____

2. Display all the records.

   COMMAND: _____

3. Display all the records but do not include record numbers.

   COMMAND: _____

4. Display the CHECK NUMBER, DATE, PAYEE, CHECK AMOUNT, and EXPENSE code fields for all records.

   COMMAND: _____

5. Display the sixth record.

   COMMAND: _____

6. Display the record for check number 108.

   COMMAND: _____

7. Display any record on which the check amount is $25.00.

   COMMAND: _____

8. Display any record on which the check amount is greater than $50.00.

   COMMAND: _____

9. Display the records for all checks written for entertainment. Include the CHECK NUMBER, PAYEE, CHECK AMOUNT, and EXPENSE DESCRIPTION fields.

   COMMAND: _____

10. Display the records for all checks written to Sav-Mor Groceries. Use the UPPER function in your DISPLAY command.

    COMMAND: _____

11. Display the records for all checks on which the name of the payee contains the word "Groceries."

    COMMAND: _____

12. Display the records for all checks written that are tax deductible.

    COMMAND: _____

Minicase 1 (continued)

13. Display the records for all checks written that are not tax deductible.

    COMMAND: _____

14. Display the records for all checks written on January 19, 1990. (Remember that you have to use the CTOD function. In this case, you would use CTOD("01/19/90") rather than simply 01/19/90 in your FOR clause.)

    COMMAND: _____

15. Display the records for all checks written on or after January 12, 1990.

    COMMAND: _____

16. Display the records of all checks written for entertainment with a check amount above $25.00.

    COMMAND: _____

17. Display the records for all checks written for household expenses or for food expenses.

    COMMAND: _____

18. Count the number of checks in the database file.

    COMMAND: _____

19. Count the number of checks on which the expense is charity.

    COMMAND: _____

20. Count the number of tax-deductible checks.

    COMMAND: _____

21. Sum the amount of checks written.

    COMMAND: _____

22. Sum the amounts of the checks written for household expenses.

    COMMAND: _____

23. Average the CHECK AMOUNT for all checks written.

    COMMAND: _____

24. Average the CHECK AMOUNT for all checks written for entertainment.

    COMMAND: _____

25. Sort the data in the view on descending CHECK AMOUNT within EXPENSE CODE, producing SORTEXP1. Activate SORTEXP1. List the records in SORTEXP1.

    COMMAND: _____

26. Create a program called CHKLIST1. This program should (a) activate the CHECK database file; (b) display the check number, date, payee, and check amount for all expenses with the expense code HH; (c) calculate the total of the check amounts for all expenses with the expense code HH which are tax deductible; and (d) calculate the total of the check amounts for all expenses with the expense code HH which are not tax deductible. Once you have done this, execute the program. Enter the commands in your program in the space below.

    COMMANDS: _____

    _____

    _____

Minicase 2: Music Library

Instructions: Use the music library database that you created in Minicase 2 of Project 1 and modified in Minicase 2 of Project 5. You should use the view, MUSVIEW, that you created in Project 5. Activate the view by typing the words SET VIEW TO MUSVIEW at the dot prompt. Once you have done this, use dBASE commands to accomplish the following tasks.

For each problem, write the command that you use to accomplish the task in the space provided. Execute the command on the computer. Obtain a printed copy of the output by holding down the Shift key and pressing the PrtSc key, or by ending the command with the clause TO PRINT.

1. Display the first record.   COMMAND: _____

2. Display all the records.   COMMAND: _____

3. Display all the records but don't include record numbers.

   COMMAND: _____

4. Display the MUSIC NAME, ARTIST, TYPE, and COST for all records.

   COMMAND: _____

5. Display the sixth record.   COMMAND: _____

6. Display the record on which the Music Name is "America."

   COMMAND: _____

7. Display the records for the music with the category of classical.

   COMMAND: _____

8. Display any record on which the cost is greater than $7.00.

   COMMAND: _____

9. Display the records for all music on compact disk (CD). Include the TYPE, MUSIC NAME, ARTIST, and COST.

   COMMAND: _____

10. Display the records on which the artist is "Judd, Mary." Use the UPPER function in your DISPLAY command.

    COMMAND: _____

11. Display the records on which the name of the artist contains "Ralph."

    COMMAND: _____

12. Display the records for all music that is on LP.

    COMMAND: _____

13. Display the records for all music that is not on LP.

    COMMAND: _____

14. Display the records for all music on which the date is February 15, 1990. (Remember that you have to use the CTOD function. In this case, you would use CTOD("02/15/90") rather than simply 02/15/90 in your FOR clause.)

    COMMAND: _____

15. Display the records for all music on which the date is after February 1, 1990.

    COMMAND: _____

16. Display the records for all classical music that costs less than $8.95.

    COMMAND: _____

Minicase 2 (continued)

17. Display the records for all music that is either classical or vocal.

    COMMAND: _____

18. Count the number of records in the database file.

    COMMAND: _____

19. Count the number of music selections in the vocal category.

    COMMAND: _____

20. Sum the total cost of all types of music.

    COMMAND: _____

21. Sum the total cost of the music in the country category.

    COMMAND: _____

22. Determine the average cost for all types of music.

    COMMAND: _____

23. Determine the average cost of music in the classical category.

    COMMAND: _____

24. Sort the data in the view on descending COST within CATEGORY, producing SORTMUS1. Activate SORTMUS1. List the records in SORTMUS1.

    COMMAND: _____

25. Create a program called MUSLIST1. This program should (a) activate the MUSIC database file; (b) display the date, music name, artist, category code, and cost for all records whose type is LP; (c) calculate the average cost for all records whose category code is CL; and (d) calculate the average cost for all records whose category code is RK. Once you have done this, execute the program. Enter the commands in your program in the space below.

    COMMANDS: _____

    _____

Minicase 3: Computer Software Store

Instructions: Use the database of computer software that you created in Minicase 3 of Project 1 and modified in Minicase 3 of Project 5. Use the view, SOFTVIEW, that you created in Project 5. Activate the view by typing the words SET VIEW TO SOFTVIEW at the dot prompt. Once you have done this, use dBASE commands to accomplish the following tasks.

For each problem, write the command that you use to accomplish the task in the space provided. Execute the command on the computer. Obtain a printed copy of the output by holding down the Shift key and pressing the PrtSc key, or by ending the command with the clause TO PRINT.

1. Display the first record.

    COMMAND: _____

2. Display all the records.

    COMMAND: _____

3. Display all the records but don't include record numbers.

COMMAND: _____

4. Display the SOFTWARE NAME field, the CATEGORY field, the MS_DOS field, the QUANTITY field, and the COST field for all records in the database.

COMMAND: _____

5. Display the sixth record.

COMMAND: _____

6. Display the record on which the software name is Image Fonts.

COMMAND: _____

7. Display any record on which the cost is $49.95.

COMMAND: _____

8. Display any record on which the cost is less than $50.00.

COMMAND: _____

9. Display the records for all software produced by Electric Software. Include the software name, category, quantity, and cost.

COMMAND: _____

10. Display the records for all software on which the category is "Database." Use the UPPER function in your DISPLAY command.

COMMAND: _____

11. Display the records for all software whose name contains "Data."

COMMAND: _____

12. Display all software that is MS-DOS compatible (the MS_DOS field is true).

COMMAND: _____

13. Display all software that is not MS-DOS compatible.

COMMAND: _____

14. Display all records with a quantity less than 10.

COMMAND: _____

15. Display all records with a quantity greater than 25.

COMMAND: _____

16. Display all word processing software (WP in CATEGORY field) that costs less than $50.00.

COMMAND: _____

17. Display all records with a category of database or spreadsheet.

COMMAND: _____

18. Count the number of records in the database file.

COMMAND: _____

Minicase 3 (continued)

19. Sum the QUANTITY field to determine the number of products on hand.

    COMMAND: _____

20. Average the COST field to determine the average cost of the software.

    COMMAND: _____

21. Average the cost of the software with the category of Education.

    COMMAND: _____

22. Sort the data in the view on descending COST within CATEGORY, producing SORTSFT1. Activate SORTSFT1. List the records in SORTSFT1.

    COMMAND: _____

23. Create a program called SRTLIST1. This program should (a) activate the SOFTWARE database file; (b) display the software name, category, quantity, cost, and on-hand value (quantity times cost) for all software produced by the company whose code is 05; (c) calculate the average cost of all the software for which the company code is 05 and that is MS-DOS compatible; and (d) calculate the average cost of all the software for which the company code is 05 and that is not MS-DOS compatible. Once you have done this, execute the program. Enter the commands in your program in the space below.

    COMMANDS: _____

    _____

    _____

Minicase 4: Home Sales

Instructions: Use the database of homes for sale that you created in Minicase 4 of Project 1 and modified in Minicase 4 of Project 5. Use the view, ZIPVIEW, that you created in Project 5. Activate the view by typing the words SET VIEW TO ZIPVIEW at the dot prompt. Once you have done this, use dBASE commands to accomplish the following tasks.

For each problem, write the command that you use to accomplish the task in the space provided. Execute the command on the computer. Obtain a printed copy of the output by holding down the Shift key and pressing the PrtSc key, or by ending the command with the clause TO PRINT.

1. Display the first record.

    COMMAND: _____

2. Display all the records.

    COMMAND: _____

3. Display all the records but do not include record numbers.

    COMMAND: _____

4. Display the PRICE field, the ADDRESS field, the CITY field, and the ZIP field for all records in the database.

    COMMAND: _____

5. Display the sixth record.

    COMMAND: _____

6. Display the record that has 10/22/90 in the DATE field. (Remember that you have to use the CTOD function. In this case, you would use CTOD("10/22/90") rather than simply 10/22/90 in your FOR clause.)

   COMMAND: _____

7. Display information about the house at 145 Oak Ave.

   COMMAND: _____

8. Display the records for all houses listed in the city of Anaheim.

   COMMAND: _____

9. Display the records for all houses in the 92641 zip code area.

   COMMAND: _____

10. Display the records for all houses with a pool (the POOL field is true).

    COMMAND: _____

11. Display the records for all houses that do not have a pool.

    COMMAND: _____

12. Display the records for all houses with a price of less than $125,000.00.

    COMMAND: _____

13. Display the records for all houses with a price greater than $150,000.00.

    COMMAND: _____

14. Display the records for all four-bedroom houses that cost less than $100,000.00.

    COMMAND: _____

15. Count the number of records in the database file.

    COMMAND: _____

16. Find the average cost of a house in Anaheim.

    COMMAND: _____

17. Find the average cost of a four-bedroom house.

    COMMAND: _____

18. Find the average cost of a three-bedroom house in Garden Grove.

    COMMAND: _____

19. Sort the data in the view on descending PRICE within ZIP, producing SORTHSE1. Activate SORTHSE1. List the records in SORTHSE1.

    COMMAND: _____

20. Create a program called HMSLIST1. This program should (a) activate the HOMES database file; (b) display the date, address, zip, number of bedrooms, number of bathrooms, and price for all homes with a pool; (c) calculate the average price for homes with a pool; d) calculate the average price for homes that do not have a pool. Once you have done this, execute the program. Enter the commands in your program in the space below.

    COMMANDS: _____

dBASE Index